SECTORS & SKILLS

SECTORS & SKILLS
THE NEED FOR POLICY ALIGNMENT

EDITED BY ANDRE KRAAK

Published by HSRC Press
Private Bag X9182, Cape Town, 8000, South Africa
www.hsrcpress.ac.za

First published 2009

ISBN (soft cover) 978-0-7969-2265-6
ISBN (pdf) 978-0-7969-2282-3

© 2009 Human Sciences Research Council

The views expressed in this publication are those of the authors. They do not necessarily reflect the views or policies of the Human Sciences Research Council ('the Council') or of the South African Department of Labour ('the DoL'), or indicate that the Council or the DoL endorses the views of the authors. In quoting from this publication, readers are advised to attribute the source of the information to the authors concerned and not to the Council or the DoL.

Copyedited by Karen Press
Typeset by Simon van Gend
Cover by FUEL Design
Printed by Logo Print, Cape Town, South Africa

Distributed in Africa by Blue Weaver
Tel: +27 (0) 21 701 4477; Fax: +27 (0) 21 701 7302
www.oneworldbooks.com

Distributed in Europe and the United Kingdom by Eurospan Distribution Services (EDS)
Tel: +44 (0) 20 7240 0856; Fax: +44 (0) 20 7379 0609
www.eurospanbookstore.com

Distributed in North America by Independent Publishers Group (IPG)
Call toll-free: (800) 888 4741; Fax: +1 (312) 337 5985
www.ipgbook.com

Contents

List of tables and figures   vii
Acronyms and abbreviations   xi

INTRODUCTION
1   The need for alignment between industrial and skills development policies   2
    Andre Kraak

HIGH-TECH SECTORS
2   On the brink? Skills demand and supply issues in the
    South African automotive components industry   24
    Justin Barnes
3   Aerospace   45
    Erika Kraemer-Mbula
4   Three new technology platforms   64
    Jo Lorentzen and Il-haam Petersen

RESOURCE-BASED SECTORS
5   Metals beneficiation   86
    Johann Maree, Paul Lundall and Shane Godfrey
6   Chemicals   110
    Rhoanda van Zyl
7   Wood, paper and pulp   132
    Thomas E Pogue

PUBLIC INFRASTRUCTURE SECTORS
8   Energy   152
    Jeff Lomey and Kent McNamara
9   Transport   174
    Jan Havenga

LABOUR-INTENSIVE SECTORS
10 Clothing and textiles   200
    Mike Morris and Lyn Reed
11 Agro-processing   219
    Duncan Pieterse
12 Creative industries   235
    Avril Joffe and Monica Newton

SERVICES

13 **Growth and skills in the financial services sector of the South African economy** 256
Sean Archer
14 **Information and communication technologies** 274
Andrew Paterson and Joan Roodt
15 **Tourism** 300
Nicci Earle-Malleson

CONCLUSION

16 **Overcoming 'one-size-fits-all' policy-making: The need for differentiated skills development policies in a highly uneven economic and labour market landscape** 320
Andre Kraak

List of contributors 353

Tables and figures

Tables

Table 1.1:	Five organisational trends in the evolution of network relations between firms	8
Table 2.1:	Summary of investment indicators amongst South African automotive component manufacturers versus international firms in the SAABC database, 2003–2006	27
Table 2.2:	Industry employment levels (average monthly figures), 2001–2005	28
Table 2.3:	Employment demand for the period 2006–2010	33
Table 2.4:	Employment demand for the period 2006–2015	33
Table 2.5:	Management and professional skills profiles for 2006, 2010 and 2015; total demand calculations for 2006–2010 and 2006–2015	34
Table 2.6:	Artisan skills profile for 2006, 2010 and 2015; total demand calculations for 2006–2010 and 2006–2015	35
Table 2.7:	Current skills gaps as identified during firm-level interviews	37
Table 2.8:	Comparative identification of scarce skills	41
Table 3.1:	Aerospace manufactures, associated value added and level of skills	46
Table 3.2:	Trade in aircraft, spacecraft and parts (R millions), 2003–2006	48
Table 3.3:	Changes in composition of aerospace employment in key occupations, 1996–2005	54
Table 3.4:	Percentage change in skills demand in the aerospace sector and the total manufacturing sector, 1996–2005	55
Table 3.5:	Supply of engineers in HET: percentage of black and female graduates, 1996–2005	56
Table 3.6:	Identified key areas for training	58
Table 3.7:	Identified scarce skills in South African aerospace manufacturing	60
Table 4.1:	Scarce and critical skills in the engineering and technical professions, 2006	66
Table 5.1:	Benefits of beneficiation: selling price, employment and investment in different stages of carbon steel	90
Table 5.2:	Stages of beneficiation and levels achieved	91
Table 5.3:	Mark-ups of basic metals prices, 2003/04	92
Table 5.4:	Employment levels in the metal and engineering industry, 1996–2005	93
Table 5.5:	Employment changes, 1996–2001 and 2001–2005	94
Table 5.6:	Employment by occupation in the metal and engineering sector, 1999 & 2005	95
Table 5.7:	Performance transmission across FET N-Level theoretical engineering courses, 1996–2005	100
Table 5.8:	Higher education enrolment, output and qualification ratio, 1996–2005	103
Table 6.1:	Average skills distribution in the different sub-sectors (%), 1996–2005	120
Table 8.1:	Occupational ratios, by NQF level, and projected skills demand for the electrical energy sector to 2012	161
Table 8.2:	Comparison and assessment of skills demand and supply in the electrical energy sector to 2012	168
Table 13.1:	Structure of output and change in sectoral contribution to GDP growth, 1960 and 2006	257
Table 13.2:	Skills breakdown of employment by sector, 1995, 2004 and 2006	263
Table 14.1:	Number of enterprises, by sub-sector of the ICT sector, 2002	277
Table 14.2:	GDP and employment in ICT sub-sectors, 1996–2005	279

Table 14.3:	Summary of ICT sub-sector growth and employment trajectories, 1996–2005	279
Table 14.4:	Level of skill by sub-sector (percentage), 1996–1999 and 2000–2005	281
Table 14.5:	Employment, by main occupation in the ICT sub-sectors, 1996–1999 compared with 2000–2005	284
Table 14.6:	Employment of ICT-related professionals and associate professionals, 1996–2005	285
Table 14.7:	Distribution of computer professionals and associate professionals, by economic sector, 2003–2004	286
Table 14.8:	Graduate trends in ICT-related fields of study in higher education, 1996–2005	289
Table 14.9:	Graduates in ICT-cognate fields of study, by qualification level (%), 2005	290
Table 14.10:	Share of graduate numbers in Computer Science and Data Processing, by qualification level, 1996 and 2005	291
Table 14.11:	Share of graduate numbers in Computer Science and Data Processing, by race, 1996 and 2005	291
Table 14.12:	Share of graduate production among fields of specialisation within the Computer Science and Data Processing field of study, 1999 and 2005	292
Table 14.13:	Output of new graduates needed to address demand for CPAPs, 2005–2015	295
Table 15.1:	Domestic and foreign tourism, compound annual growth rate, by percentage, 2005–2006	303
Table 15.2:	Comparisons of estimates of total enterprises, by tourism sub-sector, 2000–2007	305
Table 16.1:	Criteria used in the allocation of sectors to specific labour market segments	327

Figures

Figure 2.1:	South African automotive components industry's employment composition, 2006, and projected levels, 2010 and 2015	30
Figure 2.2:	Projected employment composition of the South African automotive components industry, 2006 versus 2010 and 2015	31
Figure 2.3:	Employment demand based on employee turnover, 2006 to 2010 and 2015	32
Figure 2.4:	Average industry recruitment lead times	37
Figure 2.5:	Training expenditure as a percentage of remuneration: South African average (2001–2006) versus international average (2006 only)	38
Figure 3.1:	Aerospace industry's domestic linkages to other economic sectors in South Africa	49
Figure 3.2:	Occupational profile of the aerospace industry relative to the total manufacturing sector, average 2001–2005	54
Figure 3.3:	Intake of apprentices to the DCLD, 1990–2007	57
Figure 3.4:	Immigration and emigration of engineers and related technologists, 1998–2003	59
Figure 4.1:	Skills supply and demand in engineering and engineering technology, 2000–2006	68
Figure 4.2:	Skills supply and demand in chemistry, 2000–2006	69
Figure 4.3:	Skills supply and demand in physics, 2000–2006	69
Figure 4.4:	Skills supply and demand in mathematical sciences, 2000–2006	70
Figure 4.5:	PhD graduate output in the life sciences, 1996–2005	72
Figure 4.6:	PhD enrolments in the life sciences, 2000–2005	73
Figure 4.7:	PhD graduate output in agricultural and renewable resources, 1996–2005	76
Figure 4.8:	PhD graduate output in engineering and engineering technology, 1996–2005	77
Figure 4.9:	PhD graduate output in the pharmaceutical and mathematical sciences, 1996–2005	77
Figure 4.10:	Skills supply and demand in agriculture and life sciences, 2000–2006	78

Figure 4.11:	Skills supply and demand in chemical engineering and engineering technology, 2000–2006 78
Figure 4.12:	Skills supply and demand in pharmaceutical sciences, 2000–2006 79
Figure 5.1:	Trends in employment in the metal industries, 1996–2005 93
Figure 5.2:	Employment by occupation in metal & engineering, 1999 and 2005 95
Figure 5.3:	Higher education enrolment and output, 1996–2005 102
Figure 6.1:	Strategic sub-sector and standard industrial classifications of the chemical sector 112
Figure 6.2:	Chemical sector value chain 113
Figure 7.1:	Management objectives for plantation forests, by area, 1994–2004 134
Figure 7.2:	Sales of forest timber (real 2000 rand values), 1994–2004 135
Figure 7.3:	Primary processing exports (real 2000 values), 1994–2005 136
Figure 7.4:	Primary processing imports (real 2000 values), 1994–2005 137
Figure 7.5:	South African paper milling capacity, by company, 2005 138
Figure 7.6:	Domestic paper sales (real 2001 rand values), 2001–2006 139
Figure 7.7:	Paper exports (real 2000 values), 1994–2006 139
Figure 7.8:	Paper imports (real 2000 values), 1994–2006 140
Figure 7.9:	Wood furniture exports (real 2000 values), 1994–2005 140
Figure 7.10:	Wood furniture imports (real 2000 values), 1994–2005 141
Figure 8.1:	Formal employment levels in electricity-related sub-sectors, 1996–2005 157
Figure 8.2:	Energy sources for electricity generation in South Africa, 2001 158
Figure 8.3:	Eskom capacity status and maximum demand forecast, 1996–2008 159
Figure 8.4:	Projected maximum energy demand, 1951–2031 160
Figure 8.5:	Least-cost combination of the 10 000 GWh renewable energy target 162
Figure 8.6:	Changing NQF levels of Electrical Trades Theory output from FET colleges, 1996–2005 165
Figure 8.7:	N6 output in engineering studies from FET colleges, 1996–2005 166
Figure 9.1:	Transport, storage and communication industry demarcation system 175
Figure 9.2:	Relationship between employment demand, employment supply, skills and labour productivity 176
Figure 9.3:	Formal employment growth of the TSC industry, 1996–2005 177
Figure 9.4:	Comparison of formal employment in the transport, postal and telecommunications sub-sectors, 1996–2005 177
Figure 9.5:	Estimated formal employment split between passenger and freight transport, 1995–2005 178
Figure 9.6:	Fields of study in engineering and transportation, 1996–2005 180
Figure 9.7:	Distribution of skills bands for the TSC industry (formal employment), 1996–2005 181
Figure 9.8:	Low skills distribution of occupational category for the industry (formal employment), 2000–2005 182
Figure 9.9:	Growth in tonkilometres per worker compared to growth in real GDP, 1995–2005 183
Figure 9.10:	Tonkilometres per employee (two components of SA Rail compared to global railways) 184
Figure 9.11:	Growth in tonkilometres per worker compared to growth in real GDP per worker, 1995–2005 185
Figure 9.12:	Growth in passenger journeys per worker compared to growth in real GDP, 1995–2005 185
Figure 9.13:	Growth in passenger journeys per worker compared to growth in real GDP per worker, 1995–2005 186
Figure 9.14:	Mode comparison, passenger journeys per worker for short-distance transport, 1995–2005 187

Figure 9.15:	Growth in long-distance passenger journeys per worker, 1995–2005	187
Figure 9.16:	South African freight transport as a percentage of world figures, 2004	189
Figure 9.17:	South African freight transport network segments (with mode differentiation)	189
Figure 9.18:	Long-haul surface journeys as a percentage of world figures and expected shift in long-haul journeys if economy matures	193
Figure 9.19:	Degree of skills shift required to enable step change from long-haul road to long-haul rail freight transport	196
Figure 11.1:	Agro-processing output (constant 2000 rands), 1995–2006	220
Figure 11.2:	Agro-processing employment, 1995–2006	220
Figure 11.3:	Agro-processing exports (constant 2000 rands), 1995–2006	221
Figure 12.1:	Composition of the creative economy	236
Figure 12.2:	The film and television value chain	239
Figure 12.3:	The craft value chain	243
Figure 14.1:	Relationship between the ICT producer sector and ICT 'user' sectors	276
Figure 14.2:	Employment trends in the major subdivisions of the ICT sector, 1996–2005	280
Figure 14.3:	Employment in the ICT sector, by sub-sector and main occupation, 1996–2005	283
Figure 14.4:	Average provincial distribution of computer professionals and associate professionals and GDP, 2000–2005	287
Figure 14.5:	Graduates in ICT-cognate fields of study, 1996–2005	288
Figure 14.6:	Graduation trends in Computer Science and Data Processing, by qualification level and race, 1996–2005	290
Figure 14.7:	Comparison of changes in remuneration between all professionals and associate professionals and CPAPs, 2000–2005	296
Figure 15.1:	Foreign tourist arrivals to South Africa, 1966–2006	301
Figure 15.2:	Domestic versus foreign tourism value contribution, 2005–2006	302
Figure 15.3:	Contribution to national GDP and employment per tourist category, 1994, 2000 and 2005	302
Figure 16.1:	A six-part segmentation of the South African labour market	326

Acronyms and abbreviations

ABET	adult basic education and training
ACSA	Airports Company of South Africa
AIDC	Automotive Industry Development Centre
Asgisa	Accelerated and Shared Growth Initiative for South Africa
ATRAMI	Artisan Training and Recognition Agreement for the Metal Industry
AU	African Union
BPO	business process outstanding
BTech	Bachelor of Technology
CCDI	Cape Craft and Design Institute
CHIETA	Chemical Industries Training and Education Authority
CMT	cut-make-and-trim
CSIR	Council for Scientific and Industrial Research
CSP	Customised Sector Programme
CTFL SETA	Clothing, Footwear, Textiles and Leather Sector Education and Training Authority
DAC	Department of Arts and Culture
DACST	Department of Arts, Culture, Science and Technology
DEAT	Department of Environmental Affairs and Tourism
DEEM	design, engineering, entrepreneurial and managerial
DME	Department of Minerals and Energy
DoE	Department of Education
DoL	Department of Labour
DoT	Department of Transport
DPE	Department of Public Enterprises
DST	Department of Science and Technology
DTI	Department of Trade and Industry
ECSA	Engineering Council of South Africa
ESETA	Energy Sector Education and Training Authority
EU	European Union
FASSET	Financial and Accounting Services Sector Education and Training Authority
FET	further education and training
FIETA	Forest Industry Education and Training Authority
FoodBev SETA	Food and Beverages Sector Education and Training Authority
GCI	Gauteng Creative Industries Co-operative
GDP	Gross Domestic Product
GEAR	Growth, Employment and Redistribution
GET	general education and training
HET	higher education and training
HMO	Hermanus Magnetic Observatory
HR	human resources
HSRC	Human Sciences Research Council
IBSA	India-Brazil-South Africa
ICT	information and communications technology
IDC	Industrial Development Corporation
IPP	independent power producers
IT	information technology
Jipsa	Joint Initiative on Priority Skills Acquisition
LFS	Labour Force Survey

MAPPP-SETA	Media, Advertising, Printing, Publishing and Packaging Sector Education and Training Authority
MERSETA	Manufacturing, Engineering and Related Services Sector Education and Training Authority
MIDP	Motor Industry Development Programme
NAACAM	National Association of Automotive Component and Allied Manufacturers
NAC	National Arts Council
NASA	National Aeronautics and Space Administration
NASSP	National Astrophysics and Space Science Programme
NECSA	Nuclear Energy Corporation of South Africa
NIPF	National Industrial Policy Framework
NQF	National Qualifications Framework
NTFP	non-timber forest products
OECD	Organisation for Economic Co-operation and Development
OEM	original equipment manufacturer
OHS	October Household Survey
PBMR	pebble bed modular reactor
PPP	purchasing price parity
PV	photovoltaic
PWR	pressurised water reactor
R&D	research and development
RE	renewable energy
SA Tourism	South African Tourism
SAABC	South African Automotive Benchmarking Club
SAAO	South African Astronomical Observatory
SACTWU	Southern African Clothing and Textile Workers Union
SADC	Southern African Development Community
SADRI	South African Defence-Related Industries
SALT	Southern African Large Telescope
SANHARP	South African Human Asset & Research Programme
SARS	South African Revenue Service
SET	science, engineering and technology
SETA	Sector Education and Training Authority
SIC	Standard Industrial Classification
SKA	Square Kilometre Array
SME	small and medium enterprises
SMMEs	small, medium and micro enterprises
Stats SA	Statistics South Africa
TEI	tertiary education institutions
THETA	Tourism, Hospitality and Sport Education Training Authority
TSC	transport, storage and communication industry
UIF	Unemployment Insurance Fund
UK	United Kingdom
UNIDO	United Nations Industrial Development Organisation
USA	United States of America
WCM	world-class manufacturing
WTO	World Trade Organisation
WTTC	World Travel and Tourism Council

1 INTRODUCTION

CHAPTER 1

The need for alignment between industrial and skills development policies

André Kraak

Introduction

This book argues the case for greater alignment between industrial and skills development policies. Alignment is important for two reasons. Firstly, at a pragmatic level, a number of micro-economic, science, technology and industrial strategies have recently been adopted by government. This has provided the first opportunity since 1994 for a stronger alignment between these new policies and education and training policies approved several years ago.

Secondly, the case for greater alignment can be made conceptually. This possibility arises because of the increasing primacy of 'learning' in both education and industrial contexts. The greatest value-added in production today is increasingly generated by the dynamic capabilities of firms and their ability to absorb new technologies and work organisation techniques, introduce new processes and products, and operate in newly diversified fields of the economy. The new emphasis on 'learning' in industrial policy is also directly related to the need to compete on the basis of 'quality' and not purely in terms of cost.

The task of alignment is not easy. It is not a simple question of matching one relatively homogeneous policy environment with another and hoping for a comfortable one-on-one fit. Indeed, quite the opposite is true. Policy alignment will require a detailed disaggregation of the national economy to the sectoral and enterprise levels, which in turn will reveal high levels of differentiation and unevenness between and within sectors of the economy. This meso- and micro-level heterogeneity within and between sectors 'on the ground' suggests that the state's current and highly aggregated 'one-size-fits-all' skills development policy is inappropriate when applied equally across all sectors of the national economy. Stronger alignment with sectoral policies will require that skills development strategies are far more attuned to the specific needs of each sector and their variegated sub-sectors.

This book examines several of the priority sectors, sub-sectors and technology platforms identified by government in its recent policy texts. The book segments the national economy across five differing clusters of sectors:
- high-tech sectors (automotive; aerospace; 'big science' technology platforms such as space science, nuclear energy and biotechnology);
- resource-based sectors (metals; chemicals; wood, paper and pulp);
- public infrastructure sectors (energy; transport);
- labour-intensive sectors (clothing and textiles; agro-processing; creative industries);
- services sectors (financial services; information and communications technology (ICT); tourism).

All of these sectors and technology platforms are reviewed in this book. The chapters describe highly differentiated socio-economic conditions and divergent prospects for future growth and development in the sectors on which they focus. They show that each of these sectors will require skills development strategies that are uniquely customised to meet specific sectoral conditions. This differentiation will require a paradigmatic shift in the way in which skills development strategies are formulated by government, and in the way they are implemented by intermediary agencies such as the Sector Education and Training Authorities (SETAs), the myriad small business development agencies operating in the national economy, and other bodies that apply training strategies as part of their developmental programmes. The work of all of these bodies will have to be far more informed by sectoral conditions than has been the case in the past. Agency officials will need to acquire higher levels of sectoral expertise – a capability which is termed 'situated knowledge' later in the chapter. This level of sectoral expertise is currently lacking in the SETAs and small, medium and micro enterprise (SMME) agencies operating in the South African economy.

The purpose of this introductory chapter, then, is to contribute to the national 'rethink' about the way in which skills development strategies are conceptualised with regard to the national economy. The structure of the chapter is as follows: the first section provides a very brief overview of the new micro-economic and industrial policy frameworks which necessitate a realignment of approaches to skills development; the chapter then examines the theoretical literature on globalisation and the knowledge economy and highlights the way in which 'learning' in both education and enterprise contexts has become the new competitive advantage. Alignment and co-ordination between these two policy domains is now a crucial policy objective for all governments across the globe.

Thirdly, the chapter foregrounds the need to take cognisance of sectoral differentiation, and the need for skills and industrial policies to be appropriately customised and attuned to the wide array of sub-sectoral needs. And lastly, the analysis highlights the important role of government in promoting the alignment of cross-departmental policies. This is to be achieved through two key institutional mechanisms: firstly, improved horizontal co-ordination between participating government departments, and secondly, the effective utilisation of intermediary agencies which facilitate communication between government and employers and co-ordinate the implementation of industrial and skills development policies 'on the ground'.

The new policy environment

Space constraints do not permit a comprehensive analysis of new policies in the science, technology, micro-economic and industrial policy environments published by government since 2005. A few observations will suffice.

A new micro-economic orientation

An important shift in government economic thinking has taken place in recent years. A key factor in producing this shift has been the emergence of a more expansive state stance on expenditure on socio-economic policies. This new emphasis has become possible largely because of two particular features of government's macro-economic policy, namely, the elimination of state debt and the highly effective collection of tax revenues.

A second critical factor was the resolutions adopted at the Growth and Development Summit held in June 2003 by representatives of government, business and labour – resolutions which sought to fight the scourge of unemployment, under-development and poverty. A number of key decisions were made at this tripartite meeting, including halving poverty by 2014 and offering learnership training opportunities to 80 000 unemployed youth. Other resolutions dealt with socio-economic policies aimed at developing both the first and second economies. These included: functioning more effectively as a 'developmental state'; building stronger linkages between the formal and informal economies; increasing infrastructural investment; promoting broad-based black economic empowerment; promoting the Expanded Public Works Programme; and building a stronger social safety net for the poor.

However, the most significant shift has been government's recognition of the importance of micro-economic reform (see DTI 2002). The new micro-economic logic emphasises the fact that production of competitive manufactured goods now depends not only on the actual production process involved in transforming natural products into merchandise, but also on the 'value matrices' that incorporate the technology used in production, the efficiency of communications, logistics and distribution systems, and issues related to packaging and marketing (DTI 2002: 37–39; Lowitt & Altman 2007: 17).

By 2005, a strong consensus had emerged across government on what was required to promote growth and development. Central tenets of this consensus included:
- A commitment by government to halving unemployment by 2014. First expressed in a resolution adopted at the Growth and Development Summit in June 2003, it has now become government's top economic and political priority.
- A stronger emphasis being placed on industrial policy as a key government lever to target particular niche areas and economic sectors which are likely to contribute to economic growth and increased job creation in the future.
- Government's determination to get education and skills development more effectively aligned to its wider social and economic objectives. The prioritisation of this issue across government is a major gain – it represents the first time that a large collectivity of government departments recognises that education and training is a critical precondition for success in all other governmental socio-economic programmes. In the words of the Deputy-President, Phumzile Mlambo-Ngcuka, failure to improve education and training will constitute a 'fatal constraint' on the ability of the economy to grow over the next decade (Mlambo-Ngcuka 2006).

All of these socio-economic sentiments have now coalesced into one core political programme under the banner of the Accelerated and Shared Growth Initiative for South Africa (Asgisa) that has been led by the country's Deputy-President, Phumzile Mlambo-Ngcuka, since its launch in July 2005. The main purpose of Asgisa as an economic and industrial policy campaign is to identify the major bottlenecks to attaining a six per cent growth rate by 2010. Crumbling public infrastructure and skills constraints have received the most attention. Government has already begun to ramp up public-sector investment, which at one point fell below four per cent of GDP but has in recent years risen above six per cent. In order to eliminate the backlog that has emerged in public infrastructure, public-sector investment is planned to rise to around eight per cent of GDP (PCAS 2006: 5).

The most recent addition to government's micro-economic armoury has been the National Industrial Policy Framework (NIPF) which was approved by Cabinet in July 2007 (DTI 2007). The overall vision of the NIPF is to facilitate diversification of the economy away from its traditional reliance on minerals and mineral-processing towards increased value-addition. Key activities will include: increased downstream beneficiation, participation in value chain segments, and technological leadership in specific technologies. The strategy aims to promote a more labour-intensive industrialisation pathway characterised by sustainable, labour-absorbing manufacturing and service sectors and economic linkages which catalyse employment creation (DTI 2007: 2).

The NIPF adopts Rodrik's concept of 'self-discovery' (Rodrik 2004). It argues that due to rapid technological and other changes in the global economy, new areas of global growth frequently emerge or can be created. Countries and firms that are able to identify these trends early on have a 'first-mover' advantage in new markets. The ability to identify and act upon these opportunities requires complex processes of 'self-discovery which match new potential areas of global growth with existing or potential capabilities in order to overcome the fundamental information market failures involved' (DTI 2007: 27). The NIPF is suggesting that this process of self-discovery should occur within a clustering framework. The department proposes five broad sectoral groupings within which further sectoral diversification and 'self-discovery' can take place:
- natural-resource-based sectors;
- medium-technology sectors (including downstream mineral beneficiation);
- advanced manufacturing sectors;
- labour-intensive sectors;
- tradable services sectors (DTI 2007: 33).

Prioritising science and technology

The Department of Arts, Culture, Science and Technology (DACST) passed its flagship policy framework in a *White Paper* in 1996 (DACST 1996); this established the idea of a 'National System of Innovation' (NSI). Government has since expended significant effort in building key components of the NSI, including new technology missions in ICT, biotechnology and advanced manufacturing. The DST has also launched several intermediary agencies as the primary mechanism to work in areas such as technology transfer and small business development. Regional agencies have been launched to promote government's Biotechnology and Advanced Manufacturing Technology Strategies (DST 2001, 2003).

More recently, the DST has launched a new Ten-Year Plan for the period 2008–2018 which introduces additional technology platforms to the NSI framework. These platforms are viewed as 'grand challenges' in South Africa's transition towards a knowledge-based economy. They include:
- a space satellite programme;
- a nuclear energy programme; and
- the development of an indigenous pharmaceuticals sector (DST 2007).

Resolving the 'policy gap'

All of these micro-economic, technology and industrial policy frameworks were absent in the period 1994–2005, when the core national education and training policy frameworks were formulated and passed through parliament. For example, the *Green Paper on a Skills Development Strategy* (DoL 1997) was formulated in 1996–1997 and became the Skills Development Act (No. 97 of 1998). This policy framework argued strongly for a demand-led strategy which was attuned to the skill needs of firms (DoL 1996: 21). However, establishing such an alignment between training policy and firm needs was not feasible in the 1997–2005 period, given the absence of an industrial policy which could more clearly articulate the demand-side requirements of priority sectors of the economy. More problematically, this policy gap meant that the establishment of the 25 SETAs in March 2000 occurred without these intermediary bodies becoming informed regarding the key economic needs of the sectors.

Similarly, the 2001 National Plan for Higher Education spoke of the need to develop a system that would 'meet national development needs including the high-skilled employment needs presented by a growing economy operating in a global environment' (DoE 2001: 9). The National Plan set a target to shift the balance of enrolments between (i) humanities, (ii) business and commerce, and (iii) science, engineering and technology from 49%:26%:25% in 2001 to 40%:30%:30% by the end of the decade (DoE 2001: 27). Yet the Department of Education (DoE) has never been able to test the usefulness of these policy objectives through drawing up detailed correspondences between specific academic programmes at particular higher education institutions and actual sectoral needs located in specific regions of the country.

This 'policy gap' has had a negative effect, handicapping the ability of education and training institutions to offer courses customised to particular industrial development trajectories or technology platform needs. The fact that the stranglehold of this policy constraint may now be significantly reduced – because of the launch of new policy frameworks such as Asgisa and the NIPF – represents a very important opportunity for improved policy alignment.

The discussion now shifts to the second reason for greater alignment between industrial and skills development policies – this being the increasing emphasis in the international literature on the primacy of 'learning' in both educational and industrial settings.

'Learning' in education and enterprise settings

There is now a significant international literature which specifies the relationships between the global economy, the new knowledge and skills it requires, and the changed roles expected from education and training institutions. Most influential in this regard is the literature on new forms of work organisation, the 'National System of Innovation' literature and the entire field of 'evolutionary economics'. The latter has grown rapidly in the past two decades to challenge the conservative orthodoxies of neo-liberal economics and the 'Washington Consensus'. This new literature has become very influential in many of the world's multilateral agencies such as the United Nations Industrial Development Organisation (UNIDO), the Organisation for Economic Co-operation and Development (OECD) and the European Union (EU). Indeed, a recent study of South Africa's innovation system completed by the OECD has adopted this analytical lens to examine South Africa's science and technology base (see OECD 2007).

Four criticisms of neo-liberal orthodoxy dominate this new literature. Firstly, evolutionary economics argues that the success of the newly industrialised economies of the Pacific Rim over the past three decades did not arise because of the policy prescriptions of neo-classical economics. Rather, these economies succeeded because of strong state intervention in the economy, primarily through the establishment of effective non-market institutions which, through appropriate industrial, technology and human resources development strategies, acted to steer these Pacific Rim market economies along very successful growth trajectories. This growth did not occur because of unregulated market economics (Chang 2004; Hollingsworth & Boyer 1997).

The second criticism has to do with the idea in neo-classical economics that the economy is always at rest (equilibrium), or is undergoing well-anticipated changes; in terms of this idea, key decision-makers can calculate in a rational manner 'what is going on based on what they know securely' (Nelson 2006). These conditions simply do not hold in the real world. The new evolutionary theory argues that the economy is always in the process of change, with 'economic activity almost always proceeding in a context that is not completely familiar to the actors, or perfectly understood by them' (Nelson 2006: 2). The heightened state of flux which characterises most market transactions requires a more 'behavioural' and 'social' theory of firm-level activity – hence the rise of 'evolutionary' economics. Economic growth must be understood as an evolutionary process, driven endogenously by continuous change within the firm (Nelson 2006).

Thirdly, neo-classical economics postulates an extremely 'thin' institutional environment. The neo-classicist view is that if the market mechanism is allowed to work unrestrained by government, fewer institutional 'props' will be needed to ensure progress and growth (Chang 2004). Nelson maintains that this overly spare institutional picture fails to recognise the complexity of market relations, in particular, their embedding in broader social and institutional structures and the elements of co-operation and trust required if markets are to work well (Nelson 2006: 5–6).

And lastly, neo-classicism's treatment of 'technology' is by far the most flawed. It is seen as an exogenous variable (external to the firm), or in Lundvall and Borras's (1999: 43) terms, as 'manna from heaven' freely available for everyone to use 'off the shelf'. Firms optimise by choosing from this shelf according to their factor and product prices. The selected technology is 'absorbed costlessly and risklessly by the enterprise and used at efficient (best practice) levels' (Lall 2004: 95). Yet in the real world, we know that technological capabilities are largely firm-specific and societally determined. For example, technology's effective utilisation is largely dependent on, firstly, the tacit knowledge capabilities embedded in firms, and secondly, the way in which the firm is internally structured. Neo-classicism cannot address these questions. It has fallen to an emergent new economic discourse, 'evolutionary economics', to put the social element back into economic analysis.

It is significant that the primary focus of evolutionary economics is the study of the firm as a social as well as an economic institution, and in particular, the role played by 'learning' within the firm in the new global economy. An important corollary of this new emphasis on 'learning' is that the key issue with regard to enterprise skills is not the supply-side question of their provision on a suitable scale to meet industry needs, but more importantly, their productive deployment and utilisation within firms so as to promote continuous learning and improvement.

Inter-firm co-operation

In the search for continuous improvements in process engineering and product design and quality, firms are ultimately forced into relationships with other firms that are either suppliers of parts needed in production, or users of the firm's products. They all form part of the same value chain. Lundvall et al. (2002) argue that the most important knowledge flows have been the interactive forward and backward linkages between large upstream manufacturing producers and their downstream users. Their interactions have generated information flows about the product used. Commentary from users on product quality and other specifications of customer satisfaction have become important inputs into the new product generation process (Lundvall et al. 2002: 10).

These dynamic processes of knowledge interchange, along with dramatic changes in the organisational logic of firms and in the relationships between large and small firms, have led to a proliferation of networking forms. Castells has written the definitive work on the networked society (Castells 1996). He maintains that there are five distinct trends in the reshaping of large and small firms, each with very different origins. These trends are set out in Table 1.1.

Each of these five routes represents a different response to the search for greater production flexibility and profitability. The vertically integrated firm arose under Fordism as an attempt to reduce costs and minimise all elements of uncertainty, by absorbing these elements into the large firm. However, the down side of this approach was an increasingly complex and large structure which could only be managed via a massive bureaucracy and a steep hierarchy of supervisory labour. By the late 1970s, this structure proved to be a hindrance rather than an aid to profit, and firms began to reduce costs and improve efficiency by downsizing and sub-contracting production, maintenance, specialist producer services and marketing functions to other firms.

The links established today between the large corporation and sub-contracted firms are reciprocal, preferential and mutually beneficial networking relationships. Many small firms play a crucial role in

TABLE 1.1: *Five organisational trends in the evolution of network relations between firms*

Organisational trend	Description
1. The decline of the vertically integrated large corporation	Growing use is made of contracting out a number of functions previously incorporated within the large corporation. Small and medium firms now network with the large corporation to provide these services.
2. The revival of craft production	The advent of the new computer-automated technologies has allowed small and medium manufacturing companies to rejig equipment with minimal downtime to produce a wider variety of customised goods.
3. Toyotism	There has been adoption and adaptation of new methods of management and work organisation imported from Japan – for example, team work; continuous improvement; Just-In-Time (JIT) and Total Quality Management (TQM).
4. Networking amongst small companies	This 'networking' trend is distinct from that of sub-contracting as mentioned in trend 1 above. Here, small companies themselves take the initiative in setting up joint ventures in sharing research and development (R&D), marketing and export strategies.
5. Networking amongst large corporations	In this case, large companies form strategic alliances with other large and often foreign corporations – for example, IBM, Siemens and Toshiba – to focus on joint ventures in R&D, technology improvement, market sharing and the development of new products.

Source: Adapted from Castells 1996.

providing larger firms with high-quality inputs into production. Increasingly, these relations of interdependence are cemented in long-term supplier-buyer co-operative agreements. Networking, then, has provided the large corporation with a new dynamism and renewed profitability.

The shift to knowledge intensity

Kaplinsky and Morris (2001) use value chain analysis to foreground the fundamental changes which have occurred in the global economy, and in particular, in the attainment of profitability. They argue that the value chain is an important construct for understanding the distribution of economic returns arising across the myriad sets of activities which characterise a modern firm: design, production, marketing, co-ordination and recycling.

Applying Schumpeterian insights which lie at the heart of 'evolutionary economics', Kaplinsky and Morris argue that economic rents accrue to those parties who are able to protect themselves from competition. They most often arise from control over scarce physical resources such as land and machinery and through barriers to entry (the creation of 'scarcity'). But economic rents can also accrue over intangible assets such as entrepreneurship. When entrepreneurs innovate, they create 'new combinations or conditions, which provide greater returns from the price of a product than are required to meet the cost of the innovation. These returns to innovation are a form of super profit and act as an inducement to replication by other entrepreneurs also seeking to acquire a part of this profit' (Kaplinsky & Morris 2001: 26).

Economic rents also accrue to particular capabilities within the firm itself, for example, technological, organisational, skills and marketing capabilities. Most importantly in the current period, they may also arise from purposeful activities taking place between groups of firms – these are referred to as 'relational rents' (Kaplinsky & Morris 2001: 26).

These rents are increasingly dynamic, in that they are quickly eroded by the forces of competition, after which these producer rents are then transferred into consumer surpluses in the form of lower prices to the benefit of consumers. The cyclical search for 'new combinations' that enable new forms of economic rent, and the subsequent bidding away of this economic rent by competitors, lies at the heart of the innovation process of modern-day capitalism.

An important tendency in the innovation process globally is the shift towards greater knowledge intensity in production – where the basis for new economic rents is not so much found in the material production sphere as it is in value-adding activities such as design, branding and marketing. Rents are derived both within the firm (endogenously) but also externally (exogenously). Classic endogenous rents include:
- technology rents – having command over scarce technologies;
- human resource rents – having access to better skills than competitors;
- organisational rents – possessing superior forms of internal organisation;
- marketing rents – possessing better marketing capabilities and/or valuable brand names (Kaplinsky & Morris 2001: 28).

Other rents are exogenous to the chain and arise through natural-resource endowments, particular state policies and regulatory environments:
- resource rents – access to scarce natural resources;
- policy rents – operating in an environment of efficient government;
- infrastructural rents – access to high-quality infrastructural inputs such as telecommunications;
- financial rents – access to finance on better terms than competitors (Kaplinsky & Morris 2001: 28).

Tangible resources such as land, technology and capital have become increasingly widespread. Because of this, the new competitive advantage lies with the intangible resources of firms. Kaplinsky and Morris argue (2001: 34) that in the present period we are 'witnessing a transition from rents accruing from tangible activities to those arising from intangible activities in the value chain'. Here they refer to the increasingly knowledge- and skill-intensive activities and competencies of firms. These shifts have impacted across the globe in a highly uneven way, with intangible activities such as design, R&D, branding, marketing, logistics and financial services being concentrated in the industrially developed countries and tangible activities (actual production) being contracted out to a large band of middle-income developing countries such as China, India, Mexico, South Korea and Singapore – countries with low wages and highly developed process manufacturing competencies (Kaplinsky & Morris 2001: 101).

Tacit knowledge

Tacit knowledge is the primary intangible asset of firms. It is practical, experiential knowledge which all employees in work contexts acquire – including managers, R&D specialists and shop-floor production workers. It is the opposite of codified knowledge which is formal and procedural knowledge, organised in a range of academically based disciplines, and publicly available through academic study and research. These two knowledge forms are related. They co-exist, with some forms of tacit knowledge becoming codified over time. Tacit knowledge is acquired in contexts of application, whereas codified knowledge is distributed largely via the university and science system (Gibbons et al. 1994).

Tacit knowledge is privately held expertise. It cannot be bought 'off the shelf'. It is not a tradable commodity and cannot be transacted through market exchanges (Lundvall & Borras 1999: 48). Information technologies are speeding up the process of knowledge codification, and its distribution is made more easily available. But this process will never bring to an end the existence of tacit knowledge because of the dependence of the innovation process on human ingenuity. Individuals will always be needed to close the knowledge gap between theoretical codified knowledge and the actual practical tasks that need to be accomplished.

Tacit knowledge is not only invested in individuals, but more importantly, is embedded in firms themselves, through specific managerial strategies and workplace routines, norms of behaviour, professional and institutional cultures, and codes of information employed in the design, production and marketing stages of firm activity (Gibbons et al. 1994: 25; Lundvall & Borras 1999: 46).

Networks are also repositories of tacit knowledge. In fact, they have become the principal means by which firms strengthen their new information sets. Networks open up possibilities of new ways of doing things – through the sharing, transfer and diffusion of internally acquired tacit competences across the network.

As indicated earlier, successfully harnessing this mix of individual, firm and network forms of tacit knowledge, through effective processes of knowledge circulation, has become the new competitive advantage of firms and nations in the global economy today:

> The competitive advantage of a firm lies less in its pool of proprietary knowledge than on its base of tacit competence. As proprietary knowledge is utilised it is subject to imitation, adaptation and replacement and gradually loses its market value. Tacit knowledge can only be acquired by hiring the people who possess it and it is the principal way a firm may replenish its basket of unique technologies. (Gibbons et al. 1994: 26)

A firm's ability to access these repositories of tacit knowledge has been termed its 'dynamic capabilities' (Teece & Pisano 1998: 193; Winter 2002). The winners in the global marketplace have been those firms that can demonstrate timely responsiveness and rapid and flexible product innovation, coupled most importantly with the 'management capability to effectively coordinate and redeploy internal and external competences' (Teece & Pisano 1998: 193). This twofold concept refers both to the rapidly changing economic environment and also to the 'key role of strategic management in appropriately adapting, integrating, and re-configuring internal and external organisational skills, resources, and functional competences towards the changing environment' (Teece & Pisano 1998: 194). These capabilities are distinctive and are difficult to replicate. Many firms may acquire impressive technological and educational endowments, but may fall short on dynamic capabilities because they have failed managerially to harness the tacit competences hidden beneath the formal structures of the firm. This is particularly so when environmental shifts in the market force firms to respond with speed.

Design, engineering, entrepreneurial and managerial capabilities

In a recent review of South Africa's innovation system, the OECD introduced a cognate concept to that of 'tacit knowledge' and firm-level 'dynamic capability' in a more useful and pragmatic language. The review introduced the concept of a firm's 'design, engineering, technical and managerial capabilities'. The report argued that South Africa should give greater recognition in practical terms to the importance of these non-R&D capabilities – those concerned with engineering, design and related management and technical functions. The OECD saw these activities as 'innovation-generators in their own right and as the seed-beds in enterprises from which more formally organised R&D emerges' (OECD 2007: 12).

In short, what the OECD is saying is that the education system is not the only producer of human capability and valuable knowledge. Firms achieve these outcomes as well. Indeed, the report goes as far as saying that the success of the entire innovation strategy will depend largely on the 'depth and diversity of innovation capabilities that are accumulated by, and deployed in business enterprises' (OECD 2007: 88).

The report creates the useful acronym DEEM (design, engineering, entrepreneurial and managerial) for these non-R&D, firm-based capabilities that every enterprise deploys in divergent ways, and argues that innovation policies need to support these activities.

DEEM-level activity and formal R&D co-exist in a creative symbiosis, often through dispersed networks, or as Gibbons et al. (1994) put it, in socially distributed forms of knowledge production. These activities provide a stream of incremental innovation during the operation of existing facilities. DEEM capabilities provide the basis for continuous streams of process improvement that have a major impact on productivity and costs. This requires 'in-house capabilities that are deeply embedded in the details of the specific markets and technologies of individual firms' (OECD 2007: 101).

Recognising sectoral differentiation

The argument of this chapter so far has established two things: firstly, the significance of learning processes in the workplace, and secondly, the need to align skills development policies to these enterprise learning conditions in each sector. The precise form of this alignment will vary, being highly dependent on the specificities of each sector. As such, policy alignment will be a highly differentiated process.

A number of theoretical contributions in differing disciplines assist in understanding the determinants of sectoral differentiation, in particular, value chain analysis, innovation studies and work organisation literature. Value chain analysis emphasises the full range of activities which are required to bring a product or service to market – from conception and design through to production methods and marketing, and finally, from consumption to final disposal through waste and recycling. There are two value chain typologies which give rise to differing industrial structures: buyer-driven and producer-driven value chains. Producer-driven value chains are those in which large manufacturing firms play the central role in co-ordinating production networks through their backward and forward linkages with other firms. They command vital technologies and they take responsibility for assisting the efficiency of both their suppliers and their customers. These value chains are common in capital- and technology-intensive industries such as automobiles, aircraft, computers, semiconductors and heavy machinery (Kaplinsky & Morris 2001: 32–33).

Buyer-driven value chains are dominated by large retailers or marketers. These value chains are common in labour-intensive consumer goods industries such as garments, footwear and consumer electronics. Production is generally carried out by tiered networks of contractors that make finished goods for large-scale buyers. The specifications are supplied by the large retailers that order the goods (Kaplinsky & Morris 2001: 32–33).

Another significant body of literature – on the organisation of work – argues that it is the 'business strategies' of firms that determine the extent of differentiation between firms within the same sector, and between identical sectors across national boundaries. Business strategies that prioritise value-addition through innovative uses of new technology and work organisational methods are likely to perform more strongly in knowledge-intensive markets than firms that focus only on cost and standardisation of tasks. For the latter category of employers, business strategy is based on standardised technical operations and task-focused inter-personal relations, both of which require minimal inputs of skill and firm-level learning. As a consequence, training policies that:

> …exhort employers to train more…beyond the operational level [are] pointless and counter-productive. Resources devoted to such an 'undifferentiated' skills policy are likely to be wasteful. (Ashton & Sung 2006: 25)

The differing social and cultural forms of organisation that prevail within industries, and which have emerged incrementally over time, also have a powerful influence over sectoral characteristics. Wolfe (2002) argues that if an industry already enjoys a cohesive organisational culture and has a strong set of sector-specific associations with a tradition of acting collectively to solve joint problems, there will be a stronger basis for the sector to search collectively for solutions to economic challenges. Alternatively, 'to the extent that the sector is characterised by a more fragmented and competitive business culture, the solutions chosen will most likely reflect this underlying culture' (Wolfe 2002: 232).

A third influential body of work is Pavitt's taxonomy of innovation in industry which he developed in 1984 and amended in 1990 (Pavitt 1984, 1990). In this work, he established five types of sectors based on differing sources of innovation:
1   *supplier-dominated sectors* such as textiles, where most technological innovation comes from outside the firm, where new technologies mainly come embodied in new components and equipment, where the diffusion of new know-how occurs mainly through learning by doing and using;
2   *scale-intensive sectors* such as auto and steel, which rely on economies of scale in which the production process is highly standardised/automated and capital-intensive. Innovation occurs both internally (learning by doing and in-house R&D) as well as externally (equipment producers);
3   *specialised suppliers* such as machinery and equipment producers, where innovation is based on interactive learning with lead users of their machinery, and where customisation is based on meeting exacting client specifications. The sources of innovation are both internal (the tacit knowledge and experience of skilled technicians) and external (user-producer interactions);
4   *science-based sectors* such as pharmaceuticals, which are characterised by high rates of product and process innovations founded on high levels of internal R&D as well as extensive university-industry linkages; and finally
5   *information-intensive firms*, largely in the services sector, with the main source of innovation being information processing software and systems development (Pavitt 1984, 1990).

Firms operating in each of these differing sectoral typologies are likely to stress different features of the innovation process. For example, for automobile firms, effective feedback between product design and manufacture within the firm is more important than feedback between product design and university research. For pharmaceuticals, the reverse would be true (Pavitt 2003: 20).

Irrespective of the taxonomy chosen, it is clear that sectors differ in profound ways and any industrial, technological or skills development initiative of government will have to be finely attuned to these nuances. Not all sectors are high-tech. Many remain traditional and low-tech. However, this does not mean that they possess zero potential for growth based on enhanced learning strategies: 'The learning potential may differ between sectors and technologies but in all sectors there will be niches where the potential for learning is high.' (Lundvall & Borras 1999: 35).

In recognising the importance of sectoral differentiation, this book (as mentioned at the outset of this chapter) segments the fourteen individual sector studies into five distinct groupings, influenced strongly by Pavitt's typologies but also by the cluster proposals of the NIPF.

The role of government

It is now necessary to discuss the governance and regulation of policy domains that, in the new global economic environment, need to be more effectively integrated. There are two primary mechanisms which enable governments to achieve greater cross-departmental integration. These are: the more effective horizontal co-ordination of multiple government departments at the national (macro) level, and the more effective deployment of intermediary agencies that perform brokerage functions between the state and employers at the micro level. The discussion will now turn to these two crucial institutional mechanisms.

Horizontal co-ordination

Horizontal co-ordination is necessary because of the limits of orthodox forms of political administration which tend to be hierarchical, bureaucratic and vertical. As Edler, Kuhlmann and Smits argue, current forms of political administration are characterised by the following features:

- A high degree of departmentalisation and sectoralisation of political administration exists because of low inter-departmental exchange and co-operation.
- Few governance attempts are made at linking the many heterogeneous elements which characterise the current social order.
- Several failed attempts at developing more horizontal forms of co-operation exist because of institutional inertia and stakeholder resistance.
- 'Linear' approaches to governmental intervention dominate over more 'interactive' models that are more appropriate to multi-agency contexts.
- There is a general inability to deal proactively with the challenge of increasing cross-sectoral linkages in government through, for example, the development of cross-sectoral government networks such as horizontal taskforces, sectoral councils and foresight initiatives (Edler, Kuhlmann & Smits 2003).

These problems are not new. However, the pressure to achieve horizontal co-ordination more effectively has spiralled in recent times for several reasons. The first has to do with improved communications technology which allow for more seamless public-sector communication, and therefore the promise of improved government delivery. Hence, the benchmarks for government service delivery have risen.

In addition, there are more cross-cutting social issues on the agenda than ever before – for example, climate change, renewable energy and global social policy issues such as child poverty, AIDS orphans and homelessness. In addition, international trade and global financial flows have forced different governance agencies to work together in ways unprecedented in the past.

But perhaps the most important causal factor for the increased demand for horizontal co-ordination in government has been the dramatic advances made in science and technology which have co-evolved alongside similar socio-economic and organisational changes – changes which have often taken the form of increased networking between firms and government agencies, as well as clustering, agglomeration and the consolidation of linkages along supply chains in most industries. All of these developments have intensified the need for more cross-sectoral co-ordination.

The characteristics of horizontal co-ordination

Bakvis and Juillet (2004) define horizontal co-ordination as the management of a set of activities between two or more organisational units, where the units in question do not have hierarchical control over each other and where the aim is to generate outcomes that cannot be achieved by units working in isolation. They speak of a continuum of horizontal co-ordination with 'informal networks at one end and a fully fledged secretariat at the other'. Between the two poles would be working groups and inter-departmental committees with varying degrees of institutionalisation (Bakvis & Juillet 2004: 4).

Edler, Kuhlmann and Smits specify several characteristics of effective horizontal co-ordination, which include:
- taking into account the systemic and co-evolutionary nature of issues such as 'HRD' (human resource development) and 'industrial innovation';
- developing an institutional reflexivity, understood as the capacity to think in terms of the 'whole';
- taking advantage of the interdependencies between specific policy measures and the inter-relationships between differing policy areas;
- creating and maintaining a culture of reliability and trust between competing actor groups in government;
- building an infrastructure for 'strategic intelligence' across several inter-linked sources;
- reorganising the political administration in a way that enables flexible horizontal co-ordination and exchange among formally divided entities (Edler, Kulmann & Smits 2003).

Representations of horizontal co-ordination in South African policy

South African policy texts post-1994 are replete with references to the need for horizontal co-ordination. For example, the NIPF of the Department of Trade and Industry (DTI) (DTI 2007) makes strong reference to the interdependencies between its industrial policy objectives and the impact of policies operating under the control of other departments. With regard to skills and science and technology issues, the new industrial policy framework argues that:

> ...there is a need for far greater integration between industrial and skills policy and implementation, particularly with respect to sector strategies. This is in areas such as ensuring that sector and SETA strategies and implementation are more aligned; also, with respect to the development and attraction of scarce skills and related migration issues. In relation to the latter, a strong link between industrial policy and immigration policy must be established…[And finally] the Department of Science and Technology is the key driver of technology policy in South Africa. However, there is currently inadequate integration and funding of technology related initiatives. Closer coordination will be forged. (DTI 2007: 46–47)

The cluster system implemented by President Mbeki in his management of the Cabinet is perhaps the most important example of attempts to improve horizontal co-ordination in South Africa. Cognate departments in key areas such as social and economic policy are grouped together at the level of ministers and directors-general, who are required to plan short- to medium-term strategies for achieving presidential priorities such as job creation, poverty alleviation and HRD. These plans are interrogated, adapted and finally approved by the President and Cabinet at six-monthly lekgotlas, which take place in January and July of each year. In almost all cases, acute social problems are seen as arising cross-sectorally, their reform requiring joined-up government action. The Policy Co-ordination and Advisory Services Unit in the Office of the Presidency helps to administer and co-ordinate all of these activities.

Even though the cluster system appears to have some impact, particularly in presidential campaigns such as the Asgisa strategy, proposals for a mega-co-ordinating council have continued to be made in recent policy texts. The NIPF hints at the idea of such a super-ministry (DTI 2007: 28), although ultimately it does not propose changes to the status quo. Similarly, the DST is in the process of launching a new super-co-ordinating body, the Foundation for Technology Innovation (FTI). However, this body's co-ordination mandate is restricted to technological innovation and does not cover the entire gamut of economic and industrial development (DST 2002: 38). The recent OECD review of South Africa's innovation system suggests that such a super-agency is still needed and its mandate should be wider than innovation understood narrowly:

> Research and innovation governance in South Africa appears to lag good international practice…There is no forum or arena at the highest level of government that can play a strong integrative role across the whole of government, not least in balancing the various policies and instruments that in practice combine to make up innovation and research policy. This is compounded by the normal difficulties in co-ordination across different ministries, despite the innovative use of clustering among them. (OECD 2007: 141)

In proposing the more effective co-ordination of innovation across the national economy, the OECD review uses a template to describe four key levels of governance:

- *Level 1* is the highest level. This involves setting overall directions and priorities across the whole of national government. It may be achieved through advice to government or by more binding means, such as decisions of a Cabinet sub-committee.
- *Level 2* is co-ordination amongst ministries, whose sectoral responsibilities otherwise encourage them to pursue independent policies. Sometimes an inter-ministerial group also functions as the Level 1 co-ordination mechanism.
- *Level 3* is more operational, entailing the work of intermediary agencies. This level, too, can involve administrative co-ordination as well as more substantive co-ordination, for example, of funding activities through co-programming.
- *Level 4* involves co-ordination among those who actually implement policies. Co-ordination at this level tends to be achieved through self-organisation rather than through using formal mechanisms.

According to the OECD report, the most important issue with regard to horizontal co-ordination is undoubtedly whether there is a Level 1 agency in place or not. Such bodies are common across the globe, and many are charged with the responsibility of driving national economic growth and innovation strategies:

> Science, industrial and technology policies often involve issues that cut across the responsibilities of many different government ministries and agencies and, therefore, it is useful to have a pilot agency that has the power and the legitimacy to co-ordinate activities across different agencies and resolve potential conflicts between them. In some countries, the pilot agency took the form of powerful planning ministries with formal power to over-rule other ministries and agencies (the Economic Planning Board of Korea and the Commissariat Général du Plan of France). In others, it assumed the form of a co-ordinating committee (the Industrial Development Bureau of Taiwan) or even a single ministry (the Ministry of International Trade and Industry of Japan, where the Economic Planning Agency was powerless) with more informal power over other government agencies. However, the underlying principle is the same – you need an agency that has some power to co-ordinate different interests within and outside the government. (Chang 2004)

The Singapore case of the Economic Development Board (EDB) is a good example here. Singapore set up the EDB to co-ordinate economic and industrial policy, offer incentives to guide foreign investors into targeted activities, promote education and training in fields demanded by the economy, and in general, 'mastermind industrial policy'. It played an important role in launching and promoting certain activities which the private sector would not otherwise have entered, acting as a catalyst for increased investment (Brown et al. 2001; Lall 2004).

Intermediary agencies

Horizontal co-ordination on its own will not suffice in attempts to align skills development with industrial policies. It is at the level of implementation – at the meso and micro levels – that the extent of alignment will be determined.

The state, as a large bureaucratic entity, is not well positioned to interact with employers in its attempts at implementing policy. The traditional view of the state is that it is bureaucratic, rigid in its application of rule-based operational procedures, and inflexible in the face of change. Its mode of regulation is one of 'command and control' (Wolfe & Gertler 2002). Overcoming this organisational gulf between traditional state structures and the new forms of networking between firms is a major task for modern governments, especially in key policy areas highly dependent on co-operative relations, including industrial policy, enterprise training and small business development.

The primary mechanism for achieving policy implementation 'on the ground', according to evolutionary economists, consists of strategically placed institutional intermediaries who play an interlocutor role between state and capital. Chang (2004) – from an industrial policy perspective – argues that the task of intermediary organisations is to induce private actors into new activities which they would have had no interest in entering under free-market conditions. As Chang suggests, a hypothetical electronics industry which does not exist today has nobody to advance its interests – even though it might be very successful tomorrow and beneficial to all (Chang 2004: 167). Closing this gap – between public policy (for example, a new electronics industry) and the narrower interests of the local entrepreneurial community – is no easy task.

There is now a growing literature on the characteristics needed by these intermediary bodies if they are to succeed in their task of convincing private actors about the benefits of public policy:
- A high-quality bureaucracy: Chang argues against the fallacious perception that the highly effective East-Asian bureaucracies evolved easily because of inherited Confucian cultural traditions of discipline and a strong work ethic. It should be remembered, he notes, that both Korea and Taiwan were characterised by inefficient and incompetent bureaucracies in the 1950s. Yet within a relatively short period of two decades, very competent bureaucracies had been created by the late 1970s. The same can be said of France after the Second World War, where deliberate state efforts went into creating and training an elite and highly competent modern civil service (Chang 2004: 166, 169). These purposive actions can be replicated elsewhere.
- Expert familiarity with localised interests: Crouch et al. argue that these intermediary agencies need to 'embody a model of non-bureaucratic operation, both entrepreneurial and co-operative in an attempt to get closer to local networks' than is possible in traditional relations with the state. These agencies need to be sufficiently external to the local entrepreneurial system so as not to be captured by narrow interests, but also 'close enough to work within rather than against the network concept' (Crouch et al. 1999: 174). Writing from a vocational education and training perspective, these writers argue that intermediary agencies need to advise firms from an authority based on 'constantly updated knowledge so that firm competencies can be ratcheted up and so that educational institutions and relevant government departments can be kept in touch with what is required' (Crouch et al. 1999: 232).
- Incorruptible: The staff of agencies need to commit to a professional work ethic which discourages being 'captured' by narrow sectional interests at the expense of wider, more collective public policy goals (Lall 2004: 121).

- Visionary: These agencies need to provide entrepreneurial vision which can act as 'focal points' around which private-sector decisions can be made and co-ordinated. This 'visioning' includes activities such as indicative planning, detailed industry studies, the encouragement of private actors to form collective associations such as value chains or regional clusters, and the continuation of 'dialogue' amongst private actors themselves 'to forge a common vision' (Chang 2004: 170; Crouch et al. 1999: 174).

There are several types of intermediary agencies offering a wide array of services to firms in localised, sectoral and regional settings – services that can range from enterprise training, technology transfer, venture capital provision, support for small businesses, and financial and business planning to the formation of 'dialogic' associations of firms with common interests.

As suggested earlier, the evolutionary literature sees these interactions between firms and with the state as a 'learning process'. Wolfe and Gertler (2002) argue for a more expansive view of learning to include institutions and the state itself in processes they term 'social learning':

> The capacity for social learning and increased networking may be seen as essential for tapping into the shared intelligence of both the individual firm or organisation, as well as a collectivity of firms within a given geographic space. This form of shared or networked learning assumes that neither the public sector nor individual private enterprises are the source of all wisdom; rather, the process of innovation and institutional adaptation is essentially an interactive one in which the means for establishing supportive social relations and of communicating insights and knowledge in all its various forms are crucial to the outcomes. (Wolfe & Gertler 2002: 3)

This view of the state sees its main task as that of facilitating the circulation of knowledge between private actors, and between the private sector and intermediary agencies. Knowledge circulation plays a key role in resolving the 'cognitive uncertainty' of private actors who are unsure about the consequences of their choice to change their ways of interacting with other private actors (Culpepper 2003: 22).

This transformation in the role of the state – from its traditional bureaucratic to its new learning role – requires a distinction to be made between two types of knowledge forms:
- Standardised bureaucratic information: Culpepper maintains that the 'bureaucratic tools of information gathering are very adept at summarising aggregate features of the labour market'.
- Relational information: this type of information is obtained from private actors through dialogic means – 'embedded policy making' – and seeks to change societal patterns of co-ordination by persuading wavering private actors to change their economic behaviour (Culpepper 2003: 58).

Efforts by intermediary agencies to gain relational information are important attempts at resolving the classic 'market failure' problem in neo-classical economics – that of asymmetric information and uncertainty. This occurs when one party to a transaction or potential transaction has more or better information than the other party. In the absence of relational information, private actors are reluctant to co-operate with each other or to act in certain ways because they do not know what the reciprocal action of their market counterparts will be. Apprenticeship training is the classic example. Investing in such training is risky because trained workers can be poached by other companies who 'free-ride'. The possibility of poaching limits the willingness of the company to train unless it knows that many other companies would make the same training investment to the benefit of all (Culpepper 2003: 5).

The uncertainty relating to the benefits of a reform – even when that reform will clearly improve the future income of a majority of private players – can be sufficient to block the adoption of such a reform. The actions of these private actors may well thwart the ability of governments to achieve their public policy goals (Culpepper 2003: 5).

In the age of the learning economy, uncertainty about the impact of change has grown. Metcalfe (2005) sees the process of innovation as accentuating this uncertainty and information asymmetry. Innovation is, first and foremost, a matter of experimentation. It is the principal way in which a firm can acquire a competitive advantage over its business rivals:

> As a process of experimentation, a discovery process, the outcomes are necessarily uncertain; no firm can foresee whether rivals will produce better innovations; nor, even when all technical problems are solved, can it know in advance that consumers will pay a price and purchase a quantity that justifies the outlay of resources to generate a new or improved product or manufacturing process. (Metcalfe 2005: 11)

Relations of trust go a long way towards reducing this uncertainty. Trust and social capital built between competing firms help to make the behaviour of private actors more consistent, predictable and reliable. This often entails full revelation of what private actors regard as relevant information for the other party and restraint in exploiting the temporary weakness of partners (Lundvall et al. 2002).

The state and decentralised co-operation

Public policies are often thwarted and blocked by private actor inertia or opposition. Public policies often attempt to induce change through incentives and sanctions, but these often backfire. If the majority of private actors are not persuaded that the new policies and the new institutions will work, the sanctions then apply to everybody, not a minority, and in so doing, 'sanctions lose their reputational sting. When everyone defects, it is very hard to mete out sanctions to the whole population' (Culpepper 2003: 8).

Culpepper's view on the efficacy of public policy is not all doom and gloom. As an evolutionary economist, he believes that the state can intervene constructively through industrial, technology, education, training and small business development policies to facilitate firm-level adjustments to the new conditions of competition. He argues that local information is private information that is asymmetrically held. Policy-makers hoping to secure co-operation must acquire this 'situated knowledge' – intimate, deeply proprietary knowledge. As local actors co-operate and learn from each other, their interaction and experimentation create a base of useful knowledge which helps all actors to resolve uncertainty and information asymmetry. Collective knowledge generation such as this also creates the conditions for new or improved economic activities to ensue. Networks of firms engaged in deliberative association promote common, jointly constructed interests, thereby facilitating co-ordination (Culpepper 2003: 18). Lessons learned by one firm can be passed on to other local experimenters while laggards are held accountable for failure to perform according to jointly agreed-on standards (2003: 19). Private associations, when they have these networking capacities, are 'far better at fashioning strategies than are states' (2003: 21).

How is relational information acquired?

Culpepper believes that firm-level associations are best positioned to acquire this relational information. They are the 'most reliable societal interlocutors for the state' (Culpepper 2003: 50). Not all associations can play this role. It is only those that have 'dialogic capacity' to acquire privately owned information which makes it possible to develop problem-solving strategies for a collectivity of firms

that are useful interlocutors. Culpepper segments private actors into two distinct camps in relation to any given public policy:
- 'waverers' who have a low co-operative threshold – they could be convinced of the benefits of co-operation;
- confirmed 'defectors' – their barriers to co-operation are very high and no policy incentive or sanction will work.

Culpepper's view of effective public policy is one where the state and its intermediaries apply such a 'segmentation' strategy to the collective of private actors. Once these two camps are defined, the state should concentrate on the waverers in terms of changing behaviour. Culpepper believes that through participation in various iterative rounds of co-operation, the benefits of future rounds will become more obvious to waverers. This process will create its own accelerated momentum when the benefits of collective production of goods – training, regional export support, small-firm development subsidies, joint R&D initiatives – become apparent (Culpepper 2003: 57). These deliberative associations help actors to develop solutions collectively that they might not get to on their own.

Conclusion

It is clear from this theoretical exposition of the evolutionary literature on firm-state interactions that a number of conditions are necessary if the more effective alignment of skills development and industrial policy is to be achieved in South Africa. The implementation of both policy domains will require very similar institutional conditions. The most important of these are the following:
- Such policies will need to be embedded in appropriate structures that are 'institutionally intimate' with employers and their specific sectoral needs, and which provide the state with conduits to privately held knowledge and information – 'situated knowledge' – not usually volunteered by private actors in competitive market relations.
- These institutional agencies will be required to achieve forms of 'deliberative association' with the state and other firms which succeed in moving private actors beyond points they would not normally pass on their own.

Intermediary agencies exist in both the skills development and industrial policy environments. The Skills Development Act of 1998 led to the formation of 25 SETAs. These organisations are key interlocutor agencies located between the state and the collectivity of firms in each sector. Similarly, in the industrial policy environment, a second set of intermediary vehicles has been launched since the mid-1990s, these being the plethora of small-business development agencies. The key policy question therefore, in both instances, is whether the state, operating through these two types of intermediary agencies, has succeeded in the implementation of its crucial skills and industrial development policy frameworks. Have private actors – both large and small firms – been encouraged and incentivised to act in ways that they would not normally act in the pursuit of government's new industrial and skills objectives? Has the state succeeded in acquiring 'situated knowledge' through the acquisition of highly intimate and proprietary knowledge which private firms would normally not reveal?

At the macro (national) level, similar questions need to be asked: has there been increased horizontal co-ordination between the four key departments involved in skills and industrial development: the Departments of Education, Labour, Trade and Industry, and Science and Technology? Have more 'interactive' modes of governance emerged?

The remaining chapters in this book will shed light on these crucial questions across thirteen priority sectors of the South African economy and in three technology areas. The concluding chapter will then provide an overview analysis based on the evidence derived from the sectoral case studies, which will address the key issues raised by these questions.

References

Ashton D & Sung J (2006) *How competitive strategy matters? Understanding the drivers of training, learning and performance at the firm level.* Research Paper 66, Centre for Labour Market Studies, University of Leicester

Bakvis H & Juillet L (2004) *The horizontal challenge: Line departments, central agencies and leadership.* Ottawa: Canada School of Public Service

Brown P, Green A & Lauder H (2001) *High skills, globalisation, competitiveness and skill formation.* Oxford: Oxford University Press

Castells M (1996) *The rise of the network society: The information age: economy, society and culture.* Oxford: Blackwell

Chang HJ (2004) Institutional foundations for effective design and implementation of trade and industrial policies in least developed economies. In C Soludo, O Ogbu & HJ Chang (eds) *The politics of trade and industrial policy in Africa: Forced consensus?* New Jersey: Africa World Press and Canada: International Development Research Centre

Crouch C, Finegold D & Sako M (1999) *Are skills the answer? The political economy of skill creation in advanced industrial countries.* Oxford: Oxford University Press

Culpepper PD (2003) *Creating cooperation: How states develop human capital in Europe.* Ithaca, NY: Cornell University Press

DACST (Department of Arts, Culture, Science and Technology, South Africa) (1996) *White paper on science and technology: Preparing for the 21st century.* Pretoria: DACST

DoE (Department of Education, South Africa) (2001) *National plan for higher education.* Pretoria: DoE

DoL (Department of Labour, South Africa) (1996) *Green paper on a new integrated human resources development strategy for South Africa.* Draft Version. Pretoria: DoL

DoL (1997) *Green paper on a skills development strategy for economic and employment growth in South Africa.* Final Version. Pretoria: DoL

DST (Department of Science and Technology, South Africa) (2001) *A national biotechnology strategy for South Africa.* Pretoria: DST

DST (2002) *National research and development strategy.* Pretoria: DST

DST (2003) *A national advanced manufacturing technology strategy for South Africa.* Pretoria: DST

DST (2007) *Innovation towards a knowledge-based economy: Ten-year plan for South Africa.* Pretoria: DST

DTI (Department of Trade and Industry, South Africa) (2002) *Accelerating growth and development: The contribution of an integrated manufacturing strategy.* Pretoria: DTI

DTI (2007) *A national industrial policy framework (NIPF).* Pretoria: DTI

Edler J, Kuhlmann S & Smits R (2003) *New governance for innovation: The need for horizontal and systemic policy coordination.* Report on a workshop held at the Fraunhofer Institute for Systems and Innovation Research, Karlsruhe, Germany, November 2002

Gibbons M, Limoges C, Nowotny H, Schwartzman S, Scott P & Trow M (1994) *The new production of knowledge: The dynamics of science and research in contemporary societies.* London: Sage

Hollingsworth JR & Boyer R (eds) (1997) *Contemporary capitalism: The embeddedness of institutions.* Cambridge: Cambridge University Press. Accessed 6 April 2005, http://www.aidc.co.za/index.php?pid=1185&ct=1

Kaplinsky R & Morris M (2001) *A handbook for value chain research.* Ottawa: International Development Research Centre

Lall S (2004) Selected industrial and trade policies in developing countries: Theoretical and empirical issues. In C Soludo, O Ogbu & HJ Chang (eds) *The politics of trade and industrial policy in Africa: Forced consensus?* New Jersey: Africa World Press and Canada: International Development Research Centre

Lowitt S & Altman M (2008) Overview of the economy and economic policy. In A Kraak & K Press (eds) *Human resource development review 2008: Education, employment and skills in South Africa.* Cape Town: HSRC Press

Lundvall BA & Borras S (1999) *Targeted socio-economic research. The globalising learning economy: Implications for innovation policy.* Luxembourg: Office for Official Publications of the European Communities

Lundvall BA, Johnson B, Andersen ES & Dalum B (2002) National systems of production, innovation and competence building. *Research Policy* 31(2): 213–231

Metcalfe JS (2005) *Innovation, competition and enterprise: Foundations for economic evolution in learning economies*. Discussion Paper No. 71, Centre for Research on Innovation and Competition, University of Manchester

Mlambo-Ngcuka P (2006) Address delivered by the Deputy President at the launch of the Joint Initiative for Priority Skills Acquisition (Jipsa) at the Presidential Guest House. Pretoria: Office of the Deputy President, 27 March

Nelson RR (2006) *Economic development from the perspective of evolutionary economic theory*. Working Papers in Technology Governance and Economic Dynamics No. 2, University of Technology, Tallin, Norway

OECD (Organisation for Economic Co-operation and Development) (2007) *Review of South Africa's innovation policy*. Paris: Directorate for Science, Technology and Industry, OECD

Pavitt K (1984) Sectoral patterns of technical change: Towards a taxonomy and a theory. *Research Policy* 13: 343–373

Pavitt K (1990) What we know about the strategic management of technology. *California Management Review* 32: 17–26

Pavitt K (2003) *The process of innovation*. Occasional Paper No. 89, Science Policy Research Unit, Sussex University

PCAS (Policy Co-ordination and Advisory Services, South Africa) (2006) *A catalyst for Accelerated and Shared Growth – South Africa (Asgisa): Background document*. Pretoria: Office of the Presidency

Rodrik D (2004) Industrial policy for the twenty-first century. Unpublished mimeo, Harvard University, Boston

Teece DJ & Pisano G (1998) The dynamic capabilities of firms: An introduction. In J Chytry, G Dosi & DJ Teece (eds) *Technology, organization, and competitiveness: Perspectives on industrial and corporate change*. Oxford: Oxford University Press

Winter SG (2002) Understanding dynamic capabilities. Unpublished mimeo, Reginald H Jones Center, The Wharton School of Business, Philadelphia

Wolfe DA (2002) Negotiating order: Sectoral policies and social learning in Ontario. In MS Gertler & DA Wolfe (eds) *Innovation and social learning: Institutional adaptation in an era of technological change*. New York: Palgrave Macmillan

Wolfe DA & Gertler MS (2002) Innovation and social learning: An introduction. In MS Gertler & DA Wolfe (eds) *Innovation and social learning: Institutional adaptation in an era of technological change*. New York: Palgrave Macmillan

2 | HIGH-TECH SECTORS

CHAPTER 2

On the brink? Skills demand and supply issues in the South African automotive components industry

Justin Barnes

Introduction

The automotive assembly and components industry is South Africa's leading manufacturing sector. This is evident across a range of broader economic and firm-level competitiveness Key Performance Indicators (Barnes & Black 2005). However, notwithstanding the successes of the South African automotive industry over the last few years, it is presently under severe pressure with regard to its competitiveness. As revealed in a recent *Financial Mail Special Report* (31 August 2007), titled 'On the Brink', the industry appears to be at a crossroads, with growing international competitiveness pressures, local policy issues and a perceived lack of firm-level competitiveness blending together into a dangerous cocktail that could undermine its future development.

This view of the industry's present position may sound dramatic, but the automotive industry's progress to date is no guarantee of its continued growth. Supported in large part by the benefits of the Motor Industry Development Programme (MIDP) (DTI 1995), benefits that are slowly being reduced, the industry still represents work in progress – away from its closeted past and towards a more open domestic and international trading environment. The success or failure of the South African automotive industry over the next few years is likely to serve as an indication of South Africa's capability in manufacturing high-value-added products for local and global markets. If the industry fails, serious questions are likely to be raised in respect of South Africa's manufacturing capabilities.

Given the above context, this chapter explores the South African institutional environment's ability to supply a high-value-adding manufacturing industry, with the requisite human capital to sustain its growth over the next few years. The manufacturing sector has been identified through both the Accelerated and Shared Growth Initiative for South Africa (Asgisa) and the National Industrial Policy Framework as a priority sector within the domestic economy. This is in the face of international competition, a changing policy environment, substantial domestic market growth, surging imports, South Africa's transformation imperative, and finally, increasingly demanding customers that are squeezing component firms on both price and non-price factors.

The chapter comprises five sections, the first of which outlines international and South African automotive trends, South Africa's automotive policy framework, and the profile characteristics of South African auto component manufacturers. The second section then outlines the changing nature of skills demands in the industry. Drawing on South African Automotive Benchmarking Club (SAABC) and National Association of Automotive Component and Allied Manufacturers (NAACAM) data, overall employment growth within the industry is projected to 2010 and 2015, along with a disaggregated perspective on employment growth, in particular, high-skills employment categories: management, professional staff and artisans. A breakdown of the skills profile within each of these employment categories is also presented, providing a projection on skills demand within the domestic auto components industry to 2010 and 2015.

The third section shifts the focus of the chapter to skills supply issues within the industry. It considers graduation levels from tertiary education institutions (TEIs) and further education and training (FET) institutions supporting the industry; and then, based on 12 firm-level interviews straddling each of the auto components industry's sub-sectors, considers the particular skills supply issues confronting the industry. Attention is given to recruitment lead times, perceptions of the skills levels of graduates from the TEIs and FET institutions, and general sentiments relating to skills supply into the industry. Building on these skills demand and supply issues, as well as the contextual findings presented, the fourth section interrogates the critical skills deficiencies identified by the Department of Labour (DoL) and the Manufacturing, Engineering and Related Services Sector Education and Training Authority (MERSETA), and compares them to the findings of the primary research completed for this chapter. A short conclusion that focuses on the analytical implications of the findings generated completes the chapter.

Before moving on to these sections, however, a few words are required on the research methodology employed to complete the chapter.

Research methodology

The research methodology encompassed an interrogation of firm-level data and secondary published research over the period March to September 2007. Structured qualitative interviews were conducted with human resources (HR) representatives from 12 South African-based auto component firms, representing each of the sector's manufacturing sub-sectors.[1] The primary aim of these interviews was to ascertain the formal qualifications of employees,[2] the fundamental skills shortages experienced within the industry, and which scarce and critical skills were likely to be under-supplied in the near future. Three of the 12 firms were 'small' firms, whilst interviews were also spread across the country, to limit regional biases in the findings.[3] Quantitatively, critical measurement data were extracted from the SAABC database. This database comprises firm-level benchmarking data from 75 South African auto component manufacturers. The data used in the study generally covered the 2001–2006 period, except in instances where data were unavailable. Regarding the projected employment data to 2010 and 2015, these were generated through an estimation model created by B&M Analysts (2007). Concurrent to these two primary research activities, a comprehensive auto industry literature review was also completed.

International and domestic industry profile

The automotive industry is the world's largest manufacturing sector, accounting for approximately 15 per cent of global GDP.[4] In value terms, this equated to US$645 billion in 2003, a figure which is expected to reach US$903 billion by 2015 (MPL Consulting & Bentley West Strategic Consulting 2005). Given its scale of operation, the automotive industry is one of the largest employment sectors

---

1 These sub-sectors are: discrete (i.e. completed and functional) components, electronics, foundries and forges, glass, harness assembly, injection moulding, just-in-time assembly, metal forming, metal fabrication, precision machining, trim components, tyres and rubber.
2 This includes the various tiers of management, as well as professional staff, artisans and production workers.
3 Details of the firms interviewed are given at the end of the chapter.
4 See www.oica.net, the website of the International Organisation of Motor Vehicle Manufacturers.

globally, responsible either directly or indirectly for about one in nine jobs in developed countries.[5] The automotive industry consequently generates an enormous amount of wealth, with a number of major developed and developing economies benefiting from its economic contribution. This occurs directly in the form of value-adding output and employment, but also indirectly in the form of technology spillovers, skills development and exposure to leading international practices – in respect of product development and manufacturing processes.

In recognition of the potential benefits of the automotive industry to the South African economy, the national government's Department of Trade and Industry (DTI) promulgated the MIDP in September 1995 as a means to integrate the domestic industry into the international environment, with the expectation that positive adjustments would occur and its strategic position would be re-aligned within a global, as opposed to a national framework (DTI 1995). This has largely occurred, with the South African automotive assembly and component industries taking on strong outward orientations. Evidence of this abounds – from large-scale vehicle export programmes to the substantial growth of component exports from South Africa. In addition to the economic growth of the auto industry and its growing contribution to the national economy in the form of investments, manufacturing-value addition and employment, it has also substantially contributed to the modernisation of the domestic manufacturing sector, with lean manufacturing systems and cutting-edge product technologies introduced as export programmes have expanded.

The growth of the auto industry over the last decade has not been without its pressures, however, with many of these pressures becoming more, rather than less pronounced over the last couple of years. To put it rather crudely, international demands have become substantially more severe, placing ever more pressing cost stresses on South African-based firms as their multinational corporation (MNC) parents look to purchase more from cheaper Asian producers. Despite increasing their competitiveness over the last few years, South African firms consequently remain some distance from where they need to be, in order to compete successfully without the benefits of the MIDP.

Some of the underlying reasons for the lack of competitiveness in the South African auto industry are legacy-based, relating to diseconomies of scale in the domestic market (despite its significant recent growth) and a comparatively high cost base (wages and salaries are much higher in South Africa than in competing Asian economies). Other reasons are more industry-specific, relating to its continued comparative under-investment in people, equipment, manufacturing processes and new products. B&M Analysts' SAABC database is very clear on this (B&M Analysts 2007). Whilst the industry has performed impressively since 1995 (particularly in relation to the performance of the domestic manufacturing sector more generally), a major reason for this is the MIDP and the benefits associated with its Import-Export Complementation (IEC) scheme. These benefits have been sufficient to compensate for higher production and logistics costs in South Africa, thus encouraging exports.

As the MIDP's benefits have scaled down since 2002, and as they continue to phase down to 2012, serious questions have been raised in respect of the sustainability of the industry's recent growth. These questions obviously have important policy implications and are central to the analysis underpinning the DTI's present review of the MIDP. This is likely to culminate in the establishment of a fully WTO-compliant MIDP stage loosely derived from the Australian government's Automotive Competitiveness

---

5   See www.oica.net

TABLE 2.1: *Summary of investment indicators amongst South African automotive component manufacturers versus international firms in the SAABC database, 2003–2006*

Investment indicator	South African average (n=75)					International average (n=72)
	2003	2004	2005	2006	2003–06	2006
Training expenditure as % of remuneration	1.58	1.58	1.69	1.82	1.67	3.20
R&D expenditure as % of sales	1.54	1.98	1.56	1.48	1.64	2.98
Capital expenditure as % of sales	5.00	4.29	4.16	4.96	4.60	7.13

Source: B&M Analysts 2007

and Incentive Scheme (ACIS). Based on government press statements this new stage is, moreover, likely to run from either January 2010 or January 2013 to December 2020.[6]

At a HR level, and central to the thrust of this chapter's argument, the key questions posed in relation to its sustainability suggest that the South African auto industry may not have done enough to improve its competitiveness over the last decade. This is perhaps a harsh comment, as the industry has substantially improved its competitiveness in respect of its quality performance, operational reliability and cost control parameters.[7] However, it has done so whilst spending very little on skills development, R&D, and even new capital investment. In comparison to firms benchmarked by B&M Analysts in competitor economies as part of the activities of the SAABC, South African-based component manufacturers have clearly not invested as heavily in their operations. This is summarised in Table 2.1. As revealed, South African-based firms have spent only slightly more than half the international average on training, R&D expenditure and capital equipment.

Skills demands to 2010 and 2015

The South African automotive and components industry is steadily expanding, with industry analysts projecting favourable future production growth. This anticipated expansion will necessarily have implications in respect of industry skills demands. It is also important to note that 2005 marked the beginning of a new wave of export programmes, which were announced or implemented at South African-based vehicle assemblers or original equipment manufacturers (OEMs). Completely built unit (CBU) exports increased by 27 per cent (29 405 units) from 2004 to 2005, totaling 139 912 units (NAAMSA 2006); this

---

6   The MIDP potentially contravenes the WTO's Agreement on Subsidies and Countervailing Measures. As such, the export subsidy that is deemed to exist within the MIDP has come into question. The MIDP is therefore presently under review, although it is likely that the programme will be retained in its current form until at least the end of 2009, after which major adjustments are likely to be made. The Australian automotive industry's ACIS is being studied as an alternative. ACIS principally works on the basis of a production incentive tied to duty rebates, as opposed to an export incentive. As the incentive is linked to domestic and export production and is capped at five per cent of the total sales of recipient firms, it is WTO-compliant.

7   For example, the average customer return rate at South African-based auto component manufacturers decreased from 10 790 parts per million (ppm) in 2001 to 254 ppm in 2006. At the same time, their average internal reject rate improved from 4.6 per cent to 2.6 per cent, whilst the number of deliveries to customers that are not on time and in full progressed from 10.1 per cent in 2001 to 6.5 per cent in 2006 – despite far more onerous OEM customer delivery demands. The vast majority of South African-based component manufacturers are also now International Organization for Standardization–Technical Specification (ISO-TS) 16949-accredited (86.6 per cent), whilst a further 60 per cent of firms are ISO 14001-certified (B&M Analysts 2007). This suggests that firms have fully accepted the need for international accreditations and have aligned their operating systems with global norms and standards.

TABLE 2.2: *Industry employment levels (average monthly figures), 2001–2005*

Industry	2001	2002	2003	2004	2005
Vehicle manufacturing	32 700	32 370	31 700	31 800	33 825
Automotive components	72 100	74 100	75 000	74 500	78 000
Tyre manufacturing	6 300	6 000	6 000	6 000	6 000
Motor trade, distribution, servicing	182 000	185 000	191 000	194 000	195 000
Total	293 100	297 470	303 700	306 300	312 825

Source: NAAMSA 2005

figure is expected to increase to 250 000 units in the next couple of years. Whilst the total number of different vehicle models manufactured in South Africa is projected to remain steady at 19 through to 2010, a host of new vehicle models[8] are to be assembled in South Africa over the next few years, ensuring that additional skills demands will almost certainly materialise. In addition to the direct pressures that will emerge at the OEMs, increasing customer demands will put added pressure on the industry to broaden and deepen its employee skills base. From an export perspective, South African OEMs and component manufacturers will, for example, meet with increased quality demands from their overseas customers. At the same time, imports of CBUs and components are growing steadily, ensuring that domestic customer demands increase as the public is exposed to international product offerings. Both scenarios require that local firms upgrade their skills base.

Apart from the auto industry's traditional skills requirements, which have remained largely unchanged, the growth of imports and exports of both CBUs and components is placing additional emphasis on logistics-related issues, with this becoming a key skills demand in its own right. The changing face of industrial relations has also emerged as a critical factor impacting on skills demands. The South African labour relations situation leans towards a pluralist model, wherein workplace conflicts are mediated between management and trade unions. This, too, has increasingly mandated that individual firms source well qualified HR personnel. Finally, in recent years firms have increasingly begun to comply with internationally regulated occupational health and safety standards, such as OHS18000.

Labour force composition: status quo

Table 2.2 outlines average employment levels within the auto industry for the period 2001–2005. As highlighted, aggregated employment in the components industry was 78 000 in 2005 (according to data supplied by the NAACAM).

SAABC firm-level data echo NAACAM's findings regarding increases in sector employment. SAABC members' employment figures have risen from 18 947 in 2001 to 23 549 in 2006 – despite a 0.2 per cent decline from 2005 to 2006 (B&M Analysts 2007). From 2001 to 2006, the average SAABC employment growth was therefore 4.4 per cent per annum.

---

8   These new models include the Toyota Corolla, VW Polo, Ford T6, Renault Logan (Nissan plant), and Mercedes Benz C-Class.

Labour force composition projections: 2010 and 2015

Knowing the recent employment growth rate of the South African auto components industry is obviously important, but it fails to indicate the likely growth rate in employment to 2010 and 2015, or the composition of that employment, or the skills required. And these are of course the key issues that need to be analysed if a detailed understanding of the auto component industry's future skills demands are to be adequately understood.

In this sub-section we therefore endeavour to calculate the composition of the industry's labour force for 2010 and 2015, the likely composition of the labour force, and then finally, the skills profile within each critical labour force category (i.e. management, professionals and artisans). To undertake this task, the following methodological steps were completed:

1. Based on SAABC employment growth rates over the period 2001–2006, as well as an analysis of domestic and international factors impacting on the industry's future performance, overall employment within the South African auto components industry was extrapolated to 2010 and 2015.
2. Based on the average breakdown of employment at each individual manufacturer in the SAABC, an aggregated industry employment profile was created. Employment categories encompassed management, professionals, supervisors, artisans, production workers, apprentices/learners and other (administration and clerical) staff. Holding the employee breakdown of the industry steady, employment levels were then calculated for each category for the 2006–2010 and 2006–2015 periods.
3. Based on the difference between employment levels in 2006 and 2010/2015, and factoring in average employee turnover rates at component manufacturers on an annualised basis, the aggregated growth in demand for particular employment categories could then be calculated.
4. Finally, using interview data from the 12 firm-level interviews, a 'typical' qualifications profile was created for the 'skilled' employee categories of management, professionals and artisans. This was then juxtaposed against the aggregated growth in demand for each employee category, thus providing an indication of the industry's skills demands to 2010 and 2015.

Growth trends: 2001–2006

Using the SAABC database (n=75), the rate of employment growth within member firms was first established as a building block for further extrapolation. Off a base of 18 947 employees in 2001, aggregated employment amongst the 75 members of the SAABC increased to 23 499 in 2006, a total growth of 4 552 jobs – just over 24 per cent, or 4.4 per cent per annum.

Extrapolated growth trend to 2010 and 2015

Having established the employment growth trajectory of SAABC members to 2006, the next step was to factor in the SAABC's data on the employment breakdown of member firms, thus indicating the disaggregated employment composition of SAABC member firms – in terms of management, professionals and artisans (i.e. high-skills employment categories), as well as supervisors, trainees/apprentices, operators and 'other' employees. Figure 2.1 demonstrates the findings from this exercise, revealing the proportional breakdown for each employment category. By holding the disaggregated employment profile steady to 2010 and 2015, which is a reasonable assumption to make, we then have a basis upon which we can project forward the composition of employment within the South African automotive components industry – provided, of course, that a reasonable projection of employment growth over the periods 2006–2010 and 2006–2015 can be made.

FIGURE 2.1: *South African automotive components industry's employment composition, 2006, and projected levels, 2010 and 2015*

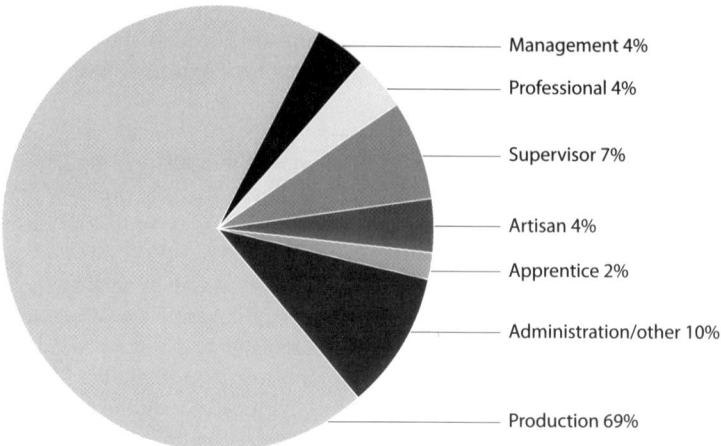

- Management 4%
- Professional 4%
- Supervisor 7%
- Artisan 4%
- Apprentice 2%
- Administration/other 10%
- Production 69%

Source: B&M Analysts 2007

Calculating employment growth to 2010 and 2015

Although the average employment growth rate has been 4.4 per cent for the period 2001–2006, this growth rate was adjusted to an annualised rate of 2.4 per cent for the period 2006–2015. This 'educated assumption' was based on an analysis of counteracting factors influencing the industry's trajectory. On balance, the analysis suggested continued employment growth, but at a reduced level relative to the last five years.

Factors likely to positively influence employment demand are vibrant domestic market demand, recent capital investments by a number of OEMs, existing MIDP benefits until the end of 2009 or 2012, and then the likelihood of similar, but fully WTO-compliant, MIDP benefits for the period 2010–2020, South Africa's Free Trade Agreement with the EU, which provides South African assemblers and component manufacturers with an advantage over their Asian counterparts when exporting into the EU, and finally, the industry's successful production track record forged over the last decade.

Despite these positive factors, there are unfortunately more negative elements that must be factored into any analysis of likely employment growth within the industry:
- growing international competition from the East – in respect of both vehicle assembly and component manufacture;
- ongoing rand strength;
- the cost of raw materials in South Africa, which makes the cost of domestic manufacture higher than in competitor economies;
- uncertainty relating to the MIDP;
- the growing import surge into the domestic economy;
- vast skills shortages, which have gained increasing attention from government, labour, and stakeholders in business.

Based on NAACAM's aggregated employment level for the South African automotive components industry of 78 000 in 2005, and based on the SAABC's recorded decline in employment of 0.2 per cent in 2006, total industry employment was calculated at 77 836 individuals in 2006. Using the anticipated

FIGURE 2.2: *Projected employment composition of the South African automotive components industry, 2006 versus 2010 and 2015*

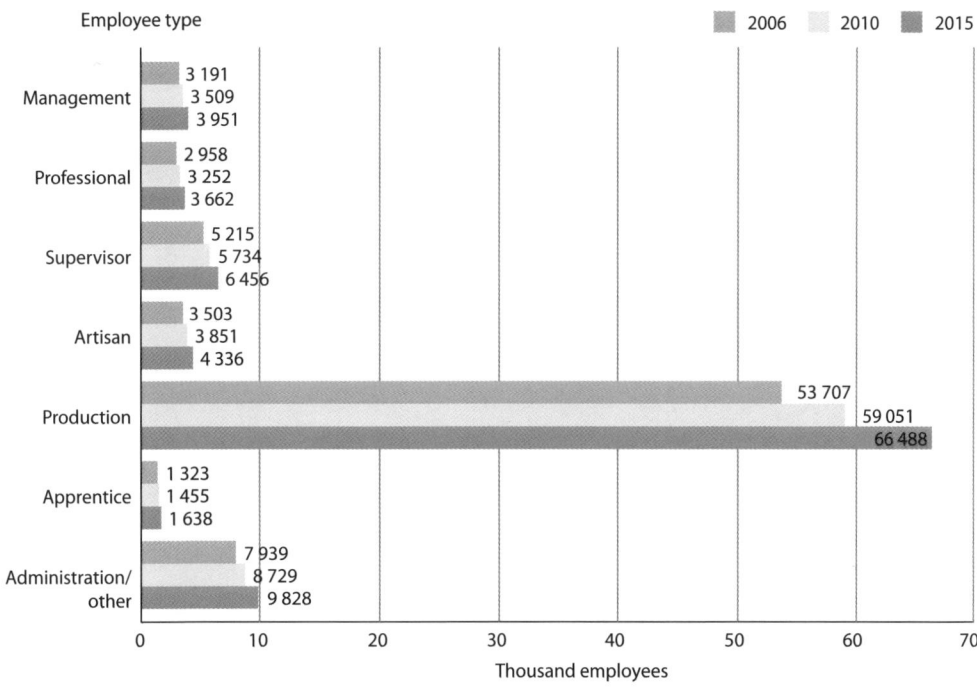

Source: B&M Analysts 2007; NAACAM 2005

growth rate of 2.4 per cent, employment is projected to increase to 85 582 in 2010 and 96 357 in 2015, translating into a total increase of 18 520 jobs from 2006 to 2015. The disaggregation of this employment (based on Figure 2.1) is presented in Figure 2.2. As revealed, the major growth in employment will be in the semi-skilled categories, although there will also be sizeable increases in management, professional staff and artisans.

Extrapolated skills demands: 2010 and 2015

In this section, aggregated and category-specific employee demands are extrapolated through to 2010 and 2015. To calculate total demand for new employees within the industry by employee category for 2006–2010 and 2006–2015, an additional calculation to that presented in Figure 2.2 was required – an estimation of the number of employees to be lost to turnover. This is because employment demand is dependent on both variables – growth/contraction in actual numbers and employee replacement, as individuals leave their places of employment and thus effectively create new demand. Based on average industry turnover rates for 2003–2006 (B&M Analysts 2007), and holding this steady through to 2015, turnover was calculated at an annualised rate of 6.7 per cent for labour, 7.5 per cent for staff and 6.2 per cent for management. Assuming that 50 per cent of this turnover remains in the industry and hence the skills are not actually lost, we then halved the turnover rates for the purposes of calculating industry-wide employee losses.[9] The findings generated are presented in Figure 2.3. As revealed,

---

9   For example, the figure we used for annualised management turnover was 3.1 per cent, or 50 per cent of the average management turnover rate of the industry for 2003–2006. Approximately 50 per cent of firm-level turnover is lost to other firms in the sector (and hence not lost to the industry) and 50 per cent to firms in other sectors, emigration, retirement or mortality.

FIGURE 2.3: *Employment demand based on employee turnover, 2006 to 2010 and 2015*

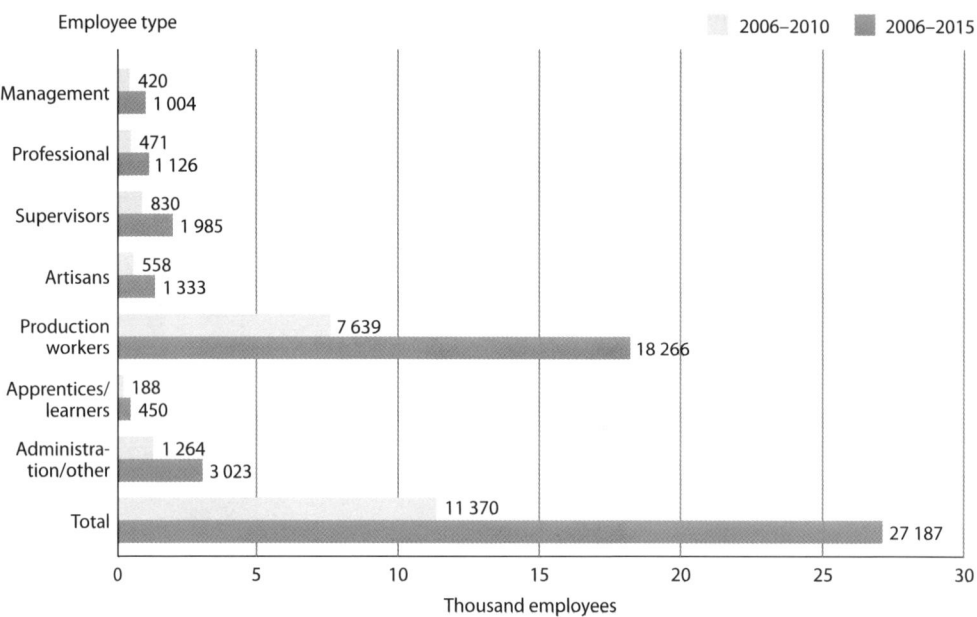

Source: Based on B&M Analysts 2007 and NAACAM database figures

total employee turnover from 2006 to 2015 is estimated at 27 187, with the majority of this turnover (18 266) in the production worker category. For management, professionals and artisans, turnover for the period 2006–2015 stands at 1 004, 1 126 and 1 333 positions respectively.

Having calculated new and replacement employment demand for the industry, we can finally calculate the aggregated demand for employees in each of the employment categories for 2006–2010 and 2006–2015. Dealing with 2006–2010, total replacement demand of 11 370 and new growth demand of 7 746 are projected to lead to aggregated demand of 19 116 persons. As unpacked in Table 2.3, in respect of the management total, aggregated demand equates to 738 persons, whilst for professionals the figure is 765 persons and for artisans 906 persons.

Whilst the 2006–2010 figures suggest growth in demand across all three high-skills categories, indicated in Table 2.3, Table 2.4 shows that aggregated demand increases significantly after 2010, with total demand for the 2006–2015 period revealing the need for the industry to recruit a total of 1 764 managers, 1 830 professionals and 2 167 artisans.

Having calculated aggregated new employment demand by employee category to 2010 and 2015, the next step is to identify the skills demands inherent in each category. To do this, we calculated a 'typical' skills profile for each 'high-skills' employee category in the industry, using firm-level data from 12 manufacturers representing each of the industry's manufacturing sub-sectors. The particular qualification of each manager, professionally employed staff member and artisan was requested from the firms, with a skills profile then created for 2006. Using the baseline employment growth calculations presented earlier, the qualifications comprising each high-skills employment category were then projected to 2010 and 2015, and then finally, based on growth and replacement demand, the total demand for new qualified employees was calculated.

TABLE 2.3: *Employment demand for the period 2006–2010*

Occupational level	Replacement demand	New demand	Aggregated demand
Management	420	318	738
Professional	471	294	765
Supervisors	830	519	1 349
Artisans	558	349	906
Production workers	7 639	5 344	12 983
Apprentices/learners	188	132	320
Administration/other	1 264	790	2 054
Total	11 370	7 746	19 116

Source: Based on B&M Analysts (2007) and NAACAM database figures

TABLE 2.4: *Employment demand for the period 2006–2015*

Occupational level	Replacement demand	New demand	Aggregated demand
Management	1 004	759	1 764
Professional	1 126	704	1 830
Supervisors	1 985	1 241	3 226
Artisans	1 333	833	2 167
Production workers	18 266	12 779	31 045
Apprentices/learners	450	315	765
Administration/other	3 023	1 889	4 912
Total	27 187	18 520	45 708

Source: Based on B&M Analysts (2007) and NAACAM database figures

Table 2.5 represents the findings from this exercise for management and professionals employed in the industry.[10] It shows that:
- Of the 6 149 managers and professionals employed in 2006, 2 023 (32.3 per cent) had engineering-related qualifications (engineering degrees or diplomas), 1 057 (17.2 per cent) had business-related degrees (business administration, business science, economics, etc.), and 1 050 (17.1 per cent) had trade certificates of some kind.
- Given the concentration of these qualifications amongst managers and professional staff, of the 3 594 management and professional positions that will need to be filled over the 9-year period from 2006 to 2015, 1 183 will need to be related to engineering-linked qualifications, 618 to business-related degrees and 614 to trade certificates of various kinds.

10 The skills breakdown of management and professionals was aggregated for this exercise, as the categories have very similar skills demands and the separation was thus deemed artificial for the purposes of unpacking the industry's existing qualification base and future demand.

TABLE 2.5: *Management and professional skills profiles for 2006, 2010 and 2015; total demand calculations for 2006–2010 and 2006–2015*

	Skills profile			Demand	
	2006	2010	2015	2006–2010	2006–2015
Engineering-related qualifications	2 023	2 225	2 505	495	1 183
Financial-related degrees	260	286	322	64	152
Business-related degrees	1 057	1 162	1 308	258	618
Social science/Humanities degrees	462	508	571	113	270
Management diplomas	260	286	322	64	152
Production diplomas	173	190	214	42	101
Trade certificates	1 050	1 154	1 300	257	614
Other diplomas & degrees	865	951	1 070	211	505
Total	6 149	6 761	7 613	1 503	3 594

Source: Based on firm-level interviews

The skills profile for artisans is presented in Table 2.6, and as revealed, whilst the largest categories of skills relate to fitters and turners (25.5 per cent) and electricians (20.9 per cent), a broad set of artisanal skills is generally required. This is reflected in the broad range of artisan skills required to 2010 and 2015.[11]

Based on this breakdown of qualifications within the skilled employment categories of the industry, we can then calculate the actual skills demands for 2010 and 2015, and not only the growth in demand for particular employee categories. As revealed, the five greatest skills demands will relate to:
- management and professionals with engineering qualifications (aggregated demand of 1 183 new positions to 2015);
- management and professionals with business degrees (618 positions);
- management and professionals with trade qualifications (614 positions);
- artisans qualified as electricians (453 positions);
- artisans qualified as fitters and turners (554 positions).

Skills supply issues

The South African auto components industry is fortunate to have a number of well established, credible TEIs and FET institutions providing it with technically and professionally skilled personnel. Less positively, a number of the TEIs and FET institutions that profess to be providers of skilled personnel for the industry are viewed negatively by manufacturers, with certain institutions having been 'embargoed' as potential sources of new recruits. The key skills issue confronting the domestic industry does not therefore appear to be the ability of good institutions to provide skilled graduates, but rather the growing gap between the absolute number of good graduates produced and the industry's growing

---

11 Unfortunately, a number of firms were unable to specify the qualifications of their artisans, hence the large proportion of 'unspecified' artisans in our calculations.

TABLE 2.6: *Artisan skills profile for 2006, 2010 and 2015; total demand calculations for 2006–2010 and 2006–2015*

	Skills profile			Demand	
	2006	2010	2015	2006–2010	2006–2015
Electricians	733	806	907	190	453
Fitters & turners	895	984	1 108	231	554
Tool jig & die	286	314	354	74	177
Millwrights	310	341	384	80	192
Tool setters	99	109	123	26	61
Electronics	124	136	153	32	77
Unspecified	1 056	1 161	1 307	273	653
Total	3 503	3 851	4 336	906	2 167

Source: Based on B&M Analysts (2007) and NAACAM database figures and firm-level interviews

skills demands – due to high attrition rates, industry growth and the advancing technological complexity of vehicle manufacture.

For example, the number of graduates in public TEIs in 2004 was 115 801 (DoE 2007a). Of this total, only 31 328 were science, technology and engineering (STE) graduates and a further 29 002 business and management graduates.[12] Calculating the number of these graduates who emerge from credible institutions with credible qualifications is, of course, a highly subjective exercise likely to be painted as extremely discriminatory to particular institutions. Nevertheless, the automotive components industry only perceives certain institutions as capable of producing employable graduates, and as such, the Department of Education (DoE) figures immediately overstate the number of graduates available to the industry. It is therefore necessary to discount the total DoE figure by 20 per cent.

Using the DoE's adjusted aggregated figures, and extrapolating these across the full spectrum of the domestic economy, the following projections can be made:
- Based on the fact that manufacturing comprised 17 per cent of the South African economy in 2005, and assuming equal demand for graduates across all economic sectors, 4 261 STE and 3 944 business management graduates would have entered the manufacturing sector in that year.
- Based on the automotive industry comprising 25 per cent of South Africa's manufacturing sector, 1 065 STE and 986 business management graduates would have entered the industry in 2005.
- Based on the components industry comprising 65 per cent of the total automotive industry's value addition, 692 STE and 641 business management graduates would have entered the industry in 2005 – 1 333 graduates.

The problem with the data generated here is that they remain far too broad. If all 692 STE graduates available to the automotive components industry held engineering-specific qualifications, then there would be no existing or future skills problems confronting the industry, but this is clearly not the case, as outlined below.

---

12 Unfortunately, the DoE does not disaggregate these two very broad fields of study any further. As such, medical professionals are classified in the same field as engineering, making the aggregated picture potentially very misleading.

A similar problem emerges when considering the number of graduates from FET institutions.[13] Whilst there may be a large number of graduates from South Africa's various FET institutions, the majority of the qualifications are (a) entirely irrelevant to manufacturers, since they focus primarily on the automotive services industry, or (b) of an insufficient standard to meet the exacting technical requirements of the automotive components industry. For example, whilst 9 726 graduates emerged from the South African FET institutions in automotive-related fields in 2005, this qualification field comprises almost exclusively automotive service qualifications. Moreover, the vast majority of these graduates are at an extremely low technical level (National Qualifications Framework (NQF) Level 1 or 2). To illustrate the magnitude of the challenge: of the 9 726 graduates in 2005, 7 104 comprised 'Motor Trade Theory' – an exclusively automotive services qualification; and of this total only 4 graduates were at Level 4 (Motor Vehicle Science), with 4 186 at Level 1 and 2 083 at Level 2. Graduation levels from FET institutions are therefore highly misleading in respect of the infusion of technical skills into the South African automotive components industry.

The industry interviews revealed that there are at least three critical shortages with regard to artisan/trade skills, as well as several severe shortages in specific management and professional skills areas. Table 2.7 categorises these shortages by employment type, specific professional skills, and finally, the frequency with which firms identified the skills deficiency. As revealed in the table, the three most frequently cited skills deficiencies relate to artisanal employment – in respect of electricians, fitters and turners, and millwrights. These were cited more frequently than management and professional skills deficiencies, the most severe of which relate to supervisors, industrial engineers, mechanical engineers and production management.

In addition to these more frequently cited skills shortages, two firms also made reference to skills gaps in respect of electrical engineers (professional staff), whilst another two firms emphasised the need to recruit artisans with tool jig and die expertise. The levels of frustration evident in the 12 firm-level interviews emphasised a mounting skills crisis in the industry, with the recruitment lead time data presented in Figure 2.4 particularly troubling.

Based on the firm-level interviews conducted, it is clear that recruiting suitably skilled personnel for technical positions is extremely difficult and becoming more so, as salary expectations rise to levels beyond the affordability of the firms. For example, 11 of the 12 interviewed firms reported that lead times for recruiting key technical staff had deteriorated over the last 2 years. Only one firm reported that lead times had remained the same, whilst none reported any improvement. Firms consequently appear to be compromising in respect of their employment of technical personnel, recruiting either less qualified or less experienced staff than they would have preferred, with this in itself leading to frustrations as the recruits struggle to perform the tasks expected of them.

Whilst a number of firms are proactively responding to the skills crisis by spending more of their own resources on training and development, as revealed in Figure 2.5, the overall firm-level response in South Africa remains lethargic in comparison to international competitors based in Central and Western Europe, Latin America and India.[14] In respect of training expenditure as a proportion of remuneration, a proxy measure for how seriously South African automotive component manufacturers are taking the development of their employees, the South African average over the last 5 years has only been 1.8 per cent, or 56 per cent of the international average – despite assertions that skills deficiencies are crippling many firms. Even more strikingly, training expenditure as a proportion of remuneration has declined since 2001. As skills supply issues have been noted as a major industry challenge, so

---

13 See DoE 2007a, 2007b.
14 B&M Analysts has 72 international firms in its international database. These firms are based in Central and Western Europe, North and South America, India and Australia.

TABLE 2.7: *Current skills gaps as identified during firm-level interviews*

Type	Profession	Score (%)[a]
Artisan	Electricians	75.0
Artisan	Fitters & turners	66.7
Artisan	Millwrights	50.0
Management	Supervisors	33.3
Management, professional staff	Industrial engineers	33.3
Management, professional staff	Mechanical engineers	33.3
Management	Production management	33.3
Artisan	Electronics	25.0

Source: Firm-level interviews

Note: a The 'percentage score' indicates the number of references made to the particular skill shortage by interviewees, (n =12).

FIGURE 2.4: *Average industry recruitment lead times*

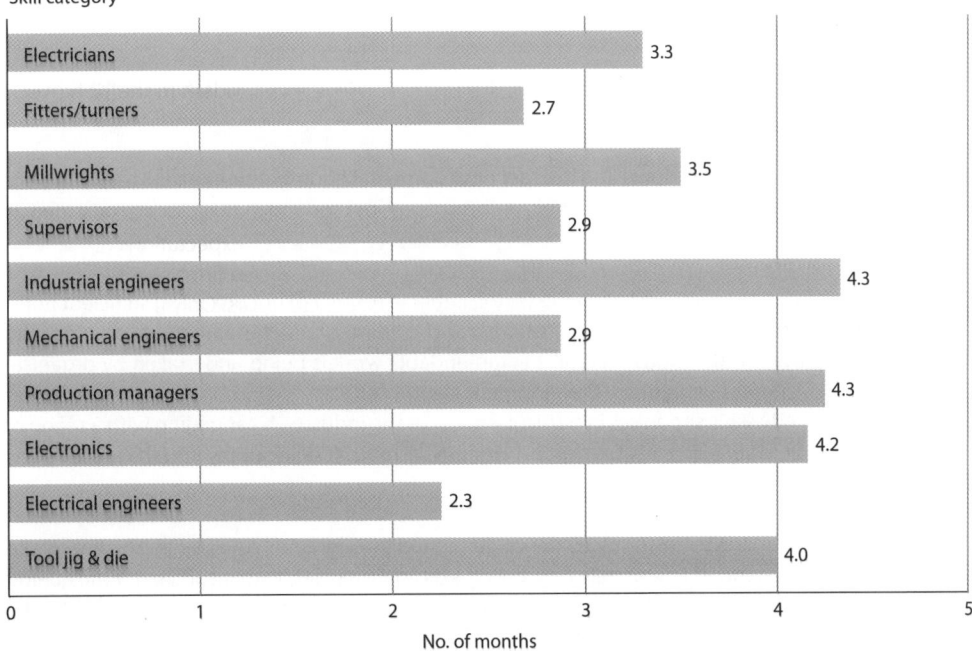

Source: Firm-level interviews

FIGURE 2.5: *Training expenditure as a percentage of remuneration: South African average (2001–2006) versus international average (2006 only)*

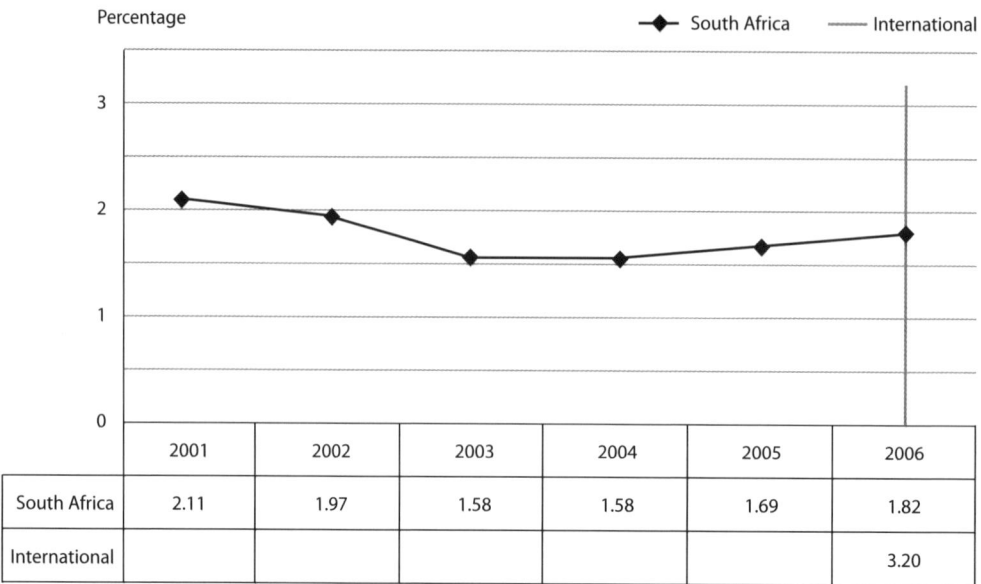

	2001	2002	2003	2004	2005	2006
South Africa	2.11	1.97	1.58	1.58	1.69	1.82
International						3.20

Source: B&M Analysts 2007

firm-level expenditure has declined rather than the inverse, as would be expected in a skills-deficient environment.

What do these firm-level, institutional and broader environmental findings therefore tell us about skills supply in the South African environment? Well, unfortunately, not too much that can be construed as positive.

Institutionally, the TEIs appear to be failing the sector, either in respect of not providing sufficient numbers of graduates (from well respected institutions), or providing graduates who are not sufficiently skilled to be employed in the industry. Whilst commendable work is being undertaken by organisations such as the Automotive Industry Development Centre (AIDC) and Durban Automotive Cluster to identify and remedy skills shortages in particular areas of the industry, by engaging with a range of academic institutions, there is a clear perception amongst firms that skills supply into the industry has deteriorated over the last few years.

Despite the criticisms made by the firms, evidence generated through the SAABC suggests that manufacturers have not responded adequately to growing skills deficiencies, with insufficient funds being allocated to skills development. Whilst firms may argue that their decreasing financial margins (in the face of growing international competition and increasing price pressures from OEM customers) limit the opportunities to spend significant amounts of money on training and development, absolute levels are poor in comparison to international competitors and hence insufficient. At least part of the skills problems in the industry consequently lies with the firms themselves.

Finally, the broader domestic economic environment is having a deleterious impact on the skills base of auto component manufacturers. As skills leave the country as a result of emigration, and as the government suddenly focuses on large-scale infrastructure projects after years of under-investment, the labour market for skilled personnel has been massively distorted. Keeping and recruiting scarce skills has therefore become an incredibly difficult and expensive process for firms – forcing sub-optimal firm-level responses, which often have negative competitiveness implications for the industry.

These issues, moreover, appear to impact on both small and large firms, multinationals and domestically owned firms alike, with no noticeable differences among the three small-firm interviews completed, or in the interviews completed at multinational and South African-owned firms. Whilst this may be surprising at face value, it is consistent with SAABC data comparisons of multinational versus South African performance, and small- versus medium- and large-firm performance levels that have been completed over the last two years.[15]

Scarce and critical skills identification

The various levels of dialogue regarding skills acquisition have led to confusing and sometimes contradictory use of terminology, such as that of 'scarce' and 'critical' skills. Moreover, the problem commonly referred to as a 'skills shortage' in South Africa is itself a nebulous concept, which encapsulates several specific issues — *shortages* in some cases (e.g. engineering and other technical skills), but skills *surpluses* in other areas (such as the social sciences).[16] In other words, there is a significant 'mismatch' between the skills sets being generated in local TEIs and the skills required by business.[17] There is, however, agreement that the demand for certain skills required to develop the domestic economy is far in excess of current supply.

For the purposes of this chapter, we will adhere to the terminology and usages provided by the South African DoL. The DoL differentiates between 'scarce' and 'critical' skills, with 'scarce skills' describing those occupations[18] experiencing a shortage of qualified or experienced individuals to form an adequate workforce. Such scarcity is typically due to an absence of appropriately qualified individuals, or to employment criteria that prohibit firms from hiring the qualified or experienced personnel available (DoL 2006a). 'Critical skills', however, describe fundamental 'top up' skills required within an occupation. The DoL identifies two types of critical skills:
- *Key or generic skills*. This includes cognitive functions such as problem-solving, literacy, mathematical skills, and ICT skills, etc.
- *Occupationally specific 'top up' skills*. These skills are required for performance within an occupation to fill a 'skills gap' that may have occurred due to changing technology or evolving forms of work organisation.

To be precise, both 'scarce' and 'critical' skills are determined by profession; however, 'scarce' skills are considered in terms of the profession itself, while 'critical' skills are regarded as the specific skill sets required of a profession in particular (DoL 2006a).

---

15 For a comparison of small- versus medium- and large-firm performance, see SAABC 2006b; and for a comparison of South African- and MNC-owned performance, see SAABC 2006a.
16 Blaine S, Government policy 'aggravates skills crisis', *Business Day* 21 June 2007.
17 Robinson V, Gedye L, Mabanga T & Tabane R, Shortage confusion mismatch surplus, *Mail & Guardian Online* 2 August 2007, accessed 29 February 2008, http://www.aidc-esdle.co.za/index.php?pid=209&ct=1&dc=3
18 The specific use of the term 'occupation' (as opposed to 'job') needs to be clarified. A 'job' is a set of functions to be executed by an employee for an employer in exchange for remuneration, whilst an 'occupation' is a set of 'jobs' or specialisations, the main tasks of which are characterised by such a high degree of similarity that they can be grouped together for the purposes of the classification (ISETT SETA 2006).

Identifying scarce and critical skills in the South African automotive and components industry

Given the context outlined above, what are the scarce and critical skills shortages besetting the South African auto components industry – as identified by the DoL, the MERSETA and the firm-level research? Moreover, are the findings consistent? Based on the recruitment lead times and skills shortages identified by the interviewed firms, as well as the skills demand profile of the industry, the following five skills categories appear of most concern: all engineering qualifications, but most notably industrial and mechanical engineering; electricians; production management; fitting and turning; millwrights; business-related degrees.

Firms moreover indicated both absolute and relative skill *scarcities*. There are generally too few qualified job applicants for advertised skilled positions, with this compounded by the aging profile of the current workforce. Whilst a number of experienced industry workers retire or are promoted to higher positions, many others are becoming increasingly redundant, due to the introduction of new technologies which have shifted emphasis from mechanical to electronic skills, and effectively increased the premium placed on computer and technology literacy (MERSETA 2006). Whilst many auto component manufacturers are increasingly seeking to replace experienced workers with a younger generation of more technology-competent and computer-literate graduates, they apparently face a major quandary – recent graduates may be computer-literate, but they do not have the core mechanical skills required. As such, filling one skills gap immediately exposes another.

Firms did not specify many *critical* skills shortages, although several respondents alluded to employee deficiencies in generic areas such as 'people skills', problem-solving skills and the inability of many professionals to complete broader tasks not specifically within their ambit of responsibility. Several firms also conveyed the view that needing to source qualified previously disadvantaged individuals was further undermining their ability to acquire sufficient skills.

MERSETA Sector Skills Plan and DoL National Scarce Skills List

In 2002, the MERSETA commissioned a study to identify and review scarce skills facing the automotive sector, with the aim of generating ideas for a practical suite of interventions. This 'Snapshot Survey' found that shortages existed in various professional and technical engineering disciplines, repair and maintenance, and manufacturing trades (Umhlaba Skills Services 2006). In 2005, the MERSETA shifted its focus to scarce skills identification in particular trade occupations. This study identified four broad occupations in which scarce and/or critical skills require immediate attention (Umhlaba Skills Services 2006).

The first of these was 'management' occupations. The study identified a scarcity of engineering and operations middle managers/supervisors at NQF Levels 5 and 6. 'Critical' skills identified in these areas included industry knowledge and understanding, financial management and understanding, and generic skills such as communication and problem-solving. According to the study, 'professional' occupations showed scarce skills in electrical, mechanical, industrial and metallurgical engineering, again at NQF Levels 5–6. Critical skills included maintenance orientation and knowledge (with this applying to engineering professionals and technicians specifically). In respect of 'trade worker' occupations, the MERSETA study showed a scarcity of skilled artisan training for NQF Levels 3–5, with this particularly evident for generic trades such as mechanical, fabrication, electrical and automation.[19]

---

19 Mechanical trades include fitter, fitter and turner, machine setter, roll turner, milling machinist and instrument technician. Fabrication trades include metal moulder, sheetmetal trades workers and welders. Electrical trades include electricians, armature winders, HT electricians, lift mechanics, air conditioning and refrigerator mechanics (Umhlaba 2006: 4).

In 2006, the MERSETA published its *Sector Skills Plan (SSP) Review 2006–2011*, which identified several cross-cutting themes occurring both nationally and across the MERSETA sectors, namely, the persistence of skills deficiencies relating to ICT and customer management. However, the *SSP Review* found that for the manufacturing sectors specifically, core technical skills continue to be urgently needed, particularly at the level of technician and artisan – skills which the MERSETA identified as both *scarce* and *critical*. The study added that there is an increasing demand for high-level, combined skills, such as those required for advanced project management, in which industry knowledge, experience, ICT and other technical skills coalesce (MERSETA 2006). In addition to the work completed by the MERSETA, the DoL issued its National Scarce Skills List in 2006, a significant proportion of which relates directly to skills priorities in the automotive industry (DoL 2006b).

A comparison of the scarce and critical skills findings identified in the firm-level primary research and the MERSETA Scarce Skills List show a high level of alignment, suggesting largely consistent findings and a broad-based understanding of critical and scarce skills issues impacting on the industry. While a number of the scarce skills identified in the DoL's National Scarce Skills List are not substantiated by the primary (firm-level) or secondary (MERSETA) findings, these, too, show a significant degree of alignment, revealing that industry bodies are 'in touch' with the skills issues plaguing the automotive components industry. Table 2.8 summarises the key skills shortfalls identified in all three studies.

A troubling question that emerges from the findings is why the scarce and critical skills situation confronting the South African auto components industry has deteriorated, when critical shortfalls were identified as far back as 2002 by the MERSETA. The firm-level research completed by B&M Analysts was unequivocal in this regard: recruitment lead times have lengthened and skills deficiencies have become more rather than less acute over the past couple of years. Whilst an awareness of the skills problems confronting the industry may be in place, this is simply the starting point for any positive set of interventions. To *effectively improve* the situation, far more still clearly needs to be done to ensure

TABLE 2.8: *Comparative identification of scarce skills*

This study (2007)	Department of Labour (2006)	MERSETA (2006)
<ul><li>Artisan/trade skills: electricians, fitters and turners, millwrights, electronics, tool jig and die</li><li>Professional: industrial engineers, mechanical engineers, electrical engineers</li><li>Management: supervisors, production management</li></ul>	<ul><li>Engineering technicians: electrical, mechanical, mechatronics, robotics, tool design</li><li>Electricians</li><li>Electronics trades workers: electronics, electronic equipment</li><li>Engineering professionals: product design, industrial, mechanical (especially mechatronics), industrial/product development technologists</li><li>Fabrication engineering trades workers: sheet metal, structural steel and welding, metal fabricators</li><li>Mechanical engineering trades workers: metal fitters/machinists, fitter and turners, machine tool setters, millwrights, mechatronics</li><li>Vehicle body builders and trimmers</li><li>Vehicle painters</li></ul>	<ul><li>Management: engineering and operations middle management</li><li>Professional: electrical, mechanical, industrial and metallurgical engineers</li><li>Trade workers: mechanical, fabrication, electrical and automation</li><li>Operator: manufacturing and engineering production operators, stationary plant operators</li></ul>

Source: Author analysis of DoL 2006b, MERSETA 2006

that the industry has the requisite skills to compete against increasingly aggressive and capable international competitors.

Conclusions

The South African auto industry has done extremely well since the mid-1990s. Sound growth rates, burgeoning exports, growing productivity, and significantly more capital investment than evident in other domestic manufacturing sectors have ensured its status as a 'stand out' performer. However, there are a number of significant challenges confronting the industry. The South African auto industry is competing against a mix of well-established developed economies and rapidly growing developing economies targeting the industry as a key economic growth enabler. As the MIDP's benefits diminish, increased pressures are therefore confronting local assembly and component operations. This is evident in respect of the import surge presently being experienced in the domestic market, the loss of recent export contracts, and in the case of the components industry more specifically, the demand by customers that they reduce their pricing, in line with Asian competitors.

Underpinning these concerns is a widely held perception that South African auto component manufacturers are simply not competitive at the firm-level, with this relating to exorbitant logistics and materials costs and comparatively low levels of productivity. Whilst the former set of issues (logistics and materials costs) can partly be addressed through increased skills acquisitions in key management line function areas responsible for procurement and logistics management, there is a broader set of structural reasons for South Africa's lack of competitiveness in these areas; and these will therefore need to be addressed at a policy and broader government level. The latter issue lies at the core of this chapter, however, with the lack of firm-level productivity and capability, at least in part, directly related to skills deficiencies in critical line function areas of operation.

Based on 2006 industry employment levels, future employment demand and 2003–2006 average rates of employee attrition, research suggests substantial skills demands to 2010 and 2015. Whilst these high levels of demand for skills suggest an extremely healthy future operating environment for component manufacturers, there is no indication that South Africa is positioned to provide the industry with its requisite skills needs. Apart from complaints relating to very significant graduate deficiencies from particular TEIs and FET institutions, and insufficient numbers of graduates emerging from credible institutions, the three most striking skills findings generated relate to:
- extended recruitment lead times, which are as high as 4.3 months for industrial engineers and production managers;
- the aging profile of professionals at South African automotive component manufacturers, and the implications of this for the absorption of cutting-edge technology, most of which is electronics-based;
- the failure of firms to invest in skills development as a means to compensate for deficiencies at TEIs and the labour market more broadly.

Existing skills demands, and associated supply constraints, are fortunately well understood by the two principal institutions mandated to support the industry's skills development, namely, the DoL and the MERSETA. These two institutions have highlighted similar skills constraints (to those identified in this chapter) in their previous reviews of the manufacturers that fall within their ambit of responsibility. The key question that emerges from this chapter, then, is why skills shortages in the industry are becoming more severe, when they are apparently well understood and have been extensively documented.

This is the exact question posed by David Kaplan in a recent *Financial Mail* article.[20] Kaplan argues that skills declines in the broader productive sectors of the economy are well understood and that the limited remedial action taken by firms and government in the face of these declines represents institutional failure. Most notably, Kaplan argues for the need to dissolve the Sector Education and Training Authorities (SETAs) and institute a training incentive for firms that more aggressively encourages skills upgrading without SETA mediation of any kind. Whilst the ambit of the research presented in this chapter does not allow for an informed perspective on the merits of such an approach to skills upgrading, Kaplan's analysis of the skills status quo in South Africa appears to be entirely consistent with the findings generated.

In conclusion, then, is the industry on the brink of a major skills crisis? Or is the very real danger for the auto components industry that skills shortages no longer remain skills shortages, because South African-based operations cease to be sufficiently competitive in the face of growing international competition (a very real threat as MIDP benefits are reduced over the next few years) – resulting in their closure, as business is lost to competitors or relocated to sister plants operating in more competitive national economies?

Strong demand for skills in the auto components industry is incredibly healthy for the South African economy, but the lead times quoted by firms, as well as other evidence generated from the firm-level and broader secondary research, do not augur well for the future of the industry. In fact, a great irony may very well be sitting in the research completed. Our projections of skills demand to 2010 and 2015 may be completely wrong, precisely because skills supply constraints grow to the point where firms can no longer grow their businesses, nor effectively compete with international competitors. If this occurs, it is entirely conceivable that demand will drop sharply and supply will no longer be an issue. Unfortunately, this would support the view of those analysts who do not believe that South Africa has the ability to manufacture high-value-added products for domestic and international markets.

References

Barnes J & Black A (2005) A strategic assessment of the South African motor vehicle, parts and accessories sector. *Metalworking News* 3(6): 43–53

B&M Analysts (Benchmarking & Manufacturing Analysts) (2007) South African Automotive Benchmarking Club database. Durban: B&M Analysts

DoE (Department of Education, South Africa) (2007a) Higher Education Management Information System (HEMIS) database 1999–2005. Pretoria: DoE

DoE (2007b) FET output data 1996–2005. Pretoria: DoE

DoL (Department of Labour, South Africa) (2006a) *National scarce skills list – Foreword*. Accessed 29 February 2008, http://www.labour.gov.za/download/11693/Useful%20Document%20-%20NSF%20-%20National%20Scarce%20Skills%20List.doc

DoL (2006b) *National scarce skills list – ASGISA aligned*. Accessed 29 February 2008, http://www.labour.gov.za/useful_docs/doc_display.jsp?id=11696

DTI (Department of Trade and Industry, South Africa (1995) *The motor industry development programme*. Accessed 17 March 2008, http://www.thedti.gov.za/midp/automotives.htm#midp

ISETT SETA (Information Systems, Electronics and Telecommunications Technologies Sector Education and Training Authority) (2006) *Isett seta scarce & critical skills training to SDFs 2006–2007*. Accessed 29 February 2008, http://www.isett.org.za/

MERSETA (Manufacturing, Engineering and Related Services Sector Education and Training Authority) (2006) *Sector skills plan review 2006–2011*. Accessed 29 February 2008, http://www.merseta.org.za/

---

20 Kaplan D, Fix for skills crunch, *Financial Mail* 24 August 2007.

MPL Consulting & Bentley West Strategic Consulting (2005) Study to explore the retention and creation of employment in the South African automobile sector.

NAACAM (National Association of Automotive Component and Allied Manufacturers) (2005) *Annual report 2005*. Meadowdale, Gauteng: NAACAM

NAAMSA (National Association of Automobile Manufacturers of South Africa) (2005) *Annual report 2005*. Accessed 29 February 2008, http://files.rgt.co.za/storage/_public/naamsa/2005%20NAAMSA%20Annual%20Report.pdf

NAAMSA (2006) *Annual report 2006*. Accessed 29 February 2008, http://www.naamsa.co.za/papers/2006ar/

SAABC (South African Automotive Benchmarking Club) (2006a) *South African Automotive Benchmarking Club Newsletter* 9(2): 2–7

SAABC (2006b) *South African Automotive Benchmarking Club Newsletter* 9(4): 2–9

Umhlaba Skills Services (2006) *MERSETA metals chamber: Scarce skills workshops April & May 2006 final report*. Accessed 29 February 2008, http://www.merseta.org.za/Documents/chamber/SkillsReport.doc

Interviews

Firms interviewed for this study are listed below. All interviews were conducted in September 2007.

Firm	Region/City	No. of employees (2007 estimates)
ATE	Gauteng	250
August Lapple	Gauteng	982
Becker	East London	52
Dunlop	Durban	1 000
Faurecia	East London	32
Kolbenco	Gauteng	340
K&S	Port Elizabeth	705
Shatterprufe Neave	Port Elizabeth	700
Smiths Plastics	Pinetown/KwaZulu-Natal	766
Webroy	Pietermaritzburg	100

CHAPTER 3

Aerospace

Erika Kraemer-Mbula

The nature of the aerospace industry

Aerospace is a very diverse industry, with a multitude of commercial, industrial and military applications. In South Africa, aerospace activities include those surrounding defence, civilian aviation, aeronautics and space. To be consistent with other existent research in South Africa, this study adopts the definition of aerospace industry as 'the research and development, design, manufacture, support, maintenance, conversion and upgrade of rotary and fixed wing aircraft; satellites, satellite launch and tracking systems; air traffic control systems; unmanned aircraft; and weapons systems as well as their relevant subsystems and components' (Hatty 2000, cited in AMTS 2004: 4). This definition focuses on manufacturing activities and excludes the operation of domestic and international aircraft or ground/flight crew, attendants and catering.

Aerospace manufacturers can be broken down into several categories according to the level of complexity of the final product. These categories are commonly referred to as 'tiers': the top tiers include tiers one and two, while the lower tiers or suppliers include tiers three to five.[1]

1. Tier one refers to organisations producing an entire aircraft with all the sub-systems already fully integrated (for example, the Rooivalk helicopter). First-tiers are also known as airframers.
2. Tier two produces major sub-systems that are made up of a significant number of sub-systems. Examples include main airframe sections such as the wing, undercarriage and complete avionics systems.
3. Tier three produces minor sub-systems. These are components that are indivisible into other systems. Examples are gearboxes, navigation systems and computer systems.
4. Tier four produces components. These are devices with a clear function that have no use unless integrated into a tier-three system. Examples are electrical circuit boards, machined engine parts, valves and pumps.
5. Tier five produces parts. These are units that can be defined as a single monolithic part. Examples include unmachined castings, shafts, rivets and electrical components.

Each of these categories can be associated with different value added and different skills requirements. These are summarised in Table 3.1.

South Africa has developed considerable capabilities and set up local companies in most of these categories, and has achieved the ability to design and manufacture tier-one complete systems, as well as

---

1 Details on this classification can be found in AMTS 2004.

TABLE 3.1: *Aerospace manufactures, associated value added and level of skills*

	Value added products	Level of skills
Top tiers or first tiers		
Tier one (complete system)	high	high level of human resources
Tier two (major sub-systems)	medium	medium level of human resources + production skills
Lower tiers or sub-tiers		
Tier three (minor sub-systems)	medium	medium level of human resources + production skills
Tier four (components)	medium	medium level of human resources + production skills
Tier five (parts)	low	medium level of human resources

Source: Adapted from AMTS 2004

lower-tier products such as parts and components. Based on these categories, this chapter examines the opportunities that exist within the South African aerospace industry and the potential to improve the industry's integration into global and local supply chains.

The aerospace industry is peculiar in several respects. The complexity of production, its intensity in regard to technology and capital, and the high risks involved in new product development have traditionally linked the industry to strong government support. The sector has been generally associated with national security and defence objectives, although aerospace technologies have also been used for commercial purposes. The aerospace industry can be divided into two main sectors: the military (or defence) sector and the civil (or commercial) sector.

Aerospace is also considered home to key skills and technologies as well as an important driver of innovation. Due to its role in transportation, communication, observation, security and defence, it has been commonly regarded as a strategic sector. Nevertheless, not many nations have managed to develop substantial aerospace industries.[2]

According to Statistics South Africa (Stats SA), the Industry Code 386 ('manufacture of aircraft and spacecraft') represents the core of aerospace manufacturing activities for both civil and military purposes, and most of the analysis in this chapter is based on information available for this sub-sector.[3] However, it is important to note that aerospace activities are spread across various other sectors such as communications equipment, instruments, special-purpose machinery and other industries. Unfortunately, available statistical sources in South Africa do not permit extraction of figures for aerospace activities across other sub-sectors.

---

2   A recent AMD study (AMD & Vuxaka 2006) states that only 19 countries in the world have achieved substantial domestic defence industries. Note that the aerospace and defence industries are closely entangled.
3   Full details of the Standard Industrial Classification (SIC) system are available at http://www.statssa.gov.za/additional_services/siccoder/siccoder.htm.

Profile of the aerospace sector in South Africa

The origin of the aerospace industry in South Africa cannot be separated from the history of its defence industry, and is related to what has been named by some authors as the 'military-industrial complex' (MIC)[4] or the 'South African Defence-Related Industries' (SADRI).[5] Designed to serve the state's military purposes in a period of economic isolation, aerospace and defence activities have largely relied on funding support from the government. During this period South Africa's aerospace industry expanded and became a first-tier manufacturer, producing complete systems such as the Cheetah fighter, a combat aircraft.

In the early 1990s, global trends, together with political transition in South Africa and economic recession, resulted in dramatic cuts in the national defence budget. As a result, many firms exited the defence industry, which became increasingly concentrated (Dunne 2006). Later exposure to international markets revealed the urgent need to formulate sustainable competitive alternatives to maintain the existing South African aerospace capabilities.

Key facts and figures of South African aerospace

Information and studies on the aerospace sector in South Africa are not conducted regularly, and in many cases they provide only a partial view of the sector. Lack of available and consistent data collection is a major constraint on an adequate assessment of the sector and ultimately, on policy formulation. This section provides a compilation of existing material on the South African aerospace industry from available sources,[6] placing domestic facts and figures in an international context.

Size and shape of the aerospace sector

Various sources suggest that there are currently between 100 and 200 domestic organisations engaged in aerospace activities in South Africa. Aerospace companies mainly operate in Gauteng province, while a smaller hub is based in the Western Cape, connected to the University of Stellenbosch.

The sector is highly concentrated in a few very large organisations, although the segment consisting of small, medium and micro enterprises (SMMEs) is rapidly growing and has been recently estimated to comprise about 75 per cent of the organisations.[7] The public-sector defence industry entities consist of Armscor, Denel and CSIR Defencetek. Private-sector companies include Aerosud (South Africa's largest private-sector aviation-industrial company), African Defence Systems (ADS), Advanced Technologies and Engineering (ATE), Grintek, and Sunspace (as the only local satellite manufacturer).

Figures on total revenue for the industry also vary depending on the source. An AMD study (AMD & Vuxaka 2006) estimated that the SADRI had total revenues of about R9.6 billion in 2005, which represented a contribution of 0.56 per cent to total GDP and 3.42 per cent of manufacturing GDP. However, a USA report on the South African aerospace industry[8] suggests that the market size for aerospace

---

4 Goldstein (2002: 522) states that aerospace differs from other components of the MIC in that the scope for diversification into civilian uses is greater.
5 As referred to in the AMD *SADRI Study* (AMD & Vuxaka 2006).
6 Data on employment were obtained from the Labour Force Survey (LFS) (Quantec 2007), and the Department of Trade and Industry (DTI) compiles detailed figures on exports and imports (DTI 2003–2006). Other information on various aspects of the sector has been extracted from international and national papers and reports. Additionally, personal communication with relevant institutions in the sector (the DTI, the Aerospace Industry Support Initiative (AISI), the National Aerospace Centre of Excellence (NACoE) at Wits University, and the Aerospace, Maritime and Defence Industries Association of South Africa (AMD)) contributed to drawing the present profile of the sector.
7 *Business Report*, Aerospace industry gets threefold boost, 28 August 2007.
8 See US Commercial Service 2004.

alone (excluding defence) in 2003 was R8.5 billion,[9] with an estimated annual projected growth rate of approximately 5 per cent until 2007.

The AMD study also revealed that about 90 per cent of total sales in the domestic market are still of a military nature, in contrast to less than 10 per cent in civilian sales. However, the study detected a significant increase in the share of civilian sales in exports, which moved up from about 1 per cent to nearly 20 per cent of the total exports in the past decade. Despite the marginal shift towards civilian sales in exports, overall sales are still clearly dominated by the military sector, which accounts for about 95 per cent of total turnover.[10]

According to the Labour Force Survey (LFS), the sub-sector 'manufacture of aircraft and spacecraft' employed approximately 1 500 people in 2005, contributing about 0.14 per cent of total employment in the manufacturing sector (Quantec 2007). However, this figure does not account for aerospace employment classified within other sub-sectors such as 'weapons and ammunition' and 'special-purpose machinery'.

Trade dynamics

The South African aerospace industry has traditionally been reliant on imports. However, following the lifting of the UN embargo in 1994, exports of aerospace and defence-related products accelerated. Opening up to international markets put pressure on domestic companies to revise their business strategies.

The latest available data from the Department of Trade and Industry (DTI) trade database, summarised in Table 3.2, reflect the recent shift in trade dynamics (DTI 2003–2006). From 2003 to 2006 exports grew exponentially, at an average annual rate of nearly 50 per cent, while imports decreased at about 13 per cent annually. The decline of imports and acceleration of exports gained momentum in 2005.

Not only has the direction of trade changed but also the origin and destination of aerospace manufactures. DTI data also show that imports have experienced a growing concentration in the USA, accounting for 51 per cent of total South African imports of aerospace products in 2006 (DTI 2006). This has been accompanied by a considerable reduction in the role of France as a major supplier (imports from France dropped from 48 per cent of total imports in 2003 to 6.4 per cent in 2006). Meanwhile, export markets have followed the opposite trend, becoming more diversified. From exporting mostly to the USA in 2003, South Africa broadened its exports in 2006 to include the EU (France, Germany and Sweden) and other sub-Saharan countries (Angola, Zambia and Kenya).

TABLE 3.2: *Trade in aircraft, spacecraft and parts (R millions), 2003–2006*

Trade	R Millions				Average annual growth rate (%)
	2003	2004	2005	2006	
Exports	796	1 210	4 254	4 018	49.9
Imports	9 336	11 806	9 510	5 379	−12.8

Source: Based on DTI 2003–2006

---

9 These latter figures were based on unofficial estimates obtained from industry sources.
10 Note that in more developed aerospace markets, such as the UK, turnover is equally shared by defence and civil sides, each representing 50 per cent of turnover (UK House of Commons Trade & Industry Committee 2005).

Upstream and downstream linkages

The overall impact of the aerospace industry must be considered in connection to other productive activities. Efficient aerospace production requires not only the obvious elements of adequate infrastructure and skilled labour force, but also access to basic aircraft production inputs such as aluminium, steel, wire, cable, fasteners, and also more sophisticated inputs such as electronic components, software, computerised parts, testers, etc. These inputs are obtained from other industries: the mining sector, composite materials, tooling, machinery, automotive, ICTs and textiles.

Upstream and downstream linkages of aerospace are represented in Figure 3.1. The figure shows that the aerospace industry is linked to more 'representative' industries – in terms of socio-economic impact in South Africa – such as metals and chemicals, which are also key suppliers to the composite materials and tooling industries. These latter sectors are suppliers not only to more advanced manufacturing sectors such as the automotive, electronics and machinery sectors, but also directly to aerospace.

Although the previous section highlighted the growing export orientation of South African aerospace manufactures, some products are still consumed domestically. Major domestic clients include the transport sector (the national carrier, South African Airways) and the defence sector (the South African National Defence Force (SANDF)). Smaller, low-cost airlines are also exploiting the fast-growing tourism sector, and are expanding their routes and fleets.

South Africa's wealth in raw materials, combined with considerable capabilities in advanced industries like automotive and ICTs, suggests that the aerospace industry is well positioned to maintain a domestic supplier base of high quality and competitive prices. There is a large potential to exploit existing advantages in composites, advanced materials and the tooling industry, which complements the country's strength in more traditional sectors such as the mining sector and the metal industry. However, locally manufactured products in less technologically advanced industries that could supply the domestic aerospace production industry have become export commodities.[11]

FIGURE 3.1: *Aerospace industry's domestic linkages to other economic sectors in South Africa*

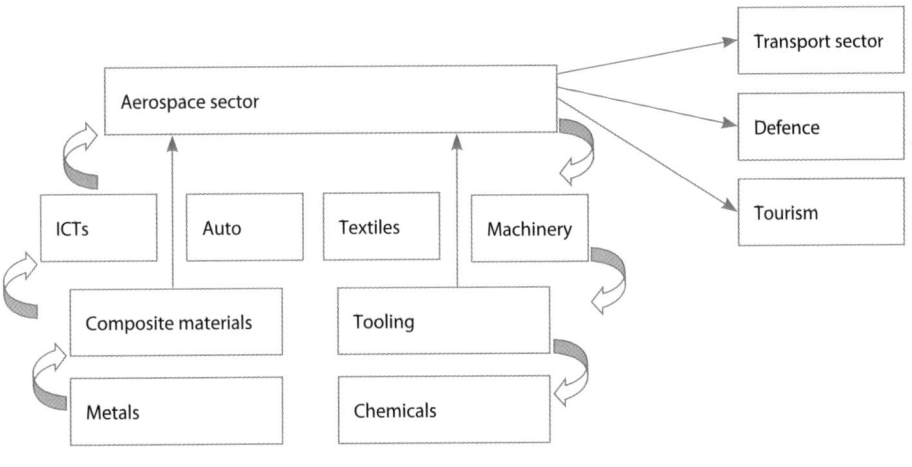

---

11 *Engineering News* gives the example of a specific reproduction material used for construction, tooling, coating and modelling which is mainly exported; while approximately 60 per cent of the raw materials are sourced in South Africa; see Heydenreych A, Opportunities emerge in aerospace, marine sectors, *Engineering News* 9 June 2006.

In summary, the strength of upstream linkages of aerospace activities with the defence, transport and tourism sectors is not matched by its downstream linkages. Integration of the aerospace industry within domestic value chains seems central to its long-term competitiveness.

Innovation and technology dynamics

Aerospace activities require enormous efforts to be expended on R&D (AMTS 2004). Therefore the sector is widely regarded as an incubator of critical technologies. Many of the technologies, methods and processes researched and developed by the aerospace industry have the potential to be employed in other economic sectors. The previous section indicated that the aerospace industry is a major absorber of technologies from other adjacent sectors (ICTs, automotive, tools, machinery, etc.). Following this argument, it is clear that the benefits from technological innovation and R&D in aerospace are not confined solely to the industry itself.

However, in South Africa, the aerospace sector has developed in isolation not only from global markets but also from the domestic economy as a result of strategic funding used for military purposes. Nevertheless, some researchers have already pointed to the increasing 'technological openness' of South African aerospace. For example, an AMD study asserts that 'the South African Defence and Related Industry (SADRI) has matured from a "technology colony" through backward industrial integration' (AMD & Vuxaka 2006).

A study by the DTI (2004) examined the strengths and advantages of South Africa in various aerospace-related technologies that were highlighted as being critically important for the continuous development and growth of the aerospace sector. The study revealed that South Africa's competitive strengths in composite materials and in health and usage monitoring systems (HUMS) technologies place it in a strong position to further develop these technologies and become a leading global player in the aerospace industry.

In particular, high-performance composites are used extensively in commercial liners by Airbus and Boeing (two first-tier global leaders) and their demand is increasing on a global scale. In 2005, the composite industry in South Africa employed about 12 000 people (Hanekom 2007). Efforts are currently being devoted to research in composite metal hybrids, nanocomposites and 'green composites'. Regarding the latter, advances in the development of green composites could have a significant impact in the agricultural sector. They have been recognised as a potential way of adding value to natural resources and creating rural employment, by growing and sustaining plantations of natural organic composites, such as hemp and flax, thereby benefiting disadvantaged groups and displaced communities.[12] Again, the widespread benefits of intense innovation and technology development in the aerospace sector seem largely dependent on the success of its integration into international markets, but equally important is its creative integration within domestic value chains. It is, however, essential that integration of the industry is entirely committed and subordinated to the country's primary goals of poverty alleviation and sustainable development.

Drivers of change in the aerospace sector

Changes in the sector are driven by multiple factors. Dramatic changes in global production chains are creating new opportunities for, and threats to, domestic aerospace companies. At the national level, new policy initiatives and emerging market opportunities also influence the direction the industry is taking. At the manufacturing level, technology intensity and innovation dynamics in the sector open new avenues of competition and production.

---

12 Naidoo B, SA composites industry needs R&D, says research council, *Engineering News* 8 June 2007.

Global changes in production

The landscape and dynamics of aerospace companies are characterised by rapid transformation. Aerospace and defence industries have experienced a decade of intense consolidation, particularly at the level of top-tier manufacturers in the USA and the EU. At the same time, liberalisation and privatisation are altering the relationships between the top-tier aerospace giants and their lower-tier suppliers.

Global decline in defence budgets and increasing privatisation of aerospace companies have provided greater room for the expansion of civil aviation. The exponential growth of low-cost airlines all over the world continues to increase purchases of aircraft. These forces are pressurising first-tiers to reduce their manufacturing costs.

These dynamics affect South African domestic aerospace companies in two ways. Firstly, first-tiers are increasingly outsourcing globally to lower-cost sites, which has clear implications for the handful of emerging economies that have managed to develop significant aerospace capabilities, such as India, Brazil, China and South Africa. Secondly, to reduce costs, first-tiers are concentrating on core capabilities and placing more design, manufacturing, risk-sharing and supply-chain management responsibilities on lower-tier suppliers (*Avionics* 2006).

In summary, global changes in production are generating large opportunities for the few developing countries that can supply aerospace products, as low-cost offshore locations. However, it is becoming increasingly difficult to survive at the lower-tier level. The ability of these countries to maintain the rapidly increasing sophistication of international demands in this technology-intensive industry has been questioned (De Bruijn & Steenhuis 2004). South African aerospace companies must multiply their efforts in order to adapt to the new terms of competition, with updated skills and technological capabilities.

New policy initiatives and key programmes under way

South Africa's government has identified aerospace as a national high-priority sector. Its vision is to develop the sector as a sustainable, growing, and internationally recognised industry by 2014 (AMTS 2004). To achieve this goal, the growth trajectory of the sector has been modelled on the successful experience of the automotive sector (SAIIA 2006). Aerospace has been recognised as both technology-driven and a labour-intensive sector, able to provide technically oriented jobs that can contribute to tackling the brain drain of skilled people. However, an overall strategy for the sector is still in progress.

Recent policy programmes reflect this vision and are oriented to different areas, although the majority of policy interventions appear to be driven by the need to fill an obvious skills gap. Most initiatives have only been operative for a few years; therefore, it is still too early to perceive their impact.

Skills-related initiatives include: (i) the European South Africa Science and Technology Advancement Programme (ESASTAP) that promotes and supports networking and partnering between scientists and institutions from the EU and South Africa; and (ii) the National Aerospace Centre of Excellence (NACoE) established in 2005. The NACoE offers skills programmes and bursary schemes with major domestic companies. It has also entered into R&D partnerships involving major global players, local universities and domestic companies.

Manufacturing-related initiatives include: (i) the Airbus A400M programme agreement, signed in 2005, whereby major domestic aerospace players became risk-sharing partners in the international manufacture of an Airbus military aircraft. So far, the A400M programme seems to have had mixed results; some companies seem to have benefited in terms of engineering capabilities, while other companies have suggested that the engineering work involved is not significant; (ii) the Aerospace Industry Support Initiative (AISI), which was established in 2006. Its most significant planned intervention will be the Centurion Aerospace Village (CAV) scheduled to open in 2010, an aerospace supplier park modelled on the automotive industry.

Key programmes under way include the South African Space Agency, which was approved in 2006. The agency is envisaged to be active by 2008 and to co-ordinate and implement the country's space science and technology programmes. In addition, new policy perspectives are contemplating the promotion of co-operation between South Africa, India and Brazil to cultivate their complementary niches in aerospace rather than competing in their low-tier supplies to developed economies.[13]

Changes in domestic conditions

The rapid growth in domestic civil airlines and the growth of tourism have had a positive impact on the sector and are raising favourable prospects of future aerospace products demand. This provides incentives for domestic aerospace manufacturers to upgrade their manufactures and eventually become first-tier producers. In addition, South Africa is well positioned to easily access new regional markets, not only in southern Africa but also on the rest of the continent. Airbus has estimated that air traffic in Africa will increase by 7 per cent annually from 2006 to 2010 (Airbus 2006).

Technology and innovation

Manufacturing aircraft and spacecraft is highly technology-intensive. Therefore technology changes have a significant impact on employment and skill requirements in aerospace production. Technological advance promotes the constant upgrading of skills in the workforce for this sector. As mentioned in previous sections, technologies affecting the sector originate both in aerospace and in adjacent sectors such as composite materials, tools and automotive.

Measuring the skills gap in aerospace manufacturing

This section examines the 'size' of the skills gap in aerospace manufacturing, comparing the demand and supply of skills as well as their changes in composition over time.

Demand for skills

The design and manufacture of technologically sophisticated products for the aerospace industry require inputs and skills from various types of workers, including managers, technicians, plant operators and assemblers, as well as administrative and support staff. However, overall the aerospace industry has a larger proportion of workers with education beyond high school than the average for all industries.

---

13 The agenda of the India-Brazil-South Africa (IBSA) working group in this respect can be found in SAIIA 2006.

Aerospace employment in South Africa

According to the LFS, South Africa's 'manufacture of aircraft and spacecraft' directly employed about 1 500 people in 2005 (Quantec 2007).[14]

This figure reflects the fact that aerospace is not a major contributor to employment in South Africa. On average, the sub-sector 'manufacture of aircraft and spacecraft' represented about 0.15 per cent of total employment in manufacturing for the period 1996–2005.

Available data show that employment in 'manufacture of aircraft and spacecraft' has consistently increased from 2003 to the present. However, growth in labour demand has not taken place homogeneously in terms of occupations, level of skills, age, race and gender. Changes in the composition of demand might be the result of various factors: the dynamic nature of the aerospace industry, the adaptation of South Africa's industry to changes in international markets, and finally, new employment dynamics at the national level following South Africa's political transition.

Figure 3.2 shows that, contrary to national dynamics,[15] in the aerospace sector employees in elementary occupations accounted for the smallest single share of total employment (3 per cent) in 2001–2005. Compared to the total manufacturing sector, aerospace has three times the proportion of managers and senior officials, and twice the proportion of professionals. The numbers of technicians, clerks, service workers and assemblers are also proportionally higher in the aerospace industry. The proportions of elementary occupations and craft-and-related-trades workers are about six times lower in aerospace than the average in the manufacturing sector.

From a gender and racial perspective, most employees in the sector are male and white. Occupations held by women, and by black (i.e. African, coloured and Indian) employees, are predominantly located at the semi-skilled and unskilled occupational levels. Yet major changes have taken place in 'senior officials and managers' occupations. This category has gone through a rapid transformation during the past decade, with the inclusion of more black, female and intermediate-skilled employees; however, the data also show that this category is rapidly aging (see Table 3.3).

Changes in other occupational categories, particularly those related to technical and advanced manufacturing skills, such as 'professionals' and 'technicians and associated professionals' have been very limited. A critical challenge facing the sector is increasing the participation of non-white, female and younger people in the technical occupational categories. Meeting the future demand of professional and technical skills in the sector largely depends on the correction of these imbalances.

Another interesting feature is presented in Table 3.4. This table shows the rapid growth of the demand for intermediate skills in the aerospace industry. From representing 43 per cent of total aerospace employment in 1996–1999, the intermediate-skilled workforce accounted for nearly 60 per cent in 2001–2005.

---

14 It must be noted that defence and civil aerospace are very difficult to separate – especially in South Africa – since the same companies often produce for both markets. Identifying the size of aerospace employment is thus largely constrained by the fact that some aerospace manufactures can be classified as 'weapons and ammunition', which fall into other categories such as 'manufacturing of special purpose machinery'. Current methods of data collection do not allow for extracting the proportion of aerospace-related employment within other sub-sectors. In this report, we suggest that the real figure on aerospace employment is very likely to be higher than 1 500 employees.

15 In 2005, elementary occupations accounted for the largest single share of employment (22.9 per cent) (MERSETA 2006).

FIGURE 3.2: *Occupational profile of the aerospace industry relative to the total manufacturing sector, average 2001–2005*

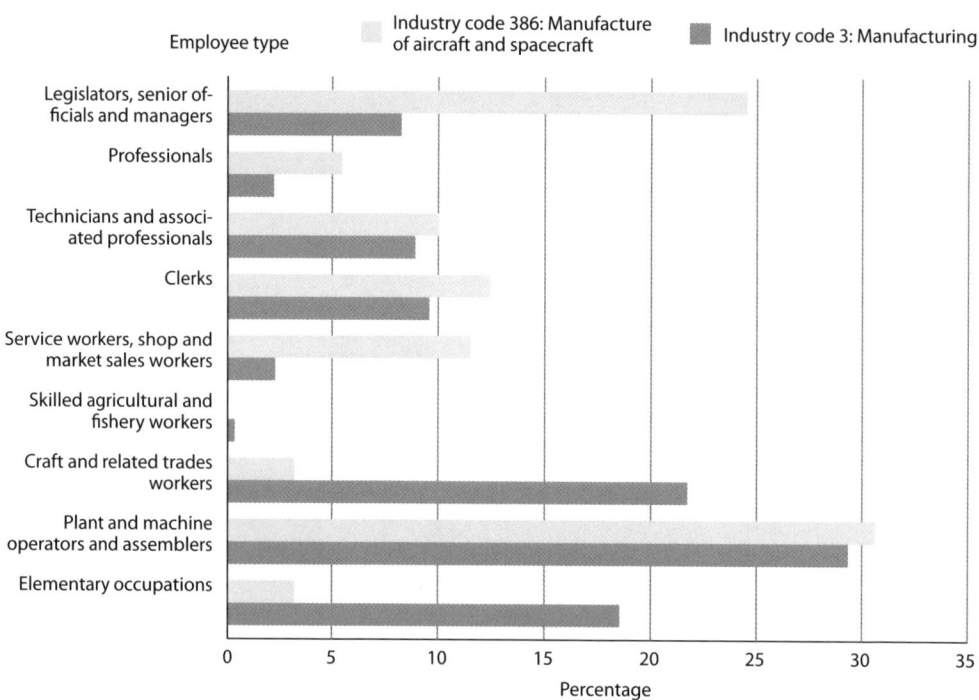

Source: Quantec 2007 (Stats SA OHS data for 1996–1999; Stats SA LFS data for 2000–2005)

TABLE 3.3: *Changes in composition of aerospace employment in key occupations, 1996–2005*

Staff composition	Senior officials & managers (%)		Professionals (%)		Technicians & associated professionals (%)	
	1996–1999	2001–2005	1996–1999	2001–2005	1996–1999	2001–2005
Black	0	46	0	0	0	27
Female	0	23	0	0	0	0
Intermediate skills	0	94	0	0	0	100
Younger than 50	100	54	0	0	100	100

Source: Quantec 2007 (Stats SA LFS data for 2000–2005)

Results also indicate that the demand for skills in the aerospace industry is converging towards the profile of the overall manufacturing sector. In aerospace manufacturing the demand for lower skills is rising, while the demand for high skills is declining. Meanwhile, the overall manufacturing sector is moving up from a low-skill base towards a higher-skilled profile.

TABLE 3.4: *Percentage change in skills demand in the aerospace sector and the total manufacturing sector, 1996–2005*

Skills level	Manufacture of aircraft and spacecraft			Total manufacturing		
	1996–1999	2001–2005	% change	1996–1999	2001–2005	% change
Low	29	35	7	65	55	–10
Intermediate	43	58	15	30	39	9
High	28	7	–21	3	5	1
Unknown	0	0	0	1	1	0
Total	100	100		100	100	

Source: Based on Quantec 2007 (Stats SA LFS data for 2000–2005)

The supply of skills

Any manufacturer of complex machinery requires a pool of available skilled labour. Moreover, a country wishing to establish and promote aerospace manufacturing must have access to a sophisticated academic system, capable of producing highly educated engineers. This is especially relevant for South Africa, which is competing as a supplier to global leaders through upgrading its aerospace manufactures. Local producers are now required to build products that meet the strictest international standards, and this has direct implications for the education and training systems in South Africa.

Further and higher education and training

An examination of the availability of further education and training (FET) and higher education and training (HET) graduates with qualifications in the aerospace and engineering fields reveals the poor state of skills supply for aerospace activities. Statistics from the National Learners' Records Database (NLRD) reveal the low number of enrolments in FET courses on aerospace subjects. Moreover, some aerospace-related subjects have been practically deserted during the last decade (DoE 2007b). The NLRD also shows that pass rates have decreased over time, suggesting that the quality of education in technical subjects has deteriorated.

In relation to HET, the total number of graduates in technikons (now called universities of technology) and universities with qualifications in engineering was 4 348 in 2004. However, only 16 of these had majored in aeronautical engineering, and just over 600 in mechanical engineering (with direct application to aerospace manufacturing). Overall, graduation rates in engineering are strikingly low, and although they show moderate improvements in technikons (from 8 per cent in 2000 to 11 per cent in 2004), they declined in universities from 19 per cent overall in 2000 to just 14 per cent in 2004 (DoE 2007a). The Manufacturing, Engineering and Related Services Sector Education and Training Authority (MERSETA) has suggested that an improved graduation rate is desirable, as insufficient numbers are coming through the system to meet demand from the industry (MERSETA 2006).

Table 3.5 illustrates the pace at which the racial and gender distribution of engineering graduates in HET has evolved. Racial equity achievements are visible at the undergraduate level (from 43 per cent black graduates in 1996–2000 to 60 per cent in 2001–2005), as well as at the postgraduate level (from 20 per cent postgraduates in 1996–2000 to 36 per cent in 2001–2005). However, white postgraduates still represented about two-thirds of the total for 2001–2005. Although female representation at undergraduate level has doubled during the last decade, in 2001–2005, 80 per cent of the undergraduates in

TABLE 3.5: *Supply of engineers in HET: percentage of black and female graduates, 1996–2005*

	Undergraduate		Postgraduate	
	1996–2000	2001–2005	1996–2000	2001–2005
Black (%)	43	60	20	36
Female (%)	10	20	11	15

Source: Based on DoE 2007a

engineering were male. In postgraduate studies, advances in gender equity were minimal from 1996 to 2005 (with female postgraduates increasing from 11 per cent to 15 per cent of the total).

Drivers of change in aerospace skills

This section examines the existing routes for new skills formation in the aerospace sector. It provides a brief description of available training providers, complemented with first-hand information on skills development practices in individual aerospace firms. This information has been collected through personal interviews with a sample of seven aerospace manufacturers[16] and also with the Denel Centre for Learning and Development (DCLD).

Supply of training

The absence of a specific training authority for aerospace manufacturing limits the amount of formal training available for companies in the sector. A number of firms have developed their own in-house training programmes, but smaller firms lack the resources to provide ongoing training. Skills development and training continue to pose a major challenge to this industry.

SETAs and domestic training providers

Two SETAs partially service South African aerospace companies: the MERSETA and the Transport Education and Training Authority (TETA). The MERSETA covers a number of manufacturing activities such as automotive, new tyre, plastics, metal and motor manufacturing, but not aerospace manufacturing; while the TETA is responsible for aerospace, but only as a transport service.

All interviewed companies reported that they belonged to either the MERSETA, the TETA or both. Nevertheless, the interviews with these companies revealed the limited use that aerospace manufacturers make of the SETAs. Grants, learnerships, apprenticeships and tax incentives can be accessed from the MERSETA and the TETA to encourage companies to increase their training activities. The SETAs' policy is to reimburse training costs, but only if the trainers are accredited training providers, that is, in possession of a qualification registered with the South African Qualifications Authority (SAQA).

Due to the complexity of aerospace manufacturing, training often cannot be found nationally. In order to fulfil the customers' requirements, aerospace companies tend to send their employees abroad or

---

16 The companies interviewed included three first-tiers (Denel, Aerosud and Sunspace), two lower-tiers (ATT Composites and CCII), and two aerospace services companies (one small, TMI Consulting, and one large, ARMSCOR). Despite the small size of the sample, the variety of companies represents the different types of organisations operating in the industry. All interviews were conducted between 10 July and 30 September 2007.

FIGURE 3.3: *Intake of apprentices to the DCLD, 1990–2007*

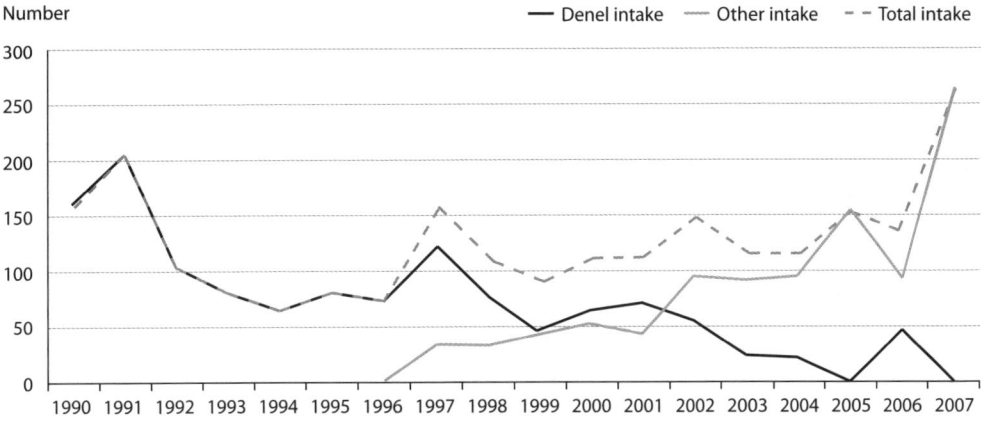

Source: Denel Centre for Learning and Development, personal communication with the author

to un-accredited training programmes. This results in a large pool of unclaimed contributions to the SETAs that remains unused, and an increase in the costs of training for domestic aerospace manufacturers.[17] The effectiveness of the SETAs, in particular for the aerospace industry, has been generally questioned and there have been several calls from industry for a reassessment of their structure.

The DCLD was established in 2002 as a separate entity to Denel. The courses provided by this training centre are accredited by the TETA and the Aerospace Chamber. According to the organisation, the DCLD is the largest public skills development and training programme in Africa for the aerospace and defence industry.

The DCLD services Denel and other national and foreign private companies. Figure 3.3 shows that the intake of apprentices from outside Denel has largely overtaken the intake from Denel since 2002.

The DCLD apprentice school holds over 250 apprenticeships, and runs a Youth Foundation Training Programme in conjunction with the Department of Defence. The majority of intakes in 2007 were African men (40 per cent of total intakes), followed by white men (24 per cent) and African women (22 per cent). Indian and coloured intakes account together for only 14 per cent of the total.

Training practices in aerospace firms

Not surprisingly, training was recognised as central to production activities in all companies interviewed for this study. Although training patterns and practices differed for individual firms, common issues were raised across the sample.

The interviews indicated that the development of skills in the workforce beyond entry level tends to be mostly undertaken by the employers. A large part of the technical and management training takes place in-house, or occasionally in collaboration with private training institutions, customers, other

---

17   For contract-specific skills training, some of the large aerospace companies have managed to negotiate a refund of a percentage of the training costs at overseas institutions, although they need to be accredited in their respective countries (some companies reported claims of up to 70 per cent of the costs of training). However, not every company is in a position to claim back these expenses.

domestic companies, universities and technikons/universities of technology. The relevance of training is reflected in companies' reported focus on training as a central aspect of their strategy. The intensity of training is also high; on average, employers devote between 5 and 10 per cent of their sales income to training expenses.

Technical training appears to be the most common form of training, including in-house, overseas and local technical training. Management training, on the other hand, is not a priority in training practices, whether local or overseas. Major international clients play a key role in training South African aerospace workers. Offset agreements imply that foreign contractors have to reinvest a certain amount of the value of their purchases in South African development. In some cases, this is achieved by establishing skills development programmes with the foreign contractor, which involves sending local technicians overseas. Overall, technicians and associated professionals seem to benefit most from training, as management training is less frequent.

Interviewed companies were asked to identify the two most important *areas of training* for each of the broad occupational categories (see Table 3.6). For managers and supervisors, training in 'soft skills' was the most commonly identified area, and also production planning and financial skills. For engineers and technicians, computer skills appeared to be crucial. Aerospace production is becoming increasingly computerised and these skills have become a prerequisite for South African manufacturers to gain international contracts.[18] Project management was also widely regarded as an important area in which to train engineers and technical staff. Other specific technical skills related to particular customer requirements, and were usually obtained on an ad hoc basis. For production workers and artisans, training appears to be more regular, and focused on specific job tasks such as moulding, composites training, design, and also on occupational health and safety.

TABLE 3.6: *Identified key areas for training*

Occupation	Most important areas for training
Managers/supervisors	soft skills: communication, leadership team-building line management occupational health and safety human resources management financial skills production planning
Engineers and technicians	computer skills: programming, application software project and contract management quality assurance production planning logistics and maintenance
Production workers/artisans	design training moulding composites training occupational health and safety

Source: Author interviews with industry participants

18 For example, CATIA is a suite of software products for PLM (Product Lifecycle Management) solutions. It covers the process of design, simulation and manufacture, allowing companies to improve efficiency with minimal errors. CATIA is continually evolving, and competence in this technology has been established as a prerequisite for awarding contracts to suppliers. See Tyrer L, Investment in technology key to competitiveness, *Engineering News* 2 June 2006.

FIGURE 3.4: *Immigration and emigration of engineers and related technologists, 1998–2003*

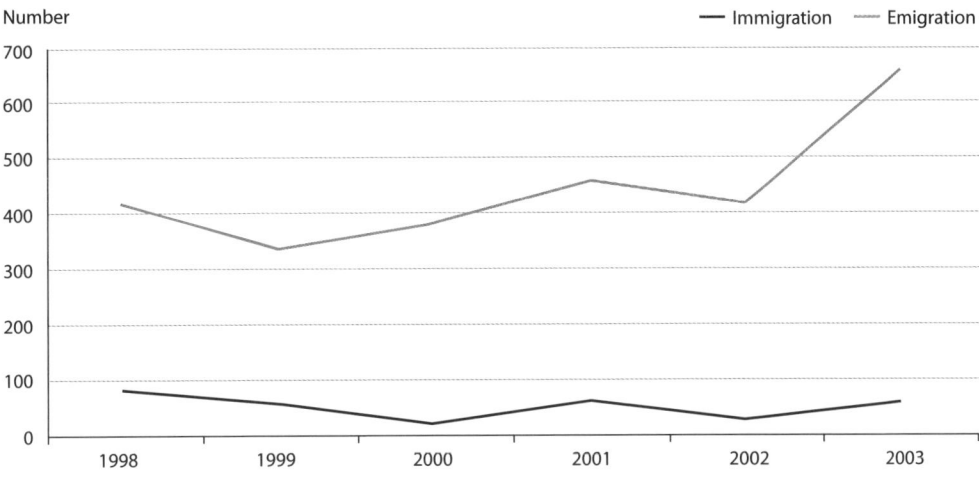

Source: Stats SA 2000; 2003

Note: In 2004, Stats SA stopped collecting and publishing emigration figures. Emigration trends can therefore not be traced beyond 2003.

Socio-economic drivers

Migration and HIV/AIDS are some of the social factors affecting the supply of skilled professionals in South Africa. Emigration trends collected by Stats SA highlight that there is an increasing loss of 'engineers and related technologists', while the immigration of skilled engineers declined during the period 1998–2003 (Stats SA 2000, 2003). These trends are shown in Figure 3.4.

In relation to HIV/AIDS, a lower prevalence would be expected in comparison to other sectors, given the occupational and skills profile of the aerospace industry. However, to date figures on the prevalence of HIV/AIDS in the aerospace industry are not available. Nevertheless, this study found a general recognition amongst employers of the need for intensified education and awareness in relation to health and safety for aerospace workers.

The skills gap: scarce and critical skills

The number of orders received by the South African aerospace industry is rapidly growing, and companies have indicated that they lack the skilled personnel to attend to current and future customer demands. In general, the shortage of technical personnel, in particular engineers, stands out. Scarce skills in the sector are mainly related to technicians and associated professionals, as well as airframe artisans, plant operators and assemblers. These occupational categories are experiencing growing demand over time, but the rate of formation of these types of workers does not seem to be keeping up with the rapid pace of change in the industry.

Scarce and critical skills are related to the processes and procedures that global contractors require from South African aerospace manufacturers. However, the capacity of local companies to compete is largely limited by the scarcity and quality of available engineering skills, as well as skills at the intermediate level of artisans and composite specialists.

Scarce skills

In general, the shortage of engineers was highlighted in all interviews. Technical skills appear to be in high demand in the South African aerospace sector (see Table 3.7). The urgency of companies' need for engineers is commonly translated into a limitation on their ability to accept orders and fulfil their customers' demands. Mechanical, aerospace, electronic, design and logistic engineers were the most frequently mentioned specialities. In addition, five out of seven companies reported that their expected future demand for skilled workforce would also be for airframe artisans, plant operators and assemblers.

These scarce skills are generally related to the processes and procedures that the first-tiers require from South African suppliers. Domestic aerospace firms seem to be adjusting to their new role in global value chains and managing to attract a considerable share of orders of aerospace sub-systems. However, their capacity to compete and expand is largely limited by the quantity and quality of the available engineering base, as well as by limitations at the intermediate level of artisans and composite specialists.

Critical skills

Interviews conducted for this study revealed that critical skills are generally the result of insufficient training prior to entry into the workplace, technological changes, and recent regulatory changes in the identification of engineering work.

In the interviews, companies were asked to rate the provision of skilled personnel by local universities and technikons. On average, companies considered the quality of the supplied skilled personnel as moderately good (rated as 3 on a scale of 1 to 5). However, many weaknesses were also identified. The most common were:
- lack of understanding of job specifications;
- lack of innovation capabilities;
- lack of adaptation to markets changes;
- lack of practical skills;
- lack of business skills;
- lack of soft skills.

TABLE 3.7: *Identified scarce skills in South African aerospace manufacturing*

Group	Sub-group
Engineers	mechanical engineers aerospace engineers electronic engineers design engineers logistic engineers
Artisans	machine sheet metal assembly composite
Computer-skilled/software developers	computer-aided design packages

Source: Author interviews with industry participants

There was widespread concern about the need to expose skilled personnel to the marketplace during their period of tertiary education and the initiation of their working life. Internships, vacation work for engineering students, mentorship programmes and bursaries inclusive of training in the company were identified as the most successful ways to ensure the readiness of the personnel and their loyalty to the company.

Critical skills listed by employers included:
- for management staff: financial skills, leadership skills, communication skills, human resources management, performance management, project management;
- for production workers: computer skills, engineering design, quality assurance, project management, soft skills.

Specialised technical skills and engineering design were identified as critical for production workers in aerospace manufacturing. However, soft skills and project management were the most important critical skills in the sector, as they cut across all occupational groups.

Conclusions and policy recommendations

South Africa is one of the few developing countries that have managed to develop capabilities in aerospace manufacturing. Changes in global production chains are bringing new opportunities and challenges to South Africa as a global aerospace supplier. Likewise, rapid growth in air traffic and civil airlines raises the favourable prospect of increasing aerospace industry demand. The number of orders in the industry is clearly growing, mostly in connection to major global players such as Boeing or Airbus.

However, these changes are also demanding higher capabilities from South African aerospace manufacturers. The growth of global outsourcing causes growing competition among low-cost sites in other emerging economies such as China, India and Brazil. Domestic companies need to respond to new challenges through upgrading their manufacturing capabilities as international suppliers. In achieving this goal, the integration of aerospace manufacturing into international and domestic supply value chains still remains a major challenge. South Africa's existing advantages in green composites, advanced materials and the tooling industry (which are key major suppliers to aerospace) remain unexploited. Most of the production in these sectors is exported instead of being incorporated into domestic advanced manufactures.

Technicians and artisans are in increasing demand, and shortages of these skills are constraining the capacity of domestic firms to expand their production and survive. Simultaneously, the quality of the supply of skilled personnel seems to have deteriorated during the last decade, reducing the ability of local aerospace manufacturers to maintain competitiveness.

The formation of new skills also appears to be limited, with domestic companies bearing a large fraction of the costs of training. Interviews with industry participants emphasised the severe skills constraints faced by South African aerospace manufacturers. Skills shortages are evident in terms of both overall skills to maintain current production, and also specific skills to be able to confront future changes in demand and markets. Accredited training providers seem to be scarce, while high training expenses threaten the sustainability of firms, particularly the growing base of aerospace-related SMMEs.

Structural problems in the composition of the skills base are reflected in persistent inequalities in terms of the demand and supply of technical personnel and engineers, which remain dominated by white men. Black, female and young employees remain marginalised. The correction of these imbalances seems crucial for the industry's long-term sustainability. The persistence of social factors affecting the supply of technicians and engineers, such as migration and HIV/AIDS, also threatens existing skills shortages. In conclusion, it is essential to ensure that objectives in aerospace are achieved, in line with key economic policies of government, such as reducing unemployment and eradicating poverty.

Policy recommendations

Effectively addressing the existing skills gap in aerospace manufacturing requires the design of a sustainable and broad strategy for the sector, in connection to adjacent domestic industries. The formulation of interventions needs to be grounded in detailed, updated and comparable information on aerospace activities. Such information is still lacking in South Africa.

Shortages of technical skills emerge in this chapter as a central concern. Careers in science, engineering and technology need to be promoted and made attractive for the young generation, especially in previously disadvantaged communities and among women. In the shorter term, firms' capacity to compete and expand can be tackled by facilitating the employment of international labour when skills are not available locally.

The development of skills beyond entry-level training at the workplace is considered critical to maintaining current competitiveness in the sector. Training was recognised as central to production activities in all the companies interviewed. The shortage of available accredited training providers in South Africa requires urgent attention. Interventions should also promote the development of training networks as well as improve mobility of skilled employees across aerospace firms.

Creating an adequate regulatory environment for aerospace activities requires co-ordination efforts among several departments, such as the DTI, the Department of Defence and the Department of Science and Technology. New initiatives have recognised the benefits that will result from reorganisation of the aerospace industry in South Africa, and the need for synchronised efforts on the part of various local actors, including industry, government and educational organisations. Integration of supply chains, strengthening of strategic partnerships and skills development are at the centre of recent initiatives. However, it is still too early to feel their impact.

Last but not least, objectives in aerospace need to be formulated in line with key economic policies of government, such as reducing unemployment and eradicating poverty. Alignment with these core development goals remains an indispensable condition for realising a sustainable aerospace industry in South Africa.

References

Airbus (2006) *Global Insight – Global Market Forecast 2004–2023*. Accessed 10 June 2007, http://www.airbus.com/

AMD (Aerospace Maritime and Defence Industries Association of South Africa) & Vuxaka (2006) *The 2006 South African Defence-Related Industries (SADRI) study*. Centurion: Aerospace, Maritime and Defence Industries Association of South Africa

AMTS (Advanced Manufacturing Technology Strategy) (2004) *ASEGAI – A strategy for sustainable, economical and growing aerospace industry*. Pretoria: Department of Science and Technology

Avionics (2006) Avionics development: Playing by the new rules. Accessed 20 September 2007, http://www.aviationtoday.com

De Bruijn E & Steenhuis HJ (2004) Freedom of choice in technology strategy? An analysis of technology strategy in the large commercial aircraft industry. *Technology Analysis and Strategic Management* 16(3): 381–393

DoE (Department of Education, South Africa) (2007a) *Higher Education Management Information System (HEMIS) database 1999–2005*. Pretoria: DoE

DoE (2007b) *FET output data 1996–2005*. Pretoria: DoE

DTI (Department of Trade and Industry, South Africa) (2003–2006) *Trade online database*. Accessed September 2007, http://www.thedti.gov.za

DTI (2004) *Aerospace sector technology development trends*. Pretoria: DTI

Dunne JP (2006) The making of arms in South Africa. *The Economics of Peace and Security Journal* 1(1): 41

Goldstein A (2002) The political economy of high-tech industries in developing countries: Aerospace in Brazil, Indonesia and South Africa. *Cambridge Journal of Economics* 26: 521–538

Hanekom D (2007) Opening address by the Deputy Minister of Science and Technology, Mr Derek Hanekom, at the third South African International Aerospace Symposium (SAIAS '07), Council for Scientific and Industrial Research (CSIR) International Convention Centre, Pretoria

MERSETA (Manufacturing, Engineering and Related Services Sector Education and Training Authority) (2006) *Sector skills plan 2005–2010*. Pretoria: MERSETA

Quantec (2007) *RSA Regional indicators database*. Accessed September 2007, http://www.quantec.co.za/data

SAIIA (South African Institute for International Affairs) (2006) *The aerospace industry: Prospects for strategic cooperation among the IBSA countries*. Trade Report No. 13, South African Institute for International Affairs

Stats SA (Statistics South Africa) (2000) *Tourism and migration*. Data Series P0351. Pretoria: Stats SA

Stats SA (2003) Tourism and migration. Data Series P0351. Pretoria: Stats SA

UK House of Commons Trade & Industry Committee (2005) *Fifteenth report of session 2004–2005: The UK aerospace industry*. London: House of Commons

US Commercial Service (2004) *Report on general aviation market in southern Africa*. Washington DC: US Department of Commerce

CHAPTER 4

Three new technology platforms

Jo Lorentzen and Il-haam Petersen

Introduction

Why undertake big science in a developing, middle-income country such as South Africa? Critics might see the requisite investments as a zero-sum game – every rand spent on advanced technology platforms is a rand less spent on the alleviation of the most dramatic manifestations of under-development afflicting large parts of the population: hunger, disease, unemployment, lack of services, and so on. In addition, they might argue that these investments are a waste of money in that a developing economy must stick to its guns rather than dabble in activities that are simply too big for its shoes.

Although there is some merit in these considerations, things are not quite as simple. Firstly, advances in earth observation can in principle of course alert poor, subsistent rural populations to adverse weather conditions, much as developments in green biotechnology can help them cope with and adjust to these conditions. Secondly, although it is true that catch-up is initially based on technological accumulation through adoption and adaptation, there is a point at which latecomer countries must venture into frontier activities so as to graduate to a higher level of technological sophistication.

Hence what matters is striking a judicious balance between big science and the other developmental activities in support of the catch-up process. Just as an exclusive focus on big science would be mistaken, its complete neglect would also be likely to deprive the country of development opportunities. In essence, therefore, the justification or otherwise of the degree of big science support is an empirical question.

In post-apartheid South Africa, big science was made part of the reconstituted national innovation system from the very beginning and it has become more prominent ever since. It co-existed somewhat uneasily with lower-tech activities in national innovation strategy documents that were remarkable more for the range of activities they proposed to cover than for the focus they established on selected activities (see DACST 1996; DST 2002). This chapter does not address the trade-off between big science and other developmental activities. Instead, it focuses on a narrower question of efficiency, namely, whether the country commands the kinds of human capital required to make big science work.

The attention of the analysis is focused on human capital dynamics in three technology fields: nuclear, space and biotechnology. The core competences in question are in engineering, astronomy and molecular or microbiology. The chapter first reviews pertinent characteristics and trends for each field separately, and establishes the relationship between the demand for and the supply of skills. It then discusses issues across the three fields comparatively, and concludes with recommendations.[1]

Nuclear power and technology[2]

South Africa is one of 30 countries worldwide making use of nuclear power, which in 2006 provided some 15–16 per cent of the world's energy in 435 reactors. Worldwide demand for electricity is forecast to grow by almost 100 per cent by 2030. The renewed interest in nuclear power is based on the increasing realisation that meeting this demand through fossil fuels would exact too high a price from the environment (IAEA 2007).

The Koeberg Nuclear Power Plant near Cape Town consists of two pressurised water reactors (PWRs), each with a capacity of 900 MW. It was commissioned in 1984 and has a design life of 40 years. Eskom owns and operates the plant, which supplies about 5–6 per cent of total electricity to the country. Koeberg employs roughly 1 200 people. Off-site jobs amount to 600, and there are 2 000 additional jobs in the nuclear supplier industry. About 100 non-nuclear firms supply equipment to Koeberg. Upstream, the country processes uranium-rich slurries produced as a by-product of gold or copper mines. Low- and intermediate-level waste from Koeberg is stored at the national radioactive waste repository at Vaalputs in the Northern Cape province. Spent fuel is kept on site at Koeberg.

The Draft Nuclear Energy Policy and Strategy of July 2007 supports the use of nuclear power (DME 2007), partly in order to mitigate the effects of climate change. It provides for an ambitious programme encompassing the entire nuclear fuel cycle. In early 2006, the government announced that it was considering building an additional conventional unit, possibly on the Koeberg site, to alleviate supply constraints in the Western Cape. Similarly, in early 2007, Eskom included 20 GW(e) of new nuclear capacity in its plan to double generating capacity to 80 GW(e) by 2025. The first phase provides for the construction of a 4 GW(e) PWR, like the current Koeberg model, which it is hoped will be commissioned in 2016.

By 2016, South Africa should be engaged in local manufacturing of nuclear components and equipment, and the country's flagship third-generation reactor, the pebble bed modular reactor (PBMR), should be commercialised and ready for export. The current energy generation strategy amounts to a construction programme of some 12 large PWR units and 24 PBMRs. Therefore the South African government is taking a major bet on nuclear technology and especially on the PBMR. So far, the country has invested almost R5 billion in a project whose demonstration plant and fuel facility are currently thought to cost about R16 billion, a figure that could easily rise.[3]

The PBMR is based on a German design (Nicholls 2002). Its shareholders include Eskom, the Industrial Development Corporation (IDC), the South African government and the reactor manufacturer, Westinghouse. Current planning foresees construction of a demonstration plant starting in 2009, with criticality scheduled for 2013. Design certification application in the USA is planned for 2008. The South African government's aim eventually to produce 4 000–5 000 MW of power from PBMRs translates into demand for some 2 030 reactors.

---

1 We are grateful to Carmen Adams, Elmari Bester, Kobus Cloete, Shirley Crawford, Reinhard Hiller, Chris Hodgson, Glenda Kruss, Anita Loots, Sipho Mdleleni, Velaphi Msimang, Sean Phillips, Johan Pienaar, Dries van Schalkwyk, Patricia Whitelock and Derik Wolvaardt for their generous help in providing us with information that was essential to completion of this study.
2 This section is largely based on background material and data assembled by the International Atomic Energy Association (www.iaea.or.at), OECD/IEA 2006, the Nuclear Energy Corporation of South Africa (NECSA; www.necsa.co.za) and the World Nuclear Association (www.world-nuclear.org).
3 K Davie, Bell the cat, *Mail & Guardian* (*Business*) 12–18 October 2007.

The national and international sales prospects of the PBMR are controversial. The PBMR company is of course upbeat (Nicholls 2002). Yet for a number of reasons the success of this technology is as yet unproven (Auf der Heide & Thomas 2002). Also, until the design has been afforded approval by the USA authorities, export prospects, which Eskom initially put at 20 units per year, are merely a theoretical possibility.

The demand for nuclear skills

Engineering skills are globally in short supply. An international survey conducted by Manpower Inc. (2007) found that in South Africa, engineers, skilled manual trade workers such as electricians, welders and carpenters, and technicians, respectively, are the three categories of skills most in demand. Industry bodies report that the shortage concerns all qualifications, from artisans to R&D staff and specialist engineers. The nature of the problem precludes quick fixes. Too few young people enter the career pipeline,[4] and skills in demand in the knowledge economy take longer and longer to acquire.[5]

It is necessary to derive the demand for skills from a variety of data sources. The list of scarce and critical skills published by the Department of Labour (DoL) is based on estimates of the Sector Education and Training Authorities (SETAs) and others, and as such, is very much a document under construction (DoL 2006). The list covers engineering and technical professions, within which it identifies a scarce and critical skills list for the nuclear sector, *not* yet reflecting Eskom's new build programme (Table 4.1).

According to estimates by the Department of Public Enterprises (DPE), Eskom needs almost 4 000 people between 2006 and 2012. This demand prominently includes intermediate skills. Over the same period, the PBMR company is short of 150 people. This is more a case of critical rather than scarce skills per se, many of which fall into the medium- as opposed to the high-skills band. An internal study by Eskom (Van Schalkwyk 2006) reported (outdated) resource needs for the entire nuclear energy sector up to 2009, amounting to 765 people across skill bands. Another DPE projection puts Eskom's demand at 2 300 artisans, 2 600 technologists and technicians, and 2 400 engineers. The PBMR company will need about 50 engineers.

TABLE 4.1: *Scarce and critical skills in the engineering and technical professions, 2006*

Specialisation	Number
Mechanical engineers	120
Process engineers	?
Chemical and materials engineers	10
Nuclear engineers & scientists	?
Specialist pipe engineering & manufacturing	500
Fabrication engineering trade workers	45
Toolmakers and patternmakers	?

Source: DoL 2006

---

4 Deane C, 'National effort' needed to tackle engineering shortage, *Engineering News* 15 September 2006.
5 Davenport J, Funding required to tackle skills shortage, *Engineering News* 17 June 2005.

The nuclear sector, of course, competes with other sectors for scientific, engineering and technical skills. Information about job vacancies derived from the *Sunday Times* database shows that over a 3-year period starting in April 2004, employers were looking for about 2 000 mechanical engineers and technicians, 1 300 electrical engineers and technicians, 600 chemists, chemical engineers and technicians, and 3 200 civil engineers and technicians (Erasmus 2008). Demand for physicists and instruments makers, by contrast, was below 50. Demands for specialists with specific nuclear skills were few and far between, at less than 20. This reflects two facts, namely, that the nuclear sector is indeed competing for generic technical skills with other sectors, and that the data do not yet include trends associated with the new build programme announced in the course of 2006.

Therefore, in general, it appears that the nuclear sector primarily experiences a lack of scarce skills at the medium-skill level and a lack of critical skills at the high-skill level. It is also clear that, in light of the very sizeable planned expansion of the nuclear sector, some of the official information, notably the scarce and critical skills list of the DoL, under-estimates the demand for expertise. What exacerbates the situation, especially at the high-skill end, is that nuclear expertise is a critical skill globally. Hence South Africa directly competes with all other countries with nuclear industries for a small pool of specialists, including its own who might be attracted by employers abroad. This puts the emphasis on indigenous skills training.

The supply of nuclear skills

In 2007, some 28 500 engineering professionals were registered with the Engineering Council of South Africa (ECSA). Of newly recruited members in 2006, 47 per cent were African. The share of Africans is generally on the increase. The South African Council for Natural Scientific Professions had registered 3 191 people in 2006, of whom just 8 per cent were African and 87 per cent white. Women accounted for less than a fifth of the membership. Scientists who could, in principle, work in the nuclear sector numbered roughly 600. By comparison, therefore, the world of science is much more in need of gender and equity transformation than the world of engineering.

According to a DPE study, in-house training by Eskom from 2008 to 2012 will add 400 artisans, 500 technologists and technicians, and 500 engineers per year to the available pool of skilled labour. In addition, the PBMR company will train some 10 new engineers per year in the same period.

Specialists in the nuclear sector primarily originate in three broad study fields, namely, engineering, physics and mathematics. Between 1996 and 2005, South Africa produced some 80 000 graduates in this area. In engineering, 57 per cent of these graduates had at least a bachelor's degree, while the remainder had pre-degree qualifications. Almost all fields experienced positive growth, but nuclear engineering did not. All three areas were dominated by men, but this diminished in engineering and mathematics. The race distribution changed more substantially in the decade to 2005.

In 2000–2005, South African training and education institutions enrolled a quarter of a million people in the engineering field, slightly more than half of whom were at the intermediate-skill level. With a few exceptions, growth rates were positive. Growth rates for female enrolments were considerably higher in engineering, but only marginally so in physics and mathematics. Thus, while the share of women in engineering improved by 4.5 percentage points between 2000 and 2005, it hardly changed in the other two areas. The share of Africans in engineering rose to almost two-thirds in 2005, while that of whites fell to below a quarter. The trend was similar in physics, but less pronounced in mathematics.

The Department of Science and Technology (DST) runs the South African Human Asset & Research Programme (SANHARP), which aims to align skill availability in the nuclear sector with the planned technology platforms. Its bursary holders numbered 160 in 2007. The bulk of these (57 per cent) studied engineering and the rest (43 per cent) studied sciences. On average, 1 in 4 were women who opted more for engineering (58 per cent) than for sciences (42 per cent), but among younger female students, the world of science is evidently much more of a career option than among their older counterparts. SANHARP originally aimed at producing 173 undergraduates and 156 postgraduate and postdoctoral students from 2005 to 2014. However, initially this only reflected the needs of the PBMR, which is why, in light of the new build programme a new skills assessment is needed.

In 2007, five students graduated from the country's only dedicated nuclear engineering programme at the University of the North West. They went to work for the PBMR, the NECSA, M-Tech Industrial, and Eskom.

Conclusion

On the basis of the available data, it does not appear that there is a material shortage of engineers (Figures 4.1–4.4). Graduates consistently exceed the number of vacancies many times over. This is true for all fields of engineering and sciences that are of relevance to the nuclear sector. It is really only in nuclear engineering proper that an admittedly very low vacancy rate is higher than the graduation and even the enrolment rate. In view of the numbers involved, this is unlikely to amount to a crisis per se, but it suggests that nuclear growth in the future might be hampered by skill availability at the specialist end of the skills spectrum.

FIGURE 4.1: *Skills supply and demand in engineering and engineering technology, 2000–2006*

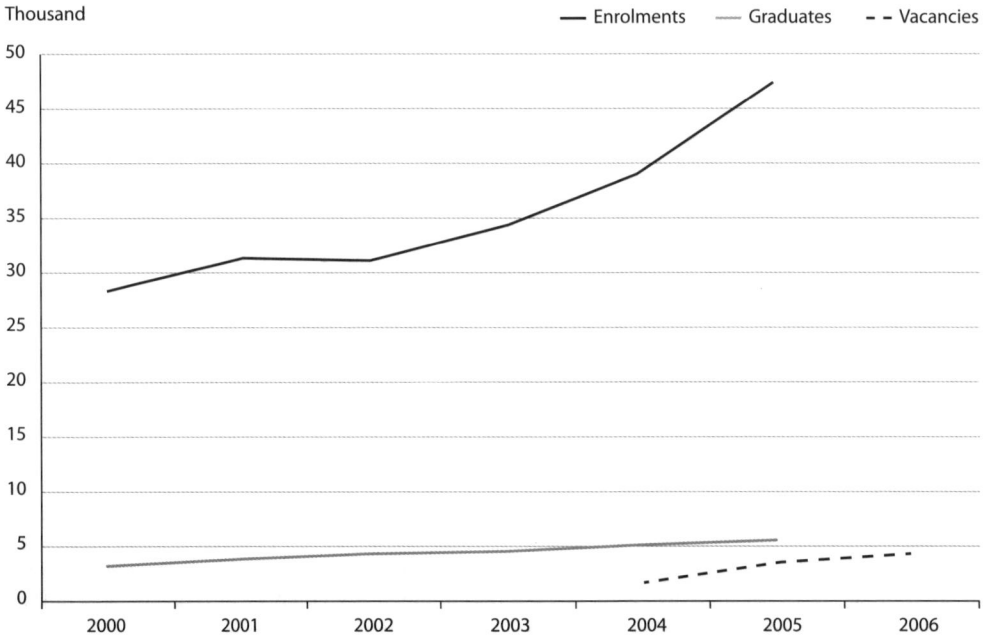

Sources: DoE 1996–2006; Erasmus 2008

FIGURE 4.2: *Skills supply and demand in chemistry, 2000–2006*

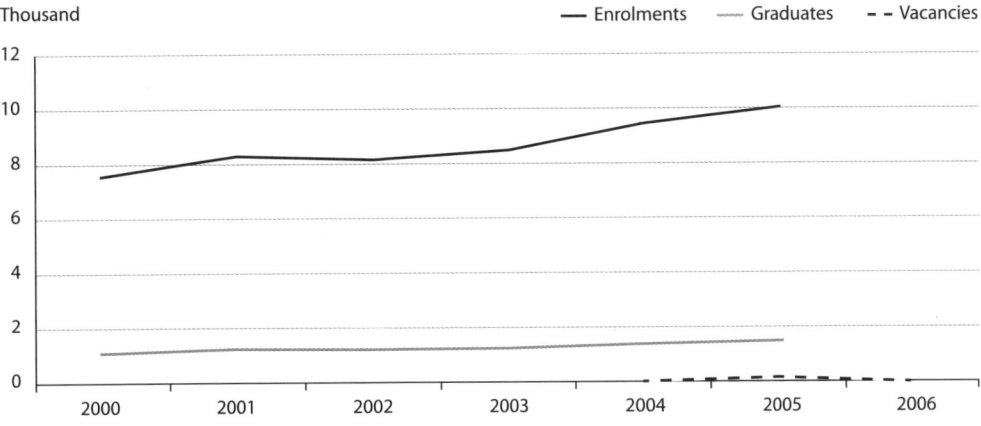

Sources: DOE 1996-2006; Erasmus 2008

FIGURE 4.3: *Skills supply and demand in physics, 2000–2006*

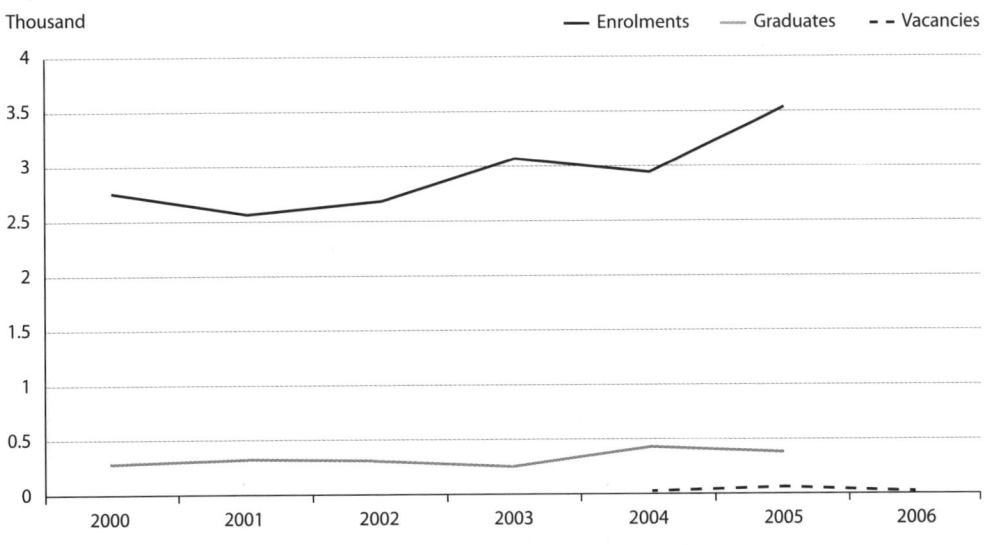

Sources: DOE 1996–2006; Erasmus 2008

Space technology

Space initiatives focus on the exploration, development and use of space. Space technology assists in this endeavour through earth observation from space (satellite technology) and space observation from earth (telescope technology). These initiatives are increasingly being pursued as multinational

FIGURE 4.4: *Skills supply and demand in mathematical sciences, 2000–2006*

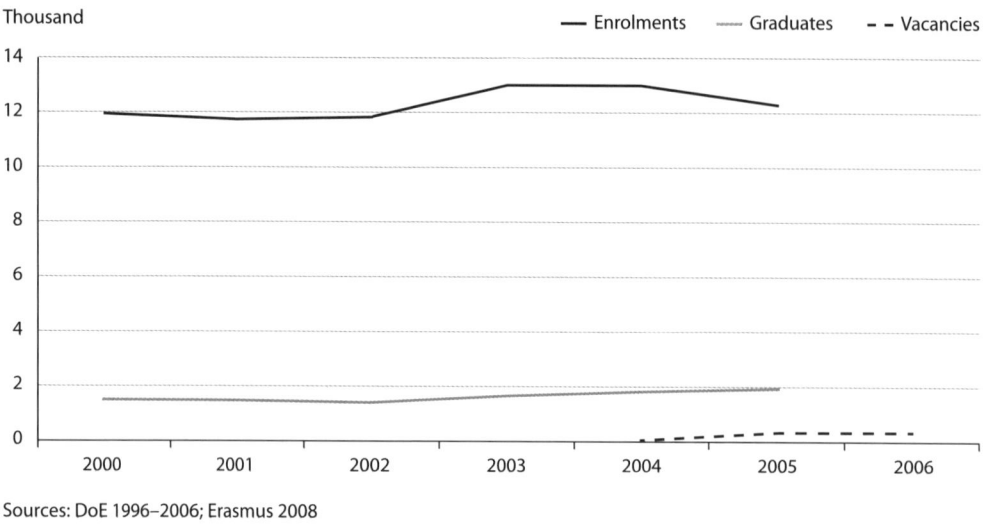

Sources: DoE 1996–2006; Erasmus 2008

endeavours[6]. There are 35 leading countries and organisations and 48 emerging national space programmes in the world (Euroconsult 2006).

The global space market is dominated by the satellite and launch industries. The satellite manufacturing industry is extremely competitive due to an imbalance between supply and demand, thus placing satellite operators in the position to impose price pressures on manufacturers (Saleh 2005). This results in less funding being available to invest in R&D. Breaking into the satellite industry is not easy, as there is a reluctance to buy satellites from companies with an unproven track record because insurance premiums are higher for unproven hardware. There is a small gap for the entry of manufacturers of micro-satellites, but even this market is highly competitive as the big, established companies have started manufacturing micro-satellites as well.

A number of mega-science astronomy projects are planned for the 21st century. The Square Kilometre Array (SKA), which will be the world's largest interferometer radio telescope, is one such mega-science technology planned for completion in 2020 (Hall & Kahn 2006). Technologies such as the SKA provide the opportunity for nations to demonstrate their scientific capabilities, share technology know-how and collaborate on innovative R&D initiatives.

South Africa is one of the best observation sites in the world. The country has a long history in space science and technology. The current government has begun to revive the space sector to enable the country to participate actively in space initiatives and to gain from the global space market. Space science and technology is one of the Frontier Science and Technology Programmes of the DST (DST 2006). South Africa has already successfully built two micro-satellites, one of which was launched in 1999 by NASA. Of the firms operating in the space industry, only one specialises in manufacturing satellite systems (SunSpace) and one operates a testing site capable of launching satellites (Denel's Aerospace Group).

6   This section is largely based on background material and data assembled by Euroconsult (http://euroconsult-ec.com), the DST's space portal (www.space.gov.za), the Square Kilometre Array (SKA) international project (www.skatelescope.org), the SKA South African project (www.ska.ac.za), and the Southern African Large Telescope (SALT) project (www.salt.ac.za).

Space science research in South Africa is mainly conducted at the national research facilities, universities and science councils. The three national research facilities focusing on space science are the South African Astronomical Observatory (SAAO), the Hartebeeshoek Radio Astronomy Observatory (HartRAO) and the Hermanus Magnetic Observatory (HMO).

South Africa is an active participant in the international space arena and collaborates with various international partners, such as NASA and the European Space Agency (ESA). The SKA project is a prominent international initiative in which South Africa plays a leading role. South Africa also hosts the Southern African Large Telescope (SALT), which is an initiative run by a consortium of a growing number of international partner institutions. SALT is the largest single optical-infrared telescope in the southern hemisphere, located near Sutherland in the Northern Cape.

South Africa only contributed about 34 per cent of the funding to build SALT, but about 60 per cent of the contracts and tenders, and many of the high-tech aspects of SALT, were awarded to South African industry. The SALT construction team included astronomers, software and mechanical engineers, software mirror and optical specialists, software developers, electronic engineers and technicians, and technical draftspersons. The SALT initiative plays an important role in strengthening South Africa's bid to host the SKA, as it demonstrates the country's ability to host 'big science' astronomy initiatives.

The SKA will be the world's largest radio telescope. It is an international endeavour operated by a consortium of 18 countries. South Africa has proposed the Northern Cape as the ideal site for the core array. The site for the SKA will be chosen in 2008 or 2009. Construction of the SKA is scheduled to begin in 2010 and the project is expected to be completed in 2020. The SKA project is currently in the developmental phase. South Africa is in the process of developing its SKA demonstrator, the Karoo Array Telescope (meerKAT). The South African government has committed R860 million to South African SKA initiatives. The meerKAT design will be one per cent of the technology of the proposed SKA design and is supposed to be operative by 2013.

The meerKAT will be a world-class radio astronomy facility which will be used to train scientists and engineers, and thus build human capital to prepare South Africa for the SKA. The meerKAT initiative will also provide the opportunity for industry in South Africa to develop and demonstrate its capability to contribute to the construction of large astronomy facilities, in this way strengthening its position in the competition for contracts and tenders for the construction of the SKA and its high-technology components. In the case of the SKA, it is imperative that industry be involved at all stages of the project, considering the scale and complexity of the technology, and in order to keep within the budget and proposed time-frame (Hall 2004). Collaboration with industry will be particularly important for the development of the antennae, and for meeting the signal transfer and processing requirements (Hall & Kahn 2006).

The demand for space technology skills

Space technologies are fundamentally based on competences in mathematics, physics and astronomy. But in addition, they require many of the same skill sets used in other areas of the economy, such as engineering and related generic, multi-use disciplines. It is not possible to isolate the precise demand for space-related skills and distinguish it from all other possible fields of occupations. Hence the data supplied in this section represent an upper boundary, effectively exaggerating skill demand in this area.

Between April 2004 and March 2007, the *Sunday Times* carried some 9 000 vacancy announcements that were potentially relevant to the space sector (Erasmus 2008). However, the core demand for astronomers and physicists amounted to fewer than 50 people, while the demand for engineers and technicians – who would probably be sought by other sectors as well – numbered in the thousands. Year-on-year demand grew by 86 and 42 per cent, respectively.

The supply of space technology skills

South Africa has a rather small astronomy community. In 2006, there were some 60 astronomers employed at universities and other research institutions in the country, up from about 50 at the beginning of the decade. This includes people who are nominally retired but still publish actively. Only eight of these people are black and only eight are women. A considerable proportion of this group is foreign-born.

Between 1996 and 2005, South Africa graduated some 51 000 engineers. It is important to underline that these graduates *might* find employment in the space sciences sector, but they would also – and conceivably more likely – end up working in other industries and with other technologies. In the fields more closely related to space sciences proper, graduates amounted to some 3 000. Significantly, average annual growth rates for astronomers were negative. Most fields were strongly dominated by men. African male and female graduates generally constituted the single largest group, except in aerospace and computer engineering, astronomy, atmospheric sciences and mathematics. All fields were strongly dominated by men except for three fields in the life sciences and physical sciences: astronomy, atmospheric sciences and general earth-space sciences.

Especially at the high-skill end, it is clear that competence can literally be counted on the fingers of one hand (Figure 4.5).

In 2000–2005, South Africa enrolled some 257 000 engineering students. Enrolments in physics, astronomy and mathematics totalled 17 500. In almost all these fields, enrolments were to varying degrees dominated by men. With few exceptions, Africans constituted the largest racial group in all fields. Again, enrolments of PhD students were few and far between (Figure 4.6).

FIGURE 4.5: *PhD graduate output in the life sciences, 1996–2005*

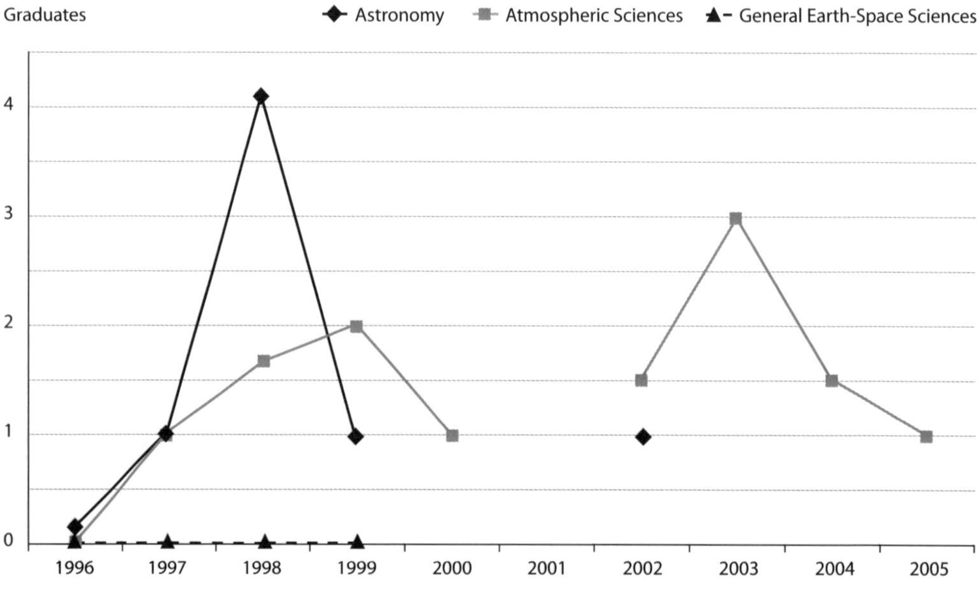

Source: DoE 1996–2006

FIGURE 4.6: *PhD enrolments in the life sciences, 2000–2005*

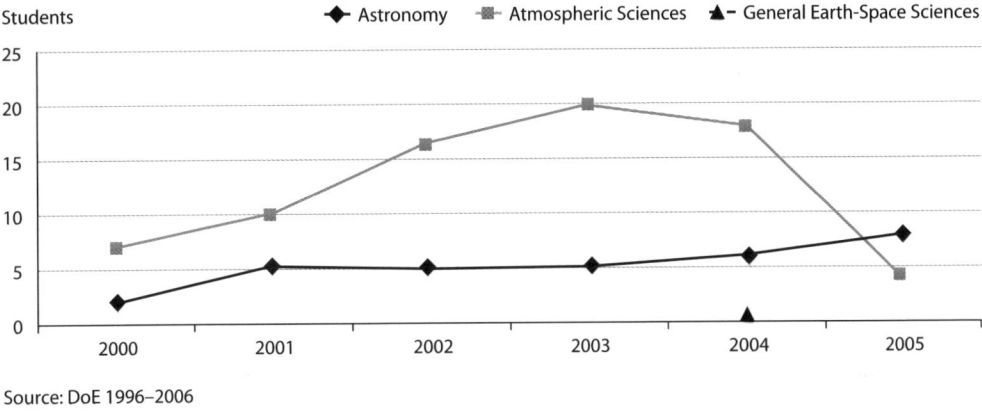

Source: DoE 1996–2006

The National Astrophysics and Space Science Programme (NASSP) was initiated in 2003 as a response to the need to build human capacity in astrophysics and space science in South Africa and the region. The NASSP graduated 49 honours students and 36 master's students in 2003–2006 (NASSP 2006; Whitelock 2007). The majority of the African graduates are from other countries in Africa. The NASSP currently has 13 students enrolled in its honours programme. Twenty-two NASSP graduates went on to PhD level; three of these students had upgraded from their master's programme and three opted to complete their PhD in the UK. The programme will need to produce 60–100 PhD students by 2012 in order to meet skills requirements.[7]

South African universities also offer postgraduate training in other areas of space science.

The South African SKA programme initiated its Human Capital Development Programme in 2004 in order to develop expertise needed in radio astronomy. It has offered a number of bursaries to students in the NASSP programme. Fifty-two bursaries have been awarded since 2004, and the programme plans to offer another 72 bursaries over the next few years.

Biotechnology

Biotechnology is the 'application of science and technology to living organisms, as well as parts, products and models thereof, to alter living or nonliving materials for the production of knowledge, goods, and services' (Van Beuzekom & Arundel 2006: 7). Relevant technologies include genetic, protein, cell and tissue engineering, with applications in human and veterinary health, agriculture, industrial processing and other fields.

In 2003, some 11 500 firms were active in biotechnologies in the OECD member states, Shanghai and South Africa, of which over 4 000 were core biotechnology companies. South African firms accounted for about one per cent of the total. Bio-active employment in these firms was just under 290 000. The USA led sales with US$50 billion (at PPP rates), while South African sales amounted to US$123 million. Approximately half the firms were active in health applications, followed by agro-food (19 per cent), and industry-environmental applications (15 per cent) (Van Beuzekom & Arundel 2006).

---

7   South Africa's input vital in space science development, *Monday Paper* 24 February 2003, www.news.uct.ac.za/print/mondaypaper/archives/?id=3544

Biotechnology has yet to become profitable; to date the sector has always run up – albeit diminishing – losses. The collective fascination with biotechnology is thus not based on delivery in terms of its commercial prospects, but on the innovative technologies it employs. When the stock market crashed in 2000, the industry reacted to the changing funding environment by accelerating product development in alliances and creating new business models. The implicit, longer-term problem for the industry as a whole is that there is now a funding gap for early-stage development. Solutions to this problem include increased mergers and acquisitions activity, including big pharmaceutical companies that move back further in the pipeline to embrace basic research. Overall, the industry structure more and more consists of system integrators – such as large pharmaceutical firms – co-ordinating a networked knowledge production system, large parts of which are outsourced (Ernst & Young 2006; see also Hopkins et al. 2007).

Biotechnology is a knowledge-intensive activity. Patent applications grew above average in the 1990s and early 2000s. The share of biotechnology patents in total patents is also on the rise (Van Beuzekom & Arundel 2006).

A recent review of biotechnology in Africa undertaken on behalf of the African Union (AU) and New Partnership for Africa's Development (NEPAD) not only concluded that biotechnology was key to Africa's development, but also identified what it would take to promote existing, disparate initiatives to a higher level, namely, recognising the importance of regional economic integration bodies, regional innovation communities, and investment in human resources (Juma & Serageldin 2007). The AU/NEPAD report therefore recommended that southern Africa be principally responsible for health biotechnology within the regional distribution of competences and concentrations across the African continent.

Within Africa, South Africa has particular strengths in food and medical biotechnology. It also leads the exploitation of biotechnology in manufacturing, notably in the replacement of synthetic chemicals with biological alternatives. South Africa has a long tradition of first-generation biotechnology. A 2003 survey (eGoli Bio 2003) identified 47 core and 59 non-core modern firms, plus some 600 research groups, organised around just under a thousand projects. Start-ups numbered about two every year. Most firms employ up to 50 people. Although a majority does not work with genetically modified organisms, firms do use modern technologies and develop new applications. Approximately one-tenth operate at the technological frontier. Subsidiaries of multinational pharmaceutical firms are active in the country, primarily to manufacture and distribute their products and undertake clinical trials. In descending order of importance, most biotechnology is concerned with human health, followed by plant biotechnology, industrial applications, and food and beverages (eGoli Bio 2003; Motari et al. 2004; Wolson 2007). The local industry does have successes to show, but there is a general consensus that on the whole the sector has not been very successful at commercialisation.

Biotechnology is a key technology platform within South Africa's national innovation system. It was given prominence in the National R&D Strategy (DST 2002). This derives from its acknowledged role in the knowledge economy more generally, and its potential to address national priorities, especially in the area of human health. It is supported by a dedicated National Biotechnology Strategy (DST 2001), which is currently being reviewed, with a view to producing an updated version in 2008. Strategic interventions have included the formation of Biotechnology Regional Innovation Centres (BRICs), which are essentially cluster facilitation bodies that were expected to set up technology platforms and gain critical mass through agglomeration economies that would attract further funding (see Wolson 2007).

The DST implements the National Biotechnology Strategy. It funds the National Bioinformatics Network and the BRICs. Initial government funding to the BRICs amounted to R450 million. In addition, there are two incubators. The Innovation Fund implements the R&D Strategy. The Department of Health runs the South African AIDS Vaccine Initiative (SAAVI) through the Medical Research Council (MRC), and – in conjunction with a group of healthcare companies – the Biologicals and Vaccines Institute of Southern Africa (BioVac). The Agricultural Research Council focuses on plant and animal research, while the Council for Mineral Technology (MINTEK) makes contributions in the mining field and the Council for Scientific and Industrial Research (CSIR) in a series of applications.

The demand for biotechnology skills

Biotechnology is a small field in South Africa. Estimates of the demand for skills are hard to come by and must be gleaned indirectly from generic vacancy posting sources and, as far as the general situation of the demand and supply match are concerned, directly from human resources (HR) practitioners in firms.

According to the *Sunday Times* vacancy database (Erasmus 2008), the fields within which demand for biotechnologists is generated yielded annually between 800 and 2 200 vacancies between April 2004 and March 2007. This is the upper boundary of the total demand for people with biotechnology skills, in that of course not all physicists, chemists, mathematicians and so on are necessarily *bio*physicists, *bio*chemists, and so forth.

In almost all sub-fields, demand in 2006/2007 was higher than in 2004/2005. For example, for chemists, mathematicians, biologists, natural science technicians and life science technicians, demand rose between three- and fivefold. So there is dynamic growth, albeit from a low base, which, if these growth rates are sustained, will over time translate into significantly larger numbers of vacancies. It is clear from the data that possible mismatches between demand and supply in biotechnology do not refer so much to sheer volumes of people as, if anything, to their exact competences or experience. Only firm-level information can illustrate the extent to which this is a problem.

The supply of biotechnology skills

Specialists in the biotechnology field principally come from the following broad fields of study: agriculture and renewable resources, engineering and engineering technology, healthcare and health sciences, and life, physical and mathematical sciences. In agriculture and renewable resources, South Africa produced some 9 000 graduates between 1996 and 2005, with positive growth rates in almost all sub-fields. The field is strongly dominated by university graduates. While in 1996 men predominated, this had by 2005 become less pronounced or even reversed in some sub-fields. The race distribution, heavily skewed towards whites in 1996, had become much more equitable by 2005.

In bioengineering and biotechnology, chemical engineering and pharmaceutical sciences, some 11 000 students graduated between 1996 and 2005. Bioengineering and chemical engineering are dominated by men, although at least in the latter case less so than 10 years ago. Women predominate in the pharmaceutical sciences, a trend that actually strengthened over time. African graduates are the largest race group in bioengineering and biotechnology as well as in chemical engineering. Only pharmaceutical sciences are still dominated by whites.

South Africa graduated some 41 000 biologists, chemists, physicists and mathematicians between 1996 and 2005. Compared to an even gender distribution in 1996, almost two out of three biologists in 2005 were female. Women also predominate in chemical sciences. They are a minority in physics and mathematics, but while this trend was exacerbated over time in physics, the situation gradually improved in mathematics. In chemistry and physics, African graduates are the single largest group.

White graduates still dominate in biology and mathematics; in biology, their predominance has actually strengthened over time.

In 2000–2005, South African universities enrolled some 36 000 students in sub-fields of agriculture and renewable resources relevant for biotechnology. Over the same period, enrolments in bio-relevant engineering and healthcare amounted to some 49 000 students. Finally, in the life, physical and mathematical sciences, enrolments reached 191 000 students. Except in agricultural food technology and pharmaceutical sciences (where women strengthened their predominance over time), soil sciences, bioengineering and technology, the gender distribution became more balanced. In terms of race, only in soil sciences did white students not reduce their share in the total contingent. In most fields, African students have become the largest group.

Some sub-fields are more successful than others at enrolling and graduating specialists at the very high end (Figures 4.7–4.9). On the whole, however, growth rates of both enrolment and graduation are rather low. Notable exceptions include plant sciences, chemical engineering and technology, and biology.

Conclusion

There is no evidence that the available volume of human capital is a constraint on the biotechnology sector. The sector is simply too small to exhaust the pool of available graduates, be they those already on the labour market or those still in training. But it is possible to differentiate this across the broad fields examined here (Figures 4.10–4.12). In agricultural and life sciences, a rise in vacancies is accompanied by a rise in both graduation and enrolment rates. The same is broadly true for chemical engineering. By contrast, in pharmaceutical sciences, a rise in vacancies is accompanied by a substantial drop in enrolments and graduations. This does not as yet suggest mismatches, because this information cannot possibly show whether there are enough jobs for all graduates. Hence, this may simply be a correction of an over-supply. Alternatively, if these trends continue, the pharmaceutical sector may be heading for supply constraints. Similar observations can be made for mathematical sciences.

FIGURE 4.7: *PhD graduate output in agricultural and renewable resources, 1996–2005*

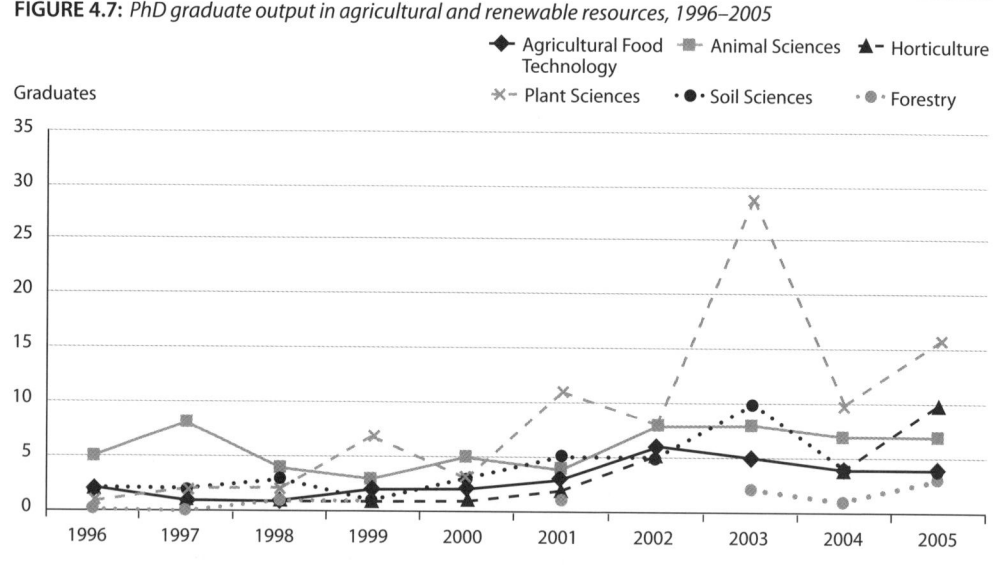

Source: DoE 1996–2006

FIGURE 4.8: *PhD graduate output in engineering and engineering technology, 1996–2005*

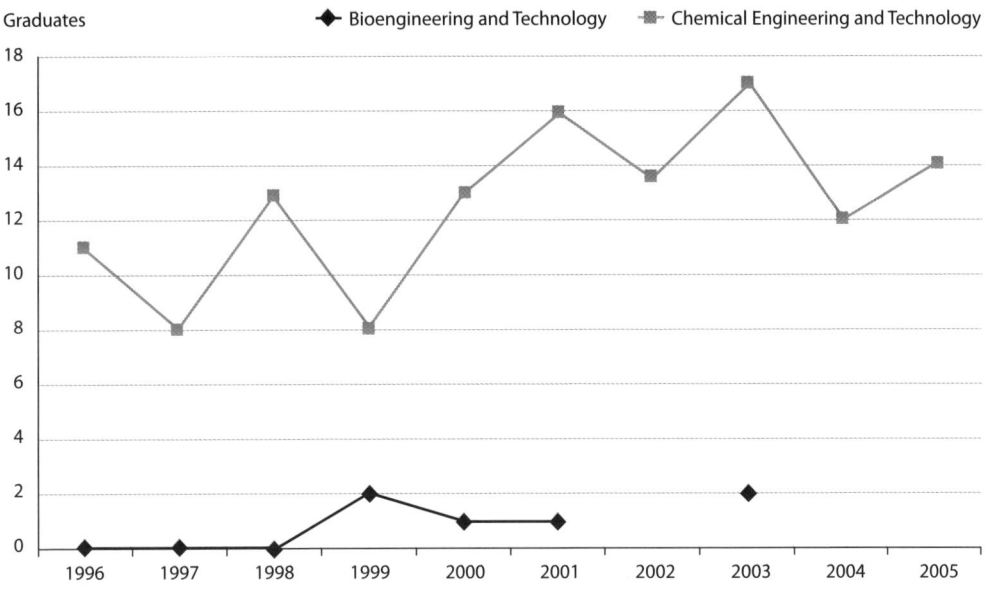

Source: DoE 1996–2006

FIGURE 4.9: *PhD graduate output in the pharmaceutical and mathematical sciences, 1996–2005*

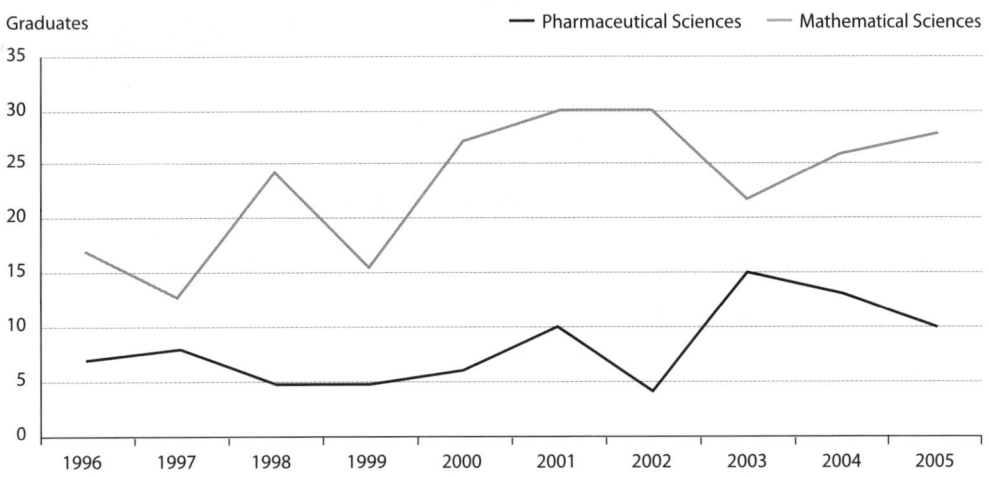

Source: DoE 1996–2006

FIGURE 4.10: Skills supply and demand in agriculture and life sciences, 2000–2006

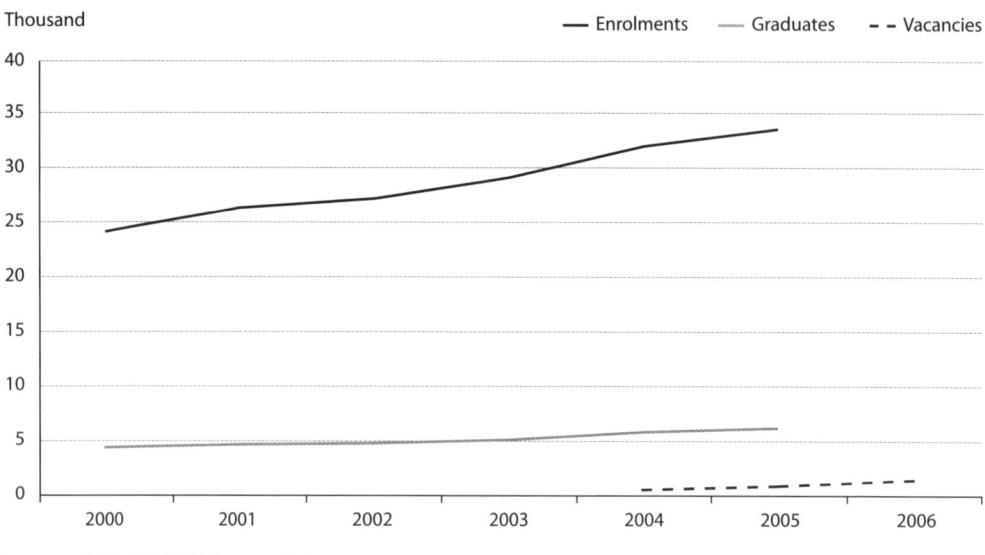

Sources: DoE 1996–2006; Erasmus 2008

FIGURE 4.11: Skills supply and demand in chemical engineering and engineering technology, 2000–2006

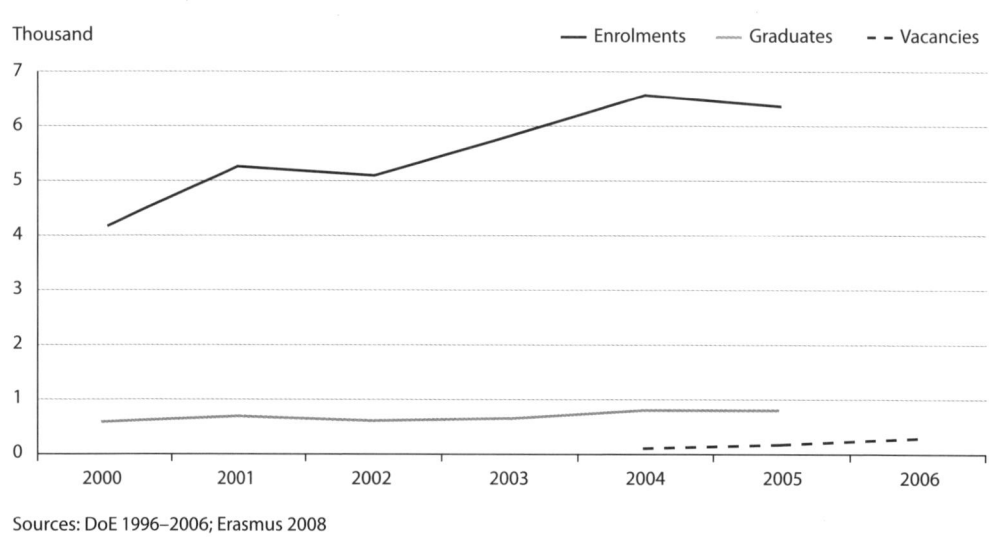

Sources: DoE 1996–2006; Erasmus 2008

Comparative issues and problems

All three technology fields reviewed here have a history, albeit an interrupted one, in South Africa. The civilian use of nuclear power has been around for more than two decades, and the apartheid state also invested in uranium enrichment as part of its creation of a nuclear arsenal. Space exploration has an even longer tradition, and was less instrumentalised for the maintenance of the apartheid regime per se. Of the three, third-generation biotechnology is the most genuinely 'new' field, even though it did exist prior to 1994, for example, as part of the old regime's biological weapons research. In the

FIGURE 4.12: *Skills supply and demand in pharmaceutical sciences, 2000–2006*

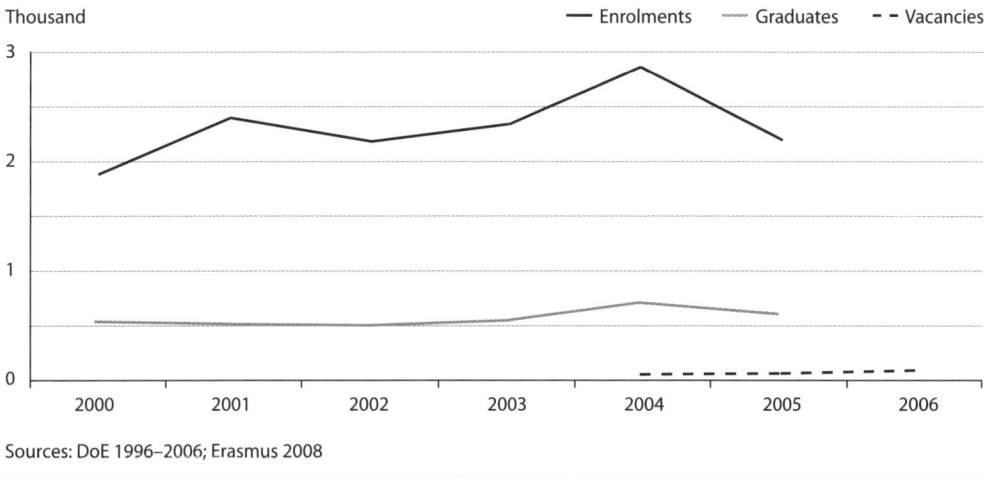

Sources: DoE 1996–2006; Erasmus 2008

early 1990s, many associated past programmes were discontinued and it would thus be somewhat misleading to claim path dependence. But it is certainly the case that because of South Africa's past, developments in these three fields from the second half of the 1990s could rely on an existing body of competence and expertise in the country, especially in the nuclear and space fields.

The prominence of these platforms in the national innovation system is intimately linked to robust government involvement. In nuclear and space technology, this is the international norm; in biotechnology, it reflects the absence of a large enough private sector, especially with respect to venture capital funding. While it is pretty inconceivable that the state would ever not be the principal in nuclear energy and large-scale space exploration, the private sector is expected to grow into a much more important role-player than it hitherto has been with regard to biotechnology. Thus, over time, government involvement – although crucial at present – might diminish.

Nuclear and space technology suffer from a global skills shortage. In biotechnology, there is a national skills shortage, especially at the very high end, but it is possible to identify the requisite talent in other countries without much difficulty. The situation in nuclear and space technology is therefore much more serious. This is reflected in a much more ambitious attempt to align skill availability with the requirements of the technology platforms in these two areas, spearheaded by the DST.

Co-ordination problems faced by nuclear and space technology are also more serious than in the case of biotechnology. In both fields, the expectation is to situate extensive and highly complex value chains, in large part *ex novo*, in the country. The scope of these initiatives is much larger than the attempt to kickstart a fledgling biotechnology industry, where the private sector can sooner or later realistically play the lead role.

In all three fields, there is a particular shortage of critical skills at the high-skill level, complemented in the case of nuclear technology by scarce skills at the medium-skill level. Reactor operators, astronomers and biotech research project leaders-cum-entrepreneurs, respectively, are the competences most in demand. They are being sought through a mixture of foreign mentoring and local training. In this respect, international technology transfer and the accessibility of global knowledge networks are key. In nuclear and space technology, attempts at forming partnerships between the demand for skills at project level, and training and education provided by some universities, are more advanced than in biotechnology, where university-industry linkages seem on the whole to be poorer.

Having said this, nuclear enterprises and space projects rather than universities are currently the single most important locus for skills development. In the nuclear field, the challenges are twofold. Downstream, they result from capacity limits in the private sector, especially in smaller companies. Upstream, they result from cohorts of school-leavers or higher-education graduates whose grounding in science or engineering is found to be wanting. This is a problem insofar as it imposes the burden of education – as opposed to training – on firms, something that they are not equipped to do. In the case of space technology, the SAAO has proven that it can operate a world-class telescope. Yet South Africa will only be able to gain maximum mileage from SALT if it manages to marry the advantages of geographic location and the ability to maintain the telescope with the sort of expertise required to design and implement scientific experiments on the installation. Hence the target is ambitious, and it is moving.

Conclusions

The nuclear sector can currently make do with the volume and quality of human resources at its disposal. This is not to say that there are no problems, but that on the whole the numbers are there to operate and maintain both the existing and future plants, and that the necessary expertise in dealing with nuclear technology exists and can be passed on to new entrants into this industry.

At the same time, however, the envisaged expansion of nuclear energy generation over the next two decades or so is unprecedented. The sector will need literally thousands of people across the skills spectrum to build and operate the new plants. This will exacerbate those problems that are already in evidence – such as poor backgrounds in science and mathematics of most school-leavers – and possibly throw up new ones. The latter include the depth of technical knowledge required to localise the component industry necessary to sustain up to 90 per cent local content of the PWRs, and possibly more in the case of the PBMR.

Likewise, South Africa's objectives in space science and technology are extremely ambitious. In short, the country wants to operate at the global technology frontier. This strategy is based on a combination of geographic and other site advantages for the location of major international collaborations in telescopes, and residual capabilities in astronomy. But in order to be able to collaborate with the world's leading space science institutions, South Africa needs to upgrade the depth of expertise and the volume of knowledge it commands in the field. Currently astronomers are few and far between, and nowhere near the levels required to ensure that South Africa does not simply end up hosting world-class institutions, without the requisite capabilities to exploit their scientific and technological potential.

This poses a series of challenges. In the nuclear field, not all firms are equally well equipped to deal with this challenge. Case studies undertaken for this study provided evidence that Eskom has plans in place to hire thousands of people so that it can be ready when the first new nuclear reactors reach criticality. But Eskom is a large local company with a proud history of massive training programmes. Smaller firms are less likely to rise to the challenge, especially for scarce skills where there are economies of scale in training. Also, either Westinghouse or Areva will have to build some five or six reactors, while gradually increasing local content. While they do have experience in working with local contractors, they – unlike Eskom – are not experienced in building up a local workforce from scratch.

Given the numbers involved, this is a co-ordination problem that the private sector by itself may not be capable of solving. Government initiatives in this area – such as SANHARP's bursaries and research chairs – address these concerns, but they do so in a piecemeal and marginal fashion. A few hundred high-school graduates with specialisations in mathematics and sciences are but a first step.

The advantage of the nuclear build programme, with respect to human resource development, is its long lead times. It is known that the first new reactor will not be built before 2010 and not be finished before 2016. The others will take even longer. Hence interventions in favour of an intensification of science and mathematics training at high-school level will produce people who in principle could be raw material for training as operators in a few years, and nuclear engineers in four more years.

What is required is not so much a change of tack as a massification of the initiatives under way. This would also address transformation most effectively. At the end of the pipeline, equity targets could be relaxed because the country relies on foreign expertise, which clearly would not address inequities anyway. For the time being it would appear that South Africa needs all the expertise it can get, regardless of race or gender. Meanwhile, the changing profile of enrolments and graduations will sooner or later see to it that at the end of the pipeline new talent reflects the demographics of the country.

In relation to space science and technology, customised graduate programmes such as the NASSP and meerKAT's bursary programmes must be expanded. It is important that higher education institutions be given incentives to co-operate with these programmes, instead of perceiving them as an encroachment upon their turf. The current financing model of higher education penalises universities for students who 'leave' their home university in order to study on a specialised joint graduate programme elsewhere. Since in astronomy and related fields no single institution by itself has the critical mass to offer a full-range training programme, this practice is detrimental to the setting up of partnerships across universities and their partners.

In addition, South Africa relies on outside skills for which there is global demand. Astronomy expertise is globally in shortage. Because of the country's location-specific advantages, international experts are in principle available to come to South Africa, boost its local expertise, mentor junior colleagues, and generally strengthen the country's claim to be a promising emerging space nation. Yet anecdotes of excellent people who were put off – and eventually lost to the country – by bureaucratic delays, obstructionism with respect to work permits for their spouses etc., abound. This must end. It requires the DST and Department of Home Affairs to get their act together to ensure that South Africa does not shoot itself in the foot when it comes to attracting and retaining global talent, without which its space ambitions are unlikely ever to become world-class.

Finally, biotechnology in South Africa has a lot of ambitions and hopes invested in it as well. It is also, for the time being, a rather small sector. Most activities in the especially interesting and challenging third-generation dimension are being undertaken by the scientific community in the public sector. A few skills that are locally in demand are not locally available, but since there is no global shortage, this is not a problem as long as the foreign experts are allowed to work in the country. Graduates from the universities do not always have the requisite experience. However, this is true for all professions and thus not specific to biotechnology. The universities could improve this situation by enriching their curricula through biotechnology-relevant laboratory experience, but most up-skilling will have to be done on-the-job by firms and research groups.

The biggest challenge faced by the sector, however, is not to find the right people for the jobs but to find the right jobs for the people. It is simply not possible to detect critical skill shortages in an industry that employs so few people. Nor does it necessarily make sense for graduates to opt for a study of biotechnology unless the sector grows considerably. The question, then, is how the sector would grow beyond where it is today. International experience suggests that entrepreneurial dynamism is prominently behind the start-ups and spin-offs from established research groups. Therefore the one skill that appears to be lacking in the biotechnological community is the ability and willingness to take risks, replete with the motivation to run one's own business instead of working in safer, corporate environments. Business acumen is certainly a skill that could be imparted in programmes of molecular or microbiology, or biochemistry studies.

At the outset, this chapter posed the question of whether the country commands the kinds of human capital required to make big science work. Based on the evidence reviewed here (and available in much more detail in a companion study to this chapter (Lorentzen & Petersen 2008)), the answer can be given in two ways: *No, but*, and *Yes, but*.

Thus, it would be preposterous to argue that the human capital currently available in the country can supply the skills and competences, both in terms of quality and quantity, to achieve the objectives of the nuclear, space and biotechnology missions. Much needs to be done to align skill availability with the demands of these three fields. However, it would be equally misguided to claim that South Africa suffered from some kind of ambitious overstretch when it decided to take a major bet on technologies that, until not so long ago, were the exclusive domain of advanced economies. There is evidence that the minimum competences are in place not only to conceive of and drive such an effort but, more importantly, also to design strategies in support of the process of catching up with the moving target of the global technology frontier in these fields.

References

Auf der Heide T & Thomas S (2002) The PBMR project: An assessment of its economic viability. *South African Journal of Science* 98: 36–42

DACST (Department of Arts, Culture, Science & Technology, South Africa) (1996) *White paper on science & technology: Preparing for the 21st century*. Pretoria: DACST

DME (Department of Minerals and Energy, South Africa) (2007) *Nuclear energy policy and strategy for the Republic of South Africa*. Draft for Public Comment. Accessed October 2007, http://www.dme.gov.za/pdfs/energy/nuclear/nuclear_energy_policy.pdf

DoE (Department of Education, South Africa) (1996–2006) *Higher Education Management Information System (HEMIS) database*. Pretoria: DoE

DoL (Department of Labour, South Africa) (2006) *Master list of scarce and critical skills*. Pretoria: DoL

DST (Department of Science and Technology, South Africa) (2001) *A national biotechnology strategy for South Africa*. Accessed October 2007, http://www.dst.gov.za/programmes/biodiversity/biotechstrategy.pdf

DST (2002) *South Africa's national research and development strategy*. Accessed 16 November 2007, http://www.dst.gov.za/legislation_policies/strategic_reps/sa_nat_rd_strat.pdf

DST (2006) *Annual report 2005/2006*. Accessed 31 October 2007, http://www.dst.gov.za/publications-policies/annual-reports

eGoli Bio (2003) *National biotech survey 2003*. Accessed October 2007, http://www.egolibio.co.za/pages/biotech_survey.pdf

Erasmus JC (2008) Vacancy analysis report. Report on phase 3: A survey of employers who have recently advertised vacancies. In *Project 4.1: A multiple source identification and verification of scarce and critical skills in the South African labour market*. Report commissioned by the Department of Labour, Pretoria

Ernst & Young (2006) *Beyond borders: The global biotechnology report 2006*. Accessed October 2007, http://www.ey.com/beyondborders

Euroconsult (2006) *World prospects for government space markets 2006/2007 edition*. Accessed 25 October 2007, http://euroconsult-ec.com/brochures/world-prospects-for-gov-space-markets-2007.pdf

Hall PJ (2004) *The international SKA project: Industry interactions paper 1 – Background, and collaborative research and development,* 2 August, SKA [Memo 52]. Accessed 1 October 2007, http://www.skatelescope.org/pages/memos

Hall P & Kahn S (2006) *The International SKA project: Industry liaison models and policies,* 28 July, EWG Industrial Liaison Task Force, SKA [Memo 80]. Accessed 1 October 2007, http://www.skatelescope.org/pages/memos

Hopkins MM, Martin PA, Nightingale P, Kraft A & Mahdi S (2007) The myth of the biotech revolution: An assessment of technological, clinical and organisational change. *Research Policy* 36: 566–589

IAEA (International Atomic Energy Agency) (2007) *Nuclear technology review*. Vienna: IAEA

Juma C & Serageldin I (2007) *Freedom to innovate: Biotechnology in Africa's development*. Report of the High-Level African Panel on Modern Biotechnology. Addis Ababa & Pretoria: African Union & New Partnership for Africa's Development

Lorentzen J & Petersen I (2008) *Human capital dynamics on three technology platforms: Nuclear, space, and biotechnology.* Research report for the Human Sciences Research Council, Cape Town

Manpower Inc. (2007) *Talent shortage survey. 2007 global results*. Accessed October 2007, http://www.manpower.com/research/research.cfm

Motari M, Quach U, Thorsteinsdóttir H, Martin DK, Daar AS & Singer PA (2004) South Africa – Blazing a trail for African biotechnology. *Nature Biotechnology* 22 (Supplement): 37–41

NASSP (National Astrophysics and Space Science Programme) (2006) *Report on activities: 2003–2006.* Accessed 26 September 2007, http://www.star.ac.za/news/nassp-report.pdf

Nicholls DR (2002) The pebble bed nuclear reactor. *South African Journal of Science* 98: 31–35

OECD/IEA (Organisation for Economic Co-operation and Development/International Energy Agency) (2006) *World energy outlook*. Paris: OECD

Saleh JH (2005) Will we see a regional or global duopoly in the satellite manufacturing industry? The European perspective. *Space Policy* 21: 277–285

Van Beuzekom B & Arundel A (2006) *OECD biotechnology statistics – 2006*. Paris: OECD

Van Schalkwyk D (2006) Estimated resource needs up to 2009. Internal memorandum, Eskom

Whitelock P (2007) *Astrophysics in Southern Africa*. Accessed 26 October 2007, http://arxiv.org/ftp/arxiv/papers/0707/0707.0921.pdf

Wolson RA (2007) The role of technology transfer offices in building the South African biotechnology sector: An assessment of policies, practices and impact. *Journal of Technology Transfer* 32: 343–365

3 RESOURCE-BASED SECTORS

CHAPTER 5

Metals beneficiation

Johann Maree, Paul Lundall and Shane Godfrey

Introduction

It is generally thought that South Africa has a serious skills shortage, and that artisanal and engineering skills are particularly important categories of scarce skills. For instance, the Accelerated and Shared Growth Initiative for South Africa (Asgisa), the government's formally growth strategy launched in 2006, has alleged that the skills shortage is hampering economic growth; it has therefore made the elimination of the shortage a priority (The Presidency 2006).

Radical changes to the primary and secondary education system and the introduction of an entirely new skills development dispensation, both of which preceded Asgisa, should be providing the foundation for efforts to address the skills backlog. However, there have been numerous problems with regard to both these initiatives and it is not clear whether they are solving or worsening the skills shortage. Certainly, after a number of years, no major inroads have been made into the skills shortage.

The second National Skills Development Strategy for the period 2005–2010 focuses much of its attention on identifying and addressing skills that are in short supply. It instructs the Sector Education and Training Authorities (SETAs) to use their discretionary funds to identify critical skills in their sectors. Thereafter, the skills development bodies must address the scarcities in line with projected demand. SETAs must provide funding for learnerships, bursaries, internships and study support to acquire identified scarce skills. There is also a commitment to assist all learners in critical skills programmes covered by sector agreements from further education and training (FET) and higher education and training (HET) institutions, to gain work experience. The aim is for 70 per cent of these learners to find placement in employment or self-employment (DoL 2005: 4–5, 12–13).

This chapter contributes to the discussion on scarce skills by examining whether skills shortages exist in one particular sector, namely, the metal beneficiation sector.[1] It does so by examining the structure of the sector and the characteristics of its production chain. It proceeds to identify the catalytic factors that led to the development of the sector and the forces that promote and inhibit its further growth. Interrogation of data on the demand and supply of skills in the sector shows that one of the inhibiting forces is the lack of provision of suitably skilled labour. The chapter examines why the necessary skilled labour in the form of artisans, technicians and engineers is not being supplied and what the industry

---

1 By beneficiation is meant the additional processing of a metal to a stage where it becomes a final product such as a machine, stainless steel utensil, or jewel. In the course of processing, value is added at every stage of production.

itself is doing to eliminate this bottleneck. It ends with some recommendations on what can be done to facilitate the dynamic expansion of the sector.

The metals beneficiation sector and its development

South Africa is remarkably well endowed with metals. It has more than 80 per cent of the known world reserves in the platinum group metals and manganese, more than 70 per cent of chrome, and around 40 per cent of gold and vanadium. In addition, it produces considerable iron ore and nickel (DTI 2005: 13–14). Combined with the abundant supply of coal and cheap electricity, South Africa thus has a considerable comparative advantage in metals beneficiation.[2] The sector is critical for economic growth. It is a significant sector in the manufacturing industry as a whole, constituting about a third of all manufacturing activity (DTI 2005: 18).

Historically, there were a number of catalytic forces that drove and shaped the metal and engineering sector to become what it is at present.[3] Initially, the large mining companies and the railways were the nodes around which a network of suppliers of infrastructure and services came to be established (Feinstein 2005: 115; Rosenthal 1981).

This initial impetus from the mining industry was followed by others at key moments in South Africa's industrial development, mostly driven by surges of foreign direct investment. The first impetus came from mining-sector capital that was raised on overseas bourses or investment houses based in London and New York. The refined and processed precious ores mined were mostly exported. The flow of investment provided the basis for the support and repair firms that were linked to the mining industry (Feinstein 2005: Chapter 8, particularly 172–176).

The second catalytic force that impacted on the structure and growth of the metal and engineering sector was the state policy to develop the automobile manufacturing industry. Motor vehicles were first sold in South Africa as fully assembled units. However, by the early 1920s, Ford and General Motors had established assembly plants in South Africa. The catalytic effect of the investment by foreign vehicle manufacturers, coupled with state policy on local content, impacted significantly on the development of the metal and engineering sector (Black 2001).

The particular form of state involvement in the South African economy has also had a strong influence on firms in the metal and engineering sector. In this sector, state-owned enterprises such as Escom and Iscor were established in the 1920s to stimulate the sector and provide a ready supply of cheap energy and material inputs (i.e. ingots and ancillary products derived from pig iron and scrap iron) to firms within the sector.

The impact of expenditure on the military, commencing in the 1940s, constituted a major impetus to the development of the metal and engineering sector, particularly through enabling specialised and sub-contracted firms to emerge. The Second World War created an opportunity for certain companies to become inserted into the military-industrial apparatus (Martin & Orpen 1979: DGWS Annexure: Factories and their Production). The apparatus continued to grow after the Second World War as the

---

2   In this chapter, the metals beneficiation sector is taken to include the following sub-sectors: manufacture of basic metals, fabricated metal products, manufacture of machinery and equipment, and office, accounting and computing machinery (Division 35 of the Standard Industrial Classification), as well as manufacture of electrical machinery and apparatuses (Division 36). It excludes the manufacture of radio, television and communication equipment, and the manufacture of all transport equipment such as motor vehicles and components.
3   The metals beneficiation sector almost inevitably entails engineering skills and processes. It is therefore appropriate to refer to it as the metal and engineering sector when wishing to highlight both aspects of metal beneficiation.

apartheid regime sought to bolster its defences. From the 1970s until the fall of apartheid, it included a wide spectrum of metal and engineering firms that were sustained by the state's armament acquisitions. The firms spawned a range of supporting firms and a skilled labour force (Lundall 2005).

These historical driving forces have resulted in a geographic distribution of the metal and engineering sector. Gauteng, where almost 80 per cent of enterprises are based (MERSETA 2006: 57), has had a strong association with the mining industry and large firms engaged in the assembly of military vehicles and gun turrets. Motor industry firms are associated with Gauteng, the Eastern Cape and Durban, while Cape Town has a concentration of precision-engineering firms, many of which tend to be medium-sized and smaller, as well as the nearby Saldanha Steel mill.

The current catalytic forces driving the metal and engineering sector include the motor industry with its strong export orientation; infrastructural expansion by the state, particularly in the provision of electricity; construction in preparation for the 2010 World Cup; as well as the upgrading of public transport. The expansion of the Angolan oil fields is also making demands on the sector.

Having considered the historical and contemporary forces that drive the metal and engineering industries in South Africa, it is necessary to understand the stages of production in the beneficiation of metals.

The value chain in the metals beneficiation sector

There are generally four stages involved in metals beneficiation.
- Stage 1 is the primary stage of mining and producing an ore or concentrate.
- Stage 2 converts the ore or concentrate into an intermediate product such as a metal or alloy. The production of intermediate products usually takes place in capital- and energy-intensive smelters and refineries (DTI 2005: 15). This stage is referred to as the *milling* stage. Milling firms in South Africa are chiefly involved in the production of pig iron and the conversion of pig iron into a range of wrought iron and steel materials.

    Arcelor Mittal SA (formerly Mittal SA and before that Iscor) is the dominant producer in the primary steel industry, with only Highveld Steel competing with it in the flat steel products market. In the long products market, Highveld Steel, Scaw Metals, Cape Gate and Cisco compete with it (DTI 2005: 24). The majority of primary steel production takes place in Mpumalanga because of the availability of raw material in the province (MERSETA 2006: 32).
- Stage 3 transforms an intermediate good into a refined, semi-fabricated product suitable for use by both small and sophisticated enterprises. This stage of transformation takes place in blast furnaces and foundries using heat-treating and/or cold finishing processes. Employment levels are high and the degree of value added increases substantially due to the inclusion of other resources and inputs such as skills and technology (DTI 2005: 15). Much of the activity takes place in South Africa in *engineering or machine shops* that are responsible for the manufacture of products, parts, components, tools, forgings and moulds.

    The foundry industry is crucial. It provides critical inputs to most of the manufacturing sectors, with mining, automotive and general engineering being the largest industries it supplies. Approximately 40 per cent to 50 per cent of South Africa's casting production in value is automotive components, while about 85 per cent of all aluminium castings are for use in the automotive industry. There has been significant restructuring and consolidation in the South African foundry industry over the past 10–15 years. The number of firms shrank from 450 in the early to mid-1980s to just over 200 in 2003. The industry is very small compared to its global competitors (e.g. in 2003, China had 12 000 foundries and India had 4 500) (DTI 2005: 35).

- Stage 4 transforms the processed metal further into finished products of a large variety. The range of employment opportunities is significantly larger at this stage and firms involved in this stage of production include small, medium and large manufacturers (DTI 2005: 15). Of particular importance are the machine builders, which generally tend to source parts and components from engineering or machine shops.

    South African firms have lower design and customisation costs in products than their main competitors in Europe and the USA. But research has repeatedly shown that the local pricing of steel has undermined the competitive advantage of steel products (DTI 2005: 40–41).

Stage 1 falls outside the scope of this chapter and is thus not discussed further. Stages 2, 3 and 4 are the focus of this chapter and their enterprises are generally referred to as the milling firms (Stage 2), engineering or machine shops (Stage 3) and machine builders (Stage 4).

Structure, training and investment in different stages

In South Africa, milling firms, almost from their inception, dwarfed general engineering shops in terms of scale of operations and size of the workforce.

The milling firms all had in-house training facilities that included workshops and in some instances, even the basic infrastructure for classroom instruction. At these different enterprises, such in-house training facilities, coupled with public or state-supported training programmes, were used to train the cohort of apprentices needed as the sector grew. While there was supporting legislation with regard to artisan training, it gradually became the norm that large firms would operate their own in-house training programmes or training schools, with dedicated instructors in various trade specialisations.

At the same time, a plethora of large, medium and small enterprises arose that were not able to run comprehensive in-house training programmes. This was because many did not have spare production machinery for the purposes of training younger workers that were indentured to the firm. It necessitated making use of public technical colleges to perform this training function (Wessels interview).

Many firms that participated in these initiatives had an ongoing programme in place. While larger firms tended to operate a company training school that was integrated into the production process,[4] firms that were not able to afford such self-initiated schemes allowed their apprentices time off from work to attend technical college instruction through a process known as 'block-release'. The industry training centres attempted to combine the function of training schools and technical colleges, and were financed through government grants or levies diverted from the Industrial Training Board.

The upstream basic metals industries (basic iron and steel and non-ferrous metals) are highly capital-intensive and have registered very high rates of growth while simultaneously reducing their labour force. They are also characterised by very large economies of scale, and a very small number of producers with monopoly powers to set prices. By contrast, the downstream labour-intensive metal products industry has grown very slowly (DTI 2005: 18).

Different levels of investment in the value chain help to explain these trends.

During most of the 1990s, investment in the upstream ferrous and non-ferrous metals sector was very high. From 1993 to 1995, gross investment in non-ferrous metals was in excess of 75 per cent of the

---

4   Some of the Cape ship repair firms continue to operate such training schools (e.g. Dorbyl). (See interview data in Lundall 2006: 34–49.)

sector's value added. Then, from 1996 to 1998, investment in basic iron and steel averaged around 50 per cent of the sector's value added. By way of contrast, investment in the metal products sector remained low throughout, never rising above 18 per cent of value added and averaging 14 per cent over the decade from 1994 to 2004 (DTI 2005: 20).

Benefits of metals beneficiation

According to the DTI (2005: 15), employment opportunities tend to be low at the milling (i.e. refinery) stage, but can become very high at the mass semi-manufacturing and final production and machine-building stages. Table 5.1 presents information on the carbon steel pipeline, the most important one in terms of volumes. It shows that Stages 2 and 3 are very capital-intensive, with investments of R1.5 million to R8.5 million required per job. The employment-output ratio is also extremely low with only 1–7 workers employed per 1 000 tons of steel produced. On the other hand, Stage 4, the finished-product and machine-building stage, is much more labour-intensive. Investment per job ranges from only R0.1 million to R0.6 million, while employment per 1 000 tons of steel output ranges from 75 to 150 workers. Thus the potential for employment creation is far greater at the downstream finished-product end of the metals beneficiation pipeline. At the same time, the selling price per unit weight of steel increases dramatically.

Currently a very small proportion of most metals is beneficiated through to Stage 4 in South Africa, where most employment creation occurs. This is quantitatively demonstrated in Table 5.2. The table clearly reflects the overall under-development of the downstream metal products industries. In each column it indicates the percentage of a particular metal that reached the stage of beneficiation indicated by the column. For instance, 100 per cent of gold mined in South Africa is refined (Stage 2), but only 2 per cent is beneficiated into a final product (Stage 4). The levels of beneficiation of chrome, platinum, aluminium, iron ore and manganese up to Stage 4 are also all extremely low. There is therefore great potential to grow the downstream higher value-added end of the metals production chain.

TABLE 5.1: *Benefits of beneficiation: selling price, employment and investment in different stages of carbon steel*

Commodity	Selling price per ton of steel (US$)	Employment per 1 000 tons of steel	Investment (R million per job)	Stage
Iron ore	30	0.12	n.a.	1
Iron	120	0.60	2.0	2
Hot rolled steel	300	1.10	6.0	3
Cold rolled steel	500	1.60	8.5	3
Pipe and tube	650	7.00	1.5	3
Structural steel	1 000	75.00	0.1	4
White goods	5 000	100.00	0.4	4
Mining equipment	13 000	150.00	0.6	4

Source: DTI 2005: 16

TABLE 5.2: *Stages of beneficiation and levels achieved*

Commodity	Stage 1 ores / concentrates (%)	Stage 2 processed / refined ore (%)	Stage 3 primary manufacture (%)	Stage 4 finished manufacture (%)
Gold	100	100	5	2
PGM (Platinum group of metals)	100	100	n.a.	6
Iron ore to steel	100	30	30	15
Chrome to stainless steel	100	85	9	3
Aluminium	0	100	30	11
Zinc	100	100	90	60
Manganese	100	50	25	22
Titanium	100	15	4	small
Copper	100	100	65	50

Source: DTI 2005: 16

The reasons for the low levels of beneficiation are wide-ranging. Probably the most important reason has been the practice of import-parity pricing by upstream metals producers at Stages 2 and 3. The market power of the basic metal firms, which produce the most important inputs in the metal beneficiation sector, has resulted in local firms being charged higher prices than firms in other countries, despite the fact that South Africa has amongst the lowest production costs in the world for basic metals (DTI 2005: 50). Import-parity pricing was repeatedly mentioned in the FRIDGE[5] survey as an impediment to growth and employment creation by the downstream sectors (FRIDGE 2003: 3). This means that the capital-intensive upstream metal industry is fundamentally impeding the growth and production of value-added, labour-intensive downstream metal products. Table 5.3 demonstrates the competitive disadvantage faced by the steel beneficiation sub-sectors.

A further aspect of pricing that impedes the development of downstream steel production is differential pricing by the dominant supplier, Arcelor Mittal SA. In the past, the company charged a US$100/ton premium on the steel it sold locally (*Financial Mail* 14 September 2007). Furthermore, Mittal charged different prices to different customers and ran a complex system of rebates, which customers got only if they proved to Mittal that they added value to the steel and exported it, rather than reselling it on the local market (*Mail & Guardian, Business* 14–20 September 2007).[6]

Another important input into the whole metals beneficiation value chain is electricity. Stage 2 of metal beneficiation, that is, the smelting and refinery processes, is very energy-intensive, as are blast furnaces and foundries involved in Stage 3. However, the pricing agreements differ at different stages

---

5 FRIDGE (Fund for Research into Industrial Development Growth and Equity) is a study conducted by the National Labour and Development Institute (NALEDI).
6 In September 2007, the Competition Tribunal imposed a fine of R691 million on Mittal for 'price fixing' and 'the manipulation of supply' (*Financial Mail* 14 September 2007: 12). The Tribunal also ordered Mittal to cease placing conditions on the resale or use of its products (*Financial Mail* 14 September 2007: 64). At the time of writing, Mittal was taking the Competition Tribunal's fine and order to the Competition Appeal Court.

TABLE 5.3: *Mark-ups of basic metals prices, 2003/04[a]*

Prices	Carbon steel	Stainless steel	Aluminium
SA net export price	100	100	100
EU price	122	120–139	107
East Asian price	101	113	104
SA buyer price	146	130	105–109

Source: DTI 2005: 51

Note: a The mark-ups are given as index numbers with the South African net export price (the base index) set at 100. The differences between the indexes can then be read as percentages above the South African net export price.

in the value chain. The primary and secondary producers get their supply directly from Eskom at pre-negotiated rates while the downstream producers have to pay higher municipal rates. The primary and secondary producers (Stages 1 and 2) are thus the main beneficiaries of the country's competitive advantage in electricity (DTI 2005: 52).

The increased price of electricity and high prices of basic steel facing the downstream producers inhibit the growth of the higher-value-added metal sub-sector. There is also a lack of collaboration between the downstream and upstream sectors (FRIDGE 2003: 7). This accounts for the fact that a very large proportion of the production of basic metals continues to be exported (DTI 2005: 51).

But there is a further question that also needs to be addressed, namely, whether skills shortages have contributed in any way to the lack of beneficiation. The focus therefore shifts to a consideration of the demand and supply of skilled labour in the sector.

Demand and supply of skills in metals beneficiation

It is commonly believed that there are severe skills shortages at artisan, technical and engineering levels of the metals beneficiation sector. It is also maintained that the shortage of skilled artisans exists across the manufacturing industry as a whole. In 1982, there were 13 000 artisan apprentices registered, but this figure had dwindled to only 2 000 in 2003 (DTI 2005: 53).

Historically, state-owned firms such as Eskom, Iscor and Spoornet used to provide apprenticeship training for young people, thereby providing a pool of skilled people from which industry could draw. But since these enterprises have scaled back their training programmes, the skills shortages have accelerated (DTI 2005: 54). Consequently, according to the Department of Trade and Industry (DTI), one of the biggest constraints faced by the metal industries is a general shortage of artisans.

However, actually establishing that there is a shortage of skills requires an examination of both the demand for and supply of skills, not only in quantitative but also in qualitative terms. In addition, it also requires a study of the perceptions and experiences of employers in the sector regarding the availability and suitability of skilled labour in order to verify the findings of the macro data.

The demand for skills

In order to try to assess the demand for skills in the metals beneficiation sector, it is useful to investigate the employment trends for different occupational levels. This provides an indication of the rate at which the demand for each occupation has been increasing. Before doing so, a broader perspective is provided by presenting the overall employment for this sector over a 10-year period. Table 5.4 depicts the Standardised Employment Series levels of employment in the metal and engineering industries in South Africa over the period 1996–2005. The data have been grouped into the stages of beneficiation identified earlier in this chapter, that is, iron and steel mills, engineering or machine shops, and machine-building firms.

Figure 5.1 (based on the data in Table 5.4) shows a significant haemorrhaging of employment in the metal and engineering sector, especially over the period 1996–2001. Overall employment for this period (1996–2005) declined by 13.3 per cent or 44 950 jobs, but a turnaround and improvement in employment growth starts to manifest from 2001 to 2002, and is sustained on aggregate up to 2005. However, in only one industry, the machinery and equipment industry (i.e. machine builders

TABLE 5.4: *Employment levels in the metal and engineering industry, 1996–2005*

Sector	1996	1997	1998	1999	2000	2001	2002	2003	2004	2005
Basic iron & steel	77 921	73 791	67 113	59 977	50 773	51 717	52 541	53 025	53 295	52 172
Metal products	108 957	106 549	100 769	91 964	89 746	89 710	93 667	95 856	99 561	98 733
Machinery & equipment	93 731	92 117	90 198	89 865	86 755	88 877	92 796	94 982	99 320	102 304
Electrical machinery	58 094	54 706	54 444	49 078	47 333	42 997	40 937	38 536	38 630	40 545

Source: Quantec 2007

FIGURE 5.1: *Trends in employment in the metal industries, 1996–2005*

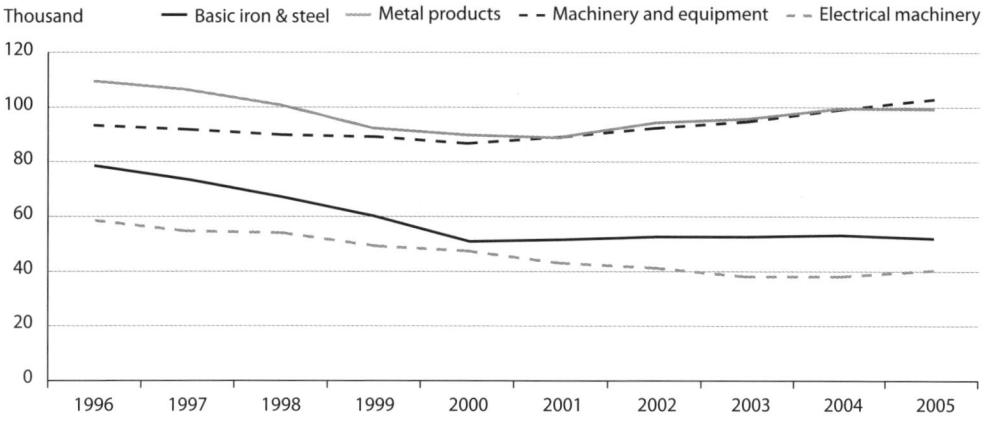

Source: Derived from Table 5.4

TABLE 5.5: Employment changes, 1996–2001 and 2001–2005

Industry sector	1996–2005	1996–2001	2001–2005
Basic iron and steel and non-ferrous metals (milling processes)	−33.05	−33.63	0.88
Metal products (engineering and machine shops excluding machinery)	−9.38	−17.67	10.06
Machinery and equipment (machine builders non-electrical)	9.15	−5.18	15.11
Electrical machinery and apparatus (machine builders electrical)	−30.21	−25.99	−5.70
Total	−13.27	−19.31	7.48

Source: Calculated from Table 5.4

– non-electrical), does employment in 2005 exceed the level recorded in 1996. Thus, in spite of high investment levels in the basic iron and steel industry (the milling stage), employment in this industry declined over the period under consideration. This confirms the observation earlier in this chapter that the capital-intensiveness of the mills has been rising.

Table 5.5 summarises these employment shifts. The overall employment change is presented in summary form in the first column. In the next two columns the period is broken down to show the downturn from 1996 to 2001 and the upturn thereafter. The table highlights the fact that the period 1996–2001 largely accounted for the decline in employment within the sector, whereas the data for the period 2001–2005 show the onset of gradual employment growth.

Occupational changes within the sector

Having examined employment trends within the industry as a whole, the occupational trends within the metal and engineering sector are investigated next. Figure 5.2 and Table 5.6 provide the necessary statistical data. However, the data should be treated with caution: sample sizes at this level of detail become small and the data are therefore somewhat unreliable.

Figure 5.2 and Table 5.6 highlight the fact that demand for the skills of technicians, craft workers and operators rose over the period 1999–2005. For craft workers it increased by 48 per cent. This is not the case for elementary workers, who are being shed from the sector as a whole. Surprisingly, if the figures are correct, the number of professional engineers dropped by almost half over the period.

However, the latter figures must be viewed with great caution. These findings are derived from household surveys conducted by Statistics South Africa (Stats SA) that have severe limitations. First, it should be noted that 'engineers' only make up a component of the total numbers for professional employment. Second, we could not derive a meaningful time series depicting the trend of professional employment for each successive year between 1996 and 2005. Third, if one uses engineering employment as the axis of analysis, the data cannot be assembled on a sector (e.g. manufacturing sector), an industry (e.g. metal and engineering industries), or an industry-specific level (e.g. machinery and equipment or machine-building industry). One can only reach such an occupationally specific level of representation for 'engineers' by discussing the aggregation of every discipline which contains engineers, from aeronautical and agricultural engineers, at the one extreme, to nuclear and transport engineers at the other. Such an analysis was done in 2003 by Steyn and Daniels. While pointing to the problem

FIGURE 5.2: *Employment by occupation in metal & engineering, 1999 and 2005*

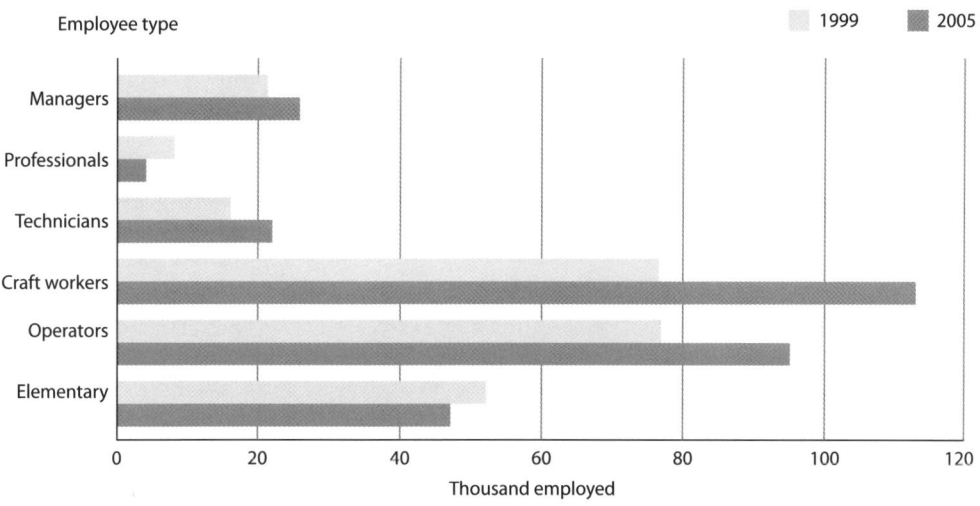

Source: Derived from Table 5.6

TABLE 5.6: *Employment by occupation in the metal and engineering sector, 1999 & 2005*

	Managers	Professionals	Technicians	Craft workers	Operators	Elementary
1999	21 093	8 090	16 170	76 298	76 886	52 062
2005	26 143	4 166	21 856	113 067	94 962	47 202
% change	24	−49	35	48	24	−9
% of total employment[a]						
1999	8	3	6	27	27	19
2005	7	1	6	32	27	13

Sources: Stats SA 1999, 2005

Note: a The percentages of total employment do not add up to 100 because Clerks and Sales & Services occupations have been omitted.

of insufficient data, they indicated that the household data suggested 'erratic fluctuations around a moderately declining trend' (Steyn & Daniels 2003: 568). They found, furthermore, that engineering employment actually hovered around the 70 000 mark between 1990 and 2001. An alternative source of data is the Engineering Council of South Africa (ECSA). Its registration figures for all classes of engineers have been relatively stable at just under 26 000 over much of this period, with a slight increase to the 27 000 mark in 2005 and 2006 (although it should be noted that not all engineers in employment are registered with the ECSA). The analysis of the educational supply level data below paints a similar picture: consistent engineering skills provision with a moderate upward trend. It therefore appears that the household survey data are providing an inaccurate picture of engineering employment. Contrary to what these data suggest, there appears to be moderate demand for engineers. Our qualitative research, however, goes further: it points to a strong demand that is not being matched by supply.

Supply of skills

This section commences with an explanation of the different routes by which a person could acquire skills in the metal sector. Then it examines the entries, throughputs and outputs in FET institutions, followed by a similar examination of acquiring qualifications through HET institutions.

Paths to becoming artisans, technicians and engineers

Individuals who are being trained in a technical occupational field and who obtain theoretical instruction through an FET institution study for national certificate qualifications such as National Technical Certificate (NTC) 3 or NTC 4 (sometimes abbreviated further as N3 or N4). The NTC 3 courses have a content and conceptual level that is equivalent to the national educational certificate or matriculation certificate. To qualify as an artisan requires that students achieve the NTC 2 level, but in the newer technology programmes this minimum requirement can be raised to NTC 3.

Similar qualifications pegged at a higher level are offered through the technikons (now called universities of technology). Although organised in a semester system, the technikon courses are whole-year courses that lead to the award of a national diploma (NDip). The first-year level of a technikon course is designated as T1 and the further levels as T2 and T3. Normally a matriculation certificate with exemption is a prerequisite to enter these courses, particularly in the scientific fields of engineering, accounting, medical technology, etc. Graduates in the engineering and scientific fields who qualify from technikons/universities of technology with a bachelor of technology (BTech) degree are usually designated as technologists and engineers.

University courses are usually divided into undergraduate and postgraduate courses. The feeder qualifications of high-level human resources that enter the metal and engineering sector from the university system are either a professional engineering degree (e.g. in metallurgy, chemistry or mechanical engineering) or an undergraduate bachelor's degree in a science discipline (e.g. metallurgy, chemistry, etc.). The university system further provides for a wide spectrum of more specialised studies that can be undertaken at a postgraduate level. Individuals who hold university engineering degrees or undergraduate or postgraduate degrees in specific science disciplines are referred to as engineers or scientists.

It is important to recognise that there are a number of different paths that can be followed to become an artisan, technician or engineer. The routes to artisan status are as follows:
- A four-year traditional apprenticeship at a firm with block-releases to attend sandwich courses (N1 and N2) in trade theory subjects at an FET college. Admission to such apprenticeship programmes at a firm would normally be a minimum of a Grade 9 general education and training (GET) school-leaving certificate with a credit in mathematics. Credits in science, technical drawing and other technology-related subjects would be a bonus. The firm is required to release the apprentice in blocks lasting for up to 4 months (15 weeks) to attend trimester N-courses in theory subjects of the trade specialisation that the apprentice is engaged in. Learnership programmes that contain equivalent theoretical and practical content will result in similar admission routes into the artisan ranks. But even under the traditional apprenticeship programme, an apprentice who reached a trade competence and fulfilled the theoretical requirements could, with the consent of the employer, undergo a trade test within the four-year apprenticeship period and gain admission to artisan status. This is the normal route that is followed to become an artisan.
- An accelerated apprenticeship programme leads to the same result but it is completed over a shorter period. Instead of taking 4 years, it can be done in just over 80 weeks. This embodies 60 weeks of in-house training and theoretical instruction, either at a training centre attached to the firm or at an FET college, coupled with a further 24 weeks of on-the-job training in a normal working

environment. Usually the on-the-job training takes place in a normal working environment in which the trade skill is largely embedded. Firms with their own training centres would merely transfer the apprentice or learner from the training centre to the factory floor. A training centre at an FET college would seek to place the apprentice or learner for 24 weeks with a reputable firm that provides the candidate with practical on-the-job experience.

- Some years ago a system of recognition was established in the metal and engineering industries for those who were not able to enter an apprenticeship programme but qualified to undergo further training and had acquired a theoretical knowledge and competence in specific areas of a designated artisan trade. Known as the Artisan Training and Recognition Agreement for the Metal Industry (ATRAMI), it has been endorsed by the new institutions of skills development such as the Manufacturing, Engineering and Related Services Sector Education and Training Authority (MERSETA). The ATRAMI system is designed for two types of learners: those who are under 21 years old and have not been able to secure an apprenticeship contract with an employer; and learners with a competence to do similar skilled work to artisans with more than five years working experience, and competence in all the prerequisite theoretical modules for the trade, who can immediately apply to undergo a skills recognition test. If successful in the recognition test, they would be granted artisan status. If not successful, the result will indicate at what level each trainee has to undergo further training. In terms of the ATRAMI, trainees have to proceed through a sequence of modules. A competence test is undergone at the end of each module. The trainee must pass this competence test before embarking on the next module. Once all the prescribed modules have been successfully completed, the trainee can apply to the MERSETA to undergo a national trade test under section 28 of the Manpower Training Act (No. 56 of 1981) at an accredited trade test centre. Success in the national trade test automatically leads to the granting of artisan status.

Across these three levels of entry into artisan occupations, there is a high degree of overlap and substitutability between the apprenticeship route and the learnership route. Both routes represent old and new institutional forms for the creation of a corps of artisan workers in the metal and engineering industries by deepening the interaction between learning and the activity of work.

Similarly, a plurality of routes can be pursued by an individual intending to become an engineer. The most prominent is through academic study in order to obtain an engineering degree. Thereafter, recently graduated engineers can acquire experience by working on-the-job under the supervision of highly experienced engineers. Such programmes are referred to as an engineering pupilage and bear some resemblance to the experiential workplace training that is recommended for individuals at the senior level of their technikon/university of technology diploma studies.

An artisan can also become an engineer, mainly through part-time studies at a technikon/university of technology. These theoretical studies are combined with applied practical work in the field of engineering that eventually culminates in sitting an examination for the government-certified engineer's ticket. This route is open to individuals in the mechanical engineering, chemical engineering, electrical engineering and marine engineering fields. Although it has lost much of its popularity, it can still be used by individuals to develop their careers in the engineering field and eventually be admitted to the engineering profession.

Having discussed the different paths to becoming a skilled worker in metal and engineering, we next consider the institutions that play a key role in providing the skills. They are the FET colleges, universities of technology and universities.

FET institutions: enrolments, throughputs and outputs

There are two major features of FET institutions that impact on the quantity and quality of education and training they provide. The first is that there has been an increase in enrolments at all levels of theoretical courses (from N1 to N6) over the 10-year period from 1996 to 2005. The second is that there has not been a systematic progression from one level to the next. Enrolment numbers for the different levels have been highly erratic.

There was a consistent increase in the number of individuals participating in engineering programmes at FET colleges for all levels between 1996 and 2005. Student retention rates over the period showed improvements. Likewise, there were improvements in pass rates in FET engineering courses, especially from the N1 to N4 levels. Pass rates at levels N5 and N6, however, showed pronounced declines. The data are shown in Table 5.7

The evidence of throughputs given in Table 5.7 suggests that the FET system does not convey the same group of learners from the lower levels to the upper levels. Enrolment progression from N1 to N2 is relatively steady and suggests that the same cohort of learners is largely involved in these levels. This is, however, marred by a dramatic decline in enrolments at N3, which shrinks to slightly less than one-fifth of the enrolments recorded at N2. A bulging-out and expansion of enrolments thereafter follows at the N4 and N5 levels: there is roughly a doubling in enrolments from N3 to N4 and a tripling of enrolments from N4 to N5. Finally, N6 enrolments decline by more than half of those at N5.

It is apparent from the data that the enrolments are not consistent. The evidence shown in Table 5.7 suggests that different cohorts of FET learners participate in the system at different levels. One group appears to undergo the trade test with the minimum education prerequisites. This group is likely to comprise learners who either do not hold a matriculation certificate or just scraped through.

The second group seems to be made up of matriculants who have mathematics and science subjects. Some of this group probably enter the FET system because that is the only entry point they have to study further and progress beyond the artisan layers of the labour force. With only minor exceptions, those who enrol at the N1 and N2 levels generally do not continue beyond this point once the theoretical requirements to be admitted to artisan status have been fulfilled. Such learners are not likely to reach the higher N4 and N5 levels.

There is a third group of learners who appear to enter the FET system as dropouts from the HET system. The entry point of this third group is the N5 level, and it accounts for the more than threefold increase in enrolments from the N4 to the N5 level. We do not have data to ascertain whether the group that enters the FET system from the HET system eventually attempts to get back into the HET system once they have made headway and acquired an FET national certificate (i.e. N5 and N6).

An interviewee confirmed that the majority of enrolled learners at the N1 and N2 levels are made up of individuals who have fallen out of the schooling system or passed with poor symbols that do not allow them to access the public higher education system (Pereira interview). For these learners, enrolment at an FET institution represents a second chance to obtain a qualification, but many do not continue beyond N2 because they cannot cope with the standard demanded by FET institutions. Their departure from the FET system after N2 coincides with the departure of learners who are indentured into artisan programmes after having fulfilled the minimum theoretical requirements. These two groups largely account for the massive decline in N3 enrolments. N3 enrolments are largely generated internally as throughputs from N2.

Enrolments at N4 level and beyond come from a number of sources: throughputs from N3, the return of previous dropouts, the admission of matriculated school-leavers, and learners transferring, either temporarily or permanently, from the HET system. The return of dropouts is generated by the demand by employers for prospective apprentices to have higher educational qualifications. The N-levels within which students from the HET system are placed depend on the types of courses that they have previously studied and the credits that they have obtained.

These three participating groups in the engineering programmes of the FET system enter the system from different avenues, which suggests that the corps of FET-trained employees in the metal and engineering industries embodies a diversity of technical and engineering education: some proceed through the artisan track, a small group makes the best use of the educational opportunities of the FET system, while others use the FET system as an educational safety net as a result of failures experienced elsewhere. This diversity poses challenges for the education and training of the intermediate-level corps that passes through the system. The engineering programmes in the FET system do not build up a coherent cadre of intermediate technical and production-related certification outputs. Until they do this, the FET system will be perceived as a stopgap measure that will have low credibility.

HET enrolments and outputs

The three higher education qualifications that contribute more than 80 per cent of technicians and engineers for the metal sector are the NDip, BTech and bachelor of engineering (BEng) degree. Figure 5.3 and Table 5.8 indicate the trend in enrolments and output of these three higher education qualifications. They show erratic enrolment figures for the NDip and BTech degree. The NDip declined by 25 per cent for the first period from 1996 to 2001, but then soared by 129 per cent from 2001 onwards to 34 874 enrolments in 2005. It accounted for no less than 62 per cent of all higher education engineering enrolments in 2005. The BTech degree displayed quite a different trend in enrolments: graduates with this qualification almost quadrupled from 1999 to 2001, only to decline rapidly from 2002 to 2004, although they did not fall below the 1999 figure. As a result, BTech enrolments more than tripled between1996 and 2005.

This trend corresponds to earlier research by Cooper and Subotzky (2001). There were significant increases in African enrolment throughout the 1990s, in particular at university and technikon levels. However, from 1997 onwards these science and technology programmes started to exhibit enrolment reversals. At the same time, new African enrolments were skewed towards the social sciences and humanities. This meant that potential African science and technology enrolments lagged behind their enrolments in non-science and technology programmes.

It is important to note that corresponding to the declining BTech enrolment in engineering and engineering technology programmes – pervasive from 1992 – BTech outputs in these programmes within the technikon system exhibited a continuous and incremental growth from a low point in 2000 to more than double this output level in 2005.

By comparison, enrolments for students registered for BEng degrees recorded a sluggish but relatively steady 41 per cent increase over the 1996–2005 period. However, registration for BEng degrees and BTech degrees in 2005 accounted for only 20 per cent and 11 per cent respectively of all higher education engineering enrolments in 2005.

TABLE 5.7: Performance transmission across FET N-Level theoretical engineering courses, 1996–2005

	Level	1996	1997	1998	1999	2000	2001	2002	2003	2004	2005
Entered											
Level 1 theoretical courses	1	2 934	2 915	3 188	3 359	2 911	2 855	2 903	3 698	4 287	4 436
Level 2 theoretical courses	2	2 066	2 271	2 294	2 392	2 119	2 135	2 606	2 967	3 509	3 817
Proportionate change: N1 to N2		-29.6	-22.1	-28.0	-28.8	-27.2	-25.2	-10.2	-19.8	-18.1	-14.0
Level 3 theoretical courses	3	597	621	511	411	427	403	489	494	640	714
Proportionate change: N2 to N3		-71.1	-72.7	-77.7	-82.8	-79.8	-81.1	-81.2	-83.4	-81.8	-81.3
Level 4 theoretical courses	4	1 115	1 994	2 033	1 625	1 479	1 442	1 363	1 332	1 544	1 609
Proportionate change: N3 to N4		86.8	221.1	297.8	295.4	246.4	257.8	178.7	169.6	141.3	125.4
Level 5 theoretical courses	5	4 396	4 631	5 117	4 653	4 978	5 044	4 922	5 288	5 476	5 406
Proportionate change: N4 to N5		294.3	132.2	151.7	186.3	236.6	249.8	261.1	297.0	254.7	236.0
Level 6 theoretical courses	6	1 795	1 922	2 019	2 093	2 206	2 504	2 440	2 376	2 358	2 619
Proportionate change: N5 to N6		-59.2	-58.5	-60.5	-55.0	-55.7	-50.4	-50.4	-55.1	-56.9	-51.6
Wrote											
Level 1 theoretical courses	1	2 521	2 517	2 735	2 946	2 493	2 516	2 522	3 266	3 735	3 891
Level 2 theoretical courses	2	1 847	2 002	2 081	2 138	1 917	1 946	2 311	2 700	3 209	3 463
Proportionate change: N1 to N2		-26.7	-20.5	-23.9	-27.4	-23.1	-22.7	-8.4	-17.3	-14.1	-11.0
Level 3 theoretical courses	3	475	506	434	338	362	373	433	429	574	642
Proportionate change: N2 to N3		-74.3	-74.7	-79.1	-84.2	-81.1	-80.8	-81.3	-84.1	-82.1	-81.5
Level 4 theoretical courses	4	915	1 652	1 698	1 447	1 301	1 280	1 214	1 189	1 363	1 419

	Level	1996	1997	1998	1999	2000	2001	2002	2003	2004	2005
Proportionate change: N3 to N4		92.6	226.5	291.2	328.1	259.4	243.2	180.4	177.2	137.5	121.0
Level 5 theoretical courses	5	3 549	3 849	4 321	4 117	4 516	4 561	4 308	4 673	4 739	4 705
Proportionate change: N4 to N5		287.9	133.0	154.5	184.5	247.1	256.3	254.9	293.0	247.7	231.6
Level 6 theoretical courses	6	1 345	1 459	1 612	1 736	1 890	2 174	2 086	2 002	1 971	2 186
Proportionate change: N5 to N6		−62.1	−62.1	−62.7	−57.8	−58.1	−52.3	−51.6	−57.2	−58.4	−53.5
Passed											
Level 1 theoretical courses	1	1 022	1 145	1 161	1 175	1 106	1 305	1 335	1 600	1 903	1 945
Level 2 theoretical courses	2	1 051	1 119	1 146	1 169	1 048	1 142	1 309	1 599	1 748	1 891
Proportionate change: N1 to N2		2.8	−2.3	−1.3	−0.5	−5.2	−12.5	−1.9	−0.1	−8.1	−2.8
Level 3 theoretical courses	3	263	313	297	235	223	211	244	305	442	494
Proportionate change: N2 to N3		−75.0	−72.0	−74.1	−79.9	−78.7	−81.5	−81.4	−80.9	−74.7	−73.9
Level 4 theoretical courses	4	526	737	844	812	782	745	736	759	772	852
Proportionate change: N3 to N4		100.0	135.5	184.2	245.5	250.7	253.1	201.6	148.9	74.7	72.5
Level 5 theoretical courses	5	1 829	1 837	1 889	2 152	2 290	2 431	1 936	2 131	2 071	2 074
Proportionate change: N4 to N5		247.7	149.3	123.8	165.0	192.8	226.3	163.0	180.8	168.3	143.4
Level 6 theoretical courses	6	664	698	834	1 004	1 203	1 164	1 146	1 065	896	950
Proportionate change: N5 to N6		−63.7	−62.0	−55.8	−53.3	−47.5	−52.1	−40.8	−50.0	−56.7	−54.2

Source: DoE 2007b

FIGURE 5.3: *Higher education enrolment and output, 1996–2005*

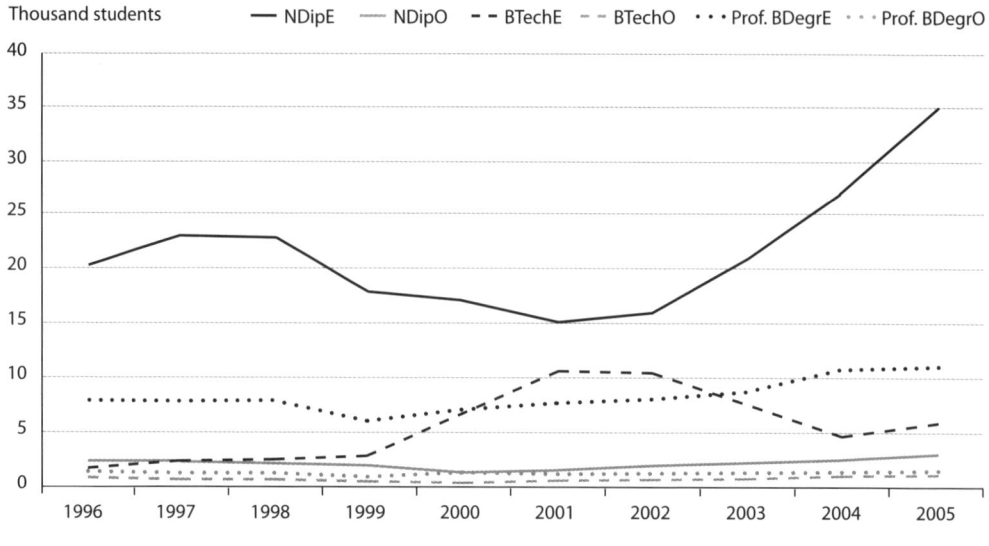

Source: Author calculations based on DoE 2007a

A matter of great concern is the low proportion of enrolled students that actually qualify each year. Figure 5.3 and Table 5.8 demonstrate that only a small proportion of enrolments for all three higher education qualifications manage to qualify. What is worse, the output-to-enrolment (O/E) ratio declined for all three qualifications over the period. The most drastic decline took place for the BTech, which dropped precipitously between 1996 and 2001. However, the ratio improved in the subsequent period: it reached 19 per cent by 2005. As the BTech and professional engineering degrees are regarded as four-year degrees, the output of qualifications would on average be 25 per cent of enrolments each year if all the students passed and none dropped out. While the qualification ratio of 19 per cent for the BTech degree in 2005 is not far from the ideal standard of 25 per cent, the ratio for the professional engineering degree declined from 17 per cent to 13 per cent over the period 1996–2005. As a result, the number of professional engineers being qualified each year only increased by 9 per cent over the 10-year period.

Over the period from 1996 to 2005, the gender distribution in the award of new qualifications in the engineering field within the higher education sector showed only a partial shift towards more female graduates. Even though the proportion of female graduates doubled, trebled and even quadrupled in the diploma and degree programmes where the largest number of students is concentrated, the gender shift amounted to roughly 10–15 per cent. The flow of newly qualified female engineering and technology graduates will need to increase significantly and remain high for a number of years before there is a discernible impact on the overall gender distribution within the high-skilled occupations in the sector.

Probably the most dramatic finding with respect to higher education qualifications within the engineering sector is the rapid growth in the number of Africans qualifying. In 2005, Africans constituted the majority of recipients of National Diplomas (70 per cent), BTech degrees (53 per cent) and Postgraduate Certificates or Diplomas (56 per cent). However, a much lower proportion of professional bachelors' degrees, that is, engineering degrees and postgraduate-level qualifications, has been awarded to Africans. In 1996, only 9 per cent of professional bachelors' degrees awarded in the engineering fields

TABLE 5.8: *Higher education enrolment, output and qualification ratio, 1996–2005*

Qualification	1996	1997	1998	1999	2000	2001	2002	2003	2004	2005
NDip										
Enrolment	20 426	23 188	22 965	17 993	17 270	15 231	16 157	20 926	27 033	34 874
Output	2 330	2 248	2 140	1 967	1 386	1 710	2 104	2 196	2 564	2 910
O/E ratio %	11.4	9.7	9.3	10.9	8.0	11.2	13.0	10.5	9.5	8.3
BTech										
Enrolment	1 840	2 503	2 599	2838	6 635	10 676	10 603	7 612	4 739	5 910
Output	812	800	691	573	433	641	687	772	952	1 131
O/E ratio %	44.1	32.0	26.6	20.2	6.5	6.0	6.5	10.1	20.1	19.1
Prof. bachelor's degree										
Enrolment	7 895	7 850	7 967	6 050	7 188	7 656	8 135	8 901	10 886	11 159
Output	1 341	1 243	1 277	1 051	1 292	1 287	1 306	1 356	1 424	1 466
O/E ratio %	17.0	15.8	16.0	17.4	18.0	16.8	16.1	15.2	13.1	13.1

Source: Based on DoE 2007a

were to African graduates. By 2005, Africans received 25 per cent of the professional bachelors' degrees in the engineering fields.

Balance between skills supply and demand

Finally, there is a delicate balance between the demand and supply, especially of skilled labour to the metal and engineering sector. While short-term conditions have an impact on the extent to which a crisis in skills availability results from demand being too aggressive, or from supply being too unresponsive to the market environment, the resolution to such disequilibria in complex systems such as labour markets is best resolved through devising a greater unity in action between demand and supply. To explicate the point with a specific example, our longer report on this sector shows that the limited size of the marine engineering industry, particularly in major port cities such as Cape Town, was a constraint to enterprise growth (see Maree et al. 2008: 58–60). Consequently, with only few exceptions, marine engineering firms in the Western Cape were by international standards almost miniscule. The inconsistency of demand for services from the marine engineering industries, particularly in the geographical proximity of Cape Town, meant that firms were only able to engage a limited permanent labour force. The pervasiveness of inconsistent market demand encouraged a higher use and dependence on contract and casual labour.

At a broader sectoral level, the evidence is not as clear-cut as that provided for the marine engineering industry. Despite the massive haemorrhaging in employment that was experienced in the metal and engineering sector nationally, unlike the situation in the marine engineering industry, there was quite a significant turnaround in employment growth after 2001. It was only in the basic iron and steel and non-ferrous metals industries (milling processes) and the electrical machinery and apparatus industry (a component of the machine-building industry) that this pattern of growth was not repeated. The employment decline in the milling processes was associated with significant capital intensification, a factor that would have resulted in changes in the occupational and skills embodiments demanded. If one examines the areas of occupational growth in the sector as a whole after 2001 (we use the time points 1999 and 2005), it is noticeable that an expansion in the employment of managers, technicians, craft workers and operators was particularly strong. This was in contrast to declines in the employment of elementary workers and professionals. However, due to sampling size, we caution against reading too much into the employment trend for professionals.

Our analysis of educational supply demonstrates a much slower response to pressures arising at the demand level. While employment growth at the operator and craft level appeared to be robust after 2001, the FET system, which largely caters for this cohort of the labour force, was plagued with erratic outputs. Furthermore, the engineering programmes in the FET system did not build up a coherent cadre of intermediate technical and production-related certification outputs.

The evidence highlights a number of serious challenges. The types of higher education qualifications generated in South Africa are still heavily concentrated at the NDip level. In 2005, only 20 per cent of higher education engineering enrolments were for BEng degrees, while 11 per cent were for BTech degrees. Equally disconcerting is the low proportion of enrolled students who eventually achieve engineering qualifications. Added to this has been the worsening of throughput rates for engineering qualifications. This has limited the impact of enrolment growth on qualifications obtained. For instance, despite a 41 per cent increase in enrolments for professional engineering degrees between 1996 and 2005, there was only a 9 per cent increase in the number of professional engineers being qualified by the South African HET system over this period. The relatively slow responsiveness at the FET and HET levels to the more rapid changes that are taking place within the metal and engineering industries thus has direct repercussions on the delivery of skills.

Having considered employment, as well as the demand and supply of skills to the metals beneficiation sector, it is important to consider the dynamics within the sector. How do employers combine their strategic objectives with the available supply of skills? The answer to this is based on primary research conducted at 11 firms in which we examine the dynamics between the firms' strategic objectives and their skills requirements.

Research findings: firms' dynamics and skills requirements

Sample of firms

Firms were selected in order to secure a spread across small, medium and large size classes. We also sought to include firms at different stages of the value adding or beneficiation processes, that is, producers of raw materials (milling firms), constructors of intermediate products (engineering and machine shops), and builders of machines.[7] It is evident that the metal processing or milling firms in the sample are generally large firms with a staff complement well in excess of 200 employees, and the engineering or machine shops, which are mostly involved in intermediate production activities, tend to occupy the medium and small employee-size class. There is variation in the distribution of machine builders in terms of size. The firms are not discussed individually, but placed within a discussion of the sub-sector within which they fall.

---

7   The firms at which interviews were conducted are as follows:
    Milling firms: Zimalco (Germiston) (100–199 employees); Saldanha Steel (Saldanha) (570 employees); Columbus Steel (Middleburg) (1 576 employees); Highveld Steel (Witbank) (3 500 employees);
    Engineering and machine shops: Hansing Engineering (Saldanha) (20 employees); Belmet Marine (Cape Town) (76 employees); CME (Cape Town) (80 employees); SP Metal Forging (Boksburg) (100 employees);
    Machine builders: Seecor (Cape Town) (12 employees); Alstrom John Thompson (Cape Town) (551 employees); ABB Transformers (Pretoria) (600 employees).

Milling firms

Managers at iron and steel mills suggest that the low number of registered students in higher education engineering programmes is a weakness in the system. The problem is one of an under-supply of skilled labour at particular levels as well as an inconsistency between quality and the credentials which measure it. The problem of an under-supply of particular levels of skilled labour arises principally because of competition between several higher educational and professional programmes for a limited pool of matriculants with a prerequisite grounding in mathematics and science. Where recruits are found to enter firm-based artisan or learnership training programmes within the engineering fields, the firms inevitably confront challenges of educational quality. For example, the milling companies that we interviewed had experienced severe problems recruiting sufficient numbers of school-leavers with mathematics and science as school subjects. This under-supply of school-leavers with these competencies reproduces the culture of poaching, with the victims being the firms that have successfully overcome such hurdles on the labour market.

Milling firms have, furthermore, been at the forefront of raising the entrance requirements for internal artisan training programmes because the schooling system was no longer guaranteeing the quality and integrity of school-leaving certificates.

Competition for potential recruits in engineering programmes within the higher education system is even more severe at the higher occupational levels.

Furthermore, operational pressures such as routine maintenance of oil refineries and power stations can aggravate the problem of inadequate skilled labour supply within the metal and engineering sector. Opportunities within the global labour market have also impacted on the availability of skilled labour in the country.

To deal with the situation, a number of milling firms have used their social responsibility interventions as a vehicle to support the teaching of mathematics and science within disadvantaged schools in their regions.

Besides the training programmes for artisans and the experiential training for technicians and engineers, all the iron and steel mills appear to have instituted operator training and other skills programmes for employees within occupational ranks lower than the artisan level. At some firms it is referred to as 'the operator programme', at others as the 'metal production learnership', and at still others as 'skills programmes'. The different designations suggest that there are a number of institutional vehicles for delivering such programmes. Some form part of the MERSETA's workplace skills development programmes, although there are also some self-funded programmes. Others are part of learnership programmes that firms are supporting for their internal labour force. Still others are provided by initiatives that FET institutions have put in place in collaboration with a SETA. The difference with respect to past programmes is that these new initiatives appear to incorporate a qualifications progression through which the recipients of the training can eventually qualify as artisans.

Engineering or machine shops: evolution and skills training orientation

Skills are critical for the growth and expansion of general engineering and machine shops. Skill, however, does not exist outside the context of the prevailing technologies. Many of the machines being utilised in the industry are operated through computerised numerical control (CNC) technology. Interviewees emphasised the importance of computerisation for the industry, which one employer described as the 'backbone of modern industry'.

The FET institutions have often lagged behind with respect to incorporating the knowledge applications of the technological advances that have occurred. One employer remarked that until the early 2000s, the FET syllabus for the theoretical preparation of artisans did not contain any theory of computing and the FET colleges did not have any CNC equipment. The transition to the new syllabus also took roughly six years to formalise (Wessels interview).

Each of the engineering or machine shops operates some form of in-house training. For those that had an apprenticeship training programme in place, there was a modest number of apprentices undergoing training in technical trades that were deemed absolutely necessary for the firm's transmission of specialised skills. In two firms, these apprenticeship programmes were for tool and die makers and fitters and turners. In the other two firms, a learnership programme was in place with the sole purpose of supplying or supplementing the internal labour supply. The educational prerequisites to enter trades in the engineering and machine shop sector appear to be somewhat uneven, with most firms requiring at least a matriculation certificate to take on a trainee in the artisan occupations. Welders are an exception: apprentices or learners with a Grade 10 or higher qualification can still find openings to be trained in this occupation within many firms.

Machine builders: evolution and skills training orientation

Machine builders in the manufacturing sector produce a wide range of products. For purposes of this research, machine builders are classified in a broad category called 'machinery and equipment manufacturers'.

Problems in the schooling system have had a detrimental impact on the availability of skills. Employers comment that the learning background that serves as an important base on which to build engineering and scientific skills is often absent in new employees. Also absent is a culture in which measurement and calculation is the basis of normal working practice. New entrants also have a poor knowledge of the metric system and have had no prior exposure to the building blocks (mathematical literacy and accuracy) that are essential to develop engineering skills. This is an urgent signal that the reproduction of the metal and engineering skills base is being compromised.[8]

The firm in the research sample that builds industrial boilers has always had a training school for apprentices at its plant. The school has been used for training apprentices as well as technicians and engineers. The envisaged construction of new power stations, upgrading of existing ones, and other infrastructural investments has encouraged the firm to plan for an expansion of its labour force. This involves finding new artisans as well as increasing the number of apprentices to be trained by the firm.

Skills development and skills upgrading were not a big concern at the small extrusion machine-building firm. However, at the two large machine-building firms, internal skills upgrading initiatives were taken very seriously. Both of these firms had recognised the importance of an extended skills development system in the country. One of the firms indicated that the skills development legislation had forced many businesses that had never done training before to become actively engaged with skills development. So, despite many criticisms about the bureaucratic administration of the SETA system, one of the consequences is that firms have become much more involved with putting skills development initiatives into operation. Many firms have also become more strategic in diverting skills development resources into areas of training that the firm is generally better at doing.

---

8   In support of this finding see Lundall 2005 and Lundall 2006.

Staff outflows from the sector

While the opening up of the world economy has meant increased foreign ownership, and with that opportunities with regard to new technologies and the expansion of production facilities, it has also meant a greater outflow of skilled labour. Interviewees identified the following countries as the principal beneficiaries of South African artisan skills: Australia, New Zealand, parts of the Middle East such as Dubai and Qatar, and the oil fields off Angola, where artisans are reputed to earn US$10 000 per month (Lister interview).

Within South Africa, the skilled labour force produced by the training programmes of the iron and steel milling firms is preyed on by smaller downstream firms. The attitude that sees poaching rather than training as the solution to skills needs is linked to the size and system constraints of firms. The large milling firms do a much larger proportion of the training of metal and engineering artisans. However, whereas previously the state-owned enterprises made big contributions to training, today private steel mills are subjected to poaching from the state-owned enterprises (e.g. Eskom). But this is less severe than the rivalry for skilled labour between steel mills themselves, as well as among the plethora of engineering firms, machine-building firms and new start-ups in the mining sector. One informant at a steel mill claimed that the high demand for skills in the economy contributed to the firm recording a staff turnover ranging from 10 per cent to 14 per cent per annum, most of which was blamed on poaching by competitors (Van der Merwe interview).

Conclusion and recommendations

The argument put forward in this chapter is that although South Africa is richly endowed with metals, it has not managed to advance the beneficiation process of most metals to the final product stage. Most of the metals are still exported after the milling stage when relatively little value has been added to the product.

Although the reasons for the lack of beneficiation of metals are numerous and complex, the main one identified in this chapter is the pricing policy of the upstream monopolistic mills. Their practices of import parity pricing and differential pricing have served to impede the growth of the more labour-intensive downstream producers.

This chapter has also interrogated whether a skills shortage has impeded the advance of beneficiation in the metal and engineering industries. It found that an inadequate supply of skills, both quantitative and qualitative, has indeed inhibited their growth and development. With regard to technical education, it has been found that there is a lack of consistent throughput of apprentices and trainees in the system. There is a drastic decline in FET institutions' enrolments at the N3 level, only to increase considerably at the N4 and N5 levels, and then another major decline at the N6 level. In higher education, a major concern has been the low and declining throughput rate of professional engineers, resulting in an extremely low growth in numbers of qualified engineers coming onto the skills market.

The MERSETA, which is often lambasted by employers as being inefficient and bureaucratic, is thus not the primary source of the skills crisis in the metal and engineering sector. The problem is deeply rooted in three fundamental areas: first, in the low quality of public education and training, particularly at the general education or schooling level; second, in the outdated equipment and curriculum of FET institutions, which results in inferior-quality education (Fisher et al. 2003: 340, 347); and third, in an enterprise training orientation that is unable to align enterprise training with the demands of a new millennium.

Our research findings provide ample evidence with respect to the first and second areas. Significant improvements are required in general education and public FET education, especially with regard to mathematics, science and communication, which will enable learners to embrace a fast-changing technological society. Most importantly, the loss of learners from the FET and HET systems is constraining the creation of a viable massified FE and HE system.

The enterprise-level training system that prevails in South Africa is a low-beneficiation training system. In other words, training is aimed at the low-beneficiation end of the value chain. This system is rooted in the past, when large state-owned and private enterprises came to dominate the milling processes in iron and steel and also did the bulk of training. Furthermore, the public technical college system mainly developed to fuel the apprenticeship training initiatives that arose in these large state-owned and private enterprises. The many engineering and machine shops could only manage to sustain a very modest level of training activity within firms. Small engineering and machine shops not able to do this depended on recruiting or poaching staff from larger firms that did undertake staff training.

The process of transforming the training system into a high-beneficiation training system has been tardy at both a policy level and at the level of the education and training institutions. It is also only in the new millennium that a modest recapitalisation of public FET institutions has been initiated by the state. However, to be successful, technical training will have to work in tandem with an industrial strategy that focuses on the downstream segments of the industry.

While initiatives such as the accelerated artisan training programme are laudable, they focus on the short-term need, and will not on their own propel the training system from a relatively low- to a high-beneficiation training system. This is because such initiatives are premised on the training outputs of large firms, many of which are in the milling sector. The challenge for the metal and engineering industry is therefore to scale up the provision of skills for the high-beneficiation end of the production chain.

References

Black A (2001) Globalisation and restructuring in the South African automotive industry. *Journal of International Development* 13(6): 779–796

Cooper D & Subotzky G (2001) *The skewed revolution: Trends in South African higher education: 1988–1998.* Bellville: Education Policy Unit, University of the Western Cape

DoE (Department of Education, South Africa) (2007a) Higher Education Management Information System (HEMIS) database 1999–2005. Pretoria: DoE

DoE (2007b) FET output data 1996–2005. Pretoria: DoE

DoL (Department of Labour, South Africa) (2005) *National skills development strategy 2005–2010.* Pretoria: DoL

DTI (Department of Trade and Industry, South Africa) (2005) *Metals sector development strategy.* Pretoria: DTI

Feinstein CH (2005) *An economic history of South Africa: Conquest, discrimination and development.* Cambridge: Cambridge University Press

Fisher G, Jaff R, Powell L & Hall G (2003) Public further education and training colleges. In Human Sciences Research Council *Human Resources Development Review 2003: Education, employment and skills in South Africa.* Cape Town: HSRC Press

FRIDGE (Fund for Research into Industrial Development Growth and Equity) (2003) *Study to facilitate the formulation of an integrated strategy for the retention and creation of employment in the South African metals and engineering sector.* Johannesburg: NALEDI

Lundall P (2005) *A first phase exploration of the dynamics of enterprise skills in Western Cape firms.* MEDS Research Paper prepared for the Western Cape Department of Economic Development and Tourism

Lundall P (2006) *Employment flows and the distribution of targeted jobs in the upstream oil and gas sector of the Western Cape economy over the medium term*. MEDS Research Paper prepared for the Western Cape Department of Economic Development and Tourism

Maree J, Lundall P & Godfrey S (2008) *Industrial structure and skills in the metals beneficiation sector of South Africa*. Research report prepared for the Department of Labour in association with the Human Sciences Research Council

Martin HJ & Orpen N (1979) *South Africa at war: military and industrial organization and operations in connection with the conduct of war, 1939–1945*. Cape Town: Purnell

MERSETA (Manufacturing, Engineering and Related Services Sector Education and Training Authority) (2006) *Sector skills plan review 2006–2010*. Marshalltown: MERSETA

Quantec (2007) *RSA regional indicators database*. Accessed September 2007, http://www.quantec.co.za/data

Rosenthal E (1981) *Girders of the veld: Structural steel and its story in South Africa*. Johannesburg: South African Institute of Steel Construction

Stats SA (Statistics South Africa) (1999) *October Household Survey (OHS)*. Pretoria: Stats SA

Stats SA (2005) *Labour Force Survey (LFS)*. Pretoria: Stats SA

Steyn G & Daniels R (2003) Engineers and technicians. In Human Sciences Research Council *Human resources development review 2003: Education, employment and skills in South Africa*. Cape Town: HSRC Press

The Presidency (2006) *Asgisa annual report 2006*. Accessed 23 March 2008, http://www.thepresidency.gov.za/docs/asgisa2006.pdf

Interviews

Lister B, Manager: NSF (National Skills Fund) Projects, South African Oil and Gas Alliance, Cape Town, 31 July 2007

Pereira C, previously principal of the Ekurhuleni East FET College, telephonic interview, 16 January 2008

Van der Merwe F, Human Resource Director, Saldanha Steel, Saldanha Bay, 23 July 2007

Wessels E, Director, Cape Manufacturing Engineers, Epping Industria, 19 July 2007

CHAPTER 6

Chemicals

Rhoanda van Zyl

Introduction

The primary aim of the research project on which this chapter reports was to contribute to the attainment of greater alignment between skills development strategies and the development requirements of the South African chemical sector, in particular with the launch of the Accelerated and Shared Growth Initiative for South Africa (Asgisa) and the release of the new National Industrial Policy Framework. The Asgisa initiative aims to halve unemployment, and set targets of annual growth rates of 4.5 per cent or higher from 2005 to 2009, and 6 per cent or higher from 2010 to 2014.

Manufacturing GDP reduced from constituting 25 per cent of national GDP in the past to about 16 per cent of national GDP in 2006, which is an indication that the services sector has been the main contributor to the high growth rates in GDP over the past few years. The South African chemical sector constituted up to 20 per cent of manufacturing GDP in 2006, which in turn constituted 16 per cent of the total national GDP (i.e. the chemical sector constituted 3 per cent of total GDP) (Stats SA 1995–2006, 1998–2006).

Growth in the consumption of chemical products has always been similar to growth in manufacturing GDP overall, because the chemical sector intersects with every other part of the manufacturing economy, for example, agriculture, automotive, construction, consumer products, food, healthcare, mining, paper, textiles and water treatment, as chemical products are used in all of these sectors (Chemical Marketing and Consulting Services [CMCS] & Ozone Business Consulting database).[1]

The growth rate of manufacturing GDP was 4 per cent on average between 2004 and 2007. Apart from a handful of individual enterprises such as Sasol,[2] the overall production growth rate of the South African chemical sector was, however, lower than that of manufacturing GDP, with an average growth rate of 2 per cent per annum between 2004 and 2006 (Stats SA 1995–2006).

The low production growth rate in the South African chemical sector is a result of a world tendency for high manufacturing volumes to be located in countries with competitive feedstock advantages, for example, crude oil and other raw materials; in this respect South Africa is at a competitive disadvantage since it needs to import many of its feedstocks.

---

1 This database has been developed over the past 22 years of market research studies for both private and multi-client studies, and specialises in the chemical and related sectors in Southern Africa.
2 See the Sasol case study in Chapter 5 of the main report on which this chapter is based (Van Zyl 2008).

The chemical sector is also stagnant in terms of job creation (Reserve Bank 1995–2005), due to efficiency improvement as well as a general trend towards automation and capital intensivity.[3] Based on Labour Market Survey data, employment in the chemical sector grew at less than one per cent on average per annum between 1995 and 2005 (Reserve Bank 1995–2005).

This highlights the need for future skills development to be directed towards areas of active investment, as well as further downstream development in sub-sectors that have proven to be feasible to develop further.

The focus of this research was therefore firstly on identifying future capital investments, together with the perceived skills constraints on achieving these investments and on operating the new production sites. Secondly, in considering prospects for the development of the downstream chemical sector, the focus was on sub-sectors prioritised for development in the Chemical Sector Development Strategy (DTI 2005b) that forms part of the broader industrial policy framework of the Department of Trade and Industry (DTI) (DTI 2007).

An analysis was made in the Chemical Sector Development Strategy of the various sub-sectors' potential, based on their economic potential and the level of difficulty involved in successfully addressing the institutional issues affecting realisation of each sub-sector's potential. This led to key action programmes to promote certain sub-sectors that showed the most potential, namely the promotion of greater production in local pharmaceutical products and the promotion of downstream plastic products production. There are also other key action programmes in this strategy whose feasibility is still being investigated.

South African chemical sector profile

Chemical sector classification

The South African chemical sector is the largest of its kind in Africa and is highly complex and diversified. The classification of the sector is based on 11 sub-sectors that were developed as part of a Customised Sector Programme (CSP) of the DTI (DTI 2005a). The CSP Business Unit comprises programmes for the development of priority sectors in support of the DTI's Manufacturing Strategy and government's micro-economic reform strategy (DTI 2007).

These 11 sub-sectors are regarded as the most appropriate method of classification of the sector from a strategic and business perspective, and are comparable with the Standard Industrial Classification (SIC), which is generally used for statistical reporting, but is not useful for a strategic analysis of the sector. The relationship between the two classifications is summarised in Figure 6.1.

Chemical sector value chain

Figure 6.2 illustrates the chemical sector value chain, which is discussed in more detail in the following sections.

---

3   CMCS & Ozone Business Consulting database.

FIGURE 6.1: *Strategic sub-sector and standard industrial classifications of the chemical sector*

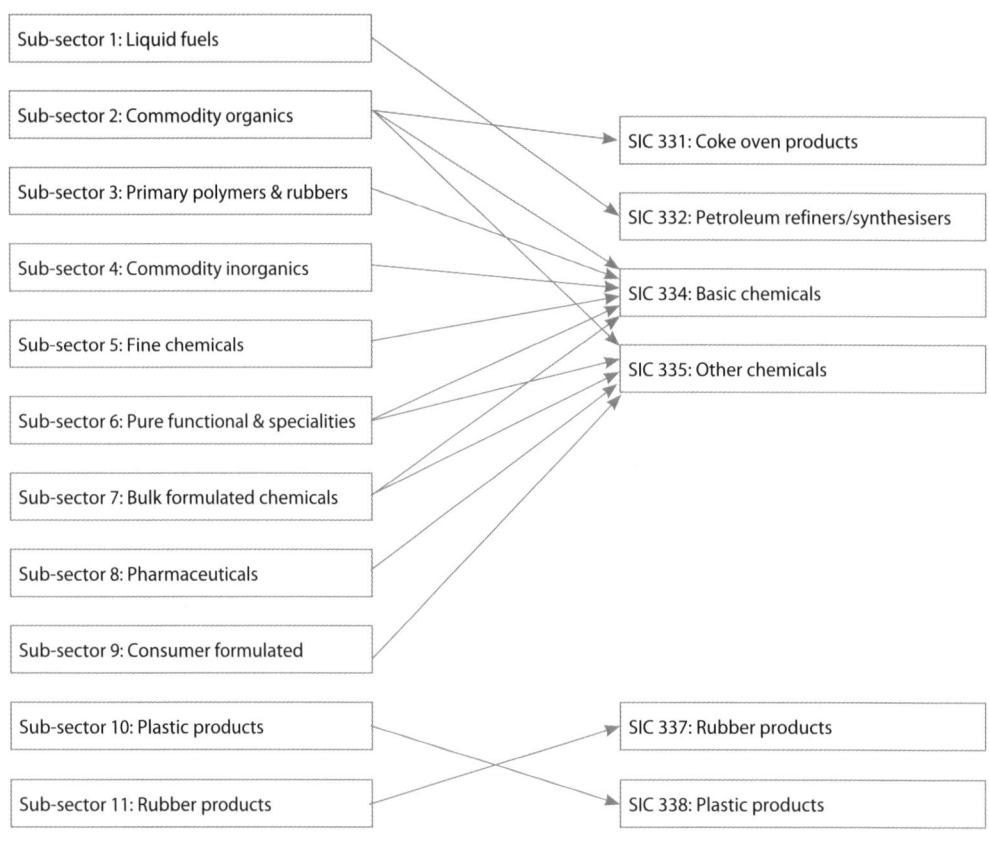

Sources: DTI 2005a; Stats SA 1993

Upstream chemical sector

Production processes

Upstream operations are typically capital-intensive and have chemical synthesis production processes (i.e. the formation of more complex chemical compounds or molecules from simpler compounds or molecules through chemical reactions) that are controlled by automated process control. World-class plants that take advantage of operational efficiencies are used.

In South Africa, upstream chemical manufacturing is concentrated among a few players, with some product categories only having one producer. The bulk of the upstream chemical sector is not well structured to accommodate small, medium and micro enterprises (SMMEs).

The relevant sub-sectors in the upstream chemical sector are liquid fuels, commodity organics, primary polymers and rubbers, commodity inorganics and fine chemicals.

FIGURE 6.2: *Chemical sector value chain*

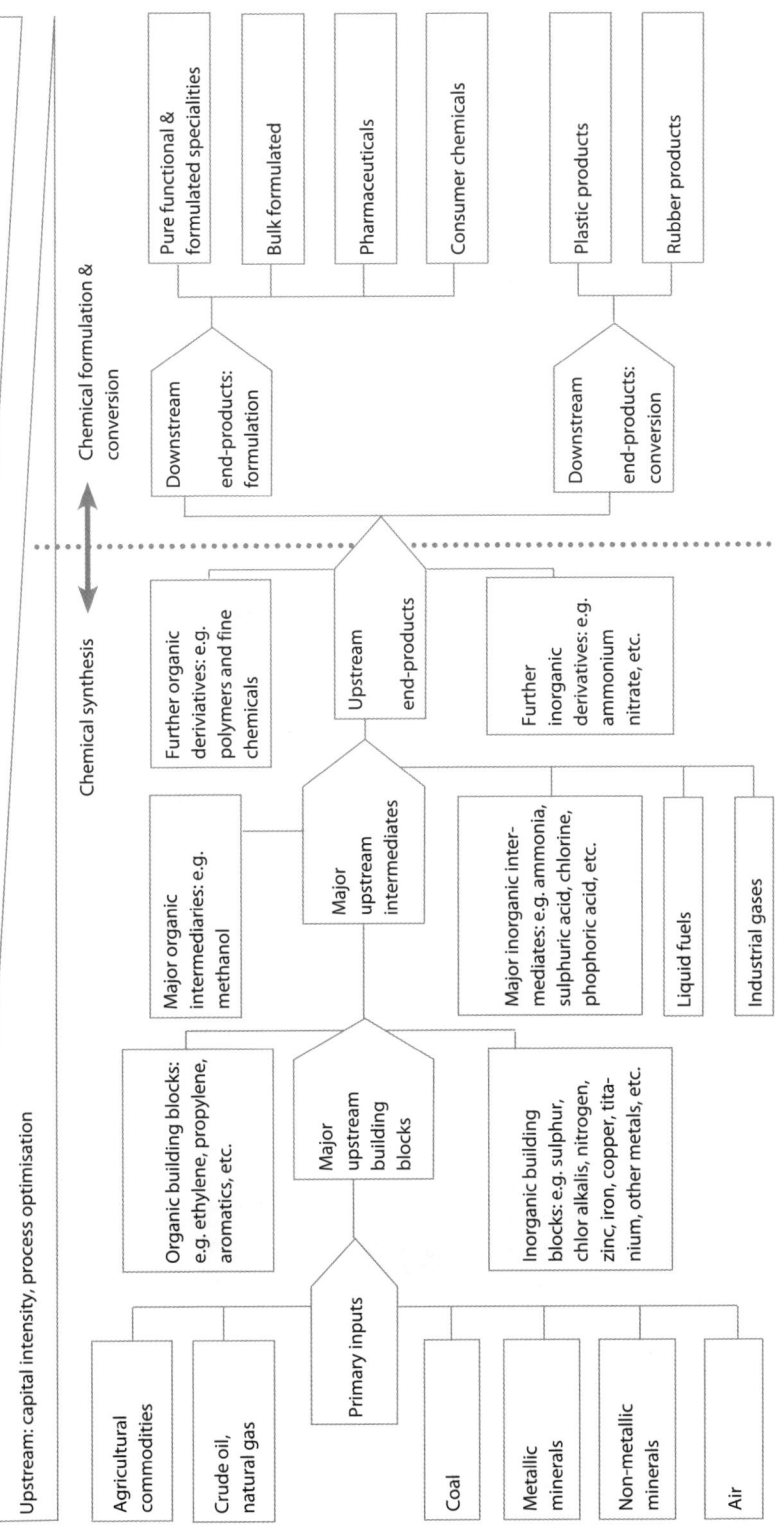

Source: CMCS & Ozone Business Consulting database

Liquid fuels and associated products

The liquid fuels sub-sector includes all manufactured fuel products such as petrol, diesel, etc. as well as associated products such as greases and lubricating oils.

Fuel products in South Africa are manufactured by four crude oil refineries and two synthetic fuel manufacturers (i.e. the manufacture of fuels from coal and natural gas). Greases and lubricating oils are also produced by the refineries and synthetic fuel operations as well as by about 20 other smaller speciality operations.[4]

The liquid fuels sub-sector is well established in South Africa; however, demand is currently outstripping supply, with the deficit being imported; this deficit is expected to increase even further in the future.[5] There are several plans to counter this trade deficit, such as Sasol's increased production of synthetic fuels and investigation of possibilities for a new coal-to-liquids inland refinery called Project Mafutha (Van Zyl 2008), as well as other investigations under way by PetroSA and Bidco for possible new developments in refinery capacity.[6]

Biofuels from renewable sources are not well developed in South Africa as yet, but the implementation of the Biofuels Industrial Strategy (DME 2007) might lead to the creation of other small agriculture-based plants. The Biofuels Industrial Strategy was developed to create job opportunities, alleviate poverty and establish developing farmers. Renewable fuels are also one of the areas identified for accelerated economic growth within the Asgisa initiative (The Presidency 2006a).

Commodity organics

Organic chemicals refer to a class of substances containing carbon and its derivatives. This sub-sector includes all pure, relatively low-cost organic-type chemicals that are used as raw materials in other chemical products as well as for direct uses in end-products.[7] Commodity organics is the best established sub-sector in upstream chemicals manufacturing in South Africa and is a growing exporter of products (SARS 2000, 2006). Sasol is the dominant player in the production of most of the major product types manufactured, while there are 15 other identified commodity organics manufacturers.[8]

Primary polymers and rubbers

A polymer is a compound whose molecule is formed from a large number of repeated units of one or more compounds of low molecular weight (monomers), while synthetic rubber is any type of artificially made polymer material that acts as an elastomer. An elastomer is a material with the mechanical (or material) property that can undergo much more elastic deformation under stress than most materials, and still return to its previous size without permanent deformation.

This sub-sector includes all polymer and synthetic rubber products in primary forms for use by converters to manufacture plastic and rubber products. There are nine manufacturers of primary polymers and rubbers in South Africa, of which the major players are Sasol Polymers and Safripol for primary polymers and Karbochem for primary rubbers.[9] South Africa is well established in certain product

---

4   CMCS & Ozone Business Consulting database.
5   Fuel retail business growing faster than industry average, *Engineering News* 27 October–2 November 2006.
6   Coega committee weighing up oil refinery bids, *Business Day* 16 January 2007.
7   See Chapter 1 in the main report (Van Zyl 2008) for discussion of typical products in this sub-sector.
8   CMCS & Ozone Business Consulting database. This number excludes captive producers that use these chemicals in other chemical end-products, as well as operations that form part of other economic sectors.
9   CMCS & Ozone Business Consulting database.

categories but does, however, still need to import others such as polystyrene, which leads to a trade deficit (SARS 2006). Some of these products could offer local manufacturing opportunities but the import figures are too low in terms of economies of scale, and therefore the export market should also be targeted. Exports would generally not be viable unless substantial protection is offered for inland sales by government (DTI 2005a).

Commodity inorganics

Inorganic chemicals are substances that are not carbon compounds, with the exception of the oxides and sulphides of carbon. These chemicals are used as raw materials in other chemical products such as fertilisers and explosives as well as for direct uses in end-products. Industrial gases such as hydrogen also fall within this sub-sector.

The variety of categories in this sub-sector (see Van Zyl 2008 for details) ensures that no single company dominates the sub-sector as a whole, although Sasol does have a prominent position in many of the categories. There are 48 identified inorganic commodities manufacturers in South Africa.[10]

Although the commodity inorganics sub-sector is well developed in South Africa, the lack of specific feedstocks drives large imports. There are, however, investment opportunities in areas where South Africa has feedstock advantages, such as titanium beneficiation into higher-value products such as titanium dioxide pigments, as well as in other mineral sectors where South Africa is a major global player. Beneficiation of these minerals into value-added inorganic chemicals for the world market should have good viability. There is also further potential to recover chemicals from waste products such as copper and aluminium scrap.

Fine chemicals

Fine chemicals are relatively high-value pure chemicals that are typically used as active ingredients (i.e. materials in a product essential for the application for which the product is designed) in products such as pharmaceuticals and agricultural chemicals.

The fine chemicals sub-sector is not well developed in South Africa, and this is not expected to change in the near future. Fine chemical products change too fast internationally to set up a sustainable local production base, and R&D would also not be feasible when competing with large multinationals (CMCS 2001). The major current local players are Fine Chemical Corporation, which makes pharmaceutical actives, and Dow Agrosciences, which makes pesticide actives; there are also other smaller operations such as essential oil producers, amongst others.

Downstream chemical sector

Production processes

Downstream operations are typically labour-intensive and generally consist of formulation production processes (that is, the mixing of compounds which do not react, in order to get a mixture with the desired characteristics) as well plastic and rubber conversion processes. Pure functional chemicals could also have synthesis reactions, but these are on a smaller scale than in the upstream sub-sectors.

The sub-sectors that form part of the downstream chemical sector include pure functional and formulated speciality chemicals, bulk formulated chemicals, pharmaceuticals, consumer formulated

---

10   CMCS & Ozone Business Consulting database.

chemicals, as well as plastic and rubber products. The majority of operations in the downstream chemical sector are small- or medium-sized.

The major bulk formulated chemical operations are, however, capital-intensive because these operations mostly manufacture captive (in-house) raw materials. The major pharmaceutical and consumer chemical producers that contribute to the bulk of the output of these two sub-sectors are also capital-intensive, as are the tyre manufacturers in the rubber conversion sub-sector and some large plastic converters.

Pure functional and formulated speciality chemicals

Pure functional chemicals are primarily used for their functional properties, such as plasticisers (i.e. various substances added to plastics or other materials to make or keep them soft or pliable). Speciality chemicals include all formulated chemicals used in industrial and non-consumer applications, for example, paints and coatings, paper chemicals and others (see Van Zyl 2008 for details).

There are more than 500 identified manufacturers of pure functional and speciality chemicals in South Africa. The largest and most diverse company in this sub-sector is Chemical Services (Chemserve), which has various manufacturing divisions. Apart from Chemserve, this sub-sector is highly fragmented in terms of products, which prevents concentration of production.[11]

Although the pure functional and speciality chemicals sub-sector is well established in South Africa, the lack of specific feedstocks drives large imports in some product categories. There is also a worldwide trend, which South Africa follows, for these types of chemicals to be tailor-made for their specific country and not for the export market. Increased R&D for new product development would be too expensive, as it would be in competition with large multinationals. The R&D is therefore focused on local conditions rather than on new products (CMCS 2001). This situation is not expected to change.

Bulk formulated chemicals

Bulk formulated chemicals are formulated products compounded from high-volume commodity-based chemicals that include explosives and fertilisers.

The major explosives manufacturers in South Africa are African Explosives Limited, Omnia and Sasol Nitro, while the major fertiliser producers are Foskor, Omnia and Sasol Nitro. There are also 20–30 smaller fertiliser manufacturers including bulk blenders, smaller blenders and organic fertiliser manufacturers.

The explosives and fertilisers sub-sector is well established in South Africa, and had a positive trade balance in 2006 (SARS 2006).

Pharmaceuticals

This sub-sector includes all formulated pharmaceuticals and other medicinal products in forms ready for final use or application.

There are about 90 pharmaceutical operations registered with the Medicines Control Council in South Africa, of which only a couple have local production facilities.[12]

---

11   CMCS & Ozone Business Consulting database.
12   CMCS & Ozone Business Consulting database.

There is a high concentration of generic pharmaceuticals production by a few companies such as Adcock Ingram and Aspen Pharmacare. Although there are many patented producers, these companies tend to dominate in specific therapeutic categories of medicines. Multinational patented producers have significantly reduced local manufacturing due to globalisation, whereby manufacturing is now focused within major global market segments and exported to smaller market regions such as Africa.

Pharmaceutical products had a trade deficit in 2006 (SARS 2006). The promotion of increased production of local pharmaceutical products is, however, a key action programme in the Chemical Sector Development Strategy which forms part of the DTI's broader industrial policy framework that could address this trade deficit in the future (DTI 2005b, 2007).

Consumer formulated chemicals

Consumer formulated chemicals include products such as soaps, household and cleaning products, cosmetics, toiletries, etc. There are about 150 identified household and cleaning-product manufacturers and about 80 identified cosmetics and toiletries manufacturers in South Africa.[13]

There is a large concentration of production in this sub-sector, in particular in the household and cleaning-products category, among a few major companies such as Unilever, Chet Chemicals and Colgate Palmolive. These operations are more capital-intensive than the rest of the operations in this sub-sector.

Although this sub-sector is well established in South Africa, the lack of specific feedstocks still drives large-scale imports in specific product categories. There is also a worldwide trend, which South Africa follows, for these types of chemicals to be tailor-made for their specific country and not for the export market. Increased R&D for new product development would be too expensive as it would be in competition with large multinationals. The R&D is therefore focused on local conditions rather than on new products (CMCS 2001). This situation is not expected to change.

Plastic conversion

This sub-sector includes all plastic products converted from primary polymers by means of various conversion processes. Typical products include packaging materials, wire and cable casings, pipes, film and sheeting, appliances, construction materials, footwear and automotive products.

Due to the fragmented structure of this sub-sector, in terms of both polymer types converted as well as product types manufactured, the concentration of production is fairly low. There are more than 800 identified plastic converters in South Africa incorporating various processes.[14]

Plastic products had a trade deficit in 2006 (SARS 2006). The promotion of downstream plastic products production is, however, a key action programme in the Chemical Sector Development Strategy that forms part of the DTI's broader industrial policy framework that could address this trade deficit in the future. The focus is on polymer types, where South Africa has excess production capacity of the primary polymers, for example polypropylene (DTI 2005b, 2007).

---

13 CMCS & Ozone Business Consulting database.
14 CMCS & Ozone Business Consulting database.

Rubber conversion

This sub-sector includes all rubber products made from primary rubbers, such as tyres, conveyor belting and other rubber products.

Production is concentrated amongst the few major tyre and belting producers, namely Bridgestone/Firestone, Dunlop Tyres, Continental Tyres and Goodyear/Tycon. There are also about 130 identified other rubber product manufacturing sites in South Africa.[15]

The rubber conversion sub-sector was previously regarded as uncompetitive, mainly due to old equipment and small production runs. This situation has been addressed by the multinational tyre companies, which have focused on investment in new equipment, rationalisation of product lines and export development (DTI 2005a). The rubber products sub-sector is more labour-intensive than the plastic products sub-sector in terms of the number of people per plant (Reserve Bank 1995–2005).[16] It is therefore recommended that this sub-sector be investigated for further development in South Africa.

Local production value and global position

The chemical sector value of production was approximately R196.5 billion for 2006, of which petroleum products accounted for 36 per cent, basic chemicals (mostly upstream chemicals) for 20 per cent, other chemicals (mostly downstream chemicals) for 25 per cent, plastic products for 13 per cent and rubber products for the remaining 5 per cent (Stats SA 2006).

Globally, there are more than 80 000 commercial unique chemical compounds or molecules, as well as countless formulated products consisting of blends of these molecules. Only about 300 of these unique compounds are produced by South Africa.[17]

While South Africa contributes less than one per cent of global GDP, two sub-sectors in the South African chemical sector contribute to slightly higher percentages in global manufacturing, namely, liquid fuels and bulk formulated chemicals. The rest of the sub-sectors contribute below one per cent of world production, with a particularly low contribution by fine chemicals.[18]

In terms of R&D, Sasol is also the only operation in South Africa that has comparable R&D levels to the rest of the world, with their proprietary coal-to-liquids and gas-to-liquids technologies in synthetic liquid fuels production (see Van Zyl 2008). The rest of the South African chemical sector's R&D levels are low compared to those of the rest of the world, and this is not likely to change in the future.

The relative cost of R&D versus the expected outcome is too high to make it feasible, as South Africa competes with large multinationals that have much higher global turnovers that can be used to fund R&D than those of local operations. For this reason, technology is mostly licensed in and modified for the local market conditions where needed, rather than developed locally (CMCS 2001). The only sub-sector where low R&D levels were identified as a specific skills constraint on future developments was in pharmaceuticals.[19]

---

15 CMCS & Ozone Business Consulting database.
16 See also CMCS & Ozone Business Consulting database.
17 CMCS & Ozone Business Consulting database.
18 CMCS & Ozone Business Consulting database.
19 See the Adcock Ingram case study in Van Zyl (2008).

Current employment

Total employment and core functions

The South African chemical sector's manufacturing operations employ between 120 000 and 130 000 people (Reserve Bank 1995–2005).[20] Although the upstream chemical sector is better developed in South Africa than the downstream chemical sector, downstream operations, being more labour-intensive, contribute about 80 per cent of all employees, with plastic products accounting for an estimated 25 per cent of the total estimated number of employees, and pure functional and speciality formulated chemicals accounting for almost 20 per cent.[21]

Core functions such as manufacturing, sales and administration are generally full-time occupations in the chemical sector, while services such as IT, catering, cleaning and security, as well as logistics, are often outsourced on a contract basis (DTI 2005a).

Gender distribution

Male employment dominates at 80 per cent or more in most of the positions in the chemical sector, except in clerical and sales positions where women account for about 60 per cent of employees. Most downstream chemical operations employ slightly fewer men at around 70 per cent, but this excludes the rubber sub-sector where men are dominant at more than 80 per cent. The gender distribution did not change much between 1996 and 2005, according to data from the Household and Labour Force Surveys conducted by Statistics South Africa (Stats SA) (Stats SA 1996–1999, 2000–2005).

There has, however, been a general increase in the contribution of female graduates in fields such as chemistry, chemical engineering and pharmaceutical science over this period that could increase the female contribution to the chemical sector in the future.[22]

Male chemistry graduates' contribution declined from more than 50 per cent of the total in 1996 to about 40 per cent in 2005, while male chemical engineering and technology graduates decreased to 58 per cent in 2005 from 78 per cent in 1996. The number of pharmaceutical science male graduates remained fairly constant at an annual average of 162 between 1996 and 2005, while the female graduates contributed to the increased number of total graduates, which rose from 401 in 1995 to 590 in 2005.[23]

Racial distribution

Higher-level positions such as managers, professionals and technicians were dominated by white employees in 2005, while the lower-level positions such as artisans, operators and elementary positions were dominated by black (African, Indian and coloured) workers (Stats SA 1996–1999, 2000–2005).

The relative breakdowns were as follows:
- 70 per cent whites as managers;
- 72 per cent whites as professionals;
- 63 per cent blacks as technicians and associates;
- 62 per cent blacks as clerks and sales people;

---

20 See also CMCS & Ozone Business Consulting database.
21 CMCS & Ozone Business Consulting database.
22 Department of Education (DoE), personal communications, April 2007 and January 2008.
23 DoE, personal communications, April 2007 and January 2008.

- 80 per cent blacks as artisans;
- 94 per cent blacks as operators;
- 91 per cent blacks in elementary occupations (Stats SA 1996–1999, 2000–2005).

There was, however, a general increase in the contribution of African graduates in fields such as chemistry, chemical engineering and pharmaceutical science between 1996 and 2005, which could mean a higher level of African employees at the higher skill levels in the future.[24]

The number of African graduates in chemistry was four times more in 2005 than in 2001, which is almost the only contributor to the increased number of total graduates in 2005. The number of African chemical engineering and technology graduates doubled between 1996 and 2005; this group also contributed the most to the total increase in the number of graduates. The contribution of African graduates in pharmaceutical science increased from 20 per cent in 1996 to 30 per cent in 2005, while white graduates' contribution fell by the same percentage.[25]

More black people were employed in the downstream chemical sector (about 70 per cent on average between 1996 and 2005) than in the upstream chemical sector (about 55 per cent on average between 1996 and 2005). The plastic conversion sub-sector employed even more black people, at an average of 85 per cent over the period of analysis (Stats SA 1996–1999, 2000–2005).

Skills level distribution

The different skill levels in the sector can be characterised is as follows:
- highly skilled: professional, semi-professional and technical occupations; and managerial, executive and administrative occupations;
- skilled: clerical and sales occupations; service occupations; transport, delivery and communications occupations; production foremen and production supervisors; artisan, apprentice and related occupations;
- semi- and unskilled: all the occupations that are neither highly skilled nor skilled occupations.

Larger volumes of highly skilled and skilled personnel are required in the sub-sectors that have synthesis and formulation processes, while fewer of these skills are required in the plastic and rubber conversion sub-sectors. The difference in the skills level distribution in the various sub-sectors is summarised in Table 6.1.

TABLE 6.1: *Average skills distribution in the different sub-sectors (%), 1996–2005*

Sub-sector/s	High	Medium	Semi- or unskilled
Liquid fuels	19	42	39
Upstream chemicals	14	33	53
Downstream chemicals	16	34	50
Plastic conversion	7	25	68
Rubber conversion	9	29	62

Source: Reserve Bank 1995–2005

---

24 DoE, personal communications, April 2007 and January 2008.
25 DoE, personal communications, April 2007 and January 2008.

The average skills level distribution remained similar between 1996 and 2005 for all the sub-sectors, except for coke and petroleum products, which includes liquid fuels and some commodity organics. The number of skilled workers increased by 14 per cent for coke and petroleum products if 1995 is compared to 2005, due to a similar decrease in semi- or unskilled workers (Reserve Bank 1995–2005). This could be due to a rise in chemical operator qualification requirements in the chemical sector, which used to be set at National Qualifications Framework (NQF) Level 2 and were increased to NQF Level 4.[26]

Supply analysis

Further education and training

Specific key subject areas related to the chemical sector at further education and training (FET) colleges include Chemical Laboratory Technology (NQF Levels 1–3), Industrial Chemistry (NQF Levels 1–3) and Chemical Plant Operations (NQF Levels 4–6).

There was a general decline in Chemical Laboratory Technology passes between 1996 to 2005, with the total number of passes declining to 108 at NQF Level 3 in 2005 from about 200 in the late 1990s.[27] This specific skill has not been identified as a constraint on active investments or further downstream development, but the latest Sector Skills Plan update on day-to-day scarce skills of the Chemical Industries Training and Education Authority (CHIETA) shows that increasingly stringent requirements for access to export markets pose significant challenges to analytical requirements, and that the DTI has begun developing a strategy to promote laboratory services in support of the chemical sector (CHIETA 2007). It is therefore anticipated by the CHIETA that the implementation of this strategy will lead to further demand for skills in this area. There is, however, a high supply of chemistry graduates at NQF Levels 5 and 6 who could fill these positions; this is discussed in the following section.

There was an increase in Industrial Chemistry passes between 1996 and 2005.[28] With chemical operators regarded by the CHIETA as a scarce skill in the current running of operations, this is a positive trend (CHIETA 2007).

There were increases and decreases in Chemical Plant Operation passes between 1996 and 2005, although the overall outcome was an increased number of passes in 2005 compared to 1996.[29] Chemical plant operators, however, do not always need this subject as they generally need a NQF Level 4 (matriculation) qualification with mathematics and science.[30]

Higher education and training

Specific key subject areas related to the chemical sector at higher education and training (HET) colleges include Chemistry, Chemical Engineering and Technology, and Pharmaceutical Science.

According to vacancy data from the *Sunday Times* (DoL 2007) the average number of chemists required was 101 per annum at NQF Level 5 for the period April 2005 to March 2007, while the supply of

---

26 Corrie Botha, Business Development Leader, NCP Chlorchem, personal communication, September 2007.
27 DoE, personal communications, April 2007 and January 2008.
28 DoE, personal communications, April 2007 and January 2008.
29 DoE, personal communications, April 2007 and January 2008.
30 Corrie Botha, Business Development Leader, NCP Chlorchem, personal communication, September 2007; Otto Pepler, Project Director, Project TalentGro at Sasol, via personal communications with Monique van Wyk, Change Management Consultant working for Project TalentGro, September 2007 and January 2008.

chemistry graduates was more than that, at an average of 400 per annum at NQF Level 5 for the period 2004–2005 and 567 per annum at NQF Level 6 between 2003 and 2005.

The number of honours, master's and doctoral chemistry graduates increased between 1996 and 2005, but showed a flat line between 2003 and 2005.[31] Due to there not being a strong focus on R&D in the South African chemical sector, this is not regarded as a concern. Sasol is the only operation in South Africa with high R&D levels, and it is also actively promoting skills development in this area (see Van Zyl 2008).

Chemical engineers with experience, pharmaceutical science graduates and other engineers required for new construction projects in the chemical sector are regarded as scarce. These scarcities, as well as the respective supplies of graduates, are discussed in the following section.

No scarcity of chemical engineering graduates at higher levels (NQF Levels 6–8) was identified during this investigation.

Skills constraints in active investments and downstream developments

Background

As discussed in the introduction to this chapter, future skills development should be directed towards areas of active investment as well as towards further downstream developments in the sector.

The focus of this investigation was therefore firstly on identifying suitable future capital investments, together with the perceived skills constraints to achieve these investments and to operate the new production sites.

Secondly, for the development of the downstream chemical sector, the focus was on sub-sectors prioritised for development in the Chemical Sector Development Strategy (DTI 2005b) that forms part of the DTI's broader industrial policy framework (DTI 2007).

As a result of this choice of focus areas, case studies selected for the research included, firstly, large identified capital investment areas in the chemical sector, namely:
- Sasol – the largest identified historical and future investor in the chemical sector (Ozone Business Consulting 2000–);
- Sasol's Project Turbo – the largest identified capital investment in the chemical sector between 2000 and 2006 – for the purpose of identifying typical skills required in large capital projects (Ozone Business Consulting 2000–);
- the Shutdown Network Forum – an initiative to counter skills constraints in active investments and maintenance projects such as refinery upgrades.

In downstream development, operations within sub-sectors in the DTI's key action programmes of the Chemical Sector Development Strategy (DTI 2005b) were chosen, namely:
- Adcock Ingram – a pharmaceutical manufacturer;
- the Plastics Federation of South Africa – an umbrella organisation in the local plastics industry.

---

31 DoE, personal communications, April 2007 and January 2008.

South Africa has three incubators that promote downstream development in the chemical sector, and therefore one of these incubators, Chemin, was also included as a case study.

Renewable fuels from agricultural sources are one of the areas identified for accelerated economic growth within the Asgisa initiative (The Presidency 2006). Grain South Africa was therefore also included as a case study because of their role in developing this industry from an agricultural point of view.[32]

In addition to the above case studies, a number of operations that are involved in active investment or developmental areas in the South African chemical sector were also responsive regarding skills constraints, namely:
- Afrox – an industrial gases producer;
- Chemical Initiatives – a commodity organics producer;
- Lurgi – a contract engineering company;
- NCP Chlorchem – a commodity inorganics producer;
- SA Tyre Recyclers – a rubber converter;
- Sasol Wax – a commodity organics producer;
- the DTI – involved in biofuels development;
- Unilever SA – a consumer chemical producer;
- the Engineering Council of South Africa, which is responsible for the registration of professional engineers.

The following sections of the chapter, drawn from the case studies and the other responsive operations, provide a summary of the identified skills constraints, as well as a supply analysis and identified training initiatives relating to these scarce skills, where available.

Areas of active investment and skills constraints

Sasol's future projects and the refinery upgrades for cleaner fuels planned to be completed by 2010 account for more than 90 per cent of identified capital investments (by value) in the chemical sector (Ozone Business Consulting 2000–).There are also investigations towards a possible new coal-to-liquids refinery for Sasol (Van Zyl 2008), a chemical cluster and refinery[33] at Coega (Coega Development Corporation 2007), and potential new biofuel plants with the finalisation of the Biofuels Industrial Strategy (DME 2007).

Identified scarce skills for active investments include artisans and engineers for the construction of these new or improved operations. There are no identified constraints in terms of operating these new plants, but there is, however, a concern about the low pass rates of African matriculants in subjects like mathematics and science that are required for operators in the chemical sector.[34]

---

32 The sources of information for each of the case studies are listed in Chapter 5 in the main report (Van Zyl 2008). The firms and associations with which interviews were conducted are listed below; all interviews were conducted between September 2007 and January 2008:
Chemical manufacturing operations: Sasol, Project TalentGro Division; Adcock Ingram; Afrox; Chemical Initiatives; NCP Chlorchem; SA Tyre Recyclers; Sasol Wax; Unilever South Africa;
Chemical incubators: Chemcity; Chemin;
Associations: Plastics Federation of South Africa; Grain South Africa; Engineering Council of South Africa;
Training initiative: Shutdown Network Forum;
Government departments: Department of Trade and Industry, Geographic Projects;
Contract engineering firm: Lurgi.
33 Coega committee weighing up oil refinery bids, *Business Day* 16 January 2007.
34 See Section 3.1 in the main report (Van Zyl 2008) for more information on this concern.

Artisans

Identified scarce artisans for chemical sector developments include boilermakers, coded welders, mechanical and pipe fitters, electricians, riggers and instrument mechanics. Coded welders are required to work on statutory equipment such as that associated with high pressures, hazardous chemicals and other specialised applications, and are required by legislation to pass a coding test.

The shortage of these artisan skills for peak refinery maintenance events and periods of peak construction activity in the South African industry has increased, due to significant capital investment programmes in numerous industries such as the petrochemical, transport and infrastructure sectors. The refineries do, however, schedule shutdowns so that they do not coincide; but the same resources are often contracted into longer-term capital construction activities and may be lost to the migrant shutdown pool of skilled labour.

The Joint Initiative for Priority Skills Acquisition (Jipsa) has set a target to train 50 000 artisans in the period 2007–2010 (The Presidency 2006b). Some of these artisans are, however, required already and these estimates also do not include any identified investments in the chemical sector.[35]

There are, however, projects running in the chemical sector as well as across the economy to fill these artisan skills gaps. Chemical sector training initiatives include the Shutdown Network Forum as well as Sasol's Project TalentGro.

Respondents from the Plastics Federation of South Africa,[36] Unilever SA,[37] NCP Chlorchem,[38] and Chemical Initiatives[39] are of the opinion that learnerships are probably not as good a form of skills development as the former apprenticeships were. Transnet, Eskom, Iscor (now Arcelor Mittal) and the mines all used to have training centres with very high standards, according to these respondents. The trainees they were exposed to supervised plant work during their training and the company was responsible for sending the apprentice to a technical college for formal learning. Currently, the onus is on the learner to develop an adequate level of skill, and the initiative and finance to do so are not always there, resulting in far fewer learners going to college to further their training.

Engineers

Engineering skills for expansion and/or construction projects are mostly provided by contract engineering companies. Engineers used in these contracts are regarded as scarce; this includes civil, electrical and instrumentation, mechanical and chemical engineers with experience.

The shortage of these engineers is not only a South African phenomenon, but is regarded as a worldwide problem, especially in the search for alternative fuels as a result of the projected future shortage of oil. Some of South Africa's engineers are going to places like the Middle East and Khazakstan to work on contracts there. Salaries are therefore becoming very high internationally, which also means that engineers can be poached easily.

Chemical engineers with experience are sourced from operations that have already provided them with the relevant experience. The problem is therefore not the number of graduates, but the number

---

35 See the Shutdown Network Forum Case Study in Chapter 5 of the main report (Van Zyl 2008) for more details on the major capital projects running in South Africa.
36 David Hughes, Executive Director, Plastics Federation of South Africa, personal communication, September 2007.
37 Mike Ngidi, Human Resources Director, Unilever South Africa, personal communication, September 2007.
38 Corrie Botha, Business Development Leader, NCP Chlorchem, personal communication, September 2007.
39 Leon Kearny, Manager, Chemical Initiatives, personal communication, September 2007.

of those with experience. This is confirmed by the fact that vacancies for chemical and materials engineers and technologists engineers at NQF Level 5, according to job advertisements in the *Sunday Times*, amounted to almost 697 in total between April 2004 and March 2007 (DoL 2007), whereas 1 311 graduates qualified at NQF Levels 5 and 6 between 2004 and 2005 who could have filled these positions.[40] The time available to train new engineers is very limited, and inexperienced engineers need to be supervised on a chemical plant site.

Black engineers are also moving around fast in South Africa. These engineers are in high demand and therefore earn very high salaries. Some will remain with one company for a year, where they go through a training period, and as soon as that is completed they are poached by other companies.[41]

The average number of civil engineering graduates at NQF Levels 5 and 6 between 2004 and 2005 amounted to 931 per annum,[42] while the demand, according to the vacancies advertised in the *Sunday Times*, amounted to 1 120 for the period April 2006–March 2007 (DoL 2007), an increase from 688 in the previous year. The large number of capital projects currently running, and therefore the increase in the demand for civil engineers in South Africa, might cause a larger supply deficit in the near future. There was also a decline in NQF Level 6 civil engineering graduates between 2002 and 2005, which is a cause for concern.[43]

The demand for electrical engineers, according to vacancies advertised in the *Sunday Times*, was 243 for the period April 2005–March 2006, and almost doubled to 430 in the following year (DoL 2007). Based on the supply data from HET institutions, there still seem to be ample numbers of electrical engineers graduating, at an annual average of 1 664 at NQF Levels 5 and 6 for 2004 and 2005.[44]

The demand for mechanical engineers in terms of the vacancies in the *Sunday Times* was 415 from April 2005 to March 2006, and jumped to 592 in the year after that (DoL 2007). These vacancies included industrial and production engineers, which might fall under other engineering professions than mechanical. Based on the supply data for mechanical engineers,[45] there still seem to be enough to meet the demand, at an annual average of 587 for 2004 and 2005 at NQF Levels 5 and 6, but a supply deficit could, however, start to form in the future.

The fact that there seem to be enough electrical and mechanical engineers speaks to the concern that due to the high artisan shortage in South Africa, technicians are used to do artisans' work, technologists are used to do technicians' work, and professional engineers are used to do technologists' work, especially in the construction engineering disciplines.[46]

Identified initiatives to increase the number of engineers in South Africa include:
- Sasol's Project TalentGro and investment in universities;
- the Technical Skills Business Partnership;
- bursaries on offer by various chemical operations;
- universities aiming to train 1 000 more engineers per annum by addressing issues that influence the current pass rates of entrants; these include the educational quality of entrants and their

---

40 DoE, personal communications, April 2007 and January 2008.
41 Corrie Botha, Business Development Leader, NCP Chlorchem, personal communication, September 2007; Peter Dewar, Engineering Manager, Lurgi, personal communication, September 2007.
42 DoE, personal communications, April 2007 and January 2008.
43 DoE, personal communications, April 2007 and January 2008.
44 DoE, personal communications, April 2007 and January 2008.
45 DoE, personal communications, April 2007 and January 2008.
46 Johan Pienaar, Manager, Registration Department of the Engineering Council of South Africa, personal communication, September 2007.

understanding of engineering, student attitudes and their social conditions, academic and social demands, training resources, and funding, amongst others.[47]

Training initiatives to counter artisan and engineers skills constraints

a) Artisan training

In 2004, some of the major oil refiners in South Africa set up a training arm of their joint Shutdown Network Forum in collaboration with the CHIETA. This was known as the Shutdown Network Forum Employment and Skills Development Lead Employer. The prime task was to manage and co-ordinate training of artisans across the South African petrochemical industry, while the CHIETA provided some funding for training. The project kicked off in 2004 and 665 learners had been trained up to NQF Level 2 by July 2007, out of an intake of 1 037 learners.

Additional funding was requested from the CHIETA for more training, but only some of it could be obtained. This led to industry supporting the shortfall. The participating companies also started to employ and train unemployed candidates by making use of tax breaks. In September 2007, there were just over 700 learners in training under this new structure, known as the Oil, Gas and Chemical Manufacturing Companies Artisan Skills Training Project.

Funding is one of the challenges that the Shutdown Network Forum is facing. Funding from the CHIETA and the National Skills Fund needs to be streamlined, as there are concerns that the approval and allocation of funding sometimes takes too long.

There is also expected to be a scarcity of suitably equipped training facilities, trainers, assessors and moderators. Another concern is host employers, where lower-level artisans can be placed for experiential workplace training, as they currently need qualified artisans and do not necessarily have the time for training.

Recruiting learners is also a challenge. Advertisements in the newspapers do not always reach the target market for potential applicants, and short-term posters and pamphlets are therefore distributed in the relevant geographical areas where artisans might be needed in the future.

There are also additional artisan training projects running across the economy, including the Technical Skills Business Partnership, at Coega, and those run by the Manufacturing, Engineering and Related Services Sector Education and Training Authority (MERSETA), the Steel and Industries Federation of South Africa (SEIFSA) and state-owned enterprises.

b) Artisan and engineer training

Sasol's Project TalentGro focuses on internal and external talent development through a multi-pronged approach that is aimed at the following:
- improving internal skills development capacity for current and future skills needs;
- contributing to external skills development initiatives, and expanding Sasol's operations support, in order to grow key talent pools; furthermore, it endeavours to influence the external skills development environment by participating in other initiatives and engaging industry leaders, in partnership with government and other organisations;
- in 2007 a new division to manage recruitment and training requirements associated with the accelerated roll-out of expansion projects was started; amongst other things, this involves the establishment

---

47 National Business Initiative, personal communication, September 2007.

of a pool of approximately 1 000 new employees to be assigned to various new projects (including foreign operations) for start-up purposes. Four hundred and thirty appointments have already been made; this pool of people will consist of about 43 per cent artisans and process controllers, and 11 per cent engineers and technicians (mechanical, electrical, chemical, process and instrumental). The rest of the pool will be made up of planners, resource consultants, trainers, managers, and others.

The Technical Skills Business Partnership is a National Business Initiative undertaking in which a partnership was formed between Sasol, Eskom, Transnet, Arcelor Mittal, Gold Fields and Anglo Platinum, which aims to deal with the national skills shortage by training 50 000 artisans by 2010 and 1 000 additional engineers per annum. These companies will make significant investments in training facilities and educators, and will also act as anchor companies in their sectors to involve other relevant companies. Consultation work is also being done with the various Sector Education & Training Authorities (SETAs) and the National Skills Fund to obtain funding for these initiatives.

Synergies and strategies required

The future of active investments in the chemical sector and the South African economy as a whole will depend on the level of commitment of all the entities involved, including government initiatives, to develop the skills required, such as artisans and engineers. Various initiatives are under way to address this problem, but better co-ordination between them is required to improve the synergy that would strengthen these efforts. Strategies to ensure the outcome of these projects should also be put in place.[48]

Downstream development and relevant skills constraints

The sub-sectors prioritised in the Chemical Sector Development Strategy for downstream development include pharmaceuticals and plastic conversion (DTI 2005b).

Pharmaceuticals

Major growth potential exists in the generic pharmaceuticals market and in efforts to increase local formulation capacity. This market, however, requires access to low-cost raw materials such as active ingredients, as well as large markets, in order to be viable for manufacturing. A harmonised regulatory regime for Southern African Development Community (SADC) countries would give South African-based manufacturers easy access to a market of nearly 200 million people (CMCS 2001).

The pharmaceutical industry is struggling to find sufficiently well-qualified people for R&D work. The resources required are qualified pharmacists with a strong background in chemistry, as it is essential for the researcher to understand the chemical reactions involved. This would normally require someone with a Master of Science (MSc) degree in Pharmacy.

Because of the shortage of these skills, all work is currently being concentrated on antiretrovirals. There is plenty of work and new ideas for development, but no staff to spare. This is particularly so for development of generic drugs and new forms of delivery of drugs to patients. Currently, the technology and background for generics are bought in from overseas, but in effect, could be generated within South Africa if staff were available. South Africa is, however, not a viable location for primary R&D, which involves the identification of new chemical entities. Multinational companies at their overseas R&D

---

48 Otto Pepler, Project Director, Project TalentGro at Sasol, via personal communication with Monique van Wyk, Change Management Consultant working for Project TalentGro, September 2007 and January 2008.

centres each employ up to 5 000 R&D specialists for primary R&D, of which typically in excess of 80 per cent would have PhD qualifications.

The number of NQF Level 6 pharmaceutical science graduates stayed fairly constant between 1996 and 2003, with a sharp increase in 2004, and a decrease to the average levels again in 2005. The average number of pharmaceutical science graduates produced at NQF Level 6 between 2003 and 2005 was 283 per annum.[49] The average number of vacancies for pharmacists as identified from the *Sunday Times* vacancy advertisements between April 2004 and March 2007 was, however, 636 per annum (DoL 2007), which shows that the average annual supply of pharmacists currently does not meet the demand.

There is also little focus on pharmaceuticals manufacturing by academic institutions. Industry-based training is provided on manufacturing best practices. Training has to be approved by the South African Pharmacy Council, which falls under the Department of Health, and the quality of courses is also controlled by the Council (DTI 2005a).

Master's graduates, however, increased between 1996 and 2005, with 128 qualifying in 2005.[50] This number sounds adequate to meet the requirements of the local pharmaceutical sub-sector, but these graduates have most probably been absorbed into other sectors of the economy such as healthcare, or do not have the necessary required chemistry background, leading to the identified shortage in supply.

Apart from assisting the pharmaceutical sector in addressing the above-mentioned skills shortages, the South African government could improve the sustainability of further local investments in generic medicines manufacturing through:
- the promotion of better local access to global information and know-how;
- the improvement of regional market (e.g. SADC countries) intelligence;
- the promotion of a local spatial cluster for the pharmaceutical industry;
- implementing a more investor-friendly and efficient regulatory environment and health policy;
- improving its sourcing through COMED, a central purchasing organisation of government, to purchase medicines in ways that favour the local industry more;
- implementing a better incentive scheme to make investment more attractive (CMCS 2001).

Plastic products

Opportunities exist to increase local beneficiation of plastic products, in particular for automotive and packaging applications. It is also recommended that the plastic conversion sub-sector strengthen its product design in order to focus on broader growth opportunities in the African and export markets.

Low mentorship levels were identified as a critical skill constraint in the plastic conversion sub-sector. There are also low levels of training by smaller operations, and a 'salary-based grasshopper' problem in that skilled people are constantly changing jobs once they have been trained, which to some extent acts as a disincentive to in-house training.

It is also not an easy process to get young people placed in the plastics industry. Somehow the industry needs to be persuaded to train staff. A particular problem that the Plastics Federation of South Africa experiences is that they have course places booked and then, because the employers suddenly realise that they cannot afford to give the staff time off to attend, there is a no-show of participants.

---

49 DoE, personal communications, April 2007 and January 2008.
50 DoE, personal communications, April 2007 and January 2008.

Cheap imports from China have also had some effect on growth in this sub-sector through displacement of local manufacturing; this is a problem that could be addressed by government.

Chemical incubators

South Africa has three chemical incubators that are involved in developing the downstream chemical sector in the country.

ChemCity, which is wholly-owned by Sasol, focuses on incubating sound business propositions into viable enterprises throughout South Africa. In the past 2.5 years, Chemcity has successfully established 30 new businesses that include biofuels, consumer chemicals, plastic conversion, effluent-to-fertiliser production, and waste management.

Chemin is a catalyst in the establishment of an entrepreneurial culture leading to the development of a successful downstream chemical industry in South Africa. Chemin therefore has a focus on developing entrepreneurial skills, amongst others. It had 33 running projects in 2007 in consumer chemicals, pharmaceutical products, and pure functional and speciality chemicals. The fine chemicals that Chemin focuses on are mainly plant extracts.

SediChem is a business and chemical technology incubator that offers entrepreneurs the opportunity for commercialisation of chemical products and services. Sedichem's focus is on the provision of infrastructural, commercial, strategic and legal support, with the aim of developing sustainable small and medium enterprises (SMEs) in Gauteng province.

Funding support from government could stimulate the further development of the downstream chemical sector, through the chemical incubators that are already in place.

Biofuels development

Apart from the skills constraints already identified in the construction of new chemical plants, namely shortages of artisans and engineers, the development of the biofuels industry faces significant constraints in terms of new upcoming farmers. Skills constraints identified include illiteracy, innumeracy, poor mathematics and science results, no practical experience in farming and poor commercial skills.

Other constraints include non-profitability, no secure access to land, lack of equipment, lack of processing materials, no fencing to protect lands, bad farm roads, no access to loans, and poor quality products.

Current commodity organisations could be used to train farmers and extension officers, and mentoring should be done by people with honourable intentions to take the farmers by the hand during the peak season. The extension support from the Department of Agriculture might not be sufficient to meet current needs.

Possible support from government could include financing for training courses provided by commodity organisations, commitment from the extension services to co-operate with the commodity organisations, and access to finance, with a special dispensation for developing farmers, such as low interest rates.

Official public/private partnerships should also be formed; for example, some of the provincial departments of agriculture give groups of farmers tractors and implements. These donations should be done in collaboration with a commodity organisation that is supporting the farmers, so that the farmers can be assisted to manage these assets.

Other constraints in the chemical sector

Apart from the sub-sectoral constraints discussed in earlier sections of this chapter, and the above-mentioned skills constraints, there are also additional overlapping constraints in the chemical sector that could limit future growth, such as transportation and regulatory constraints, as well as energy supply security; these should be addressed by government.

South Africa has high transportation costs, including those associated with roads, railways and harbours used for exports. Other disadvantages include the lack of container and bulk liquid handling facilities in ports, congestion at ports, a shortage of rail-line capacity, and the slow processing of documents at customs (DTI 2005a).

Regulatory constraints in the chemical sector include slow reactions to environmental impact assessment applications for new projects or expansions, low levels of assistance for new investors in dealing efficiently with regulatory requirements for new plants, difficulty in obtaining work permits, and high real interest rates leading to high hurdle rates for capital expenditure (DTI 2005a).

Apart from these constraints, energy supply security is a serious issue that could lead to large capital investments being held back, as well as reduce the level of foreign investment in South Africa.

References

CHIETA (Chemical Industries Training and Education Authority) (2007) *Sector skills plan 1 April 2005–31 March 2010. Version 3*. Accessed January 2008, http://www.chieta.org.za

CMCS (Chemical Marketing & Consulting Services) (2001) *Strategic analysis of the pharmaceutical manufacturing pipeline and its investment potential in South Africa*. Study undertaken for the Development Bank of Southern Africa. Midrand: CMCS & Ozone Business Consulting

Coega Development Corporation (2007) *Coega annual report 2007*. Port Elizabeth: Coega Development Corporation

DME (Department of Minerals and Energy, South Africa) (2007) *Biofuels industrial strategy*. Pretoria: DME

DoL (Department of Labour, South Africa) (2007) *Job vacancy database April 2004–2007*. Pretoria: DoL

DTI (Department of Trade and Industry, South Africa) (2005a) *Customised sector programme for the chemical sector*. Pretoria: DTI

DTI (2005b) *Chemical sector development strategy*. Pretoria: DTI

DTI (2007) *Implementation of Government's National Industrial Policy Framework: Industrial policy action plan*. Pretoria: DTI

Ozone Business Consulting (2000–) *Database: Capital investments in the South African chemical sector*. Midrand: Ozone Business Consulting

Reserve Bank (1995–2005) *Quantec labour market survey*. Pretoria: Reserve Bank

SARS (South African Revenue Service) (2000) *Export statistics*. Pretoria: SARS

SARS (2006) *Export statistics*. Pretoria: SARS

Stats SA (Statistics South Africa) (1993) *Standard industrial classification of all economic activities* (Fifth Edition). Pretoria: Stats SA

Stats SA (1995–2006) *Gross Domestic Product*. Pretoria: Stats SA

Stats SA (1996–1999) *October Household Surveys (OHS)*. Pretoria: Stats SA

Stats SA (1998 – 2006) *Manufacturing: Production and sales*. Pretoria: Stats SA

Stats SA (2000–2005) *Labour Force Surveys (LFS)*. Pretoria: Stats SA

The Presidency (2006a) *Asgisa annual report 2006*. Accessed 23 March 2008, http://www.thepresidency.gov.za/docs/asgisa2006.pdf

The Presidency (2006b) *Jipsa annual report 2006*. Accessed 23 March 2008, http://www.thepresidency.gov.za/docs/final-rep1.pdf

Van Zyl R (2008) *South African chemical sector report on skills development and the government's new economic policy priorities*. Research conducted for the Department of Labour in association with the Human Sciences Research Council. Pretoria: Ozone Business Consulting (Pty) Ltd

CHAPTER 7

Wood, paper and pulp

Thomas E Pogue

Introduction

South Africa's forestry value chain reflects a legacy of historical import-substituting industrialisation policies. It is a resource-based set of activities with significant local value addition and international competitiveness. Currently, there are several major changes occurring in the value chain. Dominant among these is the transformation of the forestry resource base, as the government privatises its plantation forestry holdings and simultaneously shifts afforestation to small growers. If not carefully managed, this change in the structure of timber production is liable to impact negatively on all the downstream users of domestic timber inputs. Skills development is critical to successful management of this change. However, several years into its implementation, the skills system remains inadequate.

The skills system also has an essential role to play in supporting and developing the value chain's competitiveness. This is especially true in prominent segments like pulp and paper. Despite advances, there are many systemic problems in the skills system. International integration induces firms to develop 'world class' operations. The associated pursuit of efficiencies concentrates resources and reduces subsidisation of skills development across the forestry value chain. Simultaneously, the search for these efficiencies is increasing skills demand within each segment as well as upstream and downstream from them. The analysis presented in this chapter identifies interventions to support these ongoing changes in the forestry value chain. After elaborating on the structure of the industry and its skills system, the penultimate section of the chapter details some priority policies aimed at strengthening the skills system.

An overview of the forestry value chain

The South African forestry value chain contains at least three distinct stages of production. The foundation of the forestry value chain is the renewable resource base; it consists of South Africa's forestry resources: woodlands, natural forests and plantation forests. In addition to growing timber, productive activities within the renewable resource base include livestock grazing, cover crops, and non-timber forest products (NTFP).

A second stage in the forestry value chain is primary processing; this involves initial value addition to timber resources. Sub-sectors within primary processing include wood fibre, sawmilling, pole processing and charcoal production. Following primary processing is a secondary beneficiation stage, which involves further value addition to timber inputs from primary processing. The components of secondary beneficiation are paper and paper products manufacturing, wood furniture manufacturing, and wood product manufacturing. While timber is the unifying factor along the forestry value chain, each stage and its components depend on a unique combination of additional inputs and skills.

Employment in the forestry value chain is estimated to be near 750 000. Formal-sector output associated with timber resources totalled R15 billion in 2004. The associated exports equalled R9.35 billion in 2005, or 2.8 per cent of total exports. Net exports totalled R2.1 billion (Pogue 2007: 11). In addition, a further R15 billion was generated across the value chain through tourism, communal livestock grazing and NTFP. Lastly, although no formal estimates of its value are available, fuel wood is a significant source of informal income for many individuals who depend on it as a primary source of energy.

Renewable resource base

Woodlands account for 93 per cent of South African forestry resources by area. Currently, besides some charcoal production, these woodland resources do not feature downstream in the forestry value chain. Nonetheless, woodlands are important economic resources. Livestock grazing and tourism are significant productive activities associated with woodlands. As an input to the informal economy, fuel wood from woodlands is also substantial output. Medicinal and traditional plants as well as craft materials are further outputs from woodlands that contribute to both the formal and informal economies.

Natural forests consist of a further two per cent of South Africa's forest area. Despite the relatively small size of the natural forests, they support great ecological diversity. Timber is harvested from natural forests for wood products as are a variety of NTFP. Fern fronds, bark, bulbs and leaves are some of the more significant NTFP produced from South Africa's natural forests. Other NTFP harvested on a smaller scale are reeds, grasses, indigenous tree fruits, mushrooms, honey, thatch, seeds and moss (DWAF 2006). Ecotourism and other recreational activities are also significant economic activities connected with natural forests.

Plantations form the remaining five per cent of forests and provide the vast majority of timber inputs to the forestry value chain. Currently, there are three types of plantation forestry growers: corporates, private farmers and emerging growers. In terms of area, corporate growers manage approximately 72 per cent of South African plantation forests. Private individuals, partnerships or family trusts account for a further 26 per cent and emerging growers for the remaining two per cent (DWAF 2007; DPE 2007). Jointly, the corporate and private growers employ about half of the total workforce directly involved with the renewable resource base. The other half is part of the emerging growers' labour force (Chamberlain et al. 2005a). In addition, another third of forestry workers are engaged as contractors for the growers. Even allowing for the fact that most of the contract foresters work for corporate and private growers, the employment intensity of the small growers is pronounced.

There are three primary species of trees used in plantation forestry: eucalyptus, pine and wattle. Constituting just over half of South Africa's total plantation forest area, pine species produce softwood used in sawmilling for timber and in pulp milling for the production of newsprint, magazines and packaging. Accounting for a further 40 per cent of plantation forests, eucalyptus is a hardwood used in pulp milling for smoother paper, fluting and corrugated cartons. Eucalyptus is also used for poles and mining timber. Wattle accounts for the remaining eight per cent of plantation forest area. Also a hardwood, wattle is used in pulp milling.

The growth cycles for all of these trees vary by sub-species, management practices and natural environmental influences. Other factors being equal, a tree that will be used for its fibre in pulp milling or as wood chips will have a growth cycle about half as long as a tree used for sawlogs. Figure 7.1 indicates changing management objectives for plantation forests between 1994 and 2004. It shows that pulp

FIGURE 7.1: *Management objectives for plantation forests, by area, 1994–2004*

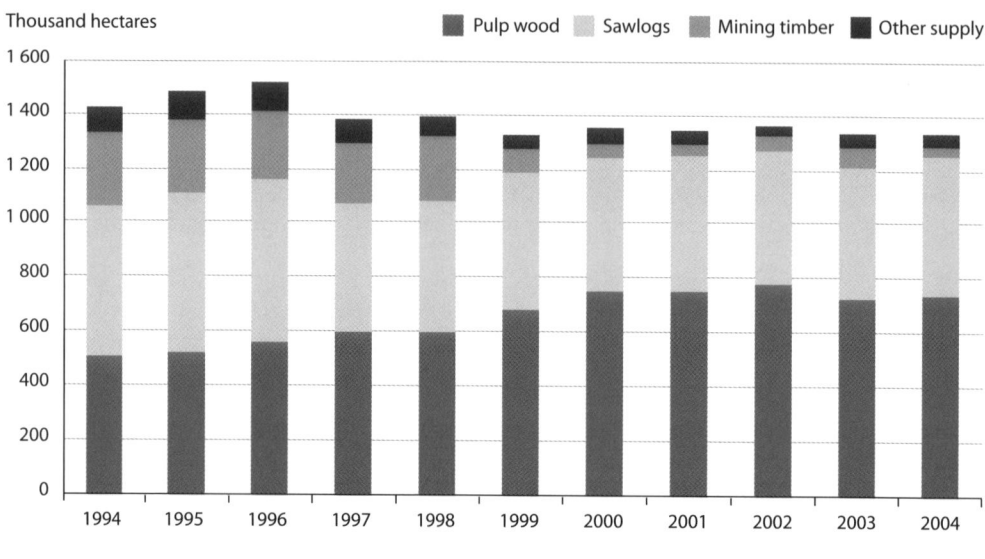

Source: FSA 2006

wood has risen in importance as a management objective over this period, and although sawlogs have remained relatively constant, mining timber has decreased.

The plantation forestry sector is characterised by a strong degree of vertical integration with downstream sectors. Therefore plantation owners also tend to be significant primary processors, and involved in secondary beneficiation. While historically state plantations were important timber sources, in 1997, the government undertook to withdraw from plantation forestry. This ongoing privatisation involves the state retaining ownership, but leasing its holdings. While these leases are focused on promoting black economic empowerment in the sector, they typically involve an established partner with downstream linkages.

Figure 7.2 shows plantation timber sales between 1994 and 2004. During this period, total sales grew at a compound real annual growth rate of 4.6 per cent. Pulp wood increased from 47 per cent of market value in 1994 to 68 per cent in 2004. In contrast, sawlogs decreased from 35 per cent of market value in 1994 to 22 per cent in 2004. South African consumption of sawn timber is relatively low by international standards. Since the early 2000s, the domestic building industry has dominated sawlog demand. However, overfelling and increasing demand for sawn timber have created a situation in which demand for sawlogs appears to be exceeding supply (Crickmay et al. 2005b).

In the pulp wood market, pulp mills account for approximately 60 per cent of demand by volume, chipping plants for 35 per cent and board mills for the remaining 5 per cent (Crickmay et al. 2005a). Because of the high capital costs, demand from pulp and papers mills tends to increase in a stepwise fashion as they pursue economies of scale within the mills. Board mills have shared in some demand growth from the domestic building industry, increasing at a compound annual rate of two per cent between 2002 and 2004. While demand for wood chip exports grew in real terms at a compound annual growth rate of 18.2 per cent between 1994 and 2002, increasing rand strength led to a real annual decline of 3.1 per cent between 2003 and 2006.

FIGURE 7.2: *Sales of forest timber (real 2000 rand values), 1994–2004*

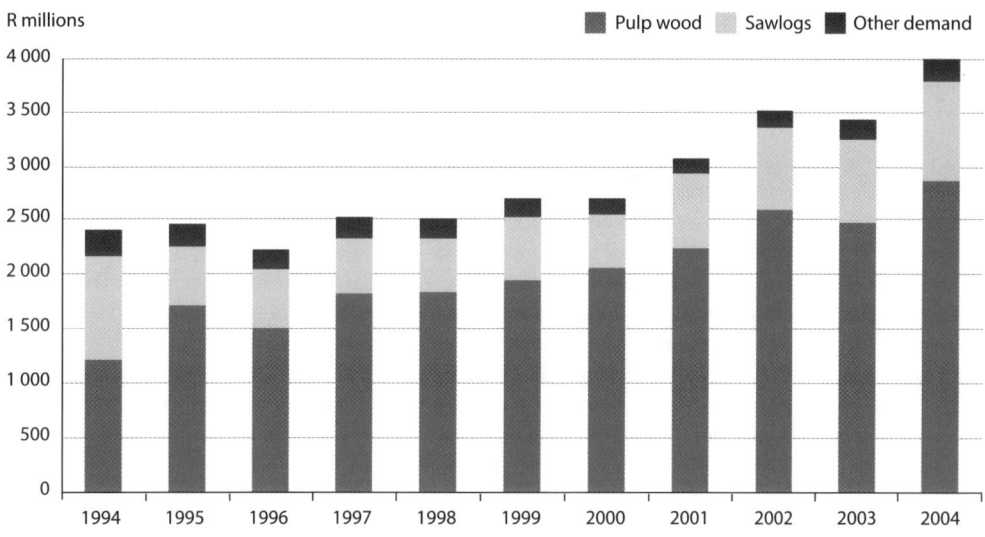

Source: FSA 2006

Some fundamental challenges face the forestry resource production system. First, there is the privatisation of state timber plantations. Historically, state plantations were a primary source of sawlogs, whose normal planting-to-harvest cycle is around 35 years. However, for a private firm to lock up its resources for 35 years is difficult, especially in an environment of relatively high interest rates. This is compounded by a regulatory environment in which companies with sufficient internal economies for these types of investments have faced anti-competitive challenges.[1] Second, under current afforestation practices there are only about 100 000 net hectares available for afforestation (Chamberlain et al. 2005b). These 100 000 hectares are less than the net 140 000-hectare increase proposed in the Department of Trade and Industry's (DTI) Industrial Policy Action Plan (DTI 2007). Third, new afforestation is targeted at small plantation community growers. These growers' current timber output is very small and does not appear likely to supply large quantities of timber for downstream users (Pogue 2007: 105).

Many difficulties confronting the renewable resource base are consequences of the established production system. Nonetheless, alternative productive structures exist locally and internationally that could alleviate the majority of these challenges to the sector. An important change would be breaking the large plantation and innovation system paradigm. If available alternative production techniques such as natural regeneration were used, and other alternatives developed, the associated decreases in investment barriers and economies of scale could significantly increase viable land for afforestation and facilitate community-based growing processes (Zwolinski & Groenwald 2004).

Similarly, systematic development of integrated livelihood enterprises among community-based growers would support the long growth cycle of timber production through symbiotic shorter-term revenue options that offer additional linkages with the formal economy. These complementary enterprises would be likely to involve NTFP, and cover crops as well as short-rotation timber and non-timber

---

1   Blom N, Komatiland faces stiff fine if tribunal finds it abused market dominance, *Business Day Online* posted 14 November 2007. Accessed 14 November 2007, http://www.businessday.co.za/

tree/shrub plantations (Pogue 2007: 63). Fuel wood and livestock fodder can be important products derived from these non-traditional plantations, and with innovations in established practices, downstream users could also utilise short rotation timber.

Primary processing

Primary processing of timber can be divided into fibre, sawmilling and other processing activities. Fibre processing encompasses pulp milling, wood chipping and fibre board production. Between 1994 and 2004, fibre processing accounted for 80 per cent of all primary processing output by value, of which pulp milling comprised 83 per cent, wood chip milling 10 per cent and board production 7 per cent. Sawmilling processes timber for lumber and mining timber. In the 1994–2004 period, sawmilling comprised 12 per cent of primary processing output. Other processing activities such as charcoal and pole manufacturing accounted for the remaining eight per cent of output (FSA 2006).

Pulp milling is the most important component of fibre processing and is integrated, through the Mondi and Sappi duopoly, with downstream paper manufacturing in South Africa and abroad. Wood chipping is a smaller, but significant, component related to the pulp and paper production stream. Export-focused chipping plants independent of the pulp mills were created in the 1970s to check the domestic buying power of Mondi and Sappi (Chamberlain et al. 2005b: 77). However, it was only with the reintegration of South Africa into the international economy after the end of apartheid that demand for wood chips became significant. Figure 7.3 documents the growing value of wood chip exports since 1994.

Currently, chip milling is not limited to non-integrated growers as it has become an established outlet for pulping timber supplies that exceed domestic pulp processing capacity. As a result, Mondi operates one of the largest chip mills, but it plans to use this chipping capacity in future pulping. Given the latent demand for wood chips by pulp mills, all wood chip exports could eventually form part of the domestic value chain. Nonetheless, Japan is currently the primary market for South African wood chips. In fact, between 2003 and 2006, Japan purchased 98.6 per cent of all South African wood chip exports.

Three distinct types of sawmill can be distinguished within sawmilling: formal sawmills, low-cost mills and micro mills. Formal mills produce about two-thirds of South Africa's sawn timber, which is all kiln-

FIGURE 7.3: *Primary processing exports (real 2000 values), 1994–2005*

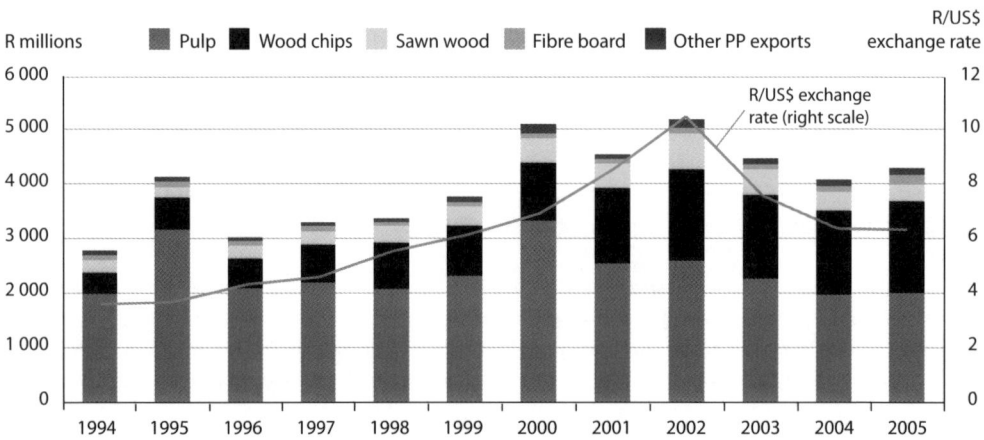

Source: Quantec 2007

FIGURE 7.4: *Primary processing imports (real 2000 values), 1994–2005*

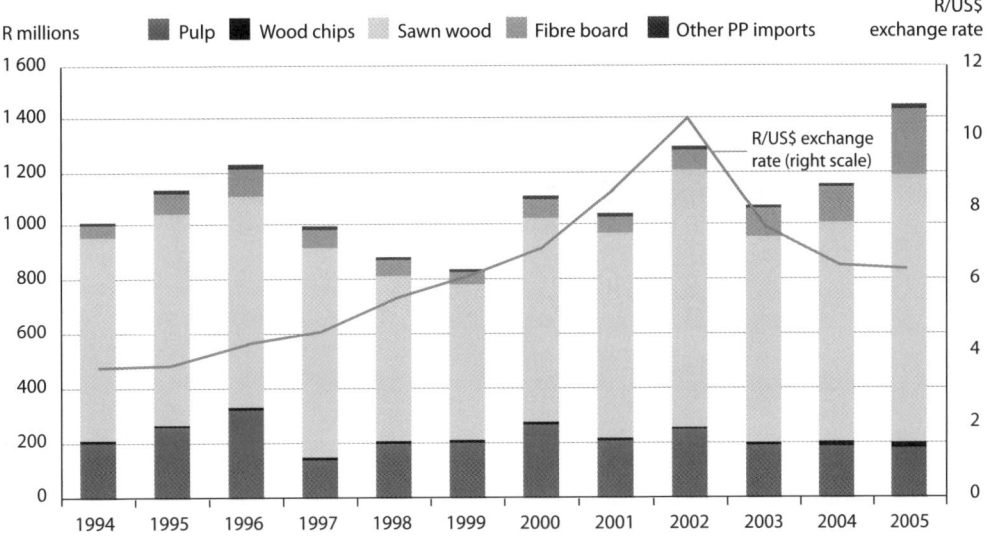

Source: Quantec 2007

dried and graded by the South African Bureau of Standards (SABS). Consolidation for greater efficiencies has characterised the formal mills. Between 1988 and 2004, the number of formal mills declined from 188 to 45, but the remaining mills produce more lumber than before (Crickmay et al. 2005b). Low-cost mills constitute 27 per cent of sawn timber output. These mills are continuously operating location-specific mills that often kiln-dry their timber, but do not necessarily produce SABS-graded timber. Micro mills produce the remaining seven per cent of domestic lumber output. These mills are mobile processing facilities that often work fire-damaged areas. Typically they produce wet or air-dried timber for local communities, pallets and cable drum manufacturers.

A primary constraint on the sawmilling industry is sawlog availability. As mentioned above, there is a growing shortage of sawlogs in South Africa that is liable to continue to increase unless alternative production systems are developed. Figure 7.4 illustrates that significant sawn wood imports are not a recent feature. Nonetheless, particularly as building demand has increasingly dominated domestic demand, the need for sawn timber imports appears likely to grow. If this increasing need for imported sawlogs continues, it will be likely to impact disproportionately upon the small and micro mills, because of the costs of importing and the associated need for greater productive efficiencies.

Secondary beneficiation

In the forestry value chain, there are three distinct manufacturing segments of secondary beneficiation: paper and paper products, wood products and wood furniture. Since the late 1990s, building growth has supported wood product manufacturers. Paper manufacturers have seen increasing internationalisation of their operations. Wood furniture manufacturers appear to be increasingly focused on niche production for domestic and international markets as import competition increases.

South Africa's paper-milling capacity is also dominated by Mondi and Sappi; there are few other companies with significant capacity. Figure 7.5 shows capacity by company. The 7 enterprises included in the figure own 21 mills, which account for 97 per cent of the total 2.94 million tons of domestic paper-

FIGURE 7.5: *South African paper milling capacity, by company, 2005*

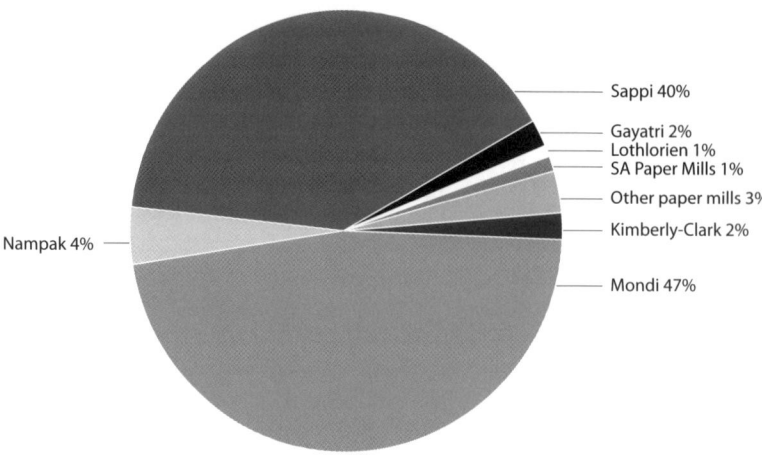

Source: PAMSA 2007: 7

milling capacity. Paper milling is concentrated along the KwaZulu-Natal north coast and in Gauteng. Paper mills that are not located near to pulp mills tend to use a higher recycled-paper content in production.

The tonnage of South Africa's paper production output has grown at a constant rate. In the 7-year period between 1999 and 2006, tissue paper output grew at a compound annual rate of 3.9 per cent, followed by packaging paper at 3.5 per cent, and printing and writing paper at 3.4 per cent. Over the same period, packaging papers accounted for 53 per cent of output, printing and writing papers for 40 per cent, and tissue papers for the remaining 7 per cent of output (PAMSA 2007: 7).

The value of paper output between 2001 and 2006 is indicated in Figure 7.6. Printing and writing paper accounted for 47 per cent of paper sales, followed by packaging paper with a further 41 per cent and tissue paper with the remaining 12 per cent of sales. In contrast to the growth in the volume of paper produced, real paper sales were largely constant.

The real values of paper exports are reported in Figure 7.7. Correlation between exports and the exchange rate may indicate that South African paper competes on a commodity price basis internationally. In terms of composition, paper and paper products appear to be an increasingly significant component of recent exports. Paper and paper product exports accounted for 70 per cent of total exports during the period, with other non-corrugated and non-container paper and paper product exports accounting for the remaining 30 per cent.

The composition of paper imports is shown in Figure 7.8. Given that domestic paper production has increased, the constant growth in paper imports appears to indicate that paper imports are not a substitute for domestic production. This suggests that increasing income, as indicated by sustained GDP growth, is an important market driver. In this context, domestically produced paper products are apparently not a suitable substitute for imported products. While skills and technological capabilities may contribute, high fixed costs associated with establishing new productive capacity may also form a considerable barrier to South African paper manufacturers' ability to meet this growing demand.

FIGURE 7.6: *Domestic paper sales (real 2001 rand values), 2001–2006*

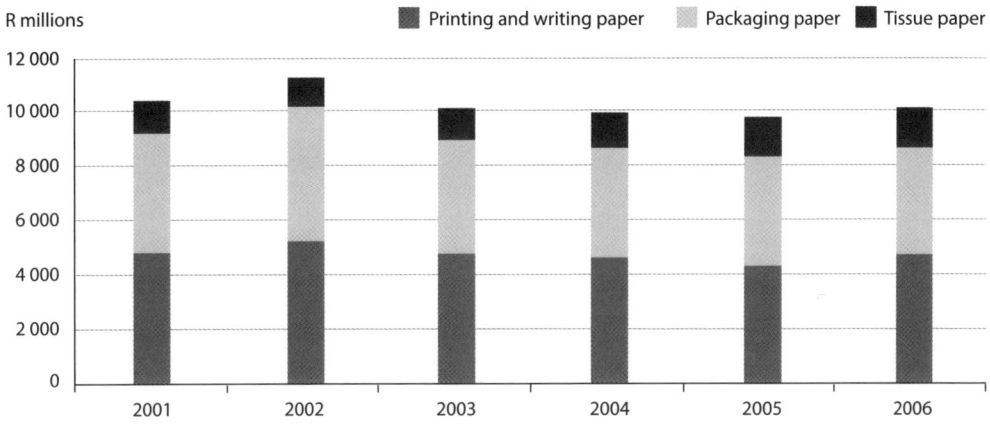

Source: PAMSA 2007: 10

FIGURE 7.7: *Paper exports (real 2000 values), 1994–2006*

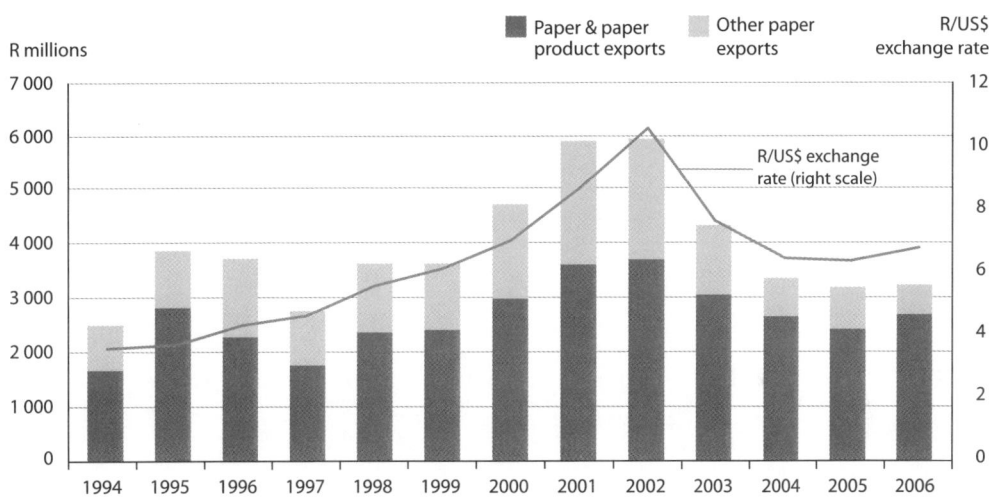

Source: Quantec 2007

The wood furniture sector relies on sawn timber inputs from the primary processing sector as well as on plastic, metal, leather and cloth inputs. The real value of wood furniture exports is reported in Figure 7.9. These exports are again closely correlated to exchange rate fluctuations. Between 1994 and 2005, the share of general wooden furniture exports increased at the expense of wood office furniture and bedroom furniture.

The composition of wood furniture imports is shown in Figure 7.10. There is little correlation between imports and the exchange rate. In fact, rand appreciation since 2002 coincides with an acceleration of wood furniture imports. Between 1994 and 2005, the value of wood furniture imports grew at a compound annual rate of 17.6 per cent. The strong growth in imports has led to a rapid decline in the

FIGURE 7.8: *Paper imports (real 2000 values), 1994–2006*

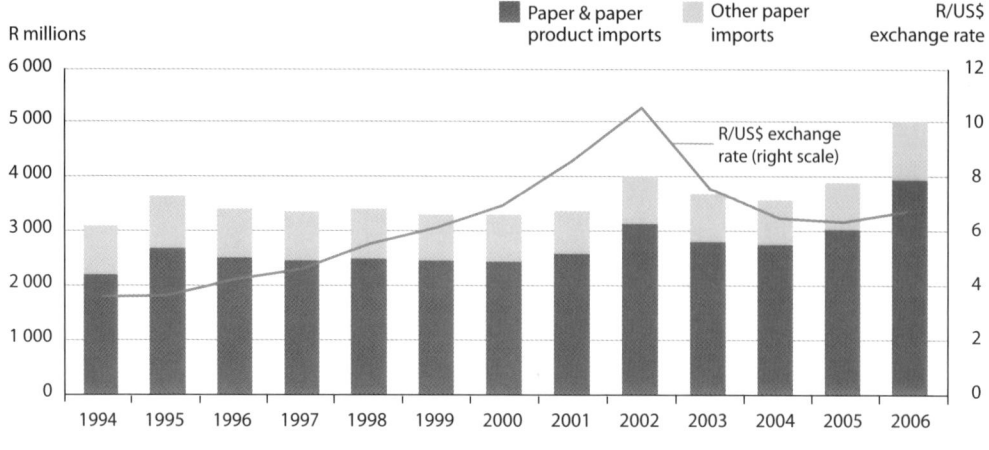

Source: Quantec 2007

sectoral balance of trade, with a trade deficit being registered for the year 2005. These trends seem to parallel those discussed for the paper market, and suggest that domestic wood furniture is an imperfect substitute for imported varieties.

Wood furniture manufacturers are mostly small and medium enterprises. Analysis suggests that 95 per cent of the estimated 1 085 wood furniture companies are small and medium enterprises (Erasmus 2004: 68). These companies are concentrated near urban centres in Gauteng, the Western Cape and Kwazulu-Natal. Since 1994, producers have transformed their orientation from an inward market focus reinforced by trade sanctions, to an increasing focus on export markets with higher volumes and variety (Moodley 2002: 31).

FIGURE 7.9: *Wood furniture exports (real 2000 values), 1994–2005*

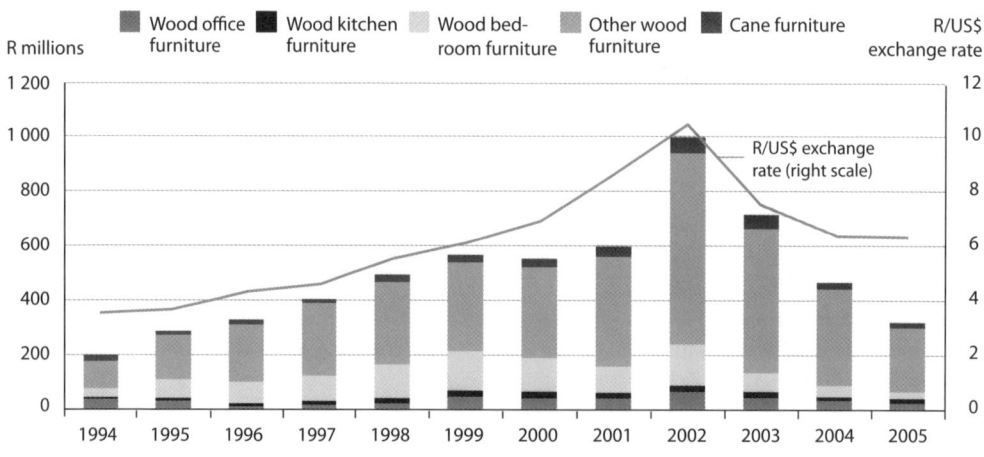

Source: Quantec 2007

FIGURE 7.10: *Wood furniture imports (real 2000 values), 1994–2005*

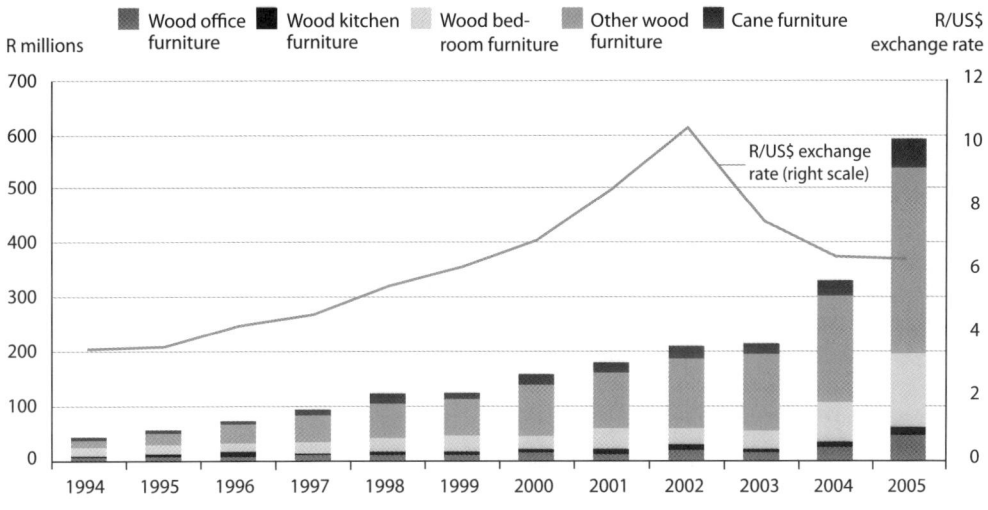

Source: Quantec 2007

A difficulty with the small and medium enterprises' (SME) predominance in the sector is that they may find it difficult to commit resources to funding R&D activities. Evidence of this is found in the R&D expenditures reported for the furniture manufacturing sector, with the 2003/04 *National R&D Survey* reporting sector R&D expenditures equal to R6.3 million and declining in the 2004/05 survey to R4.2 million (DST 2005, 2006). That gives the sector an R&D-to-revenue ratio of 0.09 per cent; nationally, South Africa's total R&D expenditures-to-GDP ratio was 0.87 per cent. In comparison, forestry and primary processing had an R&D-to-revenue ratio of 0.65 per cent.

This is not to say that wood furniture manufacturers are not innovative. Given their ability to compete in an increasingly international market it is likely that a significant quantity of innovation occurs in these firms, but it is not explicitly established as formal R&D expenditures. Interviews with wood furniture manufacturing firms also indicated that technical services were a primary resource from the national system of innovation for their operations.[2]

The recent growth of imported wooden furniture appears to indicate strengthening domestic demand. There is also a general trend in the sector internationally to connect within global value chains that require an export focus. The primary export markets for South African wooden furniture are the UK and Germany (Moodley 2002: 34). In these international markets, there is also significant competition from developing nations in Asia and Eastern Europe. In this context, international retailers are able to dictate costs, designs and quality conditions to a much greater extent.

---

2   Interviews for this study were conducted with the following organisations:
    Forestry and primary processing: Southern African Institute of Forestry (Pretoria); Council for Scientific and Industrial Research – Natural Resources and the Environment (Durban); University of KwaZulu-Natal – Institute for Commercial Forestry Research (Pietermaritzburg); Hans Merensky Timber (Johannesburg);
    Paper and pulp: Mondi (Richards Bay); Sappi (Johannesburg); Paper Manufacturers Association of South Africa (Johannesburg);
    Furniture: Furniture Bedding and Upholstery Manufacturers Association (Johannesburg); Salinga Furniture (Rosslyn); U-Niche Furniture (Meyerton).

The South African forestry value chain is internationally competitive and developed to high standards. At the same time, aspects of its production system are linked to less economically developed groups. As a result of this structure, the forestry value chain is faced with significant challenges and opportunities. In mitigating the former and enhancing the latter, the skills system plays a central role.

The skills system in the forestry value chain

The forestry value chain's skill system incorporates both the formal and informal economies. While these linkages offer opportunities to improve the livelihoods of many impoverished South Africans, they also increase the difficulty of changing established practices. This section reviews some key features of the skills system within the forestry value chain, with particular attention given to differences in skill regimes. Owing to their operational integration, the pulp and paper segments are taken as a single activity.

Renewable resource base

There are an estimated 100 000 individuals working in the renewable resource base of the forestry value chain (Chamberlain et al. 2005a: 34). There are three significant productive components in the renewable resource base: traditional growers, contract foresters and emerging growers. Traditional private and corporate plantation growers utilise artificial tree regeneration in large-scale operations. This segment was the historic driver of the timber industry's growth in South Africa, but its operations are increasingly outsourced to forestry contractors. Demand and supply of skills among traditional growers are established and typically linked to one or more downstream segments in the forestry value chain.

Currently, contract foresters make up a further third of employment in the renewable resource base. During the 1980s, forestry operations such as harvesting, silviculture and transport were increasingly outsourced. Outsourcing transformed what was a permanent workforce into a highly competitive market of contracting firms whose internal competition increases upstream and downstream authority over contractors (Khosa 2000).

Many workers view the development of forest contracting as casualisation of the labour force. These workers are now employed by contractors rather than by growers, but the same work on the same plantation is being done for less pay and fewer benefits. As a result, the contract labour force is characterised by low levels of loyalty and increased alienation. The disappointment in this transformation is also reportedly manifest in arson attacks on the plantation forests (Mayers et al. 2001: 110).

Transformation efforts appear to be reinforcing upstream and downstream authority, as emerging black entrepreneurs are caught in a drive for competitiveness based on lower margins than their established white counterparts. Given this situation, forestry contracting has severely constrained opportunities for sectoral investment that might enhance efficiencies and decrease upstream and downstream market authority. Many of the new firms are formed from employees in established contracting firms who have operational knowledge, but often have limited business skills and financial training (Clarke & Isaacs 2005: 14–20).

As a result of relatively low barriers to entry, a majority of forestry contractors are SMEs. These SMEs typically lack land or other fixed assets that they can use as collateral for new equipment, so outdated and poorly functioning equipment is often retained, further contributing to inefficiencies and potential health and safety dangers. Even larger firms find it difficult to make these investments as they face a highly competitive cost-focused market (Lewis et al. 2004: 22–24).

Currently, forestry contracting appears locked into a low-skills investment dynamic. Contractors' services are important to the forestry value chain's overall productivity. Upstream and downstream markets do not seem to value the contribution that enhanced skills amongst contractors could contribute to their own products' value. As a result, there is limited demand for a transformation of the skills system. However, at least in regard to business and financial skills, there is a need to enhance initiatives for skills development if transformation efforts are to succeed.

Community-based growers constitute the final third of employment. Under current afforestation policies, community-based growers will play a greater role in the supply of timber to the forestry value chain. This should increase employment intensity across the renewable resource base. Enhancing the role of community growers will also increase employment in both the formal and informal sectors as a result of associated trade in goods like NTFP and services like tourism.

As mentioned previously, the viability of community-based growers appears to depend on development of a new system of timber production. This system will consist of small plantations playing an enabling, but dependent, role in the broader economic development of the community. Provision of 'forestry' skills to these community growers therefore needs to encompass more than a narrow focus on plantation forestry, silviculture or entomology.[3] Skills development must holistically embrace the range of livelihoods that the entire forestry environment can provide to these rural and frequently impoverished communities (Shackleton 2004).

The importance of this complementary education and training of individuals who have not historically participated in the forestry sector is recognised in the new afforestation policy. However, providing this skills development is a challenge, particularly given that the learnership and skills programmes in the sector education and training authorities (SETAs) are often highly inflexible and centrally managed, which limits their uptake within the informal sector (DoL 2007: 15). Efforts to realise skills development within the broader forestry sector have an institutional champion in the Department of Water Affairs and Forestry's Directorate of Forestry Development.

The directorate is tasked with supporting the sustainable use of forests and forest resources to serve the livelihoods of the poor. It supports a range of programmes aimed at fostering enterprise development. A few projects have already been initiated by the directorate. However, these projects have failed to reach a point of self-sustainability and it appears that they are not a viable model for the systemic development of complementary forestry livelihoods (DWAF 2006: 31).

Primary processing

Primary processing, excluding pulp milling, has a total employment of 35 000 (Chamberlain et al. 2005a; Crickmay et al. 2005a). Sawmilling is a critical source of demand for skills in primary processing. While large sawmills have a developed skills development system, enhancing production efficiencies within the more than 500 low-cost and micro mills creates substantial demand for skills development. In this regard, there is a substantial need for development of skills in the informal economy. While there have been efforts to enhance the efficiencies of low-cost and micro mills, these programmes usually deal with a few enterprises on an ad hoc basis rather than systematically developing their skills system (Pogue 2007: 91).

Entrenching the supply of skills from these pilot initiatives on a larger scale needs to be carefully considered. Otherwise, there does not appear to be a future for these mills in the forestry value chain.

---

3   The author would like to acknowledge J. Zwolinski from the Forestry Programme at the University of KwaZulu-Natal for highlighting this point in his comments on an earlier draft. The usual disclaimer applies.

Currently, little is being done to target these mills' linkages to areas of secondary beneficiation like furniture or building products. Skills shortages and limited networks are reportedly important reasons for not developing these potential opportunities (Heyl et al. 2000: 11). Despite its relatively small share of total output, small-scale sawmilling is a critical source of income and employment in many rural areas (Horn 2000). Therefore, skills development is necessary if a significant source of living is not to be lost to already impoverished rural communities.

Secondary beneficiation

Employment in secondary beneficiation is estimated to be 123 000 individuals. This is divided into 38 000 workers in wood products, 40 000 in pulp and paper, and 45 000 in wood furniture manufacturing (Pogue 2007: 57–58). Paper and pulp is a critical component in South Africa's forestry value chain. While the informal economy is supported by over 11 000 informal paper recyclers, the skills system associated with formal paper and pulp operations is critical to the competitiveness of the entire forestry value chain.

Following democratisation in 1994, the paper and pulp sector rapidly transformed to take on international significance. In this context the industry has identified skills training as a critical dimension of developing their South African operation's competitiveness. Historically, the industry had a strong dependency on parastatals such as Iscor and Eskom to generate the supply of operators that they needed. As the parastatal training system collapsed, the industry began to further develop its own training programmes. An early initiative in this regard began in the late 1980s at Natal Technikon, which is now part of the Durban University of Technology (DUT). Both Mondi and Sappi collaboratively supplied staff to teach the programme, which was very successful. It was so successful in skills development that its graduates were rapidly promoted out of operator occupations. Although it was a testament to the sector's ability to collaboratively provide high-quality training, the programme was discontinued in the early 1990s in an environment of changing labour legislation.

With the advent of the Skills Development Framework, the sector's training programmes were institutionally vested as learnerships within a SETA, the paper and pulp chamber of the Forest Industry Education and Training Authority (FIETA). Currently, two programmes are descendants of the collaborative training initiative developed at Natal Technikon. Building on the original programme, the DUT now offers a BTech degree in Pulp and Paper Technology at National Qualifications Framework (NQF) Level 7. The other programme is a learnership modelled on the collaborative training and distance learning structure of the Natal Technikon qualification. Using a pool of instructors from both Mondi and Sappi, lectures are offered in pulp and paper centres across the country in support of the primarily correspondence-based programme. Institutional administration of the programme and examinations are run through the University of South Africa (UNISA), where this National Diploma qualification is registered.

While bureaucratic difficulties were noted in all the learnerships that the sector has developed, the UNISA programme was highly problematic because of the co-ordination it required between the Department of Labour (DoL) and the Department of Education (DoE). The industry's drive to increase the knowledge intensity of its production led to it targeting this qualification at the National Diploma level or NQF Level 6. As a learnership, the programme had to be recognised and registered by both the DoL and the DoE. In effect, two distinct systems of skills development appear to exist, rather than an integrated system. Besides bureaucratic challenges, the change to outcomes-based education required substantial review and revision of the established curriculum. As a result, there were delays in the development of learnership registration despite their having existed before the new system came into being.

Under the outcomes-based system, mentorship is a critical component of learning. Mentorship is premised upon an existence of social capital shared by instructor and learner. In the context of equity-based advancement and transformation, there is a shortage of social capital to underpin the trust and common cause that facilitates effective mentorship. The racial division that characterised the occupational hierarchy in South Africa before democratisation appears to be a cause of this dysfunctionality. In the current system, a predominately white hierarchy is now expected to mentor individuals who were previously treated as adversaries occupationally, socially and institutionally.

In the modern learning environment, knowledge and practice are intertwined. Improved knowledge relating to competency development has shortened the time in which competencies are expected to develop. However, this expectation conflicts with traditional systems in which an individual was expected to serve a prescribed time in a particular job, regardless of skills development. This tradition leads to mentors withholding knowledge transfers to learners until 'sentences' in certain roles or occupations are completed. Another barrier to effective mentorship is a learning environment characterised by a belief that knowledge development and practical skills are separate activities. In this context, conflating learning and practice is resisted by both mentors and learners. Combined, these factors severely constrain the uptake of outcomes-based education and thereby the current learnership and skills development initiatives undertaken by the paper and pulp industry. Despite these impediments, however, the industry has managed to develop a well-co-ordinated and coherent skills development system.

The diffused production structure is a critical challenge to skills training in the wood furniture sector. Despite numerous learnerships targeting skills development, there do not appear to be strong linkages with these and established or emerging participants in the sector. A significant portion of skills training originates within the context of development policies and donor aid. Therefore it appears that the supply of skills is focused on beneficiaries' own enterprise development rather than on alignment to the needs of the numerous existing SMEs and the smaller number of large enterprises.

The structure of the wood furniture SME sector creates major challenges in identifying skill demand. There is little co-ordination among the SMEs and there are not any significant industry associations that represent their interests. In an effort to address this difficulty, some initiatives have attempted to build complementary business skills within the SMEs and their training providers that would facilitate inter-firm co-operation (Pogue 2007: 112).

A Furniture Industry Industrial Training Board previously oversaw skills training for larger and more established producers in the sector. These firms currently provide significant guidance within the wood furniture chamber of the FIETA. Skills training used to be offered directly through centres run by the training board, but currently they have been transferred to learnerships at further education and training (FET) colleges. As with general skills development in manufacturing, many of these firms are working to establish a market niche for their products in the global environment. This is a challenge because of competition from better resourced, skilled and equipped manufacturers in more economically developed countries and lower-priced labour from other economically developing nations. These factors combine to create severe challenges for all segments of the wood furniture industry.

The forestry value chain's skill system incorporates both the formal and the informal economies and therefore provides a useful illustration of problems and benefits that can be derived from these linkages. Even in segments where there are no internal linkages, there are typically upstream and downstream dependencies. Significant challenges characterise the value chain as it is currently constituted, as well as its likely structure in the future. In addressing these challenges, the skills system is a critical instrument to promote development.

Policy recommendations

The forestry value chain spans a range of activities with differing priorities and interventions. The three interventions identified below are an initial attempt to facilitate the alignment of skills training to the broader strategic priorities and growth of the value chain.

Sustainable and empowering resource base

A critical challenge facing the forestry value chain is the transformation of the historical production system. Ultimately success equates to meaningful output of timber from community-based growers. Largely marginalised communities will then be integrated into an international market. However, if the decades-long growth cycles characterising plantation timber are not to be a barrier, harmonised livelihoods need to be created to support long-run plantation timber cultivation. Realising this will require development of a new holistic timber production paradigm.

This holistic forestry production system would view traditional timber growth for downstream markets as complementary to shorter-cycle timber growth for other uses, such as fuel wood. In addition, non-timber products and services would form another basis of complementary livelihoods. In order to realise this holistic production paradigm, a concerted and systematic skills development programme must be established. These skills would ensure that communities are able to grow timber for traditional markets, but at the same time develop complementary livelihoods with business, marketing and other production skills.

Currently, a range of development programmes are working on ad hoc interventions to develop these kinds of complementary skills (Shackleton 2004: 34). However, transformation of the timber production system requires sustained development of skills and other productive resources. Identifying and delivering these resources cannot be done without ongoing consultation with the communities themselves (Tyler 2006). The development of complementary business support is critical in this regard. While a community might develop some NTFP, their impact will be minimised unless they have business support (Kapila & Mead 2002).

A new extension service model appears to offer considerable promise in delivering these skills and other services in a sustained manner. Such an extension service would perform a range of roles beyond narrow tree-growing, and focus on local specifics rather than formulated answers. This type of extension service is increasingly common internationally and would form a critical vehicle for monitoring, evaluating and learning from the experience of the community-based growers (World Bank 2007: 172–176).

Complementing and related to the skills development and extension services for the segments' transformation is the need for co-ordination among communities. Enhanced co-ordination and partnership development should also be encouraged through initiatives like diffused production competencies, in which complementary business skills are developed and fostered across a network of communities. Economies of scale for productive equipment could also be realised through this network. These community-based co-operatives could also foster social capital among communities and facilitate increased market co-ordination and authority.

Entrenching monitoring, evaluation and learning systems

Many of the key challenges facing the forestry value chain are recognised, and most are being addressed through one or more interventions. Nevertheless, the interventions are often not co-ordinated, despite focusing on the same challenges. Frequently these interventions are also ad hoc and supply-driven, leading to solutions being pursued that are ineffective or even destructive. Further, there are difficulties associated with well-designed interventions impacting differently than intended, as well as inadequacies in resources, especially skills, for implementation.

Monitoring, evaluation, and learning (MEL) systems are a critical tool to address these difficulties and ensure that lessons from interventions become part of a learning process. There are key challenges in each segment of the forestry value chain where entrenching an integrated MEL system could deal with this critical dimension of implementation. In the resource base, an MEL system would seem to be a priority in guiding the transformation of plantation forestry and its associated increased usage of community-based growers. It would facilitate assessment of long-term development impacts as well as ensuring that the expected timber supplies are being delivered. The MEL system would also provide a critical source of information and feedback for the interventions to learn and improve their performance.

In primary processing, an important area is ensuring that low-cost and micro mills develop their production processes and business capabilities. Success in this regard is necessary if they are to remain viable in the forestry value chain, and if they are not, to become further marginalised from a production system that is increasingly consolidated around large-scale sawmills. In this regard, an MEL system would complement ongoing initiatives by creating a co-ordinating institution that diffuses information and builds awareness of these efforts' relative success and failure. The MEL system would also facilitate identification of gaps in initiatives addressing these challenges.

There are two areas in secondary beneficiation where MEL systems hold significant promise. In the wood furniture sector, an important challenge exists in ensuring that the skills supplied are meeting the demands from existing producers. Within this sector, there is also a critical challenge to ensure that complementary business skills are developed to support the current focus on production skills.

Paper and pulp is the other area where an MEL system could make an important contribution to the sector's challenges generally, and especially in regard to skills development. Despite resources and intra-industry co-ordination, skills development remains a large concern for the sector. An MEL system would make a significant contribution in addressing the challenges of skills development by generating and diffusing information and learning amongst key agents in the skills system.

Systemic development of critical skills in priority segments

The paper and pulp industry is a critical feature across the entire forestry value chain. Therefore its current efforts to enhance training and skills development must be supported and obstacles removed, to ensure its competitiveness. A collaborative skills planning model would mark a major step forward in this regard. Focusing on critical skills needed in the pulp and paper sector as a pilot exercise in priority skills delivery, this model should be useful for skills development across the forestry value chain.

Introducing innovations in relation to established planning and strategy software, this initiative would bring key agents across the skills system together to codify the structure of the skills system, identify critical delivery nodes, and prioritise interventions needed to enhance delivery. The model would also improve the skills development network by bringing together labour, the private sector and the public sector to develop evidence-based policies supported by their co-ordinated efforts. Premised on an evolving understanding of the skills system, with an inherent ability to update and re-design underlying relationships, the planning model would have flexibility and utility uncommon in traditional forecasting models.

By design, it would also incorporate systematic communications flow among stakeholders to facilitate consensus on priorities and challenges. The inclusive nature of the model's development and refinement thereby supports knowledge transfer to all stakeholders. The paper and pulp sector offers a terrific opportunity in this regard because of the concentrated ownership structure and evident commitment of the sector to finding practical solutions for skills development. Many challenges, such as overcoming barriers resulting from mentorship and needing to realise greater co-ordination across the skills system, are concerns that exist beyond the paper and pulp sector. Hence, the lessons learnt from the initiative will be significant for a much broader audience interested in dynamic issues of skills provision and policy formulation.

Conclusion

This analysis has focused on major changes occurring throughout the forestry value chain, their influence on the skills system and opportunities they have created for this system. The analysis has highlighted the transformation of this renewable resource as a critical development for the entire forestry value chain. Several years into the new afforestation policy, the new production system appears to be stagnating. Shortcomings in skills development were shown to be a critical aspect of successful management of these changes, but they must be accompanied by a broader contextualised focus on skills needs. The skills system was also shown to play a central role across the forestry value chain in supporting and developing domestic and international competitiveness. Systemic problems such as a limited culture of mentorship were identified as barriers to further changes in the skills system.

While the tremendous potential of the forestry value chain has been demonstrated, its ability to deliver growth and development is far from certain. Strong leadership is needed if the ongoing transformation of the value chain is to become a favourable development rather than a corrosive one. Interventions around the skills system identified in this analysis appear to be important steps forward in securing this promising future.

As pressure increases for action on climate change, there is a strong probability that an entrenched emissions trading scheme will be established. Afforestation initiatives could be given a significant boost if carbon projects linked to these schemes are translated into tangible and sustained benefits for tree growers. If South Africa can succeed in these efforts it can offer a renewable resource model that is inherently inclusive and dramatically in contrast to exclusive enclaves that historically feature in the region's development experience.

References

Chamberlain D, Essop H, Hougaard C, Malherbe S & Walker R (2005a) *The contribution, costs and development opportunities of the forestry, timber, pulp and paper industries in South Africa – Part One.* Report commissioned by Forestry South Africa. Johannesburg: Genesis Analytics

Chamberlain D, Essop H, Hougaard C, Malherbe S & Walker R (2005b) *Market analysis – Part Two.* Report commissioned by Forestry South Africa. Johannesburg: Genesis Analytics

Clarke J & Isaacs M (2005) *Forestry contractors in South Africa: What role in reducing poverty?* London: International Institute for Environment and Development

Crickmay DG, Le Brasseur J, Stubbings JA & Daugherty AE (2005a) *Study of supply and demand of industrial roundwood in South Africa.* Report commissioned by the Department of Water Affairs and Forestry. Pietermaritzburg: Crickmay & Associates

Crickmay DG, Le Brasseur J, Stubbings JA & Daugherty AE (2005b) *Study of supply and demand of softwood sawlogs and sawn timber in South Africa*. Report commissioned by the Department of Water Affairs and Forestry. Pietermaritzburg: Crickmay & Associates

DoL (Department of Labour, South Africa) (2007) *State of skills in South Africa, 2006*. Pretoria: DoL

DPE (Department of Public Enterprises, South Africa) (2007) *The future role of South African Forestry Company and its operations subsidiary Komatiland Forests*. Fact Sheet 26 March 2007. Pretoria: DPE

DST (Department of Science and Technology, South Africa) (2005) *National survey of research and experimental development (R&D): High-level key results (2003/04 Fiscal Year)*. Pretoria: DST

DST (2006) *National survey of research and experimental development (R&D): High-level key results (2004/05 Fiscal Year)*. Pretoria: DST

DTI (Department of Trade and Industry, South Africa) (2007) *Implementation of government's National Industrial Policy Framework: Industrial policy action plan*. Pretoria: DTI

DWAF (Department of Water Affairs and Forestry, South Africa) (2006) *South Africa's state of the forests report (Draft November 2006)*. Pretoria: DWAF

DWAF (2007) *Companion to the draft forest sector transformation charter*. Pretoria: DWAF

Erasmus J (2004) *A profile of the wood, paper, and pulp sector in South Africa*. Report commissioned by the Department of Labour. Pretoria: HSRC

FSA (Forestry South Africa) (2006) *Forestry and forest products industry facts 2006*. Johannesburg: Forestry South Africa

Heyl L, Von Maltitz G, Evans J & Segoale R (2000) *Issues and opportunities for small-scale sawmilling in South Africa: an Eastern Cape case study*. London: International Institute for Environment and Development

Horn J (2000) *The role of small-scale sawmilling in household and community livelihoods: Case studies in the Eastern Cape*. London: International Institute for Environment and Development

Kapila S & Mead D (2002) *Building businesses with small producers*. Ottawa: International Development Research Centre

Khosa M (2000) *Forestry contracting in South Africa*. London: International Institute for Environment and Development

Lewis F, Horn J, Howard M & Ngubane S (2004) *Small and medium scale enterprises in the forestry sector in South Africa: An Analysis of key issues*. London: International Institute for Environment and Development

Mayers J, Evans J & Foy T (2001) *Raising the stakes: impacts of privatisation, certification and partnerships in South African forestry*. London: International Institute for Environment and Development

Moodley S (2002) Global market access in the Internet era: South Africa's wood furniture industry. *Internet Research: Electronic Networking Applications and Policy* 12(1): 31–42

PAMSA (Paper Manufacturers Association of South Africa) (2007) *Paper Manufacturers Association of South Africa 2006–2007: A perspective on South Africa*. Johannesburg: PAMSA

Pogue T (2007) *A sectoral analysis of wood, paper and pulp industries in South Africa*. Research report prepared for the Human Sciences Research Council. Pretoria: Institute for Economic Research on Innovation

Shackleton C (2004) *Assessment of the livelihoods importance of forestry, forests, and forest products in South Africa*. Grahamstown: Rhodes University

Tyler S (ed.) (2006) *Communities, livelihoods, and natural resources*. Ottawa: International Development Research Centre

World Bank (2007) *World development report 2008: Agriculture for development*. Washington DC: World Bank

Zwolinski J & Groenewald W (2004) Natural regeneration of pine plantations in South Africa as a cost-effective way of stand re-establishment. *Forestry* 77(5): 483–493

4 PUBLIC INFRASTRUCTURE SECTORS

CHAPTER 8

Energy

Jeff Lomey and Kent McNamara

Introduction

The research report on which this chapter is based provides a high-level review of the current and future skills demand and supply situation for the South African energy sector, specifically in relation to the generation, transmission and distribution of electrical energy. The report highlights the critical skills shortages, likely blockages to skills development and potential opportunities for job creation, based on current government and industry policy and strategy. The report contains a synthesis of the research findings and implications, and concludes with policy and strategy recommendations for the next five years.[1]

The report aims to:
- contribute to the better alignment of skills development policies with industrial or sector initiatives/policies;
- provide policy and strategic input for government's Accelerated and Shared Growth Initiative for South Africa (Asgisa) and Joint Initiative on Priority Skills Acquisition (Jipsa) initiatives;
- provide projected quantifiable data on the match between education institution output and industry skills requirements;
- make a contribution to the Sector Education and Training Authority (SETA) community by providing an up-to-date analysis of the critical inter-relationships between industrial policy, sector (or economic) growth and skills development.

The report presents a summary of the research covering:
- a contextual overview of the sector;
- a review of current and projected demand for skills, based on sector trends and occupational data;
- an assessment of current and projected supply of skills from educational and training institutions, based on educational data;
- an analysis of the degree of match-up between skills supply and demand to 2012; and
- a concluding section identifying possible bottlenecks and barriers affecting the supply of skills, together with proposed remedial action.

---

1 This chapter is based on the full HSRC report, Projected skills demand and supply for the electrical energy sector, completed in October 2007.

Research method

The research methods applied in this study included perusal of primary and secondary literature, access to a variety of databases made available by the Human Sciences Research Council (HSRC), use of recent news reports, website scans, interviews and case study contacts.

The information presented in this report has been based mainly on available employment data from the household and labour force surveys conducted by Statistics South Africa (Stats SA) (Stats SA 1996–1999, 2000–2005), and educational data on further education and training (FET) and higher education and training (HET) output from the Department of Education (DoE 2007a, 2007b).

Sector scope

The sector concerned includes all forms of electricity generation, ranging from non-renewable to renewable sources, transmission and distribution of electrical energy, and key electricity-related sub-sectors. The review excludes consideration of biofuels and natural gases, except where they are utilised to produce electrical energy.

The time frame of the review covers trends in historical statistical data for the period 1996–2005. As far as future strategic projections are concerned, the report will mainly review implications for skills demand and supply up to 2012.

The skills requirements will be assessed in terms of the levels established within the National Qualifications Framework (NQF).

The skills debate

The so-called 'skills shortage' has been dominating news headlines in South Africa for the past few years. Recently, the annual International Business Report Survey produced by Grant Thornton found that a shortage of skilled workers was regarded as the main impediment to business expansion by 58 per cent of 200 respondents in medium-to-large businesses (*Business Day* 16 July 2007).

The skills debate has not been without controversy. The Commissioner for Employment Equity, for example, has been on record as saying that the 'shortage' is artificial and a result of the unwillingness of many employers to hire black people. By contrast, the trade union Solidarity has claimed that affirmative action contributes to the skills shortage by failing to recruit or retain skilled white people (*Business Day* 8 July 2007).

Many independent commentators and business leaders believe that there is indeed a skills shortage.[2] The legacy of 'Bantu Education' is recognised by many as having stunted the development of skills in the country.

For government, acknowledgement of this legacy led to the drafting of the Skills Development Act (No. 97 of 1998) and Employment Equity Act (No. 55 of 1998) (among others), with a view to promoting the training, development and advancement of previously disadvantaged people. More recently, government has launched Asgisa (The Presidency 2006a), and Jipsa (The Presidency 2006b), which reflect its

---

2   See comments by Ann Bernstein of the Centre for Development Enterprise and Wiseman Nkuhlu in the *Sunday Times* 10 June 2007.

twin concerns about skills and job creation, particularly the shortage of professional engineers and artisans.

The demand for skills, especially intermediate and high-level engineering and artisan skills, appears to be intensifying. According to the most recent report of the Department of Labour (DoL), *The State of Skills in South Africa* (DoL 2003), there has been a shift towards capital-intensive production, calling for more skilled labour associated with an export-led economy. The DoL report quotes Sasol's claim in 2003 that the country was already short of at least 20 000 artisans at that time.

A number of current developments in other sectors can be identified which could be placing pressure on the supply of skills. A major drive is under way to boost the transport infrastructure across South Africa, focused mainly on upgrading Transnet's railways and ports, which needs engineers and technicians. For the next few years at least, the infrastructural work on the Gautrain and facilities for the 2010 World Cup soccer tournament is also drawing away seemingly limited engineering and technical skills. Furthermore, a global commodities boom has been taking skilled artisans and engineers away from South African mining operations to other countries, including parts of Africa and Australia.

Government's Jipsa anticipates that the number of engineers produced each year will need to be almost doubled, from 1 400 to 2 400, while production of artisans will need to more than double from 5 000 to 12 500 every year over the next 4 years.

The related question of job creation and unemployment must also be considered, given government's concern about the abundance of marginalised youth in the unskilled, semi-skilled and small business sectors, including the 'informal sector', 'Sufficient employment creation remains the most crucial and most difficult of the ASGISA objectives.' (The Presidency 2006a:2).

This chapter is informed by the perspective that skills development in South Africa cannot be tackled separately from job creation and poverty alleviation. The next section describes the current sector statistics and dynamics.

Sector overview

The Department of Minerals and Energy

The electricity sector falls under the responsibility of the Department of Minerals and Energy (DME). According to the latest DME website and policy report, energy comprised about 15 per cent of South Africa's GDP in 2003.[3] DME policy, as set out on its website, is based on attainment of the following goals:
- providing universal access to energy by 2014;
- providing accessible, affordable and reliable energy, especially for the poor;
- diversifying primary energy sources and reducing dependency on coal;
- good governance;
- promotion of private-sector investments;
- environmentally responsible energy provision.

---

3   See http://www.dme.gov.za/energy/overview.stm#1, accessed in June 2007 and February 2008.

The National Energy Regulator of South Africa

Overseeing the role of Eskom and the independent power producers (IPP) is the National Electricity Regulator of South Africa (NERSA) which, together with the DME, strives mainly to ensure that electricity tariffs and capital expansion plans are aligned with national policy and development objectives.

Eskom

Eskom has dominated the energy production sector as the main supplier of electricity since early in the 20th century, producing 96 per cent of the total energy consumed in South Africa. It currently operates 24 power stations, 13 of which are coal-fired and located mostly in Mpumalanga province, within the coal fields of the north-eastern highveld region the country. There are also six hydro-powered stations, two gas-fired operations, two pumped storage schemes and one nuclear station (located just north of Cape Town).

Eskom's national transmission grid carries power to the cities, other parts of the country and neighbouring territories. As of March 2007, South Africa had a total of 27 770 km of high-voltage transmission lines and 325 000 km of distribution lines.

South Africa supplies more than half of the electricity used on the African continent, including direct power supplies to Lesotho, Swaziland, Botswana, Namibia and Zimbabwe. The country also imports some power from Mozambique's Cahora Bassa hydro-power station.

Local government – municipalities

The distribution of electricity in urban areas is shared between Eskom and municipal councils. Municipalities are by law entitled to sell and distribute power in their demarcated areas.

Independent power producers

Partly because of the large start-up capital costs associated with generation capacity and transmission infrastructure, and the recent (temporary) restrictions preventing Eskom from building new power plants, there are only a few small IPPs in the country. At the time of writing, a number of such IPPs are either being planned or under construction.

Electrification

In 1994, the inaugural year of South Africa's new democracy, the average level of electrification countrywide was 36 per cent. By 2004, this had risen dramatically to 72 per cent (Eskom 2007). The number of rural households electrified countrywide rose from 12 per cent in 1994 to 52 per cent by 2005. While this is a significant historical achievement, close to half of the rural population still does not enjoy access to grid-based electricity, partly due to the size of the country and the long distances between towns.

Rural households

Rural households comprise the majority of poor homes in the country, and are characterised by 'energy poverty', which is exacerbated by the increasing scarcity of fuel-wood. The cost of providing an extended national grid to rural areas becomes increasingly expensive, given that low levels of consumption by the end-users make the investment in power lines not economically viable. In these areas, alternative sources of (renewable) energy become more attractive.

Employment

The research undertaken for this chapter indicates that, as of 2005, the electricity sector in South Africa formally employed an estimated 114 726 people, of whom 70 206 were directly involved in the core production, collection and distribution of electricity; an additional 44 520 people provided electrical equipment and other services to the core elements of the sector (including the manufacture of motors and transformers, wires and cables, distribution and control apparatus, and related research services).

A small informal sector can also be identified, which in 2005, employed only 1 115 people in electricity production, distribution and research. The informal sector in South Africa's electricity industry is small and undeveloped.

Figure 8.1 shows the trends in formal-sector employment, both in the core electricity production, collection and distribution sub-sectors, as well as in the various supporting industries.

As the premier electricity-producing, transmitting and distributing entity, Eskom employed 29 697 people in 2006, of whom approximately 40 per cent were in generation, 10 per cent in transmission and 50 per cent in distribution (Eskom 2006). The municipalities also employed an estimated 16 000 people in distribution, bringing the total number of distribution personnel in South Africa to approximately 31 000 (EDI Holdings 2008).

The electricity distribution industry has been characterised by some duplication. For example, Eskom maintenance personnel look after sub-stations and lines in metropolitan areas, while skilled municipal workers are doing the same in residential suburbs. The planned formation of Regional Electricity Distributors (REDs), which involves a merger of Eskom distribution with that of the municipalities, is expected to partly address these overlaps, but to date, the six planned REDs for the country have not yet been implemented, mainly due to policy uncertainty and lack of capacity.

As far as the informal sector is concerned, there was a small increase in activity, reaching a peak in 2000 of 4 530 recorded jobs in energy production, collection and distribution, as well as in the supply of motors, transformers and wire cabling. This growth spurt may also have been stimulated by Eskom's electrification programme. However, the initial impact of the electrification programme on the informal sector was not sustained, with a fall-off recorded in informal and self-employment from 2001 onwards, down to 1 115 jobs in 2005 (Stats SA 2000–2005).

The available data on the informal sector in South Africa must be accepted as being incomplete and less reliable than data obtained from formal sources, but they do suggest that informal employment in the electricity supply sector is weak and undeveloped in South Africa.

Energy use

In 2004, industry consumed the lion's share (38 per cent) of electrical energy, followed by mining (15.9 per cent) and the domestic residential market (16.8 per cent) (NERSA 2004). Most household energy is obtained from fuel wood (50 per cent of net household energy, primarily in rural areas), with the remainder coming from coal (18 per cent), illuminating paraffin (7 per cent) and a small amount from liquid petroleum gas (GCIS 2006).

FIGURE 8.1: *Formal employment levels in electricity-related sub-sectors, 1996–2005*

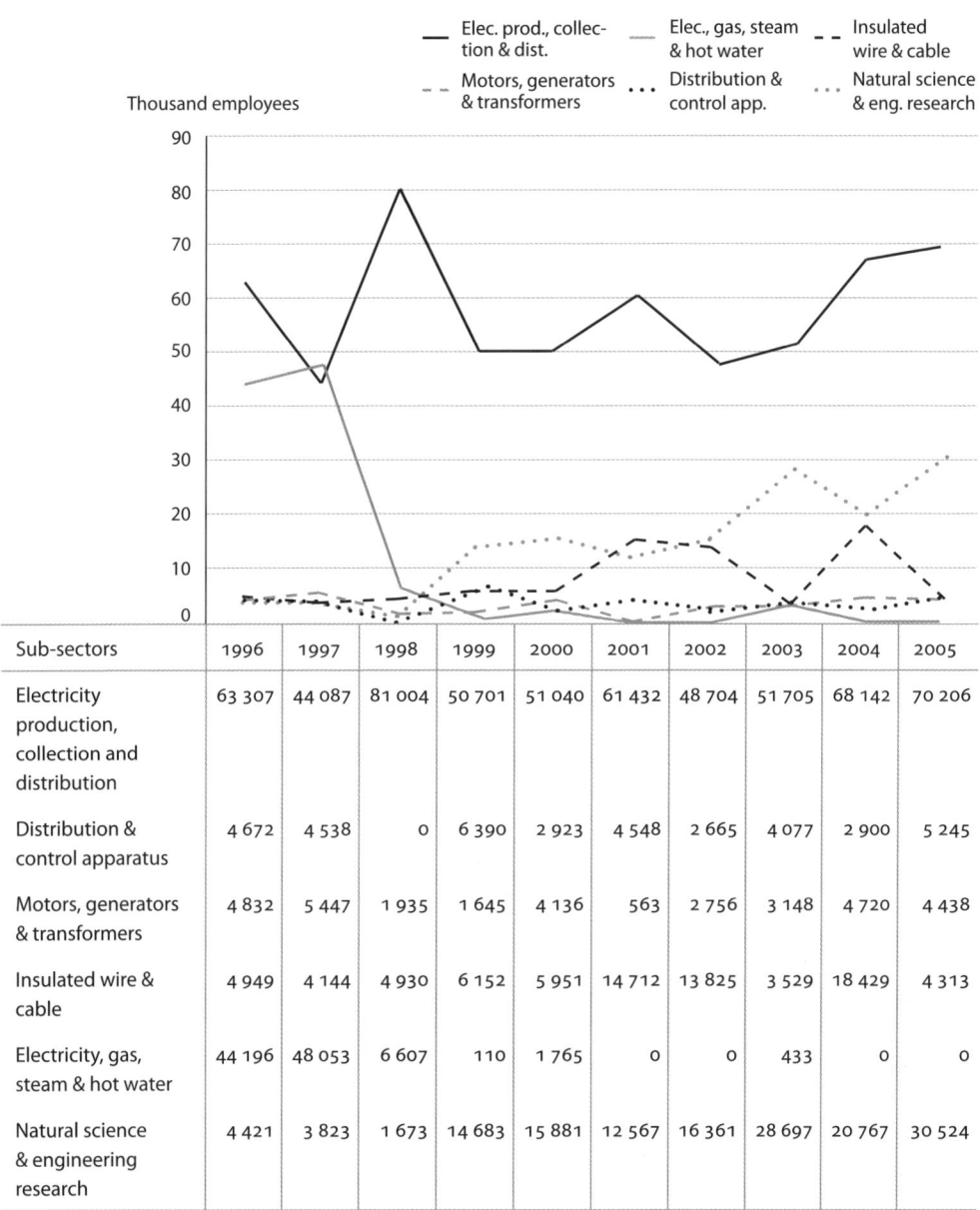

Sub-sectors	1996	1997	1998	1999	2000	2001	2002	2003	2004	2005
Electricity production, collection and distribution	63 307	44 087	81 004	50 701	51 040	61 432	48 704	51 705	68 142	70 206
Distribution & control apparatus	4 672	4 538	0	6 390	2 923	4 548	2 665	4 077	2 900	5 245
Motors, generators & transformers	4 832	5 447	1 935	1 645	4 136	563	2 756	3 148	4 720	4 438
Insulated wire & cable	4 949	4 144	4 930	6 152	5 951	14 712	13 825	3 529	18 429	4 313
Electricity, gas, steam & hot water	44 196	48 053	6 607	110	1 765	0	0	433	0	0
Natural science & engineering research	4 421	3 823	1 673	14 683	15 881	12 567	16 361	28 697	20 767	30 524

Sources: Quantec 2007; Stats SA 1996–1999, 2000–2005

FIGURE 8.2: *Energy sources for electricity generation in South Africa, 2001*

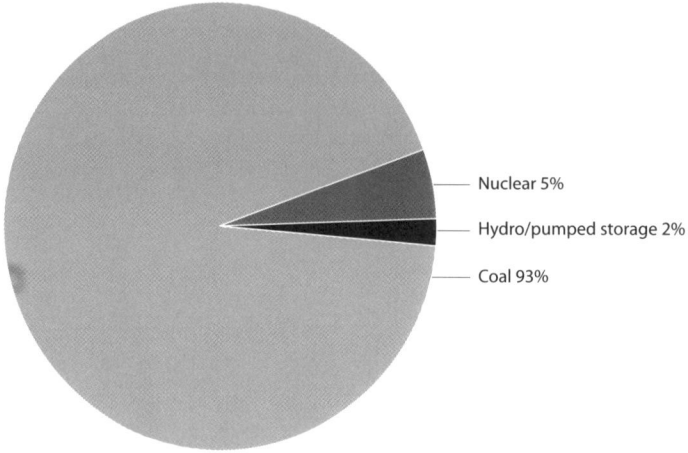

Source: NERSA 2004

Alternative energy sources

Electricity generation in South Africa has long been dominated by coal, which makes up 93 per cent of the total (Figure 8.2).

Eskom also has some pumped storage and hydro generation capacity. Renewables currently make up a negligible part of the total supply. There are co-generation, wind, solar, landfill gas, bagasse and other projects, which are experimental, planned or in use. The low cost to date of electricity produced through burning fossil fuels (and the fact that external environmental, social and economic costs are not built into the price), has mitigated against the use of renewables, which can only become more attractive options as the price of fossil fuel-based power rises in response to reduced supply or increased demand.

Renewable resources currently in use include:
- biomass: natural woodlands in communal rural areas estimated at 12 million tons;
- wind: approximately 300 000 windmills for watering livestock and supplying communities with water;
- solar photovoltaic (PV) panel assembly: capacity totalling 5 megawatts (MW) per annum;
- solar water-heaters: annual PV panel assembly capacity totalling 5 MW;
- hydro-power: 2 061 MW (ESETA 2005a: 25).

Energy supply and demand

For decades, electrical energy in South Africa has been among the cheapest in the world. Fossil fuel (coal) makes up 93 per cent of the energy source. During the late 1970s and early 1980s, Eskom committed itself to building excess generation capacity which lasted until 2007 (Figure 8.3). As the economy has expanded, power demand has been increasing, hitting a record high of 35 479 MW in the winter of 2007.

FIGURE 8.3: *Eskom capacity status and maximum demand forecast, 1996–2008*

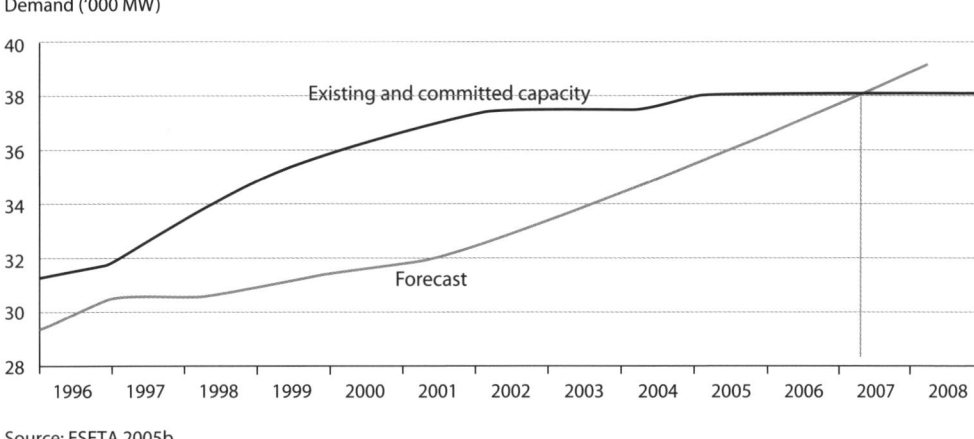

Source: ESETA 2005b

The frequency of power blackouts and load-shedding, and the prospects of increased prices for electrical energy in future, have become a matter of national concern. It is clear that Eskom's current installed capacity will be insufficient to meet forecasted demand, as Figure 8.3 shows.

Four reasons have been advanced for inadequate generation capacity, namely policy uncertainty, poor co-ordination, inaccurate planning assumptions and poor maintenance.[4] To address the challenge, Eskom is embarking on a programme to establish new generation capacity over the next 5 years, at a cost of R97 billion. Beyond 2012, with an average expected growth in demand of 4 per cent, roughly 2 000 MW will be added every year to 2025, to eventually double existing capacity by that date (Eskom 2006).

Renewable energy supply to 2013

Looking to the future, the DME in 2003 set a target of 10 000 gigawatt-hours (GWh) of renewable energy contribution to final energy consumption by 2013, to be produced mainly from biomass, wind, solar and small-scale hydro-power sources (DME 2003).

Summary

In summary, this contextual overview of the electrical energy sector in South Africa has indicated that the country is currently investing in the expansion of energy supply, mainly through the further use of fossil fuels, but also with some consideration for nuclear and renewable options. The industry's expansion plans, together with its preferred energy 'mix', will shape the demand for skills for the future. Accordingly, the current and projected demand for skills in the context of these changes in electricity supply will be considered in the next section. In the future, pressure will be placed on skills and resources as a result of the fact that rapid planning has now had to be done on a large scale to respond to the current challenges.

---

4   Eberhard A, Plugging into source of the failures, *Business Day*, 14 March 2007.

The demand for skills in the electrical energy sector

Rate of economic growth

The rate of economic growth is a key determinant in energy demand planning, and must feature in any analysis of energy sector demand forecasting. This rate will also influence the sector skills growth requirements.

In its 2006 *Annual Report*, Eskom indicated that it had revised its original expansion programme (based on a 3 per cent annual growth in demand), in the light of the government's drive to boost economic growth to 6 per cent per annum by 2010. Eskom estimated that this would result in an average growth in electricity demand of 4 per cent per annum, requiring approximately 47 252 MW of new capacity by 2025 – more than double the total existing capacity (Eskom 2006). From this point of view, the 'average high growth' curve of 3.6 per cent shown in Figure 8.4 is now being applied.

Over the five years to 2012, an estimated 10 909 MW of generation capacity will be developed, mainly by re-commissioning three older 'mothballed' stations (3 800 MW), constructing 2 open-cycle gas turbines (1 050 MW), commissioning an additional pumped storage facility at Ingula (1 322 MW), upgrading the Arnot and Gariep stations (380 MW), achieving the current DME target for renewable energy sources (1 667 MW by 2013), involving IPPs (1 000 MW), and securing some initial power from the new Medupi coal-fired station (estimated at 1 000 MW by 2012).

Sector skills demand forecast to 2012

Three alternative scenarios are presented for forecasting the projected growth of jobs in the electrical energy sector over the next five years.

FIGURE 8.4: *Projected maximum energy demand, 1951–2031*

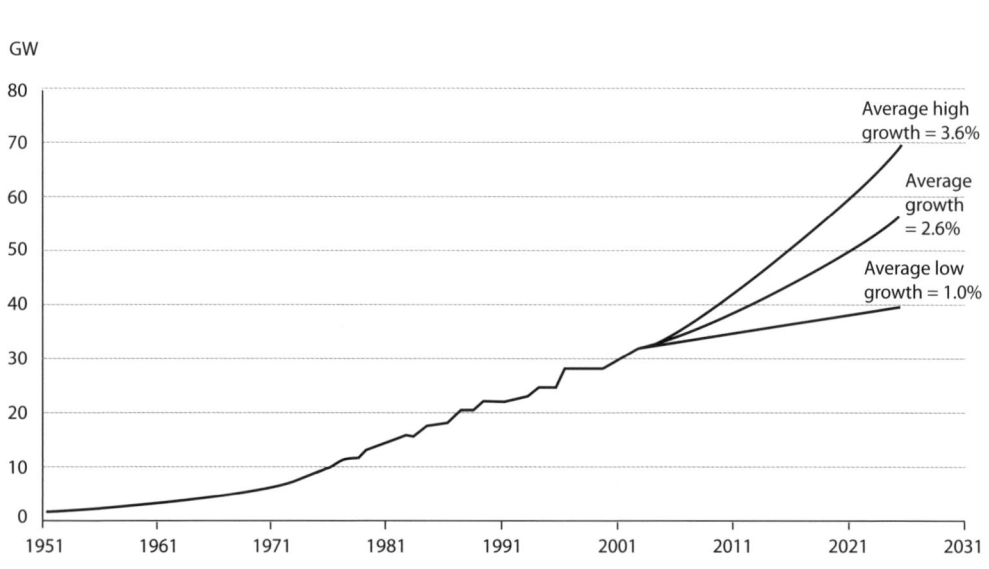

Source: Stone & Webster 2005

1 Arithmetic projection

- The current ratio is 1.85 jobs per MW in the core and 1.17 jobs per MW in the supporting sub-sector.
- 10 909 MW of planned expansion creates an additional 33 284 jobs, 20 182 in the formal core organisations and 12 775 in supporting industries, plus 327 informal-sector jobs; of the core formal 20 182 employees, 8 537 would be Eskom employees.

2 Efficiency projection

- Employment levels in coal-based electrical generation have declined by 5.4 per cent per annum, mainly due to increased efficiencies (Agama Energy 2003).
- 10 909 MW of planned expansion creates a net additional 29 879 efficient jobs, of which 7 709 would be Eskom employees.

3 Eskom-linked projection

- Eskom's own internal estimate is that 9 594 new jobs will be created by 2012.
- By combining the efficiency projection with Eskom's forecast, 10 909 MW of planned expansion would create an additional 31 764 jobs in the sector.

Projected number of electricity sector jobs per NQF level

Table 8.1 provides the current ratios for different occupations and then projects the likely demand in jobs to 2012, based on the number of jobs projected under Scenario 3 above.

Skills demand projection for renewable energy

Forecasting skills requirements for renewable energy (RE) technologies is more complex, in that the mix of RE types as well as the occupation categories may vary, depending on DME policy, the job

TABLE 8.1: *Occupational ratios, by NQF level, and projected skills demand for the electrical energy sector to 2012*

NQF level	Occupations	No. employed (2005)	Occupational ratio (proportion of total)	Projected new jobs (n)
1–3 (Low-level – pre-matric)	elementary operators	16 187	0.14	4 447
4–5 (Intermediate – matric/post-school)	crafts and trades clerks technicians service workers	73 244	0.64	20 329
6–8 (High-level – degree equivalent)	senior managers professionals	25 296	0.22	6 988
Total		114 727	1.0	31 764

Source: The occupational ratios applied in the table are based on data obtained from Stats SA 2000–2005, as given in Quantec 2007.

FIGURE 8.5: *Least-cost combination of the 10 000 GWh renewable energy target*

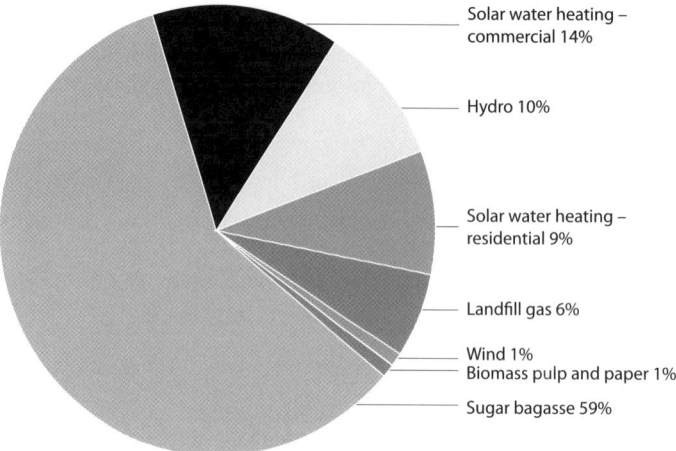

Source: DME 2004

creation potential of each RE type and financial viability. In addition, no adequate baseline skills profile exists in the current energy mix.

Potential renewable energy contribution

In its *White Paper on Renewable Energy*, released in 2003, the DME set a target for 2013 of 667 MW or 4 per cent RE contribution to total energy consumption (DME 2003).

The 2004 DME report concluded that the future RE energy mix should ideally be based on least-cost technologies, as shown in Figure 8.5 (DME 2004).

The DME's model suggests that sugar bagasse, solar water heating and hydro would dominate the RE market, although this RE 'mix' was implied rather than adopted as a formal policy target. The specific mix that is implemented by government will have an impact on the projected skills requirements. Since the policy is not yet firm, projecting an accurate skills mix is not yet possible.

Renewable energy mix

An in-depth study of the employment potential of RE, conducted by a private agency, described the *White Paper*'s target as 'exceedingly modest' and called for a higher target, mainly to derive the maximum employment benefits (Agama Energy 2003). The Agama Energy report operated on the assumption of a particular 'mix' of RE technologies, with wind contributing 50 per cent, biomass 30 per cent and solar 10 per cent.

For the RE sector as a whole, the total number of direct (and indirect) jobs which could be created by 2020 would be much larger, in the opinion of the Agama Energy researchers. The employment potential of bio-diesel and solar water heating was highest of all the renewable technologies.

Should government agree to setting a higher target of 15 per cent for the development of renewable electricity-generating energy technologies by 2020 (a target suggested by the Energy and

Development Research Centre of the University of Cape Town (Agama Energy 2003:34)), at least 36 400 net, direct jobs in renewables would be created in the South African economy.

Renewable energy occupations

The types of skills or occupations required to support the expansion of the RE sector are indicated as follows (based on a summary of the Agama Energy proposals; see Agama Energy 2003):
- general: engineering, environmental, planning, financial, legal, mechanical and electrical technicians, civil engineering and construction, consultants, academics, policy analysts, economic managers;
- wind: meteorology, surveying, structural engineers, metalworkers, mechanics, computer operators, fitters and welders, underwater marine engineering;
- solar PV: glass and steel manufacturing, electrical and plumbing contracting, architecture and system design, battery and electrical equipment manufacture;
- biofuels: mainly semi-skilled and unskilled, contract and seasonal labour, small-scale farming;
- solar water heating: artisans, 'bakkie and ladder' people.

Summary

Within existing electrical energy organisations, both in the core and supporting sub-sectors, an estimated 31 764 new jobs can be expected in order to meet power demand requirements to 2012. The potential for small business, the informal sector and the unemployed has to date been negligible in the sub-sector.

For RE, in weighing up the macro-economic benefits of different approaches, the DME report concluded that because of the high capital intensity of RE technology and the relatively limited gains which would flow from subsidising job-rich technologies, 'least-cost principles should guide the selection of RE technologies'. It also concluded that it was 'probably not advisable for government to use RE as a tool for creating jobs' (DME 2004: 16).

If the social (clean green energy) and job creation benefits are considered as critical for South Africa, then in the long term, the RE forms have potential for job creation equal to and greater than traditional 'dirty' energy sourced from coal. Even in the short term, with appropriate government subsidies, premium prices paid by high-income energy-conscious citizens and businesses, or other forms of financial investment, renewables are an attractive future source of energy and therefore of job creation.

In conclusion, the specific skills required to support RE are dependent on what targets are set, and whether government will eventually adopt a least-cost approach or a hybrid model supporting job creation.

Given the intensifying global debate on climate change, shifts in policy remain possible and could even extend to embracing higher targets for RE. In the 2003 *White Paper*, the DME committed itself to re-evaluating its RE targets and objectives after five years, to determine whether the policy direction remained appropriate; that is, that review can be expected in 2008. The preferred mix of RE technologies and related job and skills requirements can then be determined with greater confidence.

The supply of skills for the electrical energy sector

Enterprise training in South Africa

The *Human Resources Development Review* conducted by the HSRC and published in 2003, revealed that enterprise training fell from a high of 260 000 on average in 1986–1990 to a low of under 60 000 between 1996 and 1998 (HSRC 2003). At the same time, the training of apprentices in terms of the 'structured apprenticeship model' declined from 10 758 in 1991 to 3 129 in 1999 (Kraak 2007).

The Skills Development Act and the Employment Equity Act, as well as the 23 SETAs, established a single national regulatory framework for sectoral training and skills development processes.

A rapid rise in learnerships showed a fourfold increase in the number of learners achieving NQF Level 1, from 111 367 in 2002/03 to 433 437 in 2003/04 (DoL 2005). Enrolment in structured training also increased, and the number of registered learnerships almost tripled to 69 308 in 2003/04. This number fell just short of the 72 908 targeted by the Growth and Development Summit (Daniels 2007).

Two-thirds of companies surveyed by the National Business Initiative early in 2007 were found to be accredited skills training centres, although the 'vast majority of programmes are not directly related to SETA initiatives' (NBI 2007: 84).

On balance, it is clear that substantial progress has been made in reversing the historical decline in enterprise training in South Africa over the past decade or so, but it is also clear that much work remains to be done.

Supply of graduates from further education institutions

There has been a dramatic upsurge in enrolments from the FET colleges since 1990, as well as from the universities. The DoL observes that universities of technology (formerly known as technikons) produce more engineering, science and business graduates than the universities (DoL 2003).

At NQF Levels 0–3, between 1996 and 2005, the low-level pre-matric output of engineering studies courses saw a steady increase in electrical trade theory qualifications, almost doubling from 12 688 to 21 097. Most of the output in electrical trade theory was at NQF Levels 1 and 2, with NQF Level 3 output being very small and in decline (Figure 8.6).

At NQF Levels 4 and 5, engineering studies have been dominated by industrial electronics and engineering science, with an output of approximately 14 000 qualifications per annum. Of these, engineering science has been showing an upward trend.

At NQF Level 5, Industrial Electronics also dominated N6 output, as shown in Figure 8.7.

Supply of graduates from higher education institutions

At NQF levels 1–3 graduate output of electrical engineers and technologists from the HET institutions (NQF Levels 6–8) has shown an encouraging upward trend since 2001, particularly with regard to the National Diploma (NDip) qualification, which in 2005 boasted 1 179 graduates.

FIGURE 8.6: *Changing NQF levels of Electrical Trades Theory output from FET colleges, 1996–2005*

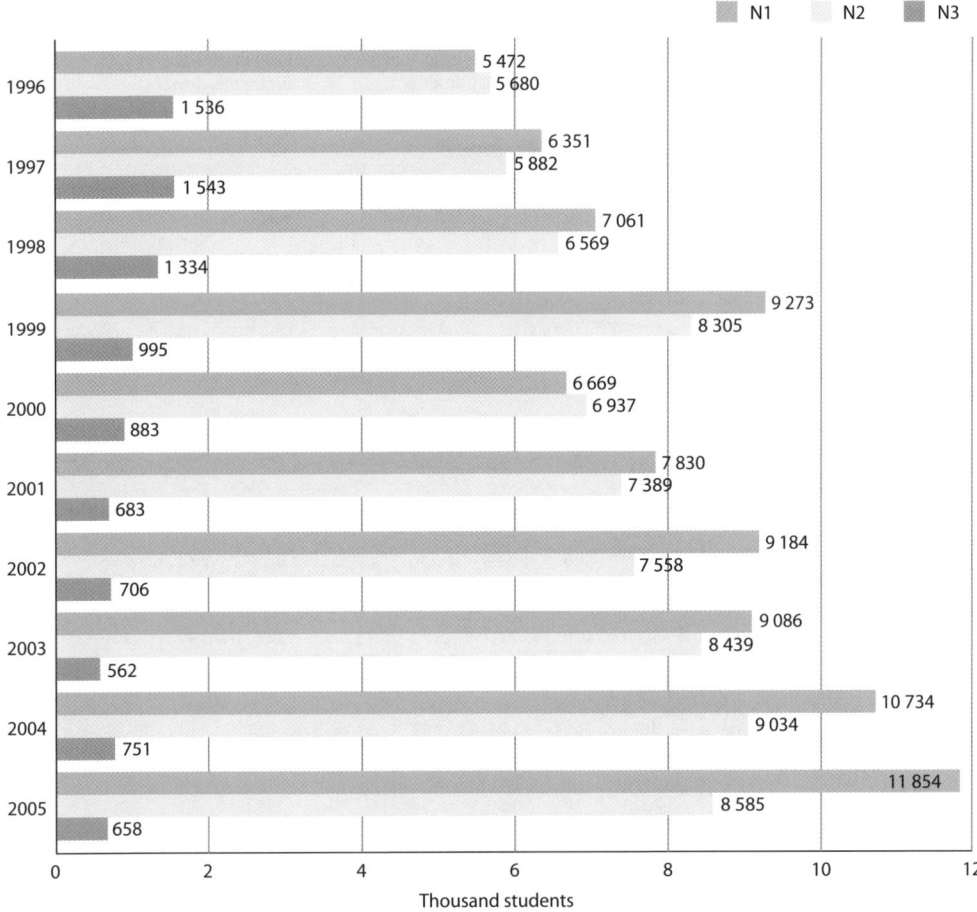

Source: DoE 2007b

A steady increase has taken place since 2001 in respect of the Bachelor of Technology (BTech) degree (264 graduates in 2005) and the master's degree (182 graduates in 2005). By 2005, over 65 per cent of NDip graduates in Electrical Engineering and Technology were African.

Africans made up only 11 per cent of professional bachelor's degree graduates in 1996, but that proportion had more than doubled by 2005 to 27 per cent of 447 graduates. The same trend was observed in respect of the third-most popular degree, the BTech. Whereas Africans made up 14 per cent of BTech graduates in 1996, that proportion had risen to 52 per cent by 2005.

The annual combined output of postgraduates in electrical engineering increased from 118 in 1996 to 239 in 2005, of whom 32 per cent in 2005 were black (i.e. African, Indian and coloured). The proportion of women graduating with the popular National Diploma in Electrical Engineering and Technology had increased from 5 per cent in 1996 to 19 per cent in 2005.

FIGURE 8.7: *N6 output in engineering studies from FET colleges, 1996–2005*

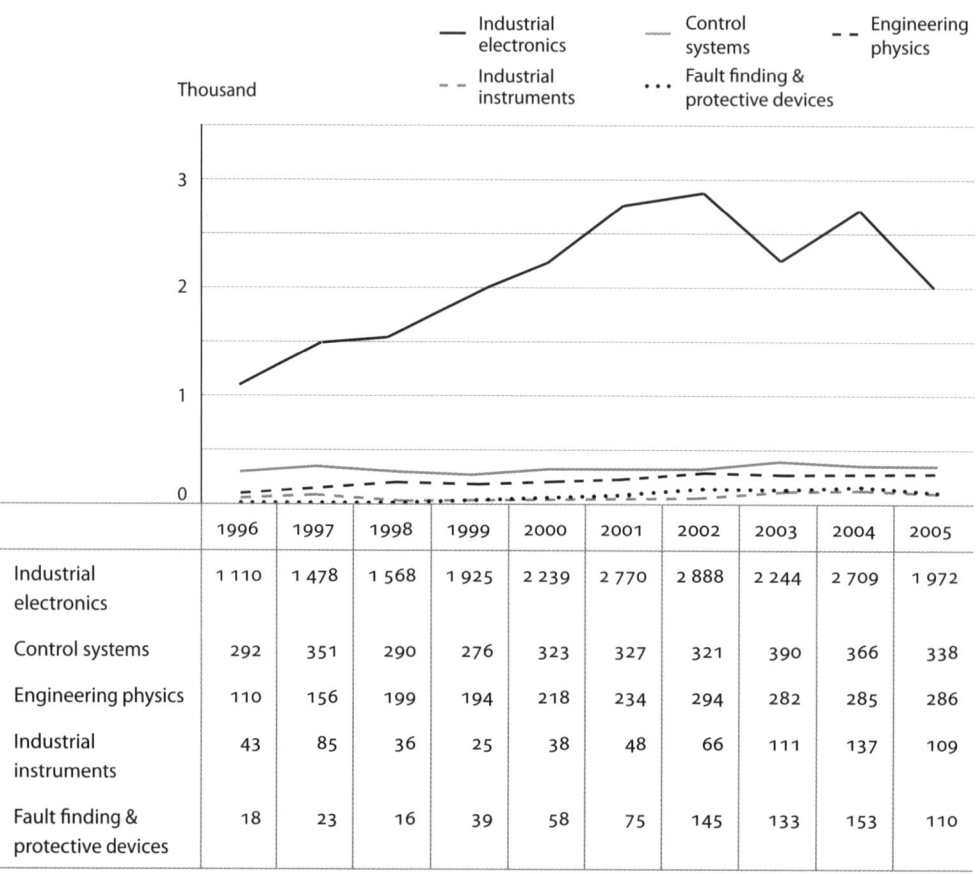

	1996	1997	1998	1999	2000	2001	2002	2003	2004	2005
Industrial electronics	1 110	1 478	1 568	1 925	2 239	2 770	2 888	2 244	2 709	1 972
Control systems	292	351	290	276	323	327	321	390	366	338
Engineering physics	110	156	199	194	218	234	294	282	285	286
Industrial instruments	43	85	36	25	38	48	66	111	137	109
Fault finding & protective devices	18	23	16	39	58	75	145	133	153	110

Source: DoE 2007b

Higher education outputs for renewable energy

In 2005, only 80 candidates graduated with the National Diploma in Renewable Energy, 75 with the professional bachelor's degree and 52 with the BTech, although a strong upward trend has been evident since 2003. There have been no graduates in nuclear engineering and technology over the past 10 years.

Implications

The implications of these supply trends in the output of graduates from FET and HET institutions over the past 10 years are as follows:
- The greatest bulk of engineering output from FET colleges is at the pre-matric skills level, NQF Levels 1 and 2, suggesting that further up-skilling may be needed in the work environment before these students can perform effectively.
- Most of the intermediate matric/post-school (NQF Levels 4–5) FET output has been dominated by industrial electronics and, to a lesser extent, engineering science, suggesting that the electricity sector will need to look to these disciplines for skilled resources at this level.

- There has been a substantial improvement over the past five years in the supply of electrical engineering diplomates from HET institutions, particularly among Africans and, more recently, women; there has also been a modest improvement in numbers of postgraduates of all racial categories.
- The supply of graduates skilled to support renewable and nuclear energy technology sources is low, but may contribute to meeting the limited demand of four per cent of energy requirements; however, if the demand for resources escalates rapidly in response to growing awareness of environmental issues, the available skills output will probably not be sufficient to meet such an escalation.

Matching skills supply and demand

As part of the present research, a matching exercise was conducted, drawing together the findings in respect of occupational demand data and those relating to the supply of output from educational institutions. The results are presented in Table 8.2.

Table 8.2 indicates that:
- the supply of NQF Level 3 low-level skills may not meet demand and will need to be boosted through in-house training;
- the quantity of supply of output from FET and HET institutions will be more than adequate to meet the intermediate skills needs of the electrical energy sector over the next five years;
- there will be a shortage of high-level professional and managerial skills in the first few years of the expansion programme, but this situation can be expected to improve over time;
- in respect of renewable and nuclear options, a shortage of skills can be expected, as these options come to enjoy increasing attention in future energy policy.

Linkages in the labour market

The alignment of supply and demand for skills in the energy sector is not just a question of matching numbers, but is also dependent on effective governance in the labour market to 'join up' learners and graduates with jobs.

The South African labour market is characterised by the paradox of a widely claimed skills shortage, together with high levels of unemployment among skilled and semi-skilled work-seekers.

The DoL's 2003 report on the 'State of Skills' noted that at least 1.3 million unemployed people had a Grade 12/matriculation or equivalent qualification, mainly in the age group 15–34 years (DoL 2003). The same point was made in its 2005 review of the labour market – matriculants made up 34 per cent of the pool of registered unemployed, and 21 000 unemployed people were qualified in the manufacturing-engineering-technology field alone (DoL 2005).

The HSRC has also established that only 34 per cent of all FET graduates have found employment after graduation (Kraak 2007). Tertiary graduates make up 2.6 per cent of the unemployed, and most unemployed graduates (85 per cent) are African. Of the 134 223 learnerships registered between 2001 and 2005, 66 per cent of those who registered were unemployed (Kraak 2007).

Kraak ascribes this state of affairs to the absence of an effective 'structured pathway into employment'. Formerly, many students were sponsored by employers and had access to shop-floor training. Today, however, most students study full-time without sponsorships, and then move into the vast, unstructured labour market to find work.

TABLE 8.2: *Comparison and assessment of skills demand and supply in the electrical energy sector to 2012*

NQF levels	Demand (estimated no. of new jobs)	Supply (annual output from FET/HET institutions)	Assessment
1–3 Low-level (pre-matric)	4 447	Fewer than 1 000 qualify annually with NQF Level 3. Close to 20 000 qualify annually with NQF Levels 1 and 2.	Poor supply of NQF Level 3 graduates. However, Eskom has an established learnership programme for Levels 2 and 3.
4–5 Intermediate (matric/post-school)	20 329	Over 20 000 people qualify annually from FET institutions in electrical trades, power station science and theory.	Supply likely to meet demand. However, the quality of output and relevance of training materials are concerns, and are partly being addressed through Jipsa working groups.
6–8 High-level (degree equivalent)	6 988	Over 1 000 people qualify annually with the National Diploma in Electrical Energy from HET institutions. Over 400 graduates qualify annually with the professional bachelor's degree in electrical engineering, over half of whom are African. Over 200 graduate annually with the BTech. There are over 200 electrical engineering postgraduates per annum from HET institutions. There are up to 21 000 unemployed graduates in engineering and manufacturing. Fewer than 100 graduates qualify annually with the National Diploma in Renewable Energy, the professional bachelor's degree and the BTech, respectively. There have been no recorded graduates in Nuclear Engineering and Technology since 1996.	For conventional electrical technology, there will be an initial shortage of high-level skills, given the rapid expansion of the sector to address electricity supply problems. The cumulative year-on-year supply of graduates should approach demand by 2012 or later. In respect of skills for renewables and nuclear options, there is a poor match, which may not be sufficient to meet (increased) demand.

Note: The demand estimate was obtained by multiplying the Eskom-linked projected growth of the sector (discussed earlier in the chapter) with the occupational ratios developed in Table 8.1. The supply projections were based on an analysis of the DoE 2007a HEMIS and DoE 2007b FET databases.

To remedy this 'dysfunctionality', Kraak (2007) argues that there is a need for better co-ordination between the DoL and the DoE, together with improved alignment between the SETAs, local and provincial government and employers. One solution, in his view, could be the promotion of localised structured labour markets.

A review by the Development Policy Research Unit (DPRU) at the University of Cape Town observed in this respect that the SETAs provided a (potentially) coherent framework for linking training across national, sectoral and enterprise levels, mainly through workplace skills plans (WSPs), and argued that this was an 'under-valued' aspect of SETA functioning (Daniels 2007). The DPRU report also called for improved co-ordination between the DoL and the DoE, together with partnerships between government, FET colleges and industries to resolve the problem.

The problem of co-ordination has also been acknowledged in the National Industrial Policy Framework, released by the Department of Trade and Industry (DTI) in 2007 (DTI 2007). In the section of the framework dealing with skills (Section 10), the need for greater co-ordination between the development and implementation of sector strategies and the corresponding SETAs was emphasised.

As far as the labour market for electrical energy is concerned, the sector is dominated by one major entity, namely Eskom. Compared to other sectors, co-ordination between the utility, the Energy Sector Education and Training Authority (ESETA), FET institutions, universities and government, should not pose too great a challenge.

However, one cause for concern is the fact that the ESETA as a whole has had among the lowest training rates of all the SETAs. Only 13 per cent of workers in the energy sector underwent training in 2002/03 (the average is 24 per cent; the mining SETA ranks highest at 59 per cent; see McGrath & Paterson 2007). Furthermore, only 28 per cent of companies in the ESETA claimed training grants in 2002/03, which was also below the national average of 41 per cent. There were also comparatively fewer companies with WSPs in the ESETA (DoL 2003).

It should be noted that the ESETA differs from the electrical energy sector being reviewed here, in that gas and water supplies, sanitation and services are included in the ESETA.

According to the ESETA's Energy Sector Skills Plan for 2005–2010, the electricity, gas, steam and hot water supply industry was expected to grow at 3.2 per cent per annum (the plan did not consider the need for increasing generation capacity in its scope). The sector was expected to need computer skills, as well as renewable and nuclear expertise. RE in particular was expected to call on engineers, environmentalists and technicians, among others (ESETA 2005b).

A wide range of skills was described in the ESETA plan as critical or scarce, including project management, financial management and information technology, artisans, fitters, computer operators and others, together with the 'softer' skills of leadership, change management and HIV/AIDS awareness, among others.

The ESETA report also noted that RE offered the greatest opportunities for electricity-related ventures involving small business and entrepreneurial opportunities, especially in the rural context (ESETA 2005b: 47).

In summary, it is clear that more needs to be done with respect to building closer working relationships between the different stakeholders in the South African electrical energy sector, so that defined linkages can be established to ensure the effective linking up of learners, diplomates and graduates with job opportunities for mutual benefit.

Overall sector outlook

The most outstanding feature of the electrical energy sector is the planned expansion of the sector to meet the country's growing energy requirements.

The country's premier utility, Eskom, is embarking on a capital investment programme to boost generation capacity by at least 10 909 MW by 2012 and to eventually double current generation capacity by 2025. At the same time, government plans are to ensure that at least 4 per cent of the projected megawatt target for 2013 is sourced from renewable forms of energy. Thereafter, renewable targets could be extended to represent a more substantial part of the new capacity planned for 2025.

A twofold skills challenge is therefore presented: on the one hand to support conventional generation expansion, and on the other, to make the first significant shift towards new technologies for harnessing RE. On the face of it, the skills requirements seem daunting. Will the country be able to supply the necessary skills for the expansion and technological transformation of the electrical energy sector over the next five years?

This research has found that in the case of low-level skills, there will be insufficient Level 3 trainee output from FET colleges, which will need to be remedied with workplace learnerships and on-the-job training.

In the case of intermediate skills in crafts, trades and technical skills, the quantity of supply from educational institutions is likely to meet demand over the next five years, although the quality of the training received may vary and would require further shop-floor up-skilling to upgrade competencies.

In the case of high-level skills, an initial shortage of graduate managers and professionals can be expected as the sector undergoes rapid expansion over the next five years. Over time, however, the year-on-year supply of high-level managers and professionals should start approaching demand towards 2012 or later.

The research has also established that there will be a significant shortage of skills to support the increased use of RE in the foreseeable future. The same can be said for nuclear options.

Bottlenecks and remedies affecting supply of skills

Certain key bottlenecks have been identified with respect to the provision of skills for the electrical energy sector. These bottlenecks relate to three key themes, namely:
- the development of the informal electricity sector and small, medium and micro enterprises (SMMEs);
- co-ordination between stakeholders and market linkages;
- skills for renewables and nuclear energy.

The informal sector and SMMEs

This research has found that the informal and self-employment sector in the South African electricity industry is poorly developed, and the initial impact of the electrification process on informal employment has not been sustained.

Going forward, it is vital that the informal sector becomes directly engaged in providing appropriate services to support the industry's capital expansion programme. Any failure to ensure growth in informal employment in the context of the expansion of the industry will represent a crucial loss of opportunity for job creation in the country.

To address this blockage, a start should be made by obtaining more reliable information on the informal energy sector, on the one hand, and SMMEs on the other.

There is very little information available on the number and type of SMMEs in the electricity sector, covering products and services, skills bases, challenges and opportunities. In the course of surveying SMMEs, the linkages between them and a wider network of informal suppliers and smaller businesses can be tracked, with a view to improving knowledge of the informal sector in general and identifying the skills and services which are on offer and which can be boosted and incorporated into the formal economy.

Apart from the need for further research on this aspect, ways also need to be found for the informal sector and SMMEs to link up more directly with the formal sector, as part of the process of identifying new opportunities and services in the context of expanding electrical energy supplies. These opportunities can be identified in both the conventional and the RE supply markets, including the supply and maintenance of insulated wire and cable, motors and transformers, and distribution apparatus on the one hand, and solar PV, solar water heaters and biofuels on the other.

Co-ordination

Thus far, co-ordination between stakeholders in the electrical energy sector has reportedly been poor. As the sector embarks on a massive expansion programme, there is a clear need for closer alignment and co-ordination between government, the Eskom utility, the ESETA, IPPs, SMMEs, colleges and universities.

From this perspective, it is heartening that Eskom and the ESETA have developed a closer working relationship in recent times, but also clear that more needs to be done, including the following:
- pool resources for training;
- collaborate to ensure a better quality of output from educational institutions;
- establish more partnerships with SMMEs with a view to assisting in extending skills training and development through the sector;
- develop more effective linkages for connecting learners, diplomates and graduates with available job opportunities.

Skills for renewables and nuclear energy

This research has found that there are insufficient diplomates and graduates from FET and HET institutions respectively, with qualifications relevant to RE.

It is clear that interest in the field of renewable and nuclear energy has yet to take root among prospective students, with the result that skills shortages can be expected in these areas as alternative sources of energy become more widely developed and applied.

One barrier in this respect is the lack of clarity on the future direction that the country should take in respect of renewables, and nuclear energy, for that matter. The current target for RE development is widely accepted as being too modest, and pressure is likely to grow to set higher targets for renewables in the context of global warming.

Government will need to commit soon to a firm policy on the desired target, together with a vision and objectives for nuclear energy.

It is recommended that in the course of conducting its scheduled follow-up review in 2008 of the renewable energy target, the DME should be requested to propose a firm 'mix' of RE technologies, so that the specific skills requirements can be identified and planned for by the sector, within the relevant WSPs and the overall skills plan for the sector. Until that happens, the specific skills requirements cannot easily be determined and renewables will not be viewed as a recognised career and field of study among potential students.

A campaign can then be mounted by the DME, in collaboration with the ESETA and Eskom, to promote student enrolments in the field of renewable and nuclear energy across FET and HET institutions.

References

Agama Energy (2003) *Employment potential of renewable energy in South Africa*. Cape Town: Agama Energy

Daniels RC (2007) *Skills shortages in South Africa: A literature review*. DPRU Working Paper 07/121, Development Policy Research Unit, University of Cape Town

DME (Department of Minerals and Energy, South Africa) (2003) *White paper on renewable energy*. Pretoria: DME

DME (2004) *Capacity building in energy efficiency and renewable energy*. Report No. 2.3.4–19. Pretoria: DME

DoE (Department of Education, South Africa) (2007a) *Higher Education Management Information System(HEMIS) database 1999–2005*. Pretoria: DoE

DoE (2007b) *FET output 1996–2005*. Pretoria: DoE

DoL (Department of Labour, South Africa) (2003) *The state of skills in South Africa*. Pretoria: DoL

DoL (2005) *Labour market review*. Pretoria: DoL

DTI (Department of Trade and Industry, South Africa) (2007) *A National Industrial Policy Framework*. Pretoria: DTI

EDI Holdings (2008) *The electricity distribution industry*. Accessed February 2008, http://www.ediholdings.co.za

ESETA (Energy Sector Education and Training Authority) (2005a) *ESETA Annual report for 2005*. Johannesburg: ESETA

ESETA (2005b) *Energy sector skills plan 2005–2010*. Johannesburg: ESETA

Eskom (2006) *Annual report for 2006*. Pretoria: Eskom

Eskom (2007) *Eskom's electrification programme in South Africa*. Accessed August 2007, www.eskom.co.za

GCIS (Government Communication Information Service, South Africa) (2006) *South Africa yearbook 2005/06*. Johannesburg: STE Publishers & GCIS

HSRC (2003) *Human Resources Development Review 2003. Education, Employment and skills in South Africa*. Cape Town: HSRC Press

Kraak A (2007) Three pathways to intermediate skilling. In A Kraak & K Press (eds) *Human resources development review 2008: Education, employment and skills in South Africa*. Cape Town: HSRC Press

McGrath S & Paterson A (2007) Enterprise training. In A Kraak & K Press (eds) *Human resources development review 2008: Education, employment and skills in South Africa*. Cape Town: HSRC Press

NBI (National Business Initiative) (2007) *Skills development: The role of business*. Johannesburg: NBI

NERSA (National Electricity Regulator of South Africa) (2004) *Electricity supply statistics*. Pretoria: NERSA

Quantec (2007) *RSA regional indicators database*. Accessed June 2007, http://www.quantec.co.za/data

Stats SA (Statistics South Africa) (1996–1999) *October Household Surveys (OHS)*. Pretoria: Stats SA

Stats SA (2000–2005) *Labour Force Surveys (LFS)*. Pretoria: Stats SA

Stone & Webster Management Consultants Incorporated (2005) *Efficiency and capital expenditure/investment plan study of Eskom transmission*. Consultancy report prepared for the National Electricity Regulator of South Africa (NERSA)

The Presidency (Republic of South Africa) (2006a) *Annual report of the Accelerated Shared Growth Initiative for South Africa (Asgisa)*. Pretoria: The Presidency

The Presidency (2006b) *Annual report of the Joint Initiative on Priority Skills Acquisition (Jipsa)*. Pretoria: The Presidency

CHAPTER 9

Transport

Jan Havenga

Introduction

Any economy that wants to perform (usually described as aspiring towards growth, employment and a stable balance of payments) requires specific inputs or production factors. These are usually identified as infrastructure and resources, labour and training, capital and innovation and enterprise management (Samuelson & Nordhaus 1989: 24, 77). South Africa's performance in terms of these factors is often reported in various international benchmark studies, of which the *Global Competitiveness Report* is probably the most well known (WEF 2007–2008). In terms of this report, the country does not perform well and recent ratings have deteriorated, especially for labour elements. (South Africa slipped from overall 36th place to 44th place out of 122 countries over the last two years, with education and health in 56th place, labour market efficiency in 78th place and health and primary education in 117th place). The infrastructure issue has been discussed in detail in recent times, as South Africa faces increasing challenges in regard to electricity supply, transport infrastructure, sanitation, water management and telecommunications. Various investment programmes have been announced to address these deficiencies. Labour, and the training programmes that are required to improve this production factor, are not yet considered on this level and programmes such as the Sector Education and Training Authority (SETA) system have not been entirely successful (*Mail & Guardian* 24 April 2007, 30 July 2007).

This chapter considers the state of the labour production factor specifically in the transport, storage and communication (TSC) industry, which is especially important in this context as it relates directly to, amongst other things, the transport infrastructure issue. In fact, many observers are concerned about the success of the investment programme in this industry, in the absence of skills to drive investment and operations.

This chapter proposes a macro-economic framework for such an analysis, considers performance in terms of this framework, and suggests approaches to be taken in order for future improvements to occur.[1]

Methodology

In order to achieve the required objective, a data-driven approach is crucial, but as is common for many studies concerned with these issues (DoT 1998: 3, 5, 11, 178–179), data are scarce and in many

---

1   The chapter was prepared with assistance from collaborators Betty Simpson, Ilse Hobbs and Neil de Jager.

instances unavailable. This is compounded by the fact that the statistical data available from official sources such as Statistics South Africa (Stats SA) are poorly constructed and categorised incorrectly, and are therefore not useful in their current format. For the purposes of this study, it was therefore necessary to conduct interviews, specifically to obtain some of the data required to enable a critical evaluation, and to undertake desktop research and modelling of the data (based on secondary test cases) in order to fill the numerous gaps that existed. Apart from constructing the data sets, interviews and surveys were performed together with further desktop analysis to inform the critical analysis of the constructed data for the various components of the industry.

Industry utilities

It will not be possible to discuss the various components of the TSC industry, which includes many utilities, without a thorough demarcation of these utilities. Stats SA uses the standard industrial classification (SIC) system as a framework for data collection (Central Statistical Services 1993), which is an inherently sound approach (it facilitates comparisons with other studies), but the system has two major drawbacks: it is not new (and therefore does not reflect current realities); and each economy in the world has different accents.[2]

Figure 9.1 compares the actual utilities provided in the TSC industry with the SIC system on the second level and proposes a demarcation system that would be logical for discussion purposes.

The proposed system is utility-based, that is, 'needs'-based, which in this case refers to the need for the transport of either freight or people (as far as the transport sub-sector is concerned). 'Needs' translates into a utility that is provided by a service provider, solution or system. Any system that is evaluated in terms of its inputs and outputs has the measurement of output productivity at its heart (relating to the inputs consumed). In the transport sub-sector, for instance, this productivity can only be defined as tons shipped and passenger journeys.

The same argument can be used to demarcate the relationship between post and telecommunications, where outputs that can be used to analyse productivity are completely different for postal and telecommunications services, and these two sub-sectors are completely different from the transport sub-sector.

FIGURE 9.1: *Transport, storage and communication industry demarcation system*

Utilities in the TSC	Passenger transport	Freight transport	Other logistics and storage activities	Tele-communications	Postal services
SIC	Transport sub-sector			Communications sub-sector	
		Storage sub-sector			
Proposed logical demarcation	Transport sub-sector			Telecommunications sub-sector	Postal sub-sector

---

2 A complete discussion on the deficiencies of the SIC system, and the demarcation and analysis problems created by Stats SA's application thereof, is included in the full report on the TSC prepared for the HSRC (Havenga 2008).

On the highest level the most logical demarcation in the industry should be between transport, telecommunications and postal services, followed by a high-level split between passenger and freight transport.

The status quo

The current performance of the TSC industry production factor is considered here by looking at employment demand, employment supply, skills levels and labour productivity factors (Figure 9.2).

'Demand' describes actual current employment levels, 'supply' considers the quality of training input and availability of skills, 'skill levels' analyses the actual level of skills of current employment, and 'productivity' analyses outputs to try and establish how labour productivity is performing in this sector.

Demand

Figure 9.3 depicts formal employment growth in the TSC industry according to official statistics. (Index measures are used in many of the graphs in this chapter. An index measure shows variance in a key variable – such as employment or tonkilometre per worker – across a number of years following the baseline year of 1996. A decline in the index implies an equivalent increase of the baseline value of 1996. The actual numbers of the variable are also provided in the tables below figures.)

Figure 9.3 shows that, after an initial decline that lasted until 2000, formal employment has risen steadily, but is still below 1995 levels.

Employment according to the three logical sub-sectors is depicted in Figure 9.4.

The changes in the distribution of the workforce relative to the three sub-sectors over the last decade show that only the transport sub-sector grew to levels higher than those of a decade ago. By 2005, 79 per cent of formal employment in the sector was in transport. The remainder of this chapter will focus mainly on analysis of the transport industry, as demarcated in this way.

The telecommunications sub-sector in South Africa has shown considerable growth, especially in terms of technology concomitant with global improvements in communication technology such as enhanced bandwidth and broadband, wireless technology and fixed wire/wireless and voice/data

FIGURE 9.2: *Relationship between employment demand, employment supply, skills and labour productivity*

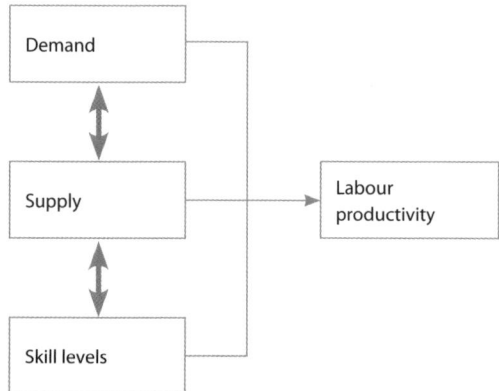

FIGURE 9.3: *Formal employment growth of the TSC industry, 1996–2005*

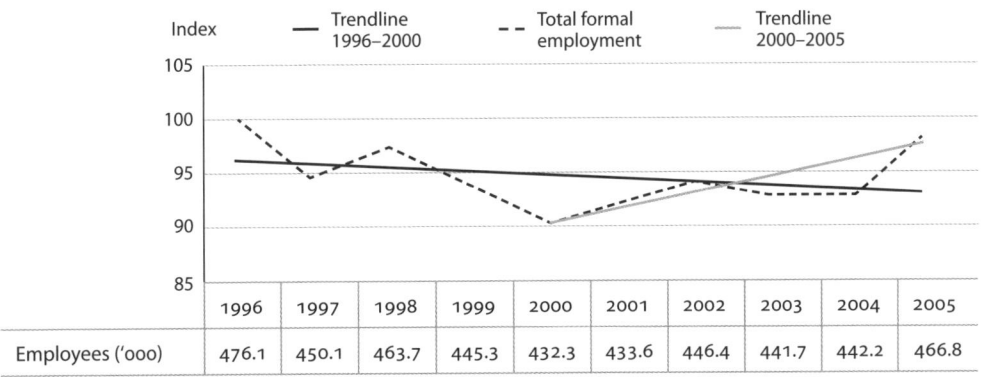

	1996	1997	1998	1999	2000	2001	2002	2003	2004	2005
Employees ('000)	476.1	450.1	463.7	445.3	432.3	433.6	446.4	441.7	442.2	466.8

Source: Stats SA 1996–2005

FIGURE 9.4: *Comparison of formal employment in the transport, postal and telecommunications sub-sectors, 1996–2005*

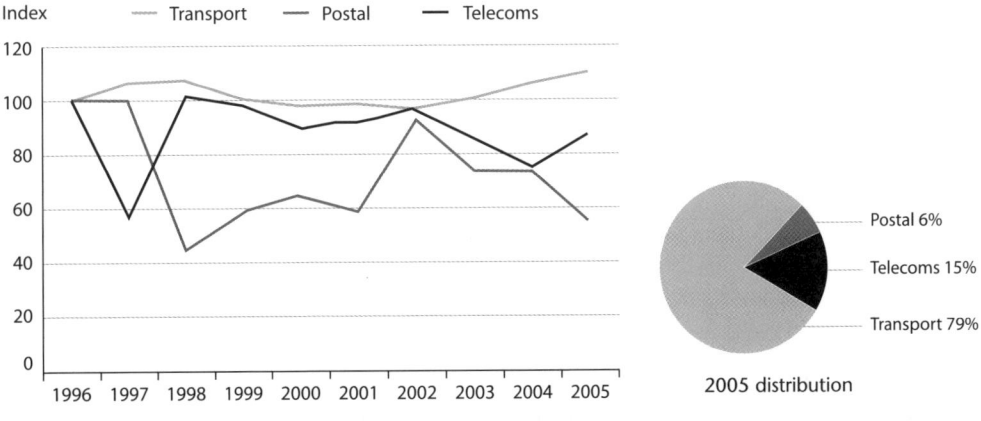

	Employees ('000)									
Sub-sectors	1996	1997	1998	1999	2000	2001	2002	2003	2004	2005
Transport	340.0	356.3	359.9	336.9	327.1	330.3	323.3	336.3	355.4	368.8
Postal	49.4	48.5	21.6	28.5	31.8	28.5	45.1	35.8	35.8	27.1
Telecoms	82.2	45.3	82.3	80.0	73.3	74.9	78.1	69.6	60.9	70.9

Source: Stats SA 1996–2005

conversion. South Africa's transport sub-sector benefits less from global improvements, and is experiencing serious congestion, cost and capacity challenges. This situation might explain why transport employment growth is faster than for the other two sub-sectors, where automation is more prevalent.[3]

---

3   For a full discussion on the ICT industry, which includes telecommunication, see Chapter 14 in this volume.

FIGURE 9.5: *Estimated formal employment split between passenger and freight transport, 1995–2005*

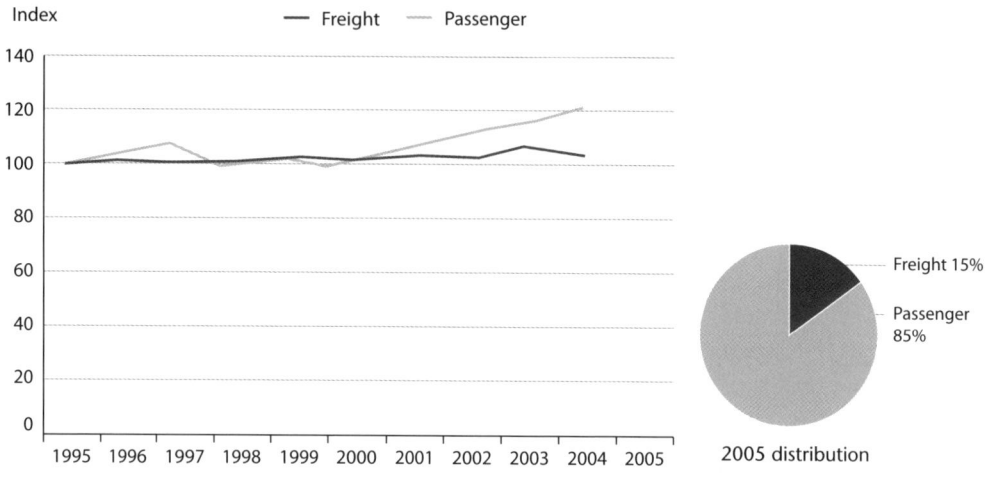

	Number of employees (thousands)										
Transport	1995	1996	1997	1998	1999	2000	2001	2002	2003	2004	2005
Freight	61.4	61.6	61.8	62.0	62.3	62.5	62.7	62.9	63.2	64.9	63.5
Passenger	302.0	312.0	321.9	298.4	303.6	298.6	311.7	324.7	337.8	350.9	363.9

Sources: De Wet 2003: 19; Stats SA 2002; University of Stellenbosch modelling 2008; unpublished Transnet statistics

Postal employment is declining as a result of the declining nature of the original technology for postal services. Advances in postal technology are included in the telecommunications sub-sector and sometimes even in the business services group of the SIC system, leaving the postal sub-sector with a declining usage base.

Many of the service components of postal services (e.g. hardware and software supplied for faxing, video conferencing, etc.) are also excluded from the SIC code and included in other groups, further explaining the declining nature of the sub-sector.

The transport sub-sector is further disaggregated in the freight and passenger utilities, as depicted in Figure 9.5.

Passenger transport is driven by a growing second economy supported by migrant labour and porous borders. Freight transport remains constant as a result of structural problems in the freight transport market that have not yet been addressed.

Informal employment in the transport sub-sector is high, but only a small portion of this is reported in recorded official statistics. Unrecorded statistics (such as statistics for taxis) suggest that 10 times more people work in road passenger transport than the numbers reflected in recorded official statistics and that total informal employment for the TSC industry is around 50 per cent (Stats SA 2006).[4]

---

[4] Ntuli Z, Move to regulate taxi industry, 25 May 2005, http://www.southafrica.info/what_happening/news/taxidrivers.htm

Transformation strategy successes are mixed. Female employment is rising fast and an overall level of 22 per cent was reached by 2005, when fewer men were working in the industry than 10 years before, but the number of women had grown by 60 per cent. The employment distribution for all races has remained flat, except in the case of Indians, whose number has doubled from a low base (by 2005, 6 per cent of all workers were Indian). Between 1995 and 2002 the workforce became progressively older, but this trend was reversed in the last three years of the period.

In summary, demand-side analysis indicates that employment figures remained mainly flat or even declined slightly for the TSC industry, driven by declines in postal and telecommunications employment. Transport employment is growing slightly, but mostly because of passenger transport employment growth, which is the area with the most informal employment. The informal nature of employment (about half of employment in the TSC industry and almost all employment in passenger transportation is not measured) is disturbing, and poses a major challenge for planning. Female and Indian employment is rising, but other transformation challenges are not being met.

Supply

Supply-side challenges manifest themselves to a large extent in the mismatch of skills, insofar as the characteristics of the available pool of potential employees do not satisfy labour demand regarding specific qualifications and skills. This is the result of, amongst other things, the debatable quality of training institutions and teaching capital, incorrect and/or inappropriate fields of study offered by training institutions, the lack and/or incompleteness of over-arching management information on the labour market (this is fragmented and incomplete), the inability of learners to make the transition from school to further education and training (FET) facilities, universities and universities of technology, as well as insufficient communication and collaboration between enterprises and training institutions.

While approximately 25 per cent of South Africa's budget is allocated to education, some schools still lack basic services, learning materials and teachers (The Presidency 2007).[5] A major deficiency is teacher skills; a substantial number of South Africa's public-school teachers are under-qualified and only 12 per cent have a postgraduate degree (DA 2006). The number of teachers has increased by 12 per cent, but the percentage with only a Grade 12 qualification has increased by 17 per cent and the percentage with a postgraduate qualification has decreased by 6 per cent (DA 2006).

Grade 12 pass rates have been improving steadily for most of the research period, though recent decreases have been recorded. The low learner skill levels caused by poor teaching skills are a bigger concern, and the actual number of learners who have passed mathematics decreased from 1995 to 2005, to very low levels (The Presidency 2007). Science, engineering and technology (SET) pass rates are better, and higher-grade pass rates have improved from 15 per cent to 25 per cent, which means that the actual number of SET graduates increased from under 4 000 in 2001 to over 11 000 in 2005 (DoL 2006).

It is often argued that the quality of South Africa's Grade 12s is not acceptable in a global context and could have negative effects on the economy. The low quality of Grade 12 education causes unemployment of school-leavers. Many school-leavers do not have marketable skills or training opportunities, meaning that, while young people suffer debilitating unemployment, there are half a million job vacancies that cannot be filled (DA 2006; Pandor 2005).[6] Grade 12-level unemployment rates have

---

5 Sapa, Skills survey slams SA education, 20 June 2007, http://www.iol.co.za/index.php?set_id=1&click_id=105&art_id=nw20070620131754606C434318
6 Sapa, Skills survey slams SA education, 20 June 2007,
   http://www.iol.co.za/index.php?set_id=1&click_id=105&art_id=nw20070620131754606C434318

increased from 25 per cent to 40 per cent since 1995 and tertiary-level unemployment rates from 6 per cent to 15 per cent (JCP International 2005).

Once learners with a Grade 12 certificate leave school, the next challenge is to receive a tertiary science and technology education. Businesses often report having to bring in skills from overseas for major projects, not because South Africa lacks the relevant skills, but because the quality of those skills is so poor that people needs to be retrained (DA 2006).

Figure 9.6 reflects the fields of study in engineering and transportation that contributed to graduate output from universities and technikons (now universities of technology) over the decade 1996–2005.

The growth rates for all fields (except marine engineering, growing fast from a low base) are unacceptable, and for many disciplines, they are lower than the growth rate of the economy over the same period. The percentage of students who obtained a tertiary qualification did, however, improve. The relative proportions of African and female graduates are improving as well.

FIGURE 9.6: *Fields of study in engineering and transportation, 1996–2005*

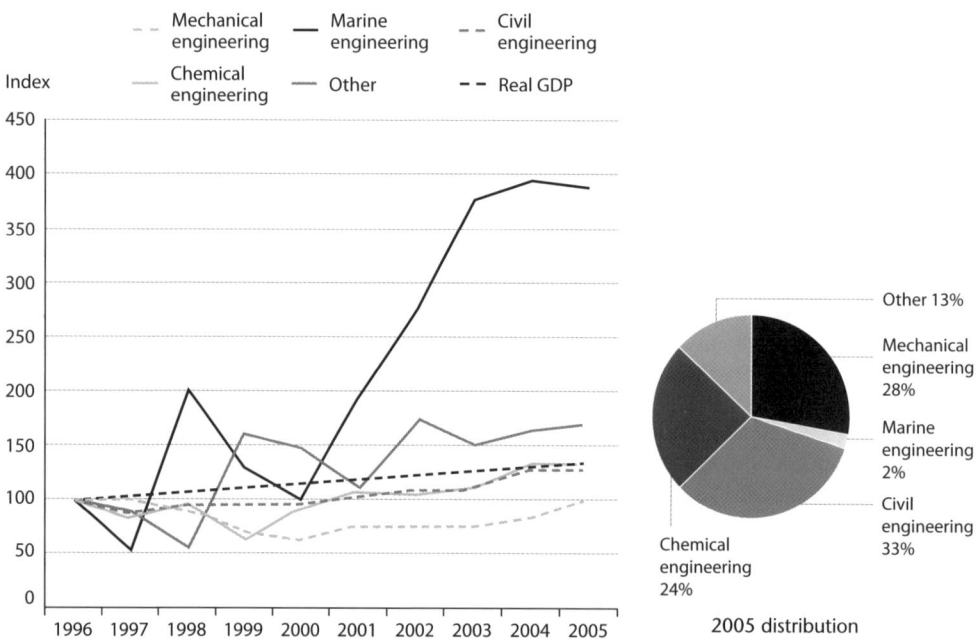

	Number of graduates									
Fields of study	1996	1997	1998	1999	2000	2001	2002	2003	2004	2005
Mechanical engineering	872	853	766	631	577	706	695	718	765	856
Marine engineering	13	7	26	17	13	25	36	49	51	50
Civil engineering	817	747	767	787	731	811	901	886	1043	1036
Chemical engineering	554	463	523	351	520	596	575	615	737	738
Other	244	210	130	392	353	272	421	364	397	413

Source: DoE 2007

In summary, supply-side analysis suggests that all indicators, in relationship to the economy, are declining. Grade 12 teaching inputs are poor and mathematics pass rates are still unacceptable. Numbers of engineering higher education and training graduates are far below what is needed in the economy, and the gap between current growth, required growth and what is actually being delivered is widening. At the same time, life expectancy is dropping and net migration is worsening over time. The TSC industry is, in fact, critically under-supplied in terms of skills.

Skill levels

Skill levels refer to current skills of workers already in the TSC industry. Skill bands have been identified in accordance with the National Qualifications Framework (NQF) schema by Kraak (2005).

The data drawn from the Stats SA October Household Surveys (OHS) and Labour Force Surveys (LFS) (Stats SA 1996–2005) indicate that half of the collective workforce holds less than a Grade 12 certificate, while 44 per cent hold a Grade 12, college and/or technikon/university of technology National

FIGURE 9.7: *Distribution of skills bands for the TSC industry (formal employment), 1996–2005*

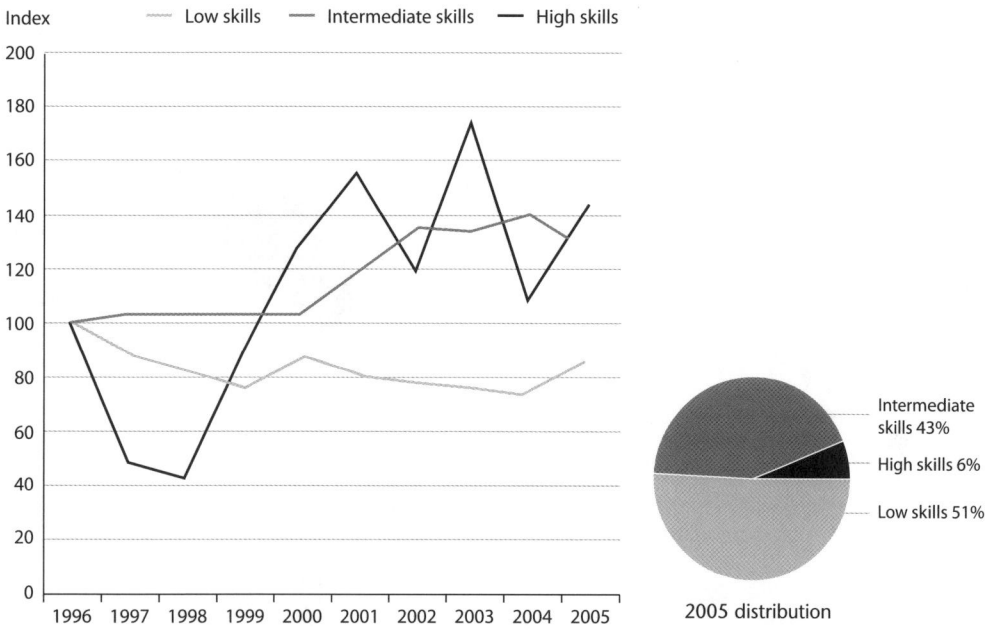

	Number of employees (thousands)									
Skills bands	1996	1997	1998	1999	2000	2001	2002	2003	2004	2005
Low skills	272.8	240.0	220.0	209.7	239.0	218.1	212.6	201.2	201.2	235.4
Intermediate skills	155.4	157.0	158.0	159.3	159.4	180.4	208.4	207.1	215.9	198.3
High skills	18.6	8.8	7.7	16.3	23.7	28.9	21.8	32.2	20.0	26.4

Source: Stats SA 1996–2005
Note: Values for 1997 and 1998 have been estimated for low and intermediate skills.

Certificate and/or Diploma. The remaining 6 per cent hold a higher educational qualification (that is, a bachelor's, honours, master's or doctoral degree).

Figure 9.7 reflects the average distribution of skills across the low, intermediate and high skills bands presented over the 10-year period 1996–2005.

The relative level of high skills has been improving since 1998. The persisting number of workers with low skills is a concern and requires consideration. This is also reflected by occupational category (Figure 9.8).

The low skills level of especially the large volume of operational employees, which includes drivers, engineers, machine operators and technicians, is of great concern.

FIGURE 9.8: *Low skills distribution of occupational category for the industry (formal employment), 2000–2005*

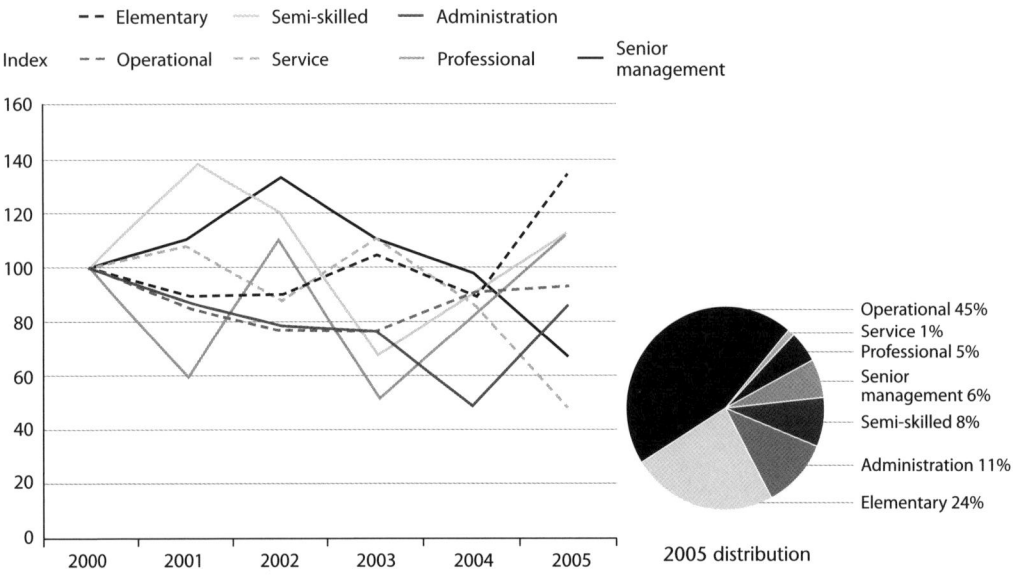

	Number of employees (thousands)					
Skills distribution	2000	2001	2002	2003	2004	2005
Elementary	40.4	35.9	36.5	42.1	35.4	54.4
Operational	112.5	95.5	86.5	86.7	101.3	104.9
Semi-skilled	16.8	22.8	20.0	11.3	15.1	18.3
Service	8.3	8.9	7.2	9.1	7.1	4.0
Administration	30.9	27.0	24.9	23.8	14.6	26.9
Professional	10.2	6.2	11.1	5.3	8.5	11.2
Senior management	19.8	21.8	26.1	21.8	19.2	13.3

Source: Stats SA 1996–2005

Labour productivity

Understanding labour productivity in the TSC industry, in order to inform scenarios for the future, proved to be a challenging task. It was possible to create freight and passenger transport productivity data with statistics from different sources and some modelling, which is helpful, since 79 per cent of TSC employment is in the transport sub-sector.

Freight transport labour productivity can be analysed by looking at road and rail freight tonkilometre produced per employee (Figure 9.9). (Other freight modes are very small and statistics even more difficult to obtain.)

The gap between rail and road freight productivity (which was half a million tonkilometres in 1995), had decreased to merely twenty thousand in 2005. When it is considered that rail freight input includes the infrastructure development and maintenance of the mode (not the case for road), rail freight employment productivity has improved the most and is now probably much better than that for road freight. Rail's capacity for automation is much higher than that of road, and as South Africa faces unique challenges in the next 50 years, this could pose a unique skills-set challenge.

Although rail freight productivity is slightly less than that for road freight, given that rail owns and maintains its own infrastructure, it is far higher than the global average (Figure 9.10).

FIGURE 9.9: *Growth in tonkilometres per worker compared to growth in real GDP, 1995–2005*

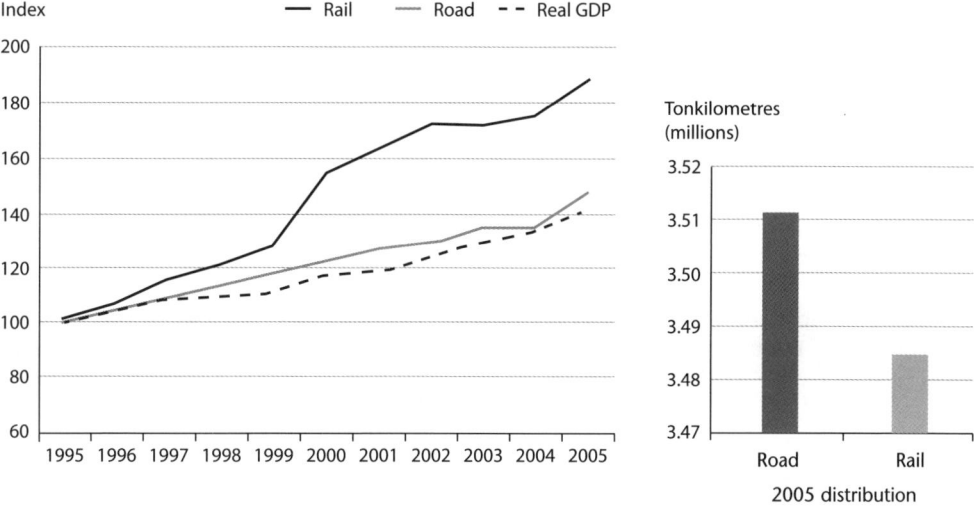

Tonkilometres (millions)	1995	1996	1997	1998	1999	2000	2001	2002	2003	2004	2005
Road	2.4	2.5	2.6	2.7	2.8	2.9	3.0	3.1	3.2	3.2	3.5
Rail	1.9	1.9	2.1	2.2	2.4	2.8	3.0	3.2	3.2	3.2	3.5
Real GDP (billions)	725.7	756.5	776.4	781.8	802.7	838.2	862.3	894.7	923.0	967.5	1 016.1

Sources: Havenga 2007: 147; University of Stellenbosch modelling 2008

FIGURE 9.10: *Tonkilometres per employee (two components of SA Rail compared to global railways)*

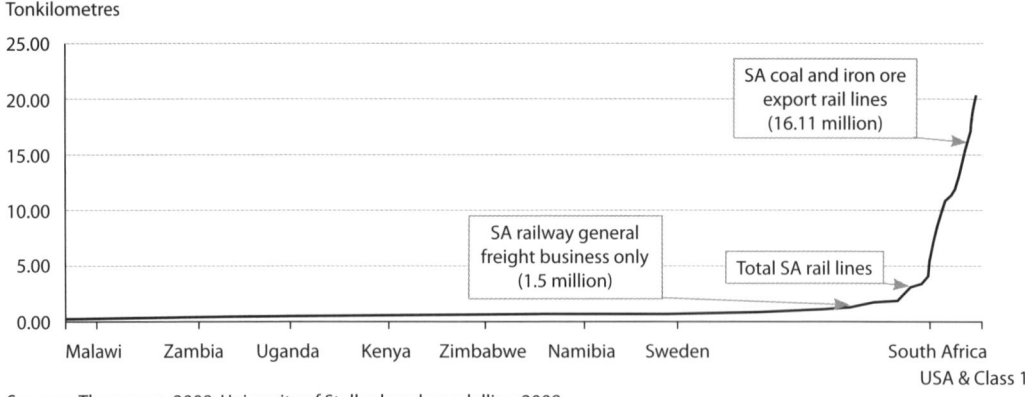

Sources: Thompson 2008; University of Stellenbosch modelling 2008

South Africa ranks fifth in the world in terms of rail employment productivity but unfortunately, because of our spatial challenges, probably needs to improve this position to be closer to that of USA Class 1 railways, in order to be globally competitive. (Except for perhaps Russia, South Africa is the most spatially challenged country in the world; the effects of this are discussed in relation to the future scenarios presented later in this chapter.) One solution proposed in the 1990s was to rationalise the railways and only retain highly densified portions of the network. As an extreme case in point, the tonkilometres per employee are depicted for a scenario in which the railroad is split into two parts, which in this case would be highly densified coal and iron ore export lines, and a less dense general freight business (GFB) railway.

Clearly the coal and iron ore export lines are highly competitive, but the challenge is to reconfigure the GFB business to achieve the same levels of employee productivity. As the railways rise to this challenge and achieve higher levels of density through regaining market share, intermodal solutions and some rationalisation, profound effects on productivity will be experienced, but equally profound skills level needs will arise.

This means that South Africa's freight transport system is currently focused on a highly effective road transport system, but this is not sustainable and growth in railway traffic will eventually have to be engineered.

The best available benchmark for overall economic productivity would be GDP produced per formal worker in South Africa compared to tonkilometre output for surface freight employment. In this regard, surface freight employment labour productivity outstrips overall economic productivity by far (Figure 9.11).

This means that whereas overall labour productivity in South Africa has declined (which in this case, unfortunately, has to be measured financially), road freight transport employment output has tracked real GDP, and rail freight employment output has surpassed it, mainly as a result of labour productivity. GDP improvements for the country are generally engineered by factors other than labour productivity.

This behaviour is caused by three drivers, that is, the capacity to improve, opportunities to rationalise labour, and the drive to exploit opportunities in a spatially challenged economy.

The position for passenger transport is quite different, as depicted in Figure 9.12.

FIGURE 9.11: *Growth in tonkilometres per worker compared to growth in real GDP per worker, 1995–2005*

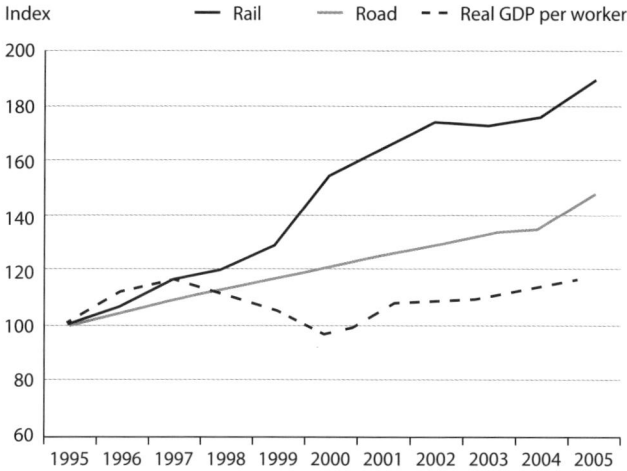

	1995	1996	1997	1998	1999	2000	2001	2002	2003	2004	2005
Road	2.4	2.5	2.6	2.7	2.8	2.9	3.0	3.1	3.2	3.2	3.5
Rail	1.9	1.9	2.1	2.2	2.4	2.8	3.0	3.2	3.2	3.2	3.5
GDP per worker (millions)	0.08	0.08	0.09	0.08	0.08	0.07	0.08	0.08	0.08	0.08	0.09

Sources: Havenga 2007: 147; Stats SA 2007; University of Stellenbosch modelling 2008

FIGURE 9.12: *Growth in passenger journeys per worker compared to growth in real GDP, 1995–2005*

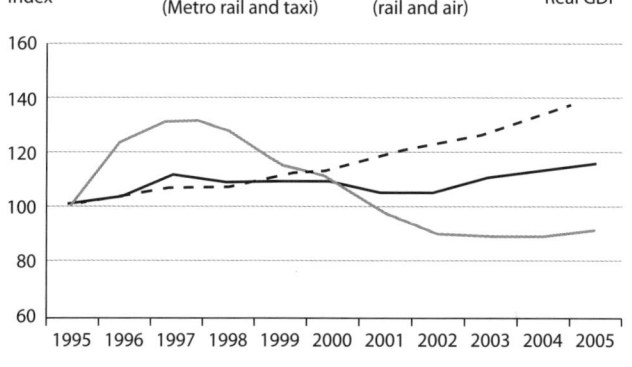
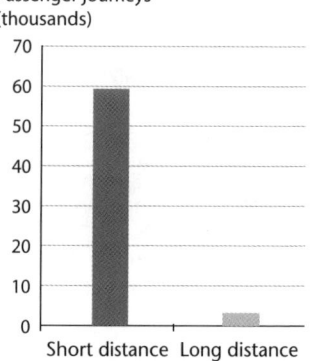

	1995	1996	1997	1998	1999	2000	2001	2002	2003	2004	2005
Short journeys (thousands)	51.6	53.1	56.7	55.6	56.1	56.0	53.8	53.6	56.7	58.1	59.6
Long journeys (thousands)	3.5	4.4	4.7	4.4	4.0	3.8	3.4	3.1	3.1	3.1	3.2
Real GDP (billions)	725.7	756.5	776.4	781.8	802.7	838.2	862.3	894.7	923.0	967.5	1 016.1

Source: University of Stellenbosch modelling 2008

FIGURE 9.13: *Growth in passenger journeys per worker compared to growth in real GDP per worker, 1995–2005*

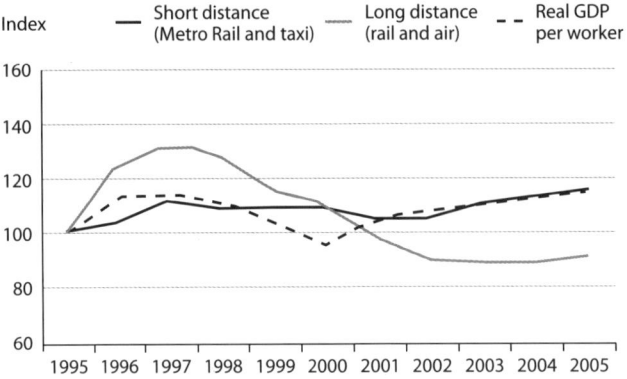

	1995	1996	1997	1998	1999	2000	2001	2002	2003	2004	2005
Short journeys (thousands)	51.6	53.1	56.7	55.6	56.1	56.0	53.8	53.6	56.7	58.1	59.6
Long journeys (thousands)	3.5	4.4	4.7	4.4	4.0	3.8	3.4	3.1	3.1	3.1	3.2
Real GDP per worker (millions)	0.08	0.08	0.09	0.08	0.08	0.07	0.08	0.08	0.08	0.08	0.09

Source: University of Stellenbosch modelling 2008

Passenger transport in South Africa is sub-optimally configured, with private car transport escalating and public transport services being under-developed and under-utilised. The congestion problems associated with this transport behaviour are well known, but the inefficiencies that it causes in the economy are not always noticeable.

Long-distance passenger transport productivity is largely responsible for the negative correlation with GDP (Figure 9.13).

Short-distance passenger transport is mostly provided by solutions such as taxis. The demand for taxi journeys will correlate well with GDP because the shift from poverty to affluence has not yet materialised in the South African economy. It is also easy to increase capacity of this mode of transport. In addition, taxi drivers also have to work longer shifts, with the obvious related negative employment satisfaction and safety implications (Figure 9.14).

For long-distance transport (Figure 9.15), the rail solution is close to collapse and a growing number of people use private cars for long-distance travel. Air travel employment productivity, as depicted by passenger journeys per worker, remains constant.

Air passenger transport productivity improvements are technologically difficult to achieve, given the complexities of the industry. Aircraft sizes remain the same and the same crew size is always required.

Theoretically, railway productivity as depicted by long-distance railway journeys per employee should improve in the same way as for railway freight, but the railway authorities made a conscious decision

FIGURE 9.14: *Mode comparison, passenger journeys per worker for short-distance transport, 1995–2005*

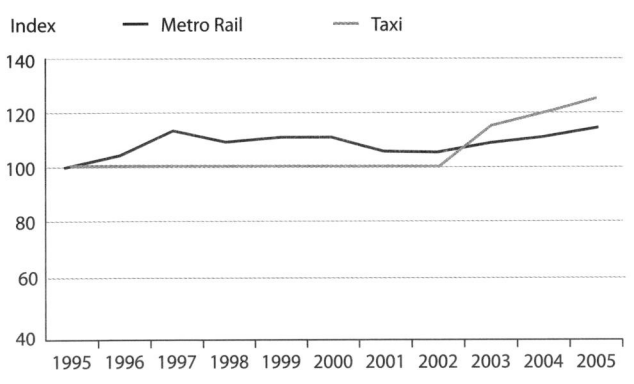
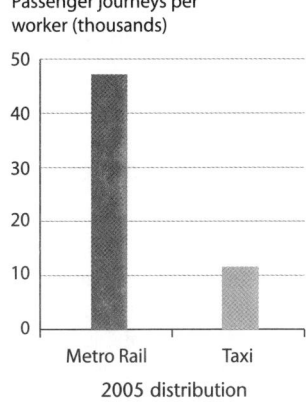

Journeys ('000)	1995	1996	1997	1998	1999	2000	2001	2002	2003	2004	2005
Metro Rail	42.0	43.4	47.0	45.9	46.4	46.3	44.1	44.0	45.5	46.5	47.6
Taxi	9.7	9.7	9.7	9.7	9.7	9.7	9.7	9.7	11.2	11.6	12.0

Source: University of Stellenbosch modelling 2008, inter alia, based on values for taxi fleet from DoT 2001.

FIGURE 9.15: *Growth in long-distance passenger journeys per worker, 1995–2005*

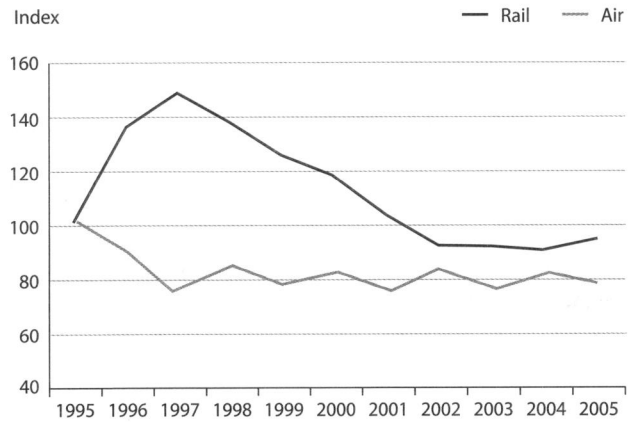
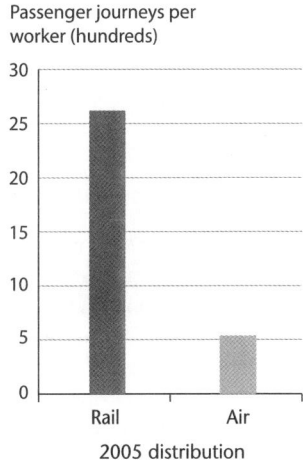

Journeys ('000)	1995	1996	1997	1998	1999	2000	2001	2002	2003	2004	2005
Rail	2.8	3.8	4.2	3.9	3.5	3.3	2.9	2.6	2.6	2.5	2.6
Air	0.7	0.6	0.5	0.6	0.5	0.5	0.5	0.5	0.5	0.5	0.5

Source: University of Stellenbosch modelling 2008

not to invest in this mode of transport. This means that supporting technology that could have led to productivity improvements was not installed.

In summary, productivity indicators confirm that the rail mode is more productive (given that the necessary densities exist). If a switch to rail is contemplated over the next two decades, the impact on skills demand will be significant in terms of the complexity and changing pattern of skills required.

Status quo summary

The status quo of employment in the TSC industry indicates that employment levels for the transport sub-sector are rising slightly, with a decline in other sub-sectors (driven by automation in telecommunications and the decline of the postal utility). Transport employment growth is primarily taking place in passenger transportation, but this is also the sub-sector with the most informal employment. Supply is unacceptable, and the gap between skills required and what can be delivered is widening. Productivity is challenged most in passenger transportation, the area that is primarily unmeasured and where the most informal employment exists. In short, the position is worsening in all areas, and most in those areas where the least formal information exists.

Scenarios for the future

As industries in the third world mature, power in the value chain moves downstream. This means that consumer demand increasingly dictates flow through the value chain and primary producers such as mining and agriculture and even manufacturers (beneficiators of primary products) have less control over prices and delivery of products.

This trend increases the complexity of the logistics system, which has a significant impact on transport. It requires more reliability, higher speed and lower costs from South Africa's transport system, which is already under severe pressure because of historical imbalances. This section of the chapter considers scenarios for the future, arising from the effects of this trend.

Freight transport

The discussion of freight transport scenarios focuses on freight transport over land. Three modes have been excluded from this part of the analysis, that is, water, air and pipeline; they are briefly summarised later in the section. Freight transport by water accounts for less than 0.25 per cent of domestic freight transport, whilst freight transport by air accounts for less than 0.1 per cent. In addition, the country's domestic pipelines are responsible for less than 1 per cent of freight transport, meaning that the three excluded freight transport modes together account for less than 1.5 per cent of total freight transport and do not contribute much to this utility.

Freight transport over land

The current structure of freight transport in South Africa and its future challenges are informed by its history, in which intrinsic geo-spatial considerations played a smaller role than in most countries in the world. Developments in most countries are aligned to natural physical characteristics of the geography, in that the positioning of rivers, valleys and mountains, and the availability of drinking water and arable land, inform such development. In South Africa, however, some harbours are not positioned in the right places, most of the population and industry are incorrectly located, and major population concentrations arose far away from water sources. This situation arose because infrastructure development was driven by extrinsic factors rather than by geography.

FIGURE 9.16: *South African freight transport as a percentage of world figures, 2004*

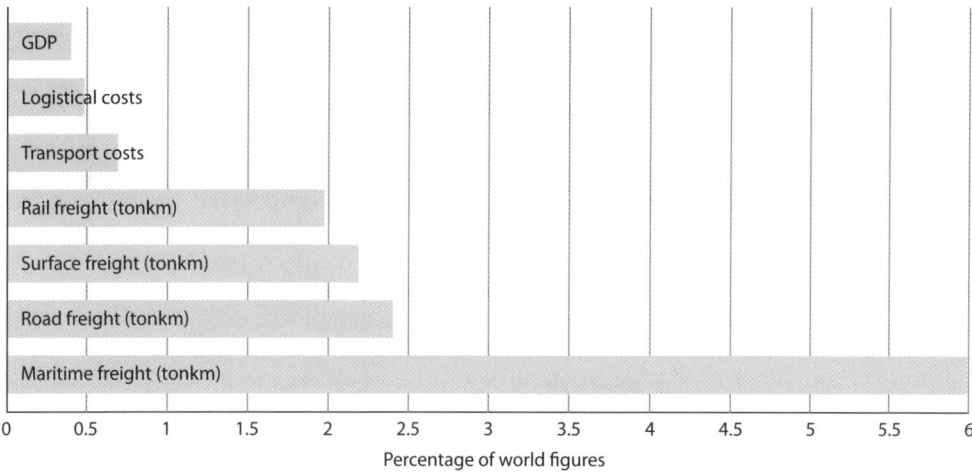

Source: University of Stellenbosch modelling 2008

Today South Africa generates 0.4 per cent of global GDP, but consumes 2.2 per cent of the world's tonkilometres and 6 per cent of maritime tonmiles. The country is freight-transport hungry, and produces only US$0.64 of GDP per tonkilometre, compared to the average production of US$3.34 for the world in total (Figure 9.16).

South Africa currently ships 1 416 million tons of freight in essentially 4 different network segments, that is, rural, metropolitan, corridor and primary segments (Havenga 2007: 146, 152–157) (Figure 9.17). Primary transport refers to the export of bulk low-value raw materials, metropolitan short-haul deliveries of high-value commodities in cities, and rural linkages between rural communities and between rural communities and export/metropolitan markets, whilst corridor transport includes the highly

FIGURE 9.17: *South African freight transport network segments (with mode differentiation)*

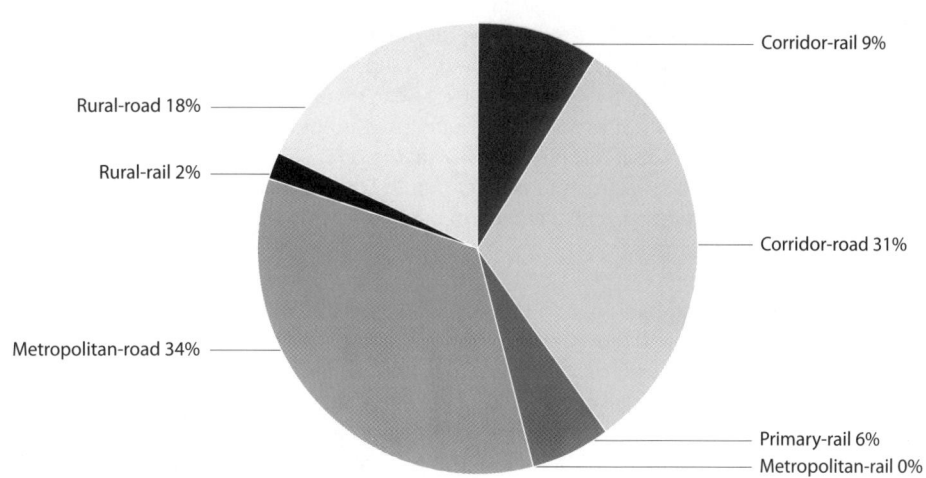

Source: Thompson 2008; University of Stellenbosch modelling 2008

densified links between major areas such as Gauteng, Cape Town and Durban. A discussion on the challenges of these typologies is included in the full report (Havenga 2008). Primary and corridor transport will be rail-bound in most economies.

The current and expected future usage of these modes plays an important role in defining the specific skills challenges involved (present and future). The current mode structure of South Africa's freight transport market is not tenable. Forecasts done by the University of Stellenbosch for Transnet indicate that freight transport demand will grow by between 200 per cent and 250 per cent (Transnet 2006: 27) over the next 20 years. Some corridors, such as the corridors between Gauteng, Johannesburg and Cape Town (which amount to 50 per cent of all corridor transport) will densify even faster than this. Even in a low-growth scenario, the challenges of alleviating congestion in metropoles, providing cheap corridor transport and developing rural infrastructure cannot be met with the current configuration.

Freight transport by road over long distances is too expensive, and it is clear that a shift from freight transport by road back to rail could solve some of the high-cost-related problems of road freight transport, and provide opportunities for a more competitive position for South Africa as a whole.

Long-distance truck travel is, in addition, also a contributing factor to socio-economic problems within the driver population, as is evidenced by the prevalence of HIV/AIDS and other social problems amongst truck drivers (*Fleetwatch* September 2002). The road freight transport sub-sector acknowledges in discussions that required future adherence to safety, health, environment and quality standards and road transport quality standards will put more pressure on the sub-sector in terms of driver education and working conditions.

The debate around how and when this step change will be facilitated is not the subject of this chapter, but the fact that a shift is required back to the railway corridors, and the need for rail-dedicated metropolitan solutions and more effective rural road infrastructure with intermodal nodes, cannot be disputed. Interestingly enough, the road transport sub-sector reports in interviews that the shift is possible and might become a reality as soon as the middle of the next decade.

The above-mentioned shift will require that the industry's Sector Skills Plan (based on skills shortages and training needs identified by the Transport Education Training Authority through analyses and aggregation of company Workplace Skills Plans) will have to be aligned closely to the Transnet national infrastructure plan, the national transport master plan of the Department of Transport (DoT) and the deployment of Moving South Africa (DoT 1998), as well as the National Freight Logistics Strategy (DoT 2005) (an alignment which has not yet been achieved), to support a skills demand shift from long-haul road to long-haul rail. Although the timing is not yet clear, more certainty is expected to emerge over the next 5–10 years. Presently, however, the required shift is not widely recognised (for various reasons – including a shortage of strategic planning skills at the DoT, a lack of integrative master planning thinking between the two infrastructure owners, that is, Transnet and the DoT, and the scarcity of market intelligence), which makes it challenging to prepare for this and deters current operators from raising the necessary alarms.

A skills demand shift from long-haul road to long-haul rail transport will have a specific impact on skills categories. As market demand grows, and even where different skills will be required because of a supply-side shift in modality, it is still relatively easy to re-skill elementary, service and administrative employees. It is more difficult to re-skill operational, professional and senior management employees. Within this group, operational re-skilling is the most critical problem, as the current levels of skills are very low and the degree of shift expected very high. This correlates with the responses received from infrastructure owners (Transnet and the South African National Roads Agency Limited (SANRAL)), large operators (Imperial, Unitrans, Bidvest, McDonalds and Safmarine), upstream providers (Robhitech) and freight owners (Tiger Brands). The degree of shift is, however, not always recognised.

Interviews and analysis of questionnaires undertaken as part of the research for this study indicate that the most critical areas of concern are in the operational fields, which include drivers', technical and engineering skills.

During interviews, the trucking industry reported that long working hours for drivers were causing them to seek alternative employment. The shortage of drivers is also reported as being the most critical skills shortage, with too little investment in the proper education of drivers. The shortage could reach levels as high as one-third, according to the industry, before the expected shift results in the alleviation of this problem, but it gives rise to new challenges in the rail freight sub-sector. This means that the shift will solve some problems, but at some stage will require the retraining and skills development of operational transport workers in a totally new direction. The sub-sector also cites mechanisation as a major future trend, but interestingly enough, this trend will not impact on truck drivers as much as the shift from road to rail will.

In addition, confusion surrounding learnerships and apprenticeships caused by new educational systems is causing skills migration and shortages amongst diesel mechanics.

Other critical skill concerns are in the area of adult education for elementary workers and the degree of competency of professionals.

The road freight sub-sector is also concerned about available technical and engineering expertise. Training standards and processes exist, which means that average skills levels of existing employees are reasonable, but supply is far too low.

Management and administration skills are another concern, with low levels of skills noted in especially generic areas such as computer literacy, customer service and communication. These challenges are caused by the reconfiguration of the South African workforce, which is beginning to take hold in these areas, with a certain training backlog. The most critical skills shortage in this area is in commercial contract management, for which training programmes do exist, but once again the lack of numerical abilities in the available workforce remains a challenge.

Future solutions to South Africa's surface freight transport problems will have to consider a return to rail. This means development of highly technical skills in an area in which the country is already behind, and falling more and more behind over time.

Freight transport by water

The development of super-ports around the world, such as Dubai and Singapore, and densified global maritime routes have resulted in a reclassification of world ports into long-distance-connected and short-distance-connected transhipment ports. In terms of container capacity and handling, the port of Durban ranks as the fiftieth-largest port, that is, although large in the southern African context, it is quite small in a global context. The issue of super-port versus feeder-port development for southern Africa has not yet been settled, and could have a profound impact on skills requirements. South Africa's port infrastructure is well developed, but various initiatives such as Nacala and Lobito could impact on the landscape in the sub-continent.

The major shift in port demand is caused, firstly, by a shift in the economy from raw material export to export of beneficiated products. A second cause is the propensity to containerise more and more of the beneficiated products. This means that dry bulk and break-bulk exports will grow at rates slower than the economic growth rate, but containerisation growth will outstrip economic growth by far. The international shipping container business, which is currently underpinning global (and of course South African) trade, is growing at approximately 10 per cent per year. It is estimated that container volumes will double in the next 8 years and that the global container shipping fleet will grow by 60 per cent over the next decade. One of the fundamental obstacles inhibiting growth and efficiency is the lack (worldwide) of port infrastructure capacity. Most major ports in Asia, the USA and Europe, as well as in South Africa, are experiencing bottlenecks owing to a lack of infrastructure capacity, and in South Africa also a lack of intermodal system efficiency. Both Safmarine and Maersk Line indicated in responses to questionnaires that significantly more skills in intermodal system development and management will be required in the future. These skills are mostly lacking (in fact nearly non-existent) in South Africa at present. In addition, closer working partnerships are required between carriers, suppliers and customers to increase efficiency.

Productivity in a port is measured, amongst other things, by the average number of containers handled per gantry crane per hour. The present number of containers handled varies between 17 and 23 containers (Van Dyk 2004: 21, 26), whilst the international benchmark is a minimum of 23 containers and sometimes cited to be as high as 40 (Wong 2007: 3). Productivity in South African ports therefore seems to be below the international norm. Inefficient cargo handling seriously impacts on South Africa's ability to compete internationally. It is expected that these problems will multiply exponentially in the next 15 years if solutions are not found and the necessary skills developed.

In summary, it will be easy to re-skill elementary and administrative employees, but more difficult to re-skill service, semi-skilled, operational, professional and senior management employees. Re-skilling operational employees, as well as training professionals and senior management, is the most critical problem, as the current levels of skill are very low and/or non-existent. If South Africa wants to play a significant maritime role in the future, skills will have to be developed to achieve the correct positioning. Some growth in maritime technical expertise has been recorded, but more impetus is required in this regard.

Passenger transport

South Africa's commitment to the Millennium Development Goal of reducing poverty and unemployment by 50 per cent and creating a larger middle class will have a profound effect on passenger transport. The current solution of choice is for middle-class South Africans to use private transport (that is, private motor cars). Previously disadvantaged citizens use public transport systems which are mostly unregulated (that is, taxis) and poorly maintained, whereas a small group of wealthy citizens make use of public air transportation.

Domestic air journeys, used for mostly business reasons but including tourism applications, amount to more than 9 million flights per year, and international flights with the same application to more than 3.4 million flights per year. Long-distance rail and bus journeys, used mostly for family visits and tourism, amount to close to 6 million journeys per year. More than 6 billion commuter journeys take place every year, which means that more than 20 per cent of the population, on average, make use of public transport to commute. (In fact, the average South African will do 70 public commuter journeys per year and do one public long-haul domestic trip every third year.)

The same spatial challenges that exist in freight transport in South Africa exist in passenger transportation, with the added dimension of spatial imbalance that is external to normal geographical characteristics. The long-distance Gauteng-to-Cape Town and Gauteng-to-Durban routes are highly densified and abnormal, given the size of the South African economy, and like the unnatural freight demand, are caused by the location of industries and mining activities in Gauteng.

In metropolitan areas, large numbers of workers have no choice but to use public transport, because they are displaced far from places of work as a result of the apartheid-era government's policies.

Long-haul passenger transport by air

The passenger air transport dimension is described by the number of domestic and international flights per year, that is, 12.9 million flights originate or depart from a South African airport each year. In global terms, 0.2 per cent of all international passenger journeys originate in or depart from South Africa, with 0.4 per cent of all domestic air passenger journeys in the world taking place within the borders of South Africa.

The growth curve for domestic flights is high, and future demand growth for Africa and especially South Africa will outstrip world growth. Domestic passenger numbers have more than doubled in the 10-year reporting period; in fact, the numbers have grown by 130 per cent, compared to world growth of 40 per cent (measured for the 1998–2007 period).[7]

This state of affairs will place huge pressures on air transport-orientated skills, especially in air traffic control and aircraft maintenance (both professions that have been reporting extremely high emigration trends in recent years). As far as the upgrading of airports is concerned, civil engineering and technical building skills will also be put under pressure in the foreseeable future.

Surface long-haul passenger transport

Long-haul surface public passenger journeys are unnaturally low. In comparison with rail and bus journeys, rail has a 56 per cent market share, but only 0.01 per cent of long-haul rail journeys in the world take place in South Africa. This is an incredibly low figure and needs to be put into perspective (Figure 9.18).

FIGURE 9.18: *Long-haul surface journeys as a percentage of world figures and expected shift in long-haul journeys if economy matures*

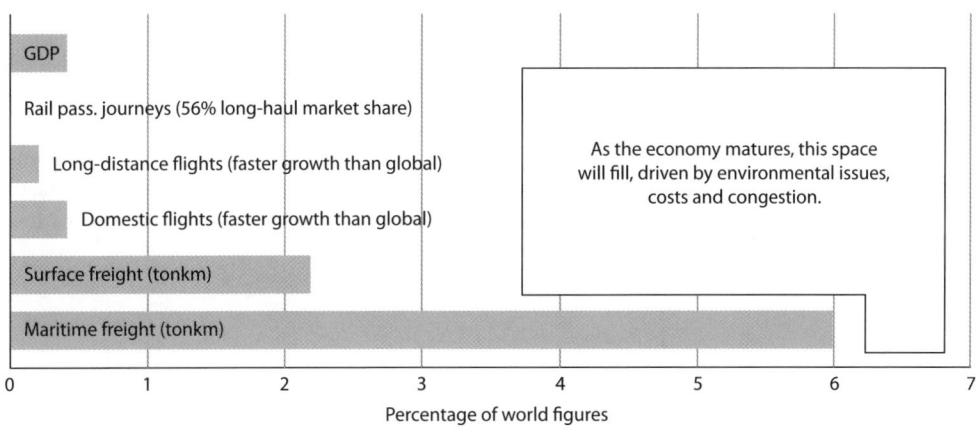

Source: University of Stellenbosch modelling 2008

---

7   ICAO (International Civil Aviation Organisation), *Buoyancy in Airline Traffic Continues in 2007*. ICAO News Release PIO 13/07, http://www.icao.int/icao/en/nr/2007/pio200713e.pdf

Most South Africans still do long-haul passenger journeys by private car (although the percentage of taxi journeys is unknown). If the economy matures in the way that the government's Accelerated Growth Initiative for South Africa (Asgisa) and Growth, Employment and Redistribution (GEAR) policy aspire to do (Department of Finance 1996; PCAS 2006), and poverty and unemployment are halved, this picture could change dramatically (Figure 9.18).

The critical argument in this regard is that demand will grow much faster than economic growth (much more so than for freight), as a growth in personal wealth for the middle class is expected, in addition to the mode switch from private to public transport for long-haul travel from a much lower base than for freight transport. This means that an extremely high growth of long-haul public transport could take place in 10–20 years' time, which is mostly not foreseen, though some service providers to the industry already report a backlog in rail capacity, even with the current unnaturally low rail demand. At the same time, the current solution most often cited is to extend working hours; this is one of the major reasons why employees leave the industry, therefore creating a classic vicious circle.

Approximately 1 200 employees work in the dedicated service section of rail long-haul. As new rail solutions are developed in the next decade, the country will have to deal with the fact that even with the current configuration, an extreme shortage of graduates from railway-orientated engineering disciplines is experienced. At the same time, and also with the current configuration, providers report that unnaturally high salary expectations are created by this shortage, and at the hint of new projects. The fact is that the country cannot afford the shortage, which will stunt growth, as has happened in the case of electricity, and the exorbitant salaries expected cannot be afforded, even with the shortage.

Surface short–haul passenger transport

Short-haul public-transport journeys are mostly commuter-orientated, with two-thirds taking place by taxi, a quarter by bus and only one-twelfth by rail. This trend needs to be reversed, however, as congestion debilitates all the major metropolitan areas in South Africa. This means that skills requirements will have to be considered in relation to two complex issues, which are the formalisation of taxi industry employment and the extreme engineering/operating skills gap in various disciplines, such as those that will be required once the Gautrain is implemented.

Massive structural changes are necessary in this sub-sector. Whereas growth in the country's economy is difficult without engineering, technical and management expertise, no growth is possible without infrastructure; and the expertise to do just that, that is, build and maintain the necessary infrastructure for the first half of this century, is dangerously depleted.

The expected skills shift in the passenger transport sub-sector is even higher than that for freight transport, and it will occur in an area where productivity is declining and statistics are unrecorded. A major challenge will be to better understand future public-transport needs in terms of the timing of certain shifts, and to prepare for these changes.

Conclusion

The skills challenges facing the TSC industry in South Africa are not immediately apparent, because of a lack of data, the absence of a logical macro-economic framework within which to analyse the data, and the inordinately high level of informal labour in the industry. Employment has remained flat, but telecommunications employment has declined as a result of high levels of automation. Transport employment has risen, but mostly in the informal sector and mostly in the passenger transportation sub-sector, where it is inefficient and unproductive. Transport is one of South Africa's biggest challenges, but the debilitating effect of the country's current configuration is not always known or understood. Major changes will have to be contemplated over the next two decades, which will require a step change in skills requirements in exactly those areas where the country is lagging, and where the gap between what is required and what can be supplied is widening.

An important deduction that follows from this analysis is that there are differences in employment supply and demand issues for various industries, especially when the future is considered. In many respects, supply challenges are the same for most industries, that is, in South Africa a large gap is opening up between the demand and supply for technical/operational skills for all industries in general. In some cases, however, industries change because of external factors, and sudden demands for some skills will grow exponentially (not merely in line with GDP), with the result that significant shortages can be expected.

The systemic effect of such a skills shortage can be described by the following cumulative process, and a comparison can be made between the present electricity shortages and possible future passenger transport employment skills shortages:
a) The first level of shortage arises when inadequate investments are made for a low-growth scenario. (This is especially true in South Africa for energy and transport infrastructure.)
b) The shortage is compounded by higher-than-expected growth (true for both electricity and transport).
c) This is further compounded by structural changes on the demand side which cause most infrastructure types to outgrow GDP (also true for both). Examples are a growing black middle class, a lowering of the Gini coefficient, specialisation in the economy, etc.
d) This is further compounded by structural changes on the supply side. For energy, this will also be required eventually, driven by environmental concerns and causing skills demand changes, but this trend is much further in the future. For transport, this change is critical, driven by corridor densification, metropolitan congestion, rural backlogs, export competitiveness concerns and, obviously, also environmental concerns.
e) This cumulative effect is at its worst for passenger transport in South Africa (even more than for freight), where a propensity to outsource will grow suddenly as most South Africans will not be able to use private car transport in cities any more.
f) And in the final case of major change, industries will need to reconfigure themselves, as is the case for the railways, where the various engineering disciplines (which are already quite complex) will need to integrate with each other as well as with the value chains of customers (Le Roux 2008: 4).

The over-arching effect of this step change on employment categories is illustrated in Figure 9.20.

The x-axis of Figure 9.20 depicts current skills levels in the industry, which were analysed as very low for elementary and operational employees. The y-axis depicts the degree of change that will occur if industry modalities should change. This means that, for instance, although elementary employees are poorly skilled, they will be the least affected, in terms of job content, if the shift occurs. At the same time, although service employee job content will change with such a shift, the current skills levels are high, which means that changes could be more easily accommodated. The major area of concern is therefore operational employees, with poor current skills and large shifts expected. Professional employees, on the other hand, are well trained but too few in number and will lack sufficient skills, especially in the integrative disciplines of engineering and logistics.

Policy recommendations are difficult to formalise due to the unique structure of the industry. Infrastructure is owned by various entities, that is, the government directly, through agencies such as the Airports Company of South Africa (ACSA) and SANRAL, and indirectly through Transnet. In road

FIGURE 9.19: *Degree of skills shift required to enable step change from long-haul road to long-haul rail freight transport*

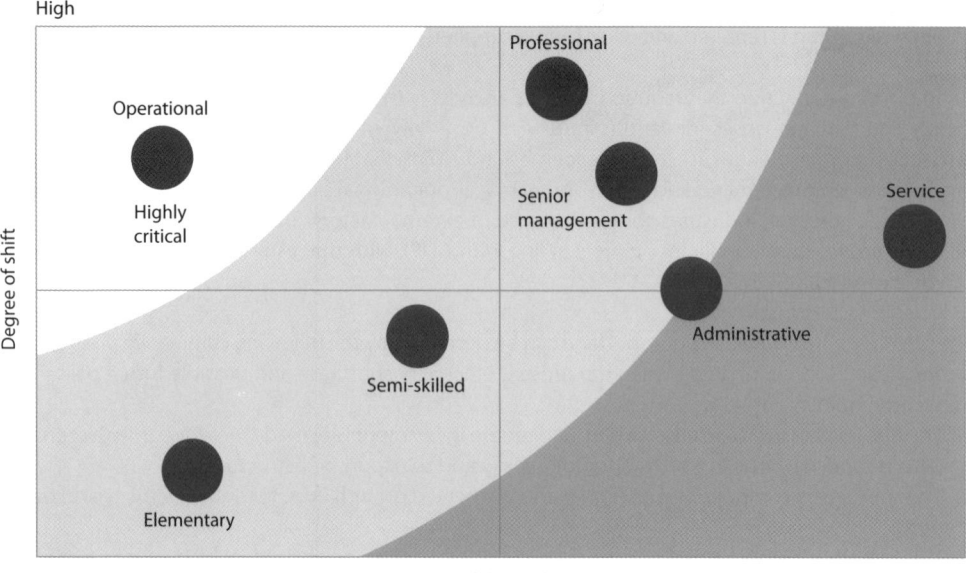

Source: University of Stellenbosch modelling 2008

and air transport, only private undertakings operate on this infrastructure, but for rail, pipelines and harbours, operations are mostly effected by the infrastructure owner. The National Freight Logistics Strategy (DoT 2005) calls for a separation of these responsibilities, but there is no clear-cut agreement on this issue and many obstacles exist that could make vertical separation and open access difficult. The DoT's ability to strategically manage the various transport utilities is varied, with some successes in certain areas but poor performance in others. This will have a profound effect on strategy formulation, as statistics and market intelligence remain scattered and unorganised, strategies unfocused and entities taking accountability for the industry do not communicate on a strategic level.

Central control will be difficult to achieve and probably unsuccessful, but policies could enforce central participation, harmonised statistics and combined planning systems. These should seek solutions for both the utilities and the inputs required, such as labour. Solutions will only be found through a credible central planning agency that can manage the many transitions that will be required.

References

Central Statistical Services (1993) *Standard industrial classification of economic activities.* Pretoria: Central Statistical Services

DA (Democratic Alliance) (2006) *Skills and vacancies project.* Accessed 15 January 2008, http://www.da.org.za/da/Site/Eng/campaigns/DOCS/SkillsVacancies_Project_2006.doc

Department of Finance (1996) *Growth, employment and redistribution: A macroeconomic strategy (GEAR).* Pretoria: Department of Finance

De Wet TJ (2003) The effect of a tax on coal in South Africa: A CGE analysis, submitted in partial fulfilment of the requirements for the degree of PhD (Economics), University of Pretoria

DoE (Department of Education, South Africa) (2007) *Higher Education Management Information System (HEMIS) database 1999–2005*. Pretoria: DoE

DoL (Department of Labour, South Africa) (2006) *State of skills in South Africa 2006–2007*. Accessed 15 January 2008, www.labour.gov.za

DoT (Department of Transport, South Africa) (1998) *Moving South Africa: A transport strategy for 2020*. Accessed 25 September 2007, http://www.transport.gov.za/projects/msa/msa.html

DoT (2001) *Transport statistics 2001*. Accessed 29 September 2007, http://www.transport.gov.za/library/index.html

DoT (2005) *National freight logistics strategy*. Released by JT Radebe, Minister of Transport, September 2005. Accessed 23 March 2008, www.rra.co.za/.../docs/national_freight_logistics_strategy_sept._2005_condensed_final_051018_to_website.doc

Havenga JH (2007) The development and application of a freight transport flow model for South Africa. Dissertation presented for the degree of Doctor of Philosophy (Logistics Management), University of Stellenbosch

Havenga JH (2008) *HSRC sector case studies: Case study report on the transport, storage and communication industry*. Stellenbosch: University of Stellenbosch

Havenga J & Pienaar W (2005) The case for development logistics. In H Ittman (ed.) *The second state of logistics report of South Africa, 2005*. Pretoria: CSIR

JCP International (2005) *Employment trends in South Africa*. Johannesburg: JCP International

Kraak A (2005) Human resources development and the skills crisis in South Africa: The need for a multi-pronged strategy. *Journal of Education and Work* 18(1): 57–83

Le Roux A (2008) Railways 2030: Extinction or regeneration. Paper presented at the Indian National Academy for Engineering Annual Conference, 29 February–1 March 2008

Pandor N (2005) Address by the Minister of Education, Naledi Pandor, MP, at the launch of the National Qualification Framework Support Link, 6 June, CSIR Convention Centre, Pretoria. Accessed 30 September 2007, http://www.saqa.org.za/show.asp?include=docs/sp/sp0606-05.html

PCAS (Policy Coordination and Advisory Services, South Africa) (2006) *A catalyst for Accelerated and Shared Growth – South Africa (Asgisa): Background document*. Pretoria: Office of the Presidency

Samuelson PA & Nordhaus WD (1989) *Economics*. New York: Mcgraw-Hill

Stats SA (Statistics South Africa) (1996–2005) *October Household Surveys* and *Labour Force Surveys*. Pretoria: Stats SA

Stats SA (2002) *The transport industry*. Statistical Release P7101. Pretoria: Stats SA

Stats SA (2006) *P7000 – Transport, post and telecommunication industry, 2006*. Pretoria: Stats SA

Stats SA (2007) *Gross Domestic Product*. A statistical release. Pretoria: Stats SA

The Presidency (2007) *Development indicators mid-term review*. Accessed 29 September 2007, http://www.info.gov.za/otherdocs/2007/developmentindicator/education.pdf

Thompson L (2008) *World Bank railway database*. Accessed 18 February 2008, http://www.worldbank.org/transport/rail/rdb.htm

Transnet (2006) Transnet freight demand model: Final report. Unpublished report. Johannesburg: Transnet

Van Dyk E (2004) *National fruit logistics strategy*. Pretoria: Council for Scientific and Industrial Research

WEF (World Economic Forum) (2007–2008) *Global competitiveness report for 2007–2008*. Accessed 13 February 2008, http://www.gcr.weforum.org/

Wong WH (2007) *Port benchmarking study for assessing Hong Kong's maritime services and associated costs with other major international ports*. Accessed 6 February 2008, http://www.mardep.gov.hk/en/publication/pdf/pocp2_07.pdf

5 | LABOUR-INTENSIVE SECTORS

CHAPTER 10

Clothing and textiles

Mike Morris and Lyn Reed

Introduction

The South African clothing and textiles industries have undergone difficult restructuring processes over the past decade under the combined impact of domestic and international factors. The negative impact of this transformation is manifest in the declining contribution of the sector to total manufacturing output, its falling export share and its significant contraction in sector employment. The outcome might have been different had this process of restructuring been pre-empted and accompanied by a concerted effort to up-skill remaining workers and promote innovation. This could have enabled the sector to pursue a skills-led competitiveness strategy and assist a move towards higher-cost, high-quality items. Paradoxically, under-investment in both human and physical capital in the South African clothing and textiles sector has deepened the crisis precipitated by globalisation and currency weakness, and the sector has been incapable of dealing with rising import penetration. Government policy designed to address the effects of liberalisation on the sector has largely been regressive and reinforces the perception of global trade as a threat rather than an opportunity. Instead of creating a paradigm shift up the value chain, it would seem that interventions such as the quotas on imports from China are driving local firms in the opposite direction, that is, down the value chain towards basic, low-value-added garments (Morris & Einhorn 2008; Morris & Reed 2008).[1]

In the new global economy, a country's successful participation in the global value chain for clothing is contingent on its ability to flexibly and reliably respond to customers' needs, which requires local manufacturers to upgrade their design and marketing skills and demonstrate world-class manufacturing capabilities (Barnes & Esselaar 2005). Amongst other factors, the US International Trade Commission (US ITC) has identified skilled labour and management as a critical success factor which provides countries with an advantage (US ITC 2004); consequently, there is a serious need to develop skills in the clothing and textile industry. The global trend has been for less-skilled tasks to be moved to low-cost locations while higher-value-added and higher-skilled tasks remain in developed countries. This is also accompanied by outsourcing to informal economy enterprises. In this context, increasing emphasis is placed on the need for developing countries to upgrade their technical and production capabilities so as to compete in terms of quality, design and delivery, rather than simply on price (Roberts & Thoburn 2002).

South Africa faces numerous general challenges which could potentially protract and deepen the skills crisis. The global skills market has become increasingly competitive. Whilst other countries have

---

1   See the full report on which this chapter draws (Morris & Reed 2008) for detailed data on the sector.

exploited this to their advantage, South Africa continues to act defensively, seeing it as a threat rather than an opportunity. A legacy of discrimination has resulted in a (disproportionately white) skills base, particularly vulnerable to emigration and aging. Finally, transformation policies have had the unintended consequence of misdirecting and wasting skills.[2]

The performance and dynamics of the clothing and textile industry in South Africa

The South African clothing and textiles industry is highly diverse, mature and centred on a sophisticated domestic market. In 2005, the South African market for clothing and textile products combined was R45 634 million, up 34.5 per cent from R29 887 million in 2001. However, domestic sales by local producers have declined. Between 2002 and 2005, total local sales declined by 18.1 per cent, clothing sales by 13.4 per cent, and textiles sales by 22 per cent. The increased domestic demand has clearly been taken up by an increasing reliance on imported clothing and fabric. Products range from inexpensive mass-produced basics to higher-value-added fashion and tailored garments, and specialised textiles. The exchange rate is crucial to the industry's competitiveness and sustainability. In addition, South Africa's clothing industry is dominated by a small number of large retailers, wielding considerable value chain power, with the power to set prices as well as make demands on quality and delivery.

The price pressures from trade liberalisation, currency strengthening, and the exercise of local retailers' power within domestic value chains has resulted in clothing firms following a number of different survival strategies. In line with global trends, there has been a restructuring of the industry and recomposition of labour, with a move towards sub-contracting and informalisation as parts of their production, which are outsourced to cut-make-and-trim (CMT) enterprises that provide production services at lower costs due to lower overhead structures. In addition, formal factory downsizing and closures have resulted in the establishment of micro-enterprises, home industries and unregistered firms, causing an increase in the number of people employed in the informal sector of the clothing industry and making it difficult to accurately calculate employment figures (Edwards & Morris 2007).

Firms that are well integrated into local retailer value chains have been adopting world-class manufacturing (WCM) techniques to upgrade their operational performance – speeding up delivery and lead times, cutting inventory levels, reducing defect rates, introducing new work practices, and creating value chain alignment between retailers and suppliers. The Cape and KwaZulu-Natal Clothing and Textile Clusters have been pivotal in driving competitiveness and upgrading in the industry. The result has been a change in the types of skills demanded and utilised on the factory floor.

Primarily in KwaZulu-Natal, firms have been relocating from urban to rural areas, where wages are lower, a more flexible labour regime operates, and lower rates of unionisation are evident. Some firms have gone as far as relocating across borders to Lesotho and Swaziland, where the wage and regulatory environment is even less onerous.

Firms have been confronting cheap imports from trade liberalisation, rising costs, and pressures related to lower prices and more stringent quality demands. Textiles firms have moved to focusing on core products, curtailing non-core functions and following vertical disintegration strategies. Many have chosen to focus on niche markets, and restructuring has resulted in greater specialisation and longer production runs. These textile survival strategies have been criticised by the clothing industry because

---

2   Bernstein A & Johnson S (2007) Skill needed to face up to real needs, *Business Day* 1 March.

they have resulted in firms moving away from the production of apparel textiles and towards production of higher-margin technical, industrial and household textiles.

The trade performance of the two sectors has been disappointing, with exports collapsing and Chinese imports growing at a prodigious rate. Clothing exports jumped phenomenally, from R995 million in 1999 to R2 590 million in 2002, and then, when the exchange rate stabilised and the rand strengthened, plummeted to R837 million by 2006. Likewise over the same period, textiles exports grew from R2 430 million to R4 511 million, and then fell back to R3 464 million by 2006. Consequently, exports are no longer a substantial component of the clothing and textile industries. Imports accelerated dramatically from 2002. Imports of textiles (consisting overwhelmingly of fabric feeding into clothing production) almost trebled, from R5 069 million in 1999 to R14 370 million in 2006. The surge in imports has, however, been most stark with respect to clothing, where imports jumped sevenfold from R889 million in 1999 to R6 898 million by 2006.

The dynamics governing this dramatic rise of imports and collapse of exports are tied to a reaction on the part of the retailers that dominate the domestic market to the brief flourish of exports at the turn of the millennium. When the rand suffered a major devaluation in 2000/2001 (from US$1 = R6.10 in 1999 to R12.11 in 2001), local clothing manufacturers signed up numerous export orders. Lacking sufficient stock for both markets, many reneged on orders to local retailers. The latter consequently went offshore, discovering Chinese imports. The strengthening of the rand after 2003 (with US$1 = R6–R7) turned the scenario around. Local manufacturers could not service export orders, and sought vainly to return to their domestic customers, but large-scale Chinese imports had become entrenched.

The lack of firm-level operational competitiveness exacerbated pressures; the industry was failing to extensively incorporate WCM standards. The failure of competitiveness pertains to the industry's global 'betwixt and between' position. It is neither a high-value-added, fashion-oriented, first-world player competing through cutting-edge technologies, highly skilled personnel and specialised market knowledge; nor is it a low-cost, mass-based, developing-country industry competing via scale economies, low-cost labour and aggressive government policies. Indeed the lack of skills has become a major issue. Given the changing demands resulting from pressures to achieve international competitiveness, this problem will not be solved through absorbing unemployed workers as the industry contracts.

How has government handled the skills issues in the industry?

The Clothing, Textiles, Footwear and Leather Sector Education and Training Authority (CTFL SETA) argues that the decrease in employment has occurred only in semi-skilled and unskilled positions, implying that there is great potential to create employment in medium- to high-skilled occupations (CTFL SETA 2004). The main conclusions of its skills audit of the industry are that there are:
- shortages in upper occupational strata (senior managers, professionals and technicians);
- shortages of artisans and skilled workers (e.g. machine mechanics);
- no skills shortages in the lower occupational strata (CTFL SETA 2004).

The SETA aims to raise skills levels through i) increasing the number of employees on learnership programmes; ii) training middle managers in work-planning and process management; and iii) boosting the number of technologists employed.

The consensus on education and apprenticeship training is that, at current graduation levels, the skills base of the industry cannot be maintained, let alone broadened. This in itself justifies efforts to encourage participation in formal programmes. The education profile of employees presents an opportunity to up-skill those in the further education and training (FET) band to the higher education and training

(HET) band. The Skills Audit has shown that the supply does not satisfy the demand for skills, in terms of both numbers and categories of worker demanded. The HET infrastructure, despite capacity to train more students, has had very low graduate rates since 2000, and these need to be increased to maintain international competitiveness. The FET infrastructure, which operates through learnerships and apprenticeships, is not generating enough graduates to decrease the skills shortage significantly, despite having enough capacity to increase enrolment rates significantly.

Several other relevant points emerge from the literature. Firms need to use their own labour resources more efficiently and conduct in-house training of low-skilled workers. Short-term solutions are also demanded to save the industry. Kaplan (in *Business Report*) and Bernstein and Johnson (in *Business Day*) suggest aggressive recruitment policies targeting skilled immigrants.[3] Although 9 000 skilled immigrants were required in 2004 to maintain the skills base at 2003 levels, only 194 were actually registered – a mere 12 of whom were recruited into the CTFL sector (CTFL SETA 2004). Finally, there is a need to isolate which specific skills are lacking in each category of firm. Daniels (2007: 2) suggests that 'skills shortages are not only about scarce and critical skills', but should encompass advanced qualifications and elementary qualifications alike. In this context, skills development may be needed for different people at different stages of their life cycle, or over the business cycle, or both.

To address the gap between skills supply and demand, the CTFL SETA's Sector Skills Plan 2005–2010 (CTFL SETA 2006) introduced the following strategies:
- training of technicians and artisans as a critical intervention;
- mandatory grant funding to member companies to train 400 production managers in 5 years;
- small, medium and micro enterprise (SMME) training clusters to up-skill owner-managers and workers;
- strategic partnerships with the Cape Peninsula University of Technology, Durban Institute of Technology and University of Johannesburg.

The Skills Development Levies Act (No. 9 of 1999) taxes enterprises at one per cent of payroll expenditure. The logic of this measure is that public provision of training is necessary to correct the market failures associated with historically poor levels of investment by enterprises in training. The National Skills Development Strategy reiterated the importance of learnerships as a complement to apprenticeships (Daniels 2007), and as a key method to improve skills development for high, intermediate and low skill levels. In addition, skills development has been linked to the National Qualifications Framework (NQF).

Rasool (2006) outlines process and administration difficulties with apprenticeship training – poor support from Technisa and the Department of Education in examination administration, lack of monitoring by the SETA, SETA staff possessing insufficient knowledge about apprenticeship schemes, neglect of apprenticeships in favour of learnerships, onerous marking of assignments by firms that train multiple apprentices, and non-compliance by firms with stipulated procedures. Daniels' (2007) findings indicate that the majority of firms do not value the SETA's role and capacity. The Department of Labour (DoL) survey conducted in 2005 revealed that the majority of respondents thought that the SETA was not doing a good job (Daniels 2007). Indications are that the SETA lacks industry credibility and is not supported, rendering its programmes ineffective (Barnes & Esselaar 2005).

---

3   Kaplan D, Labour is like tomatoes: the greater the shortage, the higher the price, *Business Report* 29 May 2007; Bernstein A & Johnson S, Skill needed to face up to real needs, *Business Day* 1 March 2007.

Evidence from the firms

The SETA's view is that scarce skills demands are for highly skilled technical people in occupations which fall into the upper strata; furthermore, there are no skills shortages in the lower strata of the occupational sphere. According to the SETA, this is congruent with the massive job losses in semi-skilled and unskilled occupations (CTFL SETA 2004). For the research on which this chapter is based, firm-level evidence was compared with this view, so as to examine the SETA's effectiveness in addressing the skills crisis.

Between July and September 2007, 15 clothing and 5 textiles firms in the Western Cape and KwaZulu-Natal were interviewed to:
- establish a current profile of the skills distribution in firms;
- distinguish between, and identify, industry skills gaps and skills shortages;
- identify firm strategies to address these skills gaps/shortages;
- evaluate government sectoral interventions in alleviating skills shortages/gaps;
- assess future skills needs.

The sample covered the entire spectrum of firm sizes and types – full-package clothing manufacturers (FPMs), CMTs, and textile firms supplying large domestic retail chains, with the smaller FPMs servicing small chains and independents.[4] The CMTs feed primarily design houses for South Africa's major retailers. The clothing firms cover a wide range of items. The textiles firms all manufacture fabric. The key distinguishing feature, though, between the firms, over-riding size or type, was their strategic vision for the future. The particular vision driving a firm's production methods to a large extent dictates that firm's skills requirements and thereby also its ability to meet its skills needs. In terms of this criterion, two types of firm can be distinguished:
- those explicitly differentiating between skills shortages and skills gaps, and addressing problems by internal recruitment and training or external recruitment of potential staff within this new mould;
- those trapped in old management and production processes, and continuing to recruit from the industry labour pool with diminishing success.

Skills gaps exist when employers recognise that their existing workforce has lower skill levels than are necessary to meet business objectives (Pye 2002). Skills gaps therefore refer to a lack of proficiency of existing staff or an inability to perform their roles to the optimum level. Skills gaps are an important indicator, as they can signal a lack of business efficiency or inappropriate recruitment strategies. They may also be symptomatic of skills shortages, if inappropriate or unqualified recruits are employed in the absence of qualified people.

Both clothing and textile firms experience wide skills gaps. For clothing, the main concern is at both ends of the occupational spectrum – in management and in operative areas. Technical skills gaps occur mainly at production operative level. Without exception, firms identified the shortage of machinists as their greatest problem, with other production-related positions also becomingly increasingly difficult

---

4 The sample of firms comprised:
Five large full package manufacturers with 1 500+ employees;
Four medium full package manufacturers with between 500 and 1 000 employees;
One small full package manufacturer with approx. 150 employees;
Two large CMT firms with 350+ employees;
Three small CMT firms with between 100 and 150 employees;
One large textile manufacturing firm with 1 500+ employees;
Two medium textile manufacturing firms with 350+ employees;
One small textile manufacturing firm with less than 100 employees;
One large trimmings manufacturer with 450+ employees.

to fill. In terms of management, skills gaps are identified overwhelmingly at mid-management level, mainly relating to problem-solving and team-leading. For textiles, technical skills gaps are manifest in insufficient numbers of machine operators, particularly knitters and creels. Similar to the situation in clothing firms, there is a chronic shortage of upper management skills, although gaps are encountered at all levels of the management ladder.

Skills shortages exist where there is a lack of adequately skilled and/or qualified individuals in the accessible labour market *and* it is difficult to find people with the skills required (Pye 2002: 13). Recruitment difficulties can be symptomatic of skills shortages, but they may also reflect uncompetitive labour conditions or policies which discourage work. Firm data suggest that skills shortages occur overwhelmingly at the operative and technical occupational levels, although in some cases firms report difficulties with recruiting professionals such as engineers.

Whilst the demand for skills varies across occupations and firm size, it is fundamentally defined by the firm's particular strategic vision of the future. That is, *skills gaps are more evident in those firms – irrespective of size or market orientation – which have actively engaged in the transition to WCM and explicitly recruit labour within this new mould.* Skills shortages are less important to these firms. The creation of new skills gaps occurs because the WCM redefines production activities, supplementing them with new, and often greater, skills requirements. Furthermore, skills gaps may indicate future skills shortages, if firms do not immediately address exposed gaps. Conversely, there are fewer skills gaps, and more shortages, reported by firms imbued with traditional modes of thinking.

Firm-level interviews unpacked skills shortages and gaps in specific occupational positions, providing empirical support for the view that WCM has redefined many of the traditional occupations and thereby also the skills profiles of those occupations. The main implication is that firms who aspire to WCM practices face growing skills gaps in their existing workforce. Simultaneously, these firms face growing skills shortages, since recruitment of 'old-style' staff from the industry with the old skills arsenal is increasingly unfeasible. This suggests that i) the skills profile of an occupational position is defined by the firm's particular manufacturing model, that is, the extent to which it practises WCM; and ii) this particular skills profile shapes the firm's perception about whether there is a skills gap or a skills shortage in that occupational area. The interviews also identified whether perceived skills shortages relate to quantity (that is, insufficient numbers of qualified people to meet demand), or quality (that is, qualified people are available but do not meet the standard demanded).

Skills gaps/shortages by occupational category in the clothing sector

Twenty per cent of firms highlight operatives with gaps in their skills portfolio. Since machinists are the 'engine room' of the business, shortages here impact negatively on efficiency, productivity and profitability, and are of overwhelming and immediate concern. Most firms, irrespective of size or orientation, reported that the shortage of skilled machine staff represented the *single binding constraint* on their ability to grow their business and that the shortage has drastically increased in the last two years:[5]

> In the past 4 months, we have opened up 4 new lines with 84 machinists. In the next few months, we are planning to open another 3 lines for which we will need another 100 machinists and we are struggling to find qualified machinists from the industry.

---

5   All quotations are from the firm-level interviews conducted as part of the research study on which this chapter draws (Morris & Reed 2008).

> I have been approached with a lucrative offer to expand my business but I had to turn it down because I cannot find machining staff…
>
> It has become much more difficult to recruit [qualified machinists] over the past two or three years…Actually, we don't know what to do…
>
> We have been short 15 machinists since July. For every 1 that comes in, we lose 2…We can lose up to 15 machinists a month.
>
> When Singer closed down 18 months ago, they retrenched 130 machinists. I went and offered them all jobs. Only two pitched…

The shortage of machinists increases with the skills requirement. Most firms report commercial 'extinction' of highly skilled operators who can conduct specialist multi-skilling operations:

> If 30 skilled machinists walked through the door and they were all pocket machinists and collar setters, I would take them all!
>
> The type of work at this factory is specialist since most of the garments that we produce are elasticated so it's more cover seam work. We just cannot get anyone any more.

For the majority of firms, the shortage of skills in this occupational sphere translates directly into an insufficient *number* of machinists available to the industry. They simply cannot find machinists. However, 27 per cent of firms argue that there are machinists available for employment, but they have the wrong mindset and attitude. This implies that the shortage also relates to quality of skill, personal attributes and experience.

This occupational level is particularly susceptible to change during industrial restructuring, and is most affected in terms of skills advancement as the old mould is broken and new processes are introduced. Already, progressive firms are identifying new skills gaps at operator level. Current identifiable skills gaps at the operator level in clothing firms relate primarily to multi-skilling capabilities, while textile firms report skills gaps at the technical level. This is exacerbated by the high proportion of learners and newly qualified operators currently in the industry. In addition, firms expressed concern about team-building and communication skills, arising mainly from low levels of literacy and numeracy. This is more pronounced in textiles than in clothing, due to the greater technological dependency and the technically advanced production process involved in textile manufacture.

Eighty per cent of firms reported cutting-room shortages, although mechanisation may address these. Fifty-five per cent reported difficulties in recruiting layers-up, sorters and fusers in the cutting department, but not on the scale of cutters and machinists. All firms reported a severe shortage of suitably qualified sample machinists who construct a garment 'prototype' without the aid of a pattern, hence lying at the higher skills-proficiency end of the spectrum and requiring experience and multi-skilling capabilities. Sample machinists are generally over 50 years of age, since it takes at least 10 years to become proficient. The average minimum reported fill time for a sample machinist is eight weeks. Patternmaking demands a high level of proficiency and skill and is at the upper end of the skills spectrum. This role also tends to be filled by older staff with a minimum of 10 years' experience. All firms, without exception, reported a 'huge' shortage of patternmakers. Furthermore, firms reported problems in filling positions for other less skilled production staff (e.g. ironers and markers), although this was primarily attributed to high labour turnover.

Fifty per cent reported a shortage of machine mechanics, ranging from moderate to 'chronic'. Twenty-seven per cent experienced extreme difficulties in recruiting welders and electricians, reflecting a general countrywide shortage of artisans. Fifty per cent reported a shortage of technologists – they were available, but at a prohibitive price. This skills shortage related not to the quantity of qualified people available, but more to the quality and type of skills available relative to firms' requirements. Firms describe a skills requirement which goes beyond that of quality advisors, who currently masquerade as technologists. The latter, however, require skills which include capabilities such as garment construction, as well as understanding the entire value chain.

> There are a lot of technologists available but they tend to be quality advisors. Technologists, in the true sense, are very rare and if available at all, very expensive.

Larger firms encountered a greater degree of skill problems in management. However, the gap is not exclusively a large-company issue, but relates to most firms that aspire to WCM standards, have made the transition from individual to team-based performance, and are driving efficiency through the production chain from the top down. As a result, the management function profile has changed and the quality of management required has been upgraded. The skills needs of firms have thus changed, with a mismatch between the quality and type of skills available and those which they require to make the transition to WCM.

> The problem is that you get a lot of soldiers. We need people who can think and innovate. These people are in short supply…

Less than 30 per cent of firms reported skill-related vacancies across managerial occupations, suggesting that skills in this domain relate more to existing managers than to the recruitment of new managers into the sector. Most firms expressed a view that there is a declining amount of quality management material available relative to the past, and that the number of new graduates entering the sector is also decreasing.

> There are not enough people in the technikons and even of those who do graduate, many move out of the clothing sector and out of the industry…

This is due to the generally negative image of the industry, as graduates opt for employment in the more glamorous, lucrative and thriving clothing retail or design sectors. Furthermore, the poaching of management skills from other economic sectors is limited. Given that managerial skills are generic, this skills pool is particularly vulnerable to attrition from skills migration.

> Another question is how we offer a person who has reached the upper bound of his responsibility a career path which compares with what competition can offer to take him further up the ladder…

All textile firms in the sample reported their greatest skills shortages in technical areas (technicians and technologists) as well as in middle and upper management. Furthermore, firms report a large amount of 'churning' in the labour pool for technical staff. In other generic skills areas (e.g. HR) there seems to be significant migration from the industry altogether. The shortage of management skills, particularly production managers, was the greatest area of concern for all textile firms. Few new people are coming through, and current incumbents are over 55 years old. Textile firms also reported a shortage of machine operators, particularly knitters. The shortage of high-level technical skills is pervasive, with larger textile firms reporting massive shortages of all artisans, and wages that are 'going through the roof'.

How does the firm-level evidence compare with the SETA's Sector Skills Plan (CTFL SETA 2006)? In summary, it differs substantially from the view of the SETA:
- Most job movement occurs at operator level, but this is not due to natural attrition or rationalisation at the bottom end of the occupational spectrum. Instead there is a massive operator flight into the informal sector.
- The rise in the proportion of staff at the management occupational level is consistent with consolidation of the management structure, responding to deteriorating market conditions.
- It is important to distinguish between skills gaps in the existing workforce that compromise their ability to perform to the level required by the firm, and skills shortages which arise from insufficient numbers of recruits in the industry labour pool. The former may become of increasing importance to firms which make the transition to WCM. If left unaddressed, these skills gaps may become skills shortages in the future.
- Skills shortages arise not solely due to insufficient numbers of people, but also because of the quality of people available – principally because there is a mismatch between their qualification and 'ability to do the job'. This is particularly the case in respect of designers, patternmakers and technologists.
- Skills gaps, rather than shortages, are more of a problem at management level, with huge implications for up-skilling. Most firms believe that institutions are ineffective at aligning management training with their needs.

Strategies to overcome skills shortages

In order to overcome skills gaps, firms were faced with several strategic options:
- recruit qualified people from the industry;
- recruit new unqualified (and mainly unemployed) people from outside the industry;
- source people internally and promote them;
- recruit people from outside the industry with generic skills;
- recruit graduates from technikons and other formal institutions;
- outsource production to CMTs.

In addition to shaping a firm's skills needs, its vision also ultimately defines the strategies it adopts to address skills shortages and gaps. Progressive firms are more likely to recognise skills factors, such as the absence of strong management capabilities, as a key constraint in attaining WCM levels, and choose fundamentally different strategies to augment the skills base of their workforce than those firms which remain locked in the old mode of thinking. Progressive firms have all but ceased to recruit people from the industry, opting instead to recruit unqualified people and train them in the new mould or to fill positions via internal recruitment and training. In effect, the fill-time for vacancies in most firms now gets translated into training time. The traditional firms, however, continue to recruit from the industry, albeit with diminishing success.

Firms reported a low success rate for efforts to procure qualified people from the industry, especially for semi- and low- to medium-skilled staff. Numerous recruitment methods were tried, including approaching the bargaining council and unions, advertising in regional or national newspapers and community newspapers, word-of-mouth, and posters placed in public areas. Some firms reported going to 'extraordinary lengths', even making church announcements. All met with low success rates. One desperate owner drives home the futility of advertising strategies:

> We advertised in the *Argus* [a major daily newspaper in Cape Town] and in community papers. We even went on radio at huge expense. *Not one single applicant*!

An important pattern emerging from the interviews was the negligible role that the bargaining council plays in recruiting critical production staff, and the lack of assistance in this regard from the SETA.

In certain occupational areas (that is, machinists), the labour pool is diminishing at an alarming rate. Firms offered several explanations for the extreme difficulties they had encountered in recruiting machinists and more recently, other production staff. It is widely thought that these people are:

1. collecting their substantial provident fund payments to pay off debts, as well as drawing from the Unemployment Insurance Fund (UIF) and living off the proceeds, and are thus unavailable for employment;
2. leaving the industry to seek work in other, higher-waged sectors;
3. using their accumulated provident payment to set up their own informal CMT operations or working for an informal neighbourhood CMT:

> At the end of the day, all people care about is take-home pay. So if they can work from home where they can take care of their kids and not have to expend money for travel, avoid deductions for UIF, union dues, industrial council contributions etc., they probably earn more by working in the informal sector than they do working in the formal sector.

> Of all the thousands and thousands [of machinists] that have lost jobs, none want to come back into the formal industry. Bottom line is they get more money working for backyard CMTs than they would get working for a formal enterprise…

> What people want is flexibility. When they join a CMT, they can work four days a week if they want to. There is very high absenteeism in CMTs for precisely this reason…

The implication is that skills are not being lost to the industry but rather to formal-sector firms (and union membership). Instead, we are witnessing a recomposition of labour and a restructuring of the industry.

All firms reported supplementing their skills requirements in low-skilled positions (machinists and knitters) by sourcing unqualified people from outside the industry and training them. However, the recruitment strategies pursued, as well as the motivation behind each strategy, differ. Thirty-eight per cent of firms explain the decision to recruit from outside as a voluntary move motivated by a conscious decision to move away from employing people in the old mould, instead recruiting and training new people in terms of WCM practices. For the rest, this strategy was largely precipitated by the shortage of recruits available in the industry.

Larger clothing firms have created a 'feeder pool' for machining staff consisting of their lowest-skilled staff, including ironers, line feeders, cleaners and layers-up. Junior machinists and cutters are sourced internally from this pool, usually against some internal assessment criteria. Recruitment for new machinists on this basis was evident in 30 per cent of firms. Positions on the next occupational level on the shop floor (senior and multi-skilled machinists), in turn, are filled by promoting junior machinists.

The dominant strategy that firms adopt to address skill shortages, especially for machinists, is to train young people as quickly as possible. However, a new machinist does not add value until she starts producing, and even as a qualified worker, it takes between 6 and 12 months before she starts to add value, thus impacting negatively on efficiency and profitability in the short term. Nevertheless, firms report a high success rate with this strategy, and that machinists from their training programmes are superior to industry recruits. Similarly, internal promotion is currently the most immediate option chosen to overcome skills shortages at supervisory and management levels, given the critical shortage of suitably qualified candidates. Despite the purported large reserve pool of labour, firms suggest that there are difficulties involved in drawing from it, as these people have low motivation levels and very little work experience.

Firms are also addressing shortages in line management positions through internal sourcing and promotion. Once again, the ways in which firms have addressed skills shortages and gaps at this occupational level distinguish between progressive and traditional firms. The former believe that they could recruit experienced staff from outside the industry, but choose not to, since they are set in their own ways and resistant to change – the antithesis of WCM methodology. Within this new methodology, firms ascribe a completely new role to the 'team leader' – who was traditionally seen as a 'supervisor':

> To achieve fundamental quality-at-source, there is a fundamental need for line supervisors [aka team managers] to possess the combined skills that traditionally are associated with quality engineers and technologists. That is, they should not only be able to recognise faults but identify why the flaws occur; for instance, when the wrong thread is used. In other words, they examine the entire supply chain, not just the quality of work. We need to incentivise this person by empowering them with responsibility for the entire value chain.

Talent-spotting has become an integral part of firm vision – this involves acknowledging the potential and aspirations of existing staff members, identifying suitable candidates, and providing formal training. These firms actually regard outside recruitment as a failure on the part of the company:

> Our system is such that when we recruit from outside, it is seen as a failure of management because there is no seeding. A cleaner needs to believe that she can become a cutter…

> From a skilled machinist, you become a supervisor. The idea is to start talent-spotting right from the start to identify who will become a supervisor…

Those firms not championing WCM strategies are also compelled to source internally to overcome skills shortages at supervisory and management levels because of the shortage of industry recruits. However, promotion is often not accompanied by additional training or formal skills development to effect the transition.

Sixty per cent of full-package clothing manufacturers (FPMs) reported that they were side-stepping shortages of machining staff by outsourcing an increasing portion of their production to CMTs. This strategy involves hiving off production of non-complex, cost-based garments to CMTs, while maintaining production of complex garments in-house. It is regarded as key to their future survival in a shrinking market, since it permits expansion and contraction of the workforce in tandem with seasonal demand.

> The rise of CMTs is very important given that the clothing business is so seasonal. Businesses try to hang on to their core staff like sample machinists and patternmakers and let the others go, because labour is a fixed cost. The only way to survive is either by having a brilliant production manager, at exorbitant cost, or to retrench and CMT. We took the latter option. We now have the same amount of people employed as before but as owner-managers.

Furthermore, this trend is escalating and is unlikely to reverse even if shortages are addressed, since it also provides firms facing production capacity constraints with an expansion path.

> We could run 60% of production through CMTs. In the last 6 months, turnover increased by 15% with a 25% growth in the proportion outsourced to CMTs. In other words, the growth has been accommodated entirely through the CMT industry.

Although outsourcing is an important future strategy for some firms, it does have limitations where firms are supplying large chains, due to reliability and quality problems which are generally associated with CMT operations.

Training and the SETA

Skills shortages and the transition to WCM practices demand increased training within firms. So how do the firms interviewed evaluate the usefulness and effectiveness of the SETA in addressing skills shortages? The CTFL SETA governance structure is based on a 50 : 50 split between labour and business – with the Southern African Clothing and Textile Workers Union (SACTWU) holding 50 per cent, and 16.6 per cent for each of the 3 business sectors. Strategic collaboration with any other sector gains SACTWU a controlling share. A prevalent view (particularly among clothing firms) is that SACTWU's *modus vivendi* on the body undermines the credibility of the SETA as a training and skills development initiative, illegitimately channels needed sector skills training funds for union training purposes, and exposes it as a political tool which is being used to solve compliance issues. This view is reinforced by the fact that the SETA marshals its resources around low-end skills development (adult basic education and training (ABET)), despite explicit requests by firms for high-level technical skills training.

All firms pay the SETA a skills development levy equal to one per cent of their wage bill, half of which forms the Mandatory Grant to refund training expenses, claimable on submission of the Workplace Skills Plan and Annual Training Report. Five per cent of collected funds are paid to the South African Revenue Service (SARS), 10 per cent towards administration, and 15 per cent towards the National Skills Fund. SACTWU claims a flat amount of R2 million from each sector for training of its shop stewards. The remaining funds are distributed between the sectors in proportion to their contribution. This forms the discretionary fund, which is used to fund projects to address 'scarce skills' identified by the SETA. These include i) skills programmes (short courses), ii) learnerships (allocated to companies) and iii) bursaries (allocated to individuals). All funding is dependent on Skills Development Participation, which prescribes that firms allocate 3 per cent of turnover to training and maintain a complement of learners equal to 3 per cent of the total workforce.

Firms say that the SETA directs the large bulk of its discretionary fund resources towards the provision of ABET, including assistance with HIV and life skills, in response to the chronically low levels of literacy and numeracy. Just over a quarter of firms expressed approval for the ABET programme, while the vast majority regard ABET as a waste of the SETA's limited resources. Of those who support ABET provision, three-quarters experience practical difficulties in motivating staff enrolment. In a significant move, in over one-third of firms, the ABET issue has been side-stepped by ensuring that new applicants have an education level of Grade 10 or above. The general sentiment is that, whilst ABET is important, it has run its course. The industry needs to re-focus and adopt a new strategy to deal with literacy and numeracy issues:

> We can do ABET training through the SETA but I want technical training.

The SETA offers technical training through learnerships for machine operators. There are two categories of learners (18.1 learners employed in the firm, and 18.2 learners not permanently employed), and two levels of technical training (basic and advanced multi-skilling). Both types of course are conducted by SETA-accredited service providers. The 18.2 course (12 weeks long) equips learners with basic theoretical and practical knowledge to address skills shortages. The advanced course has a small theoretical component but mostly involves on-the-job training for six months and aims to address skills gaps in the workforce. The firm claims reimbursement for training facilitators, but it is restricted in the amount of funding it can claim for the learners. A quota applies and the level of funding received is determined by the past number of learnership grants. A firm gets R15 000 per 18.1 learner up to 10 per cent of its workforce, and R7 500 per learner thereafter, up to a maximum of 20 per cent of its workforce. Firms stressed that the quota creates a one-off amount. The quota on 18.2 learners is not defined, and grants appear to be made at the SETA's discretion.

Twenty-seven per cent of firms, and exclusively those employing over 1 000 workers, conduct a greater proportion of their technical training through in-house programmes, which are SETA-accredited but not SETA-funded, than through learnerships or other SETA grants. These firms have expanded their training capacity significantly over the past two years, particularly amongst machining staff:

> We tried to recruit from the industry. After two months without success, we reverted to plan B, to train ourselves. We increased our training capacity in our two skills centres which we usually use for multi-skilling and decided to use the centres as basic training schools to get people for our new lines.

Large firms do not find the restriction of 20 per cent problematic. Of greater concern to these firms is the limitation on the number of learners that may be trained at any one time due to space and availability constraints, and the length of time that it takes for new recruits to qualify on a SETA course. Consequently, the urgency with which firms require skills is not being adequately addressed through SETA programmes:

> The SETA has a learnership programme for machinists; we get R7 500 per learner as well as R200 000 for a service-provider. But it took 16 weeks to train these learners where we are doing the same amount of training in a month.

> Only some of our line-feeders go on the full SETA course. 20–25 people who are line-feeders enter our training centre but not on learnerships. Another 20–25 people go on the SETA learnerships courses but we cannot afford in terms of time to do all our training through learnerships.

For smaller firms, the quota is a binding constraint on training through 18.1 learnerships. All of the smaller firms in the sample – those employing 150 people or less – conduct all formal workforce training through the SETA and train their machinists exclusively through SETA learnerships. Eighty per cent have exhausted their quota, some as early as 2002. Principally due to financial constraints, no formal training has taken place since then, although some on-the-job training has occurred. Having been granted an additional quota in 2007, these firms are resuming their learnerships but face future problems, predicting that they will have used up their quota by 2008.

> The problem with the SETA is the quota on funding. We get our staff all motivated, they see people coming back from the learnerships feeling empowered and then the SETA says that there is no more funding.

The upshot is that most firms regard the SETA as a thinly disguised business tax.

There are numerous other problems with the learnership mechanism. First, although the idea behind the 18.2 learnerships is job creation, employment is not guaranteed. Only 36 per cent of firms applied for learnerships in parallel with actual job opportunities within their organisation. Even those firms who place people on learnerships with genuine intentions of providing employment have no alternative but to release them if the vacancy is filled. There is no industry system disseminating information about qualified learners requiring placement. Every firm should be obliged to circulate a list of learners available for uptake; otherwise the resources are lost to the industry.

> The problem lies in the fact that we train learners with specific skills, in our case narrow fabric weaving, and then utilise them in another capacity, for instance, as a packer, so they don't stick around. The fact that the learnership does not guarantee them a job is a big problem.

Second, the average attrition rate amongst learners is 40 per cent.

> The problem with the learnerships is that because they are free and people are not paying for them out of their own pocket, they are not committed. We have learners that have completed 75 per cent of the course and then drop out because they get pregnant or decide that it is not what they want to do.

Third, 37 per cent of firms question the quality and content of the 18.1 programme, which claims to achieve multi-skilling capabilities on 3 machines in 5 operations.

> …[c]ertain things must be embedded…You could maybe achieve three operations, but five is not possible…We are looking to set up our own internal training programme which is better aligned with skills shortages.

Finally, whereas previously learnership payment came in two equal payments, it now dribbles in in a 20/40/40 split. This increases the immediate financial burden of training, which many smaller firms can ill-afford.

The SETA pays grants towards higher-skills development for specific FET diplomas which carry national certification. The purpose is to promote people from the FET to the HET band to fund skills development where skills supply shortages exist, as identified by the National Skills Audit. These include training for patternmaking and design, technology, general management, HR relations, marketing, clerical skills, bookkeeping and accounting, education and training and IT. Forty per cent of firms receive grants of R15 000 per learner for training in one or more of these categories. Where the grant is a bursary, educational institutions are directly reimbursed. Twenty-six per cent of firms receive funding for Bachelor of Technology (BTech) students at Cape Peninsula University of Technology, although they report that the SETA was reluctant to fund this, possibly due to the higher rate of reimbursement for these learners (R40 000).

> We had to do a lot of fighting to get this. They [the SETA] said that they didn't fund BTech students but they were talking about a new type of technologist so we pushed it from that side by saying that we believed that a person on that level has to have a BTech qualification.

There are, however, issues surrounding the quality and content of courses run by technikons/universities of technology, and the quality of graduates produced. Whilst 90 per cent of firms are satisfied that they are adequately addressing skills shortages for designers, this is not the case for patternmakers. Consequently, skills shortages in these areas persist and translate into excessively high wage rates.

> The technikons are generating such ineffective patternmakers that they are driving the price up to R19 000 per month. You need a world-class accreditation to justify this salary…Technikons are producing basic garden-variety patternmakers, so good ones are scarce.

There are similar misalignments between the quality of technologist graduates and those sought by firms. WCM envisages a technologist function surpassing mere quality assurance and encompassing an understanding of the entire value chain. Firms argue that technikons/universities of technology are basing their curriculum on the old methodology, not on WCM principles, creating a mismatch between the skills required by firms and those acquired through formal learning. In essence, the 'piece of paper' does not accurately reflect an 'ability to do the job', causing the firms to place less and less weight on formally acquired qualifications and increasingly rather on experience and practical know-how. This may be due to poor relationships between institutions and industry players – lecturers seldom enter the industry environment and thus are unaware of new methods, products etc. In an effort to marry the theoretical and practical elements of graduate training and equip graduates with on-the-job experience, textile firms have invited the technikons/universities of technology to allow graduates to do technical training within factories, and expressed overwhelming support for a distance-based learning initiative to allow individuals to learn on-the-job while also completing a tertiary degree.

When asked to comment generally on the SETA's usefulness, the response was decidedly negative. Among the smaller firms, the greatest problem area is the restriction on the number of learnerships. This is further complicated by the SETA's employment equity agenda embedded in the learnerships. Smaller firms tend to have a high proportion of coloured machining staff for which they urgently require funding, whilst African staff are mainly in unskilled positions. The greatest issue for larger firms is the waste of resources – the SETA is giving them money to do what they would do anyway, that is, invest in workforce training.

A major source of dispute is the allocation to SACTWU of a substantial sum for shop steward training from SETA discretionary funds which are meant for the up-skilling of workers, to make the industry more competitive. Firms legitimately feel that such utilisation of SETA funds for shop steward training does not upgrade the industry's competitiveness. However, the SETA's consensus-based governance structure makes firms feel that they have no choice – if they do not support this project, they fear being blocked on other firm-based training projects.

The division of funding between the respective sectors for training in FET and HET bands is also a prickly issue. Clothing firms feel that their sector receives a disproportionately small share of funding relative to the textiles industry:

> The way in which the system operates at present is not to attack the skills problem since the funding gets diverted along the way. It's like a bucket with holes in it, by the time you get to funding skills development, there is nothing left.

Accordingly, complaints against the SETA were lodged overwhelmingly by clothing firms. Textile firms, it would appear, have fewer problems with the SETA.

A major complaint is the lack of provision in the current SETA funding structure for high-level technical skills training. The main thrust of the SETA is towards the provision of basic education, rather than higher-skills development. This places the onus of up-skilling the bulk of their workforce squarely upon firms.

In the view of clothing firms, the SETA is not adequately addressing skills shortages. Interviews with individual firms suggest that the SETA is providing insufficient technical training assistance, choosing instead to marshal its resources around low-skills training. This is a direct contradiction of the stated objectives of the National Skills Plan to provide resource assistance to firms to overcome critical and scarce skills shortages in the industry. Some firms argue that the SETA and its funding programmes are little more than a weapon to wield against non-compliant firms.

> In present industry support structures SMMEs are starved by Big Business and SACTWU of resources and training desperately needed to improve their efficiencies as a consequence of their non-compliance. These efficiencies are sorely needed by them to become sustainable before they can afford the cost of the regulation imposed on them. It's a Catch-22 situation. The purpose is to ensure that through starving them of resources, the compliance managers of the bargaining council and the threat of gaol, they will eventually be forced to comply. The fact is as much as they want to…they have no means to…

Conclusion

The CTFL SETA identified scarce skills in high-end technical and management areas, and a shortage of artisans and skilled workers (mechanics). No scarce skills shortages were detected in the lower occupational strata. The SETA's priority interventions are increasing the number of learnerships, up-skilling of middle management, increasing the number of technologists, and upgrading the educational level of the workforce through ABET.

However, the firm interviews reveal that there is a major skills shortage of machinists, contradicting the SETA's argument that there are no scarce skills at operator level. Clothing firms overwhelmingly report difficulties with recruiting qualified machinists and plant operators from the industry, such that demand far outstrips supply. Firms also distinguish between *skills gaps* and *skills shortages*, which refer to fundamentally different skills problems. The former indicates a shortage of potential or available candidates in either number or quality, or both. The latter refers to the skills base of the existing workforce falling short of firms' needs. Skills gaps are of more immediate concern than skills shortages. Furthermore, future skills gaps are avoided by accompanying recruitment and promotion with appropriate and timeous training.

Firms are fundamentally differentiated by their strategic approaches to addressing skills shortages and gaps, based on their response to industry restructuring. In particular, firms embracing WCM principles in their operational performance platforms recruit new staff using criteria based on the new methodology. These firms have all but abandoned recruiting from the industry, and either source internally or recruit new outside people with the potential to fit into the new mould.

Alternatively, firms trapped in the old methodology, reproducing a historically obsolete operational platform, unsuccessfully try to recruit machinists and production staff from within the industry. They are compelled to fill vacancies in higher occupational categories by promoting existing staff into more senior positions. In this scenario, in contrast to that above, internal recruitment *creates* skills gaps, since people are promoted without the requisite attributes or capabilities to become effective managers.

Evidence from firms suggests (particularly in the case of clothing) that some unemployment in lower occupational spheres, and a large proportion at operator level, is voluntary – motivated by debt and the ability to access accumulated provident funds, accessing UIF payments, and the growth of the informal economy which provides the ability to maintain a certain level of disposable income. Hence, whilst many firms have closed and retrenched workers, there has been a concomitant (but not equal) rise in demand by surviving firms for semi-skilled workers, particularly machinists, which is not met through recruitment in the labour market.

There is a significant movement of operators/machinists into the clothing informal economy because it provides job opportunities closer to their homes, and access to immediately available disposable income. This implies that the employment problem at this level is fundamentally a *formal*-sector problem. Indeed, a large part of this problem is a problem experienced by the union and superimposed on the industry – union membership losses presenting as a loss of clothing-sector employment. It would seem that net involuntary job loss in the sector is significantly less than the official numbers imply. Instead we are witnessing the twin processes of industrial restructuring and a recomposition of labour.

With regard to addressing the skills problem in technical, professional and management occupations, recruiting 'new blood' is also frustrated by the poor quality of graduates entering the industry. In particular, there is a mismatch between qualification and the 'ability to perform'. This is blamed largely on misalignment of the curriculum with the practical needs of firms. Firms interviewed used the KwaZulu-Natal and Cape Clothing and Textile Clusters as sources of training for their medium- to high-skilled staff, using them to introduce WCM principles into their firms.

There is significant clothing-sector unhappiness with the SETA's operating activities, but this is not necessarily echoed in the textile sector. Firms argue that its fund allocation is inconsistent with the rhetoric of the Sector Skills Plan. The latter recognises the urgency of up-skilling and multi-skilling, whilst the former privileges basic skills and education. Furthermore, firms claim that the SETA gives insufficient emphasis to the need for low-end skills embedded at operator level.

The SETA's focus on ABET and learnerships as the dominant intervention in respect of lower-end training is not supported. They feel a disproportionate amount of funding is allocated to ABET, which has played a historical role but has run its course, and should not be critically prioritised. Instead, the available funding should focus on improving productivity through competitiveness training.

Furthermore, the learnership programme is not fulfilling the aims of firms, in terms of quantity trained, quality of training, funding availability, and learnership graduates being employed. Clothing firms were also very critical of the restrictions placed on the amount of funding available.

The shortage of artisans has been identified by all as a critical, scarce skills shortage. However, there is a major problem with the industry training new artisans. The current SETA programme (as in most industries) is simply not adequately addressing this problem.

A majority of firms expressed deep dissatisfaction with the way the SETA is training shop floor workers. When resources are scarce, interventions need to be prioritised. In the context of the massive problem of skills facing the industry, the critical importance of raising the skill levels in production, and the scarce available resources to undertake this task, the allocation of SETA funds for shop steward training (albeit to sensitise them to the importance of skills) seems highly problematic indeed. There seems to be little rationale for prioritising the allocation of much-needed funds to the union rather than to the firms themselves to undertake competitiveness training of their workforce.

In the eyes of many clothing firms, the SETA is further undermined by its practice of denying training funds to non-compliant firms in the Bargaining Council. The latter's massive problem of non-compliance should be solved within its own parameters. It is simply illegitimate to use the SETA for this purpose, and unacceptable that the government and some industry partners have acquiesced to union demands to do so. This is all the more so, given the critical and crying need for training in the industry, when the firms being penalised are the smaller enterprises struggling against international competition.

In conclusion, there is a desperate need for a large-scale, government-funded training programme to raise and upgrade skills levels. Moreover, firms require different skills interventions and a 'one size fits all' programme is doomed to failure. Finally, the current institutional structure sucks up resources. Whilst textile firms and the union may be content with the current structure, the SETA in its current form and role is not addressing the diverse needs of clothing firms.

This is not a situation unique to this sector. Kaplan argues that SETAs are government bureaucracies tying up managerial resources, diverting financial resources, and imposing an unnecessary bureaucratic layer between firms and training providers/activities:

> An alternative system would allow firms to determine their training needs without intercession of any state bureaucracy. Firms could approach any licensed training institution, public or private, and determine their training programme. Firms would pay the training provider for their services. Training expenditures would be specified in the firm's tax return. The firm would receive a tax deduction…Government would be a postbox – payments made by firms to licensed training providers would automatically attract subsidy. Government would not scrutinize training programmes. Its substantive role would be confined to licensing training institutions, with considerable saving of scarce management resources.[6]

Ultimately the future of the industry depends on its ability to upgrade firm production capabilities and create successful value chain alignment so as to achieve systemic competitiveness. This requires rethinking policy to address the skills gaps and skills shortages. Otherwise the industry will not take the upward step along the ladder to international competitiveness.

References

Barnes J & Esselaar J (2005) Customised sector programme: Clothing and textiles draft research report. BM Analysts report prepared for the Department of Trade and Industry

CTFL SETA (Clothing, Textiles, Footwear and Leather Sector Education and Training Authority) (2004) *An assessment of skills needs in the clothing, textiles, footwear and leather sectors: CTFL SETA skills audit.* Pinetown: CTFL SETA

CTFL SETA (2006) *Sector skills plan 2005–2010 (5th edition).* Pinetown: CTFL SETA

Daniels R (2007) *Skills shortages in South Africa.* Working Paper 07/21, Development Policy Research Unit, School of Economics, University of Cape Town

Edwards L & Morris M (2007) Undressing the numbers: The employment effect of import quotas on clothing and textiles. *Journal of Development Perspectives* 2(2): 121–140

Morris M & Einhorn G (2008) Globalisation, welfare and competitiveness: The impacts of Chinese imports on the South African clothing and textile industry. Mimeo, Policy Research in International Services and Manufacturing (PRISM), School of Economics, University of Cape Town

---

6   Kaplan D, A fix for skills crunch, *Financial Mail* 24 August 2007

Morris M & Reed L (2008) *A sectoral analysis of skills gaps and shortages in the clothing and textile industry in South Africa*. Report for the Human Sciences Research Council of South Africa

Pye M (2002) *An assessment of skill needs in the clothing, textiles, footwear and leather and furniture, furnishings and interiors industries*. UK Skills dialogue: Listening to employers, 12. Nottingham: Dept for Education and Skills. Accessed 29 March 2008, http://www.dfes.gov.uk/skillsdialoguereports/docs/SD12_%20Clothing.pdf

Rasool H (2006) Re-positioning textiles apprenticeship training in South Africa: Policies, practices and future directions for the CTFL SETA. Unpublished paper, September, Durban

Roberts S & Thoburn J (2002) *Globalisation and the South African textiles industry*. Discussion Paper 9, UK Department for International Development Research Project 'Globalisation, Production and Poverty' (R7623). Accessed 29 March 2008, http://www.gapresearch.org/production/DP9%20SAf%20textiles.pdf

US ITC (US International Trade Commission) (2004) *Textiles and apparel: Assessment of the competitiveness of certain foreign suppliers to the U.S. market*. Volume I, Investigation No. 332-448. Washington DC: US ITC

CHAPTER 11

Agro-processing

Duncan Pieterse

Overview of the agro-processing sector

Agro-processing refers to the subset of manufacturing that adds value to raw materials and intermediate products derived from the agricultural sector (agriculture, forestry and fisheries). It includes processes that follow harvesting, including those activities that do not necessarily change the form of the product but improve its value (DTI 2006a). There is a high degree of interdependence with forward and backward activities in the agro-processing value chain. In developing countries, the interest in agro-processing is associated with its potential for generating demand for primary produce from small-scale farmers, upgrading primary production through small-scale food processing and improving food price stability and food security (Cardoso 2000; Saasa 2000).

Agro-processing is suited to developing countries because processing plants are not always scale-dependent – small operations can be as economically efficient as larger plants which benefit from economies of scale (FAO 1997). Therefore, agro-processing could play an important role in supporting economic development and thus contribute to poverty reduction and economic inclusion. As a result of its potential to contribute to broad-based economic development, various strategies have been developed at a national level to optimise the impact of agro-processing.

Output in the agro-processing sector increased between 1995 and 2006, as illustrated in Figure 11.1.

Food is by far the largest agro-processing sub-sector, followed by paper and paper products and beverages. The food sub-sector also showed the largest growth in output between 1995 and 2006.

However, despite this growth, the agro-processing sector's share of total output steadily declined from 9.7 per cent in 1995 to 7.8 per cent in 2006, and its share of manufacturing output declined from 29.5 per cent to 24.7 per cent over the same period. This decline can be explained by output growth in the motor vehicles and vehicle parts, chemicals and televisions, and communication equipment sub-sectors (Mather 2005). At 24.7 per cent of total manufacturing output, agro-processing still represents a significant proportion of the total manufacturing sector.

The food sub-sector is the largest employer within the agro-processing sector – contributing 1.4 per cent and 11.5 per cent to total and manufacturing employment respectively. Beverages and wood are the only sub-sectors that experienced increased employment between 1995 and 2006, contributing 7 281 and 15 769 jobs, respectively (Figure 11.2).

FIGURE 11.1: *Agro-processing output (constant 2000 rands), 1995–2006*

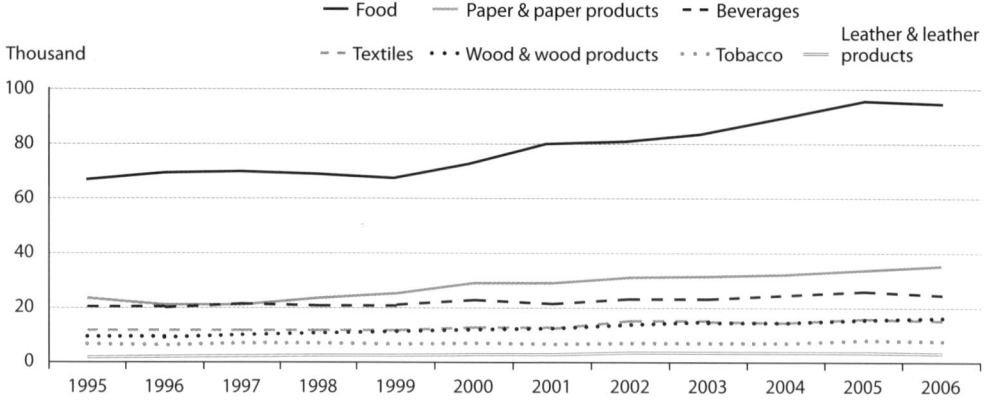

Source: Quantec 2007

FIGURE 11.2: *Agro-processing employment, 1995–2006*

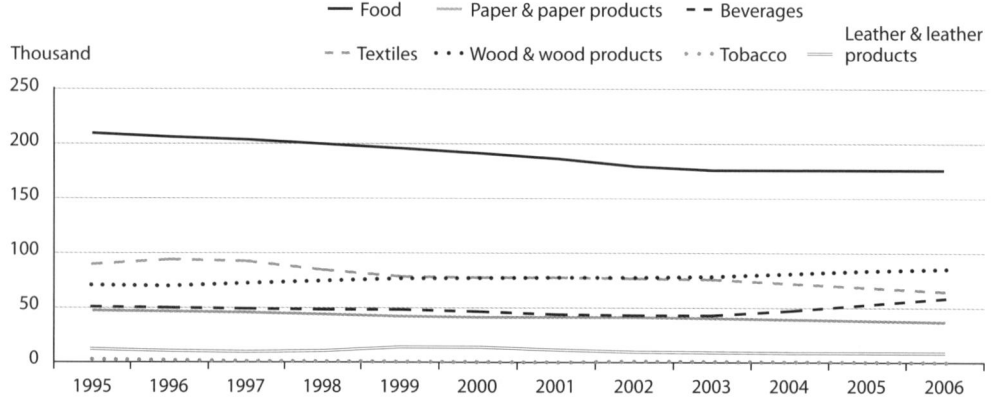

Source: Quantec 2007

Although the economy as a whole gained 975 941 jobs between 1995 and 2006, the agro-processing and manufacturing sectors lost 45 977 and 130 867 jobs respectively. Most of the employment growth came from the tertiary sectors (in particular, financial and business services and internal trade), which added 2.5 million jobs between 1995 and 2005, and the secondary sector (in particular, construction, which added 488 000 jobs over the same period) (DoL 2006).

The declining employment in agro-processing is largely caused by the restructuring of the sector in response to greater competitive pressures associated with lower tariffs and a freer trade regime. In the last 10 years, South Africa's tariff structure has changed dramatically (Vink & Kirsten 2002). The result has been a rapid increase in cheaper imports that have had a significant impact on several agro-processing sub-sectors.

FIGURE 11.3: *Agro-processing exports (constant 2000 rands), 1995–2006*

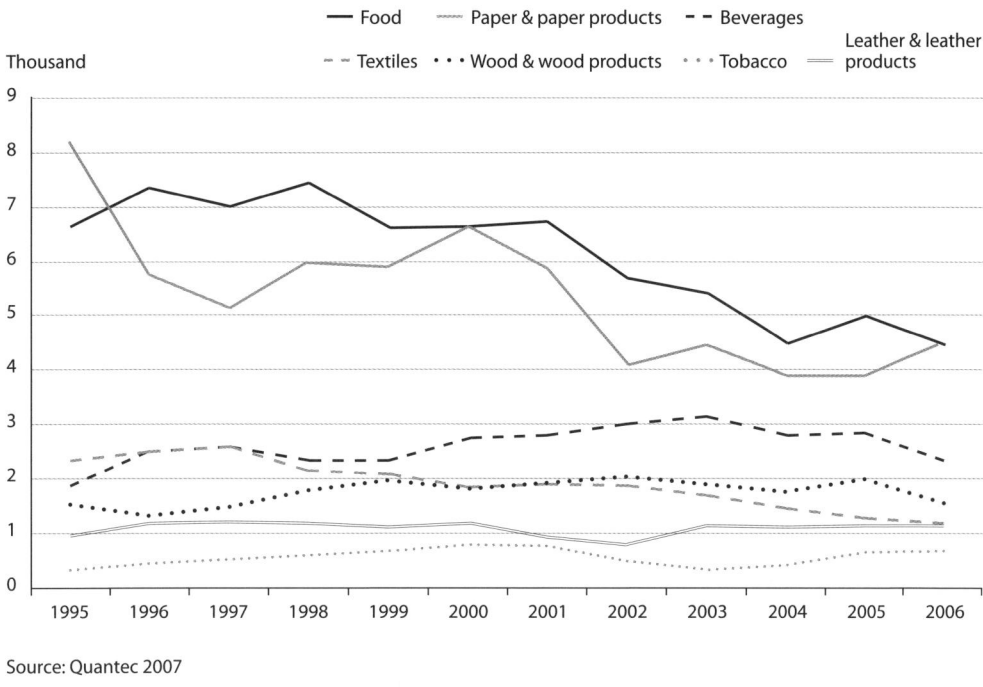

Source: Quantec 2007

The agro-processing sector's share of total employment declined marginally from 4 per cent in 1995 to 3.6 per cent in 2006, and its share of manufacturing employment declined from 29.1 per cent to 28.2 per cent over the same period.

The competitive pressures on agro-processing mentioned before also played a role in the decline of exports for the food, textiles and paper sub-sectors (Figure 11.3), as firms in these sectors increasingly compete with lower-cost producers, particularly in China and India. Increased exports from the beverages, tobacco, wood and leather sub-sectors over the period are probably the result of the presence in South Africa of large dominant firms within these sub-sectors that have managed to protect themselves from foreign competition.

The agro-processing sector's share of total exports declined significantly, from 10.7 per cent in 1995 to 5.1 per cent in 2006, and its share of manufacturing exports declined from 21.1 per cent to 10.4 per cent over the same period. However, research has shown that exports of processed food products to Southern African Development Community (SADC) countries – mainly in the form of cereals, milling products, dairy and sugar – increased dramatically (Vink et al. 2002). This regional market is becoming increasingly important for exporters of South Africa's processed food products (Mather 2005).

Prioritised agro-processing sub-sectors

This sector study will focus on the following sub-sectors within the agro-processing sector: food, beverages, and leather and leather products. These three prioritised sub-sectors feature in the labour-intensive sector cluster, which is one of six clusters proposed by the National Industrial Policy Framework.

As a number of sectors face similar challenges and therefore require similar support, clustering allows government departments to optimise administrative resources needed to develop these sectors (DTI 2006b).

Food and beverages

South Africa is active at all stages of the value chain, although basic agro-processing products dominate production and exports. In the food sub-sector, the major exports (by value) are fresh fruit and nuts, sugar, processed fruit and vegetables, fish products and cereals and grains (USDA 2004). Milled grain products constitute the largest food sub-sector, as these contribute 17 per cent to total output (USDA 2004). The major food products (by volume) are refined sugar (1 232 mt), bread flour (812 112 t), sunflower seed oil (438 720 t) and fish meal (142 654 t) (Stats SA 2003).

The beverages sub-sector comprises three industries: malt and beverages, distilleries and wineries, and soft drinks; these constitute 41 per cent, 32 per cent and 27 per cent of total production, respectively (USDA 2004). The major beverages (by volume) are natural wines (211 210 kl), brandy (18 144 kl) and sparkling wines (9 654 kl) (Stats SA 2003). Although there are more than 7 297 food and beverage companies (FoodBev SETA 2007), the top 10 companies are responsible for 70 per cent of the industry's turnover (USDA 2004). These large companies tend to be vertically integrated into both primary production and retailing – for example, Tiger Brands has a controlling interest in the Spar retail group as well as interests in grain milling (Mather 2005).

Leather and leather products

South African leather value chains have undergone a substantial transformation over the last decade as a direct result of the effects of a more liberal economy; from being relatively untraded before liberalisation, when each stage of the value chain was oriented to a domestic market or supply base, leather has become highly traded and exported at various stages of beneficiation (Ballard 2002).

Total exports of leather and leather products (including footwear) amount to US$485.94 million (Ballard 2002). This is shared between automotive upholstery (58 per cent), leathers, skins and hides (38 per cent), and general goods (e.g. exotic leather handbags) and footwear (5 per cent). Exports of exotic leather are valued at US$62 million, compared to exports of bovine leather of US$43.8 million. Therefore it is the most important component of exports of raw materials by value, despite the fact that almost 14 times less volume of exotic leather is exported than tanned bovine leather.

South Africa produces about two million cattle hides and five million sheepskins (Turvey 2002). Fifty per cent of the total production is exported in wet-blue form and the remaining 50 per cent is split between the automotive leather and footwear industries (with the automotive leather industry consuming about 80 per cent). South Africa currently produces 70 per cent of the global ostrich leather output, down from 100 per cent in the late 1990s.

In the past, most tanneries were oriented towards producing leather for the footwear industry; however, with the decline in footwear production and increased use of imported footwear leather, many of these tanneries either closed or switched to manufacturing leather for the automotive upholstery industry. As a result, there have been massive job losses in the general leather goods sector. However, growth in new sectors, in particular, automotive upholstery, has compensated for these declines. At least one large company is vertically integrated across both tanning and semi-finished goods – KAP International Holdings Ltd owns both the largest tannery in South Africa (Mossop-Western Leathers) as well as the largest manufacturer of automotive leather goods (Feltex Automotive Leather).

The demand for skills

Employment trends in the prioritised sectors

As mentioned earlier, although the food sub-sector is the largest employer of the prioritised agro-processing sectors, the beverages industry is the only sub-sector in which employment levels increased between 1995 and 2006.

Formal employment in the three prioritised sub-sectors and informal employment in the food and leather sub-sectors decreased between 1995 and 2006. However, informal employment in the beverages sub-sector showed a significant increase during the same period. In the beverages sub-sector, informal employment, as a share of total employment, increased from 9 per cent to 34 per cent and formal employment, as a share of total employment, decreased from 90 per cent to 65 per cent (Quantec 2007).

In the food sub-sector, high-skilled and semi- and unskilled employees, as a share of total employment, remained stable between 1996 and 2005, whereas skilled employees, as a share of total employment, declined from 36 per cent to 32 per cent. The beverages sub-sector experienced similar dynamics, with skilled and semi- and unskilled workers most affected by job losses. However, it is clear that the skilled and semi- and unskilled workforce recovered after 2003. High-skilled, skilled, and semi- and unskilled employees, as shares of total sector employment, decreased from 9 per cent to 7 per cent, 28 per cent to 20 per cent and 52 per cent to 38 per cent, respectively. This confirms the decline in formal employment in the beverages sub-sector, as most of the employment growth in the sub-sector came from the informal sector (Quantec 2007).

Employment in the leather sub-sector peaked in 2000, after which consistent job losses were experienced, in particular, in the skilled and semi- and unskilled sections of the workforce. The peak in employment coincided with the highest level of exports for the leather sub-sector between 1995 and 2006 (Quantec 2007). It is likely that restructuring in the industry and the closure of some manufacturing plants contributed to the decline after 2000.

These job losses were mostly confined to the general leather goods and wet-blue industries, because employment in the automotive leather industry increased in response to recent demand resulting from the automotive industry incentive programme, the Motor Industry Development Programme (MIDP), which encourages automotive manufactures to use local products.

High-skilled and semi- and unskilled employees, as a share of total employment, increased from 4 per cent to 5 per cent and 40 per cent to 47 per cent, respectively, while skilled employees, as a share of total employment, decreased from 42 per cent to 41 per cent (Quantec 2007).

In all three prioritised sub-sectors, high-skilled labour was the least affected by job losses between 1995 and 2006. The primary factor behind this is increasing capital intensity in production, which is occurring simultaneously with the expansion of exports in the beverages and leather sub-sectors. South Africa has a remarkably low, and declining, share of exports that use unskilled labour, and a relatively high share of exports using more skilled labour (Lewis 2002). This reflects a change in the structure of the South African economy away from primary towards tertiary or services-based output (Bhorat & Oosthuizen 2007). This explains why the manufacturing sector as a whole has lost jobs at a rate greater than the growth of the labour force, despite the rapid growth in exports (Altman & Mayer 2003; McCord 2003; McCord & Bhorat 2003).

Recent employment trends by occupation

In the food and beverages sub-sectors, the majority of employees are male and can be found in the lower skill categories as labourers and machine operators and drivers. The single largest category of food and beverages employees is male machine operators and drivers. Most machine operators and drivers and labourers are African and coloured, while white employees are generally found in the higher skill bands as managers and professionals. Gender equality decreases significantly as one moves from the lower skill bands to higher skill categories, such as managers and professionals. For example, women constitute 15 per cent of all labourers, 6 per cent of all machine operators and drivers, and 7 per cent of all clerical and administrative workers, but only 1 per cent of all managers and professionals.

African employees in the food and beverage sub-sectors are less qualified than their coloured and Indian counterparts and make up the highest share of workers with no proof of qualification (32 per cent of the total African workforce). Indian employees have the highest share of workers with qualifications below the General Education and Training (GET) certificate (54 per cent), compared to 34 per cent of Africans. For National Qualifications Framework (NQF) Levels 4–8, the pattern is standard: white employees have the highest share of workers at each NQF level, followed by Indian, coloured and African employees. This pattern is essentially reversed for NQF Levels 1–3: African employees have the highest share of workers at each NQF level, followed by coloured, Indian and white employees. This confirms that the historical relationship between race and skill level is still very evident in the food and beverages sub-sectors (FoodBev SETA 2007).

In the dairy industry, the majority of employees can be found in the lower skill bands, in two occupational categories: plant and machine operators, and assemblers and elementary occupations.

The remainder of employees are in the middle-skill bands, such as technicians and associate professionals, clerks and service workers, and shop and sales workers. All of these occupational categories in the lower and middle-skill bands experienced growth between 2000 and 2005. Overall, according to these data, employment in the dairy industry grew between 2000 and 2005. Although men represent the majority of the workforce in the dairy industry, most of the growth has been at the low-skill levels, and African and coloured female employees have benefited most from growth in this sector. This is consistent with an increase in demand for dairy products by an emerging class of consumers in South Africa who are now able to afford dairy products such as yogurt and cheese, as their incomes grow (Stats SA 2000–2005 with author calculations).

In the clothing, textiles, footwear and leather sub-sectors, the majority of employees are female and work as plant and machine operators and assemblers. These figures are slightly skewed by the number of women working in the clothing and textiles sub-sectors, which represent 89 per cent of the total workforce included in the Clothing, Textiles, Footwear and Leather Sector Education and Training Authority (CTFL SETA) Sector Skills Plan (CTFL SETA 2006). Plant and machine operators and assemblers represent 53 per cent of the total workforce – most of these are African and coloured, while white employees are generally found in the higher skill bands as managers and professionals. Male and female Indian employees are relatively well represented in higher skill categories such as managers and technicians.

The African workforce in the clothing, textiles, footwear and leather sub-sectors are less qualified than their coloured and Indian counterparts, and have the highest share of workers with qualifications lower than the GET certificate (2 per cent of the total African workforce compared to 0.2 per cent for Indian and coloured employees). A similar qualifications pattern to the food and beverages sub-sectors emerges: for NQF Levels 5–8, white employees have the highest share of workers at each level, followed by Indian, coloured and African employees. Again, this pattern is essentially reversed for NQF

Levels 1–3, confirming that the historical relationship between race and skill level is still very evident in the clothing, textiles, footwear and leather sub-sectors (CTFL SETA 2006).

In the leather sub-sector, where the female employees outnumber the male, the majority of employees are trades workers and technicians. As a result, 84 per cent of the leather workforce is classified as having intermediate skill levels. As mentioned earlier, most tanneries were previously oriented towards producing for the footwear industry; however, with the decline in footwear production and increased use of imported footwear leather, many of those tanneries either closed or switched to manufacturing leather for the automotive upholstery industry. As a result, there have been massive job losses in the general leather goods and wet-blue industries. However, employment amongst white employees has grown – this suggests that with increasing capital intensity and consolidation of manufacturing capacity, white employees, who are presumably more skilled, were retained despite an overall decline in employment (Stats SA 2000–2005 with author calculations).

The supply of skills

This chapter focuses on data for graduates from further education and training (FET) and higher education and training (HET) institutions to understand the provision of skills that are relevant to the prioritised sub-sectors (DoE 2007a, 2007b). It also identifies bottlenecks and constraints in skills development as well as scarce skills within the prioritised sub-sectors.

Graduates from FET institutions

The highest number of FET graduates in natural sciences subjects is in the mechanical engineering trades (59 per cent of the total number of graduates), followed by the electricians (19 per cent) and manufacturing trades workers (11 per cent). With the exception of mechanical engineering trades and electricians, all occupational fields experienced declines in numbers of FET graduates between 2000 and 2005. In terms of the prioritised sub-sectors, there were no graduates in food trades work in 2005 and 2 834 graduates in the textile, clothing and footwear trades. Both these occupational fields experienced a decline in FET graduates from 2000 to 2005 of 30 per cent and 13 per cent respectively. Several technical occupational fields, including waste water plant operators, mechanical engineering trades, manufacturing trades, electricians, chemical technicians and air-conditioning and refrigeration mechanics, exhibited very low average pass rates between 2000 and 2005.

The highest number of FET graduates in general subjects is in the management studies (27 per cent), accountancy (22 per cent) and communication (20 per cent) fields. With the exception of accountancy, agricultural technicians and economics, all occupational fields experienced declines in numbers of FET graduates between 2000 and 2005. In terms of the prioritised sub-sectors, there were 2 617 graduates in the clothing trades, 395 agricultural technicians and 3 382 graduates in hospitality. On average, the pass rates for general subjects were much higher than those for natural sciences subjects.

It should be noted that employment prospects for FET graduates remain very low (DoL 2005). In South Africa, only 33.6 per cent of FET students found employment after graduation, with 69.7 per cent of African graduates unemployed but only 24.2 per cent of white graduates unemployed (Cosser et al. 2003). In addition, research conducted by the Development Policy Research Unit at the University of Cape Town showed that there are approximately 200 000 unemployed graduates in South Africa, with a mix of certificates, diplomas and degrees. Unemployment among African graduates, in particular, rose faster than any other category of the unemployed: between 1995 and 2005, the unemployment rate for graduates increased by half from 6.6 per cent to 9.7 per cent (The Presidency 2006).

Graduates from universities and universities of technology

Higher education in South Africa plays a major role in the development of a high-skilled workforce, in the form of professionals and managers, as well as producing the scientists and knowledge base critical to the national system of innovation (DoL 2005).

In agricultural food technology, there were no certificate, diploma or Bachelor of Technology (BTech) graduates in 2005. The largest numbers of graduates were those who obtained bachelor's degrees; graduates obtaining these qualification also increased between 2000 and 2005. Graduates were mostly white and female, with no coloured graduates in 2005. There were significantly more graduates in food and nutrition (595 graduates, compared to 72 graduates in agricultural food technology). The majority of these graduates were African and female, and these categories grew by 22 per cent and 11 per cent between 2000 and 2005, respectively. Most food and nutrition graduates obtained a national diploma, with very few obtaining higher qualifications – it is likely that provision of this qualification is skewed towards universities of technology. However, albeit from a low base, there has been significant growth in the number of graduates obtaining a bachelor's degree – indicating that universities are becoming more active in the provision of this qualification.

In engineering and technology qualifications that are relevant to the prioritised sub-sectors, namely, agricultural engineering and technology and manufacturing engineering and technology, there were very few graduates at all levels. This is particularly significant, given that these qualifications are most relevant to the intermediate skills required by these prioritised sub-sectors in the form of trades workers.

In addition, the graduates in agricultural engineering and technology were split between higher qualification levels, that is, professional bachelor's degree and master's qualifications, highlighting the fact that this qualification is generally provided by universities and often feeds into specialist agricultural programmes (such as the viticulture programme for winemakers at the University of Stellenbosch). In contrast, graduates in manufacturing engineering and technology obtained national diplomas, which indicates that these are the intermediate qualifications required by the prioritised sub-sectors. However, given that there were only 16 graduates in 2005, this may be insufficient to meet needs.

Business, commerce and management (BCM) graduates were more evenly split between the various levels of qualifications (and therefore more evenly split between universities and universities of technology). There were 1 864 marketing, 1 416 personnel management, 1 894 other management, 12 267 accounting, 799 administration and 6 998 management graduates in 2005, with a significant number of these obtaining postgraduate qualifications – this is also where most of the growth in graduates between 2000 and 2005 occurred.

Progress has been made in shifting the balance of enrolment in HET institutions across the humanities, social sciences and education (HSSE), BCM sciences, and science, engineering and technology (SET), as proposed by the National Plan for Higher Education (DoE 2001).

The ability of the higher education system to produce sufficient skilled graduates to meet South Africa's needs is constrained by the high rate of student dropout (DoL 2006). Of the 120 000 undergraduates who entered higher education for the first time in the year 2000, half of the cohort dropped out before completing their degree and only 22 per cent of the total cohort had graduated at the end of their third or fourth year of study (DoE 2005).

Recommendations

This chapter contains recommendations based on an analysis of the demand and supply data, as well as the case studies, aimed at proposing sector and skills development initiatives that respond to the current and future trends in the prioritised sub-sectors.[1]

Food and beverages

The food and beverages sub-sectors are expected to be underpinned by significant growth in food sales, which will drive higher prices for many food and beverage products, including wheat, maize and milk. While developed economies, such as the EU, are experiencing continued upgrades away from staples (such as bread and rice) to higher-value food products (such as organic alternatives), current global growth in food and beverages is linked to the growing wealth of emerging economies like China and India.

In addition, increasing global demand for food and beverages, as well as subsidies for biofuel production in many developed economies such as the USA, are driving increased food prices throughout the world. Biofuel subsidies have the effect of pushing up prices for maize, sugar and other feedstock for biofuel as well as the general prices of food throughout the economy. When governments subsidise biofuel feedstocks such as maize, farmers switch from other produce such as grain to maize, in order to benefit from the subsidy. This results in a decline in the supply of grain, which increases the grain price if demand is unchanged. Also, when biofuel plants compete with food producers for biofuel feedstock such as sugar cane, this increased demand has the effect of pushing up prices for these products.

Small-scale markets, including South Africa and Latin America, experienced the fastest overall regional growth in food and beverages for 2004, at 10 per cent and 7 per cent respectively. Europe experienced the slowest growth, with only 2 per cent growth in sales in 2004, while the Asia-Pacific region grew at 5 per cent. North America (that is, the USA and Canada) grew at 4 per cent over the same period, but showed the largest growth in absolute value terms. According to the FoodBev SETA (2007), economic growth in South Africa's food and beverages sub-sectors is projected to match that of the wider economy, which is expected to grow at 4–5 per cent between 2007 and 2010.

Sector development

In general, the requirements for the development of the food and beverages sub-sectors to serve highly competitive export markets are high. Based on the challenges faced by the food and beverages firms interviewed as part of the case studies (see note 1) and the wider industry dynamics, it is evident that local firms should focus on the following areas:

Competitive cost structure: cost competitiveness is initially driven by the availability of key primary inputs (e.g. crops and chemicals) and key secondary inputs (e.g. labour, electricity and water) at competitive prices. However, for local and export market penetration, transport and logistics costs can be substantial. Therefore cost-to-market needs to be competitive for firms to grow within their respective industries.

---

1   Interviews were conducted with the following firms during October 2007:
    Food firms: Epic Foods (Aeroton) (170 employees); Langeberg and Ashton Foods (Wellington) (371 employees);
    Beverages firms: Ceres (Ceres) (450 employees); Distell (Stellenbosch) (4 237 employees);
    Food and beverages firms: Fairfield Dairy (Howick) (220 employees); Illovo Sugar (Mount Edgecombe)
    (2 352 employees);
    Leather and leather products firms: Mossop-Western Leathers (Wellington) (261 employees); African Hide Trading
    (Port Elizabeth) (229 employees); Swartland Tanning (Wellington) (19 employees).

Product safety and quality control: to meet increasingly stringent local and international requirements on the part of consumers, retailers and regulators, food and beverage manufacturers need to run appropriate quality procedures, such as hazard analysis critical control point (HACCP) methodology, in their operating environments. There is also increasing emphasis on tracking-and-tracing systems through which ingredients and their handling can be monitored across the entire supply chain.

Economies of scale for retail and export supply: food and beverage manufacturing operations in South Africa are clearly sustainable at all levels of operation, from small-scale local to large-scale national manufacturing. However, to serve retailers and participate in export opportunities, significant production volumes and economies of scale are required. The ability to consistently produce the required volume at the right quality and price, and just-in-time (JIT) to meet tight supply windows, are key supplier selection requirements for retailers and exporters.

Highly efficient supply chain management: food and beverage manufacturing involves complex supply chain management to ensure availability of raw material inputs and to meet the increasingly stringent delivery windows demanded by retailers and export/import agents. In addition to the required management capability, the use of ICT for supply chain management is now a key driver of competitiveness. The trend is towards ICT system integration across the entire food supply chain.

High quality of transport infrastructure: processed foods range from perishable to non-perishable products, all with their own storage requirements and sell-by dates. Transport infrastructure that can cater to the needs of the entire range of processed food products to ensure they reach markets timeously and in saleable condition is therefore crucial. The extent to which the quality of infrastructure can minimise transport costs (during processing and delivery of final goods) is important, as it enhances the overall competitiveness of food producers.

Ability to tailor products, packaging and marketing strategies to suit varied consumers: consumer and retailer needs vary by region; hence producers cannot adopt a standardised or uniform approach to all their market segments. As the regional SADC market is becoming increasingly important for South African exporters of food and beverages, manufacturers should focus on understating the tastes and preferences (including packaging, etc.) of regional customers.

Innovation and customer applications and processes expertise: there has been a shift in the relationship between industrial users and ingredients suppliers. Industrial customers in the fruit and beverage processing industries now look for more knowledge and expertise, rather than just the products. Increasingly, this important buyer group is looking to suppliers to sell them a product concept that is closely tailored to their needs. Accordingly, products increasingly need to be provided with product specifications, instructions for use and storage, product presentation, and information on quality assurance (e.g. HACCP). Suppliers need a strong understanding of the industrial manufacturer's applications and processes to ensure that the products they supply are tailored to the customer's operations and complement their business and R&D strategies. As a result, there is an increased focus on the supply of value-added products and related business services.

Professional business-to-business (B2B) transactions: international retailers in key consumer markets are driving industry consolidation and an increased focus on standards throughout the entire food supply chain. This requires suppliers to become more sophisticated business partners to the retailing and food processing industry. In terms of business management, there is an increasing focus on professional logistics, strong supply chain management capabilities and electronic data exchange, in order to facilitate a seamless supply chain.

Trademarks, market relationships and institutions: in the processed fruit and vegetable industries, intangible assets such as brand trademarks are often more important than capital or technology and may drive higher returns (USDA 2005). Other intangible issues that are important are the relationships with increasingly global retailers. To achieve this, it is often beneficial for food and beverages firms to have significant product category expertise, as retailers are increasingly organised according to category management practices. Strong relationships with retailers are particularly critical for entering new markets and launching new products. Institutional support is particularly important as a driver of better co-ordination and co-operation between market players across the food supply chain (that is, growers, manufacturers, market intermediaries, retailers, etc.).

Skills development

Several skills development themes emerge from the case studies as well as the wider industry dynamics discussed earlier; this section contains recommendations for skills development based on these dynamics.

Matching supply and demand: there were no graduates in food trades worker fields from FET institutions in 2005 and a decline of 30 per cent from 2000 to 2005. With regard to HET institutions, there were no certificate, diploma or BTech graduates for agricultural food technology in 2005. There were significantly more graduates in food and nutrition, a course provided largely by FET institutions, compared to graduates in agricultural food technology (a course provided largely by HET institutions). Also, in the relevant engineering and technology qualifications, such as agricultural engineering and technology and manufacturing engineering and technology, there were very few graduates at all levels. This is confirmed by the vacancy data presented earlier. Given that skills are demanded at the higher NQF levels, HET institutions in particular should introduce more courses related to food technology and chemistry, and companies should promote on-the-job coaching, mentoring and guidance to address the graduates' lack of work experience.

Producing employable graduates: current supply from tertiary institutions does not provide adequate skill sets to meet the requirements of the food and beverages sub-sectors. HR managers have indicated that many graduates, particularly African graduates, lack the 'soft skills', such as communication and writing skills, required in the work environment. There should be a greater degree of partnership between training providers and industry. For example, courses could be jointly designed by employers, FET and HET institutions and professional bodies and funded through the National Skills Development Strategy (NSDS) or bursary schemes to deal with any skill deficiencies evident amongst graduates, in particular, those graduates who are currently unemployed. The provision of work orientation and life skills programmes should be introduced by employers to address the lack of 'soft skills'.

Greater private-sector involvement: the private sector should become more proactive in signalling the types of skills they require to training providers such as HET and FET institutions. For example, manufacturers should provide a greater number of bursary schemes that are aligned to their own scarce skills to ensure that there are fewer mismatches between supply and demand, and therefore improve the employability of graduates. Currently, there is insufficient investment by companies in bursaries and internship opportunities to develop skills at the higher occupational levels. In addition, private-sector firms should ensure industry participation in public education initiatives, curriculum development, field trips and career fairs for students, and provide short work experience opportunities and internships on an ongoing basis.

Addressing racial inequalities: African employees in the food and beverages sub-sectors are less qualified than their coloured and Indian counterparts and have the highest share of workers with no proof of qualification (32 per cent of the total African workforce). Indian employees have the highest share of workers with qualifications below the GET certificate (54 per cent), compared to 34 per cent of Africans. White employees have the highest share of workers at higher NQF levels (4–8), followed by Indian, coloured and African employees. Skills development initiatives must continue to focus on improving racial equality in the workplace through the use of grants offered by the FoodBev SETA and learnerships and apprenticeships offered by the private sector. Also, the FoodBev SETA must ensure that its recognition of prior learning (RPL) processes are working and are widely understood, in order to ensure that workers with no proof of qualification, but significant practical experience, are brought into the NQF framework.

Increasing the number of private service providers: there is currently a shortage of private providers of industry-specific training, for example, in the dairy industry. In addition, some firms have mentioned that specific courses, which could be provided by private service providers, are currently not being offered widely enough by private or public training providers. This includes training on aspects related to sanitary and phyto-sanitary requirements for specific food and beverages industries, the workings of contracts, and futures and currency forecasting and cash flow management.

Targeted training interventions: the greatest potential opportunities in food and beverages can be found as one moves further downstream in the value chain to advanced food and beverage processing (e.g. health foods, naturally-derived food ingredients, organic products and ready-made meals). This end of the value chain tends to be increasingly technology-intensive and therefore requires specific high-skilled workers, such as food technologists, chemists and quality assurance managers, to ensure its sustainability. Training interventions by the FoodBev SETA and other training providers should be linked to identified growth areas and the emergence of new occupations as the emphasis shifts to food safety, food quality and environmental sustainability.

Achieving gender parity: in the food and beverages sub-sectors, the majority of employees are male and can be found in the lower skill categories as labourers and machine operators and drivers. Gender equality decreases significantly as one moves from the lower skill bands to higher skill categories, such as managers and professionals. For example, women constitute 15 per cent of all labourers, 6 per cent of all machine operators and drivers and 7 per cent of all clerical and administrative workers, but only 1 per cent of all managers and professionals. Skills development initiatives must continue to focus on improving gender parity in the food and beverages sub-sectors through the use of grants offered by the FoodBev SETA and learnerships and apprenticeships offered by the private sector.

Leather and leather products

In recent years, European tanners have experienced significantly reduced order volumes and the continued strength of the euro has eroded some of their international market share. However, low-cost tanners in Asia are experiencing much better market conditions; tanners in China, in particular those who are selling their products into the Chinese market, are expected to continue experiencing significant growth. Most of the demand in the leather industry is driven by upholstery manufacturers and other high-value products.[2]

In South Africa, the leather and leather products sub-sector has undergone significant transformation in recent years. There has been significant decline in the wet-blue industry – many of these tanneries have either closed or switched to manufacturing leather for the automotive upholstery industry. As a result, there have been massive job losses in general leather goods.

---

2   Friedrich Sturm GmbH & Co. KG, Market Report: 30 November 2007, http://www.frsturm.com

However, growth in new sectors, in particular automotive upholstery, has compensated for these declines. Greater certainty about the future of the leather industry will be obtained at the end of 2007, when some detail on the revised MIDP is made public (further details on the revised MIDP will be released in 2008). If the revision of the MIDP results in an increase in demand from the automotive sector for seat leather, this should significantly improve the growth prospects of the automotive leather industry. At the same time, in order to hedge against possible loss of leather upholstery business from South Africa, some firms are diversifying into the export of cloth seat covers (Ballard 2002).

In addition, there is growing demand for high-end, niche leather products, such as exotic leather handbags and clothing. Ostrich leather manufacturers based in South Africa may be able to break into the automotive upholstery sector in the future if this becomes an alternative to the leather used in vehicles at the moment – in particular for higher-end vehicles and sports cars. The market for low-grade leather and leather products is expected to continue its decline.

Sector development

As with food and beverages, due to the existence of competitive, low-cost producers throughout the world (particularly in India and China), the requirements for the development of the leather and leather products sub-sector to serve highly competitive export markets are high. Based on the challenges faced by the leather and leather products firms interviewed as part of the case studies and on wider industry dynamics, it can be concluded that local firms should focus on the following areas:

Improving cost competitiveness: South African tanners face severe competition from low-cost producers in Brazil, China and India. In addition, South African manufactures of leather products compete with producers in the EU (in particular, Italy), whose industries are often heavily subsidised. This results in a difficult global trading environment for South African tanners and manufacturers. Therefore it is important for local leather manufacturers to have the ability to absorb increases in input costs (e.g. hides and chemicals – hide prices have increased by 25 per cent over the last 2 years and the wet-blue chemicals used to tan leather are imported and therefore subject to currency pressures). Increasing efficiency (through capital investments and capacity-building of staff, for example) is the only way to remain viable under increasing price pressures.

Competing against entrenched 'preferred suppliers': local manufacturers of footwear and other leather products (such as handbags and belts), as well as retailers, have preferred suppliers that are entrenched within these markets. This is largely because downstream manufacturers and retailers prefer to maintain existing relationships with larger-volume suppliers that are able to meet their quality and quantity demands. As a result, many retailers do not allow significant price increases, despite increases in input costs (raw materials and transport costs). Again, improving productivity is the only way to remain viable under increasing price pressures.

System improvements: given the requirement for traceability and certification demanded by manufacturers of leather products and retailers, tanners need to ensure that their systems and processes meet traceability requirements. There is increasing emphasis on tracking-and-tracing systems through which raw materials can be monitored across the entire supply chain, right back to the producer. This requires putting in place the necessary record-keeping, production management and IT systems to meet certification requirements. Systems improvements should also be aimed at overcoming cash flow constraints related to large volume orders and long payment cycles (e.g. financial management and cash flow management systems).

Access to raw materials: bovine hides represent the major part of raw materials used in the tanning industry. Access to such raw materials is a great concern for South African tanners, in particular because cattle are generally not reared for their hides, but for their meat. Also, the best hides are currently consumed by the automotive leather industry. Therefore, the relevant industry associations (e.g. the Skin, Hides and Leather Council) may need to discuss their requirements with producers through a relevant forum, such as the Footwear and Leather Cluster Initiative. (This initiative is a joint exercise between the Department of Trade and Industry (DTI) and the leather and footwear industry, to define a strategy for growth for the industry. It includes the following six working groups: customs, industrial relations, materials procurement, marketing (export and local), manufacturing and training. The cluster is represented by manufacturers, suppliers, labour, government, the Industrial Development Corporation (IDC), retailers and the Skin and Leather Council producers.)

Improving market access: South African tanners are exposed to increasing competition from a large number of low-labour-cost leather manufacturers such as China and India. Therefore it is important that the South African government, through the DTI and structures such as the India-Brazil-South Africa (IBSA) agreements, should ensure fair and reciprocal market access to allow South African tanners to access new markets; this should include strengthening the lobby effort for the removal of trade-distorting quotas and other trade barriers, through the completion of the Doha round of trade talks.

Improving preferential trade access: in addition to ensuring fair and reciprocal market access to allow South African tanners to access new markets, as mentioned above, due to South Africa's developing status and given that some of its industries (such as automotive leather producers) are infant industries, preferential trade arrangements should also be negotiated. This includes the finalisation of preferential trade agreements such as the new SADC Economic Partnership Agreement and changes to the African Growth and Opportunity Act and the MIDP, which have underpinned growth in the automotive leather sector until now.

Skills development

In contrast to the food and beverages sub-sectors, due to the consolidation of the leather industry and subsequent retrenchments, the pool of available skills in the industry is much greater. The firms interviewed for the case studies indicated that scarce skills have had very limited impact on their operations. However, these firms have indicated that more employment equity candidates need to be employed in key positions.

Despite this, some skills development themes have emerged from the case studies as well as the wider industry dynamics discussed earlier; this final section of the chapter contains recommendations for skills development based on these dynamics.

Producing higher value leather products: it is important for South African producers to move further down the value chain towards the production of leather products, including niche high-value leather products, instead of retaining their current narrow focus on low-grade leather. However, at the moment, many tanneries suffer from old and obsolete equipment and lack of spare parts, a shortage of technical skills and, on the marketing side, poor design capabilities and international exposure. In particular, design skills will have to be improved, in order to allow South African companies to capitalise on indigenous products and knowledge – e.g. ostrich leather, exotic leather and gameskins and related products. This requires investment in improvements in the capabilities of local designers, to encourage downstream activity in niche products that use indigenous materials.

Addressing racial inequalities: African employees in the clothing, textiles, footwear and leather sub-sectors are less qualified than their coloured and Indian counterparts and have the highest share of workers with qualifications below the GET certificate (2 per cent of the total African workforce, compared to 0.2 per cent for Indian and coloured employees). A similar qualifications pattern to the food and beverages sub-sectors emerges: at higher NQF levels (5–8), white employees have the highest share of workers at each NQF level, followed by Indian, coloured and African employees. Skills development initiatives must continue to focus on improving racial equality in the workplace, through the use of grants offered by the FoodBev SETA and learnerships and apprenticeships offered by the private sector.

Improving provider responsiveness: NQF unit standards and training courses have to be updated to ensure that these respond to future scarce skills that may exist in the sub-sector. For example, training interventions should be linked to demand for technicians (e.g. fitter and turners) as the sector becomes more technology-intensive and the supply chains become more complex (e.g. logistics management). In addition, the CTFL SETA has to ensure that its RPL processes are working and are widely understood, in order to ensure that workers without qualifications, but with significant practical experience, are brought into the NQF framework.

References

Altman M & Mayer M (2003) Overview of industrial policy. In Human Sciences Research Council *Human resources development review 2003: Education, employment and skills in South Africa*. Cape Town: HSRC Press

Ballard (2002) *Exporting and upgrading in South African leather Industries*. CSDS/SODS Research Report No. 55, School of Development Studies, University of Natal

Bhorat H & Oosthuizen M (2007) Employment shifts and the 'jobless growth' debate in South Africa. In A Kraak & K Press (eds) *Human resources development review 2008: Education, employment and skills in South Africa*. Cape Town: HSRC Press

Cardoso M (2000) *Small-scale food processing sector in Mozambique*. CTA Working Document No. 8013, Imani Development and Technical Centre for Agricultural and Rural Cooperation

Cosser M, McGrath S, Badroodien A & Maja B (eds) (2003) *Technical college responsiveness: Learner destinations and labour market environments in South Africa*. Cape Town: HSRC Press

CTFL SETA (Clothing, Textiles, Footwear and Leather Sector Education and Training Authority) (2006) *Sector skills plan 2005–2009*. Pinetown: CTFL SETA

DoE (Department of Education, South Africa) (2001) *National plan for higher education*. Pretoria: DoE

DoE (2005) *Student enrolment planning in public higher education*. Pretoria: DoE

DoE (2007a) Higher Education Management Information System (HEMIS) database 1999–2005. Pretoria: DoE

DoE (2007b) FET output data 1996–2005. Pretoria: DoE

DoL (Department of Labour, South Africa) (2005) *State of skills in South Africa 2005*. Pretoria: DoL

DoL (2006) *State of skills in South Africa 2006/2007*. Pretoria: DoL

DTI (Department of Trade and Industry, South Africa) (2006a) *The South African agro-processing sector overview*. Presentation at the Kwazulu-Natal Trade and Investment Fair and Conference, Durban Exhibition Centre. Accessed September 2007, http://www.kznded.gov.za

DTI (2006b) A National Industrial Policy Framework. Draft document. Pretoria: DTI

FAO (Food and Agriculture Organisation) (1997) *The state of food and agriculture*. Rome: FAO

FoodBev SETA (Food and Beverages Manufacturing Industry Sector Education and Training Authority) (2007) *Sector skills plan 2005–2010*. Johannesburg: FoodBev SETA

Lewis J (2002) Promoting growth and employment in South Africa. *South African Journal of Economics* 70(4): 338–358

Mather C (2005) *SMMEs in South Africa's food processing complex: Development prospects, constraints and opportunities*. Working Paper No. 3, Trade and Industrial Policy Secretariat.

McCord A (2003) Overview of the South African economy. In Human Sciences Research Council *Human resources development review 2003: Education, employment and skills in South Africa*. Cape Town: HSRC Press

McCord A & Bhorat H (2003) Employment and labour market trends. In Human Sciences Research Council *Human resources development review 2003: Education, employment and skills in South Africa*. Cape Town: HSRC Press

Quantec (2007) *RSA regional indicators database*. Accessed September 2007, www.quantec.co.za/data

Saasa O (2000) *Small-scale food processing sector in Zambia*. CTA Working Document No. 8015, Imani Development and Technical Centre for Agricultural and Rural Cooperation

Stats SA (Statistics South Africa) (2000–2005) *Labour Force Survey (LFS)*. Pretoria: Stats SA

Stats SA (2003) *Manufacturing statistics: Products manufactured – Food and beverages: Statistical release P3051.1*. Pretoria: Stats SA

The Presidency (Republic of South Africa) (2006) *Jipsa annual report*. Pretoria: Office of the President

Turvey H (2002) Holding on to our seats. *Pursuit Magazine* October/November. Accessed September 2007, http://www.pursuit.co.za

USDA (US Department of Agriculture Foreign Agricultural Service) (2004) *Food processing ingredients sector: South Africa's food processing industry*. GAIN Report No. SF4010, Global Agriculture Information Network

USDA (2005) *New directions in global food markets*. Agriculture Information Bulletin No. AIB794. Economics Research Service

Vink N & Kirsten J (2002) *Pricing behaviour in the South African food and agricultural sector*. Pretoria: National Treasury

Vink N, Tregurtha N & Kirsten J (2002) *South Africa's changing agricultural trade regime*. Paper presented at the 2002 annual TIPS forum, Glenburn Lodge. Accessed September 2007, http://www.tips.org.za

CHAPTER 12

Creative industries

Avril Joffe and Monica Newton

An overview of the creative industries

Globally, the creative industries are recognised as a significant component of trade and at the heart of the knowledge economy. It is estimated that the global creative economy is growing at 5 per cent per annum and is likely to triple in size by 2020 (Howkins 2001). In the UK, for instance, between 1997 and 2003, output of the creative industries, measured as value-added, grew at 6 per cent per annum, compared to 3 per cent growth for the rest of the economy. Employment in these industries grew at a rate of 3 per cent per annum compared with 1 per cent growth for the whole of the economy (DCMS 2005).

Characteristics of the creative industries

The creative industries include music, film and television, publishing, craft, visual arts, multimedia, heritage, design and the performing arts. From industry mapping efforts in the city-state of Singapore, a useful model for describing their activities and relationships has emerged (Heng et al. 2003). This model has been adapted by the authors of this chapter to include further elements of the creative economy, more broadly understood (CAJ 2007).

The creative industries comprise two distinct groups of activities (Figure 12.1): basic or 'upstream' arts that are traditional art forms such as the performing, literary and visual arts, shown in the figure as 'cultural industries'; and 'downstream' arts that are the applied arts such as advertising, design, publishing and media-related activities. While 'upstream' art activities may have commercial value in themselves, 'downstream' art activities derive their commercial value principally from their applications in other economic activities. The value of this model is that it allows for a more holistic approach to the sector, which incorporates all activities, commercial and non-commercial, and emphasises the symbiotic relationships between them. As the model makes clear, growth or decline in one area will have a concomitant effect on another.

The industries that comprise the sector are complex and diverse, but generally have the following common characteristics:
- They are project-based, comprising a range of time-bound opportunities linked to specific initiatives such as a film or theatre production or a specific commission or order. The potential of the creative industries lies in their ability to provide short-term income-generating opportunities, either for the application of high-level creative skills such as design or in the form of more labour-intensive contracts for films, festival organisation or big concerts.

FIGURE 12.1: *Composition of the creative economy*

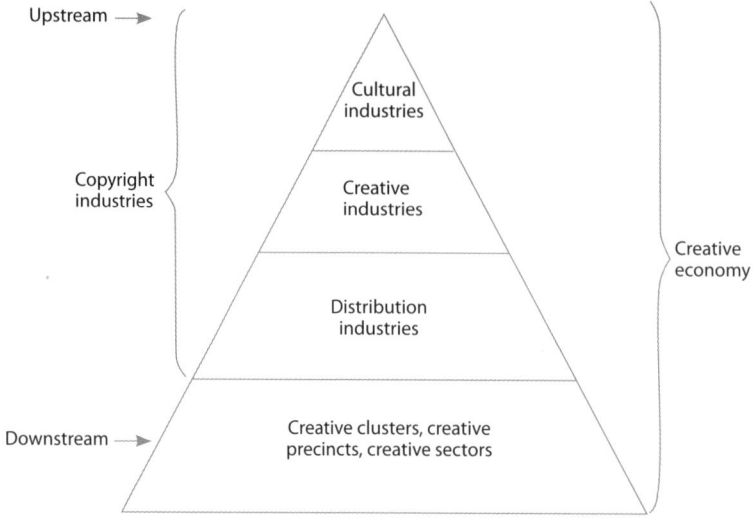

Source: CAJ 2007, adapted from Heng et al. 2003

- They comprise a set of knowledge-based economic activities making intensive use of creativity and innovation as primary inputs to produce marketable, value-added creative products.
- Creative products and services are centred in, but not restricted to, arts and culture, and are often found in purely commercial sectors such as clothing, textiles and furniture.
- The outputs are tangible products or intangible services with creative content, economic value and market objectives.
- They are able to generate income from trade and property rights.
- Products and services are produced in value chains that are often non-linear (for example, a film and television producer ties up the distribution deal prior to production). All activities in a value chain can also be performed by the same person or company in smaller markets.

The policy environment for creative industries in South Africa

In South Africa, all creative industries have strong relationships with the state to differing degrees, from reliance on the provision of infrastructure (theatres, music venues, concert halls) to institutional arrangements for funding (for example, via the National Arts Council (NAC) and the National Film and Video Foundation). The broader cultural sector in South Africa is supported by the *White Paper on Arts, Culture and Heritage* published in 1996 by the Department of Arts, Culture, Science And Technology (DACST) (DACST 1996). This policy document highlights the value of the cultural industries[1] in meeting broader government objectives relating to job creation and economic development.

Many of the sectors comprising the creative industries are heavily dependent on public-sector investment. This is especially true for the heritage and performing arts sectors. Any growth in these sectors, and resultant demands for labour, are dependent on increased public-sector investments. The South African experience has shown that organisations are so dependent on this funding that core business operations are changed, depending on the nature of the funding that is available, for example, focus-

---

1   The *White Paper* refers to 'cultural industries', which was the common terminology at the time.

ing exclusively on training to access funding for this purpose made available by the Media, Advertising, Printing, Publishing and Packaging Sector Education and Training Authority (MAPPP-SETA), which covers all industries in this sector.

Despite their inclusion in the *White Paper*, recognition of the value of the cultural industries to the mainstream economy has taken some time to take root. Starting with the Cultural Industries Growth Strategy (CIGS) commissioned by DACST[2] in 1998, the sector has taken nearly 10 years to enter mainstream economic strategies. From a sectoral point of view, a number of important initiatives to enhance the growth of the creative industries have arisen either directly or indirectly from the *White Paper* and CIGS processes,[3] including the following:

- The formation of the Music Industry Task Team to identify and implement a range of initiatives to overcome critical challenges in the music sector. Moshito, the industry-led music development initiative, is one of the primary outcomes of this process.
- The establishment of Film and Publishing Clusters which aimed to foster collaboration across the value chain to develop the sectors. The film initiative did not last; however, the recent establishment of the South African Screen Federation (SASFED) has filled this gap in the sector. The Print Industries Cluster Council (PICC) is an ongoing project supported by industry and government.
- The establishment of the National Film and Video Foundation (NFVF), Business and Arts South Africa (BASA) and the NAC as government agencies to fund and support various sectors as prescribed by legislation.
- The Create SA project in partnership with the MAPPP-SETA, the Department of Labour (DoL) and the Department of Arts and Culture (DAC), which developed a vocational education and training framework for the sector for the first time. The MAPPP-SETA continues to support education and training in the sector.
- SA Music week, which provided a platform in collaboration with the music sector to showcase local music and promote the sector. This initiative, unfortunately, no longer exists.
- Poverty alleviation through rural craft development and other cultural initiatives as part of the Extended Public Works Programme to create employment in identified rural and urban nodes.
- The inclusion of sectors such as design and multimedia within the national framework for development, thereby linking critical cross-cutting sectors to the broader development objectives of the sector.
- The Customised Sector Programmes for Film and Craft of the Department of Trade and Industry (DTI), which aligns creative-industry development to formal industrial policy and outlines a time-bound framework for implementation.

The Accelerated and Shared Growth Initiative for South Africa (Asgisa) has now identified the creative industries, and particularly the craft and film sectors, as a driver of sustainable economic opportunities and livelihoods. The strategy particularly specifies a role for the sector in supporting local communities, whilst expanding business opportunities for small, medium and micro enterprises (SMMEs).

It is important to note that statements in the *White Paper* concerning the needs of the sector are broad and undefined. Unfortunately, a recent policy review process initiated by the DAC in 2006 continues to under-emphasise the need for clear policy regarding the development of the creative industries. The discussion document framing the deliberations at the policy review workshop in May 2007 (DAC 2007) engaged superficially with the industry, giving it only a limited focus, and did not make any substantive recommendations regarding the economic development of the sector. For example, the document does not touch on issues raised in the DTI's customised sector programmes for both craft and film, or

---

2 The department has since split into two, creating a separate Department of Arts and Culture (DAC).
3 A creative industries unit in the DAC has initiated numerous projects in many sub-sectors of the creative industries, from books and music to crafts and film.

consider how to improve government alignment of policy and co-ordination of implementation. As such, the policy and enabling environment for the sectors, which is critical to their continued success and innovation, remains weak and undefined.

Increasingly, an expanded definition of the creative industries, used in mapping studies in the UK, has influenced the South African community of researchers, consultants, policy advisors and government officials. As such, the term 'creative economy' has come into use, both in the DAC's Creative Mapping Study, in collaboration with the British Council,[4] and by the Gauteng provincial government in their branding of Creative Gauteng (Department of Sport, Arts, Culture and Recreation, Gauteng 2005). The creative industries, which include the cultural industries, as well as the broader cluster of industries which support them, are encompassed into the 'creative economy', which is:

> ...an evolving concept based on creative assets potentially generating economic growth; [i]t can foster income generation, job creation, export earnings as well as social inclusion, cultural diversity and human development; [i]t embraces economic, cultural and social aspects interacting with technology and tourism objectives; [i]s a set of knowledge-based activities with development dimension and cross-cutting linkages at macro/micro levels to the overall economy; [and] [i]t is a feasible development option calling for innovative intra-ministerial policy responses. (UNCTAD 2006)

To illustrate the diversity of the creative industries in South Africa, the following sections provide an overview of the film and craft sectors.

The film sector

In terms of the taxonomy used above, the film sector falls squarely into the category of creative industries, operating downstream from sectors such as the performing arts. Since 1994, investment in the sector, from the perspective of the state at least, has generally been a cultural project to ensure that South African content is expressed in this medium. The primary support mechanism in this regard is the NFVF, which was established as a statutory development agency in 1999. Other development support initiatives include the Industrial Development Corporation that provides finance, and provincial film commissions and offices that facilitate local and international film productions.

International trends in the film and television industries indicate that while growth estimates in 2003 were 9.4 per cent and 6.3 per cent respectively, traditional industry revenue streams are declining. Contributing factors include technology convergence, declining box office attendance and the shrinking theatre-to-DVD windows. Business models are increasingly driven not by box office sales but by new distribution channels such as online portals, with simultaneous multiple product releases more evident. Production funding models are changing, due partly to an increase in big-budget productions and increasing private equity funding, which lessens the studio's need to pre-sell rights or enter into co-production arrangements (Deloitte 2007).

Emerging markets, however, are growing, with countries such as Mexico, Thailand and Egypt reporting rising attendance figures. In South Africa, the following growth areas have been identified (DTI 2005b):
- The biggest driver of film and television is the economy, and South Africa has the largest economy of the group of countries from Africa and the Middle East for which the European demand for films is high.

---

4 There are as yet no published documents for this study.

- South Africa has the highest box office attendance levels of all its regional competitors. This is despite it having a smaller population than most of its regional competitors.
- The country is one of four countries in the world experiencing real growth in cinema-going audiences. In addition, South Africa is experiencing growth in broadcasting and cable television segments, reaching over four million households in 2004 and growing consistently since 1987.
- South Africa is well positioned to exploit the regional broadcasting base in Africa, which comprises 206 national television channels in the region and 35 per cent of the total number of national television channels in the world.
- The sector has enjoyed increasing government support over the last decade.
- South Africa has pre-existing cultural ties to the UK, which is Europe's largest film market by value.
- DVD sales are increasing at a real adjusted 12.6 per cent per annum (at a value of only R3 million for 2004, but nevertheless growing).

The film and television value chain

The film and television value chain comprises two broad networks, the producer-led project network (supply) and the distributor-led rights exploitation network (demand) (Figure 12.2). In South Africa, the focus has been on the provision of funding and development support to the supply functions and, in particular, the production side. This is not surprising, given the country's employment focus and its ability to service runaway films (big-budget foreign films) relocating to foreign locations. Real wealth from the film sector, however, does not come from production activities, but from content and the ability to sell rights to that content.

At this point, content development is not where the money is made in South Africa. More than 90 per cent of all film releases in the country comprise imported material, and local distributors are primarily engaged in the facilitation of foreign product into the local market. The problems associated with distribution of audio-visual products have been consistently identified in numerous studies, and have led to recommendations for the development of distribution infrastructure as one of the interventions recommended by the Film Customised Sector Programme (CSP) of the DTI (DTI 2005b).

FIGURE 12.2: *The film and television value chain*

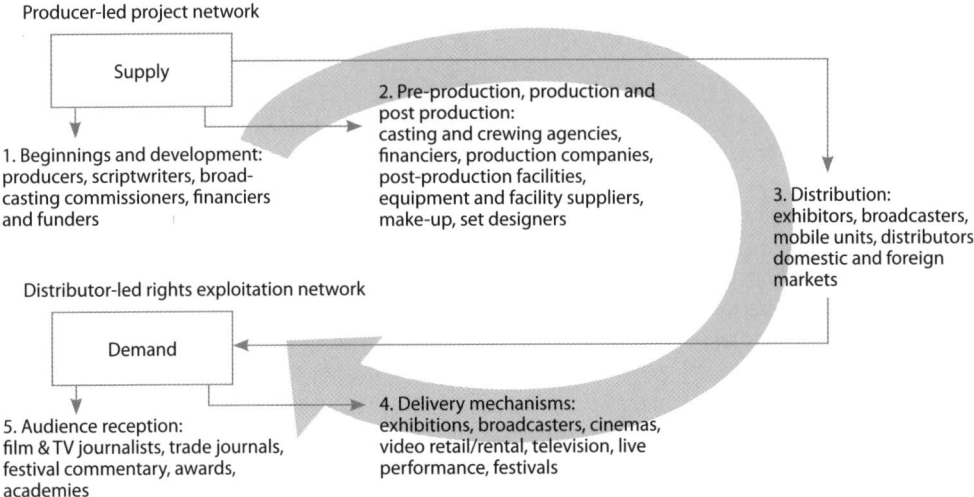

Source: Adapted from LMA/SQW 1998 with input from the Film CSP (DTI 2005b)

Key challenges for the film and television sector

The sector faces a number of constraints to growth, including the following:
- There is a lack of strategic information and research vital for industry sustainability (Joffe 2004).
- Intellectual property rights might exist but are poorly enforced, and as such, crimes such as piracy are having a negative impact on the sector (SAFACT 2007).
- The inadequate access to funding in South Africa and the requirement for revenue generation guarantee is a barrier to investment in the sector, because local producers generally cannot meet the access criteria of the DTI rebate.[5]
- The lack of seamless government services and the consequent fragmentation of government interventions and support policies remain a concern to the industry (IPO 2007; see also the TOM case study in this section).

Tom Pictures – the experiences of a small business in the film sector

TOM Pictures (TOM) is a 66 per cent black-owned independent film production company based in Johannesburg. It was founded in 2003 by Robbie Thorpe, Akin Omotoso and Kgomotso Matsunyane. The partners met through their individual work in the film and television industry and developed a friendship based on common ideas and approaches to the industry. TOM produces work in the area of film and television productions, television commercials and corporate videos. It also provides education, consultancy and international facilitation services. The primary focus is to develop projects which are exclusively South African-based and -financed.

The company is a small and flexible entity that utilises the services of freelancers and contractors on a project basis to complement the multi-faceted skills base of the partners, which are at the heart of what gives it its competitive edge. The company is a production entity that facilitates investment in ideas that ultimately are given form as films and television products. Networking is an essential business function, occupying 40 per cent of the productive time in the enterprise and ensuring that the partners have access to crucial information and business opportunities.

The company was started without any capital, and with no financial backing. The partners acknowledge that their collective business skills require upgrading. According to them, there is little or no understanding in the South African corporate sector of the film industry as a business and no clear model or system that offers reasonable guarantees for ongoing income. The partners have been systematic in their strategy over the life of the company, taking salaries only when the financial position of the company allowed and continuing with other work (such as acting) for additional revenue. Their aim is to remain as small and as light as possible. They have only recently employed the first full-time staff member, a line producer. All company earnings are project-based.

TOM, like many other production companies, depends on the national broadcaster, the South African Broadcasting Corporation (SABC) for the bulk of their work. The SABC is currently the primary consumer of local content and has very tough one-sided terms of trade. The broadcaster contracts for a very limited period, claims all intellectual property rights in the product, pre-determines and fixes profit margins, stipulates various conditions for production and delivery (the producer takes all the production risks), and yet there is almost never a pre-agreed roll-over on the contract, should all the requirements be met. TOM argues that no matter how well a company performs it has little chance to sustain or even build an independent

---

5 The DTI rebate is an incentive that was introduced to promote film-making in South Africa by providing an incentive to South African production and official treaty co-productions to increase local content production and improve location competitiveness for foreign film productions.

business under these circumstances. The partners would like to move away from dependence on the broadcaster to a 70–30 scenario, by obtaining access to the corporate sector and finding long-term projects.

TOM feels that training in South Africa is uncoordinated, fragmented and myopic, with little or no crossover from drama to commercials. In addition, the following factors act as constraints to the viability of production enterprises:
- There is insufficient opportunity for progression in the training environment.
- There is a lack of co-ordination amongst role-players in the sector and a lack of consistent investment in professional support for companies.
- Many top skills and talents across the value chain have been lost to television and the feature film industry because of a decline in big-budget productions.
- The industry is also not able to lure or retain key artistic talent, management or technical skills, as it does not offer financial rewards comparable to advertising, international production or the financial and IT sectors, and does not offer sustainability and growth.
- Declining television budgets prohibit the inclusion of assistants on a production, limiting the opportunity for learning. In addition, sound assistants are frequently eliminated from the budget, with the result that there are perhaps two or three fully qualified, expert sound editors in the country.
- There is a lack of investment in the research and development process such that only a few writers are able to live off their craft.
- Cheaper technology has facilitated both access and development, although there are many who now believe it is sufficient to be able to work the technology and 'do the job' without any obligation to learn the craft.
- The lack of accessible distribution outlets is a significant constraint to their business, as it restricts the outlets for products.

The company sees the new media explosion worldwide as an opportunity that will push content creators to the centre of the value chain. Access to technology and technological literacy will be essential to take advantage of this. In addition, master classes are needed to provide continuous professional development opportunities, and specialised training institutions (such as AFDA[6]) are regarded as the most appropriate training interventions to meet the challenges of this new opportunity.

The partners argue that while government support is vital, it is not currently meeting the needs of the sector, especially with regard to credit facilities. This is as a result of a lack of clarity regarding the roles and functions of government and the development agencies as well as a lack of financial resources. In addition, the company feels that the current funding model of the national broadcaster, which combines a commercial and a public imperative, is contradictory. They argue that profitability, as a measure of success of programmes, cannot be applied to those which have a non-commercial value and fulfil a public-service mandate.

TOM believes that there is no space for failure in the South African industry. Success is expected at an early stage, even though there is insufficient and inconsistent development support, creating enormous and unrealistic pressure.

At present, the company is focused on building its reputation rather than on making profits. The company aims to be successful locally through television, feature films, short films and documentaries. As a core marketing strategy, it targets international film festivals, as they provide exposure for product and talent, thereby adding to the company's credentials and profile and serving as an essential networking opportunity.

---

6   AFDA is a specialised film training school based in Johannesburg and Cape Town. Interestingly, approximately 60– 70 per cent of crew on TOM productions are AFDA students and graduates.

The DTI Customised Sector Programme for film and television

In response to the development constraints identified, the Film CSP proposes the following interventions:

a) Reworking of the current film and television rebate offered by the DTI to ensure greater consistency in production rates, promote collaboration amongst local producers, support broad-based black economic empowerment objectives in the sector and facilitate skills development.
b) The establishment of a market development programme, administered by an institution established for this purpose, to ensure regular information-gathering and dissemination and to promote collaboration and co-operation in the sector, in order to develop a clear market access strategy.
c) The establishment of a licensed investment company within an existing financial institution to attract private-sector investment, improve the functioning of Section 24F of the Income Tax Act (No. 58 of 1962),[7] increase the stock of domestic product and promote relations with international sales agents.
d) The development of distribution infrastructure through a public-private partnership to triple the number of cinema visits per capita over 10 years and increase the percentage of South African content consumed.

Evaluated by a range of key performance indicators attached to the individual interventions, the anticipated outcomes of the programme are an increase in the number of foreign productions and co-productions in film and television, growth in the international and local markets for South African content, an increase in the levels of private finance and an increase in the returns on domestic production to between R15 million and R25 million per annum.

The craft sector

The craft sector is aligned to the model presented in Figure 12.1, in that it is a cultural industry which operates upstream from the creative industries. In South Africa, the DTI's Craft CSP defines the sector as follows:

> Craft refers to the creation and production of a broad range of utilitarian and decorative items produced on a small scale with hand processes being a significant part of the value-added content. The production of goods uses a range of natural and synthetic materials. (DTI 2005a)

It is important to note that, from an intellectual property perspective as well as from a marketing and consumer perspective, crafts and visual arts overlap significantly. Both sectors produce essentially hand-made products, often culturally rooted, whose distinctive quality or inherent character has a primarily aesthetic appeal which is judged largely by the eye. Craft items, however, may also have functional or useful features, whereas the products of visual arts generally do not. On the whole, craft products:

- are produced by artisans, either completely by hand or with the help of hand-tools and even mechanical means, as long as the direct manual contribution of the artisan remains the most substantial component of the finished product;
- have no particular restriction in terms of production quantity;
- are unique – even when artisans make quantities of the same design, no two pieces are ever exactly alike;

---

[7] Section 24 of the South African Income Tax Act provides for tax deductions in respect of production and post-production costs by an owner of the film. Films qualifying for tax allowances include digital, video and other common formats so that the film owner can deduct from his taxable income the film allowance in respect of any film used by him in the production of his income or from which any income is received by or accrues to him.

FIGURE 12.3: *The craft value chain*

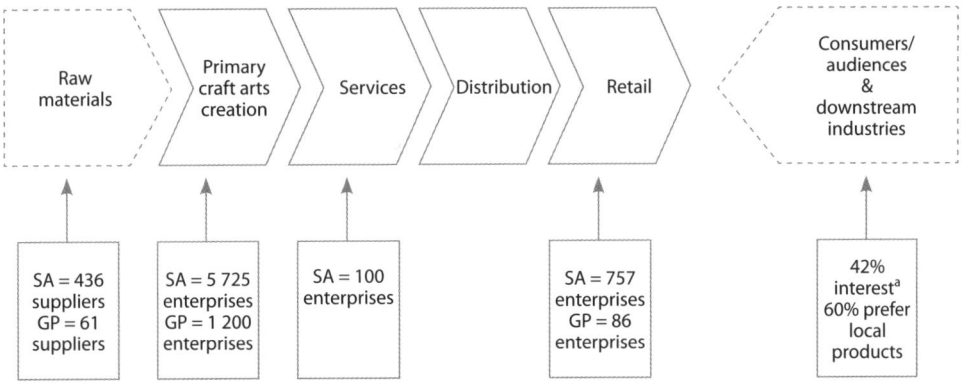

Source: CCDI 2007 using data obtained from DTI 2005a
Notes: GP = Gauteng Province;
   a. This refers to general interest in the craft sector expressed by South Africans, as reported in a survey conducted in 2001 by BASA, the Arts and Culture Trust and the NAC (BMI Sport Info 2001).

- have a special nature that derives from their distinctive features, which can be utilitarian, aesthetic, artistic, creative, culturally attached, decorative, functional, traditional, and religiously and socially symbolic and significant.

The craft value chain

Unlike many of the creative industries, and certainly film as described above, the craft sector follows a more 'classical' value chain in which raw materials as inputs are processed into tangible products that are then distributed to the market via wholesalers and/or retailers (Figure 12.3). It is important to note that some value chain functions can be represented in a single enterprise, as is the case of the Gauteng Creative Industries Co-operative (see the case study in the next section), where craft producers also retail their own products.

A study commissioned by the Indian Export Promotion Council for Handicrafts in 2005, provides the best current overview of the global market for crafts. The report argues that the world market is in a state of flux, primarily due to the flow of low-cost, mainly cloned products from countries such as China, Taiwan and Hong Kong that are slowly affecting the market for hand-made goods. The market value for crafts and decorative goods was US$235 billion in 2003, with an annual growth rate estimated at 5.1 per cent between 1999 and 2003. The USA is the largest net importer of craft, joining Germany, the UK, Japan, Hong Kong, France, Canada, Belgium and Spain in accounting for 77.5 per cent of the total imports (Frost & Sullivan 2005). South Africa is not currently a significant player in terms of world trade in craft. The Craft CSP estimates that South Africa represents only 1 per cent of global trade; with the interventions proposed in the CSP, it is expected that the country will capture 5 per cent of global trade by 2014 (DTI 2005a).

Characteristics of the craft sector

The craft sector is composed of small and micro-business, with work often conducted in studios and workshops. The 'economies of scale' that drive international competition in many goods markets are rarely a factor in the craft sector, though there are craft communities and collectives that sometimes band together for sales and marketing purposes, for example the Gauteng Creative Industries Co-operative (see case study below).

The small scale of studios and diversity of media in the sector mean that it is more difficult to create and sustain business or industry associations to service its needs. The craft community is diffuse and loosely organised, partly because it is possible for an individual to design and produce a product or range of products. A profile of crafts workplaces, like a profile of crafters, is hampered by statistical and definitional problems. Both of these issues have been recognised in the Craft CSP as constraints to growth, and as such, enterprise development programmes and a national craft and design co-ordinating forum will be established that take account of them (DTI 2005a).

Gauteng Creative Industries Co-operative

The Gauteng Creative Industries Co-operative (GCI) was founded by master crafter Peter Mthombeni for craft producers in February 2007. The GCI comprises 18 founding members, with 12 other enterprises waiting to be incorporated. The key motivation for establishing the co-operative was the many common problems facing the members, from administration to design, from sourcing material to accessing markets. The companies that comprise the co-operative are diverse, ranging from survivalists to well established micro-enterprises. The co-operative intends to share skills and knowledge amongst its members, in order to ensure the sustainability of all enterprises that are part of it.

Members of the GCI produce in the following categories: ceramics, glassware, homeware and decor, clothing and textiles, jewellery, foodware, packaging, sculpture and fine arts. One of the primary roles of the GCI is to buy in bulk, as raw materials for craft can be expensive and are often difficult to source. Most beads, some ceramic materials and ceramic colours as well as leather tools are imported. Buying in bulk qualifies the GCI for discounts and eases the cash flow burden of any one craft enterprise. A second critical function is to market itself, rather than using a shared agent, to ensure an effective and direct link with the market and also to empower its members.

Highlighting the importance of government support and facilitation in the sector, the GCI has found it particularly valuable to form strong relationships with municipalities and provincial government to showcase its work at events, hire venues for exhibitions, provide a catalogue for corporate gifts and source funds for training. In Sedibeng, for instance, the municipality provided the city hall for crafters to showcase their fashion products.

In its short life, the GCI has hosted and facilitated workshops and taken part in national exhibitions such as the Design Indaba, the Rand Easter Show, a Broad Based Black Economic Empowerment conference, a craft exhibition at the opening of the Gauteng Legislature, Beadex, Rooms on View, the Tourism Indaba and Import/Export Africa. In addition, the enterprise has been included in talks with international representatives from all over the world and has run a capacity-building programme with the National Productivity Institute.

It is anticipated that the following factors will have a major impact on the future growth and direction of the craft sector:
- the growth of fair-trade practice and products as a niche market, especially in the EU, and its resultant impact on producer and buyer relations;

- the increasing importance of cultural content in product development, and the application of handmade processes to ensure that products are easily differentiated in the global markets;
- the continued importance of skills development to meet the existing skills gaps in the sector and to ensure that access to new technologies and market opportunities are assured;
- competition from cheap imported products that flood the local market and emphasise the need for product differentiation based on the country's unique cultural and heritage resources;
- improved market access, which is likely to lead to homogenisation that will impact negatively on the viability of craft products, locally and globally;
- international and local trends in fashion and style that will continue to have a major impact on the sector, forcing it to keep abreast of these trends and invest in regular market intelligence-gathering exercises;
- greater access to new materials and new technologies that will promote continuous product innovation (Kaiser Associates 2005).

Government intervention in the craft sector in South Africa

The craft sector has been the focus of a great deal of attention by government since the publication of the CIGS report (LMA/SQW 1998). This report identified the potential of the sector to contribute to economic development and also to meeting social objectives such as the empowerment of women, poverty alleviation and black economic empowerment. The sector also has a long history of philanthropic investment for community development purposes. Some critical interventions by government in the sector have included:

- the establishment of the Cape Craft and Design Institute (CDDI) in the Western Cape (see the case study in this section);
- the national 'Craft *Imbizos*'[8] which provide a platform for communication and consultation in the sector, as well as retail opportunities;
- the mounting of the Beautiful Things Exhibition as part of the World Summit on Sustainable Development, and subsequent craft 'supermarket' initiative, that provided a retail and showcasing opportunity for the sector under the patronage of First Lady Zanele Mbeki;
- the initiation of 'One of a Kind' as part of the Decorex trade show;
- the inclusion of the craft sector as a priority in the 'Investing in Culture' programme of the DAC and the Expanded Public Works Programme;
- the registration of formal technical and vocational qualifications for the sector through the Create SA project and the MAPPP-SETA;
- the development of the national craft marketing strategy by the DTI, which has been incorporated into the CSP;
- the publication of the Craft CSP by the DTI.

Cape Craft and Design Institute

Based in Cape Town and servicing the Western and Northern Cape provinces, the Cape Craft and Design Institute (CCDI) is the only dedicated craft development institute of its kind in the country. Identified by the DTI as a leading institution in the development of the craft sector in South Africa, this model of development will soon be extended to other provinces under the auspices of the Craft CSP. Established as a joint initiative of the Cape Peninsula University of Technology (then the Cape Technikon) and the provincial government of the Western Cape, with significant start-up funding from the DAC, the CCDI opened its doors in 2001, with a number of pilot programmes before its official launch in 2003.

---

8   The *Imbizos* (meetings) were established to promote discussion and networking in the sector, aligned to market access programmes. Unfortunately the programme is no longer implemented by the DAC.

A small administrative and financial management unit supports the five core programmes of the CCDI, which has grown and changed over the last 2–3 years to service the changing needs of the beneficiaries:
- networking, communication and sector marketing;
- market access;
- enterprise development and training;
- research and resource development;
- design and innovation.

In response to the demand from the sector and expanded programmes, the organisation has more than doubled in size in the last 12 months. Over the first six years of its operations, the CCDI has influenced and changed the landscape in the Western Cape by:
- creating a visual presence for the sector, providing a referral and marketing resource and contributing to the development of provincial identity;
- establishing a physical presence and point of reference which facilitates brokering and match-making from a credible and impartial resource;
- retaining institutional memory so that knowledge and information rest in an institution that is accessible and open to all;
- collating baseline information on craft enterprises in the Western Cape, providing accurate and detailed levels of information which assist with planning and measuring impact and growth;
- increasing and broadening the marketability and market access opportunities for craft products;
- raising the profile and status of people and products by showing them in new places and in new ways;
- establishing a benchmark of excellence which has improved product ranges, product quality and business sustainability;
- impacting on income generation directly through sales at events and indirectly through creating platforms for enterprises to present themselves to the consumer and trade markets;
- developing a unique, market-driven product development process with a strong market link and training component;
- implementing an accredited and multi-faceted approach to skills training with the MAPPP-SETA, which is market-driven and responsive to crafters' needs and working conditions;
- building capacity in people and enterprises across the value chain, increasing confidence, ensuring that businesses mature and stabilise, assisting more people in choosing the sector and increasing growth and sustainability;
- laying the foundation for a representative community of Western Cape craft entrepreneurs, improving communication and increasing sharing and collaboration.

In 2006/07, the CCDI commissioned an impact study that measured the effect of the organisation's programmes and activities over a five-year period (Western Cape Craft Sector Newsletter 2007). The study showed that the CCDI had impacted on a wide range of people in a very positive way, with 53 per cent of respondents showing increased sales from improved products, 37 per cent moving from home-based production to a formal workplace and 38 per cent achieving higher income. Many more felt they had learnt new skills (94 per cent), understood markets better (86 per cent) or experienced better access to markets (85 per cent). More than 70 per cent said they would not accept regular equivalent paying jobs in place of their craft work, revealing a solid entrepreneurial focus among the targeted beneficiaries. It is interesting to note that the impact study also revealed that the CCDI was having minimal impact on the two extremes of the spectrum – the least developed and best developed entrepreneurs. This points to a need for differential strategies for the many different levels of enterprises in the craft sector.

The Craft CSP comprises a comprehensive set of development initiatives with a budget of just over R30 million. The document identifies four core obstacles to the growth of the sector:

- the lack of co-ordination of development activities in the sector as a result of a weak organisational base, fragmented activities and lack of reliable data;
- a weak skills base and uncompetitive pricing strategies which are a function of the informal nature of the sector;
- the lack of investment in research and development and infrastructure;
- the inability of the sector to capitalise on market opportunities, given a lack of market-focused product and enterprise development and a common marketing strategy in the sector.

To overcome these challenges, the following measures will be implemented:
- creation of a Craft and Design Sector Co-ordinating Body to ensure regular and constructive engagement with the sector and development agencies;
- an enterprise development programme to drive the commercialisation of the sector and build its global competitiveness;
- a research and development programme to improve products, technology and commodities in the sector;
- integrated craft development hubs in the provinces and a market access programme to capture 5 per cent of global trade in handicraft by 2014.

In doing so, the CSP anticipates supporting 180 craft enterprises and over 5 000 crafters, improving awareness of the importance of design and improving expenditure on research and development, creating strong market linkages between crafters and buyers, and increasing market share and sales.

The Craft CSP has embraced the holistic programme initiated successfully by the CCDI (see case study) over a number of years. In doing so, it focuses on the economic and market potential of the sector, as opposed to the general social investment imperative which has largely characterised government involvement. The GCI (see case study) represents an innovative response to prevailing market conditions, and a marriage, as it were, between the skills of the 'master crafter' Peter Mthombeni and others in the co-operative who are well known crafters, and the social imperatives of empowerment and skills transfer.

Skills and the creative industries

Supply of skills

Enterprises in the creative industries most often source the people and skills that they need from other employers in the sector, or in closely related sectors such as advertising, design, multimedia and the broader entertainment sector. Most people who obtain a job do so from the position of already having some work experience. The basic requirements are for people with excellent generic skills in communication, networking and teamwork; individuals who can work flexibly with good inter-personal and research skills; and of course the requisite creative and technical skills that apply to particular occupations. Recruitment of people, particularly those who have come straight from the education system (but by no means exclusively these), will generally be accompanied by some employer-based training. Feedback from employers in the Create SA project evaluation process shows that experience is the primary currency in the labour market (Create SA 2005).

In terms of recruitment, employers participating in the 2003 *National Skills & Resource Audit* report the following challenges:
- finding workers who will share the vision of the organisation or sector and a passion for the creative work that will sustain and bolster them in the face of low wages and stressful working conditions;

- finding workers with crossover skills, particularly a combination of artistic or technical and 'soft' skills, especially in new media (Create SA 2003).

In general, despite a range of scarce and critical skills, the creative industries are over-supplied, especially with new entrants. Given the small business base, however, some of these skills are absorbed into self-employment opportunities.

New entrants into the sector have a variety of access points for training at different levels, including:
- informal arts education through community-based organisations, art centres and development agencies;
- formal education through higher education and training (HET) and further education and training (FET) institutions, such as universities and private colleges, although enrolment and completion trends show a decline in this sector (especially in government institutions) that is primarily attributed to a lack of funding for students;
- technical and vocational training using new qualifications aligned to the National Qualifications Framework (NQF), which has seen over 3 900 learners registered in learnerships[9] since 2003 against a range of new qualifications.

Specific challenges relating to skills upgrading are the lack of industry-appropriate training opportunities, the degree to which training can be flexible to align with the project-based nature of careers, and the perceived costs, in terms of both time and money, of interventions. While some enterprises in the sector are large enough to benefit from the training incentives provided through the National Skills Development Framework, in general, the amounts that can be claimed back are very small, given the small size of payrolls and the costs associated with mandatory grant administration.[10]

Demand for skills

The project-based nature of work in the sector means that opportunities tend to be temporary, and generally involve a diverse range of skilled people engaging in the execution of a well defined but complex singular task or job such as a film, play or concert. As a result, the creative industries operate on a strong inter-personal, rather than inter-firm basis (MAPPP-SETA 2004). Recruitment, for example, is primarily through 'word-of-mouth' rather than formal advertisements (Create SA 2003).

Most people active in the sector have 'portfolio'-based careers which comprise complex career paths, with individuals managing several careers in different fields, often simultaneously. These careers emanate from or result in self-employment (Harvey et al. 2002). For individuals in the creative industries – whether contractual or full-time employees and whether working in the for-profit or not-for-profit sectors – employment conditions can be very difficult. This has a direct impact on the ability of the sector to recruit and retain high-level skills, due to:
- working conditions, which are often stressful because of the nature of the work, including tight deadlines and lack of capacity and resources;
- employment requirements which require flexible specialisation and a range of 'soft skills';
- the instability of organisations, given the low margins and small turnovers of companies and the intransigence of the grant-funding environment;
- turnover and mobility of experienced workers who are able to find more lucrative opportunities in other fields;

---

9   A learnership is a training intervention with a work placement component aligned to a qualification registered on the NQF, which is undertaken under contract between the learner, the employer and the training provider.
10 The National Skills Development Framework has established a system of training levies, 1 per cent of payrolls of over R500 000 per annum, of which 50 per cent can be claimed back through the relevant SETA.

- succession and the lack of adequate planning to 'upskill' younger generations;
- the high attrition of cultural managers due to poor working conditions, the lack of opportunities, limited compensation, little recognition and support and the lack of professional development opportunities;
- acute capacity problems facing historically disadvantaged communities, especially those in rural areas;
- the lack of adequate art curricula and teacher training at school level.

Most enterprises participating in the Create SA survey reported that they had experienced staff turnover in the previous three years. Respondents attributed 41 per cent of this to resignations, 36 per cent to redundancy, 18 per cent to ill-health and 5 per cent to dismissals. The high redundancy rates are linked to the short-term nature of employment opportunities but also to the financial sustainability of small- and micro-enterprises in the sector (Create SA 2003).

Occupations and scarce skills in the creative industries

There are a large number of occupations within the creative industries, many of which are specific to individual sectors, such as film production accountants and music publishers. In general, the majority of occupations in the creative industries are found in higher-skilled jobs, at professional, technical or managerial level. Almost all managerial occupations are taken up by specialist managers, who are expected to have creative and technical skills closely allied to the professional and technical occupations which comprise the bulk of employment opportunities in the creative industries. The creative industries have generally low levels of staff involved in sales, administration or elementary occupations (Create SA 2003).

In addition to a range of highly sector-specific scarce skills, such as product developers and designers in craft and experienced script and screen writers in the film sector, many in the creative industries have creative talent, and are well established in their field, but they lack the following skills (MAPPP-SETA 2006):
- marketing;
- distribution;
- legal knowledge, specifically an understanding of intellectual property;
- fundraising and sponsorship;
- public relations;
- research;
- project management.

Two contradictory trends are apparent with regard to job roles in the creative industries: an increasing specialisation of job roles, especially for freelancers, and a need for 'magnificent generalists' – people with high-level skills and experience that cross boundaries (Dumelow et al. 1999). As a result, creative workers need to constantly update their specialist art-form knowledge whilst keeping abreast of changes in such areas as government legislation (particularly copyright, data protection, health and safety and contract law), and new technology (multimedia, digitisation, Internet opportunities and sound and lighting equipment).

Technological change, which is impacting on the way in which companies produce their output, is the most important driver of skill demand. The move towards digitisation will result in digital communication over-riding face-to-face communication. This is particularly important because, increasingly, certain services such as design, post-production and editing can be carried out anywhere in the world where prices are most competitive or where the creative skills base is concentrated (Harvey et al. 2002). Often this new technology is expensive to invest in, but it is difficult to meet customer demands without its adoption. The pace of change is such that any new technology soon becomes outdated. Smaller firms, in particular, are under enormous competitive pressure. Film companies struggle to pay for new technologies (digital equipment, new advances in cameras, lighting, sound and editing equipment) and to develop the necessary skills to exploit the advantages of technology. In the craft sector, the issues are different and relate primarily to access to technology for communication and as a business tool for online retail trade.

The implications for the future are that creative workers, whether working as employees, entrepreneurs or freelancers, will need to:
- network effectively to promote themselves and generate income opportunities;
- have the skills to plan their careers and manage diverse activities;
- be able to communicate effectively, manage inter-personal relationships and conduct research;
- integrate themselves into organisations in a very short space of time, work well with others and assume responsibility very early on in their careers;
- be able to manage time and work with very little input and supervision (Bell 2003).

The importance of continuous professional development, whether formal or informal, is paramount to successful 'portfolio' careers in the creative industries.

Conclusion

The developing world contributes very little to the global market for the creative industries (UNCTAD 2008). As such, there is significant potential to develop the market share of these countries in identified niche markets globally, and also to enhance the share of the creative industries in the local market. Very little is known about the creative economy on the African continent; however, in South Africa, there is a reasonable understanding of how the value chains operate (DACST 1998). There is very little statistical information on the sector and therefore estimates relating to the contribution of the creative industries to broader macro indicators such as GDP are difficult to generate. Mapping projects, such as the current Gauteng and Western Cape studies (for which no documentation is yet available), are initiatives that have the potential to collect these data consistently and allow for a trends analysis in alignment with the needs of industrial strategy.

The major domestic markets for creative industry products and services are the tourism, services and retail sectors – all of which are showing significant growth in South Africa, in most cases, above average national growth. Research shows that most products and services emanating from the creative industries are consumed at a local and provincial level, with a small percentage accessing national and export markets (Create SA 2003). This reflects both the untapped market potential for local products and the absence of skills and resources in marketing and distributing products nationally and internationally.

There are a number of key challenges facing the creative industries:
- Competition for discretionary income has never been greater in some sectors, and it is often difficult for locally produced work to compete with internationally produced work, such as films, created with large budgets.
- Given the low-income levels for creative workers in many sectors, a large number are dependent on income from other employment to support themselves. This reduces the overall capacity of the sector to create and innovate, with only the most dedicated managing to continue long enough to create viable careers.
- There is a gap between the large number of graduates from training institutions and the limited number of opportunities in the sector. In addition, there appears to be little connection between

the education and training initiatives and the sectors to ensure that education and training meet industry needs.
- The lack of a local market for the products and services of the creative industries is compounded by a consistent lack of investment in audience development.
- The base of the creative industries is unstable, since small and micro-enterprises are predominant and often have very low income levels.
- There is a lack of co-ordination between government departments and government agencies.
- The levels of investment in the creative industries are low.
- There is a lack of access to conventional business finance opportunities.

The nature of employment and the shape of enterprises in the sector are changing. Enterprises have a need to be more flexible and more able to engage with a broad range of activities, and creative workers have to be highly innovative, creative and flexible. The nature of skills, occupations and careers in the sector is changing rapidly, primarily due to technological developments and the inconsistent nature of the grant-funding environment. Individuals entering and working in the sector will be expected to be both generalists and specialists. In addition, many will have 'portfolio'-style careers, in other words, a working life composed of numerous project-based or short-term engagements. All training will need to have an emphasis on self-employment, whether in the commercial or non-commercial aspects of the sector. From a skills perspective, the critical factor for successful training initiatives will be to develop specialisation within fields and also to allow for the development of generic competencies such as project management, financial management and facilitation that can be applied across different sectors.

Current educational and vocational efforts tend to focus on the entry level to the market, and while the vocational aspects do include experiential training, it is clear that employers would like to see a significant increase in experiential learning in the profile of potential applicants. Training needs are also changing so rapidly that in addition to the need for formal training, more informal training, which can be adapted rapidly to fill these gaps, should be supported by institutional and government funding mechanisms. Given the ever-changing context for the sector, continuous professional development, as highlighted in the TOM Pictures case study, is essential and largely absent from the current training environment.

Policy recommendations

It is important to address the general lack of business and entrepreneurial skills. The creative industries comprise mainly small and micro-enterprises, the support base for which is weak and generally not customised to meet their needs. While some agencies that provide grants-in-aid have included enterprises in their criteria for eligibility, the general lack of finance available is severely inhibiting the establishment and growth of businesses.

Technology is having a significant impact at all levels, but policy in this area is under-developed and legislation, such as copyright, is not keeping pace. An engagement with the impact of digitisation on the industries as a whole, and the identification of critical government interventions aligned to the national innovation strategies, must be initiated.

Not only is the public sector a major investor in the creative industries, but co-ordinated actions between and within government are also essential for its development. South Africa is one of the few countries in Africa that has an enabling environment comprising policy, resources, capacity and appropriate linkages to other important policy arenas, and yet the impact of this policy is inconsistent across the creative industries. The current environment would appear to be too generic to deal with the unique needs of the different sectors. A lack of clear co-ordination, overlapping responsibilities in different spheres of government, resulting in duplication at best and confusion at worst, and a constituency base that feels it is excluded from government policy-making, seem to typify the creative sector in South Africa. Core problems still relate to the lack of evaluation of policies and interventions, the lack of seamless government as well as governance issues in many of the dedicated government agencies, from the NAC to the MAPPP-SETA.

The need for public policy is well established. This is not just because the creative industries have high growth potential, as in developed countries, and some industries may need support because of their symbolic meaning, use value and intellectual property rights implications; public policy is also important because creative industries provide public benefits that cannot be captured through markets. The reason for supporting these industries needs to be clearly understood, so that government can allocate appropriate resources, financial and human, in an appropriate governance system with numerous cross-cutting areas of responsibility.

There are positive indications that the creative industries are set to take their place in the mainstream economy. Growth in the creative industries is anticipated in response to the increase in leisure spend from a growing middle class. In addition, government is developing strategic interventions such as the focused sectoral strategies of the film and craft CSPs. International experience, such as that in the UK, shows that these intersecting factors are critical for the development of a vibrant and buoyant creative economy.

References

Bell L (2003) Future directions for employability research in the creative industries. Working Paper commissioned by the Council for Higher Education in Art and Design (CHEAD), the Employability Partnership, the Design Council and the ADC-LTSN

BMI Sport Info (2001) Musictrack: The adult arts and culture and arts and culture sponsorship market in South Africa. Research commissioned by Business Arts South Africa, the Arts and Culture Trust and the National Arts Council

CAJ (Creativity Avril Joffe) (2007) Creative industries in South Africa. Report prepared for the Human Sciences Research Council, December 2007

CCDI (Cape Craft and Design Institute) (2007) Gauteng audit of craft assets. Unpublished audit commissioned by the Gauteng Department of Sports, Arts, Recreation and Culture

Create SA (2003) *National skills and resources audit*. Accessed 22 April 2007, http://www.mappp-seta.co.za/forms/CSA%20National%20Skills%20&%20Resources%20Audit%20Nov%202003%20Final%20Version.doc

Create SA (2005) Evaluation report. Prepared for the National Skills Fund. Johannesburg: MAPPP-SETA

DAC (Department of Arts and Culture, South Africa) (2007) *Arts and culture policy review: A discussion document on arts, culture and heritage policy review process in South Africa*. Pretoria: DAC

DACST (Department of Arts, Culture, Science and Technology, South Africa) (1996) *White paper on arts, culture and heritage: All our futures, all our legacies*. Pretoria: DACST

DACST (1998) Creative South Africa: A strategy for realising the potential of the cultural industries, November 1998. Report prepared for the DACST by the Cultural Strategy Group

DCMS (Department of Culture, Media and Sport, UK) (2005) *Creative industries economic estimates. Statistical bulletin*, October 2005. Accessed 3 May 2007, http://www.culture.gov.uk/NR/rdonlyres/8B1842A1-71D0-464C-9CCA-CD1C52A4D4E1/0/CIEconomicEstimatesREVISED24OCT.pdf

Deloitte (2007) Project Gaullywood: Market intelligence and sector competitiveness. Report commissioned by the Gauteng Film Commission, Johannesburg

Department of Sport, Arts, Culture and Recreation, Gauteng (2005) *Creative industries development framework of the Gauteng Provincial Government*. Accessed 12 April 2007, www.srac.gpg.gov.za/SRAC%20CIDS%20FINAL1%20narative.pdf

DTI (Department of Trade and Industry, South Africa) (2005a) *Craft customised sector programme*. Pretoria: DTI

DTI (2005b) *Film customised sector programme*. Pretoria: DTI

Dumelow I, MacLennan H & Stanley N (1999) *Planning the future: Career and employment patterns among British graduates in art, craft and design*. London: INSEAD

Frost & Sullivan (2005) Market feasibility study and business development plan for the handicrafts sector, prepared for the Export Promotion Council for Handicrafts, New Delhi, India

Harvey L, Locke W & Morey A (2002) *Perceptions of the Media Studies Curriculum and employability*. Birmingham: Centre for Research into Quality, University of Central England

Heng TM, Choo A & Ho T (2003) Economic contribution of Singapore's creative industries. *Economic Survey of Singapore First Quarter 2003*: 51–75

Howkins J (2001) *The creative economy*. London: Penguin Books

IPO (Independent Producers Organisation) (2007) *Minutes of the Annual General Meeting, 31 January*. Accessed 4 June 2007, http://www.ipo.org.za/Articles3.htm

Joffe A (2004) The sector skills plan: Film and television. Research report prepared for the MAPPP-SETA, Johannesburg

Kaiser Associates (2005) Western Cape microeconomic development strategy crafts study. First report: Crafts profile, revised draft.

LMA/SQW (Labour Market Alternative/ Segal Quince Wickstead) (1998) *The South African film industry*. Report prepared for the Cultural Industry Growth Strategy, commissioned by the DACST. Accessed 14 April 2007, http://www.info.gov.za/otherdocs/1998/mso1a2.pdf

MAPPP-SETA (Media, Advertising, Printing, Publishing and Packaging Sector Education and Training Authority) (2004) *MAPPP-SETA sector skills plan 2004–2009*. Johannesburg: MAPPP-SETA

MAPPP-SETA (2006) *MAPPP-SETA sector skills plan update 2007/08*. Johannesburg: MAPPP-SETA

SAFACT (2007) *Piracy in South Africa*. Accessed 15 August 2007, http://www.safact.co.za/piracy_facts.htm

UNCTAD (United Nations Conference on Trade and Development) (2006) *Creative economy and industries*. Creative Industries Division pamphlet. Geneva: UNCTAD

UNCTAD (2008) *The creative economy report 2008*: The challenge of assessing the creative economy – towards an informed policy-making. Geneva: UNCTAD

6 | SERVICES

CHAPTER 13

Growth and skills in the financial services sector of the South African economy

Sean Archer

In the South African economy between 1960 and 2006, the *weight* of the sector labelled 'Finance, insurance, real estate and business services' rose from 10 per cent to 19.5 per cent of GDP. In addition, its contribution to the *growth* of GDP over this approximate half-century was 1.6 percentage points out of the 5 per cent growth per annum recorded by GDP at market prices; that is, its growth contribution was 32 per cent, almost one-third. Thus, demonstrating this remarkable and ongoing expansion, in a recent period of a dozen years (1993–2005), its contribution to GDP rose by 3 percentage points (IMF 2006; INSETA 2006; Standard Bank 2007).

These figures convey the magnitude of the structural change that has occurred in our economy during the second half of the 20th century. The services sector as a whole – of which financial services are a part – increased dramatically in size, while mining and manufacturing declined in relative terms. They did not fall absolutely, which would be reflected in lowered sectoral value-added, which is not evident. Table 13.1 makes this clear, with financial services doubling in relative weight between 1960 (10 per cent) and 2006 (19.5 per cent) (Standard Bank 2007: 15).

This chapter concerns the skills profiles that characterise the financial services sector and its principal sub-sectors. It examines the possible causes of slow delivery that stand in the way of additional skills supply to the wide range of such financial activities in South Africa.

Employment in these activities is concentrated in jobs that are non-manual and either intermediate- or high-skill in character – as well as high in professional and social status – along with clerical and secretarial occupations at lower levels. Thus the jobs spectrum in this sector shows polarisation in skill requirements, in the nature of the work performed (that is, the autonomy and discretion exercised by the holder of the skill), and in payment differentials.

But this is changing. Lower-skilled work continues to be substituted, and therefore demand for it eliminated, by capital inputs that arise from advances in information technology (IT). Also, international *task trading* is a new phenomenon in services, including financial services, falling under the generic heading of *off-shoring* (Grossman & Rossi-Hansberg 2006). Much of this activity ends up in large emerging economies like India and Pakistan, where the English language is in widespread use. Currently there is speculation that South Africa may also be a contender for off-shored financial services from major industrial economies, for example, in call centres (Gelb, Keeton & Malikane 2005; Lundall 2007).

One major conclusion of this chapter meriting a clear statement at the outset is that *accountancy skills* show the strongest signs and symptoms of being in excess demand in sectors that provide and use

TABLE 13.1: *Structure of output and change in sectoral contribution to GDP growth, 1960 and 2006*

Sector	Relative size 1960 (%)	Relative size 2006 (%)	Contribution to growth (% points)
Agriculture, forestry and fishing	10.6	2.4	−0.3
Mining	11.8	7.0	0.0
Manufacturing	19.0	16.1	0.8
Electricity, gas and water	2.3	1.9	0.1
Construction	2.8	2.3	0.4
Wholesale and retail trade, catering and accommodation	13.2	12.3	0.9
Transport, storage and communication	9.4	8.4	0.5
Finance, insurance, real estate and business services	10.0	19.5	1.6
Community, social and personal services	15.7	18.6	0.6
Total value-added	94.9	88.6	4.6
Taxes on products less subsidies	5.1	11.4	0.4
GDP at market prices	100.0	100.0	5.0

Sources: SARB 2007; Standard Bank 2007
Note: Totals may not add to 100 due to rounding.

financial services. Besides companies, this includes all branches and levels of government, regulatory agencies and non-profit organisations.

By widespread agreement, South Africa is judged to have a sophisticated financial services sector by international standards. It is ranked by experts and practitioners as, in relative terms, way above its average performance in other economic dimensions. These propositions are based on the annual Global Competitiveness Report. The relevant tables are reproduced in Archer (2008).

First, these data show that South Africa ranks overall in place 44 by the combination of the scores for the 12 'pillars' used by the World Economic Forum in the estimation of *overall* competitiveness. The total sample of countries is 131.

Second, when measured by *financial market sophistication*, South Africa is ranked 25th. This means that in the judgement of the researchers, drawn from assessments by major business figures, South African financial sector performance is *markedly higher* than place 44 in the aggregate ranking of the economy's efficiency.

Conversely, it is no surprise that South Africa's assessment in certain other dimensions is dismally low. For instance, our *quality of public schools* is ranked 87th and *quality of mathematics and science education* 115th out of the 131-country sample (Porter et al. 2007; Sala-i-Martin et al. 2007; World Economic Forum 2007).

One further source of international perspective on the sophistication of South Africa's financial sector is the recent World Bank study of the investment climate in South Africa, based on 'a survey of over 800 formal private enterprises…benchmarked against firms' in six other countries that include two in Africa plus Brazil, Lithuania, Malaysia, Poland and China.

> In contrast to firms in other countries [assessed by the World Bank], firms in South Africa rated neither access to finance nor cost of financing as serious obstacles to enterprise operations and growth. Fewer than 20 percent of enterprises rated either [of these dimensions of financing] as a major or very severe obstacle. Firms rated access to finance 8th and cost of financing 11th among the 18 constraints queried in the survey. By comparison, over 50 percent of enterprises in the middle-income comparator countries of Brazil and Poland rated cost of financing as a major obstacle. (Clarke et al. 2007: 73)

What is the role of the financial services industry?

The following activities characterise the role of the financial services industry as a whole:
- *Allocating capital efficiently* to those economic activities which are of higher than average profitability. This provides a mechanism widely accepted to foster competitive behaviour and to raise the productivity of all the inputs used.
- *Managing risk* in a cost-effective way by spreading and pooling its incidence through the use of financial instruments. But the current financial crisis in the USA, spreading elsewhere, is being cited as evidence that the new methods of coping with risk developed in recent decades have failed in their purpose (*New York Times, Financial Times* and myriad other sources in 2007 and 2008).[1]
- *Managing payment systems* for banks and other deposit-receiving institutions. Minimising cost and maximising security in the transfer of money are essential for global markets. In addition, providing means for individuals to effect payments promotes their financial inclusion. The variety of systems shows continuous innovation. In contrast to more mature economies, South Africa's economically active population at lower levels of income has resort to micro-finance institutions for the supply of credit.
- *Outcome verification* by the conduct of audits in the broad sense. Corporate governance issues are central to the fulfilment of this function in organisations where owners and managers have goals that are not aligned. Equivalent procedures are essential in the public sector. State accountability for the use of resources under its jurisdiction likewise requires the upper levels of administration to demand verification of outcomes carried out by lower levels. These services are performed by accountants, auditors, actuaries and others.
- *Business process outsourcing and call centres* are a recent set of non-core financial operations to evolve within the sector. These are functional extensions of activities like capital allocation, financial monitoring and payment systems. Known also as *third party administration*, these activities are the consequence of advances in information processing brought about by major investment in IT and by technical progress in both hardware and software.

Banks in South Africa

The banking sub-sector is the largest component of any country's financial system, measured by its volume of transactions and its total employment. Yet the economic role of banks extends beyond these dimensions because of their interaction effects as intermediaries with all other sectors of economic activity in a national economy, as well as internationally.

---

1 Lanchester J, Cityphilia, *London Review of Books*, 3 January 2008.

The 'big four' commercial banks in South Africa are ABSA, FirstRand, Nedcor and Standard Bank (sometimes Investec is included in the list as a smaller counterpart, although its activities, which include merchant banking, are wider). Currently these four banks account for over 80 per cent of South Africa's total banking assets (BANKSETA 2006; Standard & Poor 2008: 2).

Their pattern of evolution in recent years has seen each bank consolidate through mergers with other financial entities, as well as by the acquisition of smaller firms providing financial services. The International Monetary Fund (IMF) describes South African commercial banks as 'conglomerates [being] large and complex financial institutions with cross shareholdings and operations that span sectors and borders' (IMF 2006: 68).

For purposes of the present concern, principally with skills problems, the issues that warrant raising are those likely to influence the evolution of retail banking in the longer term:
- First, there is a history of contention that *bank charges* in South Africa are considerably higher than similar charges levied by counterpart banks in other countries. This is vigorously denied by the retail banks themselves, so the issue remains unsettled (ABSA 2006; Falkena et al. 2004; Feasibility Report 2006).
- Second, putting banking into a development perspective, what *regulation* by authorities like the Treasury and Reserve Bank is the most appropriate for advancing the welfare of our population? Too much control inhibits growth. Too little control raises exposure to risk which causes substantial losses to large numbers of people when banks under-perform, as in the USA currently.
- Third, what *barriers* hold back the extension of banking services to half the South African population who remain unbanked?
- Fourth, do banks merit *subsidies* from the state to encourage extension of services lower down the income profile of individuals and companies? Or are state-financed or state-controlled banks the better option?
- Finally, banks everywhere chafe at regulations, and the South African banking industry appears no different (ABSA 2006). The following quotation expresses a representative attitude by the international banking community:

> This [Regulatory Working Group] is a reflection of a wide-spread concern among our sponsors and friends that the tide of ever-more intrusive micro-regulation has become irresistible, and that it is starting to do serious damage both to the financial services industry [globally] and to the City of London. We are not alone in this view; nor is our Group the only one out there. (CSFI 2006: 3)

Regulation is a policy art more than a science. *Financial contagion* is the domino effect of bank failure to repay borrowings in the interbank loan market, where such lending is integral to the conduct of the industry's business. Contagious defaults occur if the losses on the exposures to the defaulting bank exceed the capital of a creditor bank. Every default weakens the surviving bank, leading to a cascade of bank failures.

But the most prominent cause of contagion is high waves of deposit withdrawals or bank runs (Upper 2007). At the time of writing in early 2008, we are seeing contagion spreading in the USA financial sector, spurring the USA government's rescue of Bear Sterns, for instance. In the UK, in the high-profile case of Northern Rock, as well as in France and Germany, the financial authorities in recent months have rescued individual banks subject to bank runs.

In summary, *regulation* of the banking industry should comprise a selection of the following categories of policy action in any given national economy:

- Minimum capital adequacy is prescribed for banks by the central bank; locally this is the South African Reserve Bank (SARB). In 2008 South Africa is publicly committed to adopting the Basel II Accords on international standards stimulating capital provision against the financial and operational risks faced by domestic banks.
- Credit controls on individuals are instituted to protect the consumer against over-indebtedness.
- Deposit insurance is compulsory in that, in the event of bank failure, depositors receive their deposit investments back. But in some national jurisdictions the amount insured is not necessarily 100 per cent.
- Banks are stipulated to supply customers with minimal price transparency concerning their service fees, minimum balances and penalties.
- Transaction costs are minimised by regulation; examples of such costs are the cost of buying a house and registering a mortgage bond, as well as the cost of enforcement procedures in the case of defaults.
- The monetary authorities set maximum interest rates that may be levied by banks at any time, as under the South African Usury Act (No. 21 of 1968) and the Usury Amendment Act (No. 10 of 2003).
- Government ownership of banks can be a substitute for regulation of private banks. Yet there is little international evidence that government ownership means lower obstacles to the horizontal expansion of banking services to poor individuals and small, medium and micro enterprises (SMMEs) (Beck et al. 2007; Ide et al. 2007; World Bank 2006).

> South Africa has a complex, dynamic and innovative financial industry, thus skilled consolidated supervision and substantial resource availability is a constant imperative for regulatory adequacy. The financial system is sophisticated with complex legal, financial and business relationships among the various parts of the banking groups and substantial cross border operations. The SARB supervises the banking groups on a consolidated basis, but it has to constantly upgrade its regulatory framework to address emerging risks due to the complexity of the ownership structure and operations, the concentration of the sector, the global reach of these banking groups and constant product innovation. This, therefore, places heavy demands on the supervisory resources. (IMF 2006: 82–83)

The insurance industry in South Africa

Like the other major sub-sectors, South African insurance activities are conducted by a bi-polar distribution of organisations, being a small number of large firms and a large number of small firms, some with annual payrolls of R0.5 million or less. At present, 4 000 contributors pay the skills development levy and employ an industry workforce of 102 000. Yet we do not know how many small operations fall through this net, because 'estimates of the number of very small and independent intermediaries differ vastly' (INSETA 2006: iii).

What is the role of the insurance industry in a national economy? Insurers offer economic decision-makers protection against risks and the consequences of such risks. Customers buying insurance policies are covered against injury or loss, the probability of which is calculated by the insurer – usually actuaries with specialised skills for the purpose – on the basis of quantitative models derived from historical information and insurers' experience of the market (DfES 2001; FSSC UK 2007; Hartmann et al. 2007; INSETA 2006).

A premium or fee is assigned to the insurance policy, so that total premiums received will at least cover the total expected claims of the insured person or organisation. By this process, the risk of loss is transferred from customers to the insurers, who have the capacity to manage it in a more efficient way by pooling risk and spreading it over a group of similar policy-holders.

The major divide is between *life insurers* devoted to long-term risk and investment management, and *short-term or general insurers*. This terminology differs between countries but the activities conducted by each type are the same.

One striking example of the challenges that face this industry globally is climate change. Signs of atmospheric and oceanic warming exist in the present, yet in ways difficult to project on risk grounds. Insurance providers will be under pressure to provide cover through new kinds of policies, in the expectation of losses through natural events. Insurance does not decrease loss from an unexpected negative event, but it spreads the financial impact by enabling individuals and groups at risk to pay a small premium, in order to protect themselves against a large loss that has a low likelihood of taking place.

Accountancy and auditing as financial services

By general agreement, the skills shortages identified in this sub-sector are the most prominent and widely accepted. This mimics the worldwide inadequacy in the supply of trained accountants and auditors (IFAC 2007).

Any description of the accounting and auditing sub-sector in South Africa will bring out yet again the common characteristic of financial services activities, namely, a bi-polar distribution by size of enterprise. The 'big four' accounting firms have been in place in the country for many years (PriceWaterhouse, Deloittes, Ernst & Young, KPMG), although previously under other names. In addition, there are a substantial number of medium firms and SMEs which supply either the full range or a subset of auditing services to the national economy.

What is clear is the high regard internationally for the South African profession's 'strength of auditing and reporting standards'. In this, it ranks number 6 in the world out of 131 countries, scoring 6.2 against a mean for the entire sample of 4.7. It is topped by only the five countries, Germany, Sweden, the UK, Australia and Austria (World Economic Forum 2007: 391).

The following generalisations apply to the accounting and auditing sub-sector of the financial services sector at the time of writing in early 2008. Most are shared with the international profession, but some are caused by uniquely South African circumstances.
- The large firms continue to increase the weight of their *advisory and consultancy* services – in contrast to auditing services – in their total activities (Boyd 2004a, 2004b; Cunningham 2006; Financial Reporting Council UK 2007). This feature generated much public debate following the USA accountancy scandals and the disappearance of the firm, Arthur Anderson. It led directly to the passage of the Sarbanes-Oxley Act of 2002. Non-USA firms are not subject to this legislation when they operate outside the USA, but its influence on international behaviour is undeniable.
- Individuals and firms are subject to a complex mixture of *regulations*, some by the state and some by their professional associations.
- The main drivers of change are regulation, competition that is domestic and international, and technology through the communications uses of computerised information.
- There is a possible *erosion* of trust between the public users of accounting and auditing services, like companies, governments and other organisations, and the professionals providing the range of financial services now on offer (Bazerman 2007; Boyd 2004a, 2004b; Cunningham 2006).

- There is worldwide concern about auditor *concentration* – a small number of extremely large firms contributing the vast bulk of service output – which is believed to limit competition and compromise independence. Conversely, there appear to be substantial economies of scale in auditing, with wide international networks of accountancy services that require significant investment in training (International Audit Networks 2006). How this trade-off relationship is best resolved remains to be decided.
- Accountancy and auditing are uniquely *mobile* activities for professional employees, particularly those trained to meet qualification standards for which there is a major drive towards *uniformity* in international markets (FASSET 2007a; FSSC UK 2007; IFAC 2007).
- Similarly, the vast majority of national professional associations identify *human capital* problems as their most pressing concern (IFAC 2007).
- Technological change in general has reduced the demand for some conventional accountancy services because functions previously carried out manually can now be performed by the appropriate software. This inhibits job creation within the profession, but in complex ways not easily identified as trends.
- In South Africa, sector charters governing the advancement of black (that is, African, coloured and Indian) employees straddle financial services, but particularly so in accountancy activities. It is the shortage of black professionals with the required qualifications that constitutes the largest shortfall in accountancy, auditing and – as regards managers in particular – the financial services sector as a whole.
- It is easy to forget the demand for accountancy skills coming from the public sector. 'South Africa has 37 government departments and 284 municipalities. Government departments in particular need about five chartered accountants each. They are presently nowhere near that number' (South African Institute of Chartered Accountants (SAICA), cited in Johnston & Bernstein 2007: 20).
- A current regulatory proposal in early 2008 is for a Financial Reporting Investigation Panel to be set up in South Africa as a new regulatory watchdog for the financial services sector. Perception of skills shortages has, however, generated scepticism about its staffing up to the level required for efficient operation.

Asset management and financial consultancy

Financial advice covers all activities involved in the distribution for sale of financial services as products sold to the public. It includes the management of investments in financial assets for the benefit of a client community. Services sold are information and guidance supplied directly, either by providers themselves, like banks, insurance companies and pension funds, or by independent advisers and asset managers, known also internationally as IFAs (independent financial advisers).

Asset management and financial advice compete for similar work competencies with every other major sub-sector such as banking, insurance and accountancy. It is plausible to predict that ongoing product differentiation in financial services will intensify the information problem and therefore the demand for guidance skills.

Skill demand issues in the financial services sector as a whole

Financial services as a sector uses a proportion of skilled labour nearly double the average for the economy as a whole. This is the case consistently for the 11-year period covered in Table 13.2, if the mix of financial intermediation, insurance, real estate and business services in the table is accepted to be a reasonable proxy measure, as it is judged to be in this chapter.

A snapshot view of skills training can be misleading. Firms, particularly small businesses, demand skills and provide training according to their current need and are influenced by their financial position. Thus the level of their training activity can be measured only over a period of time. At the aggregate level – for an industry or sector – this problem may be less serious because above- and below-average training intensity may cancel each other out. But this depends on its unknown distribution across firms and other training organisations (Cosh & Hughes 2003).

TABLE 13.2: *Skills breakdown of employment by sector, 1995, 2004 and 2006*

Sector	Year	Skilled	Semi-skilled	Unskilled	Total
Agriculture, hunting, forestry and fishing	1995	0.01	0.22	0.77	1
	2004	0.05	0.42	0.53	1
	2006	0.04	0.48	0.48	1
Mining and quarrying	1995	0.07	0.74	0.18	0.99
	2004	0.07	0.8	0.12	1
	2006	0.07	0.74	0.19	1
Manufacturing	1995	0.12	0.68	0.19	1
	2004	0.17	0.64	0.19	1
	2006	0.15	0.65	0.20	1
Utilities (electricity, gas and water supply)	1995	0.18	0.67	0.13	0.98
	2004	0.39	0.5	0.1	0.99
	2006	0.28	0.65	0.07	1
Construction	1995	0.09	0.71	0.19	1
	2004	0.09	0.68	0.23	1
	2006	0.08	0.71	0.21	1
Internal trade	1995	0.17	0.64	0.2	1
	2004	0.14	0.56	0.3	1
	2006	0.15	0.54	0.31	1
Transport, storage and communication	1995	0.26	0.62	0.11	0.99
	2004	0.23	0.62	0.14	1
	2006	0.21	0.66	0.14	1
Financial intermediation, insurance, real estate and business services	1995	0.38	0.56	0.06	1
	2004	0.39	0.5	0.11	1
	2006	0.39	0.51	0.10	1
Community, social and personal services	1995	0.45	0.39	0.15	0.99
	2004	0.5	0.35	0.15	1
	2006	0.49	0.38	0.13	1
Private households	1995	0	0.02	0.97	1
	2004	0	0	1	1
	2006	0.00	0.01	0.99	1
Total	1995	0.2	0.48	0.31	0.99
	2004	0.22	0.48	0.3	1
	2006	0.21	0.50	0.29	1

Source: Oosthuizen 2005: 19 & update to 2008 by Carlene van der Westhuizen, Development Policy Research Unit, University of Cape Town

All demands for skilled competencies are derived demands. Together the composition of output, the scale of output, and the technology in use that determines the mixture of inputs so as to maximise profitability, determine what kinds of skilled and unskilled labour are required for efficient production. A firm's product strategy will reflect these influences, yet this dimension of the demand for skills tends to be overlooked in policy discussion.

The key influences on the financial sector's expansion, contraction or structural alteration are the following: the *macro-economic context* is of major importance: financial services are integrated with every sector of the economy: stability, together with growth, have been the symptoms of major success in South Africa's economic fortunes since the political changes of the early 1990s. But whether the future prospects for the financial services sector will continue to remain favourable is not possible to determine. There are current worries about the slowdown of the USA economy, which is highly likely to impact on middle-income countries like South Africa.

A number of other sector-wide influences on the demand and supply of skilled labour in South Africa's financial services sector can be listed briefly:
- First, one example of innovation in product rather than process is the movements in the range of pensions instruments becoming available.
- Second, what is solidly in evidence in most countries' financial services activities is the trend towards *outsourcing* and *sub-contracting*. Call centres and Internet-accessed services or business process outsourcing (BPO) increasingly rely on information and communication technology (ICT) equipment to sell by negotiation, to deliver and to service financial packages. Examples are insurance policies, differentiated banking accounts, asset management services, and medical aid programmes, claims and payments.
- Third, *globalisation*, in the straightforward sense of the ongoing increase in the volume of economic transactions across national boundaries, has particular relevance for financial activities in any national economy, and therefore for skills demand.
- Fourth, there is *competition*. Where its pressure is significant there is usually a concentrated focus on cutting costs. This includes a reluctance to hire skilled workers and the search for cheaper alternatives to such hiring, such as making do with lower levels of qualified workers, supplemented by short and dedicated training courses (Basel Committee 2008; Cunningham 2006; Falkena 2004; IMF 2006; IFAC 2007; International Audit Networks 2006).
- Fifth, in countries with well documented financial services sectors, there are shifts evident in producer strategies, from a product focus to a *client focus*. This can have contradictory effects. 'With the advent of ICT, there is no brand loyalty. But the only thing we have to differentiate ourselves with the competition is our customer care and service' (financial services employer consulted in UK research, cited in DfES UK 2001: 30; see also Leitch Review 2006).

One countervailing aspect is that a significant proportion of financial services to clients have to be produced and consumed *simultaneously*. Transactions between parties require both sides to be in place at the same time. This entails a direct relationship between personnel in the supplying entity, say an insurance company, and the consumer of a policy or pension scheme. Thus the use of ICT cannot be a complete substitute for skilled employees.

Channels for the supply of skills to the financial services sector

The supply of skills is the outcome of a set of inter-related determinants, the most important of which are the following:

Labour supply depends on:
- population changes by age, gender, marital status, urbanisation and other internal movement;
- international migration flows;
- operation of the grants or social security system which in *net* terms either encourages or discourages labour force entry;
- cultural influences on participation in the labour force.

Skills supply depends on:
- the magnitude of labour supply at any point in time;
- output volume from the compulsory schooling system;
- quality of school-leavers;
- operation of the higher and vocational education systems;
- methods of financing higher and vocational education;
- the training system;
- employer and individual investment in skills acquisition.

Individuals are trained to enter sector-specific job categories as accountants, auditors, actuaries, financial consultants, investment managers and bookkeepers, alongside a range of financial technician occupations, through channels that are a successive mixture of:
- compulsory schooling of nine years;
- voluntary additional schooling to Grade 12;
- further education in technical colleges and private training institutions leading to diplomas and a range of certificates;
- higher education in universities and technical universities for three- and four-year degrees; and
- training on-the-job in employing organisations and off-the-job in institutions dedicated to the purpose.

The *distinguishing* features of training in financial services are:
- At the upper end of the occupational, skill and remuneration hierarchy, the training is by nature 'professionally-driven, hence the presence of a significant accreditation system which is *specific* to the sector' (DfES UK 2001: 53).
- Training is delivered through in-house channels or by private-sector providers.
- The public sector has only a slight role 'in providing training and skills development support in financial services' (DfES UK 2001: 51).
- Yet higher education is predominantly in the public sector in most countries – prominent exceptions being the USA and Japan – so the provision of graduates as prerequisite preparation for specific skills training is squarely a state responsibility.
- Similarly, at lower levels of the hierarchy, the quality of school-leavers plays a particularly significant role in this sector, with its emphasis on numeracy and ICT aptitudes. Quality standards are predominantly a public-sector responsibility.

Of major importance for South African occupational markets at the high end of the skills profile in financial activities is that at least three industries – banking, insurance and accountancy – compete in overlapping ways for the existing pool of qualified professionals and managers.

The demand and supply of skills by sub-sector in financial services

Skill issues in the major sub-sectors are treated in this section of the chapter. There is no attempt at completeness, although the vast majority of skilled workers engaged in financial activities work in these half-dozen categories of identified activity or industries.

The public or government sub-sector

Government both uses and trains skilled labour in the production of financial activities. But it tends to produce qualified workers on a scale smaller than its own new and replacement needs. In consequence, it exerts a net demand for higher-level professionals trained in the private sector. This appears to be true for all levels of government.

For example, recently the Gauteng government launched a programme for the training of skilled workers to provide their services at the local government level. 'The municipal standing committees on public accounts, also known as Scopas, were launched…to promote oversight and accountability in municipalities…such committees should be provided with competent staff to study the reports and provide information on them' (*Business Day* 13 March 2008).

The share of the public sector – 'SARS [the South African Revenue Service] and Government Departments' – in total financial services employment is 13 per cent. This proportion is influenced by the way in which this sector and sub-sector are defined by the Financial and Accounting Services Sector Education and Training Authority (FASSET) (2007b: 2).

The banking sub-sector

The following brief observations apply to the major banks in the South African economy. These are commercial as well as merchant or investment banks, whether independent or controlled within the main 'big four' group.

One important dimension of skills recruitment which distinguishes South African banking is that it appears not to have an image problem among potential job applicants with high-level skills. The growth of local commercial banks in recent decades, their ability to offer competitive salary packages, and the evolution of product and process innovations has made this sub-sector an attractive employer to graduates and professionally qualified applicants.

This is not the case in certain other countries, for example the UK, where the banking sector faces a negative image problem when recruiting.

A further observation bearing on skills deficiencies is that South African banks have been net shedders of jobs in recent decades. This is the consequence of a number of influences, some being local, like the ongoing consolidation in the industry, a process already raised earlier in the chapter.

> The [South African] financial services sector has seen a range of major acquisitions, movements, repositioning and volatility. Although it is generally only the conglomerates and the high-profile groups and companies that make the news headlines, increased activity has permeated the entire sector. The forging of international alliances has already begun with Barclays acquiring a major stake in Absa. (BANKSETA 2006: 10)

The insurance sub-sector

The number of posts in the insurance sub-sector listed as those which 'organisations struggle to fill' can be ranked by occupational group from highest to lowest. These are for illustration, and are not a complete listing from the source:
- professionals, 2 209 posts, 69.5 per cent of the total number;
- clerical and administrative workers, 12.1 per cent;

- sales workers, 11.4 per cent;
- managers, 5.6 per cent (BANKSETA 2006: 47).

In summary, 'the most pressing skills shortages [in insurance] were experienced in respect of actuaries, chartered accountants and other financial professionals such as specialist portfolio investment managers, qualified financial planners and business analysts. The employment agents also reported a shortage of the higher level *numerical skills* required in positions filled by financial analysts, semi-professional and actuarial support staff, and business and management consultants' (BANKSETA 2006: 49, emphasis added).

The accountancy and auditing sub-sector

Accountants and auditors at the top of the occupational hierarchy in this sector are the best documented by numbers. But despite being the largest in total number and in number of identified deficiencies, these financial services professionals are not one of the 'five high profile priority skills' clusters identified currently by the Joint Initiative on Priority Skills Acquisition (JIPSA) as of strategic importance for economic growth (The Presidency 2007: 9). Why they are omitted and not considered priority skills is a question for future research.

FASSET data show that despite possessing post-matric qualifications in the fields of business, commerce and management studies, there is notable *unemployment* in the group that makes up the main supply stream in financial services. There are 535 600 of these, comprising 24 per cent of the total number in the economically active labour force holding post-matric qualifications, 2.2 million strong. Of this group, 88 500 or 17 per cent were unemployed at the time of the September 2006 Labour Force Survey (FASSET 2007b: 22).

This is a surprising and troublingly high number. But the rate differs significantly by *level of qualification*. It is 22 per cent for those with only a post-matric diploma or certificate, in contrast to 1 per cent for those with a postgraduate qualification.

The main strategic question concerning the production of chartered accountants, internal accountants, accounting technicians and other related skills is whether South African training procedures can be speeded up. This chapter cannot answer this question, given the differences of opinion evident in the profession, universities and government departments. But the following statement is provocative and needs wider attention; the author, John Stuttard, is Lord Mayor of London and a UK chartered accountant:

> [C]urrent structures are unlikely to produce [the accountants needed]. First, almost uniquely in the world, SA requires those wanting to qualify as accountants first to take university accounting degrees before beginning professional training.
>
> In the UK all that matters is that you master the material necessary to pass the (tough) professional exams – that is, the result and your independently assessed skills are what matter, not how you get them. This ensures the widest possible pool from which to draw the best minds.
>
> If South Africa wishes to emulate the success of other countries economically then it should reduce the time it takes to qualify and make it easier for non-accounting graduates to enter the profession. (*Business Day* 10 October 2007)

Skill shortages, skill gaps and the precision of existing estimates

Demand for skilled labour is a derived demand. The process of economic change drives demand alterations in the labour market and consequently, skill needs. The sectoral structure is itself the result of changes in the patterns of consumer demand, technology and organisational evolution, 'as well as the evolving pattern of national competitive advantage [that] continues to change the balance of occupations, qualifications and skills required in the labour market' (Campbell et al. 2001: 210). These complicated causal mechanisms, difficult to model, add up to reasons for not placing confidence in projections of skill shortages in *any* economic sector.

Strictly speaking, a fully-specified macro-economic model is required to make projections of future skilled labour demand. This forms part of the projections in a few countries like the UK, but not in South Africa. There is a case to be made that in the absence of such a model, establishing the expected performance in skills training of sectors like financial services, or sub-sectors like accountancy, banking or insurance, will be an approximation. But it will be an approximation of unknown reliability.

Because inconsistencies have crept into the operational definitions used in national surveys of skill quantities in excess demand, recent suggestions have been to minimise or even *avoid* use of the word 'shortage' in this context.

> Given the definitional ambiguity regarding skills shortages we construct four definitions from the data base:
> [1] *Current skills gap*: those respondents reporting that there exist 'gaps between the skills currently available within your workforce and the skills which your organization needs to achieve its business objectives'.
> [2] *Hard to fill vacancy (HTFV)*: those respondents that have 'experienced any difficulty in recruiting the staff you need' during the 12 months prior to the survey.
> [3] *Anticipated skill problem*: those answering 'yes' to the question 'could you say whether you anticipate that skills shortages in the next 3 to 5 years will affect your company'.
> [4] *Emerging skill problem*: employers that do not feel that they have a current skill gap, but anticipate that skill problems of some kind will emerge in the future. (Watson et al. 2006: 44)

If we apply these distinctions to South African statements of skill shortages by occupation in specific sectors, challenging questions are thrown up. We do not know with sufficient clarity (i) which concepts of deficiency underlie them; (ii) in what magnitudes; and (iii) whether the implicit definitions used are uniform across the employer sources consulted.

With the sceptical international literature in mind, it appears that the estimated shortages now circulating in the South African policy arena can have ambiguous implications for skill formation planning by companies as well as for Sector Education and Training Authorities (SETAs) and the state agencies charged with fostering skills training. Whether we will overcome this problem in the future remains to be seen. But we have to recognise it first.

> In the market for engineer-scientists or for any other commodity we expect that a steady upward shift in the demand curve over a period of time will produce a shortage, that is, a situation in which there are unfilled vacancies in positions where salaries are the same as those being currently paid in others of the same type and quality. Such a shortage we will term a *dynamic shortage*. The magnitude of the dynamic shortage

> depends upon the rate of increase in demand, the reaction speed in the market, and the elasticity of supply and demand. (Arrow & Capron 1959: 301)

It is ironic that this definition by Arrow and Capron is nearly fifty years old. It clearly states the requirement that it makes little sense to speak about the shortage of any commodity without reference to its price. We cannot identify quantities of skills or occupations as being in excess demand – for instance, a shortage of some specific skill like qualified chartered accountants – nor can we analyse the possible reasons for such a shortage without linking that shortage to its price. The concept must be of a shortage *at a stated level of the wage or salary package payable for a skill of the same type and quality currently being paid.*

Forecasting skills demand

From the date of its launch, the National Skills Development Strategy has aimed at the construction of skills plans at workplace, sector and national levels. Recently, skills planning at the national level appears to have shifted down the action agenda for reasons not clear to researchers.

Skills forecasting is subject to unknown margins of error and is no longer practised widely in other countries. In general, the international literature is sceptical after the disappointed hopes for developing country manpower planning exercises conducted in the 1970s and earlier (Ellis 2003; Heijke 1994; Hopkins 2002; ILO 1995; Woolard et al. 2003).

Forecasting difficulties show up in all national labour markets.

> As long ago as 1989 the main [UK] national employers body – the Confederation of British Industry (CBI) – argued that 'few employers are able to predict their medium term skill requirements with any confidence. The uncertainties over technology, exchange rates, and future corporate strategies are simply too great to allow traditional corporate manpower planning approaches to work effectively'. Many of these factors have with the passage of time become more, not less, uncertain. (Gleeson & Keep 2004: 56)

The subject of forecasting is large, so brief observations suffice to show the underlying difficulties. For instance, the freeing up of international capital flows and the ongoing globalisation of trade in recent decades have *widened* the range of goods and services bought and sold in the majority of commodity markets. In response, changes in tastes have accelerated, causing alterations in the mix and availability of consumption and investment goods and therefore the demand for skilled inputs (Acemoglu 2002; Crafts 2004; Rodrik 2004).

A second obstacle to effective forecasting is the relationship between technological change and the required human capital in skilled, semi-skilled and unskilled labour. The key unknowns are the substitution possibilities *within* any given technique of production in use. Substitution refers to the flexibility of input coefficients per unit of output. Is skilled and unskilled labour, capital, energy and so on required for each unit produced, an amount or a range? Can a road be built as cheaply with unskilled labour equipped with spades and wheelbarrows as it can with bulldozers and mechanical earth movers?

A modest claim is the most supportable, like the following for UK skills projections, even using a macro-economic model:

> The results presented here should be regarded as indicative of general trends and orders of magnitude rather than precise forecasts of what will necessarily happen.

> That is, they are *not intended to be prescriptive* but rather to indicate the most likely future given a continuation of past patterns of behaviour and performance…If policies and patterns of behaviour are changed then alternative futures might be realised. The results are intended to provide *a useful benchmark for debate and policy deliberations* about underlying employment trends. (Sector Skills Development Agency, UK 2006: 3, emphasis added)

International trade is a separate source of uncertainty about future skills demand that provides a simple case in support of arguments against fine-tuned skills projections. The uncertainty injected into skills projections has arguably become greater in recent decades, with globalisation. Trade entails a policy dimension that by its nature is political as well as economic. Thus it is difficult to conceive of a reliable forecasting procedure taking into account *both* changing comparative advantages on economic grounds in foreign trade patterns *and* shifts in goals and alliances with other countries driven by political considerations.

In essence, what has to be devised for usable projections of skill demands is a system of *translation* between knowledge of skills needs at an establishment or plant level and a functioning training system. But when aggregated or added together, can such a translation process operate at the sector or industry level too? It is an open question, best treated without preconception.

Certain researchers in the field are explicit in rejecting the main presumptions that underlie skills forecasting.

> [T]here is no real sense in which a given level of education in the economically active population in a country can be said to be technically 'required' to permit the achieved level of economic growth of that country. Such an argument grossly exaggerates the contribution of manipulative and cognitive skills in the performance of economic functions, ignores the fact that such skills are largely acquired by on-the-job training, and utterly neglects the vital role of suitable personality traits in securing the 'invisible handshake' on which production critically depends. In short, educational policies may be fitted to literally any level or rate of economic growth and cannot be justified in terms of those patterns of growth. Education does make a contribution to economic growth, not as an indispensable input into the growth process, but simply as a framework which necessarily accommodates the growth process. (Blaug 1995: 51)

Conclusions and policy implications

The following summary themes are of most interest to the general reader, particularly when placed in a policy context.

First, the financial services sector in the South African economy has been a major success in its growth contribution, in its stability, in the level of sophistication embodied in its supplied services, and in its established outward links with the international economy.

Where there remain serious problems, these are related to the high proportion of the population who do not possess access to financial services. Too many are denied the economic gains attendant on use of payment, intermediation, credit and saving activities in established institutions and organisations. Coupled to this failing are the relatively low numbers of skilled workers from previously disadvantaged groups employed in the major sub-sectors This has a great deal to do with the deficiencies of our schooling system, a matter which falls outside the scope of this chapter.

Second, by common agreement, the drivers of change in this sector are regulation, competition and technology. Regulation of the main sub-sectors – banking, insurance and accountancy – can import dangers. It has often been put in place with conflicting objectives in mind. Instances of this are the promotion of national financial institutions for prestige, providing exaggerated consumer protection, fostering sectoral and sometimes regional development, and 'preserving financial stability, in particular the safeguarding of the payment and settlement system' (De Serres et al. 2007: 10).

Third, overcoming *information* deficiencies will be a dominating challenge to the financial sector of any country in the future. But it will also make major demands on a country's scientific ingenuity and the law. All the following words are at root about information: *disclosure, transparency, trust, confidence, intangibles* and *intellectual property*. One major cause of the current financial crisis in the USA and other industrial economies arises from a feature as basic as the absence of the working of the price system for intangibles.

Finally, people have to bear the consequences of their mistakes. This may sound harsh but it is essential for efficiency as well as equity. One of its implications is that in practice the state cannot protect every individual and firm from losses through subsidies, guarantees, write-offs and tax holidays in the financial sector. When put in place, there is ample evidence that such cushions or safety nets encourage *moral hazard,* meaning inordinately risky behaviour.

Two examples are in banking and in accountancy. When backed by government, because they cannot lose, banks take on *higher* lending risks, as was evidenced by the Savings & Loan bankruptcies in the 1980s in the USA where deposits were guaranteed (Milgrom & Roberts 1992). Similarly, in a world of auditing and accountancy dominated currently by major companies only four in number, there is a contention that these 'big four' practitioners will behave as if they are 'too big to fail'. In 2005, KPMG broke the law in the USA and was not legally pursued by the federal government 'for crimes it admitted committing' (Cunningham 2006: 1698). In the industry, it was inferred that KPMG was *too big to fail*. This belief encourages moral hazard behaviour, runs the argument. Large firms take risks that are too high by normal business operating standards (Bazerman 2007).

These observations do not lend themselves to straightforward interpretations for the demand and supply of skills in financial services. But it seems reasonable to infer that the demand for skills, particularly in relation to professionals, professional technicians and the great variety of management skills across the sector, will continue to deepen. If it deepens ever more steeply, the deficiencies in our systems of education and training become ever more strategic to mend.

References

ABSA (2006) *Annex 6: Comments on the Falkena Report.* Johannesburg: ABSA

Acemoglu D (2002) Technical change, inequality, and the labor market. *Journal of Economic Literature* 40: 7–72

Archer S (2008) *The financial services sector and the skills development issues relevant to the South African economy.* Research report prepared for the HSRC, Cape Town

Arrow K & Capron W (1959) Dynamic shortages and price rises: The engineer-scientist case. *Quarterly Journal of Economics* 73: 292–308

BANKSETA (Banking Sector Education and Training Authority) (2006) *Sector skills plan 2007/08 update.* Johannesburg: BANKSETA

Basel Committee (2008) *Liquidity risk: Management and supervisory challenges.* Basel: Bank for International Settlements

Bazerman M (2007) Behavioral decision research: Legislation, and society. *Capitalism and Society* 2: 1–18

Beck T, Demirguc-Kunt A & Peria M (2007) *Banking services for everyone? Barriers to bank access and use around the world*. World Bank Working Paper, Washington DC

Blaug M (1995) The wage contract and education. In M Carnoy (ed.) *International encyclopaedia of the economics of education*. Oxford: Pergamon Press

Boyd C (2004a) The structural origins of conflicts of interest in the accounting profession. *Business Ethics Quarterly* 14: 377–398

Boyd C (2004b) The last straw: Book review of 'Final accounting: ambition, greed and the fall of Arthur Andersen' (Toffler & Reingold). *Business Ethics Quarterly* 14: 581–592

Campbell M, Baldwin S, Johnson S, Chapman R, Upton A & Walton F (2001) *Skills in England*. Policy Research Institute, Leeds Metropolitan University, UK

Clarke G, Habyarimana J, Ingram M, Kaplan D & Ramachandran V (2007) *An assessment of the investment climate in South Africa*. Washington DC: World Bank

Cosh A & Hughes A (2003) *The relationship between training and business performance*. Department for Education and Skills, UK, Research Report No. 454, London

Crafts N (2004) Globalisation and economic growth: A historical perspective. *The World Economy* 27: 45–58

CSFI (Centre for the Study of Financial Innovation) (2006) *CSFI director's review of 2005*. London: CSFI

Cunningham L (2006) Too big to fail: Moral hazard in auditing and the need to restructure the industry before it unravels. *Columbia Law Review* 106: 1698–1748

De Serres A, Kobayakawa S, Slok T & Vartia L (2007) *Regulation of financial systems and economic growth*. OECD Economics Department Working Paper No. 506. Paris: OECD

DfES UK (Department for Education and Skills, UK) (2001) *An assessment of skill needs in financial services and accountancy*. London: DfES

Ellis S (2003) Anticipating employers' skills needs: The case for intervention. *International Journal of Manpower* 24: 83–96

Falkena H, Davel G, Hawkins P, Llewellyn D, Luus C, Masilela E, Parr G, Pienaaar J & Shaw H (2004) *Competition in South African banking*. Pretoria: National Treasury & South African Reserve Bank

FASSET (Financial and Accounting Services Sector Education and Training Authority) (2007a) *Scarce skills in the FASSET sector*. March 2007. Johannesburg: FASSET

FASSET (2007b) *Sector Skills Plan 2005 to 2010: update for the 2008/2009 financial year*. Draft, July 2007. Johannesburg: FASSET

Feasibility Report (2006) *The national payment system and competition in the banking sector*. Financial Economic Analysis Strategy, Johannesburg

Financial Reporting Council, UK (2007) *Key facts and key trends in the accountancy profession*. London: Financial Reporting Council

FSSC UK (Financial Services Skills Council, UK) (2007) *The skills bill: Assessment of education and training provision in UK financial services*. London: FSSC

Gelb S, Keeton L & Malikane C (2005) *The scope of the financial services sector industry in the Western Cape*. Report by the Edge Institute, Johannesburg

Gleeson D & Keep E (2004) Voice without accountability: The changing relationship between employers, the state and education in England. *Oxford Review of Education* 30: 37–63

Grossman G & Rossi-Hansberg E (2006) *The rise of off-shoring: it's not wine for cloth anymore*. Working Paper, Federal Reserve Bank of Kansas City

Hartmann P, Heider F, Papaioannou E & Lo Duca M (2007) *The role of financial markets and innovation in productivity and growth in Europe*. European Central Bank Occasional Paper Series No. 72. Frankfurt am Main: European Central Bank

Heijke H (ed.) (1994) *Forecasting the labour market by occupation and education*. Dordrecht: Kluwer

Hopkins M (2002) *Labour market planning revisited*. Basingstoke: Palgrave Macmillan

Ide S, Hoj J & Lenain P (2007) *Enhancing the benefits of financial liberalisation in Belgium*. OECD Economics Department Working Paper No. 588. Paris: OECD

IFAC (International Federation of Accountants) (2007) *IFAC 2007 Global leadership survey: Summary of findings*. Washington DC: IFAC

ILO (International Labour Organisation) (1995) *World labour report 8*. Geneva: ILO

IMF (International Monetary Fund) (2006) *South Africa: Selected issues*. IMF Country Report No. 06/328. Washington DC: IMF

INSETA (Insurance Sector Education and Training Authority) (2006) *Sector skills plan for 2005–2010*. Johannesburg: INSETA

International Audit Networks (2006) *Global capital markets and the global economy*. International Audit Networks, November 2006, Global Public Policy Symposium, New York

Johnston S & Bernstein A (2007) Skills, growth and migration policy: Overcoming the fatal constraint. *CDE In Depth* Issue 5: 1–55

Leitch Review of Skills (2006) *Prosperity for all in the global economy: World class skills*. Final report, December 2006. London: HM Treasury

Lundall P (2007) *Employment flows and the distribution of targeted jobs in the call centre and business process outsourcing sector of the Western Cape over the medium term*. Cape Town: Western Cape Department of Economic Development and Tourism

Milgrom P & Roberts J (1992) *Economics, organization and management*. Englewood Cliffs: Prentice-Hall

Oosthuizen M (2005) *The post-apartheid labour market*. DPRU Working Paper 06/103, Development Policy Research Unit, University of Cape Town

Porter M, Ketels C & Delgado M (2007) *The microeconomic foundations of prosperity: Findings from the Business Competitiveness Index*. Geneva: World Economic Forum

Rodrik D (2004) Industrial policy for the twenty-first century. Mimeo, Kennedy School of Government, Harvard University

Sala-i-Martin X, Blanke J, Hanouz M, Geiger T, Mia I & Paua F (2007) *The global competitiveness index: Measuring the productive potential of nations*. Geneva: World Economic Forum

SARB (South African Reserve Bank) (2007) *Quarterly bulletins*. Pretoria: SARB

Sector Skills Development Agency, UK (2006) *Working futures 2004–2014: Sectoral report*. Institute for Employment Research, University of Warwick, Coventry

Standard Bank (2007) *Economic profile South Africa 2007*. Johannesburg: Standard Bank

Standard & Poor (2008) *South African banks balance robust growth with rising risks in 2008*. Johannesburg: Standard & Poor

The Presidency (2007) *Jipsa (Joint Initiative on Priority Skills Acquisition) 2007 annual report*. Pretoria: The Presidency

Upper C (2007) *Using counterfactual simulations to assess the danger of contagion in interbank markets*. BIS Working Papers No. 234. Basel: Bank for International Settlements

Watson D, Webb R & Johnson S (2006) Influence costs and the reporting of skill deficiencies. *Human Relations* 59: 37–59

Woolard I, Kneebone P & Lee D (2003) Forecasting the demand for scarce skills, 2001–2006. In *Human resources development review 2003: Education, employment and skills in South Africa*. Cape Town: HSRC Press

World Bank (2006) *Policy research report: Access to finance: measurement, impact and policy concept note*. Washington DC: World Bank

World Economic Forum (2007) *Global competitiveness monitor 2007–2008*. Geneva: World Economic Forum

CHAPTER 14

Information and communication technologies

Andrew Paterson and Joan Roodt

Introduction

Information and communication technologies (ICTs) are widely assumed to be an enabler of economic growth. The ICT sector is an important economic sector because it is in effect the 'producer sector' of ICT goods and services which are applied in myriad business and personal environments.

Concern has been expressed to the effect that there is a shortage of ICT skills in South Africa which will constrain government's goal of achieving a sustainable annual six per cent growth rate in GDP and halving unemployment and poverty by 2014. Claims about South Africa's apparent ICT skills shortages emanate from a range of sources such as government, training providers, industry, and writers of journal articles and media reports. We begin by briefly referring to key examples of dimensions of the ICT skills shortage from the perspective of the media.

Drivers of skills needs:
- Technology change: Technology obsolescence and changing business requirements lead to skills shortages locally and globally.
- Asgisa: Within the Asgisa initiative, business process outsourcing (BPO) is gaining momentum, but higher-level skills, such as call centre management skills, are required to achieve the competitive edge.
- Equity: There is a shortage of skilled black ICT candidates. Fulfilling the statutory employment equity requirements is a challenge in the midst of an ICT skills shortage. More investment is required in skills development. ICT companies have tended to recruit staff instead of developing human resources (HR) internally.
- Migration: The global market attracts South African skills, and there is a 'brain drain' from South Africa.

Types of skills needed:
- Technical skills: There is a continuous shortage of software engineering skills and advanced skills in hardware development.
- Project management skills: Consistent calls are made for more project management expertise across large and small ICT projects.
- Business skills: ICT workers need to go beyond systems and technologies and build their knowledge and skills in business disciplines and sectoral/industrial specificities.

- Experience: A critical shortage of experience is identified, especially for large-scale vendor projects. South African firms chase international skills among South African nationals who have gained experience abroad.

These observations reveal that skills 'shortages' or 'needs' are driven by a range of factors that are exogenous to firms (e.g global labour market pressures) and endogenous to firms (e.g. weak commitment to skilling and retaining own workers).

The observations also show that skills 'needs' or 'shortages' may be identified in a number of different dimensions (that is, 'scarce skills' as unfilled vacancies, or 'critical skills' as gaps in the skills make-up of the employed). These range from technical skills, to managerial skills, to soft skills, to experience. In addition, skills shortages may be fairly specific (e.g. to a particular industrial sub-sector or even to a particular software development environment). The severity of shortages differs by location and over time.

This chapter examines skills – in particular scarce/critical skills – in the ICT sector itself and in the cohorts of workers employed in ICT occupations across all economic sectors. Our analytical approach is based on moving from the sectoral to the sub-sectoral and then to the occupational level, at each stage obtaining a more disaggregated view of skills demand. In turn we address skills supply through considering the wider set of study fields that are relevant to employment in an ICT occupation, and then focus on computer professionals and associate professionals.

We argue that skills demands within the ICT sector as an economic sector, and in ICT occupations across all sectors, are concentrated increasingly on high skills. We review data and methods of research on the demand and supply of ICT skills, and conclude that the results are somewhat disappointing as they seem inadequate to direct policy in a particular direction. At the same time, we suggest that in order for research on skills needs to generate better data that can actually support skills development interventions, a sharper focus is needed that is based on plans by sectoral stakeholders to enter particular ICT markets.

Structure of this chapter

This chapter is structured in five main sections. The first section below serves as an introduction to the domains in which ICT skills are applied.

This is followed by a second section which investigates skills demand in the ICT sector workforce, and then in particular ICT occupations that are found across all sectors.

It is necessary to address the question of ICT skills in the economy in two ways. One approach entails examining the ICT sector labour market. In such a case, the unit of analysis is the ICT sector and its three component sub-sectors. The ICT sector workforce will contain workers from all occupational categories. This means that workers with ICT skills (e.g. computer programmers) will work alongside other workers (e.g. clerical and administrative workers) in enterprises whose core business is to produce and sell ICT goods and services. Taking a sector workforce as a unit of analysis is standard practice (e.g. ICT or manufacturing or construction) because each industrial activity will have characteristic labour demands for particular combinations of low- to high-level skills. In our analysis of ICT sector demand, we consider these issues in some detail.

Another equally important approach is to examine the demand for ICT workers across the economy. As we have observed here, workers with ICT skills are employed not only in the ICT sector but across all sectors which use ICT (e.g. especially banking and retail and financial services but also mining and agriculture). This approach will emphasise not the sector as the unit of analysis, but rather the occupational category. This is because it is necessary to consider changes in the total number of computer professionals who are employed across all sectors in the entire economy. In this way, we would be in a better position to draw out the general levels of demand in particular ICT specialist occupational categories. It is only at this level that we can begin to try to match occupational (skills) shortages with supply of workers holding qualifications with analogous skills sets.

The third section of the chapter involves a detailed analysis of the supply of skills into the labour market, particularly from public higher education institutions.

In the fourth section, the chapter considers the relationship between demand and supply through three different methodological approaches to the question: a projection, an analysis of remuneration, and a survey of vacancies.

Based on the foregoing, the final section argues for speeding up the industrial policy process so that improved alignment of industrial planning and ICT skills development can be anticipated.

Introduction to the ICT sector

The ICT sector constitutes a sub-component of the national economy which influences and is influenced by the changing shape and size of the larger economy. The ICT 'producer' sector itself consists of three sub-divisions, electronics, telecommunications and IT services, which because of their diverse activities are located in different broad industrial divisions according to the Standard Industrial Classification (SIC) system (Figure 14.1). IT services are categorised within the broader 'services', telecommunications in the broader 'transport and telecommunications', and electronics in the broader 'manufacturing' sets of economic activity.

The broader economy

During the period under review (1996–2005), as elsewhere globally, the ICT sector in South Africa experienced a concerted surge of activity and growing investor confidence, followed by a sudden

FIGURE 14.1: *Relationship between the ICT producer sector and ICT 'user' sectors*

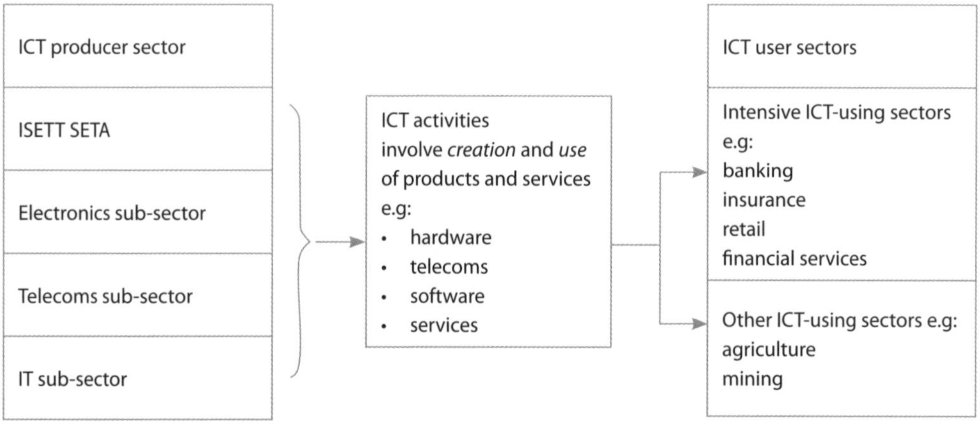

ICT producer sector		ICT user sectors
ISETT SETA	ICT activities involve *creation* and *use* of products and services e.g: • hardware • telecoms • software • services	Intensive ICT-using sectors e.g: banking insurance retail financial services
Electronics sub-sector		
Telecoms sub-sector		Other ICT-using sectors e.g: agriculture mining
IT sub-sector		

Source: Paterson 2007

turnaround in the dot.com crash, coupled with the effects of global economic slowdown. Since the turbulent millennium period, the local ICT sector has shown positive growth in tandem with the economy as a whole.

In terms of industry sector contribution to South Africa's GDP, the ICT sector was projected to reach 2.5 per cent for the period 2002–2003, while sales in the sector were estimated to be 7–8 per cent of GDP for the same period (*Leadership* 2002). Although all sectors of the South African economy – except for wholesale and retail trade – shed labour between 1997 and 2001, there were a number of positive signs for the ICT sector.

After 2001, the South African economy showed growing diversification in services exports. In particular, the category of 'other services', which includes telecommunication, financial and information services exports, expanded. In the financial services, business services, banking, and wholesale and retail sectors in particular, the information intensity of business processes is high.

Size of sub-sectors

The size of each sub-sector, in terms of number of enterprises, and in relation to the average size of enterprises, has a bearing on how much training is provided. In general, increasing size of an enterprise is associated with higher propensity to provide training to workers. In addition, training co-ordination on an industry basis should be easier in sectors where there are a few large players than in those with a large number of small players, notwithstanding competition.

Telecommunications

The telecommunications sub-sector contains the smallest proportion of enterprises in the ICT sector overall, but a few of these are very large employers (Table 14.1). Enterprises in the telecommunications sub-sector are predominantly active in landline telephony, television signal distribution and wireless telecommunications (excluding satellite), with some activity in cable network services (Paterson 2006: 54).

Information technology

As can be seen from Table 14.1, in terms of enterprise numbers, the information technology (IT) sub-sector is by far the largest within the ICT sector, and consists mainly of small organisations. About 80 per cent of enterprises had less than 5 employees, and 88 per cent had less than 10 employees, in 2002 (ISETT SETA 2002: 3). Business activities of companies in this sub-sector involve mainly deployment and support of products and technology sourced internationally.

TABLE 14.1: *Number of enterprises, by sub-sector of the ICT sector, 2002*

Sub-sector	No. of enterprises	Percentage of enterprises in the ICT sector
IT	5 597	87
Electronics	165	3
Telecommunications	612	10
Total	6 374	100

Sources: ISETT SETA 2002: 3; Paterson 2006

Electronics

The electronics sub-sector includes major enterprise players in the industrial, power, defence and telecoms electronics areas (DTI 2004). From the range of sectorally driven electronics activities, the electronics sub-sector appears to be quite diversified. Nevertheless, the majority of enterprises import pre-manufactured IT electronic components.

International performance of the ICT sector

For the ICT sector in South Africa, growth is based mainly on domestic consumption rather than on exports, and is concentrated mainly in communications and IT services, less in software development, and least in hardware. Sustained export growth remains elusive. South Africa's share of world trade in ICT products in 1999/2000, at 0.06 per cent, was lower than its share of all product exports of 0.7 per cent1[1] which can be attributed in part to the tendency for the ICT sector, in the period after 1994, to focus on supplying a small group of large domestic clients.

Steady domestic progress of the ICT sector since the millennium has been put in some doubt in 2008 with global equity market negativity, a looming economic recession in the USA, local electricity supply problems and rising interest rates. However, local ICT businesses in the infrastructure field and those with government contracts will be less worried, because government expenditure – including that for the Gautrain and the 2010 FIFA World Cup – is committed.

ICT sector demand: economic growth and employment growth

The question of skills shortages – in terms of scarce or critical skills – is part of a broader question: what are the broad trends in sector activity that are likely to be job-creating or labour-shedding? It is appropriate to first examine the macro-level trends across the ICT sub-sectors before considering fluctuations in occupational demand for skilled workers.

Historical performance of the three sub-sectors (Tables 14.2 and 14.3) reveals the following trends. The ICT manufacturing sub-sector produces a minor share of ICT-sector GDP, with a low growth trajectory. Its employment share is three times larger than its GDP share. This means that its GDP-per-worker ratio is not as favourable as those of the other two sub-sectors. Employment is in slow decline.

The communication sub-sector produces a large share of ICT sector GDP with a strong growth path. It has a moderate labour market size but has suffered significant job losses. These characteristics appear to be consistent with job-shedding, capital-intensive, technology-sector development.

The ICT services sub-sector generates a large share of GDP with good growth, though lower than that of communication. It sustained the fastest growing share of employment through the period 1996–2005.

Employment in ICT sub-sectors

We turn now to employment patterns in economic activities within each sub-sector, based on Labour Force Survey (LFS) and October Household Survey (OHS) data (Quantec 2007). We have observed that telecommunications suffered a declining share of ICT employment. We do not disaggregate this sub-sector.

---

1. Top skills, export incentives open up competitive niches. *Leadership*, August. Accessed 21 May 2003, http://www.leadership.co.za/issues/2002aug/articles/invest0802.html

TABLE 14.2: *GDP and employment in ICT sub-sectors, 1996–2005*

ICT sub-sector[a]	GDP		Employment	
	Share (%)	Average annual growth (%)	Share (%)	Average annual growth (%)
ICT manufacturing[b]	9.8	2.7	30.9	−3.5
Communication	45.6	8.8	37.0	−5.2
ICT services	44.5	4.0	32.1	3.4
Total	100.0	4.5	100	−2.0

Source: Based on data from Quantec 2007

Notes: a. Sub-sector definitions differ from official South African definitions adopted by the Information Systems, Electronics and Telecommunications Technologies Sector Education and Training Authority (ISETT SETA). However, key features will be similar between data sets. The sub-sectoral definitions applied are broader than those applied to data from the Labour Force Survey (LFS) and October Household Survey (OHS) that are used later in the analysis.

b. In our analysis, we include the manufacture of insulated wire and cable sub-division which incorporates all types of covered wire, cables and other insulated conductors. This sub-group is part of the telecommunications value chain (e.g. optical fibre for landlines). There are 3 major players and altogether about 16 players in the sub-division.

TABLE 14.3: *Summary of ICT sub-sector growth and employment trajectories, 1996–2005*

ICT sub-sector	GDP		Employment	
	Share	Growth	Share	Growth
ICT manufacturing	Small	Low	Moderate	Low negative
Communication	Large	Strong	Moderate	Strong negative
ICT services	Large	Medium	Moderate	Positive

Source: Based on data from Quantec 2007

In the IT services sub-sector, which increased its share of employment, the industry sub-group 'software consultancy and supply' was a strong employer (46 per cent). This is consistent with the importance of software to business processes in the widest possible array of organisational environments. When we group together businesses active in servicing general hardware and network needs,[2] their combined share of total employment (35.9 per cent) begins to approach the magnitude of the software consultancy sub-group. One would have expected the former to grow faster in the recovery period post-2000.

In the smallest sub-sector, manufacturing, enterprises in the manufacture of 'computing machinery' and of 'insulated wire and cable' employed 4 in every 10 ICT manufacturing workers. Big employment increases were reflected for wire and cable producers.

---

2 The sub-groups are: 'hardware consultancy', 'wholesale trade in equipment', 'maintenance and repair services and equipment rental'.

The third-biggest group, 'electronics', showed a substantial decline in employment, whereas enterprises engaged in manufacture of 'medical and other instrumentation and appliances' increased their employment share by the same magnitude.

We selected five ICT sub-sectors/sub-groups with a view to creating employment trend-lines for each over the 1996–2005 period. They are:
- ICT manufacturing;
- telecommunications;
- software consultancy and supply;
- hardware consultancy;
- maintenance and repair of office, accounting and computing machinery.

A line was drawn to show the general direction of the trend in each case (Figure 14.2). The r-squared linear regression method was applied to show the strength or consistency of upward/downward employment trends for the selected sub-sectors/sub-groups.[3] A value close to 1 indicates a high linear reliability.

FIGURE 14.2: *Employment trends in the major subdivisions of the ICT sector, 1996–2005*

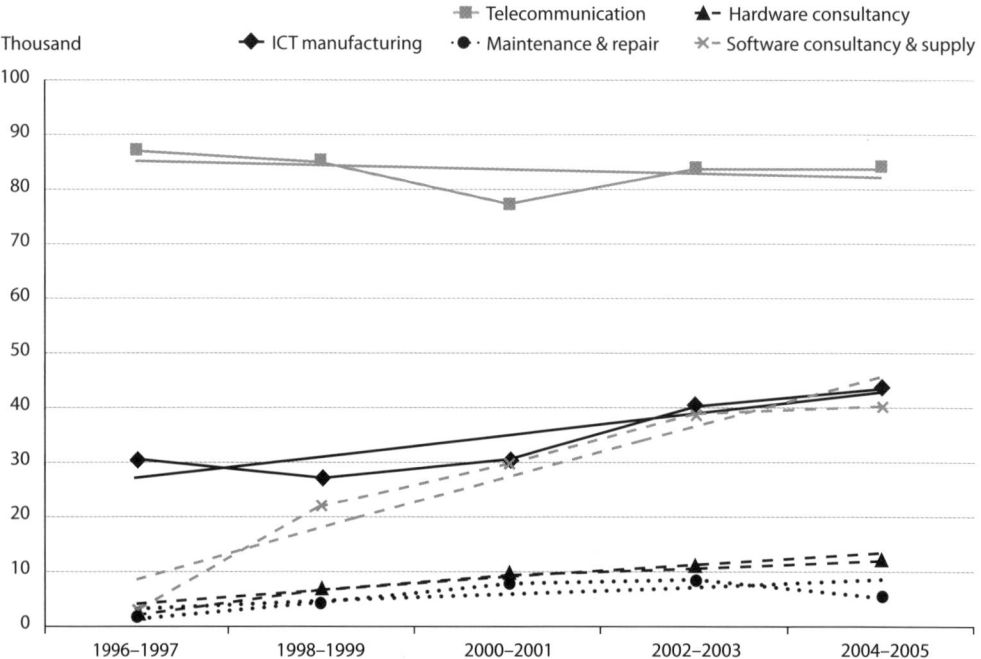

Source: Quantec 2007 (Stats SA OHS data for 1996–1999; Stats SA LFS data for 2000–2005)
Note: On account of large annual data fluctuations in the OHS and LFS, data points were calculated at two-year intervals (averaged) from which the trend-lines were drawn; Telecommunication – $R^2 = 0.1119$;
ICT manufacturing – $R^2 = 0.7632$; Software consultancy & supply – $R^2 = 0.8963$; Hardware consultancy – $R^2 = 0.9209$; Maintenance & repair – $R^2 = 0.4603$.

3   We are employing the r-value simply to obtain a measure of the linear reliability of progressive change in the phenomenon under investigation. This can serve as an indicator of whether the direction of change can be predicted in the future with greater or lesser confidence.

The two sub-groups with the strongest r-squared (R^2) values closest to 1 were: hardware consultancy ($R^2=0.9209$) and software consultancy and supply ($R^2=0.8963$). Because the trends in these two sub-groups have the highest confidence levels based on trends in employment growth in the decade 1996–2005, this suggests that the existing trends in these sub-groups are likely to be sustained in the future – barring any significant changes in the environment.

Based on our analysis of the period 1996–2005, the ICT sector as a whole is unlikely to absorb labour. The manufacturing and telecommunications sectors will in all likelihood continue to shed labour. Growth and employment prospects seem most likely to be achieved in the ICT services sub-sector. However, much will depend on the specificity of the sub-activity concerned, because the skill intensity and combinations of skills required of different services sector activities can vary quite considerably.

ICT sub-sectoral shifts in skills levels and between occupations

We have established a sense of the aggregate shape of employment change in relation to sub-sector growth. The valency of employment change is informed by the type of sectoral economic growth or decline, but this cannot only be viewed in the aggregate. To make sense of the impact of such changes on skills needs, we must investigate changes in employment with reference to skill levels and to occupational breakdown of the sub-sectoral workforce. Only a more disaggregated analysis will provide indications of possible skills shortages or job-shedding.

Changes in skill levels in the sub-sectors

Although the evidence points to a general increase in skill levels,[4] there were different patterns in each of the three sub-sectors for the periods under discussion (Table 14.4).

Between the two periods (1996–1999 and 2000–2005), the proportions of low-skill workers declined in all sub-sectors, but especially in telecommunications. In that sub-sector, a sharp decrease in low-

TABLE 14.4: *Level of skill by sub-sector (percentage), 1996–1999 and 2000–2005*

Occupation	Period	Average employed per annum			
		Low skill	Intermediate skill	High skill	Total
ICT manufacturing	1996–1999	42.9	47.0	10.1	100
	2000–2005	35.8	54.2	10.1	100
		−7.1	7.2	0.0	
Telecommunications	1996–1999	37.5	57.1	5.4	100
	2000–2005	20.9	67.1	12.0	100
		−16.6	10.0	6.6	
IT services	1996–1999	21.5	62.6	15.8	100
	2000–2005	12.8	62.1	25.1	100
		−8.7	−0.5	9.3	

Source: Quantec 2007 (Stats SA OHS data for 1996–1999; Stats SA LFS data for 2000–2005)

---

4 By 'skill levels' we refer to a method of grouping of the nine major occupations (according to the International Standard Occupational Code (ISOC) system) into three categories – 'skilled', 'semi-skilled/intermediate' and 'un-skilled' for purposes of analysis.

skill workers occurred simultaneously, with increased shares among both intermediate- and high-skill workers. This may reflect a reduced emphasis on building telecommunications infrastructure and a stronger emphasis on developing telecommunications services.

In ICT manufacturing, a shift transpired between the low- and intermediate-skill levels in favour of higher proportions of workers with intermediate skills. Although there was no increase in the proportion of high-skill workers, the aggregate skills profile of ICT manufacturing shifted upwards.

In IT services, a general rise in skill levels was apparent, through a decrease in low skills together with an increase in high skills proportions, while the proportion of intermediate skills was virtually unchanged.

The changes in the proportionate share of skill levels noted above should not be considered in isolation, but in relation to changes in relative size – in employment numbers – of occupational groups.

The changes in skill levels that we have identified across the sub-sectors confirm a palpable shift towards high skill levels across the decade. The question is: had the supply institutions been able to make skilled workers available in larger numbers, would the results of the analysis have revealed even stronger upward shifts in the skills base of the ICT sub-sectors? And a further question is, could these trends have been strengthened by employer initiatives to raise worker skills?

The evidence strongly suggests that there was an increased employer requirement for higher skill levels that was relatively independent of the demand for more skilled workers. We have shown that formal employment in the telecommunications sector declined over the decade, and formal employment in the ICT manufacturing sector was stagnant, while only the IT services sub-sector exhibited signs of employment growth and the potential to absorb labour in the future. Nevertheless, *all* sub-sectors exhibited features of rising skill levels.

Sub-sectoral shifts in occupational distribution of workers

We continue by briefly looking at the general distribution of occupational employment in the three main sub-sectors, averaged over the decade. Thereafter we examine changes in occupational shape over time within each sub-sector.

Each ICT sub-sector expressed different patterns of demand for occupational groups, as might be expected of different industrial activities (Figure 14.3). Representation of professionals and associate professionals increases from the smallest share in 'manufacturing', through 'telecommunications', to the largest share in 'IT services'.

Over the decade, managers, professionals and associate professionals together constituted 39.2 per cent, 49 per cent and 71.6 per cent of all employment in the manufacturing, telecommunications and IT services sub-sectors respectively. This demonstrates how skills intensity differed vastly across the three sectors. As expected, in the 'manufacturing' sub-sector, operators constituted a substantial group, together with elementary workers and craft and related workers.

There were also isomorphic features in the occupational profiles. The occupational group with largest representation across each of the sub-sectors is associate professionals. However, the associate professionals occupational group is markedly smaller in manufacturing than in the other two sub-sectors.

FIGURE 14.3: *Employment in the ICT sector, by sub-sector and main occupation, 1996–2005*

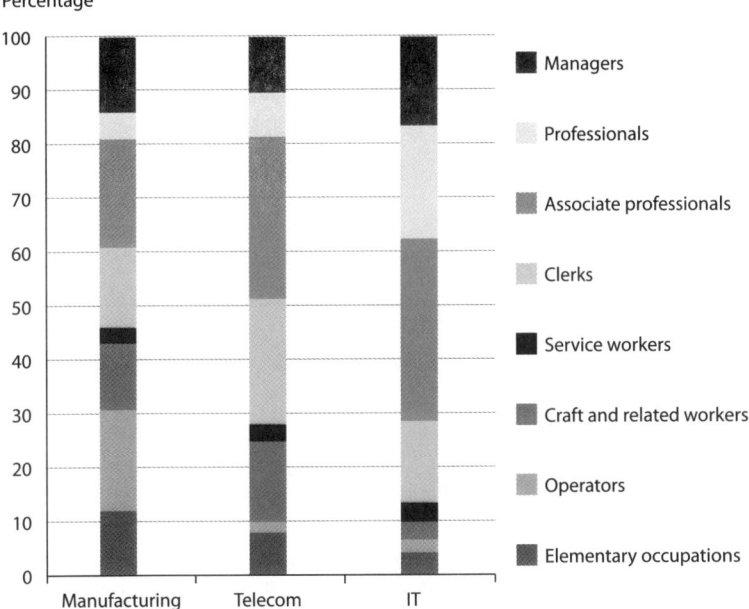

Source: Quantec 2007 (Stats SA OHS data for 1996–1999; Stats SA LFS data for 2000–2005)

The proportion of service workers was relatively small across all three sub-sectors. It is interesting that this should be the case even in the 'IT services' sub-sector. This strongly suggests that the nature of services activity in the latter sub-sector requires high-skill-level workers to service client needs (that is, professionals and associate professionals). Note that this shift places a higher premium on the capability of graduate production in higher education.

If we look at changes in the occupational share of employment between 1996–1999 and 2000–2005, Table 14.5 highlights (in grey) occupational categories whose share of sub-sectoral employment declined. This confirms a general pattern of declining emphasis on low skills, declining emphasis on intermediate technical skills, and indifferent demand for service workers. The implication is that in the near future, the ICT sector broadly will be unlikely to absorb labour in the lower technical, clerical and unskilled occupational categories. On this basis, we must conclude that general assumptions made about potential labour absorbtivity of the ICT sector in these occupational categories are not consistent with the nature of labour force change in the sector.

Occupational-level analysis

Thus far, the analysis has addressed ICT skills with emphasis on the ICT sector labour market, where the unit of analysis was that sector and its three component sub-sectors. Consequently, the analysis revealed the growth paths and labour demands that characterise the ICT sub-sectors. This approach foregrounded the occupational structures of each sub-sector and how different skills needs characterised each different industrial activity.

TABLE 14.5: *Employment, by main occupation in the ICT sub-sectors, 1996–1999 compared with 2000–2005*

Occupation	Average employed per annum 2000–2005 (%)			Difference 1996–1999 compared to 2000–2005		
	Manu-facturing	Tele-comms	IT services	Manu-facturing	Tele-comms	IT services
Managers	12.8	13.3	15.8	−4.2	7.0	6.3
Professionals	3.6	8.5	14.6	−3.2	0.6	1.1
Associate professionals	19.8	29.7	32.4	−1.5	−1.9	0.6
Clerks	15.5	26.7	21.4	1.4	8.4	5.3
Service workers	2.8	3.2	3.0	−0.4	0.6	−0.6
Craft & related workers	11.4	11.8	7.1	−2.6	−7.2	−6.3
Operators	21.1	0.9	1.1	7.8	−2.7	−2.7
Elementary occupations	12.9	5.9	4.6	2.7	−4.4	−3.7
Total	100.0	100.0	100.0			

Source: Quantec 2007 (Stats SA OHS data for 1996–1999; Stats SA LFS data for 2000–2005)

However, there are limitations to this approach when questions are asked about the demand for ICT workers across the economy. We have observed that workers with ICT skills are employed not only in the ICT sector but across all sectors of the economy. It is therefore necessary to undertake an analysis in which the occupation rather than the sector is the unit of analysis. This makes it possible to investigate demand for ICT professionals who may be employed across all sectors in the entire economy. Subject to the availability of disaggregated data, the levels of demand for certain ICT-related specialist occupational categories may be interrogated.

It is the latter approach to exploring ICT skills that will be pursued in the rest of this chapter. To confirm this shift in analytic approach: in the previous section we investigated skills needs of the *ICT sector labour force*, whereas in the remaining part of this chapter we will investigate the skills needs of the *ICT workforce*. In the preceding section, the analysis rested on a definition of the ICT sector and sub-sectors, whereas in the remaining sections, the analysis will rest on a definition of what occupations are considered part of the cross-sectoral ICT workforce.

Size of the ICT sector workforce (based on a selection of ICT occupational categories)

The combined impact of technological innovation and the re-engineering of workplace occupational structures has, over time, contributed to the creation, destruction and reshaping of occupations across industries. The range of occupations that incorporate the use of ICT, or are transformed by ICT, constantly widens. Systems of occupational classification have lagged behind these changes. Analysts may or may not agree on which set of occupations can be legitimately classified as ICT-related.

For this reason, we adopt a broad definition of ICT in order to identify and select a set of occupations that may – in our view – be taken as broadly representative of the ICT workforce as a whole. This approach suggests that the size of the intermediate and high-skill ICT workforce rose from 126 880 in the first period to 154 941 in the second period (Table 14.6).

TABLE 14.6: *Employment of ICT-related professionals and associate professionals, 1996–2005*

ICT occupations	Average employed per annum					
	1996–1999		2000–2005		1996–2005	
	N	%	N	%	N	%
Electronics & telecommunication engineering technicians	27 441	21.6	45 408	29.3	38 221	26.6
Computer associate professionals	27 652	21.8	32 154	20.8	30 353	21.1
Computer professionals	27 651	21.8	29 833	19.3	28 960	20.2
Graphic/industrial designers	21 480	16.9	28 929	18.7	25 950	18.1
Photographers & image/sound equipment operators	12 335	9.7	11 169	7.2	11 635	8.1
Broadcasting & telecommunication equipment operators	5 106	4.0	4 028	2.6	4 459	3.1
Electronics & telecommunication engineers	3 074	2.4	2 386	1.5	2 661	1.9
Mathematicians & related professionals	2 140	1.7	1 035	0.7	1 477	1
Total	126 880	100.0	154 941	100.0	143 716	100.0

Source: Quantec 2007 (Stats SA OHS data for 1996–1999; Stats SA LFS data for 2000–2005)

At the occupational level, across the 9-year period from 1996 to 2005, computer professionals and computer associate professionals constituted 20.2 per cent (28 960) and 21.1 per cent (30 353) respectively of the number of workers employed in the identified occupational categories. So, computer professionals and associate professionals constituted over 40 per cent of the ICT workforce within our broad definition of ICT workers.

The next-largest occupational group was electronic and telecommunications engineering technicians at 26.6 per cent (38 221), whereas the related electronic and telecommunications engineers group constituted only 1.9 per cent (2 661) of the ICT workforce.

'Associate professionals' and 'technicians', as intermediate-skilled workers, carry out technical tasks related to their field of expertise.[5] Usually they will work in teams under the supervision of a professional or engineer, as may be the case. It is important to note the 1:1 ratio between higher-level computer professionals and intermediate-skilled computer associate professionals. By contrast, in the electronic and telecommunications engineering field, intermediate-skilled technicians outnumber engineers at a ratio of 14.4:1. From this, we infer that the appropriate balance between workers with high skills and intermediate skills in the same occupational category may differ by field of expertise, and that this has implications for skills shortages.

Even though keeping track of national ICT workforce size is important in relation to other macro trends, it is not a statistic that can be used for occupational-level planning to inform strategies that can combat skills shortages or over-supply. The reason is that the list of occupational types used to obtain an

---

5 Associate professionals and technicians are defined as: 'People who possess technical knowledge and experience in a field of the physical and life sciences or the social sciences and humanities…[They] perform mostly technical and related tasks connected with research and the application of scientific or artistic concepts and operational methods, and government or business regulations, and teach at certain educational levels…[They] may receive guidance from senior government officials, Managers or Professionals' (THETA 2006).

aggregate picture of the ICT workforce should be disaggregated for further analysis. This is because these occupational types form part of analytically distinct occupational labour markets that are defined partly by ICT sectoral economic activity and partly by links to different knowledge fields and other practices influenced by sectoral business value chains and activities.

At the same time, there is evidence of increased convergence between the technology fields of electronics and IT, driven by ongoing product and service development in industry, which may over time lead to increased overlap between these two fields in terms of professional training. Even though the skills and knowledge profiles of electronics and IT graduates may be slowly converging, they still remain relatively independent systems of expertise which respond differently to industry needs. In particular, the demand for computer professionals derives from their participation in a range of business processes, from software development to providing consulting services. Consequently, for the time being, the drivers of demand for 'computer professionals' and for 'electronics and telecommunications engineers' will be taken as different, notwithstanding levels of convergence.

In the next stage of the analysis, we should focus in detail on the employment features and possible skills needs of only four occupations that, by common usage, may be taken less controversially to be core ICT occupations – namely computer professionals and computer associate professionals (CPAP), and electronic and telecommunications engineers and technicians (ETET). Cumulatively, this group constitutes about two-thirds of total ICT workforce employment. However, we will focus on the CPAP categories to limit the length of this chapter.

Sectoral employment of computer professionals and association professionals

The biggest sectoral employers of computer professionals in the 2003–2004 period were finance (70.2 per cent) and manufacturing (8.6 per cent) (Table 14.7). A similar proportion was evident in the sectoral employment of computer associate professionals, where the biggest sectoral employers were finance (55.0 per cent) and manufacturing (12.3 per cent). As these are the largest sectoral employers of ICT CPAPs, it would be important to investigate sectoral determinants of future employment growth through specific studies of these sectors.

TABLE 14.7: *Distribution of computer professionals and associate professionals, by economic sector, 2003–2004*

Economic sector	Professionals	Associate professionals	Professionals	Associate professionals
	N	N	%	%
Finance	21721	9076	71.0	59.2
Manufacturing	2304	2910	7.5	19.0
Trade	1445	1444	4.7	9.4
Services	2910	286	9.5	1.9
Transport	681	1164	2.2	7.6
Mining	327	441	1.1	2.9
Electricity	1209	0	4.0	0.0
Construction	0	0	0.0	0.0
Agriculture	0	0	0	0
Total	30597	15320	100	100

Source: Quantec 2007 (Stats SA OHS data for 1996–1999; Stats SA LFS data for 2000–2005)

FIGURE 14.4: *Average provincial distribution of computer professionals and associate professionals and GDP, 2000–2005*

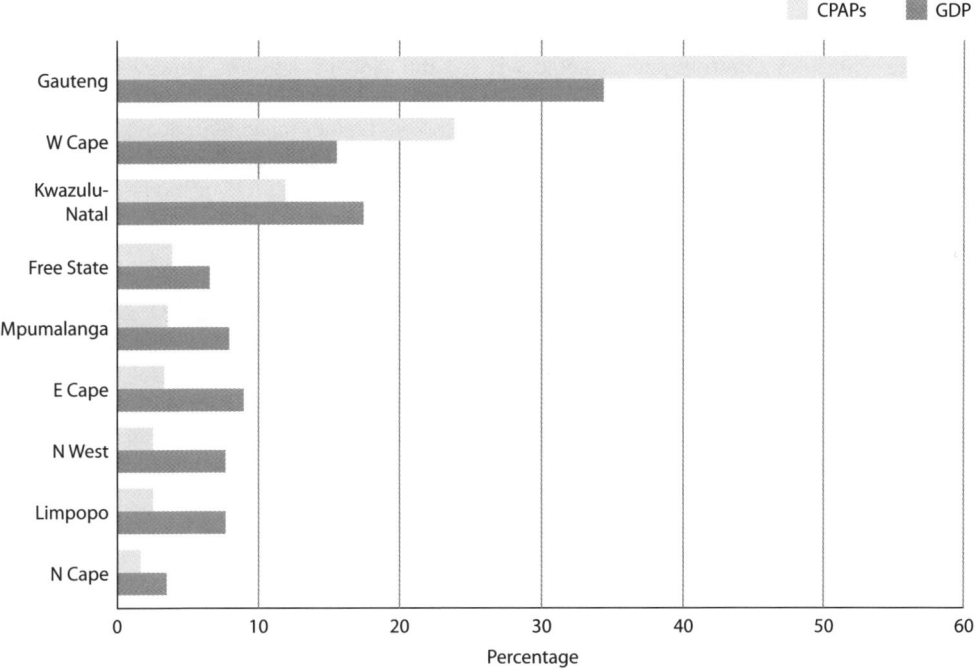

Source: Quantec 2007 (Stats SA LFS data for 2000–2005)

The distribution of ICT professionals by spatial location is also relevant to the likelihood of skills shortages.[6] Looking at provincial distribution, it is immediately apparent that practically 9 in every 10 computer professionals are located in 1 of 3 provinces: Gauteng (55.2 per cent), the Western Cape (23.0 per cent) and KwaZulu-Natal (10.7 per cent) (Figure 14.4). In each of the other six provinces the share of computer professionals is below two per cent. The future analysis of skills shortages would be enhanced if location – rural, urban and metropolitan – were taken into account. Clearly, we need to consider in more detail how spatial dimensions dictate real and perceived excess demand for CPAPs.

Supply of high-skill ICT workers

Schools, FET colleges and private training

Ordinary schools, especially high schools, and further education and training (FET) colleges have so far played a relatively small role in the development of cohorts of high-skill ICT graduates.

A small number of high school students have the opportunity to enrol for Computer Science as a subject up to the Senior Certificate (SC) examination. In 2005, 4 197 candidates passed Computer Science as a subject for the SC examination on the Higher Grade.[7] Candidates may pass Computer Science as a subject but may not qualify to enrol in higher education on their aggregate results. Computer Science as a matriculation subject is not a pre-requisite for entry into computer science study in a South African

6   The labour market for CPAP is also segmented along private/public-sector lines.
7   The higher grade and standard grade distinction has since been phased out.

higher education institution. Therefore there is not a strong link between Computer Science curriculum access at schools and at higher education levels.

In certain FET colleges, ICT-related courses offered from N4 to N6 include: Communication-Electronics, Computer Principles, Control Systems, Logic Systems and Digital Electronics. However, it was not possible to gauge what proportion of FET graduates may still be part of the ICT skills pipeline. The Department of Education supplies data on courses completed rather than on graduates with whole qualifications. In the FET colleges, a modularised course structure provides for students – and the employed – to register for vocationally useful courses on an ad hoc basis for vocational skills enrichment. Clearly, more attention needs to be paid to understanding the implications of FET college graduate output for intermediate- to high-level ICT skills production in South Africa.

In the private sector, many of the training opportunities are vendor-driven, modular and generally have a low theory component. The overwhelming majority of such training opportunities offering certification are based on global vendor-defined skills levels. As such, there is minimal alignment with national qualification systems. This said, it is estimated that a very small percentage – in the single digits – of vendor courseware is equivalent to higher education qualifications. The private sector plays a major role in skilling of ICT workers, especially in proprietary software environments.

Graduate production in higher education

Figure 14.5 provides a picture of the average share of graduate output from key ICT-cognate fields of study between 1996 and 2005, as well as average annual growth rates in graduate output for the same period. Clearly, the largest contributors are 'Computer Science and Data Processing' and 'Electrical Engineering', though in the latter case, we must note that only a proportion of such graduates would work in ICT-related occupations. It is noteworthy that two fields with relatively low graduate outputs, namely, 'Computer Engineering and Technology' and 'Business Data Systems', share high average annual growth rates along with Computer Science (Figure 14.5 and Table 14.8).

FIGURE 14.5: *Graduates in ICT-cognate fields of study, 1996–2005*

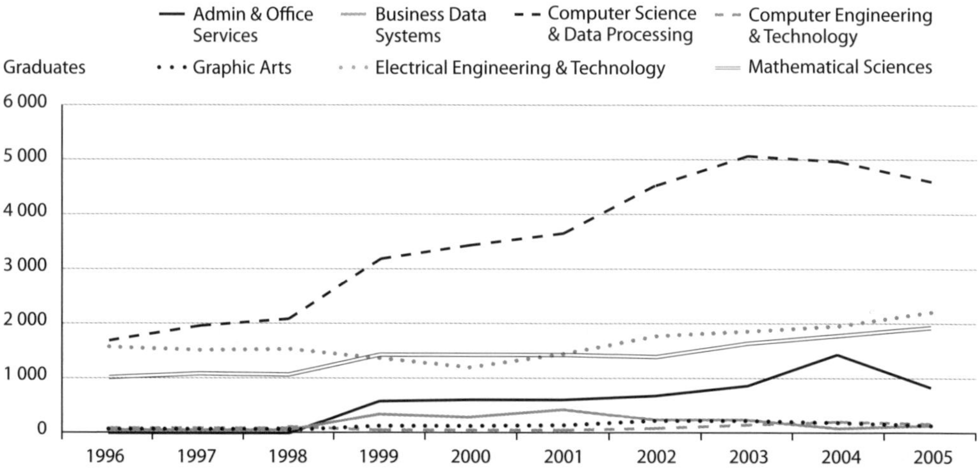

Source: DoE 1996–2005

TABLE 14.8: *Graduate trends in ICT-related fields of study in higher education, 1996–2005*

ICT-related fields of study in higher education	Average share	Average annual growth (%) (1996–2005)
Administrative & Office Services	7.3	7.0
Business Data Systems	2.1	12.6
Computer Science & Data Processing	47.4	11.9
Computer Engineering & Technology	1.0	14.3
Electrical Engineering	21.8	3.8
Graphic Arts & Technology	1.3	0.4
Other	19.0	7.3
Total	100.0	

Source: DoE 1996–2005

Graduates by qualification level in ICT-cognate fields of study, 2005

In order to obtain a more complete picture of the possible contribution from the fields related to ICT, we must consider graduate output by qualification level (Table 14.9). For instance, the field of 'Computer Engineering and Technology' does not include diplomas and certificates and for this reason can be considered a generally high-skilled group. In contrast, the graduates of 'Electrical Engineering and Technology' and 'Administrative and Office Services' are dominated by certificates and diplomas, which implies that their contribution to high-level skills is proportionately delimited, but is substantial in terms of intermediate skills.

What the above analysis tells us is that, other than Computer Science and Data Processing, the fields such as Business Data Systems and Computer Engineering and Technology may indeed contribute considerably, though unevenly, to the output of ICT field-related graduates into the labour market. At this stage, we cannot explore how this graduate production could impact on ICT employment and skills shortages. Fine-tuning the analysis would require juxtaposing graduate output at each qualification level with comparable occupational categories.

We now proceed to the next level of disaggregation, namely to consider the shape of ICT skills graduate supply through exploring one field of scholarship and training – Computer Science and Data Processing.

Graduates in Computer Science and Data Processing, 1996–2005

Over the period 1996–2005, the number of Computer Science and Data Processing graduates grew substantially. In real terms, graduate output rose from 1 645 in 1996 to 4 449 in 2005, yielding an annual average increase of 11.7 per cent.

Within this overall increase, growth in graduate output by race group was uneven (Figure 14.6). The highest growth rate was visible for African graduates, with an average annual growth of 26.5 per cent. Coloured and Indian graduate production in Computer Science and Data Processing achieved average annual growth of 14.5 and 14.0 per cent respectively. White graduate production experienced the lowest average annual increase at 3.3 per cent.

Clearly, the main locus of growth was with African graduates, whose numbers significantly exceeded those of white graduates for the first time in 2003. The share of white graduates peaked in 2002 and declined over the ensuing years. In effect, African graduate production increased sevenfold, whereas white graduate production increased by 34.4 per cent over the decade.

TABLE 14.9: *Graduates in ICT-cognate fields of study, by qualification level (%), 2005*

	Certificate / diploma	Degree	Postgraduates	Total
Computer Science and Data Processing	36.9	46.7	16.4	100
Computer Engineering & Technology	–	74.6	25.4	100
Electrical Engineering and Technology	54.7	33.3	12.1	100
Mathematical Sciences	9.0	60.3	30.7	100
Business Data Systems	–	31.6	68.4	100
Administrative and Office Services	83.9	15.4	0.8	100
Graphic Arts	41.9	58.1		100

Source: DoE 2005

FIGURE 14.6: *Graduation trends in Computer Science and Data Processing, by qualification level and race, 1996–2005*

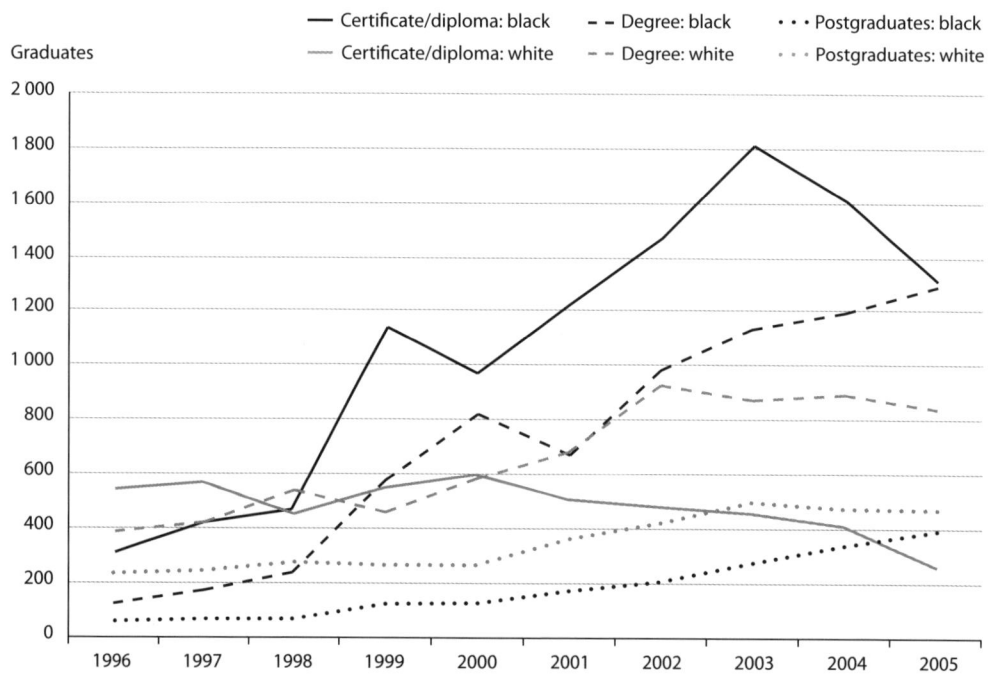

Source: DoE 1996–2005
Note: 'Black' refers to African, coloured and Indian groups combined.

Graduates by qualification level and race

This section examines graduates by qualification level and race, two important dimensions according to which we need to monitor change. In the period under consideration, a double shift occurred: degree graduate numbers increased over certificate/diploma graduate numbers, and black (that is, African, coloured and Indian) graduate numbers increased over white graduate numbers.

Firstly, changes that occurred in the overall distribution of graduates between qualification levels are shown in Table 14.10. Between 1996 and 2005, graduates holding certificates and diplomas as a proportion of all graduates declined from 51 per cent to 34.5 per cent, while the share of graduates with degrees increased from 30.8 per cent to 46.6 per cent. Postgraduates as a share of all graduates held the same proportion. This means that there was an increase in the overall qualification levels per cohort over the period that could be available to the labour market.

Secondly, in terms of the share of graduates by race, in 1996 white graduates held the majority share of graduates at all three qualification levels in Computer Science and Data Processing, as shown in Table 14.11. By 2005, this situation had shifted considerably. Black graduates were in the majority at

TABLE 14.10: *Share of graduate numbers in Computer Science and Data Processing, by qualification level, 1996 and 2005*

Qualification	1996		2005	
	N	%	N	%
Certificate/diploma	854	51.0	1 580	34.5
Degree	516	30.8	2 139	46.6
Postgraduate	304	18.2	870	19.0
Total	1 674	100.0	4 589	100.0

Source: DoE 1996–2005

TABLE 14.11: *Share of graduate numbers in Computer Science and Data Processing, by race, 1996 and 2005*

Qualification	N		%	
	1996	2005	1996	2005
Certificate/diploma				
Black	310	1 324	36.3	83.8
White	544	256	63.7	16.2
Total	854	1 580	100.0	100.0
Degree				
Black	127	1 293	24.7	60.5
White	389	846	75.3	39.5
Total	516	2 139	100.0	100.0
Postgraduate				
Black	65	398	21.4	45.8
White	239	472	78.6	54.2
Total	304	870	100.0	100.0

Source: DoE 1996–2005

the certificate/diploma level and at the degree level, while at the postgraduate level in 2005, white graduate proportions were still a slim majority.

Graduates by gender

The gender ratio of Computer Science and Data Processing graduates increased marginally in favour of women, from 32.5 to 36.5 per cent between 1996 and 2005. This means that the gender make-up of computer graduates hardly shifted during the decade.

Field of specialisation

The fields in which graduates specialise and the unevenness of graduate production across the specialisations must also be taken into account in considering the match between demand and supply. In 2005, 3 fields – out of 12 – generated nearly 66 per cent of all graduates: Information & Data Base Systems (36.0 per cent), Applications in Computer Science & Data Processing (21.0 per cent), and Programming Languages (8.8 per cent) (Table 14.12).

Supply and demand

So far, we have not explicitly addressed the interaction between demand for computer professionals in the labour market and supply of qualified graduates in Computer Science and Data Processing. In this section of the analysis we attempt to add value to the debate in three ways.

TABLE 14.12: *Share of graduate production among fields of specialisation within the Computer Science and Data Processing field of study, 1999 and 2005*

Fields of specialisation	1999 (%)	2005 (%)	Average annual growth 1999–2005
Computer Hardware Systems	1.8	3.9	20.0
Programming Systems	3.5	6.4	17.1
Computer Ops & Operations Control	6.0	9.2	13.7
Information & Data Base Systems	25.8	36.0	11.9
Applications in Computer Science & Data Processing	25.2	21.0	2.7
Education, Societal & Cultural Considerations	1.9	1.5	1.2
Programming Languages	12.7	8.8	−0.5
Other Computer Science & Data Processing	17.6	12.1	−0.7
Software Methodology	1.5	1.0	−1.3
Computer Hardware	0.5	0.0	−36.0
Theory of Computation	0.8	0.0	−37.7
Numerical Computations	2.5	0.1	−39.9
Total	100.0	100.0	

Source: DoE 1996–2005

First, we attempt to bring together the demand and supply data that we have assembled and analysed in the first two parts of this chapter. Typically, projections of labour market demand and supply are deficient if used in isolation. For this reason, we have obtained information from the labour market itself in order to enrich our analysis of the question of demand and supply of computer professionals.

Consequently, our second approach is to analyse *data on the remuneration* of CPAP in South Africa. In so doing we observe that changes in remuneration of computer professionals are evidence of a labour shortage in these occupations.

Third, we use *data from a recent survey of vacancies* conducted by the Human Sciences Research Council (HSRC) (Erasmus 2008) to formulate some tentative hypotheses about labour shortages in ICT professional occupational fields.

Projection of future demand and supply: computer professionals and associate professionals

It should be acknowledged that this is a very simple methodology and does not incorporate applied non-linear dynamic models of labour forecasting (e.g. econometric models such as the general equilibrium model or other complex input-output models) which depend on harvesting rich national data sets. Also, the methodology derives estimates for demand and supply separately, when in reality demographic trends and participation rates are interdependent.

We use historical data on the size and other dimensions of the occupational labour market of CPAP to generate assumptions about future behaviour of the market for these occupations. We then create a model that projects possible demand into the future. A similar approach is applied on the supply side which involves generating a predicted graduate production output curve into the future. The curves of demand and supply are then juxtaposed so that a putative shortage/oversupply figure is produced.

We build two scenarios which provide a quite different perspective on the demand-supply equation. That is, we include the occupational category of ICT managers in our model. We do so for two reasons: firstly, because industry players claim that there is a shortage of ICT managers, and secondly, because we assume that ICT managers will be frequently sourced from the CPAP occupations. In other words, we suggest that CPAPs will frequently be promoted to ICT management positions. There is a loss of CPAPs once they are appointed or promoted into management positions. In effect, this represents a further source of demand on the CPAP workforce.

On the side of graduate production from higher education, we do not simply take the total number of CPAP graduates at face value. Rather, we give recognition to a major factor affecting the accuracy of supply-side calculations, namely, that new graduates from a particular study field do not necessarily practise professionally in that field. For this reason, we cannot presume a simple direct relationship between graduate output and entrants into a particular professional field such as CPAP. Our study on demand for ICT workers showed that 26.4 per cent of those who have obtained a high-skill qualification in an ICT-related field of study, do not work in an ICT field. This is an important factor that must impact on supply-side calculations. Therefore, we deducted this percentage against the output from higher education for each year.

Projection

We simply calculate the following for demand:

> Scenario 1: CPAP + ICT managers – retirement – mortality – emigration = annual demand[8]

In terms of this scenario, the total demand for CPAPs by 2015 to cover losses due to retirement, mortality, emigration and new demand (including CPAPs who become ICT managers) is 93 452.

> Scenario 2: CPAP – retirement – mortality – emigration = annual demand[9]

In terms of this scenario, the total requirement of new CPAPs by 2015 to cover losses due to retirement, mortality, emigration and new demand is 74 103.

Then, in Table 14.13, the higher education Computer Science and Data Processing graduate supply is compared to the demand for CPAPs and ICT managers arising from new demand over the period 2005–2015.

If ICT managers are included (Scenario 1), a shortage of 29 027 CPAPs by 2015 is predicted by the model, assuming no changes in the assumptions.

If ICT managers are excluded (Scenario 2), a shortage of 9 679 CPAPs by 2015 is predicted by the model, assuming no changes in the assumptions.

We should note that both projections of shortages are based on a very low assumption of CPAP demand of 0.4 per cent, which was based on a period when the whole ICT industry went into a slump at the time of the millennium. Demand is likely to be higher in the next five years, which means that the above projection is probably an under-estimate.

However, projections of labour market demand and supply are deficient if used in isolation. For this reason, we have obtained information from the labour market itself in order to enrich our analysis of the question of demand and supply of ICT professionals.

Remuneration and occupational demand

Dramatic growth in employment in a particular occupation over time is likely to reflect a significant rise in demand for candidates in the labour market with the requisite skills. Likewise, rapidly rising relative remuneration in a particular occupation may imply that the demand for workers exceeds the supply (Veneri 1999). When demand exceeds supply in an occupation, compensation may rise relative to compensation in other occupations that are associated with similar education, effort and working conditions.

We compare growth in the remuneration of CPAPs to growth in the remuneration of all professionals and associate professionals in the economy.

---

8   CPAPs (0.4 per cent average annual growth) + ICT managers (25.6 per cent of CPAPs) – retirement (8.6 per cent of ICT workforce) – mortality (14.9 per cent average annual growth) – emigration (3.35 per cent of ICT workers) = annual demand.
9   CPAPs (0.4 per cent average annual growth) – retirement (8.6 per cent of CPAPs) – mortality (14.9 per cent average annual growth) – emigration (3.35 per cent of CPAPs) = annual demand.

TABLE 14.13: *Output of new graduates needed to address demand for CPAPs, 2005–2015*

Scenario 1 (including manager demand)		Year	N
A	ICT workers (including managers)	2005	62 388
B	ICT workers (including managers)	2015	64 811
C (B–A)	Growth in demand for ICT workers		2 423
D	Demand arising from death and retirement		69 685
E	Demand arising from emigration		21 344
F (C+D+E)	Total number of positions that need filling		93 452
	Total number of new graduates[a]		64 425
	Shortage		29 027
Scenario 2 (only CPAP demand)		Year	N
A	ICT workers (excluding managers)	2005	49 688
B	ICT workers (excluding managers)	2015	51 618
C (B–A)	Growth in demand for ICT workers		1 930
D	Demand arising from death and retirement		55 174
E	Demand arising from emigration		16 999
F (C+D+E)	Total number of positions that need filling		74 103
	Total number of new graduates[a]		64 425
	Shortage		9 679

Source: Author calculations based on Quantec 2007 (Stats SA OHS data for 1996–1999; Stats SA LFS data for 2000–2005) data and DoE (1996–2005) data.
Note: a The assumptions for higher education supply can be expressed as follows: Computer Science and Data Processing graduates in 2005 × average annual growth (1996–2005) 11.9% − graduates who will not work in an ICT field − graduates who will work as managers = graduates who will work as CPAP

There was growth in the remuneration of all professionals and associate professionals over the period 2000–2005, as shown in Figure 14.7. Importantly:
- The remuneration of CPAPs increased faster than the remuneration of all professionals and all associate professionals.
- The remuneration of all professionals grew at 0.9 per cent per annum; while the remuneration of *computer* professionals grew at a rate of 7.4 per cent per annum over the period 2000–2005.
- The remuneration of all associate professionals grew at 2.9 per cent, while the remuneration of *computer* associate professionals grew at 10.8 per cent per annum over the same period.

This is a strong indication of increasing scarcity/demand for CPAPs relative to demand for other professionals. We may hypothesise that increasing information intensity in business processes and buoyant economic growth in the period 2000–2005 drove the demand for computer science and data processing qualifications.

The remuneration evidence suggests that there was a shortage of computer professionals and associate professionals. But these are very broad categories. Could other forms of data also corroborate

FIGURE 14.7: *Comparison of changes in remuneration between all professionals and associate professionals and CPAPs, 2000–2005*

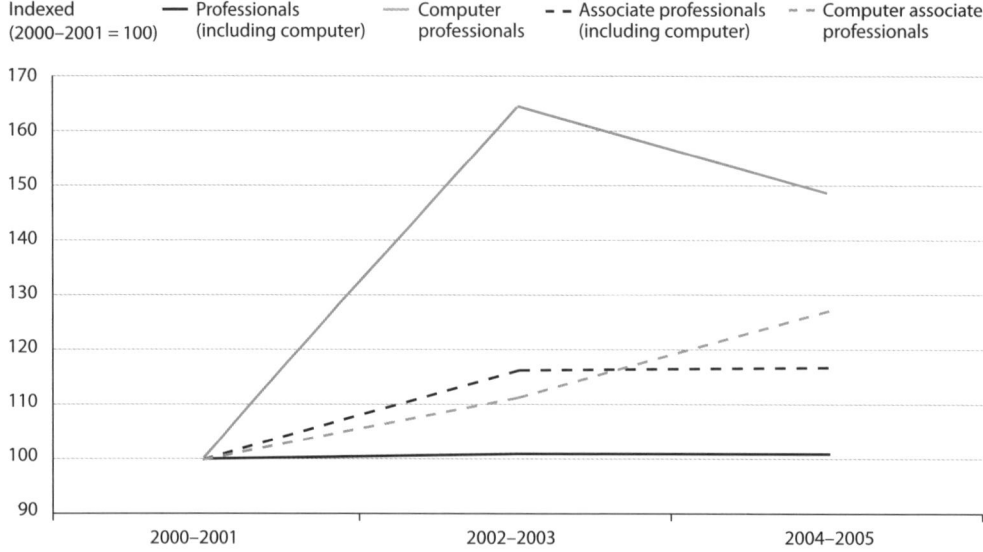

Source: Quantec 2007 (Stats SA OHS data for 1996–1999; Stats SA LFS data for 2000–2005)
Note: Remuneration data are averaged over two-year intervals to reduce short-term fluctuation.

the above analysis and add value, through more specific identification of occupations where such shortages may be manifested? The next section makes use of available survey and interview data to address these questions.

Features of the labour market for ICT professionals from a vacancy survey

We draw on data from a recent survey of vacancies conducted by the HSRC to present some tentative hypotheses about labour shortages in the computer professional occupational fields (Erasmus 2008).

The most prominent features of the data for the period 2005–2007 suggest that:
- Vacancies among ICT professionals are likely to continue rising.
- There was a relative shortage of ICT associate professionals that may still be evident. (We should bear in mind that ICT associate professionals work in a large variety of ICT environments and many hold qualifications suited to specific ICT operating and software environments. A more precise specification of skills would be necessary to initiate training interventions.)
- The most prominent demand among minor occupational categories was for a group called 'business and systems analysts and programmers'. However, the systems development functions that 'systems analysts' and 'programmers' perform are quite different. Certainly 'programmers' is a very wide category that covers different skill levels and domains of software expertise. This evidence would need some disaggregation.
- The data suggest that within the ICT professions, vacancies in certain occupations are harder to fill, and the quality of the pool of applicants, though often large, is weaker than employers might desire. The latter observation is sobering. It reflects the existence of sizeable populations of workseekers who – as employers see it – do not possess the requisite qualifications to begin to compete.

Making sense of supply and demand information

We have remuneration data that point to a shortage of CPAPs in the labour market between 2000 and 2005. We have a projection that points to a shortfall in graduate production from higher education between 2005 and 2015 in the study fields of Computer Science and Data Processing. Both studies point towards a general trend of relative skills scarcity in computing occupations – as long as current conditions persist unchanged.

However, neither of the above forms of evidence provides disaggregated information that takes account of the variegated nature of ICT skilling at the professional (high skills) and associate professional (intermediate skills) levels.

Although available information from a recent HSRC study (Erasmus 2008) begins to provide some direction with respect to which particular occupations are affected by vacancies, and which kinds of skills are needed, it does not go far enough. This is largely because the data obtained are not sufficiently focused to sustain reliable interpretation at the level of individual occupations. A targeted study with a larger sample may be worthwhile, but the cost-benefits of such a study, and whom it might benefit most (e.g. school-age learners, higher-education students, workseekers, businesses, labour brokers or labour market planners), should be carefully considered.

ICT sector policy development and implications for skills development

Since 1994, economic growth and employment creation have remained the fundamental challenges facing government's economic programmes. The relationship between growth and employment, and how to create economic conditions propitious for both to occur, remain contested empirical and policy terrain (Lowitt & Altman 2008). In this concluding section, we briefly consider how economic policy interventions after 2000 have envisioned a role for ICT in this environment.

Between 2001 and 2003, the government launched a series of policy initiatives which included the expansion of fiscal policy, the Integrated Economic Action Plan (IEAP), the Micro-economic Reform Strategy (MERS) and the Integrated Manufacturing Strategy (IMS) (Lowitt & Altman 2008); they were followed by the Accelerated and Shared Growth Initiative for South Africa (Asgisa) and its related Joint Initiative for Priority Skills Acquisition (Jipsa) in 2006. Soon thereafter, the National Industrial Policy Framework (NIPF) was launched in 2007. What were the implications for employment of the vision for the ICT sector articulated in these policies, and at what level of skills could workers take advantage of such employment opportunities?

At first, according to Lowitt and Altman (2008), the IEAP and MERS reflected the position of the Department of Trade and Industry on the set of fundamentals necessary for the economy to be competitive. These policy documents recognised, firstly, that high tariffs in the telecommunications subsector substantially raised the costs of doing business. Secondly, they acknowledged the contribution of ICT to generating efficiencies in business processes and value chains. In effect, their emphasis was on ICT as a contributor to the general conditions for national economic development, rather than on the ICT sector itself as a source of growth and employment.

Asgisa and Jipsa and the growth of business process outsourcing

The Asgisa policy initiative of January 2006 sought to promote sustainable economic growth and labour absorption. Particular economic sectors were targeted for interventions which in the short term included tourism, business process outsourcing (BPO) and biofuels (*Mail & Guardian* 7–12 April 2006).

In March 2006, government established Jipsa, which was tasked with addressing the question of constraints and inefficiencies in the existing legislative and regulatory frameworks and institutional arrangements for the delivery of skills. ICT and related skills were incorporated into this initial agenda in two ways. The need for skills in the broad communications industry was informed by the desire of government to increase access to good public infrastructure. And the inclusion of telecommunications along with transport and other 'network industries' makes it clear that Jipsa was primarily interested in ICT skills to service good public infrastructure.

Initially, Jipsa saw skilling as supportive of ICT in a general way. The question of how skills development would function as an input into specific sub-sectoral development, driven by a development plan, was not recognised.

The only instance from Jipsa which demonstrates a clear and direct link between planning to enter a particular market and an assessment of the skills needs to support such an initiative in the ICT-related field, is the case of South Africa's entry into the burgeoning global market for BPO service providers. BPO is a relatively straightforward service sector area to work in because the technologies are known, and because the skills requirements are relatively well defined. The challenge is to find similar sectors where entry to the market is relatively easy because the path has already been beaten, and where labour absorption potential remains positive, though not assured in terms of global competition between labour markets.

As far as the Asgisa and Jipsa phase is concerned – apart from BPO – it does not seem that further initiatives to identify an ICT sub-sector for diversification, and to formulate a set of strategies including skills development to suit such a challenge, have been undertaken.

National Industrial Policy Framework: platform for sharpening strategic focus

In January 2007, government published its NIPF, which aims to 'set out a vision for the industrial economy within the short-medium and medium-long term' (DTI 2007a:13, 14, 15).

The NIPF identifies five broad sectoral groupings 'where it is apparent that much of our sectoral diversification potential lies' (DTI 2007a: 37):
- natural resource-based sectors;
- medium-technology sectors (including downstream minerals beneficiation);
- advanced manufacturing sectors;
- labour-intensive sectors;
- tradeable services sectors.

The NIPF document adopts a more holistic approach than its predecessors to the challenges of generating a programme of sustainable industrialisation. It recognises that hitherto, South African efforts to achieve a more diversified and labour-absorbing industrialisation trajectory have been lacking in several dimensions (DTI 2007a: 26, 29, 51).

Significantly, the NIPF document highlights the importance of a 'much closer alignment between industrial policy and skills and educational development, particularly with respect to sector strategies'

(DTI 2007a: 47). The Industrial Policy Action Plan that deals with implementation of the NIPF proposes 'sectoral actions' for immediate implementation (DTI 2007b: 4). ICT – in terms of services and products – is one of four sectors that are identified as those 'for which substantial sector strategy development and perspectives is further required' (DTI 2007b: 33).

What has hitherto been lacking in order to make coherent plans regarding sector support measures, such as skills development strategies, is a properly researched decision to target particular ICT economic activities. Without such a specification, 'realistic' skills supply and demand analysis cannot be undertaken. Meanwhile, higher education institutions have been taking criticism for not meeting the needs of the ICT sector, a challenge these institutions could not address without a clear indication from government and the business sector of what specific ICT economic growth opportunities would be taken forward.

References

DoE (Department of Education, South Africa) (1996–2005). *Higher Education Management Information System (HEMIS). Annual databases.* Pretoria: DoE

DTI (Department of Trade and Industry, South Africa) (2004) *Electronics, IT and communication sector* brochure. Accessed 13 February 2004, http://www.thedti.gov.za/publications/electronics.htm

DTI (2007a) *A national industrial policy framework (NIPF)*. Accessed 9 December 2007, http://www.thedti.gov.za/nipf/niPF-3aug.pdf

DTI (2007b) *Implementation of government's national industrial policy framework: Industrial policy action plan*. Accessed 10 January 2008, http://www.dti.gov.za/nipf/IPAP%20-3august.pdf

Erasmus JC (2008) Vacancy analysis report. Report on phase 3: A survey of employers who have recently advertised vacancies. In *Project 4.1: A multiple source identification and verification of scarce and critical skills in the South African labour market*. Report commissioned by the Department of Labour, Pretoria

ISETT SETA (Information Systems, Electronics and Telecommunications Technologies Sector Education and Training Authority) (2002) *ISETT SETA sector skills plan 2002/03*. Version 3.4 October 2002. Midrand: ISETT SETA

Lowitt S & Altman M (2008) Overview of the economy and economic policy. In A Kraak & K Press (eds) *Human resources development review 2008: Education, employment and skills in South Africa*. Cape Town: HSRC Press

Paterson A (2006) The growth of information and communication technology research and development networks in South Africa: Leading or following the economic sector? In G Kruss (ed.) *Creating knowledge networks: working partnerships in higher education, industry and innovation*. Cape Town: HSRC Press

Paterson A (2007) *ICT skills in South Africa*. Colloquium on Information and Communication Technology Education and Training and the Production of Graduates. Department of Education and Rhodes University, 19 March 2007, Birchwood Hotel, Grahamstown. Accessed 12 December 2007, http://www.cs.ru.ac.za/ICTSkills/AndrewPatersonPresentation.pdf

Quantec (2007) *RSA regional Indicators database*. Accessed September 2007, www.quantec.co.za/data

THETA (Tourism and Hospitality Education and Training Authority) (2006) *Workplace skills plan: Guidelines for the period 1 April 2005 to 31 March 2006*. Accessed 12 February 2008, http://www.theta.org.za/downloads/Workplace_Skills_Plan_Guidelines2005-2006.doc

Veneri CM (1999) Can occupational labour shortages be identified using available data? *Monthly Labour Review* March: 15–21

CHAPTER 15

Tourism

Nicci Earle-Malleson

Tourism as a priority sector in South Africa

Tourism, as one of the labour-intensive, non-traditional tradable goods sectors that has demonstrated considerable growth since the re-integration of South Africa into the global economy after 1990 (DTI 2007a), has been assigned immediate high-priority status by government's Asgisa policy in recognition of both its current and increased potential future contribution to national growth and employment (Asgisa 2006). Future expectations for this sector include the increase in its GDP contribution from 8 per cent to 12 per cent and an additional 400 000 jobs.

Globally, the importance of the tourism sector is undisputed: according to the World Travel and Tourism Council (WTTC), tourism is the world's largest sector, with annual revenues of almost US$500 billion. Tourism accounts for roughly 35 per cent of global services exports and over 8 per cent of global goods exports, and employs in the region of 340 million people either directly or indirectly across the world. International foreign tourist arrivals increased from roughly 25 million in 1950 to 842 million in 2006 and are expected to reach 1.56 billion by 2020 (DTI 2006, 2007a). Worldwide, domestic tourism is estimated to be in the region of four to five times that of foreign tourism (Monitor 2007). Growth in the tourism sector is being driven by factors such as economic globalisation and innovations in transport, information and communication technologies, in addition to increasing leisure time and disposable income in the leading tourist-generating markets of North America, Western Europe and Japan (DTI 2006). Increasing South Africa's share of this globally important and growing sector has become a priority for government.

Additionally attractive for the South African government, with its focus on reducing the official unemployment level of 25.5 per cent (Stats SA 2007) that is affecting mainly the nation's large pool of rural, unskilled and semi-skilled workers, is the fact that the tourism sector has several pro-poor features. These include: its ability to create opportunities for emerging small, medium and micro enterprise (SMME) operators and entrepreneurs; its relatively high demand for semi-skilled and unskilled labour; its relatively low ratio of investment-to-job creation compared with sectors such as manufacturing, and thus its ability to create jobs in a relatively short time; its ability to reach into rural areas in which few other economic activities are viable; and the fact that its relatively low use of imported inputs gives rise to extensive forward and backward linkages for both goods and services within the local economy, and thus to economic and employment multiplier effects (DEAT 1996; DTI 2006; Lowitt 2006; Monitor 2007; Robertson & Skordis 2004).

Part of, and yet also parallel to, Asgisa's focus on the sector, is the fact that South Africa won the bid to host the 2010 FIFA Soccer World Cup. This has not only placed South Africa in the international spotlight but has also provided an opportunity to fast-track the development of a competitive and sustainable tourism sector in the country (DTI 2006).

With the aim of contributing to the unlocking of the sector's full growth and employment potential, a number of major research studies and strategy documents have been commissioned by members of the tourism governance cluster and have recently entered the public domain (see for example DTI 2006; HSRC 2006a, 2006b, 2007; Lowitt 2006; Monitor 2004; Prodigy-Grant Thornton 2007; Rivett-Carnac 2007; SA Tourism 2007a). These documents highlight various aspects of the challenges facing the sector and simultaneously put forward a range of recommendations for addressing them. By seeking to answer one primary question, 'Are skills shortages constraining growth within the tourism sector?' this chapter adds to this important body of sectoral research from which policy-makers and implementing departments may draw for direction.

Tourism sector performance

In South Africa, foreign visitor arrivals grew eightfold between 1990 and 2006 (Figure 15.1), increasing from roughly 1 million to 8.4 million arrivals. The year-on-year increase for 2005–2006 was 13.9 per cent (up from 7.4 million) – ahead of the world average of 4.5 per cent and of Africa's growth of 8.1 per cent over the same period.

FIGURE 15.1: *Foreign tourist arrivals to South Africa, 1966–2006*

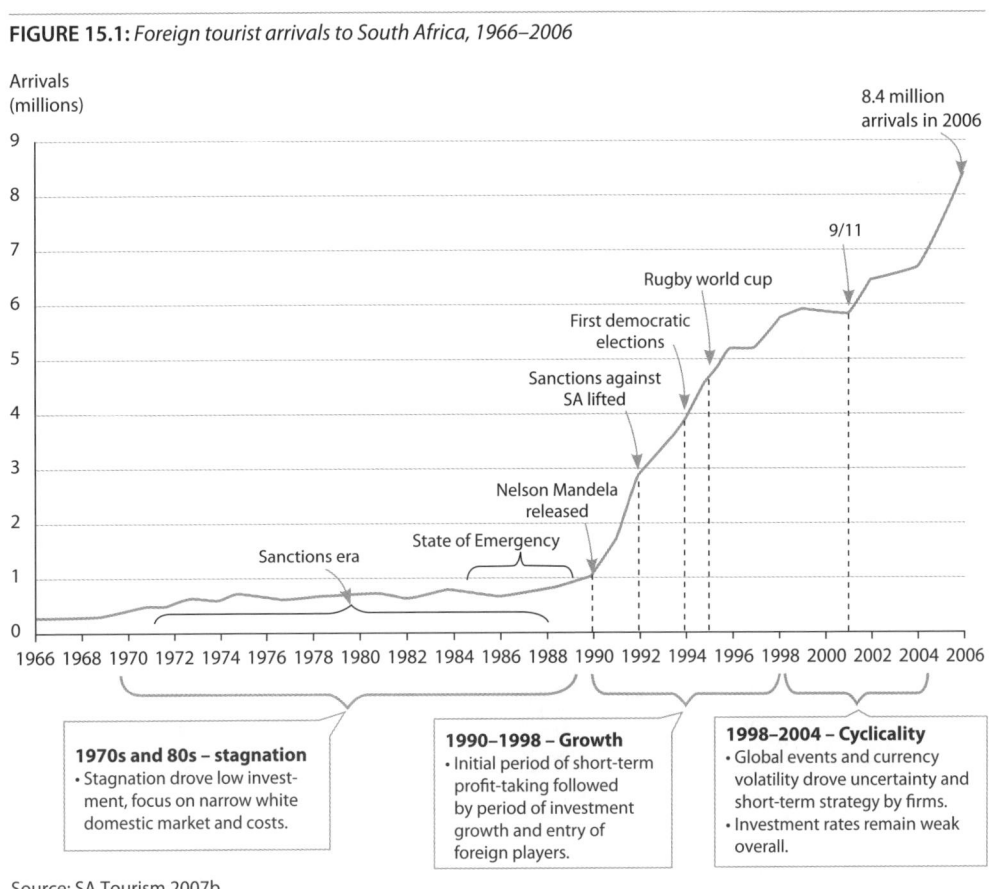

Source: SA Tourism 2007b

In 2006, the largest source region for foreign arrivals was 'Africa & Middle East', with 75.3 per cent of the total. This figure was up from 73.4 per cent in 2005. Dominating figures were arrivals from the neighbouring states Lesotho, Mozambique, Swaziland and Zimbabwe, whose reason for travel was primarily visiting friends and relatives (VFR) and/or personal shopping. Arrivals from Europe, the other major source region, represented 16.5 per cent of the total in 2006. This was, however, down from 17.6 per cent in 2005 (SA Tourism 2007b). South Africa's major competitors for long-haul European leisure tourists include Kenya, Australia, Thailand and Brazil (Monitor 2007).

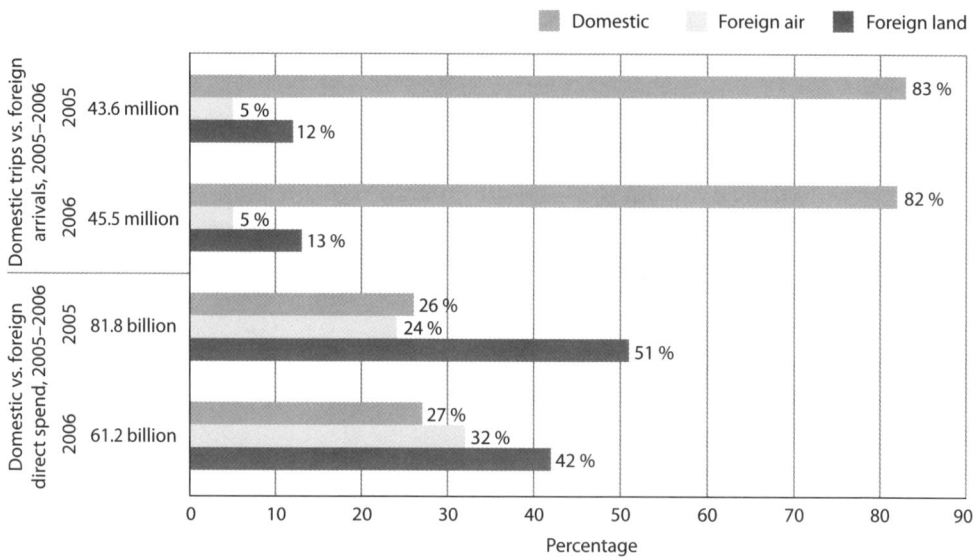

FIGURE 15.2: *Domestic versus foreign tourism value contribution, 2005–2006*

Source: Adapted from SA Tourism 2007b

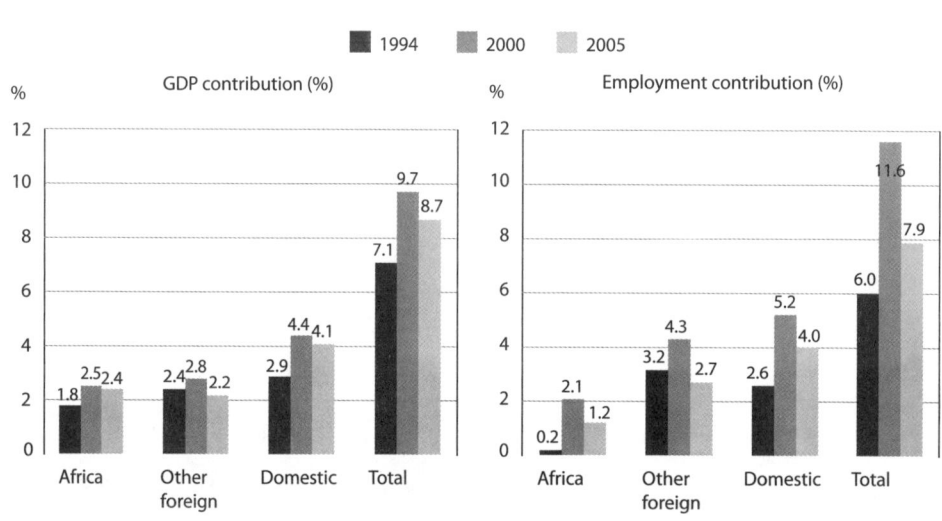

FIGURE 15.3: *Contribution to national GDP and employment per tourist category, 1994, 2000 and 2005*

Source: Pan-African 2006

TABLE 15.1 *Domestic and foreign tourism, compound annual growth rate, by percentage, 2005–2006*

	Change 2005–2006 (%)
Trips/arrivals	
Domestic	2.6
Foreign air	10.4
Foreign land	15.3
Total	4.5
Direct spend	
Domestic	−21.8
Foreign air	−0.4
Foreign land	−38.5
Total	−25.1

Source: Adapted from SA Tourism 2007b

In terms of domestic tourism, roughly 37 million trips were undertaken during 2006. These trips were undertaken by 42 per cent of the adult population of South Africa, with an average of 37.1 trips per traveller. Of this total number of trips, 29.1 million were VFR trips, 2.8 million were for holidays, 2.9 million for religious reasons, 1.9 million for business, and 0.4 million for medical reasons. Gauteng is the largest generator of domestic tourist trips and the only province that demonstrates a net outflow of travellers (SA Tourism 2007b).

The coincidence of seasonality patterns in domestic and foreign tourism results in annual sectoral activity being highest between October and February, with June being the slowest month (SA Tourism 2007b).

The direct spend generated by tourism within the South African economy was put at a figure of R61.2 billion in 2006, compared with R35.47 billion generated from the export of gold. Tourism's contribution was, however, down from R81.8 billion in 2005. And while the largest proportions of these totals were generated by foreign land arrivals, the largest value per tourist was generated by foreign air arrivals (Figure 15.2; Table 15.1) (SA Tourism 2007b).

While the importance of the tourism sector to the national economy, in terms of both GDP and employment, is well acknowledged, very little is known about the sector compared with other national sectors (Lowitt 2006). The main reason for this is that tourism, as a consumption-based services sector, which furthermore consumes both tourist-characteristic as well as non-tourist-characteristic goods and services (Stats SA 2005), is not included within the Standard Industrial Classification system on which all sectoral economic activity is collected, both locally and internationally, and is thus not explicitly captured in the System of National Accounts. Until the release of the first figures from the national Tourism Satellite Accounts (TSA) in 2008, the sector's contributions to GDP and employment are at best estimates (Lowitt 2006).

The WTTC estimates that the total direct and indirect contribution of the tourism sector to the South African GDP in 2006 was 8.30 per cent (SA Tourism 2007b). Pan-African Investment and Research Services (Pan-African 2006) suggest that the value of tourism's contribution to the national GDP has increased threefold since 1994, and in 2005 was R97 billion (in 2000 prices), with a GDP share in the same year of 8.78 per cent. Reduction in GDP share since the high of 9.70 per cent in 2000 is the result of even faster growth in other national sectors over the same period (Figure 15.3). The importance of domestic tourism to the national economy through the impact of multiplier effects is evident when comparing its relatively low contribution in terms of direct spend (Figure 15.2), with its substantially higher proportional contribution to national GDP and employment (Figure 15.3).

Estimates of the sector's contribution to total employment are even more inconsistent:
- The WTTC estimates that in 2005, direct employment in the tourism sector in South Africa was 393 650, increasing by 8.2 per cent to 425 930 in 2006. The indirect employment contribution of the sector was even larger than these direct contribution figures, bringing the overall employment contribution in 2005 to 864 460, increasing by an estimated 9.6 per cent to 947 530 in 2006 (SA Tourism 2007b).
- The Department of Trade and Industry (DTI) (DTI 2006) refers to estimates of 539 017 direct jobs in the tourism sector and an additional 699 683 indirect jobs created by the sector, with the overall contribution to employment (excluding casual labour) thus being 1 238 700.
- Pan African (2006) estimates that tourism's share of total employment has increased substantially since 1994, reaching a peak of 11.6 per cent in 2001 and declining to approximately 8.7 per cent in 2005, due to other sectors adding more jobs to the economy (Figure 15.3). Overall, the combined direct and indirect contributions of the tourism sector to employment in South Africa is estimated to have increased from 467 453 in 1994 to 1 061 169 in 2005.

Exact data on the number of firms operating within the sector are not available. The various estimations are presented in Table 15.2. The most recent estimates by Prodigy-Grant Thornton (2007) suggest a total of 28 000 hospitality enterprises, 6 200 travel and tourism services enterprises, and 3 500 conservation and tourist guiding enterprises. All three sub-sectors are dominated (in excess of 97 per cent each) by SMMEs, with many of these enterprises having no desire, or little ability, to grow.

Other than the large numbers of generally small firms and enterprises that make up the tourism industry, there are also a large number of government departments at all three levels as well as statutory bodies and other agencies involved in the sector. At the national level, key stakeholders include: South African Tourism (SA Tourism); the Tourism Grading Council; the Tourism, Hospitality and Sport Education and Training Authority (THETA); the Tourism Enterprise Programme (TEP); and the Departments of Environmental Affairs and Tourism (DEAT), Trade and Industry, Home Affairs, Transport, Arts and Culture (DAC), Land Affairs, Health, Labour (DoL), Education (DoE), and Safety and Security. Together, these make up the complex tourism governance cluster and regulatory framework.

Whether indeed the future expectations of the sector, in terms of its growth and job creation potential, are realistic, is the subject of a report by Lowitt (2006). Her calculations suggest that while the growth expectations are indeed realistic, employment creation expectations on the back of an increased 2.5 million foreign visitors (from the roughly 7.5 million in 2005 to a desired 10 million per annum) should be revised downward from 400 000 to 284 000.[1]

In sum, available data show that the direct and indirect contribution of tourism, a sector largely dominated by SMMEs, is substantial and growing, both for GDP and for employment. Employment expectations based on foreign-visitor growth may, however, have to be revised slightly downward.

---

1 On the overall desired increase of 2.5 million in foreign visitor arrivals, Lowitt (2006) suggests that a figure of 15 arrivals to 1 additional job (15:1) be used instead of the current 'golden' 12:1 ratio, and that the employment multiplier be reduced to 0.5 from the current 2.5. These changes are suggested based on open calculations using the best available tourist spend and employment data, while the 12:1 ratio and the 2.5 multiplier do not have calculations that are in the public domain and rely heavily on WTTC-simulated, rather than actual, sectoral data.

TABLE 15.2: *Comparisons of estimates of total enterprises, by tourism sub-sector, 2000–2007*

Year	Source	Quantification		Comment
		Employers	Employees	
Hospitality sector				
2000	Grant Thornton	35 830	477 800	Estimate includes both formal and informal enterprises
2004	Monitor	34 471		+/− 14 471 accommodation establishments and +/− 20 000 food and beverage establishments
2005	DoL	35 830	477 800	Based on Grant Thornton figures of 2000
2005	HSRC	6 704		Limited to enterprises listed on at least one national database that is, excluding largely informal and very small enterprises
2006	THETA SMS	14 828		Limited to those registered with the THETA
2006	Qubelisa	9 781		
2007	Prodigy-Grant Thornton	28 000	290 000	
Tourism and travel services				
2000	Grant Thornton	2 870	36 000	Estimate includes both formal and informal enterprises
2004	Monitor	> 800		Excludes all transportation providers
2005	HSRC	1 464		Limited to enterprises listed on at least one national database that is, excluding the largely informal or very small enterprises
2006	THETA SMS	1 800		Limited to those registered with the THETA
2006	Qubelisa	3 942		
2007	Prodigy-Grant Thornton	6 200	28 000	
Conservation and tourist guiding				
2000	Grant Thornton	900	30 300	Estimate includes both formal and informal enterprises
2005	HSRC	966	2 246	Limited to enterprises listed on at least one national database that is, excluding the largely informal or very small enterprises
2006	THETA SMS	1 579		Limited to those registered with the THETA
2006	Qubelisa	3 459		
2007	Government Gazette	900	30 300	Based on Grant Thornton (2000) contained in the THETA Sector Skills Plans
2007	Prodigy-Grant Thornton	3 500	30 000	+/− 8 000 registered tourist guides and +/−22 000 other employees

Sources: HSRC 2005; Monitor 2004; Prodigy-Grant Thornton 2007

Challenges and constraints to growth of the tourism industry

The challenges and potential growth constraints facing the South African tourism sector are the subject of the range of recent studies already referred to. These challenges and constraints appear to be impacting on the sector at three key levels: that of realising the desired increase in tourist volumes; that of increasing the value extraction from both current and future tourist volumes; and that of the general sustainability of the sector.

In relation to achieving increased numbers of foreign visitors, and in particular, the high-value long-haul holiday tourists from major source markets in Europe, North America and Japan, two issues require attention:
- *Seasonal limitation in airlift capacity* exists from these major source destinations, in addition to limitations on the availability of domestic flights to certain destinations at peak times. Part of this limitation relates to the high prices of airlift, particularly for direct flights on constrained international and certain domestic routes, which act as a major psychological barrier to visiting South Africa (Monitor 2007).
- Equally important, if marketing efforts and increased physical capacity are to be translated into actual tourist volume increases, will be the need to address both the *perceptions and the reality of crime* in South Africa (Dowinton 2007; SA Tourism 2007a).

Together these two factors can be seen as the most critical constraints to growth of the South African tourism sector.

In respect of maximising the value-extraction of the sector – in other words, of using tourism as a means to promote employment and achieve improved economic participation and development among the largely unskilled and semi-skilled previously disadvantaged groups – a number of challenges are highlighted:
- *Transformation of the sector is limited* and is furthermore constrained by a range of structural barriers (DTI 2006; Erasmus 2002; HSRC 2006a; Kirsten & Rogerson 2002; Monitor 2007; Oldham et al. 2000; Prodigy-Grant Thornton 2007; SBP 2006). These include: the large SMME profile of the sector; the 'lifestyle' rather than growth motivations of many established owner-managers; the lack of relevant knowledge and skills among, and the survivalist nature of, many emerging entrepreneurs; and the limited ability of large and established enterprises to attract high-level black management skills from a small pool whose remuneration prospects are higher in other sectors.
- The sector demonstrates an *unequal geographical and social distribution*. Despite its contribution to the economies of certain rural areas, the sector is still concentrated in three provinces (Western Cape, Gauteng and KwaZulu-Natal) and predominantly in the urban areas of these provinces. Furthermore, many 'pro-poor' tourism developments are criticised due to the seasonal, low-paid and menial nature of jobs that local communities are able to access and the disturbance caused to fragile rural social ecosystems. Furthermore, many other such interventions fail due to community fragmentation, in-fighting and frustration resulting from limited ability to access the jobs created, and the long turnaround time from investment to tangible benefits (Erasmus 2002; Mafunzwaini & Hugo 2005; Viljoen & Tlabela 2007).
- *Slow product and process innovation* has limited South Africa's ability to grow beyond its current international reputation of an 'adventurous wildlife destination with striking natural beauty' (SA Tourism 2007a: 37). Misaligned and unfocused product development has meant that the sector is characterised by an oversupply of certain product types in certain geographical areas, with product 'gaps' evident in others (Monitor 2007).
- The tourist sector has a *complex regulatory framework*. Related to this are high costs of 'red tape' – up to three times higher than for firms within the general South African economy. Streamlining and stricter enforcement, rather than a reduction of regulation, are however considered to be the best way forward (SBP 2006).

Compounding these value-maximisation challenges are a number of issues that impact negatively on the overall sustainability of the sector:
- There is very *limited availability of sectoral data and market-related information*, and poor dissemination of the data that do exist. This challenge underlies many of the other sectoral challenges such as misaligned product development, difficulties in accessing finance, difficulties in attracting major investors, and the high levels of start-up business failure (DTI 2006; Monitor 2007).
- The South African tourism industry is characterised by generally *poor quality of service delivery* compared with international competitor destinations – partly the result of low levels of skills within the sector, but also due to confusion between the concepts of 'service' and 'servility', and a mindset that foreign tourists have low expectations of service levels in Africa (Mills 2007; Monitor 2007).
- There are *high levels of fragmentation* within the industry – at both participant and governance levels. The impact of this is evident in short-term and reactionary thinking, destructive competition, inadequate and competitive marketing efforts, inadequate tourism education at all levels, insufficient and non-comprehensive tourism infrastructure developments, and the dominance of certain players within the tourism channel in terms of exerting authority over pricing, packaging, and the value proposition (DTI 2006; Monitor 2007; Robertson & Skordis 2004; SA Tourism 2007a).
- Most significantly, there is a *lack of strong, decisive and visionary leadership* within the tourism industry, and critically within the key national government and parastatal agencies, including the DEAT and SA Tourism. Weak intra-governmental co-ordination, staff incompetencies and lack of HR capacity, and low levels of funding combine with a lack of adequate sectoral information-generating and -capturing systems and lack of effective industry forums to limit the sector's ability to co-operatively and proactively move towards a common long-term vision (BMI 2005; DTI 2007b; Monitor 2007; SA Tourism 2007a; Viljoen & Tlabela 2007).

Demand and supply of skills in the tourism sector

Subsumed within each of these major challenge areas, and alluded to at various levels within the literature, is the notion of inadequate skills and capacity within the HR base of the sector. Due to the complex and consumption-defined nature of the tourism sector, and the general dearth of sector-related information, data on both demand and supply of skills are scarce and of a qualitative rather than a quantitative nature. The recently published *Tourism and Sport Skills Audit* (Prodigy-Grant Thornton 2007), which looks at both scarce and critical skills within the tourism sector more specifically, was commissioned in an attempt to improve the quality of information within the THETA's Sector Skills Plans. Yet even this study provides predominantly qualitative information, with the quantitative data presented being the sum of calculations based on a number of assumptions and extrapolations and thus of questionable reliability. Nevertheless, this study represents the most detailed and most recent information available and is drawn on in this section, supplemented with available primary data sources on supply.

In terms of the demand, the issues of skills gaps and skills shortages within the tourism sector largely overlap. Due to both real and geographical shortages, employers have limited choice about employing low- and under-skilled staff, with this in turn resulting in major skills gaps within the sectoral labour pool and having a major impact on the training needs of the industry. Overall, the most important skills needs of the tourism sector are identified as the following (Prodigy-Grant Thornton 2007):
- the development and strengthening of a *customer service ethic*;
- an internalisation by the sector's employees of the *importance of tourism* (both to individual jobs as well as to the welfare of the wider national economy) in order to promote the projection of a positive image of South Africa and improve visitor experiences;
- *communications skills* (including comprehension, coherence and non-verbal skills) as well as communication in English specifically;
- shortages in key *technical skills* groups – such as chefs, travel consultants and game rangers;

- shortages of available *high-level strategic managers* for recruitment into the sector (both in private and pubic spheres), and especially black managers;
- *management skills* of existing managers – especially white managers;
- *entrepreneurial skills* – especially among black entrepreneurs.

In respect of the specific sub-sectors, *hospitality* is dominated (74.7 per cent) by semi-skilled and unskilled workers. Waitrons make up 22 per cent of the sector occupationally, while a further 18 per cent are either cooks or chefs, 9 per cent are reservations/operations managers or assistant managers/supervisors, and 9 per cent are cleaners. Management positions are, however, most difficult to fill, followed by waitrons and chefs. Gaps in generic skills, rather than any sector-specific skills shortages, are most critical within this sub-sector. Foreign-language skills are not a substantial requirement (Prodigy-Grant Thornton 2007).

The *travel and tourism services* sub-sector is dominated by the highly skilled and skilled categories of workers (72.2 per cent). Travel consultants form the single largest occupational category (14 per cent), while sales co-ordinators form the second largest (9 per cent). Travel consultant and managerial positions are considered most difficult to fill; however, vacancies for tour drivers, tour operators, tour managers and tour guides are also challenging to fill. The most severe challenges are the sizeable proportion of travel agents who are unable to operate a global distribution/central reservations system, and the real shortage of skilled tourist guides and tour operators. Gaps in respect of generic skills are also critical, while roughly 50 per cent of respondents indicated the need for foreign-language skills (Prodigy-Grant Thornton 2007).

The *conservation and tourist guide* sub-sector has a roughly equal division between the highly skilled and skilled worker category (40.0 per cent) and the semi-skilled worker category (38.3 per cent). Travel and tourist guides of various descriptions make up 30.3 per cent of the sector's workforce, while security and maintenance personnel make up another 21.7 per cent. Hard-to-fill positions are considered to be supervisors/managers/CEOs, tourist guides and sales personnel. The demand for foreign-language skills is considered to be highest in this group (69 per cent) (Prodigy-Grant Thornton 2007).

Across all three sub-sectors, a comparison of the employee qualifications profile on the National Qualifications Framework (NQF) and the employment profile reveals that more people are employed within the highly skilled and skilled, and the semi-skilled, categories than would be suggested by their qualifications. This provides further evidence of both skills shortages and skills gaps within the sector. Furthermore, across all three sub-sectors, the reasons listed by employers for difficulties in filling vacancies include lack of experience, lack of suitable qualifications, lack of interest/motivation, lack of customer care ethic, and the poor salaries within the sector (Prodigy-Grant Thornton 2007).

Outside of the sub-sectoral division, three crucial areas of skills demand exist: high-level strategic management skills, and in particular, black management skills; intangible or 'soft' skills across all occupational levels; and those generic and sector-specific skills required to successfully start, operate and grow a tourism-related SMME (DTI 2006; Monitor 2007; Prodigy-Grant Thornton 2007; Rivett-Carnac 2007).

In respect of skills supply, lack of data and clear definitions means that it is currently impossible to determine with any accuracy the supply of skills into the labour market that are able and necessary to support a growing and transforming tourism sector. Available information from the DoE's Education Management Information System (EMIS) database (DoE 2007) suggests that output from schools for the Grade 12 subject Travel and Tourism is increasing dramatically, from 2 817 passes in 2000 to a total of 34 882 passes in 2006. This is, however, largely restricted to two provinces: KwaZulu-Natal (13 087 in 2006) and Gauteng (8 004 in 2006). While the information available from the DoE's Further Education and Training Management Information System (FETMIS) database (DoE 2008) does not provide geographical information, this nevertheless reveals that the total number of passes in hospitality-related courses at further education and training (FET) colleges dropped from 5 477 in 2000 to 4 385 in 2005. Travel- and tourism-related course output has remained more consistent at somewhat lower levels, rising slightly from 3 228 in 2000 to 3 557 in 2005. And while NQF Level 4 course offerings attract a majority group for both sub-sectors, hospitality output is skewed towards lower-level qualifications (38.3 per cent at NQF Levels 2 and 3) as compared with travel and tourism, where all courses are at NQF Levels 4 and above.

The dominance of Gauteng and KwaZulu-Natal in school output is mirrored by the geographical spread of THETA-registered training providers, with Gauteng having the largest number and more than twice that of KwaZulu-Natal, which has the second-largest provincial concentration. Based on the numbers of training providers focused on the various sub-sectors, output of formal skills is highest for the hospitality sector – a factor determined both by its dominant size as well as by the relatively lower level of skills required. The focus on skills output for the conservation and tourist guiding sector, which ranks second in respect of the number of sub-sector-focused training providers, is high relative to the size of the sub-sector, but not so if the mandatory registration of all guides based on formal qualifications is considered. Across all THETA-registered training providers, training is highest for NQF Level 1, with very little training taking place at NQF Level 5 or higher.

Available quantitative data on learner entry into tourism-related learnerships, specifically, support the more general information presented above, and suggest that the focus has been largely on hospitality-related qualifications and on tourism guiding: a total of 11 442 learners registered for hospitality-related qualifications, 6 916 for conservation and nature guiding qualifications, and 1 580 for travel– and tourism-related qualifications up to March 2007. The most popular learnerships were the Certificate in Food and Beverage Services Level 4 (5 405 entrants); the National Certificate in Tourism: Guiding Level 4 (5 042 entrants); and the Certificate in Professional Cookery Level 4 (2 234 entrants). The bulk of learners have registered for NQF Level 4 qualifications (80.2 per cent in hospitality, 78.6 per cent in travel and tourism services, and 72.9 per cent in conservation and nature guiding), with the prevalence of Level 5 qualifications low overall and significant only for travel and tourism services-related qualifications (21.4 per cent in the latter compared with only 0.2 per cent in hospitality and 3.3 per cent in conservation and tourist guiding). Pass rates of these learnership entrants, as well as the uptake of qualified individuals into the workplace, are unknown (HSRC 2007).

A total of 13 higher education institutions across South Africa offer tourism- and hospitality-related courses at NQF Levels 5–8. The total undergraduate enrolment for tourism and hospitality in 2006 from 10 of the 13 institutions was 6 671, while for graduations, the figure was 1 493. These overall figures are virtually unchanged from the 2004 figures of 6 687 and 1 489 respectively. Undergraduate output is dominated by the National Diploma qualification, with degree qualification numbers low. Tourism dominated both enrolments (65.0 per cent) and graduations (53.9 per cent). Postgraduate enrolments (137 in 2006) and graduations (35 in 2006) are low, dominated by tourism (78.8 per cent of enrolments and 91.8 per cent of graduations), and also relatively unchanged from 2004 figures (127 and 35 respectively).

For the majority of the tourism sector, and in particular for the dominant hospitality sub-sector, in-house training, work-shadowing and mentoring remain the most important source of skills development. Such training is, however, generally non-strategic and non-accredited (Prodigy-Grant Thornton 2007).

Yet despite the limitations of the quantitative data, the existence of a skills gap within the tourism sector is unquestionable. The mismatch between demand and supply is linked to a number of complex and inter-related factors. Significant among these is the lack of co-ordination among the stakeholders in tourism skills supply, both at the level of actual training and at the level of accreditation and quality assurance of both qualifications and training providers. Capacity constraints within the THETA are of particular importance, not only to actual sector-specific skills shortages, but also to the over-supply of under-qualified individuals in certain fields and to the lack of legitimacy of qualifications in general, and THETA qualifications in particular, within the sector. Related to this, as well as to a range of other issues within the national legislative framework, is the issue of the inadequate scope and variable quality of sector-focused training providers. The lack of adequate foundational education among South African youth, combined with a poor work ethic, an under-developed commitment to lifelong learning, and the absence of rigorous and standardised learner recruitment processes, all contribute substantially to wastage of limited national financial skills development resources as learners drop out of, and hop between, learnerships and skills programmes. The supplier-driven nature of training within the tourism sector – the combined result of industry under-valuation of qualifications and the current skills development incentive system – further serves to reinforce misalignment between skills demand and supply. Finally, the general challenges associated with skills development among survivalist, rural and time-constrained owner-operated enterprises, must be seen to apply to the sector as a whole, due to its overwhelming SMME profile.

Case studies of the tourism sectors in Soweto and Hazyview

In addition to a comprehensive review of recent literature and the analysis of available primary quantitative data, the methodology used for this study included primary qualitative research. Based on available time and resources as well as a desire to add to, rather than repeat, the work of other recent studies, it was decided to investigate the tourism industry in two case-study local geographical areas that represented opposites, in terms of the history and focus of the sector, yet to do this in a manner that would allow for comparative discussion.

The two case-study areas chosen were Soweto in Gauteng and Hazyview in Mpumalanga. Soweto, one of the largest township areas in South Africa, represents emerging urban and cultural tourism within a province and city that, while acting as the primary South African gateway for long-haul tourists of all categories, itself is marketed predominantly as a shopping and business tourism destination. Hazyview represents an established, rural, nature-based tourism destination that attracts a mix of both foreign and domestic leisure holiday and adventure tourists.

Each case-study region was assigned one week of on-site fieldwork, undertaken by the author. This consisted partly of pre-arranged interviews set up with regional and provincial tourism marketing agencies, tourism training providers based in the area, agencies and enterprises involved in local tourism development efforts, the chairpersons of the local tourism development associations, and managers of other specific local tourist attractions or products considered important for inclusion. These interviews were of a semi-structured nature. In addition, a number of unscheduled interviews were undertaken with the following categories of people: staff at the local tourist information offices; local tour operators; the owners of the accommodation establishments at which the researcher stayed; staff and managers of local restaurants and shops; craft-sellers; and other tourists in the region. While the researcher had determined in advance the types of tourism sector participants to cover during these unscheduled interviews, they were necessarily opportunistic and largely unstructured. Finally, a substantial amount of information was gathered through participant observation and the personal experience of being a tourist in each area.

Most significantly, the findings of these two case studies support the findings of the other major recent studies on the sector and outlined above in the section on sectoral challenges and constraints. Furthermore, they suggest that while some issues may be more of an obstacle to tourism development in certain areas than in others, and that other issues may be nuanced by regional factors, the challenges facing the sector are pervasive and of concern across all regions of South Africa. Overall, the findings add weight to the calls by these other studies that the following factors all need urgent attention if the sector is to achieve its full growth potential:

- *Crime,* and the perception of crime, is the single most important factor limiting growth in the tourism industry. First-time international visitors commented unequivocally on the extremely negative international perceptions of safety and security in South Africa in general, and in Johannesburg in particular: 'South Africa's reputation for crime precedes it!' Of particular concern is the criminal activity linked to OR Tambo International Airport, and the perception that Airports Company of South Africa (ACSA) is doing little to address this. Non-tourist-focused crime, however, such as armed robberies of training providers, food theft by restaurant staff, and nepotism, fraud and corruption in various government departments and agencies, also contributes to sector sustainability challenges.
- *Tourist infrastructure,* referring to the physical and public infrastructural aspects of the tourism industry and the regulations governing the use of these, requires attention in respect of quality, availability, distribution, cost and coherence of use. Arbitrary and outdated legislation is compounded by lack of resources and capacity, and general inefficiency in respect of tourism support, in Departments of Roads and Transport at both provincial and national levels. Examples include the severe challenges of compliance and value-maximisation resulting from the current fragmented public vehicle permit system, as well as the limitations on high-value self-drive tourism resulting from insufficient and outdated tourist signage. Tourist information centres demonstrate incomplete product coverage, and problems relating to industry and public accessibility. Finally, a lack of basic infrastructure such as toilets, parking facilities and safety barriers at both natural and cultural tourist attractions impacts negatively on overall visitor experiences.
- High levels of competition and mistrust, and a general lack of co-ordination between industry participants and support agencies, pointed to industry *fragmentation* at all levels. The Hazyview Tourism Association is currently inactive, with members split in terms of their support for the local private tourist information centres. There are also no established relationships between this local tourism sector and the major regional tourism draw-card, the Kruger National Park, while there is a noteworthy lack of confidence in, and support of, the provincial marketing and support agency, the Mpumalanga Parks and Tourism Agency (MPTA), which has undergone 7 restructuring efforts in the past 10 years. The Soweto Tourism Development Association, which has no formal linkages to the local community, is 'marked by squabbles, bickering and petty politics' and a general unwillingness of sub-sector participants to reach out across the barrier of market competition. Work duplication and missed opportunities result from lack of formal and institutionalised relationships defining roles and responsibilities between the Johannesburg Tourism Company (JTC) and other regional industry-focused agencies.
- *Marketing* of the South African tourism industry is generally under-funded and largely uncoordinated, despite the recent increase in funding for SA Tourism, its well-publicised marketing strategy, and its successes in increasing overall tourist numbers. The 2007 annual budgets of R7 million and R20 million for the MPTA and JTC respectively are insufficient, considering the marketing mandates and operational costs of these units. Incoherence of, tensions within, and competition between, marketing strategies, both horizontally (e.g. inter-provincially) as well as vertically (between the local, regional and provincial levels in one area), are also evident. Undermining investment in destination branding, and with significant negative industry impact, is the spree of recent place-name changes. Challenges in the area of marketing also relate to the very limited knowledge

that particularly emerging operators demonstrate of the entire concept of market demand and, because of this, of how to access appropriate markets.
- The dearth of *high-level strategic management skills* across the sector, and in particular of black management skills, emerged strongly. The most critical shortage is, however, not within the industry itself, but rather within the various government departments and supporting agencies tasked with providing the sector with strategic direction. Reasons given include the low level of industry entry; the small number of tourism-related qualifications in the higher education and training band; and greater remuneration opportunities, particularly for black high-level managers, in other sectors.

More specifically, the case-study findings add to the public debate in a number of areas:
- The demand by foreign air arrivals for *cultural tourism* products is nuanced in nature, and influenced by a complex mix of factors including fear, curiosity and respect for what is seen to be people's private lives. Furthermore, the relatively small amount of value per tourist that accrues to individual township product owners and operators is directly related to restricted tour schedules and missed opportunities. This is in turn, however, influenced by fear of crime, limited product offering, and the other more general challenges facing the sector in respect of fragmentation and lack of sufficient leadership and information.
- Widespread feelings of *'entitlement'*, compounded by government's public support of the sector as a growing employer, have resulted in the situation where many sector workers hold unrealistic expectations of both the levels and types of support available to emerging participants, and of the potential wage- and profit-related returns on involvement. This issue, which is a major factor underlying the poor service ethic, is a threat to both the growth and the current sustainability of the tourism sector.
- The industry's calls for *'attitude, passion and experience'* and its corresponding resistance to the employment of formal tourism graduates, particularly those with THETA qualifications, are part of a more complex problem that is not fully appreciated. Factors contributing to the limited value assigned to a number of (although by no means all) tourism-related qualifications include: the low level and lack of exclusivity of skills; skills that are outdated even upon graduation; the insufficient focus on sector-specific skills, considering the length of courses leading to qualifications; the still insufficiently developed foundational and cognitive skills, despite a major focus on these aspects; and the lack of guarantee that qualified individuals will demonstrate the highly prized attributes of attitude, passion, enthusiasm, commitment, honesty and being a 'people person'. The higher wages demanded by qualified individuals substantially alter the cost-benefit balance for employers. For many occupational categories, this encourages the employment of non-qualified people who demonstrate the desirable personality attributes, and who are then provided with training in-house.
- *Tourist and nature guides* act as ambassadors not only for the tourism sector, but also for South Africa more generally, due to the duration and length of direct contact that they have with foreign tourists in particular. Thus, while registration as a guide requires a relevant accredited qualification, employability demands a package of skills, many of which are not addressed in official guide training. These additional skills include good verbal and non-verbal communication skills; a broad general knowledge of both national and international issues; cross-cultural sensitivity; personal presentability and good personal hygiene; a sound and practical knowledge of physical geography; time management and organisational skills; group management skills; and high-level driving skills. Gaps within this skills set result in a number of qualified nature and tourist guides remaining unemployed, even amidst claims of shortages for this skills group.

Conclusions

Recognising the important contribution of the tourism sector to South Africa's growth and employment goals, this study has focused on the challenges currently facing the sector and the potential constraints it faces in realising its full potential. Thus returning to our original question, 'Are skills shortages constraining growth within the tourism sector?', the answer, as highlighted from this analysis, is both 'no and yes'. 'No' from the perspective that the sector's current major growth constraint is the dampening effect of the negative perceptions and reality of high levels of crime on the overall demand for the South African tourism product, and in relation to the physical limitations of meeting the demand we are able to generate through restricted airlift capacity from source markets in peak seasons. 'Yes' from the point of view that many of the other factors considered to be constraining sectoral growth at the present time are indeed underpinned by a lack of HR capacity and skills.

However, if the question asked were instead 'Are *tourism sector-specific skills* shortages constraining growth within the tourism industry?' the answer would have to be 'no'. For despite the real and critical shortages of tourism sector-specific skills such as chefs, travel agents and rangers, the negative impact of these shortages on sectoral growth is minor in comparison with shortages and gaps in generic, non-sector-specific skills such as high-level strategic and visionary leadership, general foundational education and life skills, and skills in the areas of communication, business management, customer relations, sales and marketing, and in the use of various forms of information technology. Furthermore, the intangible elements of personality, character and disposition (such as passion, enthusiasm, honesty, commitment, the ability to work in a team, the ability to internalise learning and constructive criticism, and a desire to serve) are lacking among employees at all levels of the industry, from those occupying unskilled positions to those occupying highly skilled positions, with substantially negative impacts on the sector's ability to generate positive word-of-mouth referrals and thus new as well as repeat tourism business.

Thus overall, skills challenges and shortages in the tourism industry are indeed present and are a factor contributing to many of the other current constraints on sector growth. Yet the nature of these skills shortages is generic rather than sector-specific, and can be summed up in four all-encompassing words: attitude, passion, leadership and vision. Critically, and despite its validity, government's public promotion of the sector as the place for the unemployed and the low-skilled to find work is at present severely compounding these challenges, as it has resulted in the movement into the industry of people with attitudes of entitlement, high expectations of gain and little willingness or enthusiasm to work or to serve.

Recommendations

While having focused predominantly on the challenges and potential constraints to growth facing the tourism sector, this research also provides the foundation for the identification of changes that can be made to improve the sector's overall performance and potential future growth trajectory. These range widely, from the more general to the highly specific. In order for these recommendations to be fully appreciated as arising from the evidence of this research, the full report on which this summary chapter is based needs to be considered (Earle 2007).

Most importantly, this research supports the findings and recommendations arising from other recent research work on the sector. Thus the first recommendation of this study must be that these other recommendations, most notably those of the Global Competitiveness Project report (Monitor 2004), the Customised Sector Programme (DTI 2006), and the *Skills Audit* (Prodigy-Grant Thornton 2007), be given serious consideration and that implementation plans be intensified if already in place, and developed if not. Any research on the sector in the immediate future should focus on the particular challenges of implementing these recommendations, rather than on the challenges facing the sector as a whole.

In line with the above, it is suggested that all government departments and agencies that have some role to play in terms of tourism sector support, should be well-versed in the range of issues outlined within each of these major recent studies, as well as in the part that their department or organisation will have to play in implementing the range of recommendations proposed there. Those departments and agencies whose focus on tourism is shared with a focus on other sectors, should appoint tourism sector champions to take the lead in this function, as well as in the building of relationships with relevant individuals in all other departments and agencies through which the high-level fragmentation of networks may be reduced and the dissemination of data and other sectoral information improved.

Critically, there needs to be a general acknowledgement within government that, while the tourism sector is vital to national development efforts and highly deserving of continued support, tourism can only *contribute to* reducing unemployment and poverty – it will not solve the national unemployment problem. Furthermore, many of the employment opportunities that it is able to generate will not be secure, high-quality, high-waged, 'nine-to-five' jobs with guaranteed promotion opportunities. Strategic and realistic support of the industry will most certainly contribute to national poverty reduction. However, promoting the industry as the panacea for all the problems of the nation's unskilled and semi-skilled groups, and trying to use the sector as a lever for achieving political goals that are impractical, given its nature, has already given rise to a number of tensions and contradictions within the sector's policy framework, and will ultimately lead to more harm than good being done.

This analysis has served to highlight the impact of particularly the first four of the six factors that Asgisa has identified as currently acting as 'binding constraints' for the national economy: the volatility and level of the currency; a shortage of suitably qualified labour; a complex regulatory environment and related burdens on small and medium businesses; and deficiencies in state organisation, capacity and leadership (DoL 2007). Addressing these issues more generally will undoubtedly also have a positive impact on the overall performance of the tourism sector.

The importance of addressing the issues of safety and security cannot be overstated. While there is much to be said for aligning the perceptions of crime to the somewhat lower actual levels of crime in the country, through a variety of means, the reality remains that levels of both petty and violent crime in South Africa are unacceptably high. Merely focusing on perception realignment is insufficient, as it does not address the real problem. The only viable and lasting solution will demand that government acknowledge the extent of the problem and take active steps to reduce crime levels nationally.

Improved marketing and promotion of the sector is critical for increased growth. This will, however, need to be approached from a number of different angles. Firstly, the issue of financial resources to support marketing activities must be addressed. There is a need for increased financial resources for both international and domestic marketing efforts at both national and provincial levels. It is also critical that limited resources be maximised through co-operation, rather than competition and overlap, between all the provinces and SA Tourism. Furthermore, the range of attractions that currently associate themselves with other departments, such as the DAC, needs to be brought into the tourism sector and linked to its marketing efforts. Finally, opportunities need to be sought to maximise marketing value-for-money through strategic targeting. This may include the use of the on-board entertainment system of the national carrier, SAA, for the screening of both national and provincial promotional material to a captive audience.

Secondly, it is vital that marketing efforts be informed by the reality of the tourism product on the ground, in terms of both variety and quality. This study thus supports the recommendation by the DTI (2006) for the development of a real-time product and tourism information system that can also be used as a resource by guides and tour operators, as well as to support entrepreneurs and other potential investors in the identification and filling of market gaps.

Thirdly, specific market research needs to be conducted to help create an understanding of the complex nature of demand for township and other cultural tourism-type products, in order to target marketing efforts and so improve the value-extraction of such tourism developments by emerging sector participants.

Fourthly, domestic tourism needs to be promoted vigorously, not only to increase this source of tourist spending that is more stable and less geographically concentrated, but also to increase the awareness among product owners and prospective entrepreneurs of the value of domestic tourism and to encourage product alignment.

Finally, government at all levels would be wise to consider carefully any further place-name changes, particularly in areas of high tourist significance, and if necessary, consider compromises. Should complete changes be pursued, substantial financial resources will need to be allocated to the rebuilding of relevant tourism destination brands.

Moving beyond marketing, the current skills development system needs to be reconsidered to take account of the real challenges and demands facing the sector – the shortage of highly skilled and visionary leadership, the lack of personal and working experience among graduates and emerging sector participants, and the substantial gaps in terms of learners' foundational and life skills.

Addressing the current shortages of skills at the strategic management level is vital as a first priority: without this, the industry has no hope of developing a common vision in terms of which to co-operatively address the myriad other problems it is facing. In this respect, it needs to be recognised that vocational training on a base of poor foundational, generic and life skills will only support career development to a certain level. Senior management positions demand skills that can only be provided through wider experience, and through training that focuses on cognitive and problem-solving skills in addition to sector-specific skills. As such, it is recommended that the DEAT and industry partner with the higher education institutions offering course-work programmes at the master's level, to develop a multidisciplinary programme that responds to these gaps, and that support and incentives are provided for the promotion of course uptake by those in key roles who lack such skills.

Secondly, industry's calls for 'sector experience' should be taken seriously. Increasing the level of domestic tourism will have the added advantage of increasing the exposure of the general population to the sector and should have positive spin-offs in respect of better alignment between sector demands and sector entrant expectations, as the latter will be in a position to make more informed choices. Other than this, there needs to be an increase in the number of accredited practical short courses that provide training in the skills required in everyday work, and that simultaneously take into account the challenges facing SMME owner-managers. There also needs to be an increase in the number of qualifications for which work experience prior to graduation is a prerequisite. Finally, incentives can be provided for industry itself to participate in providing highly valuable personal tourism experiences to sector students and workers.

Thirdly, the large national gap in respect of foundational education and related skills is a severe challenge for any skills upgrading effort within the tourism industry. Thus the single most important contribution to tourism sector skills will come from the overall improvement of the national school system, to the extent that the majority of people leaving school with a matriculation qualification can be assumed, with relative certainty, to have literacy, numeracy, communication and cognitive skills to at least a certain level. In parallel with such a massive task, the tourism sector can, however, support the development and utilisation of bridging and mentoring programmes, as well as free learner materials, that address communication, etiquette, problem-solving and general foundational skills but that are not linked to sector-specific training.

Turning finally to the specific issue of the THETA: while it is acknowledged that this institution is underfunded and faces substantial HR capacity constraints, in support of the *Skills Audit* recommendation that a THETA turnaround strategy be developed (Prodigy-Grant Thornton 2007), this analysis further suggests that the THETA (and the DoL) need to make a crucial decision. They should either continue along the path of attempting to compel industry to accept an output of 'qualifications' that achieve neither the sector-specific nor the foundational and generic skills requirements, and thus continue to generate little return for the expenditure of large amounts of limited resources; or they should acknowledge industry demands and move towards the provision of support that takes account of the specific nature of the sector. In summary, it is suggested that the THETA move from its current stance as the provider of tourism sector-specific qualifications, towards being the agency committed to supporting the tourism sector in meeting the full complement of its skills requirements.

References

Asgisa (Accelerated and Shared Growth Initiative for South Africa) (2006) *Media briefing by Deputy President Phumzile Mlambo Ngcuka*, 6 February. Background document, a summary

BMI (Business Monitor International) (2005) Key economic sectors. *South Africa Business Forecast Report Quarter 2*: Chapter 4. London: Business Monitor International

DEAT (Department of Environmental Affairs and Tourism, South Africa) (1996) *White paper on the development and promotion of tourism in South Africa*. Accessed 28 June 2007, http://www.info.gov.za/whitepapers/1996/tourism.htm

DoE (Department of Education, South Africa) (2007) *Education Management Information System (EMIS) database*. Pretoria: DoE

DoE (2008) *Further Education and Training Management Information System (FETMIS) database*. Pretoria: DoE

DoL (Department of Labour, South Africa) (2007) *State of skills in South Africa, 2006*. Pretoria: DoL

Dowinton S (2007) Letter to the Editor. *SATSA Tourism Tattler Trade Journal* 4: 8

DTI (Department of Trade and Industry, South Africa) (2006) *Customised sector programme, tourism sector strategy*. Pretoria: DTI

DTI (2007a) *Implementation of government's National Industrial Policy Framework: Industrial policy action plan*. Pretoria: DTI

DTI (2007b) *A National Industrial Policy Framework: Final NIPF, January 2007 Cabinet lekgotla*. Pretoria: DTI

Earle N (2007) *The tourism sector*. A report commissioned by the Department of Labour from the Education, Science and Skills Development Programme of the HSRC. Pretoria: DoL

Erasmus J (2002) *A baseline study for the INTAC project covering ten identified pilot sites: Summative report*. Pretoria: HSRC

HSRC (Human Sciences Research Council) (2005) *The THETA population: A descriptive study of needs in relation to skills training delivery*. Report commissioned by the THETA. Pretoria: THETA

HSRC (2006a) *A study of the 'Tourism Second Economy'*. Report commissioned by the Department of Environmental Affairs and Tourism. Pretoria: DEAT

HSRC (2006b) *Successes and challenges in pro-poor tourism: New models, better results*. Report commissioned by the Department of Environmental Affairs and Tourism. Pretoria: DEAT

HSRC (2007) *Learnership survey*. Data collected for the report 'The learning and employment pathways of learners in learnerships', commissioned by the Department of Labour. Pretoria: DoL

Kirsten M & Rogerson CM (2002) Tourism, business linkages and small enterprise development in South Africa. *Development Southern Africa* 19(1): 29–59

Lowitt S (2006) Translating sectoral growth into job creation: A view of South Africa's tourism industry. Draft paper, undertaken by the Economic Growth and Development Initiative (EDGI) of the HSRC

Mafunzwaini AE & Hugo L (2005) Unlocking the rural tourism potential of Limpopo province of South Africa: Some strategic guidelines. *Development Southern Africa* 22(2): 251–265

Mills J (2007) Where is the passion and pride in service? *SATSA Tourism Tattler Trade Journal* 4: 22

Monitor (2004) *Global competitiveness project for the tourism industry in South Africa 2005–2010*. Report commissioned from Monitor Group by the DEAT, DTI and SA Tourism. Pretoria: DEAT & DTI

Monitor (2007) *Global competitiveness project for the tourism industry in South Africa 2005–2010. Executive summary*, updated April 2007. Pretoria: DEAT & DTI

Oldham G, Creemers G & Rebeck T (2000) An economic evaluation of tourism: A case-study of accommodation facilities in southern Maputaland. *Development Southern Africa* 17(2): 175–188

Pan-African (Pan-African Investment & Research Services) (2006) *A framework/model to benchmark tourism GDP in South Africa*. Report commissioned by the DEAT and SA Tourism. Pretoria: DEAT

Prodigy-Grant Thornton (2007) *Tourism and sport skills audit*. Report commissioned by the NBI, DEAT and THETA from Prodigy Business Services and Grant Thornton. Pretoria: DEAT & THETA

Rivett-Carnac K (2007) *SMMEs and communities education and training task team final report including action plan*. Report commissioned by the DTI. Pretoria: DTI

Robertson P & Skordis J (2004) *International trade in services and sustainable development: The case of tourism in South Africa*. Edited by R Cassim, W Jackson & L Gavara for Trade Knowledge Network, International Institute for Sustainable Development, Winnipeg

SA Tourism (South African Tourism) (2007a) *Tourism growth strategy 2008–2010: Gearing up to be globally competitive*. Third edition. Accessed 10 July 2007, www.southafrica.net

SA Tourism (2007b) *Indaba 2007 factsheet: 2006 performance*. Accessed 10 July 2007, www.southafrica.net

SBP (Strategic Business Partnerships for Growth in Africa) (2006) *Counting the cost of red tape for tourism in South Africa*. Johannesburg: SBP

Stats SA (Statistics South Africa) (2005) *Status of the tourism satellite account in South Africa*. Discussion document D9106, April 2005. Pretoria: Stats SA

Stats SA (2007) *Labour Force Survey (LFS), September 2006*. Embargoed until 29 March 2007. Pretoria: Stats SA

Viljoen J & Tlabela K (2007) *Rural tourism development in South Africa: Trends and challenges*. Occasional Paper of the Urban, Rural and Economic Development (URED) Research Programme of the HSRC. Cape Town: HSRC Press

7 | CONCLUSION

CHAPTER 16

Overcoming 'one-size-fits-all' policy-making: The need for differentiated skills development policies in a highly uneven economic and labour market landscape

Andre Kraak

This chapter develops a conceptual device to assist in the interpretation of trends across the fourteen sector studies published in this book. The primary objective is to devise a tool which can explain the high levels of unevenness between sectors of the South African economy and the very different demands these sectors place on the education and training system.

The conceptual device privileges a labour market approach as the best means of acquiring this 'sector-skills' interactional insight. This is because labour markets play a crucial role, firstly, in establishing the institutional linkages between economic sectors and education and training providers. Secondly, they play the leading role in meeting the differentiated demand for skills across divergent sectors of the national economy.

The conceptual framework is built through borrowing from several fields of social inquiry. These influences include, firstly, 'segmented labour market theory' and its emphasis on the role of the state and market in the shaping of internal and external labour markets. A second influence is the literature on production regimes, and in particular, its focus on the need for developing economies to shift industrial structures from 'low' to 'high' value-adding production regimes. And finally, the conceptual framework is also influenced by the new school of 'evolutionary economics' which underpins 'innovation studies', particularly by its emphasis on firm-based learning as the key dynamic shaping production regimes in today's knowledge-based economy.

The structure of the chapter is as follows. Firstly, the core theoretical influences and their assumptions are briefly outlined. Secondly, the conceptual device is then constructed and explained. It comprises a six-part segmentation of the South African labour market. Each of these six segments arises as an outcome of three 'dualisms' which operate in the South African economy and society: a dualism between 'low' and 'high' value-adding production regimes within the national economy; a divide between 'state' and 'market' regulation; and finally, a divide between 'internal' and 'external' forms of labour market formation.

The analysis concludes by arguing the case for greater alignment between skills development and industrial policies in South Africa. The process of establishing such an alignment will need to overcome the limitations of the 'one-size-fits-all' policy logic which dominates current skills development thinking in South Africa.

Theoretical influences

Segmented labour market theory

The most influential school of thought contributing to the design of the conceptual framework for this chapter has been 'segmented labour market' theory. The central position of the 'Segmented Labour Market School' is the argument that labour markets are not as 'open' as neo-classical economics would have us believe. Rather, participation in labour markets is shaped by social processes of 'exclusion' and 'inclusion' which arise out of capitalism's historical evolution and through the specific needs of particular economic sectors at various stages of their development. Capital, labour and the state have struggled, historically, over the institutional and other mechanisms of control which grant or limit access to jobs and which determine the conditions of work.

Segmented labour markets are those markets which have been institutionally divided into distinct and separate employment spheres. Workers in each segment experience distinct processes and outcomes. This structural feature of the capitalist labour market has often been reinforced by racial, gender and other forms of social discrimination and exclusion.

Within the broad segmentation literature there are two schools of thought. This chapter will adopt the approach of the 'Cambridge Labour Market School' which focuses on the concepts 'internal', 'occupational' and 'external' labour markets.[1] Internal labour markets are organised around particular workplaces or employers. Jobs above entry level are generally filled by internal promotion; skills are learned as part of employment and qualifications are of secondary or no importance. The internal labour market incorporates stable and secure jobs with career paths. Workers gain security through claims upon particular employers rather than through possession of externally recognised skills. The internal labour market, historically, has been shaped by both the 'shielding' activities of skilled labour and capital's bureaucratic and hierarchical forms of labour control. Internal labour markets are about 'insiders' being treated more advantageously than those 'outsiders' who form part of the external labour market.

The second important institutional configuration within the capitalist labour market is the 'unstructured' component of the external labour market. It includes all workers who access employment independently of state support for, or employer sponsorship of, training. A major part of the external labour market, therefore, is characterised by the fact that it provides no structured pathway into employment for workers seeking employment. It comprises low-skilled workers who sometimes struggle to find opportunities for manual labour.

Thirdly, there are highly structured components to the external labour market which are often termed 'occupational labour markets' in the literature. This segment comprises all those institutions and regulations which provide workers with structured pathways from education and training into work. Occupational labour markets encourage the mobility of qualified workers amongst employers and work best with a system of standardised vocational qualifications. Workers seek security not from any particular employer but from the wider labour market, in association with certified skill and knowledge. Apprenticeship training is the classic example of such a pathway into employment. So are the organised professions such as engineering, chartered accounting, law, social work and medicine – all

---

[1] For references to the 'American' school, see: Doeringer & Piore 1971; Edwards, Reich & Gordon 1973; Osterman 1984. For references to the early work of the 'Cambridge' school see: Marsden & Ryan 1991; Rubery et al. 1987; Wilkinson (ed.) 1981. For more contemporary work on segmented labour markets see: Camuffo 2002; Grimshaw et al. 2001; Rutherford 2006. For the application of segmented labour market theory to South Africa, see Fine 1998; Kraak 1995; Webster 1985.

of which require the traversing of a highly structured pathway from school, through higher education, followed by an induction into the world of work as a 'novice', and finally, professional registration and formal employment.

The rise of 'flexible' labour markets

Much of the work of the foundational Cambridge segmented labour market school was completed in the 1980s. Even though the core principles of the Cambridge school remain relevant under contemporary conditions, there have been two major changes which have required the altering of the conceptualisation of internal and external labour market structures if they are to be applied in the present period. The first has to do with the reforms pushed through by neo-liberal governments throughout the 1980s and 1990s in pursuit of greater 'flexibility' in labour markets and production regimes across Europe, North America and East Asia. The second problem facing segmented labour market theory is the rise of the 'knowledge economy' and its failure to incorporate the new dynamics of intra- and inter-firm learning and co-operation within its typologies of labour market.

The push for more flexible labour markets and production regimes arose in the 1980s as part of the larger neo-liberal attack on the welfare state system. Neo-liberal governments across the globe perceived the so-called 'rigidities' of the welfare state labour market as being the root cause of economic decline in that period and a major brake on future growth. The solution, they believed, lay in pursuing policies of labour market 'flexibility' which included: reducing unemployment compensation, lowering or abolishing minimum wages, eliminating employment protection regulations, and, in general, weakening trade union control over labour market employment conditions (Grimshaw et al. 2001). Various forms of employment flexibility emerged in this period, but the two most important were functional and numerical flexibility. Functional flexibility leads to higher levels of worker productivity as a small core group of workers agree to a trade-off of higher productivity (as a result of the introduction of new technologies, work reorganisation and retraining) in return for employment security and higher wages. Higher productivity allows firms to employ fewer workers, and as market environments change, employers can adapt to fluctuating demand by employing more or less numerically flexible labour.

The rise of flexible labour markets has also to do with the structural shifts in the national economy away from manufacturing and towards the services sectors. New occupations have emerged, including a sizeable tranche of highly specialised information and communication technology (ICT) occupations. In addition, the financial and business services sector has grown rapidly, with an equivalent growth in specialist areas of financial management and accounting. In addition, media and advertising, tourism and hospitality, and leisure and entertainment have all become significant components of the services sector in most national economies. All of these new sectors have triggered a parallel growth in new occupations and qualifications, leading to significant growth on the supply side as public- and private-sector education providers scramble to provide qualifications for these new jobs.

These developments triggered significant changes in the structuring of external labour markets, the most important of which has been a shift in the locus of work organisation from 'permanent and stable collections of jobs to individualised, flexible employment defined by human capital portfolios' (Carnoy, Castells & Benner 1997: 27). This shift away from the standard form of contracting which guaranteed secure, long-term employment has resulted in a far higher level of labour market flux and mobility, with individual 'flexible' workers moving between workplaces, filling particular positions on demand. Many of these high-end flexible workers choose the self-employment route. Carnoy et al. estimate that flexible employment has reached as much as 40 per cent of the total workforce in countries such as Japan, the UK and the USA.

The top end

The traditional 'high professions' have always been a major component of the top end of the external labour market – doctors, lawyers, engineers, architects, accountants, and so forth. This segment of the labour market is defined by the fact that beneficiaries within it obtain the necessary education and training qualifications prior to obtaining high-level jobs – that is, independently of any employer interest in their skills portfolio or state support through scholarships and bursaries. They have acquired educational qualifications privately prior to obtaining company jobs. These employees have a class-privileged access to higher education, which enables them to afford their own education and training.

However, modes of working in these professions have changed dramatically over the past two decades. With the decline of vertically integrated corporations and the advances made with digital technology, many professional services do not need to be housed within large companies, but can be outsourced to highly skilled yet small specialist consulting firms. These activities include ICT, financial, engineering, legal, advertising and marketing consulting services. The growth in these high-tech small firms has been made easier by the mobility provided by digital technology, which allows for instantaneous connections between small firms and large client.

These two developments – new occupations and changing modes of high-end employment – have brought about equivalent changes to the high end of the external labour market. Young people now need to make their own choices about future careers. They need to invest in their own education and training. They can tap into labour market information centres through the internet to seek advice about which jobs are in most demand and which command the best salaries. Faced with this 'flexibility' of choice – choosing from a wide array of intermediate to high-end service sector jobs that are in high demand – young people with employable skills eventually find themselves in the new top-end jobs (see Grimshaw et al. 2001 for discussion of this 'individualisation' of the labour market).

The bottom end

However, the flexible labour market does not present as cosy a picture for young people from less privileged backgrounds. Their choices are less 'flexible' and 'free'. With the shift to services and the increasing automation in both manufacturing and services, many of the new jobs are positioned in the low- to-intermediate skill segment – with job descriptions that demand very little in terms of hard skill. The bulk of new jobs in the services sector are indeed in this segment and require minimal post-school education and training. A vast literature has grown on the demand for 'soft skills' in this segment – the need for certain types of personal attributes which better socialise young people into these new service-oriented roles. Qualities such as good inter-personal and communication skills are now emphasised, as well as the ability to solve problems and work in teams (Carnoy et al. 1997).

Accessing these jobs proves more difficult for young people, largely because the number of first-time entrants is far larger than the number of available jobs. Also, the fit between 'qualification' received and jobs on offer is not as neat as in the case of 'top-end' jobs, and many employers doubt the worth of the qualifications young people have received. This is acutely the case in South Africa but is also a problem elsewhere in the world.

The unstructured external labour market, in short, provides a world of opportunities for privileged youngsters who obtain a good education and training for one of the new services jobs at the top end, but it provides very little direction and support for the bulk of participants in this labour market who are less privileged, with qualifications perceived to be of inferior quality, and who do not easily find employment after having financed their own education and training.

The contribution of 'evolutionary economics'

A second source of change to the traditional model of the internal labour market has to do with the demands of innovation in the knowledge economy, and in particular, the new emphasis on enterprise-based learning, the development of tacit knowledge and the harnessing of a firm's dynamic capabilities as the basis for new knowledge generation and the incremental acquisition of innovation. The academic interrogation of these dynamics has not come from segmented labour market theory, but rather, from the work of 'evolutionary economics', which emphasises work-based learning as a critical prerequisite for innovation in the knowledge economy. It is not only intra-firm capabilities that are significant. Equally important are the backward and forward linkages between lead firms and their suppliers. These inter-firm linkages, forged through networks and cluster arrangements, act to transfer tacit knowledge between firms which then fuels new product and process development. All of these activities have the effect of extending the boundaries of the internal labour market beyond the ambit of the single firm to include all activities that develop the dynamic capabilities of firms. These inter-firm activities which enhance internal learning in individual firms comprise the 'extended' internal labour market.[2]

Labour market and production regimes

The changes in production regime described above – particularly those that have occurred during the era of globalisation – have not been uniform across all firms and in all sectors. There is a growing literature which describes distinctive variants of production regime, each defined by different labour market conditions.

For example, the 'varieties of capitalism' school articulates two distinctive pathways of contemporary capitalism – the one being the Anglo-Saxon 'free market economy' and the other the continental European 'co-ordinated market economy' (see Coriat & Weinstein 2004). Similarly, the British high-skills literature distinguishes between two ideal types of production regime: an institutional framework based on a 'low-skills equilibrium' and one based on a 'high-skills equilibrium'. A 'low-skills equilibrium' is an economic system characterised by low-cost, low-skills and standardised production (Brown et al. 2001). These ideal-type constructions in both literatures are founded on distinct labour market structures. For example, in their analysis of the differing developmental routes of three high-skill societies – Germany, Britain and Singapore – Brown et al. conclude that a major determinant of national variance between these three countries is labour market structure: a very structured 'external' labour market in the case of Germany, 'flexible' labour markets in the case of Britain, and a 'state-guided' labour market system in the case of Singapore (Brown et al. 2001).

These differences in production regime and labour market structure do not only occur between different countries but also between different sectors in a single economy. Mason (2004) illustrates this by examining the divisions within the British economy across high- and low-skill sectors. At the heart of this division is the role played by 'product strategy'. This concept attempts to capture the choices made by enterprises about product or service differentiation within particular markets. Key product strategy variables include: production volumes and product complexity; the extent to which competitive success depends on price; the extent to which the establishment competes in a 'premium quality' product market as compared to a 'standard or basic quality' product market; the extent to which the establishment provides 'a demonstrably better quality product or service than similar or competitor establishments'; and the extent to which the establishment 'tends to lead the way' in the development of new products, materials or techniques' (Mason 2004: 15).

---

2   See Manwaring 1984 for his definition of the 'extended' internal labour market; see also Chapter 1 of this volume for an elaboration of the work of 'evolutionary economics'.

Mason argues that in the UK context, many low-skill, low-wage industries remain viable and profitable, even in the era of the knowledge economy where competition is increasingly based on knowledge intensity, high-quality manufacture and product differentiation. This is because these low-skill industries operate within local or national markets where demands for basic-quality standardised goods and services remain strong. This market environment allows for profitability based upon product strategies that are low-skill and low value-adding (Mason 2004: 3).

As a consequence of this, many British firms are locked into a low-skill, low value-adding production regime. Without competitive pressures from external markets, these firms will resist government efforts to move up the value chain towards higher value-adding production. These firms 'will have little reason to change course' (Mason 2004: 45).

The six-part segmentation of the South African labour market

As indicated earlier, the primary objective of this chapter is to build a conceptual device with which to understand the uneven relationship between economic sector and skill in the South African context. The conceptual device consists of a six-part segmentation of the South African labour market, as illustrated in Figure 16.1. The device is constructed around the adoption of three powerful 'dualisms' which act to shape and differentiate labour markets. These are:
1   A dualism of production regimes between:
    - low value-adding production regimes characterised by competition established on the basis of mass-produced, standardised products based on the lowest price and made for local markets sheltered from external competition; and
    - high value-adding production regimes characterised by world class manufacturing techniques based on high-quality product differentiation and brand variation, with competition located in premium-quality export markets. Product differentiation entails highly customised manufacturing, for example, production for specific niche suppliers producing goods and services in relatively low volumes.
2   A dualism between state and market regulation of the labour market. Of great significance here is the existence of two state-sponsored segments: the 'state-guided external labour market' illustrated by Segment 1 in Figure 16.1 and the 'state-sponsored low-skills development strategy' located in Segment 6 in Figure 16.1.
3   And finally, a dualism between 'internal' and 'external' forms of labour market construction, as theorised by the Cambridge school. These two labour market structures are presented as opposite nodes on the Y–axis in Figure 16.1. Segments 3 and 4 comprise different nodes of the South African internal labour market and Segments 1, 2, 5 and 6 comprise distinct segments of South Africa's external labour market.

Figure 16.1 represents these three dualisms across the Y-axis (labour market differentiation), the X-axis (production regime), and lastly, along the left vertical side of the diagram, representing the divide between state and market regulation.

As indicated earlier, there are two important amendments to segmented labour market theory in the current period, the first being the transition to more flexible forms of employment governed through the external labour market. Segment 2 represents the top end of jobs incorporated within this flexible type of external labour market and Segment 5 incorporates all bottom-end 'flexible' jobs. The second amendment to the early Cambridge model is the need for an 'extended' conception of the internal labour market which captures those dynamics of inter-firm co-operation that lead to the enhancement of a firm's innovation capabilities.

FIGURE 16.1: *A six-part segmentation of the South African labour market*

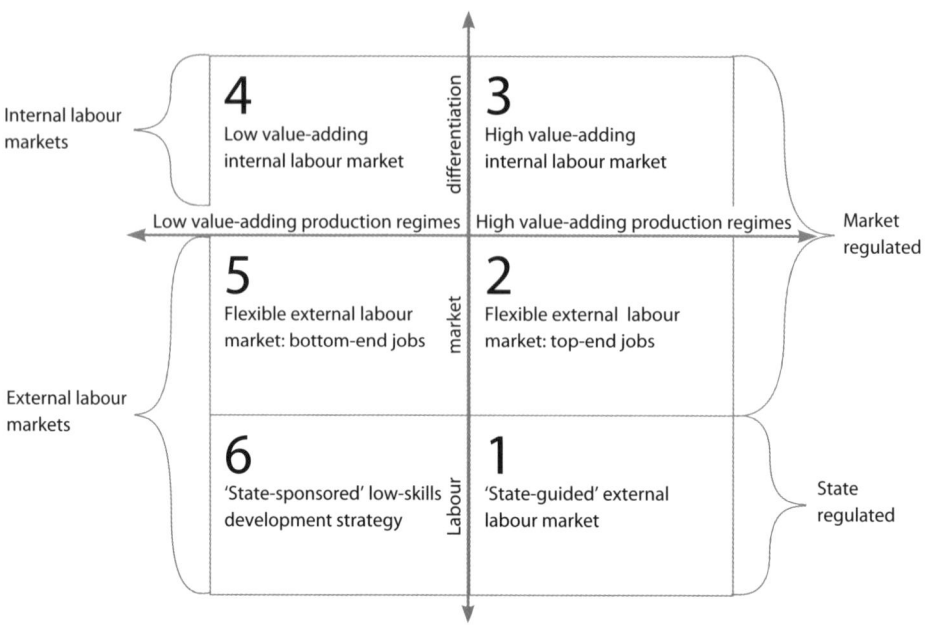

All of these 'rules of combination' produce a six-part segmentation of the labour market which is neatly captured in Figure 16.1. This six-part segmentation is a highly abstracted 'ideal-type' representation of the South African labour market. In reality, these labour market segments overlap and operate simultaneously, to a greater or lesser extent, in each sector. Each represents a different mode of allocating skills and human capital, and even though a particular sector or sub-sector of the economy can be described as exhibiting features of one labour market form – for example, high levels of enterprise-based training, which is characteristic of internal labour markets – it is also likely that other labour market practices will exist in that sector, although to a less significant degree (for example, the recruitment of professionals on the external labour market).

This is a significant amendment to the 'segmented labour market', 'varieties of capitalism' and 'high skills' literature, which tends to ascribe one form of labour market structure to one society or one sector (for example, the well-known example of Japan representing the classic 'internal labour market' route). This approach seriously ignores the uneven demand for skills across a national economy, between sectors and across sub-sectors. The approach adopted here is to assume that skills acquisition and skills distribution occur unevenly across a mix of labour market modes which operate simultaneously. Sectors are highly diverse, and particular conditions in each sector will determine the extent to which employers will draw primarily on one form of labour market provision and secondarily on others.

The next section assigns economic sectors in the South African economy to this six-part segmentation model. This allocation is determined primarily by:
- the *primary features of the sectoral production regime* itself – the extent to which value creation in the sector is dependent on the external inputs of high science (as would be the case in nuclear energy and aerospace), or is based endogenously on the dynamic capabilities of firms themselves and the incremental gains they make in moving up the value chain (as in the auto and wood, paper and pulp sectors);

- the extent to which the sector has attained *world class manufacturing* status and is competitive on global markets (as is the case with the auto and wood, paper and pulp sectors);
- the extent to which the *development and acquisition of human capital* in the sector are primarily dependent on the actions of the state, the private sector, and/or the 'flexible choices' of individuals;
- the extent to which *internal or external labour market mechanisms* determine the allocation of human capital in that sector.

Table 16.1 illustrates the allocation of a number of sectors and sub-sectors discussed in this book. It highlights the primary criteria used to allocate these sectors to specific labour market segments. In so doing, it highlights the primary labour market mechanism used to acquire and distribute skills in that sector. However, this allocation does not exclude other secondary processes of skill acquisition occurring alongside the dominant process.

Applying the segmented labour market model in South Africa

This section will draw data from only 11 of the sectors, sub-sectors and industrial niche areas covered in this book; this limited coverage is simply a result of space constraints. The coverage, therefore, does not provide a comprehensive overview of the 'sectors-skills' interaction across the entire South African economy. It does, however, provide insight into the main trends of key sectors which have been prioritised by government in its Accelerated and Shared Growth Initiative for South Africa (Asgisa) (PCAS 2006) and the National Industrial Policy Framework (DTI 2007) policy frameworks.

TABLE 16.1: *Criteria used in the allocation of sectors to specific labour market segments*

Primary feature of the production regime	Key role-players in human capital formation	Examples of sectors characterised by these core features	Labour market segment
Heavily dependent on high-science inputs. Innovation here greatly dependent on high science.	Only the state can provide the massive financial, human resource and technological inputs required by these science-based sectors.	Aerospace Nuclear energy Space science High-tech public infrastructure sectors and transport	State-guided external labour market
Production of a differentiated range of premium goods aimed at the export market. Heavily dependent on the internal dynamic capabilities of firms. The design, engineering, entrepreneurial and managerial (DEEM) capabilities of firms are crucial prerequisites for moving up the value chain into export markets. Innovation acquired endogenously and incrementally through improvements in product and process.	Building DEEM capacity is primarily the responsibility of the private sector. Attaining world-class manufacturing standards is a prerequisite for success on export markets. Employers prioritise technological upgrading, work re-organisation and skills development.	Auto Wood, paper and pulp (both successful export sectors.)	High value-adding internal labour market

Primary feature of the production regime	Key role-players in human capital formation	Examples of sectors characterised by these core features	Labour market segment
Production of standardised goods aimed at internal markets Competitiveness based on a low-wage, low-cost, low-skill production regime. DEEM capabilities under-developed in these enterprises.	These sectors operate in local and national markets, and have not succeeded in attaining world-class manufacturing standards. Low levels of beneficiation and product differentiation. Not successful in export markets. Firms do not upgrade technologically and do not prioritise skills development.	Metals Clothing Chemicals Agro-processing	Low value-adding internal labour market
Production regime shaped strongly by the growth of the services sector and digital technology. Innovation highly dependent on a dynamic 'entrepreneurial spirit' driven by highly skilled individuals. Founded on a highly mobile labour market characterised by an abundance of highly skilled professionals who are self-educated prior to seeking employment.	Allocation of highly skilled individuals in the labour market made on the basis of 'individual choice'. Many of the highly skilled seek flexible employment arrangements working from home or from small expert consulting firms. 'Experience' is a highly valued commodity in dynamic labour markets with high levels of turnover and skilled labour poaching. Highly entrepreneurial individuals start new businesses often supported by readily available venture capital.	Top end of financial and business services sector Top end of ICT sector Top end of film industry Top end of tourism industry	Top-end 'flexible' external labour market
Production regime founded on insecure, impermanent, low-wage, low-skill employment. Employment seasonal, part-time, casual.	Employment patterns are shaped by processes of casualisation and outsourcing. Workers involuntarily accept low-wage, low-skill employment because of the absence of alternative employment.	Bottom end of tourism industry Bottom end of agro-processing Bottom end of construction sector	Bottom-end 'flexible' external labour market
Increased employment in low-skill, labour-intensive sectors.	Highly dependent on the developmental role of the state to expand sustainable low-skill employment in the informal sector in areas which have strong linkages back into the formal economy.	Community forestry Paper recycling Scrap metals	State-sponsored low-skills development strategy

Segment 1: The state-guided external labour market

This segment is structured primarily through the developmental actions of the state and its various industrial, science, technology, education and training policies and agencies. Most important of all are the links the state has structured between the innovation and education systems and certain high-tech, high-skill sectors of the economy. The state has chosen a developmental path which targets these sectors for renewed growth and government assistance – assistance which would not be forthcoming if key decisions in these sectors were left to market forces operating on their own. South African sectors falling within this category and reviewed in this book include aerospace, nuclear energy and space science. The evolution of these new sectors and their dependence on state support will be briefly reviewed here.

Aerospace

The South African aerospace industry is largely owned by the public sector. The main public-sector players include Armscor and Denel. Private-sector companies include Aerosud, African Defence Systems (ADS), Advanced Technologies and Engineering (ATE) and Grintek. The Council for Scientific and Industrial Research (CSIR) – a public-sector research council – is also involved in the aerospace sector through Defencetek, which is a simulation, design, testing and evaluation facility for aircraft and air weapons. It also provides advice on and technology support for radar, artificial intelligence products, electronic systems engineering, and navigation systems technology (Kraemer-Mbula 2008).

Kraemer-Mbula in Chapter 3 of this volume[3] argues that the aerospace sector is considered one of the most advanced manufacturing sectors globally. This is because it often functions as an incubator of new technologies which, once they have fully evolved in the aerospace sector, spill over into other sectors. Aerospace is also an important absorber of technological inputs from other adjacent sectors such as telecommunications, automobiles, machinery and tooling. It therefore plays a crucial role in advancing technological upskilling in the economy (Kraemer-Mbula 2008).

The sector is also distinctive in that it functions as a single global value chain with sector leaders focusing increasingly on core business activities such as aircraft design, systems integration and sales and marketing, whilst lower-tier manufacturing has been outsourced to various developing countries. These economies face tough demands to continuously upgrade their skills base and technological capabilities because of the strict quality standards of the global value chain in which they participate. Kraemer-Mbula (2008) maintains that the supplier base of the South African aerospace sector suffers a dire lack of skills and design capabilities, which constrains it from keeping up with the rapid advances in aerospace products globally. As a consequence, it is seeking to form strategic alliances with other developing economy players in the global industry. One such alliance between South Africa, India and Brazil is planning to cultivate complementary niche capabilities in civilian aerospace.

Some of the potential that the emergent South African aerospace industry has to offer is reflected in other partnerships forged with the world's leading aerospace manufacturers, and more specifically, with the creators of the Airbus A400 programme. The Airbus A400M is a four-engine turboprop military transport and tanker, designed by Airbus Military. It can accommodate all types of loads including helicopters, light armoured vehicles, civil and military pallets and containers, and heavy earth-moving equipment. The aircraft can fly long distances non-stop without refuelling and can land on unprepared landing strips.

---

3   Each of the contributing chapters to this book has been derived from a much longer and more comprehensive study commissioned by the South African Department of Labour. References to these sector studies in this review chapter cover both the chapters and the full reports; the latter are all available from the authors or from the HSRC.

The contract to manufacture the A400M was signed in 2003, between Airbus Military and an international consortium representing Belgium, France, Germany, Luxembourg, Spain, Turkey and the UK. South Africa is one of only two extra-European partner countries in the A400M programme, the other being Malaysia.

The multinational A400M programme is considered as the most significant single contract for the South African aerospace industry and one of the most important aviation programmes currently under way in the world. Denel and Aerosud supply the A400M programme with a range of components including wing tips, wing-to-fuselage fairings, centre top shells, composite cargo holds, nose fuselage linings, and other composite and metallic airframe components (Kraemer-Mbula 2008). Furthermore, both companies will repair equipment during the programme's lifespan, and are expected to compete for the provision of aircraft maintenance and training services. The aircraft will be finally assembled in Seville, Spain. It is estimated that the A400M programme will add R859 million to South Africa's gross domestic product (GDP) each year for the next 15 years (*Business Day* 27 June 2008).

Another benefit of the Airbus A400M deal is the opening up of opportunities for technological exchange at other points along the global value chain. For example, the CSIR and two South African universities (Nelson Mandela Metropolitan University and the University of Cape Town) have struck a 'green composites' deal with Airbus to develop a natural-fibre material for aircraft interiors and, in so doing, revolutionise this area of design. The CSIR has already proven the potential of these fibres in the automotive sector, and it now hopes to extend the utilisation of the material to the aerospace industry, which has far more stringent quality and safety criteria. The material would not only be more eco-friendly, but would help to reduce aircraft weight and therefore fuel consumption. The project is also looking at ways of improving aircraft safety, using bio-resins and nanotechnology to reduce the flammability of cabin material and the amount of smoke produced in cases of fire (*Business Day* 27 June 2008).

All of these developments lead Kraemer-Mbula to conclude that South Africa's wealth in raw materials, combined with considerable capabilities in advanced industries like automotive and ICTs, suggest that aerospace is well positioned to continue functioning as a domestic supplier of high quality and at competitive prices. The potential spill-over effects into other manufacturing sectors such as tooling and composite materials are significant.

Dependency on high-technology and high skills

It is clear that this high-tech sector is strongly reliant on two inputs: large-scale state support and science-based inputs from universities. The production of high skills, and in particular, a ready supply of engineers, is a key component of this state support. Kraemer-Mbula reports that out of a higher education cohort of 4 348 engineering graduates in 2004, only 16 were qualified in aeronautical engineering. This poses a huge problem for Denel and the other companies operating in the sector.

To meet some of these high-skill demands, Denel plays a very active part in the training of its skilled workforce. Kramer-Mbula reports that the Denel Centre for Learning and Development is the largest public-sector skills development programme in Africa for the aerospace and defence industry. Denel and other South African aerospace companies also regularly send high-skill employees outside the company for formal training, often to the global head offices of the first-tier companies involved in South Africa's various international aerospace partnerships. Maintaining this high-science base is a major obligation of the sector if it wants to remain globally competitive.

Nuclear energy

Nuclear energy is a second industrial niche area promoted and supported by the South African state. Lorentzen and Petersen (Chapter 4) report that South Africa is one of 30 countries worldwide making use of nuclear power. South Africa has a small nuclear industry, having built only one nuclear power station in the mid-1980s at Koeberg in the Cape which supplies about six per cent of total electricity to the country.

Nuclear power, historically, has been an unpopular energy source, especially during the 1990s, both because of the risk of rogue states gaining access to the technology, and also because of the risk of nuclear accidents. In fact, a key part of South Africa's transition from apartheid to democracy was the decommissioning of its nuclear weapons capabilities. Ironically, almost a decade later, there has been a dramatic turnaround with regard to nuclear energy policy, both in South Africa and globally. This is due in large part to the current energy crisis facing the globe, including rocketing oil prices, the non-sustainability of fossil fuel sources and the increasing environmental damage due to high fossil fuel consumption and subsequent pollution.

South Africa's new policy on nuclear energy now supports nuclear power much more explicitly. It provides for an ambitious programme encompassing the entire nuclear fuel cycle. This involves the re-activation of conversion, enrichment, fuel fabrication and reprocessing of used fuel, all with the aim of guaranteeing energy security. It also calls for an increase in the local beneficiation of uranium ore concentrates, whether for local use or for export (Lorentzen & Petersen 2008).

The pebble bed modular reactor (PBMR) is the most ambitious of government's new science-oriented industrial projects. It is based on a German design, the rights of which Eskom bought in the 1990s. These high-temperature reactors are small, with reported advantages in terms of high thermal efficiency, great load flexibility with rapid change in power settings, on-line refuelling of expended pebbles, and modest construction and competitive generating costs. The South African government has allocated substantial funding to the PBMR since 2004. It aims to produce 4–5 000 MW of power from PBMRs in the long run, which translates into a total demand of some 20–30 reactors. Eskom also hopes to export up to 20 PBMR units per year (Lorentzen & Petersen 2008).

Eskom has proposed the formation of a nuclear training academy at Koeberg. The academy will be set up in partnership with multinational companies that win the bid to participate in the nuclear build programme. Again, the logic behind the Academy is the need to ensure a continuous flow of scientific expertise to the sector.

Space science

A third hi-tech industrial niche area being developed by government is in the field of space science. South Africa is keen to join the ranks of several developing economies that have established new national space agencies. Space science is becoming an important field not merely for space exploration purposes, but more importantly, because it can be used for humanitarian interventions such as disaster management, telemedicine and water management (Lorentzen & Petersen 2008).

South Africa is now working on moving one step up to become a country with the capability of building satellites and other space applications. South Africa has already successfully built two micro-satellites, one of which was launched in 1999 by NASA. SunSat, a 64-kg micro-satellite, was designed and built by staff and students in the Department of Electrical and Electronic Engineering at Stellenbosch University. A spin-off company, SunSpace, has been formed which manufactures small and medium satellites, satellite-support equipment, and ground-based applications. SunSpace is the only satellite manufacturing company in South Africa. It has built a second small satellite, SumbandilaSat, which was completed in November 2006. The R26 million SumbandilaSat took two years to build and is owned by the Department of Science and Technology (DST). The satellite was scheduled to be launched off a Russian submarine in June 2007 but this event was postponed and no launch has yet taken place.

Other space science initiatives

South Africa also hosts the Southern African Large Telescope (SALT), which is an international initiative jointly run by a consortium of international partner institutions. SALT is the largest single optical-infrared telescope in the southern hemisphere. It comprises a 10m-class telescope located near Sutherland in the Northern Cape.

As with the aerospace example above, the SALT initiative has led to several technological spill-over effects, to the benefit of many small high-tech South African engineering firms. The SALT construction team included astronomers, software and mechanical engineers, software mirror and optical specialists, software developers, electronics engineers and technicians, and technical draftspersons.

SALT plays an important role in strengthening South Africa's bid to host the Square Kilometre Array (SKA) as it demonstrates the country's ability to host 'big science' astronomy initiatives. The SKA is, however, a much larger project than the SALT project. The proposed SKA will be the world's largest radio telescope. It will comprise between 3 000 and 4 500 dish-shaped antennae spread across a collecting area of about 1 million square metres. In order to escape the interference of man-made radio signals, the SKA will have to be located in a part of the world that is remote yet accessible to astronomers and engineers and is large enough to position the array. South Africa and Australia were short-listed in September 2006 and are now competing to host the large telescope. South Africa has proposed the Northern Cape as the ideal site for the core array. Work has already begun on the prototype for the South African SKA telescope, which has been termed the Meerkat (Lorentzen & Petersen 2008).

These high-science astronomy initiatives are very ambitious indeed. For South Africa to succeed, it will need a vast network of highly skilled scientists who currently are not available in the numbers needed, nor with the levels of experience and expertise required. Government's response to this human capital shortfall has been to roll out a number of major human capital initiatives in addition to the industrial support it has given to the space science initiatives. For example, the National Astrophysics and Space Science Programme (NASSP) was initiated in 2003 by the DST as a response to the need to build human capacity in astrophysics and space science. The NASSP is a national master's programme aimed at increasing the pool of students, particularly black students, with a master's degree in Astrophysics and Space Science. It also acts as a feeder for PhD programmes. It is jointly run by nine universities and the various national astronomy facilities in the country. NASSP graduated 49 honours students and 36 master's students during the period 2003 to 2006. The majority of the black graduates are from other countries in Africa. Twenty-two NASSP graduates went on to PhD level. The programme will need to produce between 60 and 100 PhD students by 2012 in order to meet skills requirements (Lorentzen & Petersen 2008). This is an impressive supply-side intervention by the DST which is clearly playing a major role in 'guiding' the labour market to deliver the necessary high skills. However, it is not clear that these will constitute sufficient efforts, or whether the targets will be met.

Labour market characteristics

The aerospace, nuclear energy and space science industries share certain commonalities. For example, they were all part of the apartheid military-industrial complex and were all down-scaled at the start of the democratic dispensation in 1994. Currently, as small industrial niche areas, they all make insignificant contributions to the country's GDP. However, in the policy turnaround which has taken place in the past few years, these areas now occupy the centre stage of government-sponsored science initiatives at the high-skills level. These are initiatives which government views as having the potential, in the long run, to make significant contributions to growth and development.

Apart from the dependency on state support, each of these niche areas is also highly dependent on science-based inputs from the universities and international partnerships if they are to grow into fully-fledged industries. These inputs include research and development (R&D) activities attained through university-industry linkages and global partnerships with foreign governments and multinational corporations. The success of all these high-skill, science-based initiatives will require the production of a sufficient cadre of highly skilled personnel in specialist fields such as astronomy, astro- and nuclear-physics and aeronautical engineering.

All of these dynamics require that the state support, co-ordinate and regulate the various inputs required by these sectors. The market mechanism and private-sector role-players do not have an equivalent interest or obligation to contribute. The state must also forge strong co-operative linkages between the universities, the science councils and the state-owned enterprises – all key role-players in these state-guided initiatives. The state must also forge strong partnerships with multinational corporations and developed countries in the various global value chains that dominate these high-science sectors.

The labour market segment serving the skill needs of these sectors has acquired distinctive features which make it quite different from the more orthodox 'external labour market'. It is clearly a labour market segment where the state, institutionally, has to ensure that adequate supplies of high-tech knowledge and high-skill personnel are channelled through to these sectors in appropriate quantities.

Renewed state support for public infrastructure sectors

The discussion regarding Segment 1 has so far focused only on the new high-science sectors. But the state-guided labour market has a second and historically older responsibility, and that is to attend to the human capital and technological needs of the state-owned enterprises, particularly those high-end functions in energy and transportation that are also highly dependent on new science and technology inputs. Historically, public infrastructure sectors such as energy and transport have been very reliant on state-supported scientific know-how and financial support to overcome the high-science and investment barriers to entry in these capital-intensive sectors. Key role-players are the state-owned enterprises such as Eskom (electricity) and Transnet (tranport).

Electricity

Lomey and McNamara show in Chapter 8 how a series of problems have accumulated in the electricity sector over the past decade. Firstly, as a result of the massive rollout of electricity services to black South Africans since 1994, and the boom conditions in the economy since 2001, the consumption demand has exceeded supply on a number of occasions since 2006, leading to crippling power shortages and blackouts in the major nodes of the national economy and society.

A second problem has been that of maintenance and the deterioration of existing infrastructure. There is now an estimated R5-billion maintenance backlog which has amassed over the last 10 years. One of the main causes of maintenance neglect is that municipalities have chosen to use income from electricity to subsidise other municipal functions.

Transport

Havenga, in Chapter 9, suggests that a similar crisis awaits South Africa in the public transport system. This relates to the inordinately high levels of congestion on South Africa's roads, which are clogged up by privately owned passenger vehicles and freight trucks – all of this occurring alongside the neglect and under-utilisation of South Africa's public transport infrastructure, particularly rail. Although it is not yet part of explicit government policy, South Africa will have no other choice in the medium to long term but to bring about a paradigmatic shift from road- to rail-based passenger and freight transport modes, with an associated shift in the skills and technology base. As yet, no planning has gone into these eventualities.

South Africa's harbours are also functioning sub-optimally. Certain inefficiencies slow down transportation of goods through our ports, and increased utilisation stemming from the economic boom of recent years has increased congestion.

Skill and co-ordination challenges

Government's response to these two crises, first articulated in the Asgisa initiative launched in July 2005 but intensified by the power outages, has been to commit to a major capital investment initiative to build new electricity generation capacity and to improve public transportation, particularly rail and ports, over the next five years at a cost of several hundreds of billions of rand.

Eskom will require a massive injection of highly qualified personnel for it to succeed in this capital expansion programme. Some of the priority skills required include project managers, engineers, artisans, technicians, fossil and nuclear plant operators and technologists (Lomey & McNamara 2008).

With regard to transport, the expertise to build and maintain the new public infrastructure is dangerously depleted (Havenga 2008). Transnet has recently announced that it will need 13 846 skilled personnel in the next 5 years to underpin its growth strategy and ensure the successful rollout of its multi-billion rand capital investment programme. The state-owned enterprise will need 500 engineers, 1 500 technicians, 4 000 artisans, 100 managers, 500 specialists, 100 first-line managers and 7 146 operational staff skilled in rail, maritime and cargo transport (*Business Day* 27 August 2008). These are large numbers of skilled personnel required by only one of the several state-owned enterprises. Meeting these numbers on the supply side will be a huge challenge over the next five years.

Major turnaround in state support

Perhaps one of the most significant developments in the post-apartheid political and economic landscape has been the changing fortunes of the state-owned enterprises. In the period prior to political change in 1994, the apartheid regime sought to overcome political and economic pressures by reforming and reducing the role of the state in the market economy. In the late 1980s, it was decided that the state-owned enterprises should be commercialised to expose them to the competitive pressures of the free market system. These reforms began a decade-long process of restructuring and downsizing in all of the state-owned enterprises.

In the post-apartheid era, the market-led reforms begun under late apartheid were sustained and strengthened by the adoption of the Growth, Employment and Redistribution (GEAR) strategy in 1996 as the key framing mechanism for state involvement in the economy and labour market. Spurred on by GEAR's austerity measures to reduce the fiscal deficit, the democratic state cut back dramatically on investment in public infrastructure projects such as the maintenance and renewal of existing road, rail, port and telecommunications infrastructure (PCAS 2003). These cutbacks and restructuring efforts also affected the training functions of state-owned enterprises which at various points in their history had been considerable. What all of these downsizing measures signified was a dramatic shrinkage in the size and effectiveness of the state-guided external labour market in South Africa to produce technically trained artisans, technicians and engineers.

This is highly problematic, given that the state plays a crucial role as the lead producer and employer of high-skilled technological personnel. Smaller engineering firms, unable to train to the same extent, have always obtained their skilled workers through poaching from these state-owned enterprises. This is an important function of the state – to train in excess of its own needs so as to support the larger engineering value chain with which it interacts across several public infrastructure sectors. Du Toit and Roodt (2008) indicate that the state continued to employ almost one third (32 per cent) of all registered engineers, technicians and technologists in 2004. This figure would have been considerably higher prior to the process of public-sector downsizing and during the expansionist phase of grand-apartheid during the late 1960s and 1970s.

Downsizing was considered unproblematic for the new state until 2004, when it realised in its 10-year review of post-apartheid achievements (PCAS 2003) that the downsizing of state-owned enterprises was having the unintended consequence of depleting the stock of physical and human capital, particularly in energy and transport, but also in other spheres managed by the public sector such as water purification, distribution and preservation.

Because of these problems, government has now begun a dramatic turnaround of these rather austere circumstances. A massive financial injection (primarily through Asgisa) has been committed to rebuild energy and transport infrastructure and to re-endow the state-owned enterprises with their former human resource capabilities. Public-sector investment is planned to rise to around 8 per cent of GDP. Government and public-enterprise investment expenditure for the period April 2005 to March 2008 was planned to be about R370 billion. The main purpose of this new investment is to improve the availability and reliability of infrastructure services in response to rapidly growing demand (PCAS 2006: 5). This planned rate of growth of the capital budget of government – between 10 per cent and 15 per cent per year – is unprecedented in South African history.

What does all of this mean for the state-guided external labour market under discussion? In short, all of these dynamics suggest that major supply-side challenges need to be faced if these dual demands within this 'high-tech' labour market segment are to be met. Government will have to ensure the effective expansion of the production of skilled professionals and para-professionals on the supply side to meet the demands of its own interventions on the demand-side.

Segments 2 and 5: The 'flexible' external labour market

Discussion now turns to sectors governed by the 'flexible' external labour market. The flexible external labour market comprises two segments – what I have termed the 'top end' and 'bottom end'. The former comprises the high-professions and those high-skill jobs that have non-traditional forms of employment which are voluntarily agreed to by its beneficiaries. The latter category comprises all low-skill and insecure jobs that workers involuntarily agree to in the absence of more permanent employment. The discussion will now pursue these labour market dynamics in relation to two important components of the services industry: the creative industries and tourism.

Segment 2: Top-end jobs in the South African film industry

The case of the creative industries provides interesting evidence of some of the changing modes of high-skill work described above. The creative industries comprise several diverse sub-sectors. On the one hand, sub-sectors such as film and the formalised components of music and the performing and visual arts all comprise highly skilled jobs requiring higher education qualifications and additional practical training. On the other hand, a large component of the craft sub-sector falls more comfortably within the informal economy.

Joffe and Newton in Chapter 12 define the nature of work in the creative industries as comprising a set of knowledge-based economic activities which make intensive use of creativity as the primary input to produce marketable, value-added products and services. The outputs from the sector are tangible products or intangible services with creative content and economic value. Work in the creative industries is often 'project-based' as opposed to enterprise-located, and is often temporary (Joffe & Newton 2008).

The creative industries, including film, thus operate on a strong inter-personal, rather than intra- or inter-firm basis. This has a critical influence on the establishment of organisational structures, associations and representative bodies because those engaged in the projects are often individuals who are more loyal to their project, community or peers than to the firm. Knowledge interactions are thus intensely personal, and not based in the enterprise, making the creative industries 'people-' and not 'product-'centred. Reputation, and 'know-who', in the community are of critical importance, and more significant for success than 'know-what' and 'know-how' (Joffe & Newton 2008).

Joffe and Newton provide basic quantitative data on the size of the South African film industry, which had an annual turnover of R2.2 billion in 2003/04. The total number of commercials and feature films/television series made in 2003/04 was 570 and 46 respectively. The sector's estimated contribution to GDP was 2 per cent in 2003/04. Employment was estimated at 30 000 people.

The vision of the film sector is to be the leading producer of film and television content from Africa and the Middle East. South Africa has a comparative advantage in film, based on the size of the domestic film sector, which has grown in concert with the booming South African economy. South Africa also has the highest box office attendance levels of all its regional competitors. There is real growth in cinema, with South Africa one of only four countries in the world where this is the case. It also has the strongest growth in broadcasting and cable television segments, reaching over four million households in 2004 and growing consistently since 1987 (Joffe & Newton 2008).

The film industry has received growing support from government. For example, the establishment of the National Film and Video Foundation through an Act of Parliament in 1999 has aided the development of the industry. The focus of its work is to assist the industry to access finances through the National Lottery, private investors and international donors and to promote the industry through incentive schemes that attract international film productions.

Another support lever comes from the Customised Sector Programme (CSP) drawn up by the Department of Trade and Industry (DTI) in 2004 and the inclusion of the film sector in the Asgisa initiative. The DTI also offers a film production rebate to attract larger-budget film productions to the country and to increase the number of film producers under a co-production treatise. This, the DTI believes, will boost opportunities for employment in the film industry. The department allocated R225 million to this incentive over 3 years (Joffe & Newton 2008).

Education and training in the film industry

Human capability in the top-end flexible external labour market is acquired individually, both in terms of formal qualifications prior to entry into the labour market and also in terms of gaining diverse experience and know-how, once in the film sector. Such individuals are encouraged to acquire the widest possible set of experiences across a diverse range of film projects. These individuals then offer their diverse portfolios of experience for sale to the highest bidder at various key moments in their careers. This model of employment and career progression is obviously associated with high levels of labour market mobility, attrition and considerable poaching between competitor firms. Joffe and Newton confirm these trends in the South African film industry. Most people who obtain a job do so from the position of already having some work experience. Individual reputation and 'experience', according to these researchers, are the primary currencies in this sectoral labour market.

Two contradictory trends are apparent with regard to work in the creative industries: an increasing specialisation of job roles, especially for freelancers, and a need for 'magnificent generalists' – people with high-level skills and experience that cross boundaries (Joffe & Newton 2008). As a result, creative workers need to constantly update their specialist 'film' knowledge whilst keeping abreast of changes in such areas as government legislation (particularly copyright, data protection, health and safety, and contract law), and new technology (multimedia, digitisation, internet opportunities and sound, and lighting equipment).

Attributes of the labour market

Participation in the flexible external labour market, as occurs within the film sector, has specific attributes. Work is personalised and is focused on the creative 'project' and not the firm. Employment is seasonal, depending on the length of the project. The commodity produced and traded is the application of creative assets for commercial gain. It requires that entrants to the sector acquire formal education qualifications prior to entry, but also that they have experience of the sector and are multi-skilled – they can operate as film specialists but also as generalist managers with skills in overall project management. Work in the flexible labour market is a double-edged sword. On the one hand, it thrives on creativity, dynamism, energy and excitement. On the other, work is scarce and when it occurs, it is often highly stressful. Nonetheless, many of the creative talents who work in this sector choose these non-traditional employment lifestyles in preference to the perceived lack of stimulus in more permanent institutional employment.

Segment 5: Bottom-end jobs in South African tourism

Bottom-end jobs in tourism reflect many of the worst features of the new 'flexible' external labour market. This is true even though tourism is seen as an important component of South Africa's economic future. It has also been prioritised by Asgisa and government's new National Industrial Policy Framework (DTI, 2007).

Earle, in Chapter 15, confirms that growth has been impressive in the sector. It reached 13.9 per cent in 2005/06, a level of performance way ahead of the world average of 4.5 per cent and Africa's tourism growth rate of 8.1 per cent over the same period. Tourism's contribution to GDP has increased roughly threefold since 1994, reaching 8.8 per cent in 2005 at an estimated value of R97 billion. Government views tourism as having the potential to create over 400 000 direct and indirect jobs by 2014, although this figure is contested by Earle, who cites a more realistic projection of 284 000 new job opportunities.

The tourism sector is extensive, comprising several 'niche' areas. Although there are a few large companies that dominate part of the sector, the total industry comprises small family-owned businesses.

Recent estimates suggest a total of 28 000 hospitality enterprises, 6 200 travel and tourism services enterprises, and 3 500 conservation and tourist-guiding enterprises. Within all three sub-sectors, the proportion of small, medium and micro enterprises (SMMEs) is 97 per cent or more (Earle-Malleson 2008).

This predominance of SMMEs is a major constraint on growth and employment in the sector – contrary to the more orthodox economic logic about the job creation potential of SMMEs. The smallness and low profit margins of firms in tourism, combined with the fact that most are family-owned, makes transformation within the sector very difficult. Many of these enterprises are 'lifestyle' businesses with no desire to expand. Many operate as 'survivalist' small enterprises. There is therefore limited capacity to invest in the sector and affect change. New entrepreneurs entering the sector often fail due to lack of sector knowledge and the absence of marketing networks and channels (Earle-Malleson 2008). Other structural constraints on change in the sector include the fact that tourism is highly seasonal. In addition, the majority of jobs created by tourism are menial and low-paid and offer little chance of advancement and permanence.

A further problem for growth is the low levels of innovation in the sector. Innovation globally is based on brand differentiation – the provision of highly differentiated tourism experiences, for example, leisure tourism, business tourism, cultural tourism, eco-tourism, health tourism and adventure tourism. Innovative tourist destinations strive to differentiate themselves in respect of both marketing and product offerings. Brand differentiation is beginning to happen in South Africa, with growth in a variety of niche areas of tourism such as photography, food and wine, family, bird-watching, aviation, hiking, golfing and flowers. However, Earle-Malleson and other writers on the tourism sector highlight a number of factors that limit this innovation dynamic, including: limited levels of product and process innovation; a generally poor service delivery ethic compared with international competitor destinations; and a lack of strong, decisive and visionary leadership (Earle-Malleson 2008).

Skills development activities could be used to remedy some of these constraints. However, because of the family structure and the shaping of employment relations along familial lines, employment opportunities are often restricted to family insiders. As Moyle observes, 'for outsiders looking for a career in tourism, this family-based model provides a ceiling to progression beyond a certain level in any enterprise' (Moyle 2008: 539).

The affordability of skills development is also an issue for small firms. Training is also difficult because of the seasonal nature of work, especially in terms of employment on the lower rungs. However, the largest constraint on increases in training in the sector is the expectation amongst employers that they can recruit new employees who already have prior experience. They are reluctant to engage in any entry-level industry-specific training.

Moyle reports that at top-management level there is currently no severe shortage of qualified people. The skills gap is described in terms of 'experience' and is generally dealt with internally by the company's own managers. Family members may even fill in to cover these gaps. Foreigners are recruited by the larger companies. The implication of this approach is that innovation is limited and the potential for transformation at a senior level is curtailed. This undermines employment equity, as these jobs have historically been (and remain) 'white'.

The chronic skills shortage is at middle-management level. The skills in short supply are experience, vision, leadership and managerial skills. There is also a shortage of previously disadvantaged persons with the necessary experience at these levels. The gap is largely managed by poaching from other companies or fast-tracking internal employees – but seldom through extensive training (Moyle 2008: 531).

At the bottom end, vacancies are easily filled by lowly skilled new entrants from the external labour market. Earle-Malleson argues that the upside of this seasonal recruitment process is job creation and the resultant possibility of community upliftment. The downside, she maintains, is that employers recruit people looking for a job, but not necessarily interested in a career in tourism. There is a limited understanding of the 'business of service' amongst these recruits.

Progression is generally slow, and dependent largely on a good word put in by the employee's immediate superior rather than on increased levels of skill or qualification. It generally takes a junior employee five years to reach a supervisory level, and another twelve years to get to management level (Earle-Malleson 2008).

Typically, in the tourism sector, skills are thought of mostly in terms of personality types and experience, and not in terms of skill definitions and/or qualifications. The problem with this approach is that personality attributes are subjectively defined and hard to measure, and thus the industry believes it can only be evaluated in face-to-face situations. This undermines the possibility of creating a credible, transparent system of accreditation and qualification (Earle-Malleson 2008).

Earle argues that 'experience' rather than qualifications and skill are the key concerns in the industry. The widespread lack of generic skills across all occupations and levels is considered to be the most pressing skills-related problem. These generic skill gaps relate to communication and guest relations, in particular, but also to computer and IT skills for certain occupations.

In interviews with employers in the sector, Earle-Malleson notes that they regularly express a demand for a group of skills they struggle to define, but consider critical for the development of a culture of service excellence within the sector. These 'skills' include: being 'good with people', non-discrimination, tact, the ability to deliver information, enthusiasm, willingness to learn, productivity, reliability, conscientiousness, the willingness to go beyond the call of duty, punctuality, honesty, and presentability in both personal appearance and hygiene. These intangible factors, as well as overall levels of commitment to the sector, are considered by many employers to be lacking in employees and are seen as the reason underlying the lack of generic skills in guest relations and customer service (Earle-Malleson 2008).

According to Earle-Malleson, the large-scale provision of learnerships by the Sector Education and Training Authority (SETA) in the sector, the Tourism, Hospitality and Sport Education Training Authority (THETA), has not helped to resolve these problems. This has led to entry into the sector of unemployed learners whose personal attributes and non-enthusiasm for customer service do not lend themselves to successful outcomes in tourism, even after training. This problem is the result of the lack of other employment opportunities within the general labour market for these new entrants and the overly optimistic public positioning of the tourism sector as a job creator. This situation serves to attract a subset of people who are looking for a job, but not necessarily interested in the industry, and who have little motivation or passion to serve with excellence (Earle-Malleson 2008; Moyle 2008).

In a recent review of the training of unemployed workers destined for the tourism industry, Marock (2007) shows how the rapid rollout of this training that ensued after June 2003 provided huge opportunities for training providers to offer programmes for unemployed learners. Marock describes the environment on the supply side during this period, with providers scrambling to find trainees to fill classrooms to justify training programmes, which of course earned them significant revenues. Marock suggests that the impetus for a specific learnership programme may not have arisen because of demand-led signals from the sector, but rather from training providers who had a service to sell. She also describes some of the problematic behaviour amongst learners, who programme-hopped from one learnership to the next, desperate in their search for employment, but without much prior interest having been established or career counselling offered by the training providers (Marock 2007).

Segment overview

Employment in the tourism sector is characterised by low-skill, impermanent jobs with low volumes of training. A primary constraint on training is the structure of the industry itself – large numbers of white family-owned small firms that promote and appoint from within the family structure, or through poaching from other firms. These are non-innovative firms that pursue lifestyle or survivalist strategies in the sector. They do not consciously seek to grow employment or up-skill their workforces. This family factor restricts improvements in management and leadership styles within the sector, inhibiting the cross-pollination which would otherwise arise in a more mobile and dynamic labour market. At lower levels of the occupational structure, work is seasonal and low-skill. New recruits who enter the sector through learnerships do not possess the appropriate 'attitudinal' or 'soft-skill' dispositions to contribute to better service delivery. Attrition rates amongst low-skill newcomers are high. In short, the tourism sector, under these 'low-skill regime' conditions, is unlikely to fulfil the aspirations of government to have it act as a panacea for mass unemployment, particularly in the rural areas where unemployment is rife.

Segment 3: The high value-adding internal labour market

A key characteristic of the 'high value-adding internal labour market' is that the procurement and development of human capabilities is focused internally, largely through intensive training activities within the firm and through the reorganisation of work to maximise incremental improvements in the production process. This mode of provision also stands in sharp contrast to the state-guided external labour market discussed earlier, where high-skill labour (specialists in various advanced sciences) is procured externally by state-owned enterprises or high-tech sectors through government's deliberate construction of education and training pathways.

Knowledge generation in Segment 3 is derived internally through the strengthening of the tacit knowledge of workers and through the upgrading of the firm's dynamic capabilities. These design, engineering, entrepreneurial and management (DEEM) functions are crucial components of internal labour markets because they provide a continuous stream of incremental innovation that has a positive impact on productivity and profitability. Kaplinsky and Morris (2001) argue that it is the incremental pursuits up the value chain towards more knowledge-intensive activities that are the most rewarding, as they command the highest economic returns. Knowledge-intensive activities such as improved design, quality and product differentiation become important for access to high-income export markets. It is these activities which distinguish products from those in intermediate- and low-income markets where competition is based on mass production, lower costs and relatively standardised goods. The transition to higher knowledge intensity is derived internally, through the up-scaling of the entire production process, including human capital development, the application of new technologies and work reorganisation.

Two South African sectors will now be reviewed whose labour market conditions are best described by Segment 3. These are the 'wood, paper and pulp' and 'motor vehicle and component manufacturing' (auto) sectors. These industries can be clearly distinguished from the other sectors reviewed in this book along a number of key axes. Most importantly, they compete on global markets and are part of global value chains. They are dominated by large firms that have invested significantly in modern technologies. Production processes are highly capital-intensive. In both sectors, employer agencies and associations (often in association with regional governments) play important roles in collaboratively providing key resources needed by the sectors, including R&D and skills development. Links with education and training providers are seen as an important complement to in-house training. And in both cases, the successes on global markets achieved so far are extremely fragile, dependent, firstly, on the need to continuously upgrade internal capabilities to meet increasingly stringent global quality standards, and secondly, on the vagaries of the exchange rate and current account deficit.

Wood, paper and pulp

The wood, paper and pulp sector is one of the success stories of post-apartheid South Africa. Prior to the advent of democracy in 1994, the industry was inward-looking, focusing on domestic markets. Following the opening up of the South African economy to global markets after 1994, the sector has rapidly transformed into a significant global player under the leadership of its two primary producers, Mondi and Sappi.

According to Pogue, in Chapter 7, the sector has a number of distinctive characteristics. The first is the high degree of vertical integration along the entire value chain. Large plantation owners are also significant secondary producers of timber products. This is evident with Mondi and Sappi in pulp and paper, PG Bison in fibreboard, and York and Hans Merensky in sawn timber. The market for plantation forestry is therefore strongly linked with the downstream processing sector.

The sector has been highly successful in two areas of export: firstly, paper and pulp products, and secondly, wood chips. The pulp milling sector is highly integrated, with high barriers to entry because of high plant costs. Wood chipping is an initial stage in the pulping process, but these chip mills exist as separate production units for the export market. This sub-sector developed independently of the small number of large firms dominating forestry and paper and pulp. The wood chip sub-sector began to grow after the opening up of access to global markets in 1994. The sub-sector has now become a significant source of foreign exchange earnings, generating nominal export income of R2.14 billion in 2005 (Pogue 2008).

These gains, however, are extremely vulnerable to fluctuations in the exchange rate and increases in imported goods (which have grown since the economic boom of 2001). As a consequence of these vulnerabilities, there has been a declining balance of trade in paper and pulp since 2002. The case with furniture manufacturing is similar. Many of the small, medium and micro manufacturers operating within the furniture industry have succeeded on export markets, but imports of wood furniture continue to outstrip exports by a significant margin.

Notwithstanding the high levels of importation of wood furniture, paper products and sawn timber, the sector has clearly been transformed since 1994 and has become a globally competitive player. Part of its success has involved significant levels of in-house training and a strong emphasis on linkages with further and higher education providers. A good example of its training commitment is the South African Forestry Training College (SAFTC), a private training initiative undertaken by employers in the forestry sector. The college offers over 200 courses to users across the country on diverse topics such as management, health and safety, fire-fighting, silviculture, harvesting, and the operation of extraction equipment (Pogue 2008).

In addition to these enterprise training initiatives, the sector has evolved several close links with education providers. Five higher education institutions provide dedicated forestry qualifications. The most innovative of these is an e-learning initiative drawn up in response to the emergence of several under-qualified forestry sub-contractors in the industry in the 1990s. The initiative comprises the South African Forestry Contractors Association (SAFCA), Forestry South Africa (FSA), and the Forest Industry Education and Training Authority (FIETA) and two universities – Stellenbosch and Nelson

Mandela Metropolitan. This collaborative initiative combines distance learning with hands-on training tailored to contractors' needs in priority areas like forest engineering, business skills and machine costing (Pogue 2008).

Similarly, in the primary processing sub-sector, the South African Lumber Millers Association has taken the initiative by establishing five learnerships in primary processing. In paper and pulp, there are currently seven learnerships registered. Mondi and Sappi are the primary providers of training in paper and pulp, using several in-house training centres. Over 1 000 learners are enrolled and 450 graduates produced by these in-house facilities annually (Pogue 2008).

The sector has also been very proactive with regard to R&D activity, through the establishment of the Tree Protection Co-operative Programme and the Forestry and Agriculture Biotechnology Institute (FABI), both located at the University of Pretoria. These multi-disciplinary research programmes are aimed at controlling tree diseases and, through cloning and DNA biotechnology research, supporting initiatives that pre-empt the spread of pathogens via the cultivation of trees that are resistant to pests and pathogens (Klerck 2006: 22). Pogue indicates that two national research councils, the CSIR and the Agricultural Research Council (ARC), also generate forestry-related research. In addition, Stellenbosch University's Department of Forestry and Wood Science also conducts a variety of research for the forestry sector. The University of KwaZulu-Natal hosts the Institute for Commercial Forestry Research.

There is clearly a strong alignment between education and the skill needs of the wood, paper and pulp sector. Industry, led by the highly capital-intensive large firms that dominate the sector, has set up several industry initiatives in co-operation with education and training institutions. The sector has participated in the National Skills Development Strategy and has implemented several learnerships across the various components of the industry value chain. Paper and pulp as well as wood chip products have reached world class manufacturing standards and are being successfully exported.

The auto sector

Another South African success story has been the 'vehicle and component manufacturing' (auto) sector. According to Barnes, in Chapter 2, South Africa presently ranks nineteenth among the world's vehicle-producing nations – holding a 0.79 per cent market share of global vehicle production and recently securing growth rates ahead of China. By far the largest vehicle manufacturer in Africa, South Africa produced 525 271 units in 2005, while Egypt, the continent's second-largest producer, manufactured a mere 69 223 units. The South African automotive industry's sales, as well as indicators relating to export, employment and capital investment, all reflect robust recent performance, as well as an increasing contribution to the domestic economy (Barnes 2008).

The auto industry is the largest component of the South African manufacturing sector, accounting for approximately 28 per cent of national manufacturing output and 7.4 per cent of South African GDP in 2005, which was exceeded only by the mining and financial sectors. Furthermore, productivity has improved rapidly, and there is considerable evidence of improvement in a range of benchmarks such as quality, reliability and operational shop-floor efficiency (Barnes 2008).

Barnes provides several indices of improved efficiencies in the auto sector and its successful transition to world-class manufacturing. One such index is the average number of vehicles produced per platform, which has increased from 10 745 units to 22 594 units. Similarly, the average number of vehicles produced per employee at South African car plants increased from 11 in 2000 to 15.3 in 2005 (Barnes 2008).

It is clear that the success of this high-tech sector lies in (i) increasing economies of scale, and (ii) increases in the productivity of its workforce, as measured by the above benchmarks. Achieving these benchmarks has required high levels of the DEEM characteristics described earlier. They serve as necessary prerequisites in the transition to world-class manufacturing.

A range of programmes has been initiated to support skills development in the sector. For example, the Automotive Industry Development Centre (AIDC) has a mandate to further the skills development and training delivery for the local automotive industry. Currently, the AIDC has a strong partnership with the Nelson Mandela Metropolitan University (NMMU), a public 'comprehensive' university based in Port Elizabeth that has an automotive orientation in its various offerings. NMMU boasts a number of industry-supporting research centres, which have the stated aims of promoting technology transfer and innovation institutions, including the Institute for Advanced Manufacturing and Engineering Research, the Automotive Components Technology Station, the Manufacturing Technology Research Centre and the Advanced Mechatronics Technology Centre (Barnes 2008).

As part of the Blue IQ initiative of the Gauteng government, a number of Gauteng-based higher education institutions have provided substantial support to the auto sector. They includes Tshwane University of Technology (TUT) which hosts mechatronics facilities that have proven useful to the local automotive industry. Similar university-industry linkages have been established in the Durban automobile cluster.

Notwithstanding these successes, Barnes remains sceptical of progress made in the sector, arguing that only the upper tier of South African component suppliers operates at levels that are close to the global frontier. However, in other parts of the sector, performance is not as impressive. For example, in the components supplier domain, South African firms have not predominated, surrendering key supply chain functions to foreign-owned firms with connections to the original equipment manufacturers (Barnes 2008). This extensive foreign ownership of vehicle assemblers and components manufacturers, as well as the close links developed with parent companies, has helped the industry integrate into international markets. Furthermore, this growing global connectivity has undoubtedly facilitated technology and skill transfers, as well as other positive spill-overs. But Barnes maintains that there are drawbacks to these achievements. South African firms have not been at the core of this activity, nor have they benefited to the same extent from the spill-over effects.

One indicator of this under-performance by South African firms is their insufficient investment in enterprise training. Although training levels in the auto sector are much higher than those in other South African sectors, South African auto firms still spend far less on training than multinational corporations in South Africa and in competitor countries. Multinational corporations based in South Africa have invested more on training than locally owned firms. In 2006, multinationals were investing 2.1 per cent of payroll, with local firms trailing closely behind at 1.7 per cent. Similar scores are also evident in comparisons relating to R&D expenditure (Barnes 2008).

Barnes is also negative about the quality of courses offered by public further education and training and higher education institutions. He argues that there is a clear perception amongst auto firms that skills supply into the industry has deteriorated rather than improved over the last few years. Employers view certain higher education institutions poorly, as institutions from whom they would not source key technical staff.

Segment overview

The auto sector is by far the most successful component of South African manufacturing. It is globally competitive, participates in global value chains and exports to several international destinations. To maintain this status, the sector needs to achieve extremely high quality standards. These standards are only met through the establishment of internal labour market conditions that seek to strengthen and enhance workers' tacit knowledge and know-how on the factory floor.

The 'high value-adding' fit here between sector and labour market segment, then, is only partial and not optimal. The ideal-type labour market categories described earlier are seldom achieved in reality, 'on the ground'. In both the cases of the 'wood, paper and pulp' and auto sectors, the ideal-type conditions of high-skills, training-intensive internal labour markets are imperfectly met, with training rates well below international averages, and questionable quality of provision in some cases – for example, the poor quality of component suppliers and further education and training college providers, in the case of the auto sector. Participation in global value chains and global markets are therefore not permanently assured. High levels of importation weaken industry conditions and threaten the attainment of the ideal-type labour market conditions even further.

Segment 4: The low value-adding internal labour market

The final category of labour market to be discussed is Segment 4: the 'low-value-adding internal labour market'. This segment is defined primarily by two inter-related characteristics: firstly, the low levels of secondary beneficiation which have been achieved in these sectors to date; and secondly, the weakly evolved internal labour market mechanisms. These include low levels of training and minimal forms of inter-firm co-operation which limit the advancement of firm capabilities and the acquisition of improved sector 'know-how'. South African industries characteristic of this segment are the 'metals' and 'clothing' sectors.

The metals sector

According to Maree et al. (Chapter 5), the metals sector has a complex four-phase value chain which starts at the primary stage of mining and concludes with the beneficiation and manufacturing of finished metal products. The structure of the industry varies considerably across these four various stages of the value chain. For example, during the second stage, the production of intermediate goods usually takes place in capital- and energy-intensive smelters and refineries. This phase is referred to as the 'milling' stage. Milling firms in South Africa are chiefly involved in the production of pig iron and the conversion of pig iron into a range of wrought iron and steel materials (Maree et al. 2008).

Stage 3 transforms an intermediate good into a refined, semi-fabricated product suitable for use by both small and sophisticated enterprises. This stage of transformation takes place in blast furnaces and foundries using heat-treating and/or cold-finishing processes.

The foundry industry plays a vital role in the wider South African economy beyond its crucial contribution to the metals sector. This is because it provides critical inputs to most other manufacturing sectors, with mining, automotive and general engineering being the largest industries it supplies. For example, approximately 50 per cent of South Africa's casting production comprises components destined for the automotive industry.

Stage 4 transforms the processed metal even further into finished products of a large variety. Of particular importance are the machine builders who source parts and components from engineering and machine shops, and control systems from electrical and electronics firms (Maree et al. 2008).

As a consequence of all these divergent sub-sectors, the metals industry as a whole has a very hybrid structure, dominated on the one hand by a few large firms (mainly milling and a few large foundries), alongside several hundred smaller firms (foundries and engineering shops). Key features of the large milling firms are: dominance of this grouping by multinational corporations, capital-intensive production methods, reduced labour forces and growing export volumes. In contrast, the bulk of the foundry and engineering shops are small, characterised by short batches of products, some of them entailing complex casting and tooling and requiring highly skilled artisans and technicians with significant experience. Markets for these products are primarily local.

Beneficiation

The defining feature of the sector, however, is its low levels of beneficiation and exportation. Exports that do occur are essentially basic metals which have reached Stage 2 of the value chain. Progression further down the chain is limited in large part by the high import parity pricing of upstream metals producers, which has damaging consequences for downstream beneficiation. Occurring alongside these problems over the past two decades has been a dramatic contraction in the number of metal foundries in South Africa. Numbers shrank from 450 in the mid-1980s to just over 200 in 2003. The industry is very small compared to its global competitors (Maree et al. 2008).

Another factor in the failure to beneficiate is the weakness of inter-firm relations and the absence of cluster and network initiatives started either by firms themselves or through government facilitation. Internationally, clusters assist individual firms in developing niche capabilities and drawing on shared services, including technical and design services, skills development and the use of joint R&D facilities. The absence of these intra-industry ventures acts to rob small engineering and machine shops of the tacit learning and technological transfers that arise between firms participating in co-operative activity along the value chain.

A partial transition to world-class manufacturing

The picture in the metals sector is not entirely bleak. Maree et al. maintain that there has been a partial transition to world-class manufacturing amongst a small number of leading firms in the sector. The key factors in their success appear to be highly competent technical management teams that ensure that these firms are able to operate flexibly and harness skills needed to penetrate niche markets and win export contracts. These firms are usually run by skilled engineers who have consciously sought to establish strategic alliances with larger firms, often benefiting in the process from technological transfers as well as improved management systems.

Clothing

The clothing sector in South Africa is characterised by an 'archetypal' low value-adding, poorly performing internal labour market. This arises, in part, because the clothing sector is a buyer-driven value chain, dominated by the leading retailers in the sector, which set the specifications and standards for the merchandise to be produced and sold in the domestic sector. Production is generally carried out by tiered networks of contractors that make finished goods for these retailers, who buy in bulk (Kaplinsky & Morris, 2001: 32–33). If the industry has been low value-adding historically, it can be locked into this trajectory by the retailers, who will source high-quality garments on export markets.

However, the South African clothing sector faces additional constraints beyond the powerful grip of retailers. These include its severe vulnerability to exchange-rate fluctuations. Morris and Reed, in Chapter 10, illustrate this problem by recalling the currency crisis of 2001 which led to a dramatic devaluation of the rand. Local clothing manufacturers saw the devaluation as an opportunity to export to the USA (Morris & Reed 2008). However, the subsequent strengthening of the rand after 2003 turned the entire scenario around. According to Morris and Reed, this both created easier access to domestic markets for global competitors and simultaneously hampered the efforts of domestic producers to consolidate their position in export markets. In addition, the appreciating exchange rate and the economic boom afforded retailers greater buying power in international markets. All of these developments radically limited the capacity of domestic manufacturers to export. Exports dropped dramatically, and local manufacturers tried desperately to return to their previous customers, the domestic retail chains. However, 'the restructuring of the domestic value chain had taken a radical turn. Large-scale imports of clothing from China had become the order of the day' (Morris & Reed 2008).

Morris and Reed maintain that there have been two primary responses to the crisis facing clothing manufacturing in South Africa. The first, amongst a minority of clothing producers, has been to shift production up the value chain towards greater differentiation of brands and higher-quality, higher-priced merchandise. This has entailed significant technological upgrading of production capabilities to meet world-class manufacturing standards. However, this shift has not happened on a wide enough scale. This is because such a shift requires significant investment in capital, technology, innovation and skills. Employers have been unwilling to make these commitments. Morris and Reed argue that because of the negative perceptions of the industry, investments in new plant and machinery have not been forthcoming.

A second reaction – the dominant response to the crisis – has been to outsource through sub-contracting and informalisation to 'cut-make-and-trim' (CMT) enterprises providing production services at lower costs, due to lower overhead structures. In addition, formal factory downsizing and closure have resulted in the establishment of hundreds of micro enterprises, home industries and unregistered firms causing an increase in the number of people employed in the informal sector (Morris & Reed 2008).

Sixty per cent of firms interviewed by Morris and Reed reported that they were side-stepping shortages of machining staff by outsourcing an increasing portion of their production requirement to CMTs. This strategy involved hiving off non-complex, cost-based garments to the CMTs, whilst maintaining the complex activities and higher-quality brands in-house. The flexibility assured by the strategy is regarded by insiders in the industry as 'key to their future survival in a shrinking market, since it permits expansion and contraction of the workforce in tandem with market fluctuation' (Morris & Reed 2008).

Skills shortages plague the sector and are unresolved because of the low levels of enterprise training. Shortages are most acute with regard to skilled machinists – a category of labour regarded as the 'engine room' of the clothing business. Most firms interviewed by Morris and Reed reported that this shortage represented the single most binding constraint on their ability to grow.

Even though shortages of key operative and artisan staff are evident, training levels have remained extremely low in the sector. For example, only 88 apprentices were indentured in the combined clothing and textiles sector in the four-year period between April 2001 and March 2005. This is a rate of 22 apprentices for the entire sector per annum. This is hopelessly inadequate if the sector is to address its current skills shortages.

Higher-level technical and production management skills are also key components of the DEEM capabilities discussed earlier that should be obtained within enterprises through the effective building of internal labour markets. But in the South African clothing industry, these intermediate to high skills are also in short supply. For example, computer-aided design and manufacturing (CAD and CAM) specialists, who are instrumental in ensuring that all computerised production systems run efficiently, are in short supply. As more of these automated production systems come on line as part of efforts to upgrade technical capabilities, so these CAD and CAM shortages will become more acute. Yet, according to

Morris and Reed, South Africa's higher education institutions produce very small numbers of CAD and CAM graduates, and those that do emerge from the system are of dubious quality.

There are three higher education institutions that support the development of DEEM capabilities in the clothing sector. These are Durban University of Technology, Cape Peninsula University of Technology, and the University of Johannesburg. These institutions offer a range of courses in technology and clothing management leading to a BTech degree. However, what is lacking, according to Morris and Reed, are specialised courses in production engineering which would assist in the upgrading of technical capabilities in the sector.

National diplomas in Clothing Management and Textiles Technology can be obtained from the Cape Peninsula University of Technology, Durban University of Technology and the University of Johannesburg. These courses are supported by the Clothing and Textiles SETA. However, between 2000 and 2005, only 216 graduates completed the Diploma in Clothing Management and a further 6 completed a BTech degree in Clothing Management. This translates into an average of 37 graduates per annum over a six-year period. According to the SETA's own forecasts, these institutions should be supplying at least 67 graduates per annum. This is a serious supply-side deficit.

The problem is not merely quantitative, but also qualitative. Morris and Reed are critical of the qualifications and relevance of university of technology courses. They do not promote world class manufacturing standards which envisage a technologist function as that which surpasses one of mere quality assurance and encompasses an understanding of the entire value chain. The industry view is that universities of technology are basing their curriculum on the old methodology, not on the principles of world-class manufacturing.

The clothing sector in South Africa represents a classic example of a poorly functioning internal labour market characterised by a neglect of training and minimal investments in the upgrading of technology. Employers continue to cling to antiquated methods of production that serve a low-cost, low-quality local market. The failure to make the shift to world-class manufacturing leaves the sector highly vulnerable to the onslaught from powerful competitor nations such as China.

Conclusion

There are a number of issues that arise out of the discussion in this chapter. Firstly, the conceptual device developed, of several labour market segments cohabiting within one sector or one national economy, presents an important critique of traditional segmented labour market theory and the more recent 'varieties of capitalism' and 'high-skills' literatures. Much of this literature provides accounts of cross-national variants in economic and labour market structure – for example, the occupational labour market model of Germany versus the internal labour market model of Japan (Brown et al. 2001; Coriat & Weinstein 2004). However, this work provides little if any account of how these labour market and sectoral production regime variations co-exist within a single national economy. This is a serious flaw in the leading theoretical models, which tend to aggregate single ideal-types (such as the internal labour market model) across entire national economies and societies (for example, Japan).

In so doing, they miss the unevenness of development across sectors and within sectors. They fail to provide accounts of how several labour market segments operate simultaneously in channelling different skills and trained personnel to different parts of the same economic sector. A complex sector, for example, the metals industry, is not reliant on a single labour market structure (in this instance, the internal labour market) to meet all of its skill needs. Rather, the sector draws highly skilled professionals such as engineers and metallurgists from the top-end 'flexible' external market (Segment 2 in Figure

16.1), whilst it outsources non-core, low-skill activities such as maintenance and security to small firms in the bottom-end flexible labour market (Segment 5). These processes occur simultaneously alongside the predominant skills regimes in the metal sector, which are enterprise-based activities best characterised by the internal labour market model. The co-existence of these diverse labour market segments within one sector (and one national economy) is missed in much of the international literature.

Implications for South Africa

In addition to these theoretical advances, the analysis developed here carries several important implications for South Africa. Most importantly, because sectors are so unevenly developed, they require differentiated policies that are highly customised to sectoral needs. The characteristics of the five labour market segments discussed above, which govern the employment and skilling of workers employed in South Africa's formal economy, provide a useful start to understanding this customisation process.

Segment 1: The 'state-guided external labour market'

Each segment represents a very different set of production and employment requirements. For example, sectors governed by the state-guided external labour market (aerospace, nuclear energy and space science) will require far greater commitments from government – both financial and political – if these sectors are to succeed with their ambitious high-science objectives. Brown et al. (2001) have characterised the Singapore economy as the best exemplar of a 'state-guided' high-skills society. This has been achieved through the strong steering efforts of the state in certain key interventions in the economy, including science and technology. The Singapore Economic Development Board has been the primary instrument for achieving these goals. Its functions are to co-ordinate economic and industrial policy, offer incentives to guide foreign investors into targeted activities, promote education and training in fields demanded by the economy, and in general, 'mastermind industrial policy'. It played an important role in launching and promoting certain activities which the private sector would not otherwise have entered into, acting as a catalyst for increased investment (Brown et al. 2001: 183–184).

This is what is needed in South Africa in these new industrial niche areas, but the South African state's efforts in this regard compare poorly with those of Singapore. If they are to have any chance of success they will require far larger investments from the South African state, but also more effective co-ordination across the multitude of state departments involved in these high-science developments: Science and Technology, Minerals and Energy, Treasury, Defence, Trade and Industry, and Education and Labour. Currently, the level of inter-governmental co-ordination and co-operation is minimal.

More determined efforts will be required to produce the high skills required in Segment 1. Structured labour market arrangements will be needed to grow the number of engineers, artisans and scientists required to make these initiatives a success. The role of the state-owned enterprises will be pivotal in this regard.

Segment 2: The 'top-end flexible external labour market'

A vibrant top-end flexible external labour market has emerged in South Africa, not only in the film industry as reviewed above, but also in other key sectors such as ICT, financial services and even in high-tech micro enterprise sectors such as 'consultant engineering'. These sectors display many of the forms of non-traditional flexible employment described above. Most importantly, these sectors thrive because of the individualistic 'entrepreneurial culture' which is encouraged in this labour market. These strengths are an asset to our economy.

However, these same flexible conditions of employment represent a risk in other sectors that are more vulnerable to the impermanent forms of employment which they encourage. The entire set of top-end jobs in the creative industries is at risk through this impermanence, because these individualistic labour market conditions do not act to sustain social sectors, like music and the arts, over the long term. Joffe and Newton in Chapter 12 warn of the decline in the number of graduates emerging from the universities and colleges in these fields. This is occurring because of reductions in funding for these social sectors, a consequence of the push for increased enrolments in the commercial and technological sciences. In other parts of the world, the creative arts are sustained through significant state support and intervention – as is the case in Cuba but also in some of the Scandinavian and continental European countries. In other contexts, the creative industries are being viewed as a major trigger for growth and are receiving significant state support. In similar vein, the South African state will need to vigorously pursue the industrial policies which it has already designed that seek to support these sectors and transform them into major generators of employment and growth – as an important counter to the destructive side of the flexible labour market.

Segment 3: The 'high value-adding internal labour market'

The high value-adding internal labour market operates in the more successful corners of the South African economy. Mature industries such as the auto and wood, paper and pulp sectors already engage in world-class manufacturing and compete in global markets. The challenge for employers here, and for government which must support their further growth, is to deepen even further the pursuit of knowledge-intensive methods of production through greater inter-firm co-operation and through network and cluster development. It will also entail more intensive forms of enterprise learning and training, technological upgrading and technology transfer – the 'extended' internal labour market needs to be strengthened. To achieve these goals will require that industrial, skills and small business development policies all work in concert with one another. Policy alignment is the critical next step. Intermediary agencies working in these sectors – such as the SETAs – need to operate from the basis of possessing sector-specific expertise. They need to have 'situated knowledge' of how to take these advanced sectors several steps further along their development pathway. Unfortunately, the SETAs and small business development agencies are not yet ready to play these roles.

Segment 4: The 'low value-adding internal labour market'

Much of South Africa's traditional manufacturing sector is best characterised by the low value-adding internal labour market. This chapter has only reviewed the clothing and metals sectors but the problems described are more widespread and spread across other sectors as well (see, for example, the discussions of the chemicals sector in Chapter 6 and agro-processing in Chapter 11 of this book). The main challenge, then, is to increase the beneficiation of natural resources, move towards more knowledge-intensive activities where the rents accrued are far higher and, in so doing, diversify into export markets. This will require major commitments from employers and the state to increase training levels, invest in new plant and capital equipment, and change social relations within firms (upgrade the knowledge base) and between firms (strengthen linkages along the value chain). Government has begun this process at the policy level with the release of the National Industrial Policy Framework in July 2007. But its capacity and political will to implement and finance these ambitious plans is open to question. The commitment of business in this regard is also in doubt. From the point of view of a 'skills regime', very elementary processes still need to be put in place, like a basic commitment from employers to train workers and modernise technologies.

Segments 5 and 6: The low-skill ghettoes

Another policy challenge facing Segments 5 and 6 – the low-skill ghettoes of South African society – is to trigger sustainable economic activity that is labour-intensive and requires largely low-skill inputs. South Africa's success stories so far are in sectors which are capital-intensive and high-skill, like auto and wood, paper and pulp. The biggest economic policy challenge facing a future South Africa is to create growth and employment outside of these success stories. The sector reviews published in this book do not suggest easy solutions to this challenge, but there are important hints for sectors which have the potential to grow in low-skill, labour-intensive directions. All of these possibilities would require significant state sponsorship and steering – a development strategy which is depicted in Figure 16.1 as Segment 6.

The wood, paper and pulp sector in fact offers such potential. The possibility of significantly increased employment exists in three areas in the wood, paper and pulp sector: (i) afforestation efforts in the Eastern Cape and KwaZulu-Natal; (ii) bush-mills in both provinces; and (iii) paper recycling across the economy. With regard to the first possibility, there are already 24 000 emerging plantation farmers in the Eastern Cape and KwaZulu-Natal. There is also an estimated need to replant forests across 100 000 hectares of land if South Africa's forest resources are to be sustained over the long term. However, government's support policies to grow this sector have been ineffectual and little progress has been made, even though tens of thousands of jobs could be created. For the initiative to succeed, low-skill community foresters will need proper training and extension support to empower them to become commercially viable (see Pogue, Chapter 7).

Similarly with bush-mills and paper recycling. Bush-mills are a key form of low-skill, informal-sector activity. A dynamic initiative was launched by government in 2002 to enhance the efficiency of these small-scale sawmills which comprise about 700 firms nationally. Despite the piloting efforts of this initiative, nothing permanent was launched and the potential of the bush-mills industry remains unexploited.

Informal paper recyclers form a large base that often supports and contains bridges to formal-sector paper recycling. While state waste management policy appears to support future growth in paper recycling, there has been no clear strategy or policy designed to enhance the skills of informal recyclers, although existing paper recyclers would benefit greatly from training in basic business skills and equipment costing skills (see Pogue, Chapter 7). In short, government's policy efforts to promote low-skill, labour-intensive employment – the state strategy depicted in Segment 6 – appears to be ad hoc, short-term and terminal. There has been no major sector-based industrial and skills development policy initiative of any significant scale or endurance that has successfully sought to grow employment and create bridges between the informal and formal economies. Without growth in new jobs in low-skill sectors, workers in these low-skill labour markets are highly vulnerable to continuing low-wage and insecure employment and to unemployment.

Implications for skills development policy

It is clear from this discussion that the current 'one-size-fits-all' skills development policy of government – particularly in the form of the National Skills Development Strategy – is inappropriate, given South Africa's highly differentiated economy and labour market structure. Skills development practitioners operating in one sector will face conditions very different to those faced by colleagues in other sectors. Even within a single sector, conditions may vary widely as different labour market modes of skills provision cohabit. Practitioners will need to understand the production regime underpinning that sector, and be able to identify which labour market mode is the primary mechanism for skills acquisition and which are secondary and of lesser significance. Operating at this level of sectoral complexity will require a degree of 'situated knowledge' that does not yet exist in South Africa's skills development agencies, the SETAs. As a consequence, a greater alignment between sectoral conditions and skills development policy will need to be a necessary pre-condition for any future restructuring of South Africa's skills development architecture.

The challenges are not merely those of policy. The key role-players – the state and private-sector employers – need to amplify their efforts regarding skills formation across South Africa's diverse economic sectors. The state faces two major challenges. Firstly, it needs to massively expand its role in developing the new high-skills, science-based sectors reviewed in this book. Secondly, it needs to commit major resources to creating a more effective low-skills, labour-intensive development strategy which can provide employment and sustainable livelihoods to the millions of under- and unemployed citizens.

Employers also need to amplify their efforts on at least three fronts. Firstly, those sectors already participating in global markets – such as auto and wood, paper and pulp – need to consolidate their gains through further technological upgrading, human capital formation and the strengthening of knowledge networks and inter-firm co-operation along global supply chains. Secondly, sectors which have not succeeded in entering export markets and which remain complacent within local markets – such as the clothing and metals sectors – need to dramatically restructure production operations in South Africa so as to become globally competitive in the future. State science, technology and industrial policies need to encourage and facilitate this transformation. If they fail, global competition from China and other competitor nations will decimate what is left of these indigenous industries.

And lastly, deficits within flexible external labour markets – such as the current shortages of high-skill personnel in key professions such as accounting, engineering and project management – require creative solutions from the state and employers. Flexible labour markets will not solve these problems on their own. The state must create structured pathways between education providers and these professions with the aim of closing the supply gap in these critical fields.

A single National Skills Development Strategy will not be able to achieve all of these highly differentiated tasks within one national framework. Greater customisation will be needed so that specific skills strategies talk to the actual conditions operative in each sector.

References

Barnes J (2008) Automotive components. Report commissioned by the Department of Labour for the Sector skills research project. Pretoria: HSRC

Brown P, Green A & Lauder H (2001) *High skills, globalisation, competitiveness and skill formation*. Oxford: Oxford University Press

Camuffo, A (2002) The changing nature of internal labor markets. *Journal of Management & Governance* 6(4): 281–294

Carnoy M, Castells M & Benner C (1997) Labour markets and employment practices in the age of flexibility: A case-study of Silicon Valley. *International Labour Review* 136(1): 27–48

Coriat B & Weinstein O (2004) National institutional frameworks, institutional complementarities and sectoral systems of innovation. In F Malerba (ed.) *Sectoral systems of innovation: Concepts, issues and analyses of six major sectors in Europe*. Cambridge: Cambridge University Press

Doeringer PB & Piore MJ (1971) *Internal labour markets and manpower analysis*. Lexington: DC Heath

DTI (Department of Trade and Industry, South Africa) (2007) *A National Industrial Policy Framework*. Pretoria: DTI

Du Toit R & Roodt J (2008) Engineering professionals: Crucial key to development and growth in South Africa. Report commissioned by the Department of Labour for the Sector skills research project. Pretoria: HSRC

Earle-Malleson N (2008) Tourism. Final report commissioned by the Department of Labour for the Sector skills research project. Pretoria: HSRC

Edwards R, Reich M & Gordon D (1973) *Labour market segmentation*. Lexington: DC Heath

Fine B (1998) *Labour market theory: A constructive reassessment*. London: Routledge

Grimshaw D, Ward KG, Rubery J & Beynon H (2001) Organisations and the transformation of the internal labour market. *Work, Employment and Society* 15: 25–54

Havenga J (2008) Transport. Final report commissioned by the Department of Labour for the Sector skills research project. Pretoria: HSRC Press

Joffe A & Newton M (2008) Creative industries. Final report commissioned by the Department of Labour for the Sector skills research project. Pretoria: HSRC

Kaplinsky R & Morris M (2001) *A handbook for value chain research*. Ottawa: International Development Research Centre

Klerck G (2006) Biotechnology research and technology networks: The dynamics of competition and co-operation. In G Kruss (ed.) *Creating knowledge networks: Working partnerships in higher education, industry and innovation*. Cape Town: HSRC Press

Kraak A (1995) South Africa's segmented labour markets: Skill formation and occupational mobility under apartheid, 1979–1993. *Work, Employment and Society* 9(4): 657–688

Kraemer-Mbula E (2008) Aerospace. Final report commissioned by the Department of Labour for the Sector skills research project. Pretoria: HSRC

Lomey J & McNamara K (2008) Energy. Final report commissioned by the Department of Labour for the Sector skills research project. Pretoria: HSRC

Lorentzen J & Petersen I (2008) Three new technology platforms. Final report commissioned by the Department of Labour for the Sector skills research project. Pretoria: HSRC

Manwaring T (1984) The extended internal labour market. *Cambridge Journal of Economics* 8: 161–187

Maree J, Lundall P & Godfrey S (2008) Metals beneficiation. Final report commissioned by the Department of Labour for the Sector skills research project. Pretoria: HSRC

Marock C (2007) *Reskilling the tourism and hospitality sector: A case-study of the Tourism Learnership Project*. Johannesburg: Business Trust

Marsden D & Ryan P (1991) Initial training, labour market structure and public policy: Intermediate skills in British and German industry. In P Ryan (ed.) *International comparisons of vocational education and training for intermediate skills*. London: Falmer Press

Mason G (2004) *Enterprise product strategies and employer demand for skills in Britain: Evidence from the Employers Skill Survey*. London: National Institute of Economic and Social Research

Morris M & Reed L (2008) Clothing and textiles. Final report commissioned by the Department of Labour for the Sector skills research project. Pretoria: HSRC

Moyle D (2008) The growing skills crisis in the tourism sector. In A Kraak & K Press (eds) *Human resources development review 2008: Education, employment, and skills in South Africa*. Cape Town: HSRC Press

Osterman P (ed.) (1984) *Internal Labour Markets*/Cambridge, Mass.: MIT Press

PCAS (Policy Co-ordination and Advisory Services, The Presidency, South Africa) (2003) Towards a ten year review: Synthesis report on implementation of government programmes – discussion document. Pretoria: Office of the Presidency

PCAS (2006) A catalyst for Accelerated and Shared Growth – South Africa (Asgisa): Background Document. Pretoria: Office of the Presidency

Pogue TE (2008) Wood, paper and pulp. Final report commissioned by the Department of Labour for the Sector skills research project. Pretoria: HSRC

Rubery J, Tarling R & Wilkinson F (1987) Flexibility, marketing and the organisation of production. *Labour and Society* 12(1): 131–152

Rutherford TD (2006) 'Requiem or rebirth? Internal labour markets and labour market restructuring in the Kitchener and Sault Ste. Marie regions. *The Canadian Geographer* 50(2): 197–216

Webster E (1985) Work, worker organisation and labour market segmentation in South African foundries. *Capital and Society* 18(2): 344–371

Wilkinson F (ed.) (1981) *The dynamics of labour market segmentation*. London: Academic Press

Contributors

Sean Archer
Department of Economics,
University of Cape Town
sarcher@commerce.uct.ac.za

Justin Barnes
Benchmarking and Manufacturing Analysts
justin@bmanalysts.com

Nicci Earle-Malleson
Specialist: Policy Investigations
Secretariat for the National Advisory Council on Innovation (NACI)
Nicci.Earle@dst.gov.za

Shane Godfrey
Labour and Enterprise Policy Research Group,
Department of Sociology and Faculty of Law,
University of Cape Town
shane.godfrey@uct.ac.za

Jan Havenga
Head: Centre for Supply Chain Management
Department of Logistics,
University of Stellenbosch
janh@sun.ac.za

Avril Joffe
CAJ (Creativity Avril Joffe)
avril@caj.co.za

Andre Kraak
Education and Training Research Consultant
email: andrekraak@vodamail.co.za

Erika Kraemer-Mbula
Research Fellow, Institute for Economic Research on Innovation, Tshwane University of Technology,
Pretoria
ekmb@hotmail.com

Jeff Lomey
The Learning Event
jefflomey@yebo.co.za

Jo Lorentzen
Chief Research Specialist, Research Programme on Education Science and Skills Development, HSRC
Jlorentzen@hsrc.ac.za

Paul Lundall
Research Associate, Labour and Enterprise Policy Research Group,
Department of Sociology and Faculty of Law,
University of Cape Town
plundall@mweb.co.za

Johann Maree
Labour and Enterprise Policy Research Group,
Department of Sociology and Faculty of Law,
University of Cape Town
Johann.Maree@uct.ac.za

Kent McNamara
The Learning Event
jefflomey@yebo.co.za

Mike Morris
Policy Research in International Services and Manufacturing (PRISM),
School of Economics and
School of Development Studies,
University of KwaZulu-Natal
mike.morris@uct.ac.za

Monica Newton
CAJ (Creativity Avril Joffe)
avril@caj.co.za

Andrew Paterson
Development Bank of South Africa, Pretoria
AndrewP@dbsa.org

Il-haam Petersen
Research Intern, Research Programme on Education Science and Skills Development, HSRC
ipetersen@hsrc.ac.za

Duncan Pieterse
Kaiser Associates Economic Development Practice,
Cape Town
duncan.pieterse@kaiserdp.com

Thomas E Pogue
Research Fellow, Institute for Economic Research on Innovation, Tshwane University of Technology,
Pretoria
tpogue@wbs.co.za

Lyn Reed
Policy Research in International Services and Manufacturing (PRISM),
School of Economics, University of Cape Town
lynmead@gmail.com

Joan Roodt
Chief Researcher, Research Programme on Education Science and Skills Development,
HSRC
jroodt@hsrc.ac.za

Rhoanda van Zyl
Ozone Business Consulting (Pty) Ltd
Midrand
rhoanda@o3bc.co.za